twenty-first century leeds
geographies of a regional city

Edited by Rachael Unsworth & John Stillwell

First published in 2004
by Leeds University Press
University Road
Leeds LS2 9JT

Copyright© Rachael Unsworth & John Stillwell 2004
Book design copyright © Graphics Unit 2004

ISBN 0 85316 242 5

A CIP catalogue record for this book is available from
The British Library.

Design, art direction and production
Mark Newcombe
Production assistance
David Appleyard

BUTLER AND TANNER

Printing and binding
Butler & Tanner Limited
Caxton Road
Frome
Somerset BA11 1NF

Foreword
Sir Alan Wilson

1 Leeds: Premier City, Regional Capital
Rachael Unsworth & John Stillwell

CONTENTS

IDENTITY AND HOME

2 The City is the People: Demographic Structure and Dynamics
Phil Rees, John Stillwell & Amy Tyler-Jones

3 Multicultural Leeds: Geographies of Ethnic Minorities and Religious Groups
Debbie Phillips, John Stillwell & Amy Burrage

4 The Roofs Over Our Heads: Housing Supply and Demand
Huw Jones, Jane Kettle & Rachael Unsworth

HEALTHY, WEALTHY AND WISE

5 Healthy City? Spatial Inequalities and Health Care Provision
Myles Gould, Amy Burrage, John Stillwell & Andy Turner

6 The 'Haves' and 'Have-nots': Contrasting Social Geographies
John Stillwell & Peter Shepherd

7 Educational Attainment: What's the Score?
Robert Langley, Heather Eyre & John Stillwell

MAKING A LIVING AND MOVING AROUND

8 Creating Prosperity: Jobs, Businesses and Economic Development Initiatives
John Stillwell & Rachael Unsworth

9 Accommodating Financial and Business Services
Rachael Unsworth & Roger Henderson

10 Providing for Mobility: Transport Planning Under Pressure
Dave Milne, Guenter Emberger, John Stillwell & Rachael Unsworth

CONSUMPTION AND CONSERVATION

11 Shopping Around: the Development of Suburban and City Centre Retailing
Graham Clarke, Rachael Unsworth & Hillary Shaw

12 The London of the North? Youth Cultures, Urban Change and Nightlife
Paul Chatterton & Robert Hollands

13 How Green is My City? Environment and Sustainability: Status, Policy and Prospects
Gordon Mitchell & Rachael Unsworth

MAPPING THE FUTURE

14 Form, Movement, Space and Use: Land-use Planning and Urban Design
Rachael Unsworth & Lindsay Smales

15 Simulating the City and Alternative Futures
John Stillwell, Mark Birkin, Dimitris Ballas, Richard Kingston & Phil Gibson

16 Twenty-First Century Leeds
John Stillwell, Rachael Unsworth, Paul Stephens & Gordon Carey

III

We are extremely grateful for the sponsorship of this book by *Town Centre Securities plc*, a Leeds-based company founded by Arnold Ziff. This sponsorship is typical of the support that the Ziff family has given to numerous projects in the city, all in a spirit of generosity, asking nothing in return — something that is typical of great benefactors. The University, being a symbol of academic life in the city, has regularly received great support from the Ziff family, ranging from advice on corporate matters to funding lecture theatres and more recently, a Steinway grand piano.

The firm was led by Mr Arnold Ziff until 2004. A graduate of the University of Leeds and holder of two honorary degrees, Arnold Ziff maintained a close interest in the work of the University, seeing it as an integral part of the city which he loved so much. Arnold Ziff died in the summer of 2004, with his passing mourned in the city and beyond.

David Sugden, Pro-Vice Chancellor
September 2004

We are grateful to the *University of Leeds*, through the Office of the Vice Chancellor, for supporting the publication of this book as part of its centenary celebrations.

In 1904, the Yorkshire College of Science, founded in 1874, was awarded a royal charter. The new University of Leeds had 800 students and 99 academic staff members. In 2003–2004 there were over 31,500 students enrolled on 700 different first-degree programmes and 330 post-graduate degree programmes. A further 52,000 men and women were taking short courses with the University. Academic staff numbered 2,400 with another 4,300 in supporting roles.

Leeds is now among the top ten universities for research in the UK and is internationally acknowledged as a centre of excellence in a wide range of academic and professional disciplines. Its broad research and skills base and facilities attract interest from major multinationals and small local businesses.

The *School of Geography at Leeds*, one of the largest Geography departments in Britain, has over 30 academic staff involved in teaching an annual intake of around 230 undergraduate students. The School also provides Masters programmes and doctoral training. In the last HEFCE assessment of teaching quality it was graded "excellent".

The School has an international research reputation and was awarded Grade 5 in the 2002 Research Assessment Exercise. The interests of the Research Groups span a wide range of subject areas, one of which is concerned with urban development and modelling, with a special focus on Leeds.

DLA, solicitors, kindly supported the launch of this book.

We are grateful to the following organisations for ordering copies of *Twenty-First Century Leeds: Geographies of a Regional City* in advance of publication:

Carey Jones Architects, designers of many buildings in Leeds since the practice was formed in 1987. Amongst their most prominent achievements are Princes Exchange (featured on the cover of this book), The Quays, the Nuffield Hospital, the Western Campus for the University of Leeds, offices at 15–16 Park Row and their own offices in the converted flax mill of Rose Wharf. Still under way are Clarence Dock, Whitehall Riverside, Trinity One and West Central. Wellington Place, City One and the new premises for the Northern Ballet School are future projects. The firm also kindly made available some photographs of Leeds architectural work (see photo credits).

Landmark Development Projects Ltd a Leeds-based development company founded in the 1970s. Projects include residential development at Dock Street and in Bramhope, refurbishment of historic buildings in Angel Inn Yard, Victoria Gate (a call centre), the Travelodge hotel in Blayds Court and South Leeds Trade Centre (industrial/retail starter units). Also a partner in the development of Bridgewater Place, Landmark kindly provided the images used in Chapters 9 and 11.

St James Securities, a Leeds-based property development company, has been delivering new projects in the city since 1982. Amongst the most prominent developments have been The Embankment, The Light, The Round Foundry and Wellington Place. Schemes currently under construction include Bridgewater Place and The Electric Press, Millennium Square.

GMAP Ltd was established in 1983 by geographers from the University of Leeds. The company specialises in providing market intelligence and decision support solutions to global retail organisations which are looking to improve the efficiency of their networks, their sales territories and their channels to market.

The Lord Mayor's office, Leeds City Council.

The creation of this book owes a great deal to the funding that was awarded by the Office of the Deputy Prime Minister under the Local e-Government Programme to Leeds Initiative to create LIKNET, the Leeds Initiative Knowledge NETwork. Resources allocated to the Futures Group strand of this project under the guidance of *Gill Holt* (Knowledge Transfer Support Unit, University of Leeds), *John Stillwell* (School of Geography, University of Leeds) and *Steve Littlewood* (School of the Built Environment, Leeds Metropolitan University), were used to support two research assistants in working to build a collaborative research network and to undertake a series of collaborative research studies utilising the Virtual Knowledge Park (VKP) developed at the University of Leeds. The book is therefore the outcome of collaborative endeavour between members of the academic and policy-making communities; it is one of the key deliverables of the LIKNET project, demonstrating that collaborative research can work to good effect.

Amy Burrage and *Amy Tyler-Jones* were appointed as the two research assistants in summer 2003 for nine months, and were responsible for supporting the project both through their activities in liaising with participants and providing presentations and tutorials on how to use the VKP, and also through their careful research work on accessing, analysing and displaying data sets for chapter authors. The book and the other activities of the Futures strand of the LIKNET project would not have been achieved without their dedicated efforts, for which we are immensely thankful.

The huge tasks of designing and producing the book were shouldered by *Mark Newcombe* and *David Appleyard*, members of the Graphics Unit at the School of Geography. In particular, a massive debt of thanks is owed to Mark, whose design contribution was outstanding and whose enthusiasm for the project was demonstrated by the many extra hours of hard work that he put in.

Many people have supported this project either by providing data and information or by making useful comments. We are particularly grateful to the following:

Liz Minkin (Leeds City Council) for 'opening doors' at the Council and thereby facilitating access to information, statistics and images; Liz also commented on Chapter 1, as did *Martin Dean* (Leeds Initiative); *Jacky Pruckner* (Leeds City Council) for providing the boundaries of the communities defined by the Council; *Pete Shepherd* (School of Geography, University of Leeds), *Dimitris Ballas* (Department of Geography, University of Sheffield) and *Richard Kingston* (School of Planning and Landscape, University of Manchester) also helped to create the boundaries of the 106 community areas used for mapping; *Jennifer Wright* (Residential and Commercial Services, University of Leeds) for providing the data on the residential locations of University of Leeds students used in Chapter 2; *Gary Craig* (Department of Social Policy,

University of Hull) and *Tony Stanley* (Leeds Racial Equality Council), for their comments on an initial draft of Chapter 3; *Paul Fox* (KW Linfoot plc) for market intelligence and support of the city living research; *Nigel Tapp* (Allsop & Co) for market intelligence; *David Haigh* (Leeds City Council) for supporting student project work on affordable housing reported in Chapters 4 and 14; and *John Devine* (Neighbourhoods and Housing, LCC) for making photographs available; *Nick Emmel* (Nuffield Institute, University of Leeds) for his useful comments on Chapter 5; *Angie Grain* (School of Geography, University of Leeds) and *Harminder Suri* (The Met Office, Leeds Metropolitan University) for providing data on the parental addresses of undergraduates at each of the respective universities in Chapter 7, and *Chris Newton* (University of Leeds Careers Centre) who provided data on University of Leeds graduate retention rates; *Steve Clark* (Development Department, Leeds City Council) for allowing us to use his Excel spreadsheet containing estimates of personal income by output area in Chapter 8, *Caroline Kirby* (Yorkshire Forward) for providing foreign direct investment data for Leeds, and *Christine Leigh* (School of Geography, University of Leeds) gave comments on an earlier draft of the chapter; *John Ansbro* (Leeds Financial Services Initiative), *Jeff Pearey* (Chesterton), *Alistair Russell* (Jones Lang Lasalle), *Guy Gilfillan* (CBRE), *Paul Fairhurst* (Knight Frank) and Andrew McKeon for market intelligence, statistics and comments on Chapter 9; *Tony May, Peter Mackie* (Institute for Transport Studies, University of Leeds) and *Steve Clark* (Development Department, Leeds City Council) for their helpful comments on Chapter 10; the individuals concerned with the fieldwork that underpins Chapter 12 that was undertaken between September 2000 and August 2001, and comprised focus groups with consumers of nightlife and one-to-one interviews with venues/owners/managers, promoters and DJs, police, security firms, licensing magistrates, authority representatives and various other people involved in the nightlife industry; the efforts of *Bernie Byrnes* and *Cait Reid* were very important in researching the city of Leeds; *Tom Knowland, Dave Feeney, Peter Kelly* (Leeds City Council), *Garreth Bruff* (formerly Leeds Initiative, now SIGOMA) and *Aidan While* (School of Planning and Landscape, University of Manchester) for their contributions to Chapter 13; *Mark Burgess, Alan Cranswick, Anke Otto, John Ramsden, John Thorp, John Townsend, Peter Vaughan, Andy Wood* (Leeds City Council); *Kevin Grady* and *Peter Baker* (Leeds Civic Trust) for either providing information or detailed comments relating to Chapter 14; *Leeds Initiative* for funding support to enable the development of the Micro-MaPPAS system and *Jin Jianhui* (School of Geography, University of Leeds) who worked very hard to develop the code for the system described in Chapter 15; *Dan Vickers* (School of Geography, University of Leeds) for providing graphics and details of the national 2001 Census-based national classification of output areas in Leeds presented in Chapter 16.

Digital attribute data relating to the 2001 Census have been extracted from three sources: Key Statistics (KS) comprising of 25 tables containing core data for output areas and higher level geographies; Standard Tables (ST) which include a set of 135 detailed tables, available from ward up to national level; and Census Area Statistics (CAS) containing 149 tables, which are available for output areas and their aggregations up to national level and include some Univariate Tables (UT) that involve a more detailed breakdown of counts for a single topic.

1991 Census statistical data has been drawn from both the Local Base Statistics (LBS) covering ward to national geographical levels and the Small Area Statistics (SAS), a sub-set of LBS presenting 86 standard tables covering geographic levels from enumeration districts to national level.

Census data for 1991 and 2001 covering England and Wales have been extracted from the CasWeb website and DVDs supplied by ONS. Digital boundary files for census geographies have been obtained from CasWeb and UKBorders. UKBorders is also the source of other boundary data including postal sectors. Ordnance Survey MasterMap data has been obtained through Digimap. Leeds City Council kindly provided digital boundary files for renewal areas within the district.

Mid-year population estimates, unemployment counts and data on employment collected through the Annual Business Inquiry have been extracted from Nomisweb. Data on house sales has been obtained from the Land Registry web site. Vital statistics were obtained from the UK data Archive at the University of Essex.

All tables and figures in the book that contain 2001 (and 1991) Census data and maps based on Ordnance Survey data are reproduced with permission of the Controller of Her Majesty's Stationery Office (© Crown Copyright).

For the sake of simplicity and coherence in figures and tables, sources of attribute data used throughout the book are confined to a minimum abbreviation and sources of boundary data are omitted.

Photo credits

Antonis Varadis, pages 258 (bottom right), 259 (bottom), 272 (bottom two photos)

Carey Jones, pages 119 (top), 155, 212, 260, 320–321, 324, 333, 338 (bottom right), 340

Environment Agency, page 295

Guzelian, pages 277, 278, 280 (right), 288

Harvey Nichols kindly allowed us to use a version of their storecard on the title page of Chapter 6 (page 127)

John Angerson, pages 282 (top), 283

Janet Stillwell, page 112

John Stillwell, pages, 69, 112, 145, 180 (left), 185, 385

Justin Slee, pages 275, 282 (bottom)

K W Linfoot, pages 83 (top and bottom), 336

Land Securities, page 250

Landmark Development Projects, pages 210, 375

Leeds City Council, LCC Development Department photographer, Mick Roo, kindly provided many of the images appearing in this book: pages 2 (top and bottom), 3, 7 (bottom right), 8, 10, 13 (top and bottom), 16 (top, middle and bottom), 17, 29, 45, 82, 85, 90 (bottom), 121, 129, 131, 183, 197, 198 (left), 199, 209, 223, 228, 244, 255, 256, 258 (top left), 259 (top), 266, 267, 268, 269, 272 (top), 292 (top), 293, 300, 304 (top), 310, 312 (bottom), 322 (bottom), 323 (bottom right), 330 (top and left), 332, 334 (bottom right), 335, 337 (top), 367, 380 (left), 383

Leeds City Council Neighbourhoods and Housing Department, pages 88 (middle and bottom), 93

Leeds Initiative, pages 12, 14,

Leeds Supertram, page 233

Lloyd Sturdy (Page One), page 137 (right)

Lottie Winn, pages 30, 31, 40 (left), 43, 47, 49 (all the portraits), 60, 67, 70, 132, 175, 261, 262

Netta Cunliffe, page 146

Press Agency Photos, page 140

Rachael Unsworth, pages 7 (top left, top right and bottom left), 73, 80-81, 83 (middle), 88 (top), 91, 94, 96, 97 (left, right, bottom), 100, 109, 119 (middle and bottom), 120 (right), 122 (top and bottom), 133, 136, 149, 160, 161 (top and bottom), 168, 172, 180 (right), 191, 193 (far left and left), 194 (top and bottom), 196 (right), 198 (right), 201 (left and right), 202, 204, 205 (top, bottom left, bottom right), 207 (left and right), 208 (left and right), 211, 213, 220 (left and right), 221, 245, 246, 247, 248 (top and bottom), 249 (top and bottom), 257 (top, middle and bottom), 258 (top right, middle three photos and bottom left), 270, 275 (2nd photo), 280 (left), 281, 284, 286, 289, 292 (bottom), 295 (left), 302, 304 (bottom), 312 (top), 322 (top), 323 (top left, bottom right, top left), 326, 329, 330 (bottom right), 334 (top left, top right), 337 (bottom), 338 (top left, top right, bottom left), 339, 343, 381, 385

Sasa Savic (on behalf of Crosby Homes), page 137 (left)

Simons Estates, page 374

The Yorkshire County Cricket Club, page 371

Tim Green Photography, page 90 (top)

University of Leeds Estate Services, page 231

Yorkshire Group plc, page 184

Yorkshire Post Newspapers generously allowed us to use images from their archive. Mike Fisher and Jane Marsden kindly facilitated access to the archive. Pages 35, 40 (right), 50, 61, 68, 71, 98-99, 106, 107, 111, 116, 120 (left), 123 (top and bottom), 124, 144 (top and bottom), 150, 154, 163, 285, 297, 370

Dimitris Ballas, Lecturer in the Department of Geography at the University of Sheffield (d.ballas@sheffield.ac.uk)

Mark Birkin, Senior Lecturer in the School of Geography and Director of the Informatics Institute at the University of Leeds (m.h.birkin@leeds.ac.uk)

Amy Burrage, Graduate Transport Planner, Mott MacDonald Ltd; formerly Research Assistant in the School of Geography at the University of Leeds (amy.burrage@talk21.com)

Gordon Carey, Chairman of Carey Jones, Architects, Leeds (gordon.carey@careyjones.com)

Paul Chatterton, Lecturer in the School of Geography at the University of Leeds (p.chatterton@leeds.ac.uk)

Graham Clarke, Professor of Business Geography in the School of Geography at the University of Leeds (g.p.clarke@leeds.ac.uk)

Guenter Emberger, Senior Research Fellow in the Institut fuer Verkehrsplanung in Vienna; formerly Research Fellow in the Institute of Transport Studies at the University of Leeds (guenter.emberger@tuwien.ac.at)

Heather Eyre, Research and Information Officer at Education Leeds Limited (heather.eyre@educationleeds.co.uk)

Phil Gibson, Research Assistant in the School of Geography at the University of Leeds (philg@comp.leeds.ac.uk)

Myles Gould, Lecturer in the School of Geography at the University of Leeds (m.i.gould@leeds.ac.uk)

Roger Henderson, Reader in International Finance and Deputy Director, European Regional Business and Economic Development Unit (ERBEDU), Leeds Business School, Leeds Metropolitan University (r.henderson@leedsmet.ac.uk)

Robert Hollands, Senior Lecturer in the School of Geography, Politics and Sociology at the University of Newcastle-upon-Tyne (robert.hollands@ncl.ac.uk)

Huw Jones, Neighbourhood and Housing Strategy Manager at Leeds City Council (huw.jones@leeds.gov.uk)

Jane Kettle, Associate Dean and Head of the School of the Built Environment at Leeds Metropolitan University (j.kettle@leedsmet.ac.uk)

Richard Kingston, Lecturer in the Department of Planning at the University of Manchester (richard.kingston@man.ac.uk)

Robert Langley, Head of ICT and Information Management at Education Leeds Limited (robert.langley@educationleeds.co.uk)

Dave Milne, Lecturer in the Institute of Transport Studies at the University of Leeds (dmilne@its.leeds.ac.uk)

Gordon Mitchell, University Research Fellow in the School of Geography and the Institute of Transport Studies at the University of Leeds (g.mitchell@leeds.ac.uk)

Debbie Phillips, Senior Lecturer in the School of Geography and Deputy Director of the Centre for Ethnicity and Racism Studies at the University of Leeds (d.a.phillips@leeds.ac.uk)

Phil Rees, Professor of Population Studies in the School of Geography at the University of Leeds (p.h.rees@leeds.ac.uk)

Hillary Shaw, Sessional Lecturer at the Nantes Business School; formerly PhD student in the School of Geography at the University of Leeds (hillshaw@aol.com)

Peter Shepherd, ESRC-funded PhD student in the School of Geography at the University of Leeds (geo1pjs@leeds.ac.uk)

Lindsay Smales, Senior Lecturer in the Centre for Urban Development and Environmental Management at Leeds Metropolitan University (l.smales@leedsmet.ac.uk)

Paul Stephens, Chief Economic Services Officer, Leeds City Council (paul.stephens@leeds.gov.uk)

John Stillwell, Professor of Migration and Regional Development in the School of Geography at the University of Leeds (j.c.h.stillwell@leeds.ac.uk)

Amy Tyler-Jones, formerly Research Assistant in the School of Geography at the University of Leeds. (amy-tylerjones@yahoo.co.uk)

Andy Turner, Research Assistant in the School of Geography at the University of Leeds (a.g.d.turner@leeds.ac.uk)

Rachael Unsworth, Lecturer in the School of Geography at the University of Leeds (r.unsworth@leeds.ac.uk)

The book is a tribute to the City from the University on the occasion of the latter's centenary and it will be read by all those with an interest in Leeds.

Urban and regional geographers are very lucky to live in their laboratories! It is entirely appropriate therefore that their skills should be applied to their own cities.

The University of Leeds' geographers have joined forces with other specialists from their neighbouring university, Leeds Metropolitan, and from the City Council, to produce this book. It combines a presentation of the highest levels of academic skills with a rich portrait of the city. It is particularly impressive that the collaboration was facilitated by the University's Virtual Knowledge Park, and that itself is an indication of how very large projects such as this can be organised in the future. The list of acknowledgements shows the scale of effort — and willing commitment — that has been deployed.

I have long argued that the study of cities — seeking a full, comprehensive understanding — represents one of the major intellectual challenges of the last hundred years. Enormous progress has been made. But the results of that progress are usually presented in a very fragmented form, in specialist papers on this or that aspect of urban development. This has also led me to argue that urban science ought to be seen as 'big science': worth a considerable investment to generate an integrated knowledge base which would provide more effective guidance for the future. This kind of project is rarely attempted and is a significant step in that direction.

It also demonstrates the power of research collaboration. In fields like this one, where substantial resources are needed for success, collaboration becomes key. It is easier to pay lip service to this objective than to achieve it — but the contributors to this volume have shown the way in this respect too.

Leeds is sufficiently large and complex to illustrate all the development issues of western cities. It has been hugely success-ful in recent times, but still exhibits major challenges: managing a rapidly changing economy, tackling problems in parts of the city that remain poor and providing services effectively. These are all represented here. The authors have skilfully arranged their chapters to cover each facet, but the pulling together in one book enables the reader to grasp the interdependencies.

The book is a tribute to the City from the University on the occasion of the latter's centenary and it will be read by all those with an interest in Leeds. Its quality is a tribute to the editors, authors and designer. Above all, it will be important to a much wider audience in urban geography as a demonstration of something which is very difficult to achieve: a bringing together in one place of all the methods which offer key insights into the processes that have produced our cities, and what this means for the planning of their futures.

Alan Wilson
Department for Education and Skills, London

After leaving the post
of Vice Chancellor
of the University of Leeds
in 2004, Sir Alan Wilson
joined the DfES
as Director General
for Higher Education

This book is dedicated to the memory of

Joanna Stillwell
(1981–2004)

who was born and bred in Leeds and who loved her city

1

Leeds: Premier City, Regional Capital

RACHAEL UNSWORTH & JOHN STILLWELL

Leeds is the second largest metropolitan district in England and serves as the administrative and employment centre for the Yorkshire and Humber region.

Right, the Civic Hall towering above Millennium Square and one of the Portland stone obelisks supporting a gilded owl — the emblem of Leeds. Far right, Town Hall, designed by Cuthbert Brodrick and, left, one of the lions at the foot of the classical portico.

1.1 Introduction

This book is about Leeds — its people, its economy and its fabric, the built and natural environment within which residents, commuters and visitors live, work, shop, study and spend their leisure time. We describe and interpret socio-economic patterns across the city, based on up-to-date information from a wide range of sources, including the 2001 Census of Population in particular. We consider the national, regional and local policy contexts within which these patterns are generated and influenced, assess the variety of efforts to improve the city, and offer ideas on future directions of change on various issues.

Overall, the book presents a detailed portrait of Leeds at the start of the twenty-first century. It shows a major regional city that has areas of great dynamism characterised by prosperity, renewal and optimism; areas of poverty, exclusion and multiple deprivation where people are trapped in a downward spiral of problems; and also areas that are positioned somewhere between the two extremes. It shows a city that continues to make great efforts to tackle its problem areas and also to encourage investment both in the old-established neighbourhoods and the new prime sites that accommodate drivers of economic growth for the city itself and for the wider region, both now and into the future. It is a city

determined to build on its strengths and continue the tradition of canny diversification into new economic opportunities, while taking into full consideration the priorities of limiting resource use, output of waste and pollution and preserving (and adapting) the best of its built heritage.

The capacity to progress and the pace and direction of change are always affected by a number of constraining factors, including the wider economic environment, central government policy and local politics. Conflicts arise over how to use scarce resources to the best effect where area sustainability is paramount and how to encourage and support economic growth without causing local and more widely felt environmental damage. The built environment cannot be changed fast

Figure 1.1 Leeds in its national and regional context

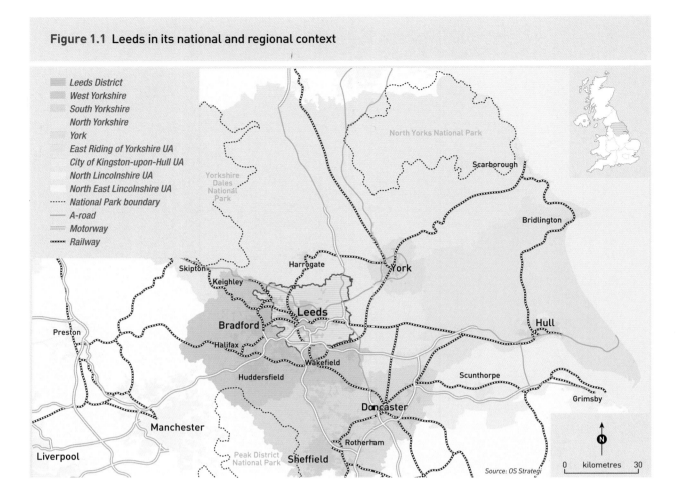

Leeds District
West Yorkshire
South Yorkshire
North Yorkshire
York
East Riding of Yorkshire UA
City of Kingston-upon-Hull UA
North Lincolnshire UA
North East Lincolnshire UA
National Park boundary
A-road
Motorway
Railway

Source: OS Strategi

enough to keep up with evolving needs. Despite some lofty aspirations and much demonstrable progress, there remain many challenges to address in improving the city's fabric and functioning and thereby enhancing the quality of life of its inhabitants, workers and visitors.

1.2 Leeds Metropolitan District

Leeds is the second largest metropolitan district in England and serves as the administrative and employment centre for the Yorkshire and Humber region (Figure 1.1). The Leeds Metropolitan District has boundaries that are set well beyond the built-up area of the city itself: the district covers an area of approximately 550m² and includes separate small towns such as Otley and Wetherby and many villages (Figure 1.2).

The extent of the built-up area of Leeds is evident from Figure 1.2 and various land uses across the district, estimated

from the *Unitary Development Plan,* are summarised in Table 1.1. It is perhaps surprising to discover that almost 62 per cent of Leeds District is designated as green belt, with 36 per cent classified as developed urban areas. The percentages in the final column of Table 1.1 do not sum to 100 per cent because of the overlap between the categories; much of the green belt is also designated as special landscape area, for example.

The present administrative boundaries of the Leeds Metropolitan District have changed relatively little since they were designated in the 1974 reform of local government and the creation of the West Yorkshire Metropolitan County. In 1986, West Yorkshire County Council was abolished and Leeds became a single tier metropolitan district with enhanced powers and responsibilities, notably in planning, transport and economic development (Haughton and Williams, 1996, p. 4). With a budget of over £1,000 million and around 35,000 employees, Leeds City Council is the largest employer in the district.

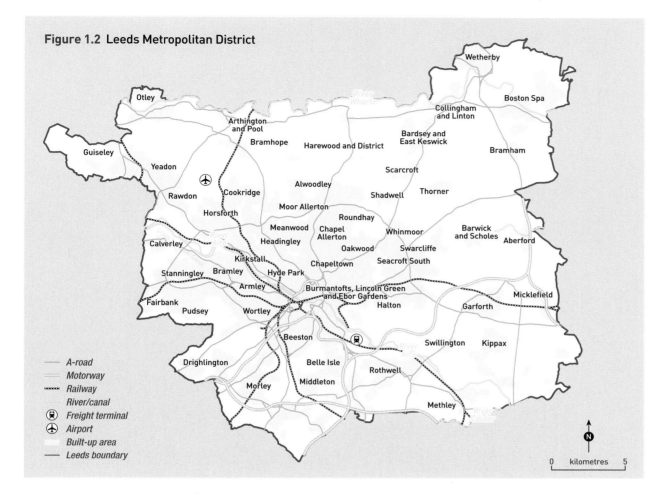

Figure 1.2 Leeds Metropolitan District

Legend:
- A-road
- Motorway
- Railway
- River/canal
- ® Freight terminal
- ✈ Airport
- Built-up area
- Leeds boundary

0   kilometres   5

Where is Leeds in the urban hierarchy — the ranking of cities? It is a city with a relatively large population (715,400 in 2001), a wide range of economic activities and a number of head offices and regional offices; it is a major provider of higher education, healthcare and cultural and sporting activities; it has a significant concentration of high quality shops; it has an important strategic location midway between London and Edinburgh, is well-connected to the rail and motorway network and shares an expanding international airport with Bradford at Yeadon. This combination of characteristics makes for a significant city, but how significant in European, UK and regional terms?

Leeds in Europe

From 1990, Leeds has aimed to be seen as a major European city. Economic re-orientation, redevelopment of buildings and remodelling of the central street scene and the urban 'gateways' (the main road entrances to the city centre) have changed the image of the city. It is no longer a place that can be summarised in the old Yorkshire phrase 'where there's muck there's brass'. It is now a more cosmopolitan, service-based city. The pavement café culture has arrived, admittedly limited by the climate at nearly 54 degrees north. Many international retail and leisure companies are now represented in the prime shopping quarter and companies have been encouraged to forge links with European partners, especially those in twin cities of Lille, Brno, Dortmund and Siegen. The local authority belongs to the Eurocities group and takes its turn in hosting events.

But despite much rhetoric on the European city theme, Leeds ranked only 53rd in Jones Lang LaSalle's European Regional Economic Growth Index in 2002 (Llewellyn-Davies *et al.*, 2002), though this was a considerable improvement on the previous year's ranking of 66th. Its relatively low position in the European urban hierarchy is further illustrated by the fact that when 150 senior business people in Germany and France were

Table 1.1 Land use summary

UDP code	Land use	Area (km²)	Percentage Leeds Metropolitan District
–	Developed land — urban areas	199.0	36.2
N32	Green belt	338.7	61.5
N37	Special Landscape Areas	172.1	31.3
N1	Green space	30.1	5.5
N38	Washlands	19.5	3.5
N50	Leeds Nature Areas — 120 sites	14.6	2.7
N50	Sites of Ecological or Geological Importance (SEGI — 33 sites	10.6	1.9
N6	Protected playing pitches	7.9	1.4
N50	Local Nature Reserves — 6 sites	6.0	1.1
N50	Sites of Special Scientific Interest (SSSI) — 17 sites	5.6	1.0
N1A	Allotments — 96 separate sites	1.3	0.2
–	Conservation areas	2.2	0.4
–	Parks and gardens of special historic interest	11.2	2.0
–	Total	550.3	100.0

Source: UDP, LCC (2001); English Heritage (1984)

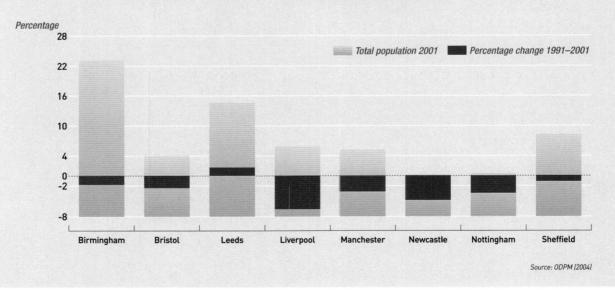

Figure 1.3 Core city populations, 2001 and percentage population change, 1991–2001

Source: ODPM (2004)

asked to name major European cities, only 3 per cent mentioned Leeds (Brahm Research, 2003). In many respects, Leeds' role is as a regional UK city, not as high-performing as many of the regional cities on mainland Europe (Leeds Initiative, 2003a). There is a recognition within Leeds that the city will have to broaden and deepen its functions and raise its

Leeds District encompasses several market towns and villages including Barwick in Elmet (top left) Otley (top right), Shadwell (bottom left) and Wetherby (bottom right).

profile if it is to be considered as a major player on the European scene, and indeed at the global level.

Leeds in UK

Since 1994, Leeds has been classed as an English 'core city', one of eight outside London that are the foci of larger city regions. Figure 1.3 indicates the size of the populations of the core cities and allows comparison of changes in population between 1991 and 2001. Unlike its counterparts that have seen population declines over the decade, Leeds has grown by 1.3 per cent over this period according to figures reported by the Office of the Deputy Prime Minister (ODPM, 2004). Over the last two years of this period, Manchester grew by 6.8 per cent whilst Leeds managed only an of increase 0.3 per cent, on a par with growth in Birmingham and Bristol. The other core cities all experienced population declines of between 0.5 per cent and 1.2 per cent from 1999 to 2001.

Whilst Haughton and Williams (1996) have argued that Leeds can be deemed a successful second tier city, a more recent study of the urban hierarchy in England and Wales (Hall *et al.*, 2001) showed that Leeds had been in the same category (2b) through the entire period from 1913 to 1998, below London (category 1) and also below Birmingham, Manchester and Bristol. Other cities classified in the same category as Leeds were Cardiff, Liverpool, Newcastle and Nottingham. However, Robert Huggins Associates (2002) provide possibly the most comprehensive index of urban economic competitiveness, covering business density, knowledge-based industries, economic activity rates, productivity, GDP *per capita*, unemployment and average earnings. According to these criteria, Leeds is in 30th position, behind Manchester, Bristol and Nottingham but ahead of the other core cities. Inevitably, all exercises that attempt to rank cities have to be read critically, but as the Leeds Core Cities Prospectus concludes: "Leeds

compares favourably across a range of measures and is a city where people continue to make a positive choice to live. However, it needs to do more not only to assert itself in the hierarchy of British cities, but also to compete internationally" (Leeds Initiative, 2003a, p.12).

Leeds in its region

Leeds has long been considered the regional capital (Burt and Grady, 1994), though of a region that has not been consistently and clearly defined. The term 'region' is highly versatile, as Brown (1967) emphasised over 30 years ago, but is most frequently used to signify political or administrative divisions. The city falls within the Government Office Region of Yorkshire and the Humber, whose internal administrative boundaries equate with those of the metropolitan districts of West and South Yorkshire, the unitary authorities of the East Riding of Yorkshire, Kingston-upon-Hull, North Lincolnshire and North East Lincolnshire as well as York, and the rural districts of North Yorkshire (Figure 1.4). However, the Leeds city region can be identified as containing those local authorities whose boundaries are contiguous with those of Leeds together with

Craven, Calderdale and Barnsley (Leeds Initiative, 2004).

As Leeds' economy has become stronger over the last decade or so, it has become an even more dominant element of the regional economy (CURDS, 1999). It has the largest population and labour force of all the districts in the region (19 per cent of the regional total) and accounted for 62 per cent of the net additional jobs in the region between 1992 and 2002. GDP per head and average household income are higher in Leeds than elsewhere in the region and unemployment is lower. It has a disproportionately large share of business in key growth areas: over a quarter of the region's finance and business services employment is based in Leeds, and a third of the employment in legal services (LCC, 2003b). Its economy has expanded at approximately twice the rate of Yorkshire and the Humber as a whole (Llewellyn-Davies et al., 2002).

The impact of regional decision making has expanded significantly following the creation of Yorkshire Forward (the Regional Development Agency (RDA) for Yorkshire and Humber) and the Yorkshire and Humber Regional Chamber in the later 1990s. The decentralisation of central government functions to Leeds, such as the Department of Work and Pensions

Figure 1.4 Leeds and the local authorities in the region

economic growth, and that the benefits of growth can be spread more equitably across the districts to ease some of the possible stresses associated with excessive focus of growth in Leeds. Work is in progress to suggest alternative ways of achieving these aims (Llewellyn-Davies *et al.*, 2002).

The newly emerging focus on the city region may help to counteract the deep-seated rivalry between Leeds and the major urban settlements within West Yorkshire which include Wakefield, Bradford, Huddersfield (Kirklees) and Halifax (Calderdale). Leeds stands out amongst the five local authorities of West Yorkshire in having 34 per cent of the population but 40 per cent of the GDP. There is a relatively low density of VAT registered businesses per capita and it does not differ as much as might be expected in terms of employment rate or level of unemployment; only Bradford has a lower level of pupils attaining five or more GCSE passes (Leeds Economy Partnership, 2003).

located on Quarry Hill, and the city's attractiveness as a business centre, accounting for 32 of the 96 plcs with headquarters in the region, have meant an escalation in local investment decision making. Tom Riordan, Yorkshire Forward's Executive Director of Strategy and Policy, has suggested that "Leeds is already a Premiership city and compares well with its UK counterparts. We want to take it into the Champion's League of cities" (Yorkshire Evening Post Supplement, 17 September, 2003). The RDA recognizes that the success of Leeds is crucial to the region's economy. It has become a magnet for investors' capital, as exemplified by the property market, but the challenge is to maintain the buoyancy whilst ensuring that significant sums of investment reach those parts of the city that are doing comparatively less well. This imperative is embraced by the Core Cities programme, in which each core city is charged by the ODPM with the task of working out how to deliver greater prosperity to the people of their own cities, to those living within their wider regions, and to the country as a whole (Leeds Initiative, 2003a). The aim is to strengthen planning and collaboration across this city region (Figure 1.4) to ensure that Leeds can maximise its role as the main driver of

1.3 Government and governance

Since New Labour came to power in 1997, the city has been solidly Labour in terms of parliamentary representation, though four out of five of the MPs received a smaller percentage of the vote in 2001 than they had achieved in 1997 (Table 1.2). At a local level, the city was under a Labour administration from 1979 to 2004. Keith Wakefield became the Leader of the City Council in 2003, taking over from Brian Walker who succeeded John Trickett in 1997. All these Labour council leaders presided over a period of great change in local government. During the 1980s, as the 'corporate city' evolved, the role of local government was transformed from that of main direct provider

Leeds Town Hall, opened by Queen Victoria in 1858, is home to Leeds International Concert Season's orchestral series and the Leeds International Piano Competition. It will re-open in 2005 after refurbishment.

of all local services to that of a major player in a public-private partnership in which action to encourage economic growth became of paramount importance (Haughton and Williams, 1996). In the local elections in 2002 and 2003, Labour secured 57 and 52 seats respectively of the total of 99, with Conservatives taking 18 and 20, the Liberal Democrats taking 20 on each occasion and the remainder going to the Greens and Independents. However, the local elections in 2004 saw the end of Labour's majority as it won only 40 seats. The Conservatives, Liberal Democrats and Green Party have formed an alliance to take control of the administration.

New Labour's modernising local government agenda led to fundamental changes in the City Council, including the introduction of new political structures, which currently comprise a cross-party executive board, six scrutiny boards, two strategy panels, three regulatory panels and 16 Community Involvement Teams (CITs). In the past, the local authority had been less than open in its operation, with a tendency towards paternalistic service provision and a lack of transparency in decision making (I&DEA, 2000). The various changes that have occurred signal Leeds City Council's intention to be seen as a more transparent and open organisation, in line with central government philosophy. The introduction of CITs in 1999, for

instance, is intended to provide an opportunity to facilitate an improved relationship with local communities and for citizens to take part in decision making (While *et al.*, 2002). Each CIT has a locality co-ordinator and brings together all the local elected members for a designated area. They have responsibility for producing a local community plan for their area, the first series of which was published in 2001. This reorganisation was

Table 1.2 Parliamentary election results, 1992, 1997 and 2001

Constituentcy	1992		1997		2001	
	Party	Percentage of vote	Party	Percentage of vote	Party	Percentage of vote
Leeds Central	Labour	62.2	Labour	69.6	Labour	66.9
Leeds East	Labour	57.7	Labour	67.5	Labour	63.0
Leeds North East	Conservative	45.4	Labour	49.1	Labour	49.1
Leeds North West	Conservative	43.0	Labour	39.9	Labour	41.9
Leeds West	Labour	55.1	Labour	66.7	Labour	62.1

Source: http://www.election.demon.co.uk/1983EB.html for 1992 results and http://www.election.demon.co.uk/1997EB.html for 1997 and 2001 results

Table 1.3 Leeds City Council structure

Departments before 2003	New departments
Chief Executive's Department	Chief Executive's Unit
Environmental and highways services; waste management; catering and cleaning; property maintenance and facilities management; transport services; enforcement; support services	City Services
Financial and customer services for benefits, revenue collection and student support; IT; human resources	Corporate Services
Planning; Highways; Leeds Development Agency; City Centre Management; Design Services Agency	Development
Leisure Services; services to children and young people not included within Education Leeds or Social Services	Learning and Leisure
Housing; Environmental Health; Community Safety; regeneration	Neighbourhoods and Housing
Social Services	Social Services

Source: LCC (2003a)

followed by restructuring of the major departments that deliver council services across the city, reducing the number of departments from 16 to only seven (Table 1.3). Some functions have been devolved down to local level, such as many elements of the former Housing Department's work which is now done in Arms Length Management Organisations (ALMOs).

A significant change in the nature of governance in Leeds has been the partnership structure initiated in 1990. The Leeds Initiative was launched as a way of bringing together all the main interest groups in the city so that economic success and policy development and delivery could be achieved by partnership between the public, private and voluntary sectors. Leeds Initiative responded to the local Chamber of Commerce's pressure for a stronger role in local governance, and recognised that such partnerships were becoming increasingly important in levering regeneration funds from central government. Leeds Initiative's objectives are to:

- promote the city as a major European centre;

- ensure the economic vitality of the city;

- create an integrated transport system for the city;

- enhance the environment of the entire city;

- improve the quality and visual appeal of the city; and

- develop the city as an attractive centre for visitors.

Each of these objectives has been pursued through a period of much change in central government policy and in local government structure and functioning. The progress of the sub-groups has been overseen, facilitated and largely financed by the City Council. But the partners involved in the sub-groups have been able to make decisions according to their own agreed principles and agendas. The Initiative has been more structured since the mid-90s, with a more formal (though slim) secretariat and an identity which stresses that it is very much not under Council direction.

Also in the mid-1990s, a series of internal and external changes — including changes in national urban policy, growing concerns about the distributional impacts of growth, and the Government's invitation for Leeds to prepare a long-term 'City Pride' strategy — provided opportunities to rethink the structure and ethos of the Leeds Initiative. Although the City Pride process was launched under John Major's Conservative Government, the election of a New Labour Government in 1997 certainly opened possibilities for a more radical approach than had been possible under the previous round of City Pride in London, Manchester and Birmingham (Haughton and While, 1999).

While the impact of the change in approach can be overstated, the resulting *Vision for Leeds* set out an integrated approach to economic, social and environmental issues in the form of a ten-year strategy, with arrangements for annual action plans and continuous monitoring and review (Leeds Initiative, 1999). It was also based on an unprecedented consultation process with stakeholders and residents, and an audit of the current city position — the Leeds Trends Report. Framed as a *Strategy for Sustainable Development,* the central theme of the *Vision* was the need to rethink urban management in order to respond to the challenges of sustainable development. In this sense, the *Vision* was very much about looking for 'win-win-win' opportunities in terms of ensuring that economic development, which remains the key priority, is balanced with social and environmental issues: "Even with its relative prosperity Leeds, too, needs to consider new approaches — not only to respond to new pressures but also to manage change in translating the principles of sustainable development into practice. We need to plan to achieve the simultaneous ambitions of economic prosperity, social equity and environmental protection" (Leeds Initiative, 1999, p.5).

The *Vision for Leeds* was organised around six strategic themes as follows:

- making the most of people — covering education, skills and training and employment, and the contribution of arts, sport and culture to the quality of life of people in the city;

- competing in the global economy — highlighting the importance of Leeds as a regional centre, together with the need to compete economically at the national and international levels;

- integrated transport;

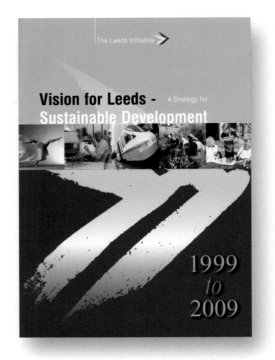

- looking after the environment — protecting the natural environment, ensuring better use of natural resources, improved waste and energy management and the regeneration of environmental damage;

- better neighbourhoods and confident communities — housing, local areas that are safe and free from crime, access to good health facilities, and encouraging community involvement in the provision of local services; and

- information and communications technologies.

In order to develop and deliver the *Vision*, the Leeds Initiative refocused its partnership arrangements. This included broadening the partnership to include the full range of private, public, community and voluntary organisations, facilitating a strategic umbrella group for company and voluntary sectors (Leeds VOICE), increasing the Leeds Initiative's staff base and appointing a chief executive. In addition, individual strategy groups were created to take responsibility for developing and monitoring the six key themes. Each of the separate groups developed a 'daughter strategy', based on consultation with partners and the requirements of government, and containing

an outline of the policy framework and a detailed action plan to take forward the *Vision* theme. Each sub-group reports back to the main Initiative board and executive, which undertake an annual monitoring view of progress on the *Vision for Leeds*. Progress by each group within the Initiative has not been uniformly rapid and far-reaching (While *et al.,* 2002) and there have been some difficulties in ensuring that all the various strands of policy — thematic and area-based — link up effectively.

Since 2001, each local authority has been asked to set up a Local Strategic Partnership (LSP) with the aim of delivering better-targeted, "sustainable economic, social and physical regeneration" through "bringing together at a local level a range of stakeholders from the public, private, voluntary and community sectors. Local partners working through a LSP will be expected to take many of the major decisions about priorities and funding for their local area" (http://www.neighbourhood .gov.uk/partnerships.asp). The Leeds Initiative is nationally regarded as an excellent example of partnership working (I&DEA, 2000) and it is said that the concept of LSPs that has been rolled out nationally was based partly on the Leeds model. The reformulated Leeds Initiative has become the city's LSP with the updated *Vision for Leeds* (Leeds Initiative, 2004) as its Community Strategy, identifying a range of future issues to be considered, including that of narrowing the gap between the 'haves' and the 'have nots'.

II Cities are the backbone of our economy; they are centres of learning, of culture, sport and invention.[1] II

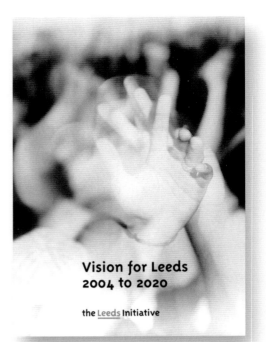

**Vision for Leeds
2004 to 2020**

the Leeds Initiative

Vision II, **the current** *Vision for Leeds* **strategy document published in 2004 that sets out the strengths upon which to build and the problems that need to be addressed over the next two decades.**

1.4 High speed change; two speed city?

Leeds' long history of industrial diversification (Bateman, 1986) helped to ensure that the city did not suffer devastating effects from the downturn in manufacturing from the 1960s to the 1980s (Leigh *et al.,* 1990). Indeed, there remains a varied manufacturing base of mainly small and medium-sized firms. As well as this historical legacy of economic strength, public and private sectors have come together to enhance the appeal of the city. Although it is impossible to determine exactly how much success has been achieved through these deliberate actions, it is undeniable that the fabric of the city has been improved[2] and that a wide range of businesses and activities has been attracted, generated and retained. These then act as a further lure to firms, employees, residents, students and visitors and the cumulative effect of these changes has been the emergence of a new kind of regional capital with a strong basis in financial and business services. This phenomenon of Leeds' transition into the post-industrial age as a 'corporate city' of public-private partnership has been the subject of a previous study (Haughton and Williams, 1996).

A number of significant changes have occurred since the mid-1990s. The arrival of Harvey Nichols in 1996 (into the already impressively refurbished Victoria Quarter) was hailed as a great coup for Leeds and a sign of confidence: it was the Knightsbridge store's first venture outside the capital. The retail area of the city centre continues to attract large numbers of shoppers, and for local people, shopping comes top of the list of the 'good things about Leeds' (Brahm Research, 2003). Further major redevelopments are planned for the retail quarter. The Royal Armouries, a museum containing the nation's collection of arms and armour that relocated to a new building in Leeds in 1996, helped to raise the profile of the city as well as start the re-development of the neglected dockland area. Very few potential waterfront development sites remain. The number of café bars, clubs and restaurants in the city centre has expanded dramatically over the last decade and Leeds is getting closer to its avowed aim of being a '24 hour city'. Not only do many more people now come to or stay in the city after

working hours, but there are new residents inhabiting a high percentage of the 2,000 or so high quality modern apartments that have been built in the city centre over the last few years. A total of around 12,000 apartments could be available for purchase or rent if all proposed schemes go ahead and this could mean up to 18,000 city centre residents (Fox and Unsworth, 2003). Many of these residents work in new and expanded business and financial services companies that are accommodated in new offices in the extended city centre. The upgrading and redevelopment of the physical environment, the growth of the business base and the spread of international brands has undoubtedly given Leeds a cosmopolitan feel that would be surprising to any Leeds native who had been exiled for 20 years. Leeds now has a star in the *Michelin Guide to Great Britain* and two Michelin-starred restaurants. It was voted the UK's most popular destination in September 2003 by readers of the upmarket magazine, *Condé Nast Traveller.* Moreover, in a recent study of 'urban behaviours' that examined professional and recreational practices of eight cities (http://www.henleymc.dk/Newsletter/UrbanBehaviours.pdf), Demetriou (2003) reported that Leeds was the city with the highest percentage of residents who were happy: 68 per cent described their quality of life as being 'excellent'.

Many elements of progress during the *Vision I* period

Table 1.4 *Vision for Leeds* indicators

<table>
<tr><th colspan="2">Headline</th></tr>
<tr><td colspan="2">

- Qualifications of 19-21 year olds
- Total output of the Leeds economy
- Generation and disposal of household waste
- Voter turnout at local election
- Number of crimes reported
- Percentage of households with an internet connection

</td></tr>
<tr><th colspan="2">Supporting</th></tr>
<tr><td colspan="2">

- Training and strategy — movement towards *Vision* objectives
- Spread (difference) of unemployment across Leeds
- Business innovation through information technology
- Number of jobs
- Public transport use during peak hours
- Urban air quality and traffic pollution — meeting Government targets
- Number of people living in Leeds city centre
- Variations across Leeds in people dying from coronary heart disease and strokes

</td></tr>
</table>

Source: Leeds Initiative (2001)

business people was asked which cities in the UK they would consider major centres for business, Leeds came fourth, with 38 per cent of the sample spontaneously mentioning the city (Brahm Research, 2003).

Monitoring and review of the city are also based around six headline, and nine supporting, indicators that were developed by a working group of the Leeds Initiative to track the progress of the city and identify areas where more work is required (Table 1.4).

are quite obvious, but in order to provide a sound basis for setting priorities in *Vision II,* the Leeds Initiative commissioned independent consultants (URBED) to carry out a thorough critical review of progress in economic, social and environmental development in Leeds. It was found that an overwhelming majority of those who took part in the original *Vision for Leeds* process, or who have since been involved in the Leeds Initiative, considered that *Vision I* had influenced the city for good and that with the *Vision,* the city had achieved more than it would have done without it. It was considered that good progress had been made on several of the themes of *Vision I* and that "Leeds has succeeded in changing its image in many quarters from that of a declining northern industrial town to a go-ahead city which is good for business, good for shopping and entertainment, and a good place to live in" (URBED, 2002). One of the key strengths associated with the city is its reputation as a powerful, commercial centre, precipitated by an entrepreneurial culture, with support from the local authority. When a sample of senior

The indicators reflect the dominant emphasis on continued economic growth but also demonstrate a clear commitment to tackling social, health and environmental problems. Several of the indicators show positive trends: quality of life and opportunities are in many respects improving (Leeds Initiative, 2001; 2003b). But this story of prosperity and improving quality of life is not the whole story. Leeds, in common with other cities, is not successful through and through: it has been called a 'two-speed city' described as "up and coming but also down and out" by a participant in a *Vision II* workshop (ibid., p.37). There are significant problems, and these tend to be concentrated in particular areas where there are high levels of unemployment, high incidence of children living in poor households, low educational attainment, poor housing, high levels of crime and anti-social behaviour. Yet the Council — directly and via the Leeds Initiative — has already poured much effort into 'closing the gap' between the less privileged and the more

privileged elements of the population: devising strategies, involving local people, drawing in and using funding and attempting to deal with many of the interconnected factors that make for a low standard of living and a low quality of life. Much of what has been done has followed central government guidelines on neighbourhood renewal and social exclusion, and some successes have been achieved.

The URBED report commented that while there had been "brave, even spectacular examples of community involvement in *Vision I* ... they tend not to be replicated" (ibid, p. 21). "Publicity surrounding successful initiatives may give the impression that the impact is greater than is in fact the case, and it may be assumed that one success will easily breed others. But replicating success requires continuing commitment and energy and rather different mechanisms from those that encourage pioneers" (ibid., p. 21).

As well as these issues of deprivation and the way that it has been tackled, there are also some negative indicators associated with the success of the economy: increased road traffic and congestion and continuing growth in waste. Employers and employees value access by car and parking provision, yet this clashes with the need to reduce congestion, air pollution, accidents (to drivers, pedestrians and cyclists) and to improve viability of public transport. The main investment over the decade has been in improved bus services and a rebuilt bus station, rationalising circulation of traffic around the city centre and closing off some streets to traffic, upgrading of the main railway station, and provision of improved routes and other facilities for cyclists. By 2007, it is intended that a supertram system should be in place to alleviate congestion and to improve economic prospects for some of the less prosperous areas of the city. Waste continues to grow (though at a slightly lower percentage rate), outpacing the progress made in diverting waste from landfill, so the amount of rubbish being dumped each year is still going up, despite efforts to improve recycling rates.

The rise in house prices across much of the city in recent years can be taken as a sign of success: prices are fuelled by

rising incomes of the growing numbers of people working in the strong sectors of the economy. North and north-west Leeds and some of the outlying towns and villages have seen above-average growth in property prices. But in some neighbourhoods, values have stagnated, reflecting low demand. Ten out of 180 communities were classed by the Council as being 'in significant decline' in 2002 and another 41 areas were 'vulnerable'. As well

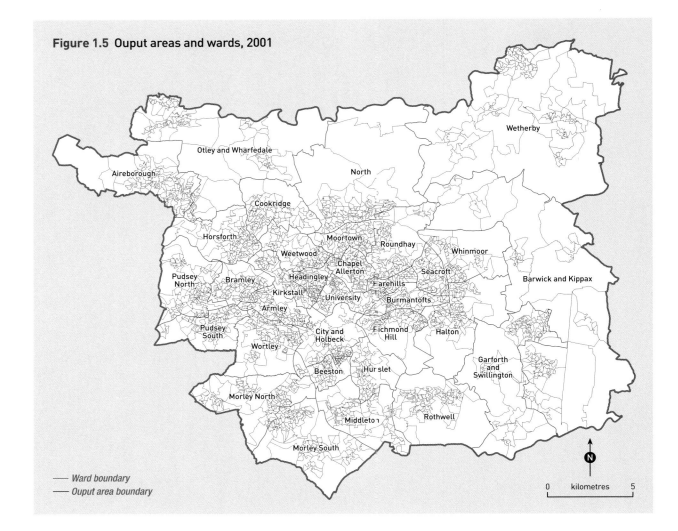

Figure 1.5 Ouput areas and wards, 2001

Wetherby

Otley and Wharfedale

North

Aireborough

Cookridge

Horsforth

Moortown

Roundhay

Whinmoor

Weetwood

Chapel Allerton

Seacroft

Pudsey North

Bramley

Headingley

Farehills

Barwick and Kippax

Kirkstall

University

Burmantofts

Armley

City and Holbeck

Richmond Hill

Halton

Wortley

Pudsey South

Beeston

Hurslet

Garforth and Swillington

Morley North

Middleton

Rothwell

Morley South

N

—— Ward boundary
—— Ouput area boundary

0   kilometres   5

as the issue of what to do about areas of low demand there has also been concern over the lack of appropriate affordable housing for young people, families with children and keyworkers. This mismatch of supply and demand is not unique to Leeds, nor is it as acute as in some other northern towns and cities, but it is a priority area for future policy focus.

1.5 Using the 2001 Census

The results of the 2001 Census began to become available in 2003 and these data represent a huge resource on which to draw in extending our understanding of the small area geographies of Leeds. The results have been produced by the Office of National Statistics (ONS) for a finer spatial scale than ever before: there are 2,439 output areas (OAs), each of which

meets threshold populations of 100 persons and 40 households. The OAs nest into 33 Census wards (Figure 1.5) each with an average population of 21,500 in 9,100 households. The OAs in 2001 compare with the 1,388 enumeration districts (EDs) that constituted the Leeds District in 1991 but which also aggregated into 33 wards (Figure 1.6). A detailed comparison of the ward boundaries between the two censuses indicates very significant correspondence but with parts of the 1991 wards of North, Pudsey, Morley South, Middleton and Rothwell lying outside the 2001 ward designations. Since the 2001 Census, changes have been made with respect to Leeds electoral wards, but the latter have not been used in this book.

Since mapping at OA/ED scale is often impractical for the whole district and because wards are relatively large

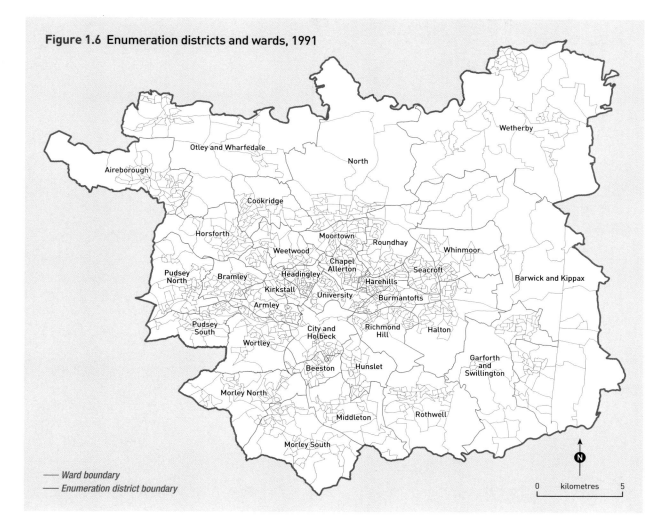

Figure 1.6 Enumeration districts and wards, 1991

Wetherby

Otley and Wharfedale

North

Aireborough

Cookridge

Horsforth

Moortown

Roundhay

Weetwood

Whinmoor

Chapel
Allerton

Pudsey
North

Bramley

Headingley

Seacroft

Barwick and Kippax

Kirkstall

Harehills

University

Armley

Burmantofts

Pudsey
South

City and
Holbeck

Richmond
Hill

Halton

Wortley

Garforth
and
Swillington

Beeston

Hunslet

Morley North

Rothwell

Middleton

Morley South

—— Ward boundary
—— Enumeration district boundary

0   kilometres   5

geographical areas with little functional cohesion, we have chosen to define a further set of small areas through aggregation of OAs to create a set of 106 'community areas' (Figure 1.7) that have spatial coherence and whose names are meaningful to Leeds people. Previous work by the City Council had identified the boundaries of 100 'communities' and the digital version of these data were overlaid on the OA boundaries. Using standard geographical information systems (GIS) intersection routines, each OA was assigned to a community if it fell wholly within a community boundary or if over 50 per cent of its area fell within that boundary. New 'community area' boundaries were then defined by merging the OA polygons in each community. Some OAs were reassigned where community area boundaries clashed with boundary features such major roads, railways or rivers; others were reassigned to improve the 'smoothness' of certain irregularly-shaped areas. Finally, in the more rural suburbs, some of the largest community areas were subdivided using topographical and communication features and parish boundaries.

Census wards, community areas and OAs are used for mapping much of the attribute data contained in the pages that follow. However, super OAs were not defined by ONS in time for their inclusion in this book. There are, however, various other geographical units in Leeds that are used by service providers, including postal sectors and districts, Primary Care Trust (PCT) areas, Arms Length Management Organisation areas (ALMOs), Police Divisions, Single Regeneration Budget (SRB) areas, parliamentary constituencies and Neighbourhood Renewal Areas (NRAs). These will be outlined in further detail where appropriate.

Figure 1.7 Community areas, 2001

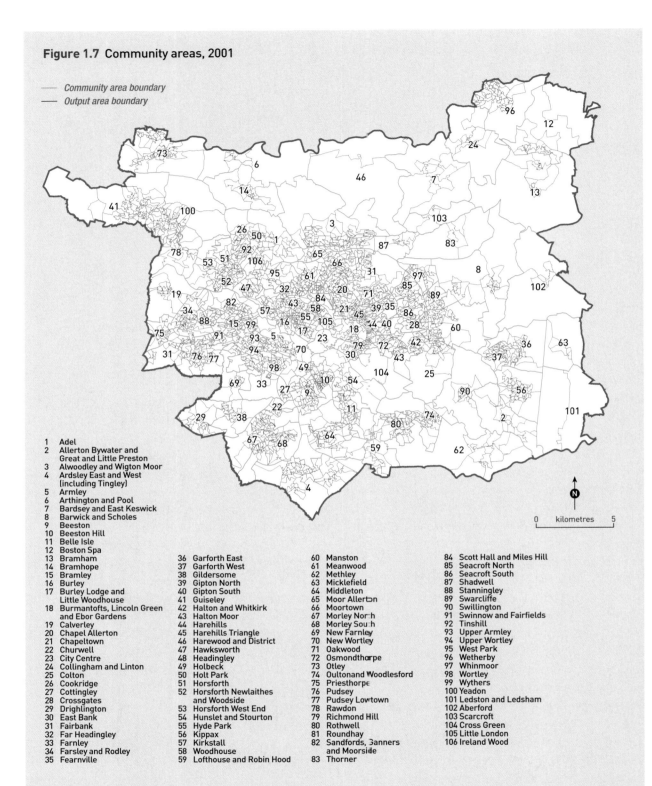

— Community area boundary
— Output area boundary

1	Adel
2	Allerton Bywater and Great and Little Preston
3	Alwoodley and Wigton Moor
4	Ardsley East and West (including Tingley)
5	Armley
6	Arthington and Pool
7	Bardsey and East Keswick
8	Barwick and Scholes
9	Beeston
10	Beeston Hill
11	Belle Isle
12	Boston Spa
13	Bramham
14	Bramhope
15	Bramley
16	Burley
17	Burley Lodge and Little Woodhouse
18	Burmantofts, Lincoln Green and Ebor Gardens
19	Calverley
20	Chapel Allerton
21	Chapeltown
22	Churwell
23	City Centre
24	Collingham and Linton
25	Colton
26	Cookridge
27	Cottingley
28	Crossgates
29	Drighlington
30	East Bank
31	Fairbank
32	Far Headingley
33	Farnley
34	Farsley and Rodley
35	Fearnville

36	Garforth East
37	Garforth West
38	Gildersome
39	Gipton North
40	Gipton South
41	Guiseley
42	Halton and Whitkirk
43	Halton Moor
44	Harehills
45	Harehills Triangle
46	Harewood and District
47	Hawksworth
48	Headingley
49	Holbeck
50	Holt Park
51	Horsforth
52	Horsforth Newlaithes and Woodside
53	Horsforth West End
54	Hunslet and Stourton
55	Hyde Park
56	Kippax
57	Kirkstall
58	Woodhouse
59	Lofthouse and Robin Hood

60	Manston
61	Meanwood
62	Methley
63	Micklefield
64	Middleton
65	Moor Allerton
66	Moortown
67	Morley North
68	Morley South
69	New Farnley
70	New Wortley
71	Oakwood
72	Osmondthorpe
73	Otley
74	Oulton and Woodlesford
75	Priesthorpe
76	Pudsey
77	Pudsey Lowtown
78	Rawdon
79	Richmond Hill
80	Rothwell
81	Roundhay
82	Sandfords, Ganners and Moorside
83	Thorner

84	Scott Hall and Miles Hill
85	Seacroft North
86	Seacroft South
87	Shadwell
88	Stanningley
89	Swarcliffe
90	Swillington
91	Swinnow and Fairfields
92	Tinshill
93	Upper Armley
94	Upper Wortley
95	West Park
96	Wetherby
97	Whinmoor
98	Wortley
99	Wythers
100	Yeadon
101	Ledston and Ledsham
102	Aberford
103	Scarcroft
104	Cross Green
105	Little London
106	Ireland Wood

A printable version of this map is available at www.leeds.ac.uk/publications/21stCentury Leeds/

*So what exists in cities? How can we hold
onto their potential and variety?*[3]

1.6 Coverage

Description and analysis of any city must attempt to take into account that it is not a closed system: materials, goods, people, money, ideas, information and pollution are constantly crossing city boundaries and over time, sources and destinations of many elements of city life are increasingly distant from the city itself. Resources are drawn in from across the globe and outputs travel to far away places or connect into complex regional, national and international networks, both physical and virtual. However, we can still attempt to describe and analyse those elements of the city that can be pinned down within its physical boundaries as well as adding to the portrait some commentary and comparative data about Leeds in its wider context. This book attempts to embrace the main themes of urban structure and life and is a progression from Haughton and Williams's earlier volume. There is a stronger focus on the geographical dimension and we have used the 2001 Census and other databases to generate detailed maps of a wide variety of attributes of the city. The analysis of the current scene and the processes of change help us to formulate ideas about likely future directions of change.

"In a large populous town like Leeds, the changes which are constantly taking place are such as to render a directory nearly obsolete at the expiration of two years" (Preface to Slade and Roebuck Trade Directory, 1851, p.iii). Cities never stand still, and certainly since the onset of the Industrial Revolution, each successive generation has probably had the sense that the pace of change in their own time is uniquely and unsurpassably rapid. Technological, demographic, organisational and economic changes and their impacts on the built environment and the patterns of occupation and movement within it, occur at a bewildering pace. Even for those thoroughly caught up in and acting as principal agents of the whirl of physical and organisational change, the city is never knowable in its entirety at any point in time. Despite a massive range of analysed data sets and the combined knowledge of a long list of researchers and practitioners whose experience has been drawn on to produce this book,

we cannot contrive to be comprehensive. Some might argue that sophisticated manipulation of large amounts of data and its presentation in maps gives a sanitised and therefore inaccurate picture of the city: it becomes a series of annotated 'butterflies in a cabinet'. Even a version of this publication provided on the web with regular updating would not address all the inadequacies of the approach. What is needed perhaps is a companion volume of experiences of female and male residents of different ages and social backgrounds, workers, students and visitors at the opening of the twenty-first century. Keith Waterhouse (1994), for example, provides us with a vivid example of a personal perspective on life in Leeds from the 1930s. A contemporary volume focusing on personal experiences might discuss the way that individuals contribute to and apprehend the structures and processes that build and energise the city, the ways that people move through and use the different spaces, their connections into the physical, electronic, political and social networks, and the multiple layers of meaning that are part of the thousands of versions of Leeds which are held in the heads of those who live, work and play in the city. Maybe some of these elements of Leeds will be represented in the new City Museum.

Our selection of topics and ways of presenting and interpreting them are not simply objective portrayals of a fully grasped reality; we bring our experiences, prejudices, selectivity and particular skills and enthusiasms to the task. However, we have attempted to focus primarily on presenting a factually-rich account which nonetheless is much more than a fact file and an advertisement for the city: we have analysed and criticised elements of the way the city has changed and the way that it is facing the challenges of the new century.

The chapters of this book are organised according to broad themes of population, well-being, economy, consumption and planning for the future, and three chapters are presented under each theme.

Notes

1   Quotation from Leeds Initiative (2003a).
2   Over the ten years to 2003, £2.3 billion of property investments were completed. Office developments accounted for about one third of this sum and retail and leisure investments for another third. Schemes under construction represent investment of a further £759 million. Developments amounting to £2.5 billion are proposed (LCC, 2003b).
3   Quotation from Amin and Thrift (2002).

References

Amin, A. and Thrift, N. (2002) *Cities: Reimagining the Urban,* Polity Press, Cambridge.

Bateman, M. (1986) Leeds: a study in regional supremacy, in Gordon, G. (ed) *Regional Cities in the UK 1890–1980,* Harper and Row, London, pp. 99–115.

Brahm Research (2003) *Towards a City Image Marketing Campaign for Leeds: A Regional, National and International View,* research findings prepared for the Leeds Initiative, October.

Brown, A.J. (1967) What is the Leeds region? in Beresford, M.W. and Jones, G.R.J. (eds.) *Leeds and its Region,* Leeds Local Executive Committee of the British Association for the Advancement of Science, Leeds, pp. 200–214.

Burt, S. and Grady, K. (1994) *The Illustrated History of Leeds,* Breedon Books, Derby.

CURDS (1999) *The Economic Links between Leeds and the Yorkshire and Humber Region,* report commissioned by Leeds City Council, CURDS, University of Newcastle-upon-Tyne, Newcastle.

Demetriou, D. (2003) Pride of the north: Leeds is best place to live in the UK, *The Independent,* 30 November.

English Heritage (1984) *Register of Parks and Gardens of Special Historic Interest in England, Part 45: West Yorkshire,* London.

Fox, P. and Unsworth, R. (2003) *City Living in Leeds: Here to Stay,* report published by KW Linfoot plc and School of Geography, University of Leeds, Leeds.

Hall, P., Marshall, S. and Lowe, M. (2001) The changing urban hierarchy of England and Wales, 1913–1998, *Regional Studies,* 35: 775–807.

Haughton, G. and While, A. (1999) From corporate city to citizens' city? Urban leadership after local entrepreneurialism in the UK, *Urban Affairs Review,* 35(0): 3–23.

Haughton, G. and Williams, C.C. (1996) Leeds: a case of second city syndrome?, in Haughton, G. and Williams, C. (eds) *Corporate City? Partnership, Participation and Partition in Urban Development in Leeds,* Avebury, Aldershot.

Improvement and Development Agency (I&DEA) (2000) *Report: Leeds City Council,* report based on visit to Leeds City Council as part of the Local Government Improvement Programme, 5–9 June.

Leeds City Council (LCC) (2001) *Leeds Unitary Development Plan,* LCC, Leeds.

Leeds City Council (LCC) (2003a) *Leeds City Council Plan 2003–2004,* LCC, Leeds.

Leeds City Council (LCC) (2003b) *Leeds Economy Bulletin,* February, LCC, Leeds.

Leeds Economy Partnership (2003) *Leeds Economy Handbook 2003,* Leeds City Council Development Department, Leeds.

Leeds Initiative (1999) *Vision for Leeds,* Leeds Initiative, Leeds.

Leeds Initiative (2001) *Vision for Leeds Indicators,* Leeds Initiative, Leeds.

Leeds Initiative (2003a) *Leeds: The Business City. An Interim Prospectus for a Competitive European City-region in a World Class Region,* Leeds Initiative, Leeds.

Leeds Initiative (2003b) *Making Progress: Indicators for the Vision for Leeds,* Leeds Initiative, Leeds.

Leeds Initiative (2004) *Vision for Leeds 2004 to 2020,* The Leeds Initiative Office, Leeds.

Leigh, C.M., Stillwell, J.C.H. and Wilson, A.G. (1990) *Manufacturing Under Pressure: Yorkshire and Humberside in Profile,* report for Barclays Bank plc, School of Geography, University of Leeds, Leeds.

Llewellyn-Davies, Steers Davies Gleave, Jones Lang LaSalle and University of Leeds (2002) *Leeds and Environs Spatial Strategy,* Final Scoping Report for the Yorkshire and Humber Assembly and others.

Office of the Deputy Prime Minister (ODPM) (2004) *Competitive European GHPs: Where Do the Core Cities Stand?,* Urban Research Summary 13, ODPM, London.

Robert Huggins Associates (2002) *The State of Urban Britain — UK Competitiveness Index 2002: City, Metropolitan and Ward Benchmarking,* Robert Huggins Business and Economic Policy Press, Pontypridd.

Slade and Roebuck (1851) *Directory of the Borough and Neighbourhood of Leeds 1851,* Slade and Roebuck, Leeds.

URBED (2002) *Vision for Leeds II: Lessons from Vision I,* draft report for Leeds City Council (unpublished).

Waterhouse, K. (1994) *City Lights: A Street Life,* Hodder and Stoughton, London.

White, A., Gibbs, D. and Jonas, A. (2002) *Environment as good governance: sustainability and the Vision for Leeds, Governance and Regulation in Local Environmental Policy Making,* Case-study Working Paper Number 5, Department of Geography, University of Hull, Hull.

Yorkshire Evening Post (2003) *Supplement,* 17 September.

2

The City is the People:
Demographic Structure and Dynamics

PHIL REES, JOHN STILLWELL & AMY TYLER-JONES

...Leeds was the only one of the core cities to experience growth during the last decade.

2.1 Introduction

According to the 'One Number Census', the population of Leeds had reached 715,000 individuals by 29 April 2001. The Office of National Statistics (ONS) produces annual mid-year estimates which, when revised in the light of the 2001 Census results, indicate that the population grew by around 1.3 per cent over the decade. This rate of change was less than half the Great Britain average of 2.7 per cent between 1991 and 2001 and suggests a degree of demographic stability, particularly when compared with the seven other core cities. As indicated in Chapter 1 and in Champion (2004), Leeds was the only one of the core cities to experience population growth during the last decade; the populations of Liverpool and Newcastle declined by 7 per cent and 5 per cent respectively, whilst more modest falls in population occurred in the other core cities. On the basis of population size, Leeds is second to Birmingham in the provincial city league table. By April 2001, with the exception of around 10,200 individuals living in communal establishments, the people of Leeds were living in 301,600 households with an average household size of 2.34 residents, slightly lower than the average for England and Wales.

There is, in fact, considerable uncertainty surrounding the exact population of Leeds in 1991 because of problems relating to census underenumeration and because students were enumerated at their place of parental domicile rather than their term-time address. However, in this chapter, we attempt to make comparisons between Leeds and England and Wales at different points in time, beginning with an examination of demographic structures using population pyramids in 1991 and 2001. Thereafter, spatial variations in broad age groups of the population and dependency ratios between 1991 and 2001 are examined. A classification of community areas based on age

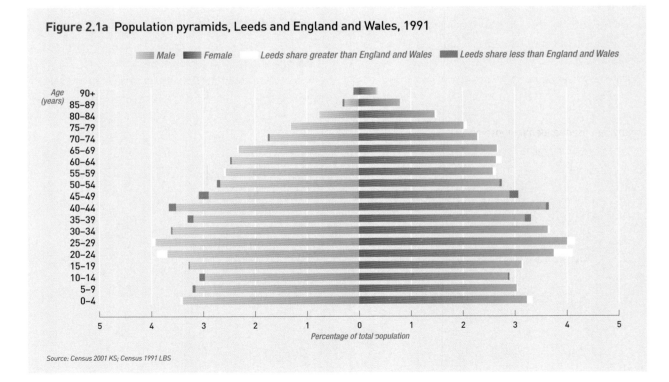

Figure 2.1a Population pyramids, Leeds and England and Wales, 1991

Male   Female   Leeds share greater than England and Wales   Leeds share less than England and Wales

Age (years): 90+, 85–89, 80–84, 75–79, 70–74, 65–69, 60–64, 55–59, 50–54, 45–49, 40–44, 35–39, 30–34, 25–29, 20–24, 15–19, 10–14, 5–9, 0–4

Percentage of total population

Source: Census 2001 KS; Census 1991 LBS

Figure 2.1b Population pyramids, Leeds and England and Wales, 2001

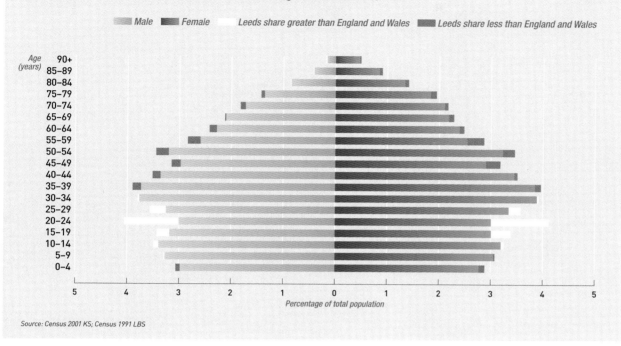

Source: Census 2001 KS; Census 1991 LBS

structure is outlined and a brief analysis of household characteristics in 2001 is followed by an exploration of two selected aspects of Leeds' population dynamics. First, life expectancies at birth are computed for wards in 1991 and 2001 and their relationship with deprivation indices is used to estimate life expectancies for community areas. Second, flows of migrants between Leeds and other parts of the country during the 1990s derived from NHS patient re-registration systems are used to identify those areas with which Leeds has major net losses or gains. Finally, the presentation of future trends in population change based on the ONS 1996-based projections to 2021 enable us to explore some of the challenges facing the city in the coming decades.

2.2 Demographic structure

The population size and demographic structure of an area are determined by the components of natural change — births and deaths — and by the flows of migrants that enter and exit that area in the course of time. Migration has been the key driver of population dynamics for different parts of the UK (Stillwell *et al.*, 1992) since fertility and mortality levels have tended

towards a stable equilibrium. However, the legacy of variations in the size of birth cohorts is evident in many of the pyramids of contemporary populations. We can track the bulge in the population caused by the post-war baby boom in the population pyramids for England and Wales and Leeds between 1991 and 2001 (Figure 2.1). Those cohorts of men and women aged 40–44 in 1991 and 50–54 in 2001, who were born in the late 1940s and early 1950s, are larger in size than the younger cohorts aged 35–39 in 1991 and 45–49 in 2001, whilst those in their 30s in 2001 were born during the 1960s when birth rates were at a post-war high. The demographic structure of Leeds shows some differences from the national structure in 1991, most noticeably in the 20–24 age group for males and females, where there is over-representation, and in the 45–49 age group where there is under-representation. Increasing student numbers during the 1990s and their enumeration at their term-time address in the 2001 Census explains why the 20–24 age group proportion for Leeds in 2001 is larger than in 1991 and in the corresponding cohort for England and Wales. The reduction in cohort size that has occurred over the last 15 years at the national level is also apparent at the local level.

The balance between males and females in the

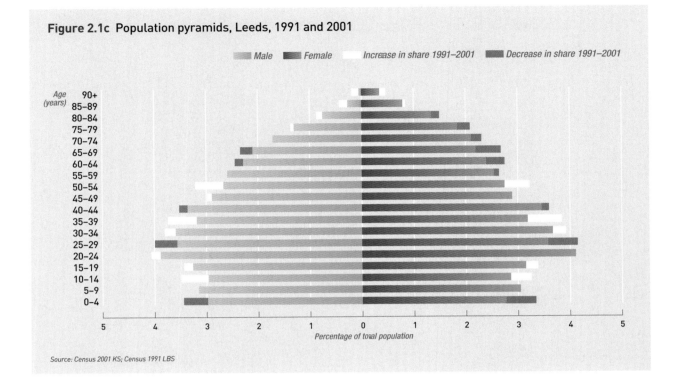

Figure 2.1c Population pyramids, Leeds, 1991 and 2001

Male ▮ Female ▮ Increase in share 1991–2001 ▯ Decrease in share 1991–2001

Age (years)

90+
85–89
80–84
75–79
70–74
65–69
60–64
55–59
50–54
45–49
40–44
35–39
30–34
25–29
20–24
15–19
10–14
5–9
0–4

5   4   3   2   1   0   1   2   3   4   5

Percentage of total population

Source: Census 2001 KS; Census 1991 LBS

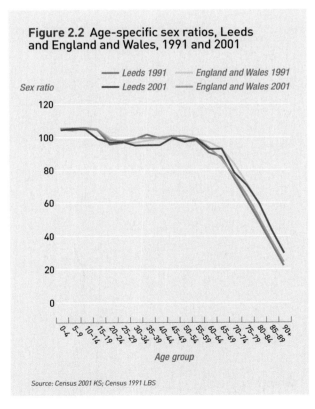

Figure 2.2 Age-specific sex ratios, Leeds and England and Wales, 1991 and 2001

—— Leeds 1991   —— England and Wales 1991
—— Leeds 2001   —— England and Wales 2001

Sex ratio

120
100
80
60
40
20
0

0-4 5-9 10-14 15-19 20-24 25-29 30-34 35-39 40-44 45-49 50-54 55-59 60-64 65-69 70-74 75-79 80-84 85-89 90+

Age group

Source: Census 2001 KS; Census 1991 LBS

population can be examined using sex ratios (males per 100 females) (Clarke, 2000). In aggregate terms, there are approximately 93 males for every 100 females in the Leeds population, which is lower than the national average. The age-specific sex ratios for Leeds compared with England and Wales in 1991 and 2001 are shown in Figure 2.2. Higher death rates for men post-retirement are responsible for the reduction in the sex ratio in older ages, such that by age 75–79, there are 70 men to 100 women and after the age of 90, there are only 30 men in Leeds to every 100 women. To sum up, the city of Leeds exhibits an age-sex profile close to the national average, except in the student ages.

2.3 Geographical variations in population structure

Before we examine the spatial patterns of age groups in Leeds, we outline some expectations based on many decades of work on socio-economic sorting within cities by researchers in the USA and Europe. One key finding is that different housing areas attract families at different stages in the life course — crudely, suburbs provide larger homes for families with children, whilst

Figure 2.3 Percentage of the population aged 0–15, by community area, (a) 1991 and (b) 2001

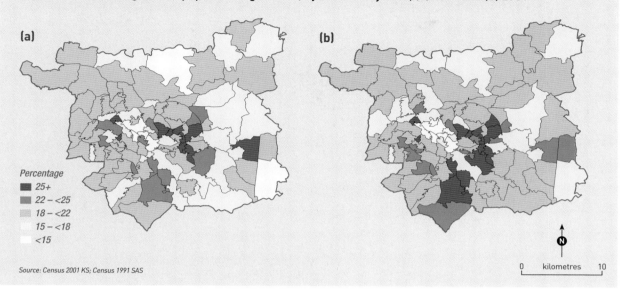

(a)

(b)

Percentage
- ■ 25+
- 22 – <25
- 18 – <22
- 15 – <18
- <15

Source: Census 2001 KS; Census 1991 SAS

N

0   kilometres   10

inner neighbourhoods provide smaller dwelling units for single, couples or multi-member households. But this very simple picture is altered through several processes including ageing-in-place, invasion-and-succession, and the emergence of different fertility behaviour (and numbers of children per family) in different social classes or ethnic groups.

Ageing-in-place occurs when families settle in a neighbourhood in the first stage of child rearing, raise their children there, and stay on as 'empty nesters' and into retirement. Invasion-and-succession may occur when one age cohort displaces others. The settling of students into inner city neighbourhoods close to their places of education has been an on-going phenomenon in may UK cities and Leeds is no exception. The process involves purchase of family accommodation by landlords and letting after conversion at higher rents to multi-adult households. Different fertility behaviours have emerged between the social classes as a result of the second demographic transition — the movement to permanently low replacement fertility rates by western developed country populations. Middle class women now have good working career prospects and the means to control their fertility, which has been either postponed into their thirties or abandoned altogether (increasing childlessness). Lower class women with less good prospects are likely to raise larger families.

Geographical variations are therefore to be expected in demographic structures and, in this section, we compare the percentage distributions of the population in three broad age groups: children age 15 and under, the population of working age defined as 16 to 64; and the elderly population aged 65 and over. In order to identify change over time, broad age

The city comes to life; citizens and visitors of all ages enjoy the ambience of Millennium Square, the public space in front of the Civic Hall that regularly becomes the focus of commercial and cultural activities.

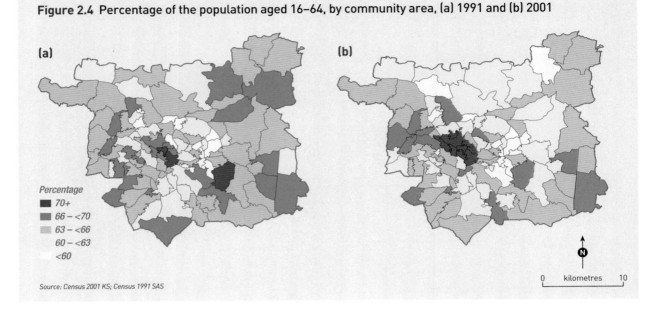

Figure 2.4 Percentage of the population aged 16–64, by community area, (a) 1991 and (b) 2001

(a)

(b)

Percentage
- 70+
- 66 – <70
- 63 – <66
- 60 – <63
- <60

N

0   kilometres   10

Source: Census 2001 KS; Census 1991 SAS

group populations for enumeration districts (EDs) in 1991 have been aggregated to create best fit community areas as defined in 2001. ED populations have been added together when their centroids fall within the same community area using a point in polygon technique. The distribution of children and young teenagers (Figure 2.3) as a percentage of total population shows concentrations in the east and to the south of the city centre and children comprise 25 per cent or more of the populations of an increasing number of community areas.

The working population distributions (Figure 2.4) include the student age groups, whose expansion between 1991 and 2001 is visible in those community areas to the north west of the city centre that include Hyde Park, Burley Lodge and Little Woodhouse and Headingley. Data from the University of Leeds Residential and Commercial Services for the locations of 23,500 students at the University of Leeds in 2003 confirm this concentration. The pie charts shown in Figure 2.5 represent the number of students resident in community areas in this part of the city, differentiated according to whether they are first year undergraduates, second, third and fourth year undergraduates or postgraduates. There is a strong coincidence, of course, between the locations of halls of residence (shown also in Figure 2.5) and first year undergraduates.

Finally, we note the emerging contrast between the south and west of Leeds and the north and east in terms of the proportion of the population that is aged 65 or over (Figure 2.6). The pensioner populations have increased in the north and east and the geographical pattern in 2001 is less fragmented than it was in 1991. Many of the community areas in the outer suburbs now have over 20 per cent of their populations in this post-retirement age range.

Pedestrianised areas in the city centre attract young teenage skateboarders. In 2001, there were high concentrations of those aged 0–15 to the east and south of the city centre.

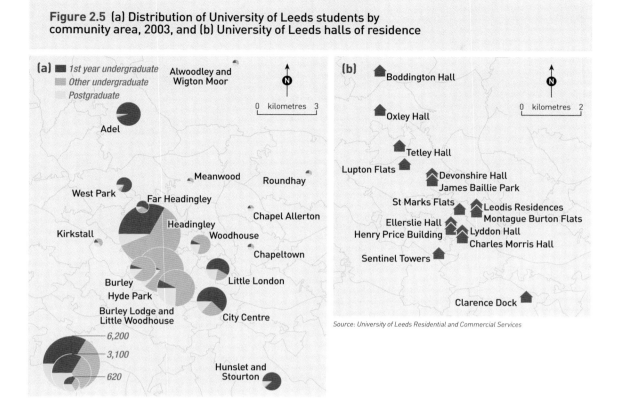

Figure 2.5 (a) Distribution of University of Leeds students by community area, 2003, and (b) University of Leeds halls of residence

(a) ■ 1st year undergraduate
▨ Other undergraduate
▨ Postgraduate

Alwoodley and Wigton Moor

N

0   kilometres   3

Adel

Meanwood   Roundhay

West Park   Far Headingley

Headingley   Chapel Allerton

Kirkstall   Woodhouse

Chapeltown

Burley   Little London
Hyde Park

Burley Lodge and   City Centre
Little Woodhouse

6,200

3,100

620

Hunslet and
Stourton

(b)   Boddington Hall

N

0   kilometres   2

Oxley Hall

Tetley Hall

Lupton Flats

Devonshire Hall
James Baillie Park

St Marks Flats

Leodis Residences
Montague Burton Flats

Ellerslie Hall

Henry Price Building   Lyddon Hall

Charles Morris Hall

Sentinel Towers

Clarence Dock

Source: University of Leeds Residential and Commercial Services

An alternative way of examining the spatial variations in age that characterise the city is to compute dependency ratios; measures of the proportions of the population composed of dependants (people who are too young or too old to work). Dependency ratios can be defined for children and the elderly respectively as the number of individuals aged 15 or under or 65 and above divided by the number of individuals aged 16 to 64, expressed as a percentage. A rising dependency ratio is a major concern where the population is ageing, since it becomes difficult for pension and social security systems to provide for a significantly older, non-working population. The highest child dependency ratios in Leeds form a ring within the inner suburbs whereas the highest ratios for the elderly are found in the outer suburbs to the north and east of the city centre.

Between 1991 and 2001, the total dependency ratio increased but this change was not consistent across the city (Figure 2.7). In fact, the growing volume of students living in the Leeds 6 area of the city is responsible for the reduced dependency ratios in several of the community areas to the north west of the city centre. The largest increases in

The student population of Leeds has increased significantly in line with the expansion of higher education in the 1990s. An increasing number of students are now living at home during their undergraduate years.

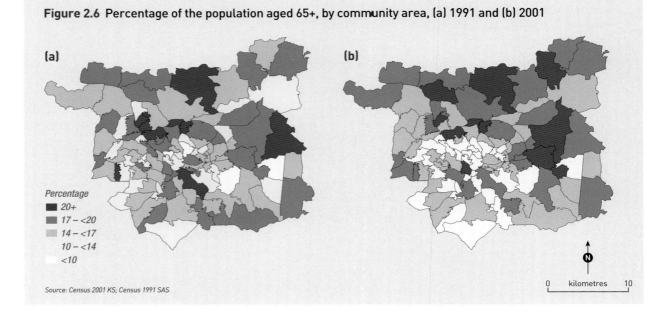

Figure 2.6 Percentage of the population aged 65+, by community area, (a) 1991 and (b) 2001

(a)

(b)

Percentage
■ 20+
■ 17 – <20
■ 14 – <17
   10 – <14
   <10

Source: Census 2001 KS; Census 1991 SAS

0   kilometres   10

Table 2.1 Populations of communal establishments in Leeds, 2001

Type of communal establishment	Residents	
	Number	%
NHS Psychiatric hospital/home	157	1.54
NHS Other hospital/home	144	1.42
Local Authority children's home	113	1.11
Local Authority residential care home	809	7.95
Housing Association home or hostel	118	1.16
Nursing home	1,920	18.87
Residential care home	1,630	16.02
Psychiatric hospital/home	73	0.72
Children's home	36	0.35
Prison Service	1,179	11.59
Probation/Bail hostel	68	0.67
Education establishment	3,251	31.95
Hotel; Boarding house; Guest house	61	0.60
Hostel	189	1.86
Other	427	4.20
Total	10,175	100.00

Source: Census 2001 CAS

dependency are apparent in Bardsey and East Keswick, Collingham and Linton, and Cookridge in the northern suburbs, Cross Green, Colton, Swillington and Crossgates in the east and Wythers in the west.

The increasing burden of dependency is likely to result in an increasing number of older people in nursing and residential care homes. The Census recorded over 3,500 people in these homes in Leeds in 2001, representing over one third of all those in communal establishments in the local authority area (Table 2.1). Figure 2.8 illustrates the distributions of those living in medical and care institutions (the first nine categories in Table 2.1) across the community areas of Leeds. A further third consists of students in halls of residence and the other major group is the prison population, which is about 12 per cent of the total, although this figure is likely to be an underestimate. In fact, HM Prison Service statistics indicate that there were 1,248 people at Armley jail in November 2003, 604 at Wealstun and a further 287 at the Young Offenders Institution in Wetherby.

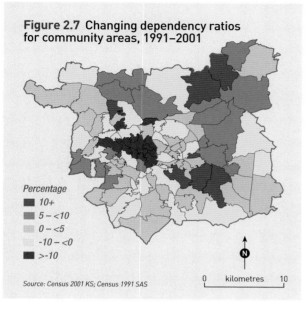

Figure 2.7 Changing dependency ratios for community areas, 1991–2001

Percentage
- ■ 10+
- ■ 5 – <10
- ■ 0 – <5
- ■ -10 – <0
- ■ >-10

Source: Census 2001 KS; Census 1991 SAS

0   kilometres   10

N

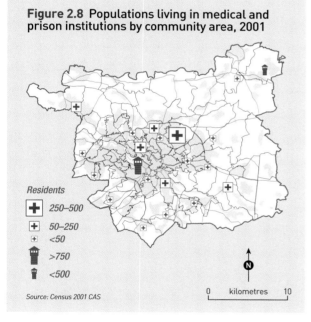

Figure 2.8 Populations living in medical and prison institutions by community area, 2001

Residents
- ✚ 250–500
- ✚ 50–250
- ✚ <50
- ♜ >750
- ♜ <500

Source: Census 2001 CAS

0   kilometres   10

N

Finally, the sex ratio varies geographically across the city. Very few community areas have a surplus of men over women. The only exceptions are in the centre of the city where hostels for the homeless are found. The highest ratios of women to men are also those areas with the highest proportion of older residents. Women's better survival experience to older ages means that the older the age group after retirement, the greater the surplus of women (though this is likely to reduce somewhat as men are catching up in the life expectancy stakes).

2.4 Demographic classification of community areas

To investigate further the geographic variation in demographic structure across Leeds, a statistical clustering method can be used to classify small areas according to their demographic structure. The K-means approach can be used to identify relatively homogenous groups of small areas which demonstrate similar characteristics of a given variable, age in this instance. Thus, we use K-means to construct a classification of community areas in Leeds according to their population age structures.

For each community area, a breakdown of population structure is provided by the proportion of the population within five-year age groups. The K-means function in the statistical package SPSS uses an algorithm to group areas with similar distributions of the population in five-year age groups. This process requires the user to initially determine the desired number of clusters. Two considerations are made when determining the desired number of clusters. Firstly, similarity within clusters should be maximised. Average distance from cluster centre indicates similarity within the cluster. The optimum number of clusters should minimise the average distance from cluster centre. The results suggest that for less than eight clusters, the average distance rises more steeply but beyond 12 clusters there is little further decline in average distance, therefore the optimum number of clusters will be between 8 and 12. The second factor to consider when determining the number of clusters to use is the number of community areas within each cluster. It helps if there are a relatively even number of community areas in each group. The problem that arises is that some clusters contain only one or two community areas because of outliers in the data set. In this case, Hyde Park, Headingley and City Centre were removed from the classification and an optimal 10 cluster solution was generated (Table 2.2).

Figure 2.9 Population pyramids for ten clusters

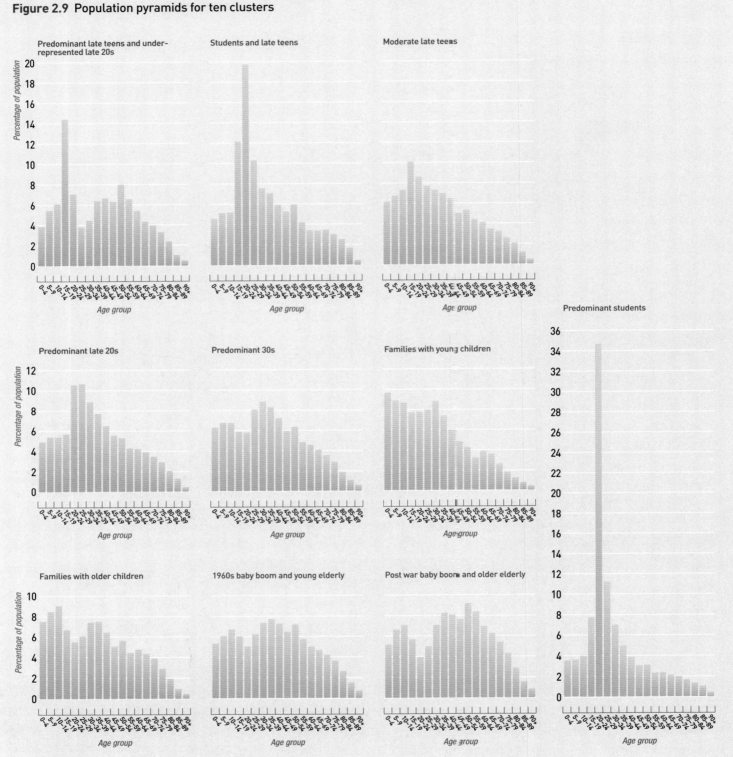

Table 2.2 Ten cluster solution with labels

Cluster	Number of cases*	Group label
1	2	Predominant late teens and under-represented late 20s
2	3	Predominant students
3	2	Students and late teens
4	4	Moderate late teens
5	2	Predominant late 20s
6	27	Predominant 30s
7	4	Families with young children
8	10	Families with older children
9	32	1960s baby boom and younger elderly predominant
10	17	Post-war baby boom and older elderly predominant

*Outliers excluded: Hyde Park and Headingley ('Extreme students') and City Centre

Population pyramids have been constructed to illustrate the contrast in demographic structure of the ten clusters and to help interpret the different cluster profiles (Figure 2.9). The pyramids have been constructed taking the final cluster centre for each five-year age group. Final cluster centres are calculated as the mean of each variable within the final clusters. The clusters have then been renamed according to the five-year age groups which are under- or over-represented within the cluster group. Thus, cluster 1, 'predominant late teens and under-represented late twenties' are community areas in which 15 per cent of the population are 15–19 years old and only 4 per cent are 25–29 years old. Cluster 2 is also characterised by a high proportion of students with 35 per cent of the population aged 20–24 years old; this cluster is labelled 'predominant students'. Cluster 3, renamed 'students and late teens', has 18 per cent of the population aged 20–24 and 11 per cent aged 15–19. Cluster 4 contained a fairly even spread of five-year age groups with a slightly higher proportion within the 15–19 age group (10 per cent) and is labelled 'moderate late teens'.

Cluster 5 has been renamed 'predominant late twenties' as 11 per cent of the population are aged 25–29. Cluster 6 is dominated by the 30 year old age groups with over 8 per cent in both the 30–34 and 35–39 year ages, and has therefore been labelled 'predominant thirties'. Clusters 7 and 8 have similar demographic structures with the distinction that and cluster 7 has a high proportion of 0–4 year olds (10 per cent) and cluster 8 has a high proportion of 10–14 year olds (9 per cent). These clusters have therefore been named 'families with

young children' and 'families with older children' respectively. Two clusters are dominated by baby boom cohorts. The first, cluster 9, is dominated by the 1960s baby boom cohort with 8 per cent of population aged 35–39 years and has been termed '1960s baby boom and younger elderly predominant'. The second, cluster 10, is 'post-war baby boom and older elderly predominant' and has 8.3 per cent of the population in the 50–54 age group and 9 per cent aged over 75.

As noted in the methodology, three outliers were removed from the analysis. Expansion of student numbers and concentration of student residence within the adjacent areas to

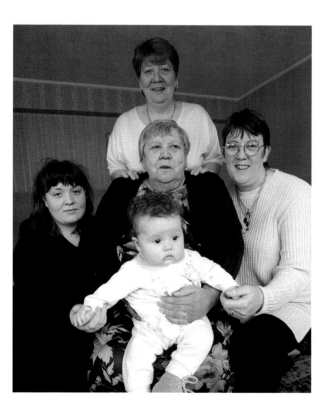

Five generations of one family from Saxton Gardens, as featured in the Yorkshire Post in 1999. This occurrence is increasingly unusual as age at marriage increases and as child-bearing is delayed.

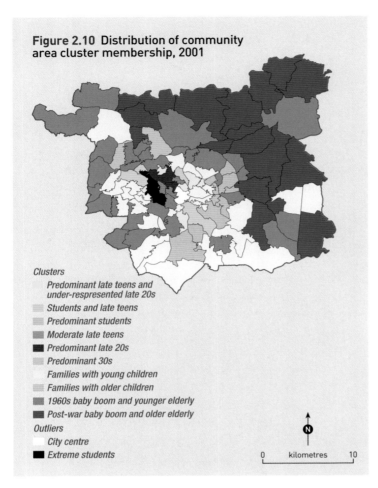

Figure 2.10 Distribution of community area cluster membership, 2001

Clusters
- Predominant late teens and under-respresented late 20s
- Students and late teens
- Predominant students
- Moderate late teens
- Predominant late 20s
- Predominant 30s
- Families with young children
- Families with older children
- 1960s baby boom and younger elderly
- Post-war baby boom and older elderly

Outliers
- City centre
- Extreme students

0   kilometres   10

the two universities in recent years has had a profound impact on the demographic structure of these areas. Two of the outliers removed from the K-means analysis, Headingley and Hyde Park, contained the highest proportion of students and have consequently been grouped together and labelled 'extreme students' with 38 per cent and 58 per cent of the population in the 20–24 age group respectively. The third outlier was the city centre and, as might be expected, this area has a very youthful population structure with 75 per cent of the population aged between 15 and 35.

The age structure derived clusters are distributed in a clear spatial structure (Figure 2.10). One set of clusters is characterised by greater or lesser concentrations in the student ages. Cluster 1 community areas (predominant late teens and under-represented late twenties) are found in only two locations containing two large student halls of residence/flats occupied by first and second year undergraduates. Some of this

group and older students are found in inner north west Leeds in cluster 2 (predominant students) and the two community areas removed from the cluster analysis and treated separately (extreme students). On the periphery of these inner north west Leeds clusters are found community areas belonging to cluster 3 (students and late teens). Cluster 4 (moderate late teens) community areas are adjacent to the main student age areas and contain some student residences but not at such high concentrations. Cluster 5 (predominant late twenties) areas are found to the west of the main student concentrations and are areas in which young persons beginning their careers can find starter homes.

A second set of clusters shows the distribution of couples and families at different stages in the family life course located in successive rings around the inner city. Cluster 6 (predominant thirties) are found in the next ring of suburbs and in outer areas to the south and west of the city. Then comes cluster 7 (families with younger children) community areas and cluster 8 (families with older children) a little further from the centre. Beyond these in the outer ring of the city, particularly to the north and east are the cohorts born in the 1960s (cluster 9: 1960s baby boom and younger elderly) and in the 1944–59 period (cluster 10: post-war baby boom and older elderly) with concentrations of older people as well. These areas are where the successful older generations live.

2.5 Household composition

Households in Leeds are split between three types of household: one person households (32 per cent), one family and no others (61 per cent) and other types of household (7 per cent). These categories are in turn subdivided into 15 groups (Table 2.3) that present a picture of household composition in Leeds vis-à-vis that of England and Wales. Leeds has a higher proportion of all student households, of non-pensioner one person households and of lone parent households with dependent children. A dependent child is a person aged 0-15 (whether or not in a family) or a person aged

Table 2.3 Household composition characteristics, 2001

Households comprising	Leeds		England and Wales
	Number	%	%
One person			
Pensioner	43,309	14.36	14.43
Other	52,142	17.29	15.59
One family and no others			
All pensioner	25,574	8.48	8.97
Married couple households			
no children	35,736	11.85	13.00
with one three more dependent children	47,953	15.90	17.56
all children non-dependent	16,898	5.60	5.99
Cohabiting couple family households			
no children	15,637	5.18	4.72
with one or more dependent children	10,485	3.48	3.24
all children non-dependent	1,125	0.37	0.32
Lone parent households			
with one or more dependent children	21,249	7.05	6.46
all children non-dependent	8,340	2.77	3.06
Other households			
With one or more dependent children	7,176	2.38	2.23
All student	3,563	1.18	0.39
All pensioner	1,225	0.41	0.41
Other	11,202	3.71	3.62
Total	301,614	100.00	100.00

Source: Census 2001 KS

16–18 who is a full-time student and in a family with parent(s). As one might expect in a major city, the proportions of married couples with and without children are below the national proportions, whilst those of cohabiting couples are above the national averages.

The household composition categories have been aggregated into six groups for mapping at community area level (Figure 2.11). 'One person households' are predominantly concentrated in the inner city and adjacent older suburbs. 'Family households, all pensioner' have their highest representation in a ring of outer suburbs from north west through north to the east of Leeds. 'Family households, married couples' are a feature of the whole ring of outer suburbs but particularly in the east. 'Family households, cohabiting couples' concentrate in the outer suburbs to the south west and south. 'Family households, lone parents' are most important in the inner city and suburbs except for inner north west Leeds (the student district). 'Other households' (unrelated people sharing accommodation) are most important in the inner city and suburbs to the north of the city centre.

2.6 Life expectancies

So far we have examined the demographic structure of the Leeds population, looking at the way different age groups and household types locate across the city. We now turn from structure to look selectively at dynamics or how the population is changing. One important influence on population change is the rate at which people at different ages are dying. How should this be measured? Conventional crude mortality rates, calculated as deaths in a year divided by the mid-year population, are problematic because they reflect the age structure of the population at risk rather than the intrinsic mortality experience of the population.

Figure 2.11 Household composition by community area, 2001

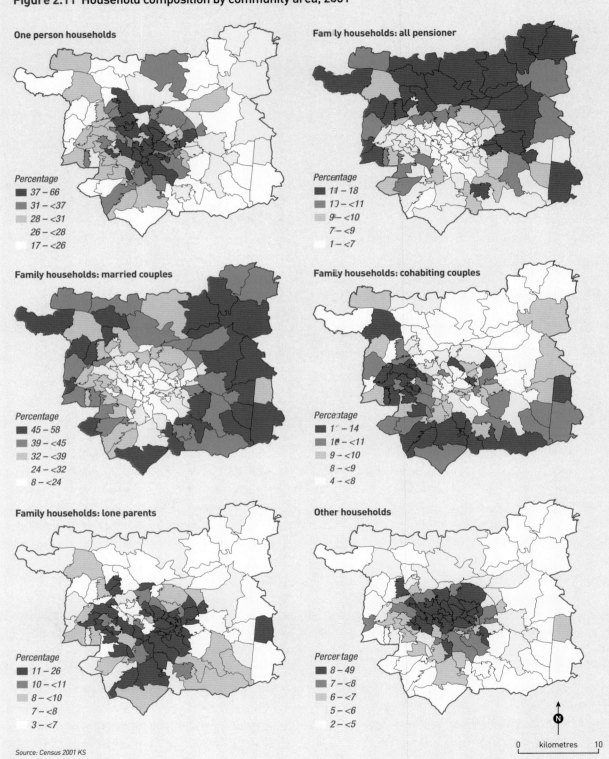

One person households

Percentage
- 37 – 66
- 31 – <37
- 28 – <31
- 26 – <28
- 17 – <26

Family households: all pensioner

Percentage
- 11 – 18
- 10 – <11
- 9 – <10
- 7 – <9
- 1 – <7

Family households: married couples

Percentage
- 45 – 58
- 39 – <45
- 32 – <39
- 24 – <32
- 8 – <24

Family households: cohabiting couples

Percentage
- 11 – 14
- 10 – <11
- 9 – <10
- 8 – <9
- 4 – <8

Family households: lone parents

Percentage
- 11 – 26
- 10 – <11
- 8 – <10
- 7 – <8
- 3 – <7

Other households

Percentage
- 8 – 49
- 7 – <8
- 6 – <7
- 5 – <6
- 2 – <5

Source: Census 2001 KS

0   kilometres   10

The solution is to use age-specific mortality rates (deaths in an age group divided by the population at risk in that age group). However, for areas with small populations, these rates, in any one year, can be erratic and therefore poor estimates of long-run mortality conditions. Two steps can be taken to mitigate these 'small number problems': first, data for several years can be combined to compute rates more representative of long-run conditions; second, a mortality measure that combines information from all age-specific mortality rates, life expectancy at birth, can be employed. This is what we do here, proposing a method to overcome the persisting small number issue characteristic of small area populations.

Having developed life expectancy estimates, we pose a number of important questions relating to life expectancy. What are the life chances of people living in Leeds in 2001? How do these differ between men and women? How do they vary across the city? How have these expectancies changed over the 1990s? How do they compare with the national averages? Have life chances of small area populations converged or diverged over the decade?

The life expectancies used to address these questions are computed for ward populations, using information on deaths by ward. However, it is also interesting to examine the variation of mortality experience for smaller populations. We estimate life expectancies for the community areas of Leeds as well, though these estimates, as will be explained later, are derived indirectly through the use of the relationship between social deprivation and life expectancy at ward scale.

Demographers measure life expectancy at birth as the number of years a person could expect to live if he or she experienced the current age-specific mortality schedule for the whole of his or her life. In order to estimate life expectancies for small areas like wards, there are four issues that need to be resolved. First, it is necessary to choose years when reliable estimates of ward populations are available because mortality rates can be very sensitive to the population estimates used (Rees et al., 2003). The years of the Census (1991 and 2001) are the most suitable time references for populations at risk.

Second, we need to use consistent mid-year population estimates as populations at risk for computing age-specific mortality rates. The 1991 and 2001 Census ward populations by age and sex are therefore adjusted to agree with the latest mid-year estimates of the population of Leeds. Note that the 1991 estimates have been revised by ONS in the light of the 2001 Census results. Third, conventional practice is to use three calendar years of deaths data rather than single year data which may be erratic; thus 1990, 1991 and 1992 mortality data is used with the 1991 mid-year population estimates and deaths in 2000, 2001 and 2002 are used with the mid-2001 populations. Fourth, because the number of deaths in a ward population is relatively small in a single year, it is necessary to adopt an estimation procedure that 'borrows strength' from a larger population. Age-specific mortality rates for England and Wales are applied to ward populations to produce initial estimates of deaths in five-year age intervals from 5–9 to 85–90 and for ages 0, 1–4 and 90+. These initial estimates are adjusted to agree with the observed ward deaths in larger age groups.

The method for estimating the ward mortality rates for use in an abridged life table and an example of the life table computation procedure are given in Rees (2003). The method produces life expectancies for Leeds as a whole which are very similar to official estimates for 1990–1992 and 1998–2000 for the local authority of Leeds (see Griffiths and Fitzpatrick, 2001a; 2001b; Fitzpatrick et al., 2000; ONS, 2001; 2003 for details of local and health authority estimates for various periods between 1990 and 2000). Life expectancies at birth for males and females in 2000–2002 were 75.9 and 80.6 and there has been a significant improvement from 1990–1992 when they were 73.3 and 78.9 respectively.

The spatial pattern of male life expectancy at birth for Leeds wards is shown in Figures 2.12. The female pattern is very similar though higher by an average of 6–7 years. The most favoured areas, unsurprisingly, are the more affluent wards in the northern and eastern suburbs. Over the decade, life expectancies improve by an average (unweighted mean of

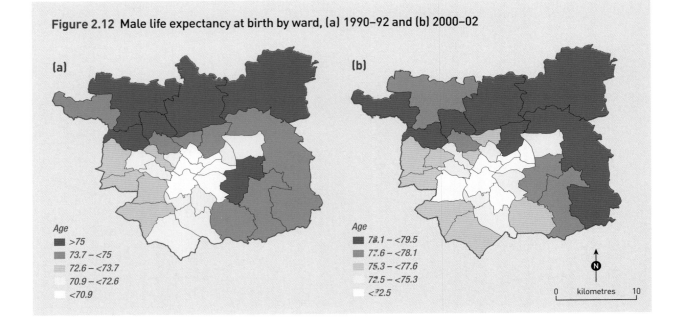

Figure 2.12 Male life expectancy at birth by ward, (a) 1990–92 and (b) 2000–02

(a)

Age
- >75
- 73.7 – <75
- 72.6 – <73.7
- 70.9 – <72.6
- <70.9

(b)

Age
- 78.1 – <79.5
- 77.6 – <78.1
- 75.3 – <77.6
- 72.5 – <75.3
- <72.5

0   kilometres   10

ward values) of 2.68 years for men and 2.50 years for women. In England and Wales as a whole, men's life expectancies improved by 2.57 years between 1991 and 2001, while women's life expectancies improved by only 1.67 years. So

evident from the maps. The standard deviation increased from 2.13 years in 1990–1992 to 3.04 years for men and from 1.48 to 2.23 years for women; the inter-quartile range increased substantially for men and moderately for women; and the

Male life expectancy (at birth) in Leeds increased from 73.3 years in 1990–1992 to 75.9 in 2000–2002 but, on average, women live five years longer. The geographical variations in life expectancy for both males and females have increased.

men in Leeds fared a little better than men in England and Wales as a whole, while women's experience in Leeds was considerably better.

Table 2.4 summarizes the variation in life expectancy

Table 2.4 Summary indicators of ward life expectancies, 1990–1992 and 2000–2002

Indicator	Male			Female		
	1990–1992	2000–2002	Change	1990–1992	2000–2002	Change
Mean	72.7	75.4	2.7	79.2	81.7	2.5
Median	72.7	75.5	2.8	79.3	81.2	1.9
Maximum	76.1	79.6	3.5	82.8	87.7	4.9
Minimum	67.9	66.8	-1.1	76.2	77.8	1.6
Range	8.3	12.8	4.5	6.6	9.9	3.1
Standard deviation	2.1	3.0	0.9	1.5	2.2	0.7
Upper quartile	74.3	77.9	3.6	80.3	83.3	3.0
Lower quartile	71.5	72.9	1.4	77.9	80.4	2.5
Inter-quartile range	2.8	5.1	2.3	2.3	2.8	0.5
Top third of wards	74.9	78.6	3.7	80.7	84.1	3.4
Middle third of wards	72.8	75.8	3.0	79.1	80.9	1.8
Bottom third of wards	70.3	71.8	1.5	77.8	80.1	2.3

Source: Census 2001 CAS

ranges increased by 55 and 30 per cent respectively. Although progress is being made across the city in life chances, it is fastest in the middle class suburbs and lowest in the inner city wards and outer city social housing estates. The average improvement for the top one third of wards is 3.7 years for men and 3.4 for women compared with 1.5 years for men and 2.3 years for women in the bottom one third of wards.

There is one ward, City and Holbeck, which experiences a substantial deterioration in its male life expectancies, probably reflecting the problems of homeless men who occupy the hostels in this ward or who sleep rough on the city centre streets. The broad geographical patterns of life expectancy for both sexes remain the same between 1990–1992 and 2000–2002 with correlation coefficients across wards, between periods of 0.88 for men and 0.82 for women. Changes in patterns are more evident for women where some of the inner city wards — Chapel Allerton, Harehills, University and Richmond Hill — have substantial gains, whereas other wards such as Burmantofts, have made relatively little progress.

For a city the size of Leeds, wards are large units in population terms, housing just over 20,000 residents each. Can we say anything about the variation in life chances at neighbourhood scale, using community areas which average

only 7,000 residents? We make indirect estimates of life expectancy for community areas in the following way. First, a measure of deprivation for ward populations is computed as a composite indicator made up of the four census variables used in the Townsend deprivation measure (Townsend *et al.*, 1988): home ownership, car ownership, unemployment and overcrowding. Second, the linear relationship between life expectancy and deprivation for wards is calibrated using linear regression. Third, we compute deprivation scores for community areas. Fourth, we predict the life expectancy for community areas using the ward regression equation. The assumption is made that the ward level relationship applies at community area scale. There is clearly considerable error introduced here, so the results should be interpreted as the life expectancy implications of deprivation for community areas. Additional life expectancy variations due to other factors (cf. Brown and Rees, 2004) are ignored. Note that the community area estimates could be improved by adjustment to the ward estimates, though this is not done here. The scatterplots and linear relationships for wards in 2001 are presented in Figure 2.13; similar equations have been computed for 1991. There is a strong inverse relationship between life expectancy and deprivation for men and a moderate relationship for women.

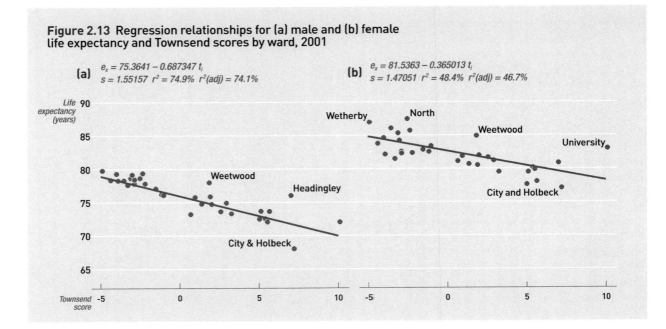

Figure 2.13 Regression relationships for (a) male and (b) female life expectancy and Townsend scores by ward, 2001

(a) $e_x = 75.3641 - 0.687347\ t_i$
$s = 1.55157\ \ r^2 = 74.9\%\ \ r^2(adj) = 74.1\%$

(b) $e_x = 81.5363 - 0.365013\ t_i$
$s = 1.47051\ \ r^2 = 48.4\%\ \ r^2(adj) = 46.7\%$

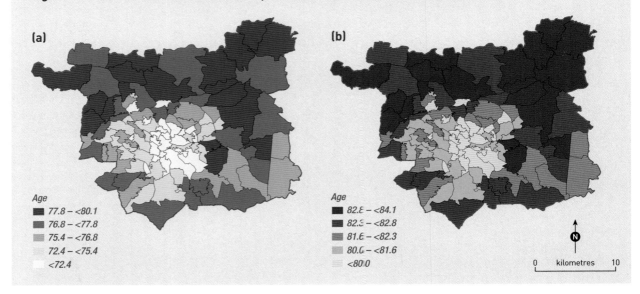

Figure 2.14 (a) Male and (b) female life expectancies at birth by community area, 2001

(a)

Age
- 77.8 – <80.1
- 76.8 – <77.8
- 75.4 – <76.8
- 72.4 – <75.4
- <72.4

(b)

Age
- 82.8 – <84.1
- 82.3 – <82.8
- 81.6 – <82.3
- 80.0 – <81.6
- <80.0

0   kilometres   10

Some of the wards such as Weetwood, Headingley and University are outliers with higher than predicted life expectancy, probably due to number of students living in area, high levels of renting and lower levels of car ownership, all of which give higher Townsend scores. Students are a healthy population temporarily living in more deprived neighbourhoods than those of their parents (on average), in order to be close to their place of higher education. The life expectancy for City and Holbeck is over-predicted by the deprivation score, probably because this score fails to pick out the especially deprived

Figure 2.15 (a) Male and (b) female years gained between 1991 and 2001, by community area

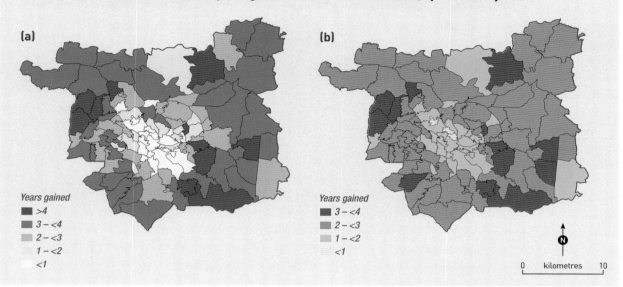

(a)

Years gained
- ■ >4
- ■ 3 – <4
- ■ 2 – <3
-   1 – <2
-   <1

(b)

Years gained
- ■ 3 – <4
- ■ 2 – <3
-   1 – <2
-   <1

N

0   kilometres   10

population living in hostels and temporary accommodation in this city centre ward. The regression equations are used to generate life expectancies for community areas (Figure 2.14).

The changes between 1991 and 2001 in life expectancies show the extent to which male gains in the expected number of life years are exceeding those of females

quite significantly in certain parts of the outer suburbs but female gains are greater than those of males in much of the inner city (Figure 2.15). The map reveals a phenomenon of considerable social concern. Although all communities are experiencing improved health (as indexed by increasing life expectancies), the poorer communities are gaining far less than the richer. Social inequalities between inner city and suburbs are widening on these measures. This was also the conclusion of the broad comparison of 1991 and 2001 Census results at local authority level produced by Dorling and Rees (2003; 2004).

2.7 Migration to and from the rest of the UK

We now turn from population exits from life itself to exits and entrances to the living population of Leeds. We examine the patterns of migration to and from the city in the 1990s. Population migration data sets from the 2001 Census are not yet available for use in analysing the interactions between Leeds and other parts of the UK or between wards within Leeds in detail. However, data on NHS patient re-registrations indicate that Leeds Metropolitan District has experienced overall net losses to the rest of the UK at an average of around 1,200 persons per year between mid-1990 and mid-1998. The aggregate net loss can be expressed in terms of migration effectiveness, i.e. the net loss through migration represents

Many more couples are living to celebrate their diamond wedding anniversary — like these octogenarians from Oulton, south east Leeds, who married in 1943.

Figure 2.16 FHSAs with which Leeds has largest net migration (a) gains or (b) losses, 1990–1998

(a) Areas to which Leeds has lost migrants in net terms during the 1990s

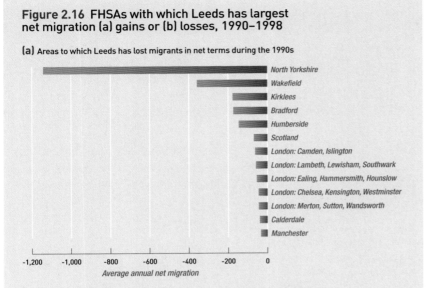

North Yorkshire
Wakefield
Kirklees
Bradford
Humberside
Scotland
London: Camden, Islington
London: Lambeth, Lewisham, Southwark
London: Ealing, Hammersmith, Hounslow
London: Chelsea, Kensington, Westminster
London: Merton, Sutton, Wandsworth
Calderdale
Manchester

Average annual net migration

(b) Areas from which Leeds has gained migrants in net terms during the 1990s

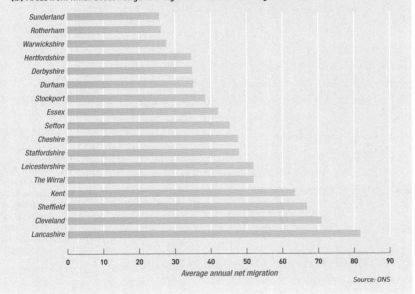

Sunderland
Rotherham
Warwickshire
Hertfordshire
Derbyshire
Durham
Stockport
Essex
Sefton
Cheshire
Staffordshire
Leicestershire
The Wirral
Kent
Sheffield
Cleveland
Lancashire

Average annual net migration

Source: ONS

Figure 2.17 Net migration flows by age group, mid-1997 to mid-1998

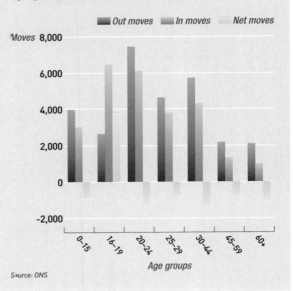

Out moves   In moves   Net moves

Moves 8,000

Age groups

Source: ONS

beyond the inner ring of adjacent areas — Lancashire to the west (82 persons per year), Cleveland to the north (71 persons per year) and Sheffield to the south (67 persons per year), as well as many of the counties of central England.

We can interpret the pattern of losses and gains as follows. Leeds loses migrants to surrounding areas as its commuting hinterland continues to develop and expand (particularly in North Yorkshire). Households choose small town and rural locales outside the Leeds boundary combined with a longer distance commute. Leeds loses to inner west London because these are the boroughs to which professional and management graduates migrate from its large civic universities to take up job opportunities in the capital. Leeds loses to traditional retirement counties on the east and south coasts and central and west Wales. Leeds gains from industrial urban northern and central England because it has a more dynamic service economy than rivals such as Sheffield, Middlesbrough, the towns of Lancashire and the Midlands.

The NHS re-registration data record the moves that take place when people change their doctor and include the movements of students when they leave home to attend college or university. This is one of the main reasons why the age-specific balances for Leeds (Figure 2.17) are positive in the 16–19 range and negative in other age groups.

approximately 2.6 per cent of the total moves into and out of the district.

In absolute terms, the most significant net losses over the 1990s have occurred to the areas adjacent to Leeds, particularly North Yorkshire which receives over 1,100 net in-migrants from Leeds per year (Figure 2.16a). There are also a group of London boroughs that gain more migrants from Leeds than lose in the opposite direction. The areas that supply Leeds with migrants, in net terms (Figure 2.16b), are those areas

Figure 2.18 Net migration balances by FHSA for (a) age 16–19 and (b) age 30–44, mid-1997 to mid-1998

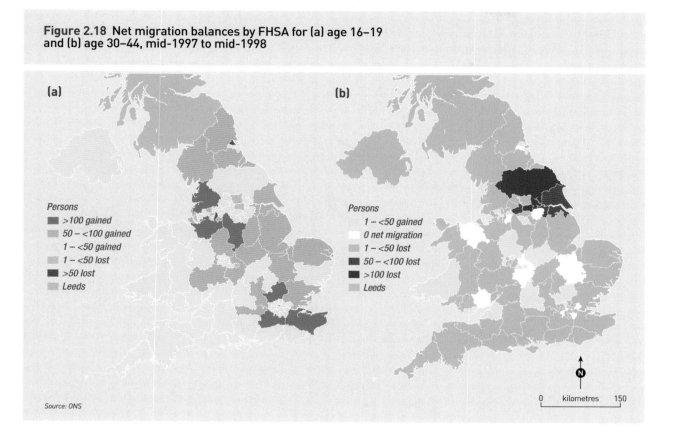

(a)

Persons
- ■ >100 gained
- ▨ 50 – <100 gained
- □ 1 – <50 gained
- ▨ 1 – <50 lost
- ■ >50 lost
- ▨ Leeds

(b)

Persons
- ▨ 1 – <50 gained
- □ 0 net migration
- ▨ 1 – <50 lost
- ■ 50 – <100 lost
- ■ >100 lost
- ▨ Leeds

0 kilometres 150

Source: ONS

The geographical patterns of net migration for areas across the rest of the UK therefore vary significantly by age. Two example net migration fields are illustrated in Figure 2.18. Leeds draws student age migrants (aged 16–19) from virtually all of England and Wales, particularly from the counties just outside metropolitan centres where middle class potential students are concentrated. In the family ages (30–44), Leeds loses families to more attractive residential areas throughout the country. The contrasts between these two maps emphasize the need always to adopt a life course perspective in understanding the pattern of population movement within a county (as emphasized in the cross-national study of internal migration by Rees and Kupiszewski, 1999).

Weekday rush hour outside city station. Leeds loses migrants to surrounding areas as its commuting hinterland expands, resulting in longer journeys to work for many workers.

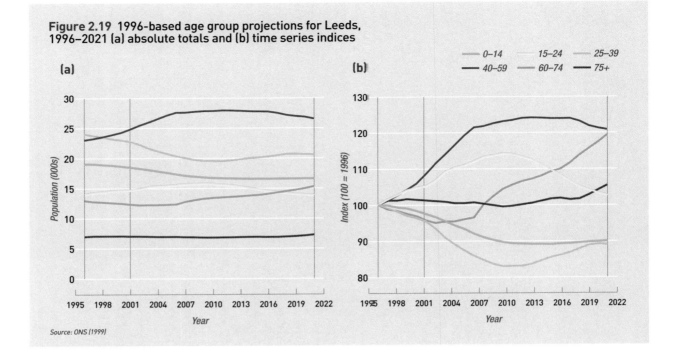

Figure 2.19 1996-based age group projections for Leeds, 1996–2021 (a) absolute totals and (b) time series indices

Legend: 0–14 | 15–24 | 25–39 | 40–59 | 60–74 | 75+

(a) Population (000s) vs Year (1995–2022)

(b) Index (100 = 1996) vs Year (1995–2022)

Source: ONS (1999)

2.8 Looking forward

We turn now from the recent past to the future and look at what prospects are held out for the Leeds population. We draw here on official projections using a 1996 population, which, although out-of-date, are the latest sub-national forecasts available. According to these projections produced by ONS (1999) for sub-national areas, whilst the total population of Leeds is due to grow by 3 per cent between 2001 and 2021, trends differ between age groups. The schedules in Figure 2.19 illustrate time series of (a) absolute totals and (b) indices computed for each year that shows the percentage change from the base year (1996=100) for six age groups.

Those aged 0–14 decline by 10 per cent over the next decade. The impact of this decline is already being felt in primary schools across Leeds where there is a huge surplus of classroom places. The situation will get worse. Education Leeds has an urgent need to develop and implement a school rationalisation policy and this is discussed further in Chapter 7. The late teenage and early adult age group is set to grow by 10 per cent over the next decade and then decline thereafter so that by 2021 it is back to its size in 2001. However, Government plans for the continued expansion of students may impact on Leeds and accentuate the demographic growth. The 25–39 worker/

family age group is diminishing in size and is projected to drop by 16 per cent by the end of the decade. This will have an impact for job recruitment in local businesses and organisations. On the other hand, the workforce is ageing and this will result in larger numbers of older workers. There are implications that employers will have to reskill and retrain older workers and provide incentives to stay on in the workforce beyond the current age, 65, at which state old age pensions can be claimed. The young elderly, defined here as 60–74 for convenience, are due to increase considerably in number from 2007. Many are likely to age-in-place within Leeds and reduce the supply of vacated housing for younger families and households. Finally, the older elderly in Leeds are projected to maintain their numbers until 2011 and to increase thereafter. There are implications for care provision and for improving the quality of life for those with different levels of material wealth. As Warnes *et al.* (2002) argue, a major effort needs to be made to improve the many less affluent residential areas of Leeds. There are many frail older people living in relatively deprived and run down areas for whom the idea of new 'retirement communities' is not very appealing, unless the planned neighbourhood regeneration schemes and the new residential developments underway are able to provide the supportive environments that are required.

clusters with two outlier groups. Each cluster has a distinct geographical distribution. Thirdly, when household types in 2001 are mapped, they show a considerable degree of spatial segregation with family and pensioner households dominating the outer ring of suburbs, and one person households, lone parent households and other households (with unrelated members) predominating in the inner ring of suburbs. Fourthly, the life expectancies of the Leeds populations have improved over the 1991–2001 decade at a faster rate than in England and Wales as a whole, but the differences between the most favoured and least favoured areas have increased, indicating both success and failure. The differences between areas are strongly related to the degree of socioeconomic deprivation. Men have improved their life chances more than women in all neighbourhoods.

In 2001, 145 in every 10,000 maternities in the UK resulted in the birth of twins, while four in 10,000 led to triplets of more. The greater use of fertility treatment is an important factor in the increased rate of multiple births.

2.9 Conclusions

This chapter has reviewed the structure and dynamics of the population of Leeds, drawing on information from the 2001 Census and other demographic sources. The key findings are as follows. Firstly, the age-sex structure of the Leeds population was very stable over the 1991 to 2001 decade and closely resembled that of England and Wales as a whole, except for higher shares in the student ages. Unusually, the population did not age significantly and there were decreases in the proportion of the population which was female and elderly. The biggest change in the demographic structure of Leeds was the expansion of the student age population and an increasing intensity of student occupation of the inner northwest of the city.

Secondly, the neighbourhoods of Leeds can be classified, on the basis of their 2001 age profiles, into ten main

Fifthly, Leeds loses population through migration, although the net out-migration rate is quite low. The city receives migrants from other urban-industrial centres and counties in northern and midland England. The city loses migrants to the North Yorkshire and other districts of West Yorkshire. It is an 'escalator' region receiving migrants climbing the initial rungs of the career ladder and sending them, once good incomes and status have been achieved, to the small towns and rural periphery of its commuting field. Finally, the future will see very modest increases in the population of Leeds but this will mask much larger swings in the populations of constituent ages. The baby boomers will age into the older working ages and then later into the younger elderly ages. The older elderly, by contrast, will increase until after 2020. The student ages will increase to 2010 but children and young workers will decrease markedly.

References

Brown, D. and Rees, P. (2004) Trends in local and small area morbidity and mortality in Yorkshire and the Humber: II explaining health inequalities, *Regional Studies,* submitted.

Champion, A.G. (2004) The census and the cities, *Town and Country Planning,* 73(1): 20–22.

Clarke, J. (2000) *The Human Dichotomy: The Changing Numbers of Males and Females,* Pergamon, Oxford.

Dorling, D. and Rees, P. (2003) A nation still dividing: the British census and social polarisation 1971–2001, *Environment and Planning A,* 35: 1287–1313.

Dorling, D. and Rees, P. (2004) A nation still dividing? Some interpretation of the question, *Environment and Planning A,* 36: 369–373.

Fitzpatrick, J., Griffiths, C. and Kelleher, M. (2000) Geographic inequalities in mortality in the United Kingdom during the 1990s, *Health Statistics Quarterly,* 7: 19–31.

Griffiths, C. and Fitzpatrick, J. (2001a) *Geographic Variations in Health,* The Stationery Office, London.

Griffiths, C. and Fitzpatrick, J. (2001b) Geographic inequalities in life expectancy in the United Kingdom, 1995–97, *Health Statistics Quarterly,* 9: 16–28.

Office for National Statistics (ONS) (1999) *1996-based Subnational Population Projections — England,* Series PP3 no. 10, The Stationery Office, London.

Office for National Statistics (ONS) (2001) Life expectancy at birth by health and local authorities in the United Kingdom, 1997 to 1999 (3-year aggregate figures), *Health Statistics Quarterly,* 11: 78–85.

Office for National Statistics (ONS) (2002) Vital Statistics for England and Wales, Table VS4 [computer file]. Colchester: UK Data Archive [distributor], December 2002, SN: 4608.

Office for National Statistics (ONS) (2003) Life expectancy at birth by health and local authorities in the United Kingdom, 1998 to 2000 (3-year aggregate figures), *Health Statistics Quarterly,* 13: 83–90.

Rees, P. (2003) Methodological innovations in the 2001 Census: a user perspective with an illustration for the demography of a big northern city, paper presented at the Office of National Statistics and Royal Statistics Society Conference, 11–12 November, Congress Centre, London. Available at: http://www.nationalstatistics.gov.uk/events/rss_ons_conf/presentations.asp

Rees, P., Brown, D., Norman, P. and Dorling, D. (2003) Are socioeconomic inequalities in mortality decreasing or increasing within some British regions? An observational study, 1990–98, *Journal of Public Health Medicine,* 25(3): 208-214.

Rees, P. and Kupiszewski, M. (1999) Internal Migration and Regional Population Dynamics in Europe: a Synthesis, *Population Studies No. 32,* Council of Europe Publishing, Strasbourg.

Stillwell, J., Rees, P. and Boden, P. (1992) *Migration Processes and Patterns Volume 2; Population Redistribution in the United Kingdom,* Belhaven Press, London.

Townsend, P., Phillimore, P. and Beattie, A. (1988) *Health and Deprivation Inequality in the North,* Routledge, London.

Warnes, T., Lowles, R. and Oh, K.M. (2002) *Older People in Yorkshire and the Humber,* study commissioned by Age Concern in Yorkshire, Sheffield Institute for Studies on Ageing, Sheffield.

3

Multicultural Leeds: Geographies of Ethnic Minorities and Religious Groups

DEBORAH PHILLIPS, JOHN STILLWELL & AMY BURRAGE

> ▋▋ *In absolute terms, Leeds has a black and minority ethnic population of just over 58,300 people.* ▋▋

Muslims at prayer in the Jamia Masjid on Spencer Place — one of about a dozen mosques and prayer houses in inner city Leeds; some are purpose-built and others are in converted premises.

3.1 Introduction

Ethnicity and religion are key determinants of people's life experiences and life chances, helping to shape people's cultural identities. While it is important to acknowledge that we cannot understand the distinctive character and geographies of ethnic groups without reference to other criteria, such as gender, age and social class, there are important and interesting differences to be observed between the groups. In this chapter, we distinguish the spatial patterns of ethnic minorities and religious groups in 2001 and then attempt to explain the processes influencing the changing distributions of the former. Some insights are provided by examining the occupational character-istics of minority ethnic groups and by the use of qualitative data to identify the importance of factors such as community ties and discrimination. In addition, we acknowledge the growing population of refugees and asylum-seekers that has arrived in Leeds in recent years following the city's designation as a dispersal centre. We begin, however, by demonstrating Leeds' multicultural complexion by mapping the incidence of ethnic and religious diversity in 2001 and by using various statistical measures to quantify the concentration of particular groups in different places.

3.2 Ethnic minorities and religious groups

Like all major cities, the population of Leeds contains a rich diversity of ethnic groups and religious persuasions. Although the black and minority ethnic proportion of the city's population (8.2 per cent) in 2001 was above the regional proportion (6.5 per cent), it was marginally less than the national average (8.7 per cent). The regional minority proportion reflects some huge variations by local authority district; the black and minority ethnic proportion amongst the Leeds' neighbouring districts, for example, varies from 21.7 per cent in Bradford and 14.4 per cent in Kirklees to 2.3 per cent in Wakefield, 1.6 per cent in Harrogate and only 0.7 per cent in Selby. Of course, the white proportions of these areas contain many who are non-UK white.

In absolute terms, Leeds has a black and minority ethnic population of just over 58,300 people. When totals of different ethnic groups as defined in the 2001 Census in Leeds (Table 3.1) are compared with the national and regional percentages, one of the most striking features of the black and minority ethnic component is the size of the Pakistani and Pakistani-British population, which exceeds 15,000 and accounts for 2.1 per cent of the total population, including those living in communal establishments. This population is relatively small in comparison to that of nearly 68,000 Pakistanis in Bradford. However, with 12,300 Indians, over 2,500 Bangla-deshis and a further 2,300 Other (South East) Asians, the Asian population in Leeds was nearly 33,000 strong by 2001, 4.5 per cent of the overall population and over half (55.4 per cent) of the city's black and minority ethnic population. A further 2,500 individuals are recorded in the Census as being Mixed White

Table 3.1 Ethnic group populations, 2001

Ethnic group	Leeds population	Leeds %	Yorkshire and Humber %	England and Wales %
White: British	637,872	89.16	91.67	87.49
White: Irish	8,578	1.20	0.66	1.23
White: Other	10,632	1.49	1.15	2.59
Mixed: White and Black Caribbean	4,603	0.64	0.37	0.46
Mixed: White and Black African	885	0.12	0.08	0.15
Mixed: White and Asian	2,516	0.35	0.29	0.36
Mixed: Other	1,733	0.24	0.17	0.30
Asian or Asian British: Indian	12,303	1.72	1.04	1.99
Asian or Asian British: Pakistani	15,064	2.11	2.95	1.37
Asian or Asian British: Bangladeshi	2,537	0.35	0.25	0.54
Asian or Asian British: Other	2,386	0.33	0.25	0.46
Black or Black British: Caribbean	6,718	0.94	0.43	1.08
Black or Black British: African	2,435	0.34	0.19	0.92
Black or Black British: Other	1,165	0.16	0.07	0.18
Chinese	3,447	0.48	0.25	0.44
Other	2,528	0.35	0.19	0.42
Total	715,402	100.00	100.00	100.00

Source: Census 2001 KS

and Asian, out of a total of 9,700 individuals of dual heritage. The Black and Black-British populations are smaller in number, with the largest group being the Black or Black-British Caribbean population that numbered 6,700 on Census night 2001. Proportions of Black minorities in Leeds are lower than the national averages. The proportion of Chinese in the Leeds population, on the other hand, is marginally greater than the national average.

The age structures of the minority populations of Leeds show some interesting variations when compared with the White British. Even amongst the white population the differences are considerable (Figure 3.1). The White Irish population is much older in relative terms than the White British, with largest proportions between ages 50 and 69, whereas the White Other contains quite a high proportion of those in their 20s and early 30s, reflecting the undergraduate

and postgraduate students coming from Europe and the USA. As we might imagine, the dual heritage minority populations are dominated by children, and teenagers, the second generation offspring of mixed marriages or partnerships. The age profiles of the two largest groups, the Mixed White Black Caribbean and White Asian are shown Figure 3.1, but the other mixed groups have similar structures. There are very few individuals aged over 50 in these sub-groups.

The profile of the Pakistani sub-population, Leeds' largest black and minority ethnic minority, also shows a preponderance of children, whilst the Indian population is more mature. This characteristic is highlighted by the place of birth statistics which, when compared with the ethnicity counts, indicate that only 39.6 per cent of the Pakistani population resident in Leeds were actually born in their homeland compared with 43.3 per cent of the Indians. In contrast and

Figure 3.1 Age profiles of selected ethnic groups, 2001

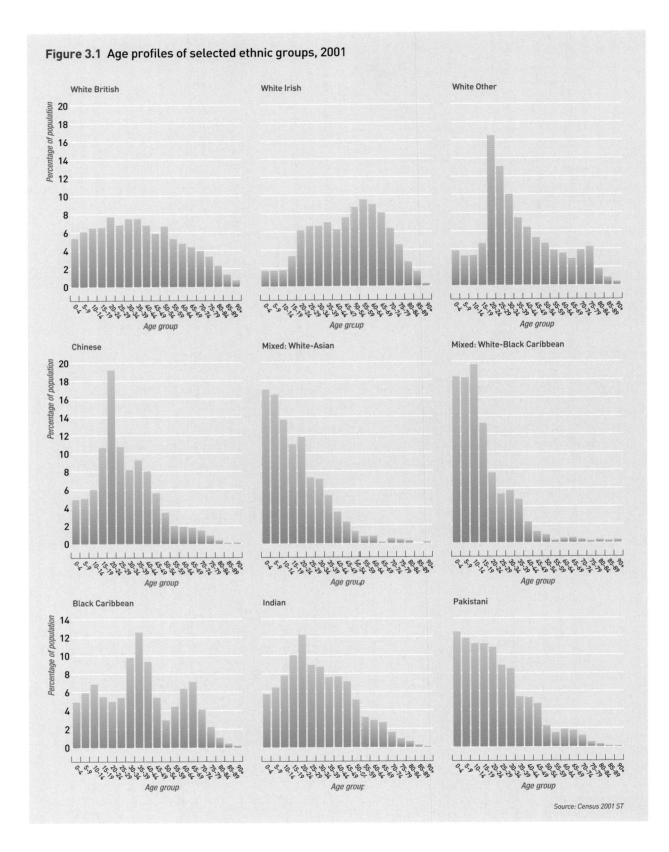

Figure 3.2 Place of birth outside UK of Leeds residents, 2001

Western Europe 27%
Eastern Europe 5%
Africa 12%
Oceania 3%
America 11%
Asia 42%

Source: Census 2001 CAS

reflecting an earlier pattern of migration and settlement, the Black Caribbean group has significant proportions of more elderly individuals with a peak at age 65-69; the peaks at ages 35-39 and 10-14 are evidence of more mature families. The Chinese minority population, on the other hand, is heavily skewed to the late teen ages and 20s, with nearly 20 per cent falling in the 20-24 age-group. This is likely to reflect the large number of Chinese students living in the city.

The birthplace data from the 2001 Census indicate that about 20,100 people living in Leeds were born elsewhere in the UK outside England and over 47,500 were born outside the UK, mostly in Asia or Western Europe (Figure 3.2). Whilst the Asian minorities are dominated by those born in Pakistan (5,900), India (5,300), and to a lesser extent, Bangladesh (1,300), there are also over 1,000 from Hong Kong, 960 from China and just over 600 from Malaysia. Nearly half of those born elsewhere in western Europe come from the Republic of Ireland (5,700) and one fifth come from Germany (2,600), the largest population sub-group from mainland Europe. The populations of those born in Italy, France, Greece and Spain vary from 830 to 480, and all the other sub-groups' populations of western and eastern European origin are below 500, apart from

the Poles, whose longstanding association with Leeds (from 1939 onwards) is evidenced by a population count in 2001 of 830 born in Poland. Most of the African born (5,600) come from South and East Africa, with Kenya (1,300) being the major country of origin. A large number of those living in Leeds who were born in North America come from Jamaica (1,300) and the other Caribbean Islands (1,800), with smaller populations from the USA (900) and Canada (580). Those born in Australia (850) are the predominant immigrant group from Oceania, recorded by the 2001 Census at just over 1,200.

The 2001 Census was the first to ask a question about religion and Table 3.2 indicates the structure of the city's population according to their stated religious affiliation in comparison with the region and with England and Wales. As expected, the large majority of the population is recorded as Christian, but Leeds differs from the national proportions most noticeably in having higher proportions of Sikhs and Jews, as well as those with no religion and those who failed to complete the voluntary question on the Census form. The second largest religious sub-group comprises of Muslims, mostly of Pakistani origin.

3.3 Changes in ethnic proportions

Various features serve to confound the direct comparison of ethnic structure in 2001 with that ten years before. The first is the changed definition in the boundary of Leeds local authority district but this is sufficiently small to have minimal effect on the comparison. The second is the definition of the categories used to record ethnicity. As indicated previously, the 2001 Census classifies the principal ethnic groups into 16 categories. The major change from that used in the 1991 Census is the introduction of four categories of 'mixed' ethnicity as well as White Irish and White Other. Following a method reported by Rees and Butt (2003), the mixed groups can be aggregated back into their constituent parentages to give estimates of the 2001 populations for the 10 ethnic categories used in 1991. The third complicating feature is the underenumeration

Table 3.2 Populations by religious group, 2001

Religion	Leeds population	Leeds %	Yorkshire and Humber %	England and Wales %
Christian	492,656	68.86	73.07	71.75
Buddhist	1,587	0.22	0.14	0.28
Hindu	4,183	0.58	0.32	1.06
Jewish	8,267	1.16	0.23	0.50
Muslim	21,394	2.99	3.81	2.97
Sikh	7,586	1.06	0.38	0.63
Other religions	1,530	0.21	0.19	0.29
No religion	120,139	16.79	14.09	14.81
Religion not stated	58,060	8.12	7.77	7.71
Total	715,402	100.00	100.00	100.00

Source: Census 2001 KS

Table 3.3 Changes in ethnic group populations, 1991–2001

1991 ethnic categories	2001 numbers*	2001 %	1991 %	1991–2001 share change
White	661,084	92.41	94.16	Decrease
Black Caribbean	9,020	1.26	0.96	Increase
Black African	2,878	0.40	0.20	Increase
Black Other	1,169	0.16	0.43	Decrease
Indian	12,821	1.79	1.45	Increase
Pakistani	15,698	2.19	1.37	Increase
Bangladeshi	2,643	0.37	0.26	Increase
Chinese	3,447	0.48	0.30	Increase
Other Asian	2,386	0.33	0.23	Increase
Other Groups	4,261	0.60	0.63	Decrease
Total	715,405	100.00	100.00	–

*2001 data converted to 1991 categories using Box 1 in Rees and Butt (2003) Source: Census 1991 SAS; Census 2001 KS

associated with the 1991 data which creates some uncertainty about the precise number of usual residents in Leeds on that date. It is for this reason that we compare only the percentage shares in Table 3.3.

The figures in Table 3.3 demonstrate the extent to which the composition of the population has changed with a reduction in the White share of nearly 2 per cent and growth in all ethnic groups except Black Other and Other Groups. The largest increases in shares have been in the two largest Asian groups, the Pakistanis and the Indians, whose populations have

grown to account for 2.2 per cent and 1.8 per cent respectively of the usually resident population in 2001.

The omission of a question on religion in 1991 means that no comparison with 2001 is possible. However, there is plenty of evidence in the urban fabric of the growing expansion of Muslims in various parts of the city as shown by their places of worship. Figure 3.3 illustrates the distribution of temples, synagogues, mosques and community centres. It is the geographical concentrations of the population by ethnic group and religion that we examine in the next section.

Figure 3.3 Main places of worship of largest non-Christian religious groups

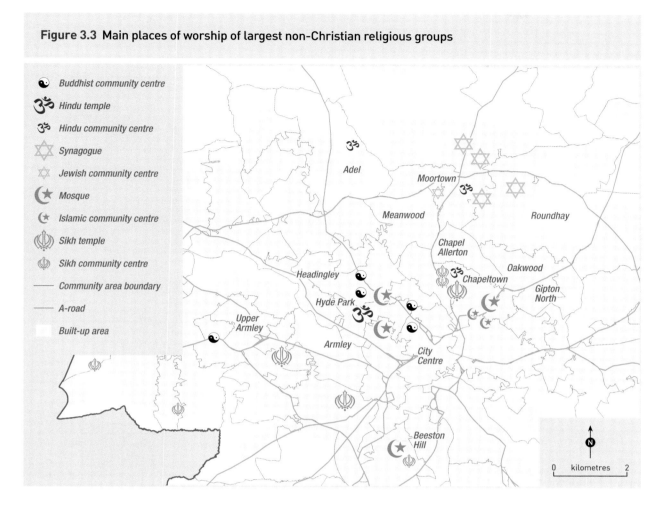

- ☯ Buddhist community centre
- ॐ Hindu temple
- ॐ Hindu community centre
- ✡ Synagogue
- ✡ Jewish community centre
- ☪ Mosque
- ☪ Islamic community centre
- ☬ Sikh temple
- ☬ Sikh community centre
- — Community area boundary
- — A-road
- ◻ Built-up area

3.4 Geographical variations in ethnic composition

Previous studies of ethnic minority populations in Leeds (Stillwell and Leigh, 1991; Rees *et al.*, 1995) have shown different degrees of geographical concentration across the city at different spatial scales. Mapping the distributions for 2001 using community area boundaries reveals how the main groups, the Pakistanis and the Indians (Figure 3.4), live in close proximity in certain parts of the city (Harehills/Chapeltown, Oakwood, Burley Lodge and Little Woodhouse) but have their own concentrations in other parts. Particularly apparent is a cluster of community areas to the south west of the city centre where the Pakistani share of the population is significant (Beeston, Beeston Hill, Holbeck) whereas Indians inhabit several community areas in the northern suburbs beyond the inner city areas, in addition to the two community areas in the far west. One of these western areas, Priesthorpe (near Pudsey), has the highest percentage of Indians in the city. This cluster has grown through the migration of Indians from the Bradford Moor area of the adjacent city of Bradford, rather than through the movement of Indians out from the inner areas of Leeds. The 2001 Census reveals that Sikhs, Hindus and Muslims live alongside each other in Priesthorpe (Figure 3.5), whereas elsewhere in the city, the major concentrations of these religious groups show less overlap.

The dispersed and multi-focal distribution pattern of the Asian minority populations is in stark contrast to the distribution of Black Caribbeans whose spatial pattern is highly concentrated around one nucleus (Chapeltown) and, to a lesser extent, the pattern for Black Africans (Figure 3.6) which has a more central city orientation (City Centre, Burmantofts, Lincoln Green and Ebor Gardens).

The Chinese, on the other hand, are distributed more

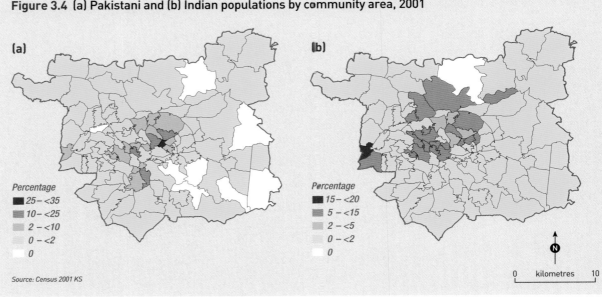

Figure 3.4 (a) Pakistani and (b) Indian populations by community area, 2001

(a)

Percentage
- 25 – <35
- 10 – <25
- 2 – <10
- 0 – <2
- 0

Source: Census 2001 KS

(b)

Percentage
- 15 – <20
- 5 – <15
- 2 – <5
- 0 – <2
- 0

N

0   kilometres   10

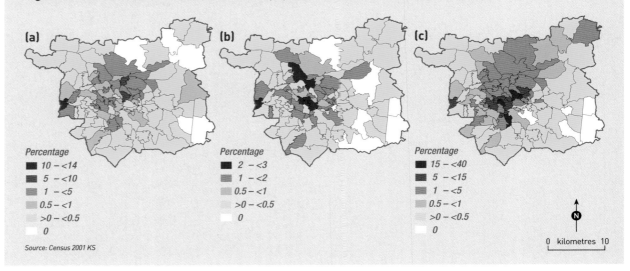

Figure 3.5 (a) Sikh, (b) Hindu and (c) Muslim populations by community area, 2001

(a)

Percentage
- 10 – <14
- 5 – <10
- 1 – <5
- 0.5 – <1
- >0 – <0.5
- 0

Source: Census 2001 KS

(b)

Percentage
- 2 – <3
- 1 – <2
- 0.5 – <1
- >0 – <0.5
- 0

(c)

Percentage
- 15 – <40
- 5 – <15
- 1 – <5
- 0.5 – <1
- >0 – <0.5
- 0

N

0   kilometres   10

diffusely across the city in a diagonal band of community areas that runs from north west to south east, whilst the Bangladeshis (Figure 3.7) also are spread quite widely but do have clusters of concentration in the centre (Chapeltown/ Harehills) and in the south (Beeston Hill).

One further ethnic minority population whose geographical distribution is distinguishable from the results of the question in the census on religion is the Jewish population. Figure 3.8 illustrates high concentrations of Jews in the northern suburbs of Alwoodley and Wigton Moor and adjacent communities.

Statistical indices can be used to compare the ethnic diversity in different community areas and the geographical distributions of minority populations across the city. The diversity index is a measure that "reports the percentage of

Figure 3.6 (a) Black Caribbean and (b) Black African populations by community area, 2001

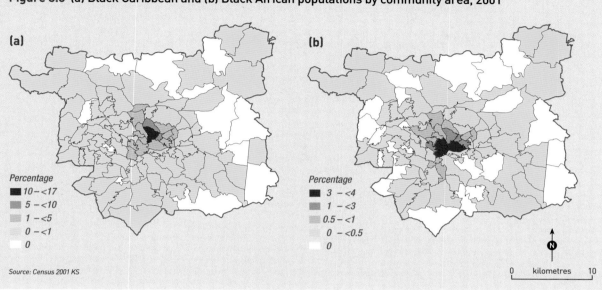

(a)

Percentage
- 10 – <17
- 5 – <10
- 1 – <5
- 0 – <1
- 0

Source: Census 2001 KS

(b)

Percentage
- 3 – <4
- 1 – <3
- 0.5 – <1
- 0 – <0.5
- 0

N

0   kilometres   10

Figure 3.7 (a) Chinese and (b) Bangladeshi populations by community area, 2001

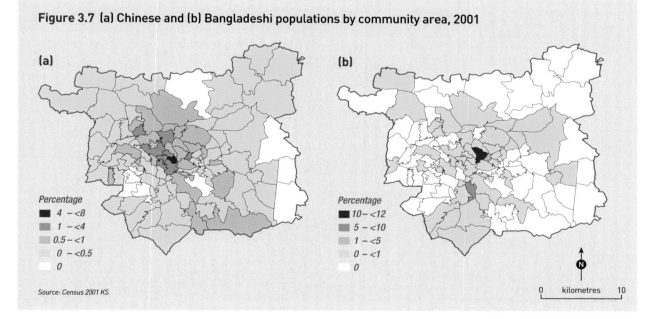

(a)

Percentage
- 4 – <8
- 1 – <4
- 0.5 – <1
- 0 – <0.5
- 0

Source: Census 2001 KS

(b)

Percentage
- 10 – <12
- 5 – <10
- 1 – <5
- 0 – <1
- 0

N

0   kilometres   10

times two randomly selected people would differ by race/ethnicity" (Brewer and Suchan, 2001, p.22). The index for each area is computed by calculating the proportion of the population of each area in a particular ethnic group, squaring this proportion and then summing up the squares across all ethnic groups and subtracting the total from 1. High values of this index represent ethnic diversity in an area, while low values indicate ethnic uniformity. The minimum value of the index of diversity is 0 while the maximum value depends on the number of groups. Thus, with 16 groups, each having an equal share of 6.25 per cent of the population, the maximum value is 93.75 per cent. In fact, the maximum diversity value in

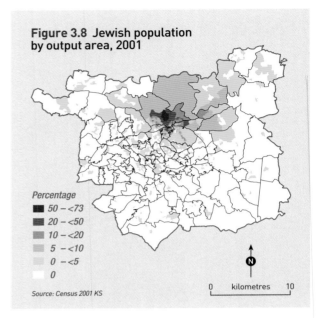

Figure 3.8 Jewish population by output area, 2001

Percentage
- 50 – <73
- 20 – <50
- 10 – <20
- 5 – <10
- 0 – <5
- 0

N

0   kilometres   10

Source: Census 2001 KS

Leeds is 83 per cent (Chapeltown) with a number of other inner city community areas including Harehills Triangle (73 per cent), Little London (61 per cent) and Burley Lodge and Little Woodhouse (60 per cent) recording high values when compared with the value of 20 per cent for Leeds as a whole. The graph in Figure 3.9 shows the extent of diversity across the city and the map illustrates the contrast between the highly diverse community areas mainly located in the inner city and the peripheral community areas in the outer suburbs to the east and south-east where the index is 5 per cent or less. Allerton Bywater has the distinction of being the least diverse of all the community areas.

Ethnic group percentages within an area are often difficult to compare because of the different sizes of the groups. A small percentage for a small group may indicate, nevertheless, that the group is concentrated in that area. Location quotients (LQs) enable us to measure the degree of concentration of a group in an area by expressing the ethnic percentage in an area as a ratio to that across the entire city. The quotient is derived for one area for one ethnic group by dividing the proportion of that area's population who are members of that ethnic group by the proportion of the population of the whole city who are members of that ethnic group. A LQ above 1 indicates a greater than average concentration of a group in that area, while a

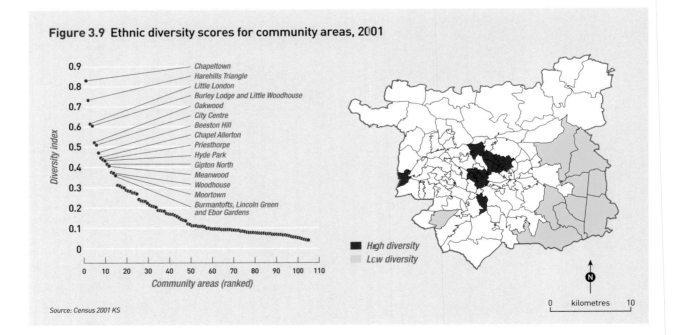

Figure 3.9 Ethnic diversity scores for community areas, 2001

Diversity index vs Community areas (ranked)

- Chapeltown
- Harehills Triangle
- Little London
- Burley Lodge and Little Woodhouse
- Oakwood
- City Centre
- Beeston Hill
- Chapel Allerton
- Priesthorpe
- Hyde Park
- Gipton North
- Meanwood
- Woodhouse
- Moortown
- Burmantofts, Lincoln Green and Ebor Gardens

Source: Census 2001 KS

High diversity
Low diversity

N

0   kilometres   10

Table 3.4 Highest community area location quotients for ethnic populations, 2001

Ethnic group	LQ/CA	Rank 1	Rank 2	Rank 3	Rank 4	Rank 5
White: British	LQ	1.11	1.10	1.10	1.10	1.10
	CA	Allerton Bywater	Kippax	Micklefield	Aberford	Ledston & Ledsham
White Irish	LQ	3.12	3.00	2.60	2.03	1.97
	CA	Gipton North	Fearnville	Oulton & Woodlesford	Scarcroft	Moortown
White: Other White	LQ	4.77	3.31	3.24	3.13	2.72
	CA	City Centre	Little London	Woodhouse	Burley Lodge	Hyde Park
Mixed: White and Black Caribbean	LQ	5.70	4.46	3.93	3.44	3.41
	CA	Chapeltown	Little London	Scott Hall & Miles Hill	Burmantofts	Gipton North
Mixed: White and Black African	LQ	6.01	4.79	4.03	3.66	3.47
	CA	Little London	Gipton North	City centre	Chapeltown	Crossgates
Mixed: White and Asian	LQ	2.94	2.81	2.65	2.55	2.55
	CA	Holbeck	Burley Lodge	Shadwell	Wythers	Chapeltown
Mixed: Other Mixed	LQ	3.93	3.44	3.04	3.01	2.94
	CA	City Centre	Little London	Moor Allerton	Woodhouse	Chapeltown
Asian or Asian British: Indian	LQ	9.46	4.17	4.11	3.55	3.13
	CA	Priesthorpe	Moortown	Meanwood	Chapeltown	Oakwood
Asian or Asian British: Pakistani	LQ	15.79	7.57	6.41	6.10	5.48
	CA	Harehills Triangle	Chapeltown	Burley Lodge	Beeston Hill	Oakwood
Asian or Asian British: Bangladeshi	LQ	31.38	16.80	7.19	1.58	1.26
	CA	Chapeltown	Beeston Hill	Harehills Triangle	Chapel Allerton	Burley Lodge
Asian or Asian British: Other Asian	LQ	5.43	5.40	4.63	4.39	4.15
	CA	Burley Lodge	Little London	Oakwood	Priesthorpe	Harehills Triangle
Black or Black British: Black Caribbean	LQ	18.01	6.27	6.10	4.56	3.81
	CA	Chapeltown	Chapel Allerton	Harehills Triangle	Little London	Oakwood
Black or Black British: Black African	LQ	11.25	11.22	9.79	5.86	5.56
	CA	Little London	Burmantofts	City Centre	Burley Lodge	Harehills Triangle
Black or Black British: Other Black	LQ	19.45	7.70	6.94	5.59	4.47
	CA	Chapeltown	Harehills Triangle	Little London	Burmantofts	Chapel Allerton
Chinese or Other: Chinese	LQ	15.11	6.86	5.08	3.07	2.90
	CA	Little London	City Centre	Burley Lodge	Harehills Triangle	Woodhouse
Chinese or Other : Other	LQ	10.74	7.76	7.54	6.06	3.78
	CA	Little London	Harehills Triangle	City Centre	Burley Lodge	Burmantofts

Source: Census 2001 CAS

location quotient below 1 indicates an under-representation of a group in that area. Table 3.4 presents the five highest LQ scores for each of the ethnic groups together with the names of the associated community areas. Thus, the highest concentrations of White British are found in the areas identified by the lowest diversity index, whilst the White Irish are most concentrated in Gipton North and Fearnville, for example. The extreme location quotient values are for the Bangladeshis (31.3 in Harehills Triangle and 16.8 in Chapeltown), Other Black (19.45 in Little London), Black Caribbean (18.01 in Chapeltown) and Pakistani (15.79 in Harehills Triangle).

Another well-known summary index is the index of dissimilarity between two population groups (A and B) across a city. This index is computed by subtracting from the percentage of group A living in one area the percentage of group B that resides in the same area. The absolute value of the difference for one area is summed with the absolute differences for all other areas and the sum is multiplied by 0.5 in order to fix the range of the index between 0 and 100. A value of 0 indicates that there is no dissimilarity between the distributions in their relative shares across the community areas of Leeds, while 100 indicates that the two distributions are completely dissimilar.

Figure 3.10 Segregation indices for ethnic groups, 2001

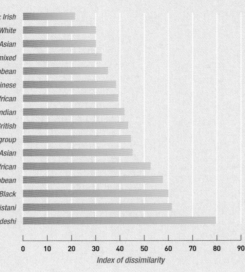

White: Irish
White: Other White
Mixed: White and Asian
Mixed: Other mixed
Mixed: White and Black Caribbean
Chinese or other ethnic group: Chinese
Mixed: White and Black African
Asian or Asian British: Indian
White: British
Chinese or other ethnic group: Other ethnic group
Asian or Asian British: Other Asian
Black or Black British: Black African
Black or Black British: Black Caribbean
Black or Black British: Other Black
Asian or Asian British: Pakistani
Asian or Asian British: Bangladeshi

0   10   20   30   40   50   60   70   80   90
Index of dissimilarity

Source: Census 2001 KS

Right, Hindu lady in traditional dress and (far right) Sikh youngsters in ceremonial costume for Vaisakhi, the celebration of the birth of the Sikh religion. Indians are represented in most areas of the city, although Sikhs are more geographically-concentrated than Hindus.

Figure 3.11 (a) Pakistani and (b) Bangladeshi populations by output area, inner Leeds, 2001

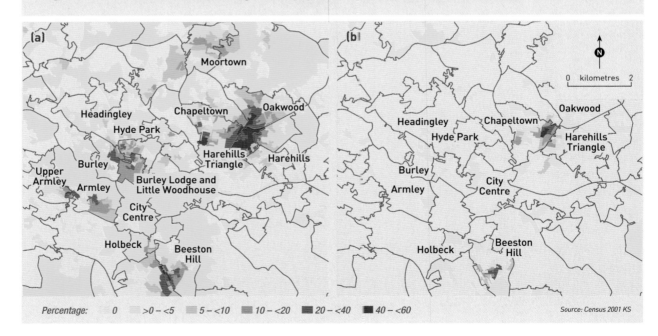

Percentage: 0   >0 – <5   5 – <10   10 – <20   20 – <40   40 – <60

Source: Census 2001 KS

Figure 3.12 Indian population by output area, 2001

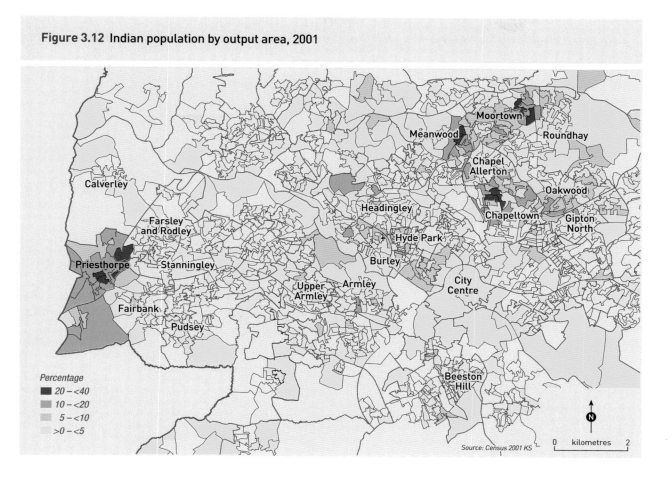

Percentage
■ 20 – <40
■ 10 – <20
■ 5 – <10
□ >0 – <5

Source: Census 2001 KS

N

0   kilometres   2

One variant of the index uses the same approach but compares the distribution of one ethnic group with the rest of the population. This is sometimes called the index of segregation and measures the percentage of the selected ethnic group that would need to move to produce exactly the same distribution as the rest of the population. In Leeds, the dissimilarity index computed for each ethnic minority against the rest of the population shows significant variation (Figure 3.10) with the White-Irish at the one end of the spectrum (21.7 per cent) and the Bangladeshis at the other end (79.6 per cent).

Although these indices provide some valuable comparative measures at community area level, the reality is that ethnic concentrations occur within community areas across the city. Thus, for example, it is the south east of Chapeltown where the proportions of Pakistanis are very high (Figure 3.11) and this pattern is in common with the incidence of Bangladeshis, although the numbers of the latter (and their proportions) are much smaller. The Indians, on the other hand,

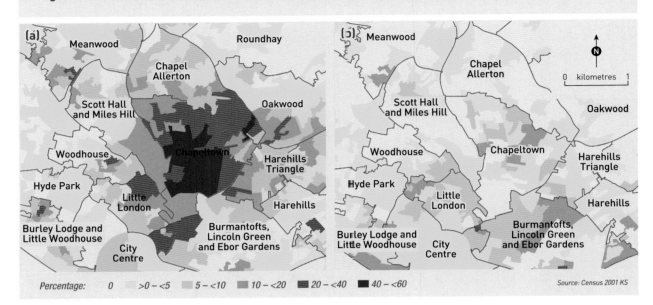

Figure 3.13 (a) Black Caribbean and (b) Black African populations by output area, inner Leeds, 2001

Percentage: 0   >0 – <5   5 – <10   10 – <20   20 – <40   40 – <60

Source: Census 2001 KS

occupy residences in the north of Chapeltown (Figure 3.12) and in the adjacent areas of Meanwood and Moortown to the north, as well as in Priesthorpe to the west.

The large concentration of Black Caribbeans, on the other hand, is found to extend across most of Chapeltown and into the adjacent or nearby areas of Chapel Allerton, Harehills, Burmantofts and Little London. This distribution contrasts with that of Black Africans that is more fragmented over the same part of the city as shown in Figure 3.13.

3.5 Processes of temporal change

The preceding discussion has provided a synopsis of the ethnic geographies of Leeds at the beginning of the twenty-first century but, as with any cosmopolitan metropolitan area, the composition of the whole population and the geographies of the component groups have changed over time. A comparison of the changes in the spatial distributions of the ethnic minority populations between 1991 and 2001 is possible by comparing the changes in the ethnic shares of populations resident in the wards of the inner city defined in Figure 3.14, whose boundaries have remained consistent between the two census dates. The choropleth shading in each of the three maps indicates the proportion of the population that is Black

Caribbean, Pakistani or Indian whilst the graduated symbols (triangles) represent changes between 1991 and 2001 in the ethnic proportions. It is evident that the relative shares of the population that are Pakistani have changed more than those of the Indians and Black Caribbeans; they have increased in wards adjacent to those with higher shares in 2001 (Harehills, Moortown and Roundhay) and decreased only in Headingley and Armley. The Black Caribbean share has declined where this minority group is most concentrated (Chapel Allerton, Harehills and University), with growth taking place in surrounding wards. Similarly, changes in the Indian proportions have occurred in areas beyond the wards of highest concentration. Collectively, these maps suggest a process of deconcentration or spreading out across the inner suburbs of the city as socio-economic status has improved.

One important factor driving the changing population has been the growth of individuals of dual ethnic heritage. As one might expect, the distributions of Mixed White and Caribbean and of Mixed White and Asian populations (Figure 3.15) follow the geographies of their respective minority populations to a certain extent but are more dispersed and without the same intensity of concentration. The vast majority of individuals in these groups are children or teenagers, as indicated in Figure 3.1.

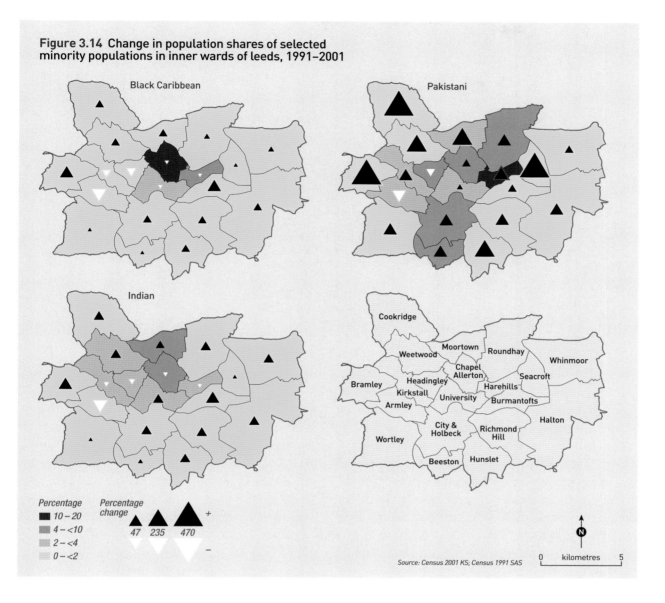

Figure 3.14 Change in population shares of selected minority populations in inner wards of leeds, 1991–2001

Black Caribbean

Pakistani

Indian

Cookridge

Moortown
Weetwood
Roundhay
Whinmoor
Chapel
Allerton
Seacroft
Bramley
Headingley
Harehills
Kirkstall
University
Burmantofts
Armley
Halton
City &
Holbeck
Richmond
Hill
Wortley
Beeston
Hunslet

Percentage
■ 10 – 20
■ 4 – <10
■ 2 – <4
■ 0 – <2

Percentage
change
47   235   470   +

–

N

0   kilometres   5

Source: Census 2001 KS; Census 1991 SAS

3.6 Explaining ethnic geographies

The distinctive ethnic geographies described in the preceding sections reflect both historical patterns of immigrant settlement in Leeds and a number of important differences in the housing preferences and opportunities of these groups in recent times. Of particular interest is the persistent but more diffuse pattern of black and minority ethnic clustering within the poorer inner city over the last 50 years. Today, the thriving Black Caribbean and Asian enclaves of Leeds still largely coincide with the relatively deprived inner areas where the first immigrants from these groups settled. In contrast, the Jewish population, which came to Leeds in the middle of the nineteenth century as poverty-stricken refugees, has migrated northwards from the slums of the Leylands (near North Street), through Chapeltown, to the affluent outer suburbs of Roundhay, Alwoodley and Shadwell.

These patterns of black and minority ethnic settlement are consistent with those found in many multi-ethnic British cities. As we have seen, in Leeds as elsewhere, ethnic clustering brings a degree of segregation from the white population, although this varies significantly across the different groups. There has been much debate in the academic literature (Ratcliffe, 1996; Phillips, 1998) as to whether these segregated

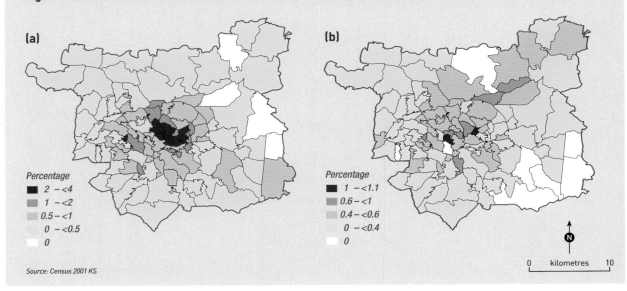

Figure 3.15 (a) Mixed White Caribbean and (b) White Asian populations by community area, 2001

(a)

Percentage
- 2 – <4
- 1 – <2
- 0.5 – <1
- 0 – <0.5
- 0

Source: Census 2001 KS

(b)

Percentage
- 1 – <1.1
- 0.6 – <1
- 0.4 – <0.6
- 0 – <0.4
- 0

0   kilometres   10

patterns reflect the different housing and neighbourhood preferences of ethnic and religious groups or whether they more accurately reflect the constraints faced by black and minority ethnic minorities, in particular, when looking for a home. In reality, members of minority ethnic groups, like everyone else, have to make their housing choices within a set of financial and other constraints. Many would argue, however, that black and minority ethnic households face more constraints than others because of racism of various kinds, although the size of the obstacle will vary within each ethnic group according to a household's social class, and the age or generation of household members. For example, as we have seen from the maps, not all Black Caribbean and Asian households live in the poorer inner areas. This means that some have managed to overcome the barriers to moving that are faced by others in their community.

The forces sustaining black and minority ethnic enclaves within the inner areas of cities like Leeds are not just of academic interest. The 2001 'riots', which involved Asian youth in Leeds, put the issue of black minority ethnic segregation back onto the agenda of both central and local governments. Many of the concerns raised were reminiscent of the 1980s, when Black Caribbean youths took to the streets of places like Chapeltown. Sensationalised media reports on the 2001 disturbances promoted alarming images of 'no-go' areas, ghettos and 'white flight' from multi-ethnic areas like Harehills.

An independent report into the disturbances across northern England also suggested that people from South Asian minority ethnic groups, especially British Muslims, were partly to blame for community tensions because of their tendency to 'self-segregate' (Community Cohesion Review Team, 2001). The report suggested that South Asians were withdrawing into their own territories and were reticent to interact with wider British society. We shall argue here that the patterns of segregated ethnic living observed in inner Leeds cannot be explained by such a simple conception.

In an attempt to understand how the distinctive geographies of ethnic settlement in Leeds have evolved over time, we will look at each of the main forces responsible for shaping the patterns of ethnic settlement in more detail. In order to illustrate the processes at work, we will draw on data from a survey of 288 South Asian households in the city conducted between 2000 and 2002. The survey included families living within the inner city and the outer suburbs and the data allow us to shed light on the issue of South Asian 'self-segregation'.

The impact of social class

The ability to compete for decent accommodation within the housing market is, most obviously, related to the disposable income of the household. In the absence of income data, we can

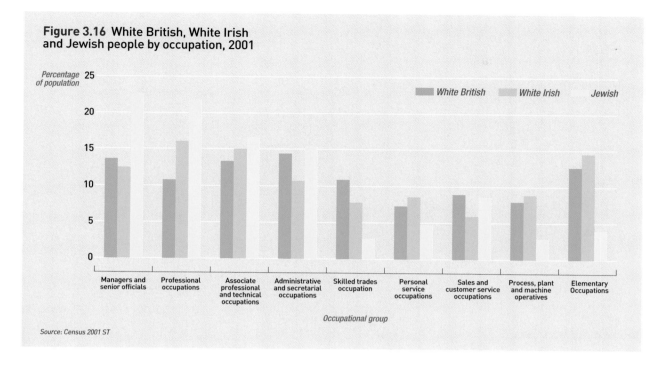

Figure 3.16 White British, White Irish and Jewish people by occupation, 2001

Percentage of population

White British ▪ White Irish ▪ Jewish

Occupational groups (x-axis): Managers and senior officials; Professional occupations; Associate professional and technical occupations; Administrative and secretarial occupations; Skilled trades occupation; Personal service occupations; Sales and customer service occupations; Process, plant and machine operatives; Elementary Occupations

Occupational group

Source: Census 2001 ST

look at differences in the occupations of the ethnic groups in Leeds as an indicator of their social class (Figures 3.16 and 3.17).

Although there is no neat relationship between social class, ethnic group and housing outcomes, it is evident that social class differences play a role in shaping the geographies of different ethnic groups in Leeds. The occupational structure of the Jewish population, with 44.5 per cent of people in professional and managerial positions, is consistent with their presence in some of the most expensive housing areas of north Leeds (especially Roundhay and Shadwell). People of Chinese and Indian origin have a wide range of occupations, indicating growing differences in social class and lifestyle within these groups. Thus, for example, whilst some Indians are likely to be trapped in the poorer inner city areas like Burley Park/Leeds 6 by their low occupational status and income, many professional Indians have been able to make the transition away from these sorts of areas to the suburbs (37.8 per cent of Indians are in professional or managerial jobs). In contrast, Pakistanis and Bangladeshis tend to have lower status occupations and relatively high levels of unemployment (Figure 3.18). This helps to explain their lower levels of movement out of the poorer inner areas. While Black Caribbeans are well represented in skilled technical and service occupations, they are far less likely to be in professional or senior manager positions at work (only

16.2 per cent of Black Caribbeans have this type of job), which limits the progress of this group into the most expensive neighbourhoods of Leeds.

Minority ethnic suburbanisation is thus clearly linked to the growth of a black and minority ethnic middle class in Leeds. It is important to note, however, that variations in social class do not fully account for the pattern of ethnic settlement. The South Asian survey data revealed that some of those moving to more prestigious suburban areas are multi-earner households in less well paid jobs. Their step up the housing ladder reflects the greater resources available to some of the larger extended-family households in this community. We also found that, in contrast to most white middle class households, by no means all economically successful minority ethnic households move away from inner areas of community settlement. This is because of fear of harassment, family obligations and/or cultural ties to the inner areas, which we will explore in more detail later.

There are clearly significant differences in the occupational status of the White-British and White-Irish population of Leeds (Figure 3.16). These wide class divisions are consistent with Leeds' image as a 'two-speed' city. Many of those living in north Leeds and the gentrified city centre are doing very well from Leeds' booming economy. Meanwhile, there are many who are excluded from this affluence by their

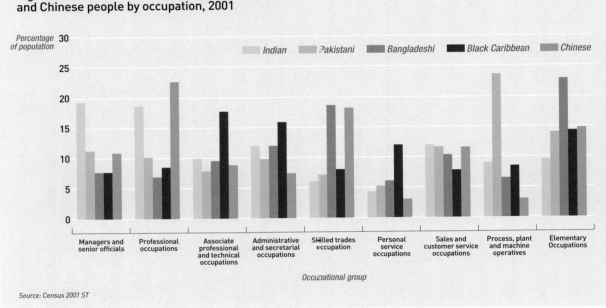

Figure 3.17 South Asian, Black Caribbean
and Chinese people by occupation, 2001

Percentage of population

Legend: Indian | Pakistani | Bangladeshi | Black Caribbean | Chinese

Occupational groups: Managers and senior officials | Professional occupations | Associate professional and technical occupations | Administrative and secretarial occupations | Skilled trades occupation | Personal service occupations | Sales and customer service occupations | Process, plant and machine operatives | Elementary Occupations

Occupational group

Source: Census 2001 ST

low paid work, unemployment and the problems of crime, vandalism and drug taking associated with the 'socially excluded' neighbourhoods in which they live (see Chapter 6). These low income white households are more likely to live in south Leeds, on the social housing estates to the east of the city, or in the poorer inner areas.

The least well off white families in Leeds, as elsewhere, are likely to be housed in the social rented sector or rent from a private landlord. This is also true for the Black Caribbean population. The large council housing estates to the east of the city (e.g. Gipton and Halton Moor) are, however, predominantly white, whilst inner city social housing is more ethnically mixed. This is clearly reflected in the map of ethnic diversity presented earlier (Figure 3.9). This pattern of ethnic segregation within the social rented sector (Figure 3.19) reflects past racial biases in allocations within the council housing sector (Law, 1996), lack of appropriate accommodation for ethnic minorities (in terms of size and level of support) as well as continuing fears about the possibility of racist harassment from white tenants living on these estates (see below). In addition, the South Asian population has traditionally followed a different route into housing from the Black Caribbean and white population; even low income Asian families have preferred to buy their own property rather than to rent. Hence, many of the Asians settling

in Leeds in the 1960s bought a property soon after arrival, usually by clubbing together with others. Properties in areas such as Hyde Park or Harehills were very cheap at the time, as white families were leaving them for the newly built suburbs.

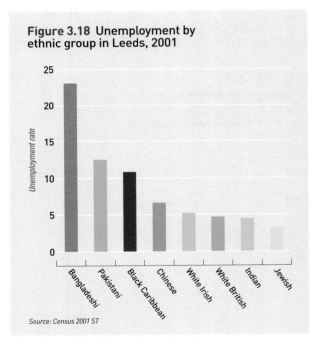

Figure 3.18 Unemployment by
ethnic group in Leeds, 2001

Unemployment rate

Ethnic groups: Bangladeshi | Pakistani | Black Caribbean | Chinese | White Irish | White British | Indian | Jewish

Source: Census 2001 ST

Figure 3.19 Ethnicity and housing tenure in Leeds, 2001

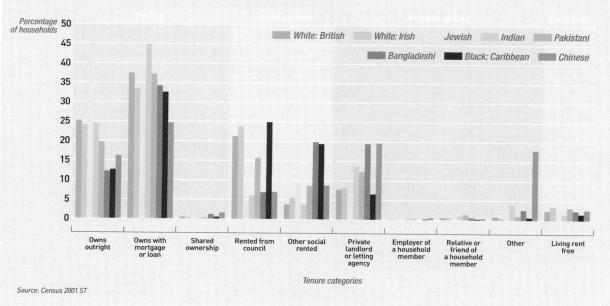

Legend: White: British, White: Irish, Jewish, Indian, Pakistani, Bangladeshi, Black: Caribbean, Chinese

Y-axis: Percentage of households (0, 5, 10, 15, 20, 25, 30, 35, 40, 45, 50)

X-axis (Tenure categories): Owns outright, Owns with mortgage or loan, Shared ownership, Rented from council, Other social rented, Private landlord or letting agency, Employer of a household member, Relative or friend of a household member, Other, Living rent free

Top categories: Owned, Social rented, Private rented, Rent free

Source: Census 2001 ST

Asians were therefore able to buy the unimproved nineteenth-century terraced houses, with cash, for a few hundred pounds. This gave rise to very high levels of owner occupation amongst this low income group, although the properties they occupied were often old and structurally poor, and suffered from problems such as damp.

Due to house price inflation, especially in areas like Hyde Park/Leeds 6, where the demand for student housing has pushed up the prices of terraced housing, less well off young Asians will now find it more difficult to buy their own homes. As a result, levels of home ownership amongst Asians are dropping so that they are now more in line with the level of white ownership. They are, nevertheless, still much higher amongst working class Asians than amongst working class whites or Black Caribbeans. The search for affordable housing is likely to draw increasing numbers of young Asians, as well as Black Caribbeans, into the social rented sector. However, the fear of harassment, and the desire for maintaining family connections within the inner city, means that their search is unlikely to take them into the white working class estates on the edge of Leeds.

The impact of culture and lifestyle
It is well known that housing and neighbourhood preferences are closely related to the desire for a certain type of lifestyle, which in turn is often associated with particular stages in the life cycle. So, for example, as shown in Chapter 2, we find students clustering in Headingley, families in the suburbs, and

Black Caribbeans are most concentrated in Chapeltown, just to the north of the city centre, where some have been resident for over 40 years.

Maintaining cultural and religious traditions is important for many people of minority ethnic origin of all generations. Above, the annual West Indian carnival in Chapeltown. Far right, The Mosque, Brudenell Grove in Hyde Park — Muslims are called to prayer five times a day. Mosques are important focal points of Pakistani and Bangladeshi Muslim communities, and have social, cultural and religious functions.

young professional people, with no children, exploiting the advantages of city-living in areas like the Calls. However, these associations between neighbourhood and lifestyle best describe the situation for white people in Leeds, and hold less well for Black Caribbean and Asian people. As we saw from the age profiles presented earlier (Figure 3.1), Asian households in particular are likely to include young children. Yet their homes are largely within the inner city and suffer from the associated disadvantages of crime, pollution, safety and lack of play space. Some households are undoubtedly trapped in these areas by their poverty and by worries about feeling isolated or falling victim to harassment if they move outwards. However, there is also a positive side to living within established ethnic enclaves, such as those in Chapeltown, Harehills or Beeston. Our survey of Asian households in inner Leeds showed that while the majority of respondents complained about the rise of crime, vandalism and drugs in these areas, they also valued the sense of community, social support, religious institutions and cultural amenities they could offer.

Hence, although there is a trend towards outward movement, many Asians still see the established community areas as important for social and cultural reasons. A sense of attachment cut across social classes, so that some middle class families opt to live in these poorer urban areas. A sense of attachment also spanned younger and older generations of Asians of all backgrounds, but was strongest amongst Muslim families.

Elderly people and recent migrants (men and women) relied most heavily on the support networks of the inner community areas of Leeds. A lady of Pakistani origin living in Harehills summed up the reasons why Asian people often continue to regard the inner city as their home: "We are safe here and a large community lives close by. All the needs of life are fulfilled".

The importance of community ties means that when minority ethnic households do make the move to the suburbs, they may well end up choosing to live near other families of a similar religious or cultural background. This is evident in the clustering of Sikh families in the Moortown area and the Jewish population in Roundhay. A survey for the Institute for Jewish Policy Research (Waterman, 2003, p. 9) described Leeds' Jews as 'a very closely bonded group of people', characterised by high levels of social interaction and a strong sense of Jewishness. For all ethnic groups, opportunities for informal socializing, maintaining ethnic/religious customs and preserving a sense of identity are often seen as important reasons for living close to people of a similar ethnic background. However, there are two sides to the coin, as the desire to cluster together can be reinforced by worries about lack of acceptance or even harassment by the majority white, Christian population. Asian respondents told us that when first moving into a predominantly white suburb in Leeds, the presence of any other "Asian face" was often felt to be reassuring in what was seen as a potentially threatening environment.

The impact of external constraints

All households face constraints when choosing their home, especially in relation to their income, journey to work, and family needs and obligations. Black and minority ethnic groups also face additional constraints in the form of discrimination by housing market institutions and the fear and experience of racist harassment. These factors have helped to shape, and continue to shape, the distinctive ethnic geographies in Leeds.

Prior to the first race relations legislation in 1965, there was overt discrimination against people on the grounds of their

race and ethnicity. Private landlords could refuse to let their rooms to people because they were Black or Asian, Irish or Jewish, and access to council housing was denied to them on these grounds (Duke, 1970). This severely limited the housing options of ethnic minority groups, and the early communities grew up wherever the immigrants could obtain housing. Despite further legislation, less overt direct and indirect discrimination by public and private housing institutions continued well into the 1980s (Law, 1996; Phillips and Unsworth, 2002). This had the effect of directing black and minority ethnic people to particular areas of the city (e.g. into existing inner city ethnic enclaves) and limiting their access to others (e.g. the suburbs and peripheral council estates).

Recent research into private housing market institutions in Leeds has shown that there are no longer so many institutional barriers to black and minority ethnic mobility as there used to be (Phillips et al., 2002). Indeed, most estate agents operating in areas of significant Asian sales and purchases welcome their business. However, it was also clear that agents saw that some streets within the inner suburbs (e.g. Meanwood) were becoming 'Asian-dominated' and undoubtedly communicated this fact to others in the market. This may have influenced white buyers' decisions on whether to look for housing in these areas. We also uncovered anecdotal evidence that the choices of both whites and Asians could sometimes be constrained by agents directing potential buyers to certain areas. Our interviews with Asian families revealed a continuing suspicion of estate agents. Most of those using agents were satisfied with the outcome, but there were perceptions of unequal treatment amongst some families and a suspicion of vendor discrimination, which could have limited their housing choices in the city.

The ethnic geographies of Leeds are also maintained by a pattern of minority ethnic avoidance of certain areas. Many white families will no doubt also avoid certain areas on the basis of their reputation, perceived social status and possibly an area's ethnic make-up. Amongst the Asian households interviewed, 68 per cent identified certain areas of Leeds that Asian people would avoid. These included "rough" areas (especially large council estates, like Gipton) and neighbourhoods that were perceived to be "white"; white working class areas in particular were thought to be out of bounds to Asians (e.g. Seacroft and Middleton). Many worried about feeling unwelcome or isolated, or feared falling victim to racist abuse or harassment.

Fear of racist harassment continues to limit Asian people's choice of housing and neighbourhood; 17 per cent of the survey respondents said they had experienced harassment in their current neighbourhood, even though they had opted to live in areas they perceived to be safe. Several interviewees recalled how they were victimised when they first moved to the suburbs. One Sikh lady in Moortown described how "our house was targeted as we were the only Asians in the area when we first moved in." Fear of victimisation was much more widespread than the experience, but still acted as a powerful constraint on housing and neighbourhood choice for some, particularly women.

Making sense of the processes

The historical legacy of forces promoting segregation in particular areas, like Harehills, Chapeltown, Hyde Park/Burley Lodge and Beeston, is difficult to ignore. Distinctive communities have grown up in particular parts of the city for a number of reasons: the poverty of early immigrants, the desire for community living and support, the importance of access to ethnic amenities (such as places of worship, as shown in Figure 3.3, and community organizations) and the effects of discrimination in the job market (which limited access to good jobs) and the housing market. These inner city communities are now sustained by community ties and the fear of racial harassment.

We can therefore see that segregated patterns of living are not just a matter of choice. Neither are they simply a matter of 'self-segregation' as implied in discussions about the recent disturbances in northern cities. While many Jews have overcome the obstacles faced by predecessors to move into one of the best neighbourhoods in Leeds over a relatively long timeframe, the future for the Black Caribbean and Asian communities is less certain. Some better-off Asians are certainly following in the footsteps of the Jews and moving northwards to Adel, Roundhay and Scarcroft. In a city like Leeds, where there are many job opportunities for the well qualified individual, the prospects for socio-economic advancement by black and minority ethnic people may be greater than in a more depressed local economy like that of Bradford. Racial discrimination and individual hostilities towards visible ethnic minorities may nevertheless remain a brake on progress.

3.7 Refugees and asylum seekers

The successful Jewish population of Leeds started out life in the city as refugees fleeing from Russia or Poland over a century ago. Freedman (1988) reports that there were nearly 8,000 Jewish people living in the city by 1891, mostly in very poor conditions in the slums of central Leeds (the Leylands). The city has received many other groups of refugees since then, including Poles, families from East Africa (of Indian origin), Iran,

Vietnam, Bosnia, Chile and Sudan. Leeds also played an important part in the Humanitarian Evacuation Programme from Kosovo, which resulted in 971 refugees being sent to the city from Macedonia in 1999. Yorkshire and Humberside as a region received the second largest number of Kosovan families under this programme, after the North West (Thatcher, 2000). Most of them stayed for about a year, and were housed first in reception centres and then in the local communities close to those centres. The majority then returned to their homeland, but some have stayed in West Yorkshire and are applying for asylum. The region launched its first ever Refugee Integration Strategy in December 2003 (Warm, 2004), aiming to provide support for new refugees, to encourage them to remain and contribute to the region's economic and cultural future.

Most of the recent refugees settling in Leeds over the last few years have arrived as part of a Home Office scheme, operated through the National Asylum Support Service (NASS), to disperse refugees away from pressure areas in the south east

of England. This dispersal policy was introduced in April 2000, and identified 12 dispersal areas, of which Leeds was one. Refugee families are given no choice about where they end up in Britain, and they are allocated housing (again on a 'no choice' basis) by the local council or a private landlord in the city to which they are sent. By the end of September 2003, 1835 asylum seekers had been dispersed to Leeds and housed in NASS accommodation under the Home office scheme. A further 280 were receiving financial support from NASS, but had found their own accommodation (Home Office, 2003).

Leeds belongs to the Yorkshire and Humberside Asylum Consortium, which has helped to accommodate and support asylum seekers across the region. There are several housing agencies in Leeds responsible for accommodating refugees under this scheme: the Angel Group, Clear Spring and Safe Haven, as well as the local authority. Families are most likely to be accommodated in neighbourhoods where there is a low demand for housing from other city residents and where there is an ethnically mixed population. This inevitably means that the refugees and asylum seekers are often directed to the poorer, less popular neighbourhoods of the city. The Kosovans were typical of many refugees in being sent to live in Beeston, Harehills, Holbeck and the Potternewton area of Chapel Allerton (Thatcher, 2000). They were, however, also housed in Bramley, a predominantly white British area of social housing in west Leeds, where there was little 'matched' ethnic support available to them.

Reactions to refugees arriving in twenty-first century Leeds have been ambivalent, just as they were when the Russian Jews arrived in the 1880s (Freedman, 1988). There was strong support from local people for the Kosovan Humanitarian Programme when it was first implemented in 1999, but the arrival of refugees and asylum seekers in particular communities is not always welcome. This is particularly true when people in the reception areas are already facing social and economic problems. As a recent survey by Onofrio and Munk (2003) documents, local residents often feel anxious about the arrival of 'outsiders' in their community and worry about the apparent strain on neighbourhood services. They may also feel a sense of relative deprivation; it is commonly believed that refugees have access to better housing, health care and social services than the local people themselves. Myths abound, not only amongst white British residents but also amongst more established minority ethnic groups too. Onofrio and Munk (2003) found that some people wrongly believed that asylum seekers were being given cars and luxury goods. Refugees and asylum seekers thus become easy scape-goats for local problems. Worries can sometimes spill over into tensions, which can bring hostility and harassment of the refugees. For example, in August 2003, a Kosovan family living on the mainly white Broadlea estate, in Bramley, were attacked with bottles and stones. They were eventually forced to move into emergency accommodation elsewhere (Yorkshire Post, 29.8.03).

Despite a fairly depressing picture of hostility towards refugees in some parts of the city, there are also some important steps being taken to break down the barriers to acceptance. Onofrio and Munk's (2003) research identified a number of local schemes aimed at overcoming people's fears and integrating refugees into housing estates and schools. In addition, the Safe Haven housing association is featured in a national report as an exemplary provider of support for refugees in the region (Chartered Institute of Housing, 2003). The Yorkshire and Humberside Asylum Consortium Citizenship Project also helps refugees to integrate by providing language classes, job training and classes in everyday skills. The work of the Consortium extends to key agencies, such as the police and housing organizations, to improve the support and services that they offer to refugees and asylum seeker in the region.

Nevertheless, the challenges are tough and a lack of experience, a shortage of resources, the Government's policy of 'no choice' of housing for these vulnerable newcomers and the negative media coverage of asylum issues, contribute to an uphill battle for all those individuals and agencies involved in the resettlement process (Onofrio and Munk, 2003).

3.8 Conclusions

This chapter has raised issues relating to the changing demographic and socio-economic profiles of the ethnic groups living in Leeds, their levels of mixing and the nature of social relations between different ethnic groups. This has particular salience at the time of writing, given the concerns about community cohesion and minority ethnic citizenship expressed in the wake of the northern riots and the aftermath of September 11th 2001. We cannot argue that Leeds is necessarily typical of other multi-ethnic cities in Britain. Each town or city has a slightly different immigration history, a different ethnic composition, and different economic fortunes. These provide distinct settings for interaction within each multi-ethnic context and a diversity of social, economic and spatial outcomes for each ethnic group. Nevertheless, the patterns and processes observed in Leeds do have resonance with those elsewhere (Modood et al., 1997; Phillips, 1998), so the city can perhaps provide a barometer of continuity and change in multi-ethnic Britain.

It is important to stress that although we can refer to Leeds as a multi-ethnic, multi-cultural city, the everyday experience for many white British people living in Leeds is not particularly cosmopolitan. Minority ethnic groups tend to be clustered in particular areas of the city, and as the diversity indices presented in section 3.4 have shown, the majority of Leeds' community areas have a low level of ethnic mixing. A visitor to Leeds' city centre might well get the impression that the city has little ethnic diversity, although only two miles away ie the distinctive ethnic landscapes of Harehills, Chapeltown, Beeston and Burley Lodge/Hyde Park. The Conway Street mosque (Harehills) is now a feature of Leeds' inner city skyline, just as the Chapeltown synagogue was in the 1940s, but the social world surrounding the mosque and its Muslim congregation is distant for many. As was explored in section 3.6, there is a myth that this social and spatial separation is the result of the desire for 'self-segregation' by South Asian (particularly Muslim) minorities, but recent research suggests that external constraints on mixing are equally powerful

Children from Black Caribbean, Pakistani and Iranian families at play in Chapeltown.

important recipient of refugees and asylum seekers, for example), the national/international arena (as a major financial and educational centre, attracting national and international migrants) and its close proximity to Bradford. The growth of the Asian population in the west Leeds area of Priesthorpe, for example, reflects the inmigration of Indians (mainly Sikhs) from Bradford. Their long established connections with the temples and cultural organizations of Bradford tend to reinforce their associations with this city rather than with Leeds. Whilst Leeds and Bradford function as a conurbation in many respects, this has more meaning for the mobile middle class white populations of each city than for their respective minority ethnic populations, especially those from the inner cities. Most of these inner city residents work locally and those youngsters in higher education often study locally. The predominantly white University of Leeds attracts more students from abroad than from Bradford's large Asian community, despite the high value placed by this group on higher education (Law *et al.,* 2002). Strong family and community associations, as well as worries about social isolation and harassment in a new setting, help to cement local connections within the minority ethnic communities. It is nevertheless clear that, despite some tensions, social interaction between ethnic communities is growing and that the old social and spatial divisions of 50 years ago are becoming increasingly blurred.

determinants of the pattern of Asian settlement in the city, i.e. 'constraint' is as powerful as 'choice'.

There are nevertheless important signs of change in the geographies of minority ethnic settlement in Leeds and in the integration of previously distinct ethnic groups. The social and spatial transition of the Jewish population from poverty stricken immigrants in the slums of nineteenth century Leeds to the affluent suburbs in the space of 100 years is remarkable, and has parallels in the accomplishments of Jewish communities in London and Manchester. Now, the Indian population also has a firm foot-hold in the inner suburbs and a toe-hold in the most affluent areas of Leeds. There is also evidence of increasing ethnic inter-mixing through mixed marriages or partnerships, especially in the Black Caribbean population. The dual heritage children in these families are, however, more likely to be growing up in Chapeltown than anywhere else in Leeds, suggesting that, for many of them, their life experiences and life chances may be similar to those of their Black Caribbean parent.

This chapter has largely focused on the city of Leeds as a separate entity. However, it is important to acknowledge that its changing ethnic profiles and geographies are inextricably related to its position in the wider context of the region (as an

References

Brewer, C. and Suchan, T. (2001) *Mapping Census 2000: The Geography of US Diversity,* US Census Bureau, Census Special Reports, Series CENSR/01-1, US Government Printing Office, Washington, DC.

Chartered Institute of Housing (2003) *Providing a Safe Haven; Housing Asylum Seekers and Refugees,* Chartered Institute of Housing, London.

Community Cohesion Review Team (2001) *Community Cohesion: a Report of the Independent Review Team,* Home Office, London.

Duke, C. (1970) *Colour and Rehousing: A Study of Redevelopment in Leeds,* Institute of Race Relations, London.

Freedman, M. (1988) *Leeds Jewry: A Demographic and Sociological Profile,* Jewish Historical Society of Leeds, Leeds.

Home Office (2003) Quarterly asylum and immigration statistics available at: *http://www.homeoffice.gov.uk/rds/immigration1.html*

Law, I. (1996) *Racism, Ethnicity and Social Policy,* Prentice Hall, London.

Law, I., Phillips, D. and Turney, L. (2003) *Institutional Racism and Higher Education Project: Final Report on the University of Leeds Case Study,* Centre for Ethnicity and Racism Studies, University of Leeds, Leeds.

Modood, T., Berthoud, R., Lakey, J., Nazroo, J., Smith, P., Virdee, S. and Beishon, S. (eds.) (1997) *Ethnic Minorities in Britain: Diversity and Disadvantage,* Policy Studies Institute, London.

Onofrio, L. and Munk, K. (2003) *Understanding the Stranger: Interim Case Study Findings,* Report of the Information Centre about Asylum and Refugees in the UK (ICAR), Kings College, London.

Phillips, D. (1998) Black minority ethnic concentration, segregation and dispersal in Britain, *Urban Studies,* 35(10): 1681-1702.

Phillips, D., Ratcliffe, P., Davis, C., Butt, F. and Unsworth, R. (2002) *Asian Mobility in Leeds and Bradford.*

Phillips, D. and Unsworth, R. (2002) Changing minority ethnic housing choices in the social rented sector, Chapter 5 in Somerville, P. and Steele, A. (eds.) *Race, Housing and Social Exclusion,* Kingsley, London.

Ratcliffe, P. (ed.) (1996) *Social Geography and Ethnicity in Britain: Geographical Spread, Spatial Concentration and Internal Migration, Volume 3 of Ethnicity in the 1991 Census,* HMSO, London.

Rees, P. and Butt, F. (2003) Ethnic change and diversity in England, 1981–2001, Paper presented at the RGS-IBG Annual Conference, London, September.

Rees, P., Phillips, D. and Medway, D. (1995) *The socioeconomic geography of ethnic groups in two northern British cities,* 27: 557–591.

Stillwell, J. and Leigh, C. (1996) *Exploring the geographies of social polarisation in Leeds,* Chapter in Haughton, G. and Williams, C.C. (eds.) (1996), Avebury, Aldershot.

Thatcher, L. (2000) *The Resettlement of Kosovan Refugees in Leeds,* unpublished BA dissertation, School of Geography, University of Leeds, Leeds.

Waterman, S. (2003) *The Jews of Leeds in 2001: Portrait of a Community,* Institute for Jewish Policy Research Report Number 4, London.

Warm, R. (2004) The region's strategy to integrate refugees, *The Yorkshire & Humber Regional Review,* 14(1): 34–35.

Yorkshire Post (2003) Pledge after Kosovars attacked, 29 August.

4

The Roofs Over Our Heads: Housing Supply and Demand

HUW JONES, JANE KETTLE & RACHAEL UNSWORTH

The housing map of Leeds has changed appreciably over the last decade, fuelled by a significant shift in perceptions, expectations and aspirations of households.

4.1 Introduction

There are around 301,600 households in Leeds (ONS, 2003) occupying approximately 312,500 dwellings (ODPM, 2003b). There is a mix of housing types and tenures that creates a complex spatial mosaic across the district. Both the supply of and demand for housing have been influenced by economic and social change, land availability, central government policy and finance, local political factors, private sector development activity and changes in architectural standards and fashions. Most recently, there have been sharply contrasting levels of demand across the city and changing perceptions of the relative attractiveness of different tenures. Also, housing is increasingly valued not just as a place to live but as a source of investment returns.

Many aspects of housing development are market-led, but the local authority, working within an ever-evolving national and regional policy context, still has an important role in the ownership, management and allocation of some of the housing stock, although council-rented dwellings account for only 21 per cent of all dwellings in Leeds (Table 4.1) and are mostly associated with semi-detached houses, flats and terraced houses rather than detached houses or other dwelling types, most of which are bedsits (Figure 4.1)

The role of the local authority has shifted to become that of an enabler: controlling private development and letting activity, encouraging private sector housing improvement and enabling the provision of affordable housing and social rented housing. More widely, action to improve housing quality and market operation is part of the overarching drive towards sustainable development, involving a range of local authority departments and partnership organisations.

Table 4.1 Dwellings by tenure, 2001

Tenure	Number	Percentage
Owned	190,405	60.93
Private rented	41,232	13.19
Council rented	66,443	21.26
Other social rented	14,425	4.62
Total	312,505	100.00

Source: Census 2001 KS

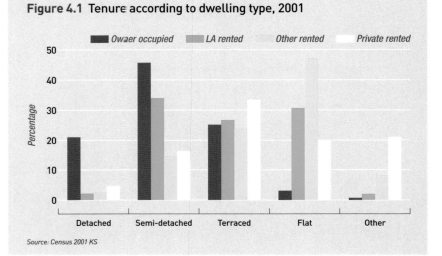

Figure 4.1 Tenure according to dwelling type, 2001

Source: Census 2001 KS

This chapter examines the patterning of housing supply and demand across the city with particular emphasis on market evolution, sub-areas, property types, tenures and prices. It offers some explanation of the trends and variations, and summarises some of the main policy interventions that aim at tackling the mismatch of supply and demand and at improving housing quality. It assesses the rapid changes in the Leeds housing landscape and acknowledges that changing community dynamics are inextricably linked to changing housing markets.

Figure 4.2 Different eras of housing development

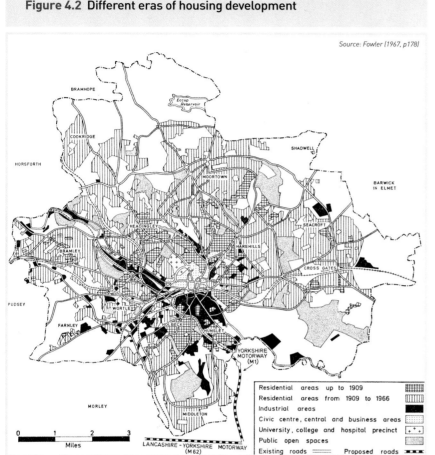

Source: Fowler (1967, p178)

clearance and rebuilding only began in earnest during the interwar years, when over 18,000 houses were built by the Council on 24 estates — places such as Gipton, Seacroft, Sandford, Halton Moor and Belle Isle. The slums of Quarry Hill were replaced by much-admired, innovative blocks of flats which initially offered greatly improved housing conditions (Fowler, 1967). However, structural faults were discovered and this addition to the urban landscape lasted only until 1975, when the flats were demolished.

The process of clearance continued after World War II, with a further 30,000 houses demolished between 1949 and 1971. Many were replaced by medium-rise and high-rise blocks of council flats — 151 blocks in all. Council building was mostly within Leeds itself — estates such as Spen Hill, Moor Grange, Armley Heights, Tinshill, Brackenwood and Cross Gates (Fowler, 1967), but all the smaller towns and villages in the district had some council housing provision, all of it originally for rent.

Almost 36,000 houses were developed by private sector builders during the interwar years, creating the suburbs of Gledhow, Moortown, Alwoodley, Roundhay, Oakwood, Weetwood and Adel (Burt and Grady, 1994). Private sector house building in the three decades up to 1979 consisted of uncontroversial extensions to existing built-up areas with no obvious restrictions on speculative development. Figure 4.2 indicates the location of different periods of housing up to the mid-1960s (within the pre-1974 city boundary) and Figure 4.3 shows illustrative examples of the housing layout in typical neighbourhoods: (a) Beeston, (b) Lincoln Green and Ebor Gardens, (c) Halton, and (d) Alwoodley.

4.2 Housing market evolution

The legacy of housing development to 1979

The need to house thousands of factory workers in Leeds during the nineteenth century was met mainly by private speculative development of terraced houses for rent. A large proportion of this was high density 'back-to-back' housing: approximately 78,000 houses were constructed and the style was only discontinued in 1937 (Dutton, 2003). Despite subsequent clearance programmes, around 15,000 back-to-backs remain in inner city wards — mainly in Harehills, University, Headingley, Richmond Hill, Beeston and Holbeck. More spacious terraced housing of the industrial era also survives in inner suburbs such as Armley, Chapeltown, and parts of University and Headingley wards. But it was in the highest density areas that the worst slum conditions developed and persisted for decades. Slum

Figure 4.3 Different housing development eras showing typical 'neighbourhood' layout

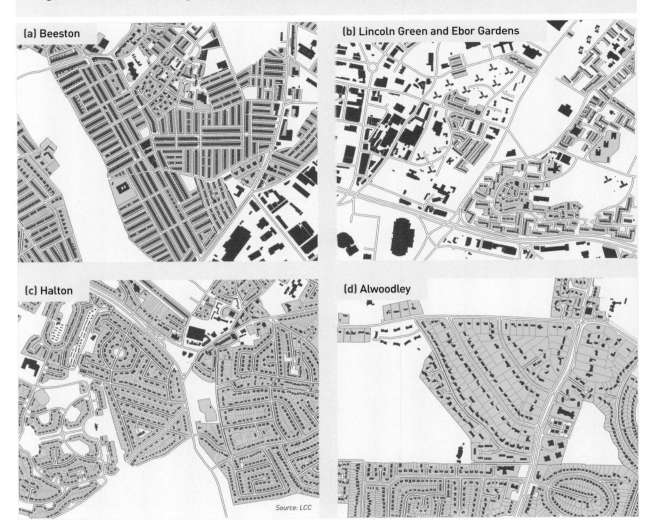

(a) Beeston

(b) Lincoln Green and Ebor Gardens

(c) Halton

(d) Alwoodley

Source: LCC

Housing development 1979–1997

Housing policy from 1979 to 1997, under successive Tory Governments, involved a reduced role for local authorities as owners and managers of housing, a growth in the role of housing associations (HAs) as providers of social housing, and an increasing emphasis on owner occupation as the preferred tenure (Balchin and Rhoden, 2002). Councils were obliged to sell houses to tenants who wanted to become owners and there was strong pressure to transfer remaining council housing to housing associations. A major housing boom in the late 1980s, followed by a slump in the early 1990s, left many recent purchasers with negative equity and led to an unprecedented rate of repossessions by mortgage companies. Adverse market conditions meant that large numbers of households presented themselves as homeless and since 1980 the responsibility for housing such households has fallen on the local authority.

In Leeds, the provision of social housing throughout the 1990s was driven by the creation in 1991 of an innovative initiative, Leeds Partnership Homes (LPH). This partnership between five housing associations and the local authority acted as a mechanism for transferring land, channelling resources and maximising the benefit of public subsidy to build social housing. By 1995, over 2,400 homes for rent or low cost sale had been completed and by 1998, the total had increased to 4,000.

Figure 4.4 Distribution of housing: (a) detached; (b) flats; (c) semi-detached; and (d) terraced, by community area, 2001

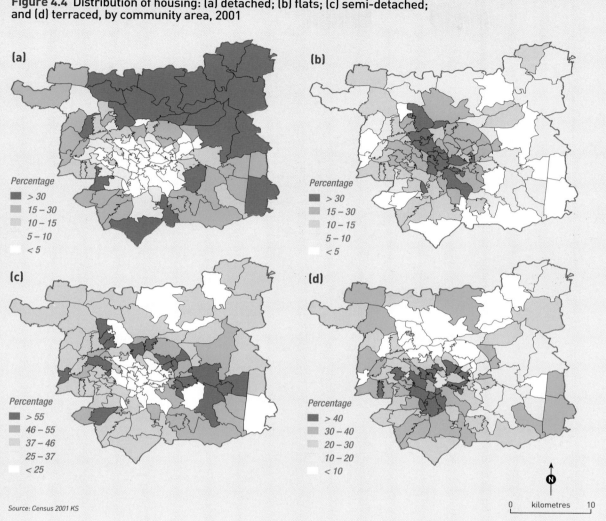

Source: Census 2001 KS

However, the operation of LPH in conjunction with the prevailing national policy environment did have a significant effect on the location and type of social development in Leeds. By the early 1990s, there was intensified competition for Social Housing Grant (SHG), a capital grant provided by the Housing Corporation to fund housing associations to develop social housing. The imperative to work with the local authority in the identification of need, combined locally with the land deals associated with LPH, resulted in a refocusing of attention on rehabilitation and infill development on peripheral and often problematic local authority estates in an attempt to diversify landlords and tenure groups.

Although Leeds pursued a collaborative, partnership approach rather than a fiercely competitive one, there was an element of competition between the partner associations for development land. Overall, this era was one that resulted in 'pepper-potting' of small developments and improvement schemes in inner areas (including the Ebor Gardens Estate in inner Leeds) and some outer suburbs (for example Crossgates) and free-standing towns (for example Otley and Morley). Arguably, many developments, while successfully providing new housing options for some households, were too small in scale to deliver a regenerative effect in the areas where investment was made (Kettle and Moran, 1999).

From the left, detached house, Weetwood, LS16; semi-detached houses, LS15; terraced houses, The Aviaries, Armley, LS12; Lovell Park (council flats) and Aspect 14 (private flats), LS7.

Into the twenty-first century

After the Labour Government came to power in 1997, national housing policy was formulated within the overarching sustainable development agenda. This meant a focus on environmental efficiency as well as on improving the quality of housing in areas of multiple deprivation and taking steps to deal with market imbalances. Arguments continue about the relative merits of area-based policies versus policies that specifically tackle the causes of deprivation for individuals and households (Moran, 1996; Anderson and Sim, 2000) and policy continues to suffer from overlaps and gaps as different initiatives and funding streams are applied without overall co-ordination and impact monitoring.

Another hotly debated topic is the extent of the need for new housing and the identification of suitable locations for such development. The amount of new housing to be developed in Leeds is decided at regional level through Regional Planning Guidance (RPG) (Yorkshire and Humber Assembly, 2003) but the locations that will accommodate new housing development are set out in the *Leeds Unitary Development Plan (UDP) Review 2003* (Leeds City Council Development Department, 2003). In the original UDP, land for housing was allocated at 65 locations around the district — enough to provide nearly 6,400 dwellings. Actual net addition to stock from 1993 to 2003, including supply by housing associations, amounted to around 25,000 dwellings. In the UDP Review, 40 sites are listed (16 of which were carried forward from the original UDP) and in addition there are seven so-called 'strategic sites' that have greater potential capacity. Chapter 14 provides more detail about land-use planning in relation to housing.

Different geographical distributions of housing in the four main type categories — detached, semi-detached, terraced and flats — are evident at the start of the twenty-first century (Figure 4.4) and conform to expectations. Detached housing is predominant in the peripheral suburbs and the surrounding rural areas whereas semi-detached properties are abundant in the outer suburbs, particularly in an arc around the north and in the east. Terraced housing, on the other hand, is important in the south and west whilst flats predominate in the inner city areas, extending diagonally from Cookridge in the north through to Hunslet in the south.

A new phenomenon of private sector residential development on formerly used land in and close to the city centre has largely been a response to the policy statements of the *Urban White Paper* (DETR, 2000a) which encourage mixed use, high density development. The requirement for 60 per cent of housing to be on brownfield sites (DETR, 2000b) supports this broad policy thrust. Leeds has exceeded this 60 per cent

threshold in every year since 2000 (ODPM, 2004), but much of the housing produced is aimed at the upper end of the private market — especially in the city centre. A few city centre residential developments took place beside the River Aire during the years of the Urban Development Corporation (1987–1995), but this amounted to no more than 500 units. After 1999, a new trend began, with local developers leading the way in the conversion of existing properties and the development of new buildings on brownfield sites. Early schemes were relatively small; the properties still in the pipeline (under construction and planned) average 100 units each and many of these later additions form part of large, mixed-used developments, some being undertaken by national house building companies. Details of the so-called 'city living' schemes are presented in Table 4.2. The majority of schemes are located in LS1 or LS2 (Figure 4.4) and many are on the waterfront — beside the river or canal — as developers are aware that a premium of up to 20 per cent can be achieved on waterside properties.

As well as the residential developments in the centre of Leeds itself (Figure 4.6), there have been conversions above shop units in town centres across the district, for example in Morley, Pudsey, Otley, Rothwell and Wetherby.

At the other end of the housing and social scale, there continues to be a problem of homelessness in Leeds, despite reduced levels of unemployment (see Chapter 6) and spare capacity in social housing. Homelessness persists not because of a lack of housing *per se,* but because the main causal factors of relationship and family break-down, often related to violence and drug abuse, continue to force people out of intolerable conditions and into temporary accommodation or onto the streets (Crisis, 2001; 2002; 2003; Bruegel and Smith, 1999).

Table 4.2 City living schemes at the end of Q1, 2004

	Total units	Total schemes	Average number of units per scheme
Completed	2,922	75	39
Under construction	2,743	20	137
With planning consent	3,210	42	76
Planning proposals	3,244	29	112
Total	12,119	166	73

Source: Author's data

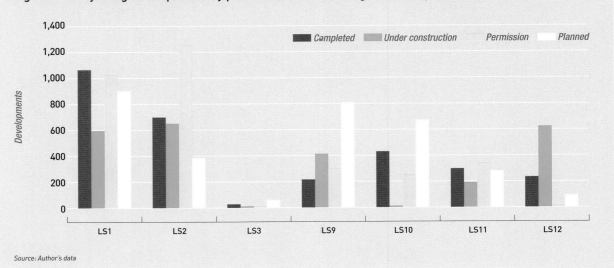

Figure 4.5 City living developments by postcode district and stage of development, 2004

Legend: ■ Completed ■ Under construction □ Permission □ Planned

Y-axis: Developments (0, 200, 400, 600, 800, 1,000, 1,200, 1,400)

X-axis: LS1, LS2, LS3, LS9, LS10, LS11, LS12

Source: Author's data

Asylum seekers and refugees have recently added to the official figures of homeless households, but much homelessness is 'hidden', with people in vulnerable circumstances staying on other people's floors in preference to seeking official help or sleeping rough (Robinson and Coward, 2003). Even where help is sought, the lack of affordable and appropriate housing in areas where people want to live can mean delays in matching applicants with suitable opportunities, though around two thirds of those accepted by the Council are found accommodation within six months.

Efforts are being made to try to reduce the incidence of households becoming homeless, and therefore the need for rehousing, by offering advice on issues such as property rights and court orders, installing additional security measures and by offering floating housing support. But for those who do become homeless, there are changes in the way that rehousing is achieved: less reliance is placed on hostels (which are unpopular, especially with the young) and bed and breakfast accommodation (the use of which has been phased

Domestic violence is the main cause of homelessness — in Leeds, 20 per cent of households accepted for rehousing are in this category.

Applications to the council from homeless people rose from 5,717 in 2001/02 to 7,999 in 2002/03 and 8,906 in 2003/04 and Leeds City Council accepted a duty to offer temporary accommodation to more than half these applicants.

Figure 4.6 Location of city centre residential developments, 2004

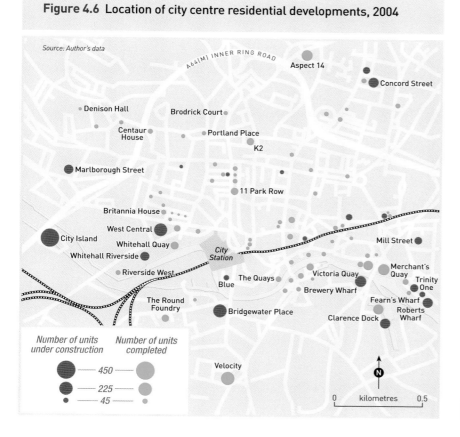

Source: Author's data

A64(M) INNER RING ROAD

Aspect 14
Concord Street
Denison Hall
Brodrick Court
Centaur House
Portland Place
K2
Marlborough Street
11 Park Row
Britannia House
West Central
City Island
Whitehall Quay
Whitehall Riverside
Riverside West
City Station
Mill Street
The Quays
Victoria Quay
Merchant's Quay
Blue
Trinity One
Brewery Wharf
The Round Foundry
Fearn's Wharf
Bridgewater Place
Roberts Wharf
Clarence Dock
Velocity

Number of units under construction | Number of units completed
450
225
45

N

0   kilometres   0.5

By early 2004, there were nearly 3,000 completed apartments in the city centre. Top, developments near Leeds Bridge. Above, 'Blue', next to the city station: 61 flats under construction. Bottom, Whitehall Quay, a new development of 193 flats.

out). Instead, emphasis is placed on rapid allocation of social housing or of temporary private rented accommodation. Support is available to enable people to overcome the hurdle of high private sector rents and private landlords' demand for deposits and rent in advance.

Other recent housing policy initiatives will be presented (in section 4.5) after discussion of the different sectors and areas.

4.3 Current housing market conditions and characteristics of residential areas

In recent years, the generally thriving local economy and a decline in average household size have combined to push up the overall demand for housing units. Low interest rates, in combination with poor stock market performance from the turn of the millennium, fuelled house price inflation, as property was regarded as the best available investment option. But this demand is not evenly spread across the city. According to figures from the Land Registry for 2003, average sales prices for

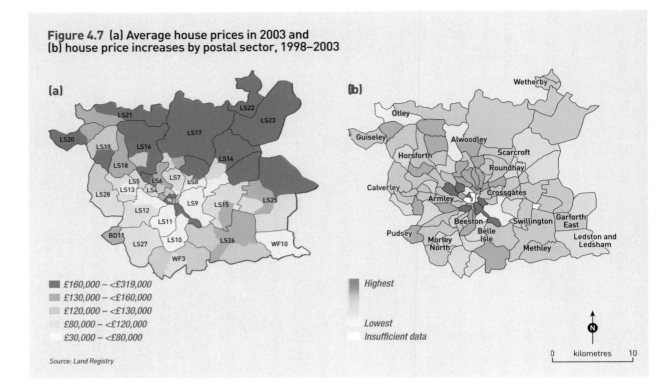

Figure 4.7 (a) Average house prices in 2003 and (b) house price increases by postal sector, 1998–2003

(a)

LS21, LS22, LS23, LS17, LS20, LS19, LS16, LS18, LS14, LS5, LS6, LS7, LS8, LS13, LS4, LS28, LS12, LS9, LS15, LS25, LS11, BD11, LS10, LS26, WF10, LS27, WF3

£160,000 – <£319,000
£130,000 – <£160,000
£120,000 – <£130,000
£80,000 – <£120,000
£30,000 – <£80,000

Source: Land Registry

(b)

Wetherby, Otley, Guiseley, Alwoodley, Scarcroft, Horsforth, Roundhay, Calverley, Armley, Crossgates, Beeston, Swillington, Garforth East, Pudsey, Morley North, Belle Isle, Methley, Ledston and Ledsham

Highest
Lowest
Insufficient data

0   kilometres   10

private properties in the district range from around £36,000 for terraced houses in inner city Cross Green to around £300,000 for properties in rural areas to the north east of Leeds. In the most desirable areas, demand pushes up prices and there is a lack of affordable housing, yet in less desirable areas, there is a low level of demand, stagnating values and some empty properties. The spatial distribution of private house sale prices by postal sector has a characteristic north-south pattern (Figure 4.7a). The pattern of changes in sale prices between 1998 and 2003 (Figure 4.7b) is less marked and more complex, reflecting patterns of new building and the relative spatial distribution of private and social housing.

The pattern of increases in prices (Figure 4.7) and the range of weekly rents (Table 4.3) reflect relative demand according to property type, area and tenure. House price trends are a reflection of the evolution of a series of inter-connected housing markets operating at different levels in Leeds.

Demand by area

Figure 4.8 illustrates the broad housing market areas in Leeds: city centre, inner urban, inner suburbs, outer suburbs and dormitory villages.

Table 4.3 Typical rents for different categories of property, 2004

Category of property	Weekly rental
Council	£47.33
Housing association	£57.05
Private rented	
Student	£50 per person*
Inner areas	£55–100
Outer areas	£90–450
City centre	£600+

*Shared house   Source: Author's data

Demand for the new developments in the city centre is predominantly from young singles without dependants who are attracted to "the city core's cultural resources, architectural sense of place, and to the concentration of single, non-attached people" (Kotkin, 1999, p.2–3).

Figure 4.8 Broad market areas

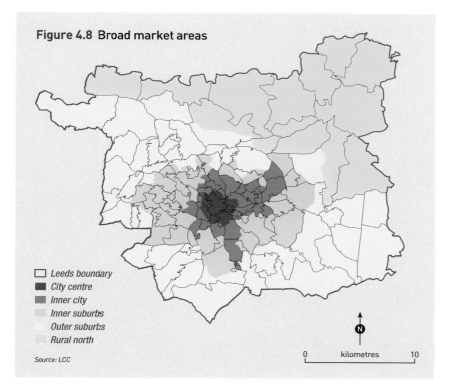

Leeds boundary
City centre
Inner city
Inner suburbs
Outer suburbs
Rural north

Source: LCC

N

0 kilometres 10

Although there is clearly strong demand for city centre apartments, vacancy levels in this sub-market are considerably higher than they are elsewhere, though precise figures are elusive because of the way that the market operates: apartments bought 'off plan' by an investor may or may not have an occupier, and full statistics of sales and lettings are unavailable. There is a bulge in supply in the early twenty-first century, but applications peaked in 2000. If all the planned apartments are indeed developed and they accommodate on average 1.5 people, as was found in the 2003 survey, this would mean a city centre population of around 18,000, representing no more than 2.5 per cent of Leeds' projected population for the year 2010. Altogether, economic forecasts, the likely geography of employment and the likely overall scale of residential construction strongly suggest that demand will be at least sufficient for the supply so far envisaged. Furthermore, as the market matures, the occupier base will widen beyond the 'yuppies' and 'dinkies'.

Inner urban areas comprise both lower quality owner occupied and rental areas and also social

Terraced housing on Beeston Hill, between Dewsbury Road and Cross Flatts Park — from the east. This part of the inner city is also illustrated in Figure 4.3(a). First time buyers now have options other than small terraced houses. Some are choosing city centre apartments.

In 2003, a survey was carried out in order to find out more about the characteristics and views of people living in the city centre (Fox and Unsworth, 2003). Completed questionnaires were received from 152 residents of 20 of the larger apartment buildings and the results are summarised in Table 4.4.

housing estates. There are peripheral estates such as Seacroft, Halton Moor and Gipton and also estates closer to the city centre such as Little London, Ebor Gardens, Lincoln Green and Richmond Hill. Low demand, high turnover and significant numbers of empty properties are reflected in generally

Table 4.4 Summary of the city living survey, 2003

Demographics
- 53 per cent of respondents were aged 30 or under and only 12 per cent were 46 or older.
- Half the respondents live on their own; the other half share with one other adult; there were no children in these households.

Tenure and property prices
- 61 per cent of respondents were owner occupiers with the remainder almost evenly split between tenants of private landlords and letting companies.
- The majority of flats in owner occupation were bought at values between £95,000 and £195,000; a quarter of all purchases fell into the £120,001–£145,000 category.
- The majority of rents fall within the broad band £500-899 per calendar month but 10 per cent of apartments cost their tenants over £1,000 a month.
- Most of the apartments are occupied as principal residences. Only 12 per cent of respondents stated that their principal address was elsewhere — mostly well beyond Leeds; most of these people were amongst the highest earners.

Living and working in the city centre
- 27 per cent of respondents described themselves as professional and a further 12 per cent were in banking/finance; media and IT accounted for another 16 per cent.
- 21 per cent of the sample comprised senior managers or partners in a business and 15 per cent owned a business; another 30 per cent considered themselves to be in middle management.
- This is an affluent section of the population: 86 per cent had a total income of more than £25,000 and over a third of the households had a total income of over £55,000.
- Most people who responded to the survey work in Leeds, and proximity to work is the main reason for living in the city centre.
- Two thirds of respondents work in the central postcode districts of LS1 or LS2.

Source: Fox and Unsworth (2003)

relatively low values and it is in such areas that there are neighbourhoods identified as requiring radical approaches to regeneration. The older areas are characterised by small terraced houses — many of which are back-to-backs — and houses in multiple occupation. The council estates in these areas exhibit high levels of social deprivation and crime (see Chapter 6). The reputation of these areas means that they are low on the list of preferences for new council house applicants and for those applying for transfers. Those that can move away do so and the remaining households are isolated in a decaying and dangerous environment. Chapeltown has benefited from a general improvement in housing market conditions. In Harehills, rising prices may reflect both rising prices across the city, continuing demand from people of Pakistani and Bangladeshi origin and an element of speculation by investors anticipating remodelling of the area. In Gipton, the Council is using a Low Cost Home Ownership Grant scheme to help tenants buy their own homes. Vacant land owned by the local authority is being sold to a developer to build housing and the money raised is used to provide grants to support tenants' purchase of the houses.

Inner suburbs include places such as Bramley, Middleton and Meanwood. Property values are lower than the average for the city and there are some patches of social and private housing that are in especially low demand. In contrast, consistently popular inner suburbs such as Chapel Allerton, Crossgates and Whitkirk maintain a buoyant market, attracting both first time buyers and aspirant households seeking to move out of inner areas. Demand in Headingley has been fuelled by the expansion in student numbers and the convenience of this area for access to the two universities. House prices rose by over 70 per cent between 1999 and 2002.

In the green belt to the north west, north east and east of the city are outer suburbs (such as Rawdon, Guiseley, Aberford, Micklefield and Morley), and dormitory villages (such as Collingham, Bramham, Scarcroft, Pool-in-Wharfedale). House prices are high here, reflecting the desirability of these areas and the strong competition for properties that come onto the market. Purchasers are mainly those trading up from smaller properties or less desirable areas, those seeking access to high-performing schools and those moving to Leeds for employment reasons. Only 14 per cent of dwellings are socially rented and these are in high demand with low turnover. Access to the sector is therefore extremely restricted.

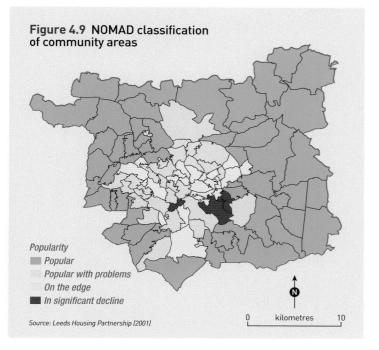

Figure 4.9 NOMAD classification of community areas

Popularity
- Popular
- Popular with problems
- On the edge
- In significant decline

0   kilometres   10

Source: Leeds Housing Partnership (2001)

Overall, two thirds of areas and housing in Leeds are at least reasonably prosperous, while one third of areas are characterised by poverty and significant problems. Precisely 61,222 properties — 20 per cent of the stock — are categorised as at risk of changing or low demand (LCC, 2002a). Two thirds of these properties are in the social rented sector and the remainder are privately owned or rented. Most are located in older housing areas and peripheral council estates at the fringes of the inner city where the least desirable housing types are found.

LCC housing researchers developed a system for categorising the relative strengths and weakness of the different markets. This is known as NOMAD, the Neighbourhood Oriented Model of Area Demand. NOMAD combines analysis of housing and social indicators to draw conclusions about the 'health' of neighbourhoods classified as follows:

- popular areas: low turnover, high demand, low benefits dependency, low crime, high levels of educational attainment;

- popular areas with significant problems: generally buoyant demand patterns but have either specific problems in relation to poverty or crime or contain estates where significant problems are evident;

- areas on the edge: high turnover, low demand, high benefits dependency, high crime, low standards of educational attainment — but not to the same extent as the areas in significant decline; and

- areas in significant decline: high turnover, low demand, high benefits dependency, high crime, low standards of educational attainment.

Originally based on 180 local lettings areas, the NOMAD scores have been transferred to the 106 community areas for mapping (Figure 4.9).

There is a recognition that the different 'neighbourhoods at risk' have experienced different combinations of factors shaping the local market. "There are contrasts in the social and mobility profiles of the populations, in the causes of dissatisfaction about the neighbourhood and in the general perceptions of residents living elsewhere in Leeds" (Cole *et al.*, 2003, p. 2–3). The corollary of this analysis is that there has to be very precise tailoring of policy responses to deal with each area. There is evidence in the 2004 NOMAD analysis that some improvement has occurred in areas where spending has been targeted: while 36 Housing Market Zone Areas showed 'low or fragile demand' in 2002, the figure was down to 25 such areas in 2004. For example, Saxton Gardens, in the East Bank regeneration area, has benefited from refurbished housing and the introduction of mixed tenure. Ebor Gardens estate continues its gradual improvement as Estate Action work affects the physical state of the housing and environment. Demolition of unpopular housing has resulted in improvements to the physical environment and perceptions on Middleton estate and Whinmoor Way. In all these places, there has also been a positive impact on demand levels following the sharply reduced crime rates that have been experienced after anti-social tenants have been moved. However, there are signs of deterioration in areas adjacent to those that have seen improved NOMAD scores: Manor Farm estate, next to

Top, before and
after improvements:
council houses in
Kentmere Avenue,
LS14. Middle,
unpopular flats in
Lincoln Green, LS9,
were replaced by
housing association
houses (bottom).

Middleton estate, has become more 'fragile' and while Saxton Gardens has shown improvements, neighbouring Cross Green has declined. These effects partly reflect displacement of problems and partly point up the need for further targeting of regeneration efforts.

NOMAD scores for Broadlea, Fairfield Wythers, New Wortley and Inner Armley have all worsened. A new public-private partnership aiming to channel investment into Armley and Wortley may help to reverse this trend. Central Headingley is another area that is moving towards being 'on the edge' of decline and will need some special attention.

Residential mobility

Overall, households who can afford to move to a more desirable area, or who have characteristics that enable them to compete successfully for the most favoured social rented housing, will tend to take the opportunity to move. Those who are unable to compete in either the private or social rented sectors are left behind in areas that are in a spiral of downward demand and declining quality. In fact, Leeds has a relatively low rate of household mobility: in 2000–2001, 8.6 per cent of Leeds' population changed addresses compared with 11 per cent of the national population. Researchers found that two thirds of Leeds residents had been at their current address for more than 10 years (Cole *et al.,* 2003). Of those who had moved within the previous 10 years, the majority had only moved once, many had been long-term residents at their previous address and half the mobile households had moved within the immediate local area. Only 11 per cent of the sample had moved from outside Leeds — a figure that is perhaps lower than might have been imagined. There are also low levels of intention to move, with 87 per cent saying that they are unlikely to move within the next five years, though it is

Mobility between tenures is most prevalent amongst under 25s and people with 'chaotic' or 'challenging' behaviour.

Table 4.5 Factors impacting on household mobility

Push factors	Pull factors
Crime	Desire to live in green areas
Poorly performing schools	Good schools
Environmental blight	Caring responsibilities
Anti-social behaviour	Making money out of housing
Negative perceptions of the area	Lifestyle aspirations
Changing life-circumstances	

Shared house

Source: Author's data

considered likely that mobility levels will in fact be higher than is indicated by stated intentions.

The innermost wards show the highest actual and potential turnover. The lowest levels of actual and planned mobility are found in the wards immediately beyond the inner city — in an arc from Moortown and Chapel Allerton in the north, through Roundhay, Seacroft and Whinmoor to Halton in the east. Pudsey North and Aireborough in the west are also notably stable. Some of the factors that influence household mobility are indicated in Table 4.5. Mobility figures are not easy to interpret: high mobility may indicate vibrancy, dissatisfaction or particular vulnerability, such as in the case of released prisoners and those with recurrent drug problems (James *et al.*, 2003). Low mobility may indicate either satisfaction or perceived difficulties in achieving a move. Mobility in Leeds is affected by the perceptions of different areas, combined with an aspiration to live in what are perceived to be greener areas. This is compounded by an overall inability of people to move up the housing ladder within inner urban and suburban areas. Movement may also be due to fear of encroaching landlords (as, for example, in Headingley) or perceptions of risk from crime.

The majority of those expressing a wish to move mostly named locations adjacent or close to their current home, further away from the inner city than their current place of residence. This echoes findings in a recent study of outward migration of minority ethnic households (see Chapter 3).

Mobility is lowest within the local authority sector and previous address is most likely to have been within the same area. Housing association tenants are more likely to have lived elsewhere in Leeds and those in private rented and owner occupied housing are more likely to have lived outside Leeds. In addition, mobility is contained within sectors of the city: for example people may aspire to move from inner south Leeds to outer south Leeds rather than across the city. Conversely, mobility aspirations for north Leeds residents extend across a larger geography, into North Yorkshire. Mobility between tenures is most prevalent amongst under 25s and people with 'chaotic' or 'challenging' behaviour (Cole *et al.*, 2003).

Findings from research in the city centre indicated that there is likely to be a much greater turnover of occupiers here than is the case with other sub-markets in the city (Fox and Unsworth, 2003). Fifteen per cent of residents, especially letting agency tenants, expected to stay at their current address for less than six months and a further 27 per cent envisaged staying between six and twelve months. But a majority of residents (58 per cent) were planning to stay in their property for over a year and of these, two thirds expressed an intention of staying for more than two years. Owner occupiers were five times more likely than tenants to state an intention of staying for more than two years.

Demand by property type

Data from the Land Registry show that while price increases for all property types from 1998–2003 were higher in Leeds than for England and Wales as a whole, the price of terraced properties and flats or maisonettes rose most rapidly. The prices of flats and maisonettes increased by 135 per cent, compared with 90 per cent for England and Wales. Prices of terraced

properties increased most rapidly in areas of student housing, both traditional (Leeds 6) and emerging (Kirkstall, Burley); in popular inner suburban areas (such as Chapel Allerton) where they may provide 'entry level' housing; in some inner areas, reflecting either purchase by private landlords of ex-Council properties or by speculator investors in areas of regeneration (Harehills, Beeston Hill). Prices of flats rose most rapidly in the city centre. In outer areas and suburban areas there are desirable new flat complexes on greenfield sites, some of which provide entry level housing in those areas.

Detached property prices showed the steepest rise in the outer areas and outer suburbs, reflecting the popularity of those areas and a desire to be close to high-performing schools, and interestingly, in some inner suburbs and inner areas (such as Seacroft, Belle Isle, Bramley, Wortley and Beeston) where new detached homes are sought after by aspirant households but where supply is scarce. Semi-detached properties increased in value most rapidly in the Headingley area, reflecting the increasing purchase by landlords and parents for student housing. Price rises for semi-detached property in the outer suburbs may reflect a connection with a desire to be close to high-performing schools (see owner occupation section below and also Chapter 7) and the desire to locate in areas where crime is less of a threat.

4.4 Housing tenure: a profile

Figure 4.10 shows how the total housing stock numbers differ across the wards, with the greatest numbers of dwellings in Morley, Wetherby, Aireborough, Wortley, Otley and City and Holbeck wards. The outer wards have the greatest numbers of owner occupied dwellings and in these areas, all the other tenures are of relatively minor importance. The inner wards have the lowest numbers of owner occupied dwellings and in several of them, renting from the Council exceeds owner occupation. Private rented properties are most numerous in the wards near the universities and in all but three wards, 'other social rented' is the smallest category of tenure type.

Figure 4.10 Tenure of households by ward, 2001

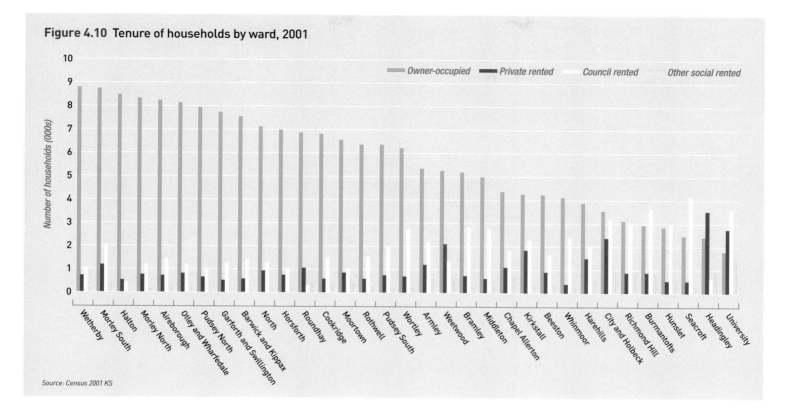

Owner-occupied — Private rented — Council rented — Other social rented

Number of households (000s)

Wetherby, Morley South, Halton, Morley North, Aireborough, Otley and Wharfedale, Pudsey North, Garforth and Swillington, Barwick and Kippax, North, Horsforth, Roundhay, Cookridge, Moortown, Rothwell, Pudsey South, Wortley, Armley, Weetwood, Bramley, Middleton, Chapel Allerton, Kirkstall, Beeston, Whinmoor, Harehills, City and Holbeck, Richmond Hill, Burmantofts, Hunslet, Seacroft, Headingley, University

Source: Census 2001 KS

Changes in tenure 1991–2001

This section reviews the developing tenure patterns within the city and explores some of the dynamics of change within and between sectors (Table 4.6). Overall, in terms of percentage growth, the private rented sector has seen greatest expansion since 1991. While the numbers of people in dwellings owned and managed by the local authority declined, there was a growth in the number of housing association tenants. Owner occupation continued to expand, but at a much slower rate than the rental sectors.

Owner occupation

Around 70 per cent of the 20.6 million households in the UK are owner occupiers, either owning their properties outright or having a mortgage. In Leeds, the level of owner occupation is lower but this sector accounts for by far the greatest proportion of households. The market is very spatially differentiated with desirable and less desirable areas sometimes extremely clearly demarcated. In the outer north-west and north-east areas of the city (Figure 4.11), the housing market has been overheating and conditions are approaching those of the South East region.

Conversely, in Beeston Hill, "people want to live above (south of) the park but no-one wants to touch the other side of the park" (a property developer quoted in Cole *et al.,* 2003, p.25), though this remark ignores the considerable continuing demand from Bangladeshis. Within Leeds 7 postal district there is a great contrast between Chapel Allerton, which is much sought-after, as the agents would say, and Chapeltown, just to

Table 4.6 Changes in tenure, 1991–2003

	2003	Percentage	Numerical change 1991–2003	Percentage change 1991–2003
Council housing	66,443	21.3	-15,920	-19.3
Housing association	14,425	4.6	4,751	49.1
All social housing	80,868	25.9	-11,169	-12.0
Private rented	41,232	13.2	20,953	103.3
Owner occupied	190,405	60.9	18,130	9.5
All homes	312,505	100.0	27,914	8.9

Source: ODPM (2003a)

the south, which is stigmatised as an area of minority ethnic group concentration, drug dealing and associated crime.

In the past, first time buyers would have had little option but to purchase in the areas with the lowest house prices. They might not have stayed long before upgrading — typically by moving outwards to the adjacent, more desirable suburbs — but their gaining the first rung on the property ladder in the inner city helped to keep all areas integrated within a single market. In recent years, increasing numbers of well-paid first time buyers, with access to attractive financing deals, have been able to afford to purchase in better areas, missing out the traditional first time buyer territory. The consequent reduced demand is manifest in stagnating and even falling prices in inner city areas (Cole et al., 2003).

When they start a family, many couples aspire to move to larger property, often with a garden, and try to ensure that they are in a suitable location to secure places at favoured schools. They prefer not to be in areas that have a reputation for crime, vandalism and anti-social behaviour. The premium for desirable areas is significant, with a house in Headingley commanding perhaps four times the price of a similar property in Holbeck (Cole et al., 2003). Figure 4.12 shows that house prices in relation to income are highest in the outer areas. There

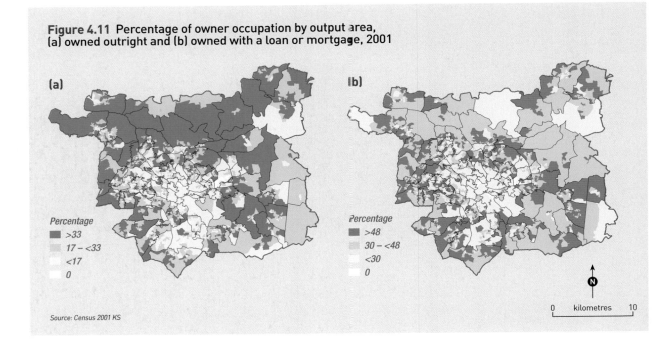

Figure 4.11 Percentage of owner occupation by output area, (a) owned outright and (b) owned with a loan or mortgage, 2001

(a)

Percentage
- >33
- 17 – <33
- <17
- 0

Source: Census 2001 KS

(b)

Percentage
- >48
- 30 – <48
- <30
- 0

0   kilometres   10

Figure 4.12 Location of affordable housing developments, 2002, 2003 and proposed

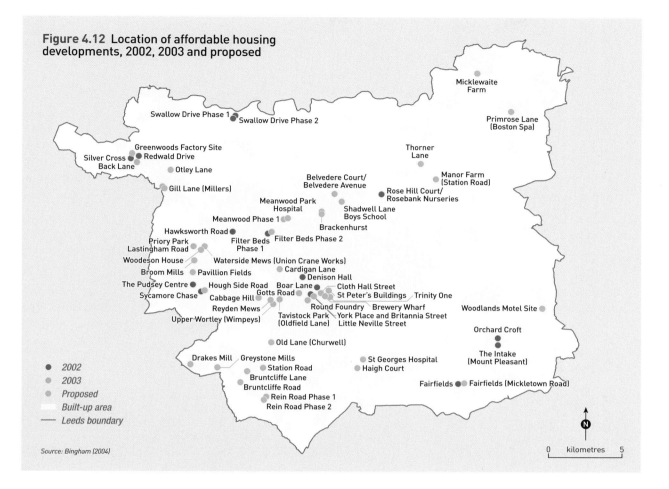

Micklewaite Farm

Swallow Drive Phase 1
Swallow Drive Phase 2

Primrose Lane (Boston Spa)

Greenwoods Factory Site
Redwald Drive
Silver Cross
Back Lane
Otley Lane

Thorner Lane

Manor Farm (Station Road)

Belvedere Court/ Belvedere Avenue

Gill Lane (Millers)

Rose Hill Court/ Rosebank Nurseries

Meanwood Park Hospital
Shadwell Lane Boys School
Meanwood Phase 1
Brackenhurst

Hawksworth Road
Priory Park
Lastingham Road
Filter Beds Phase 1
Filter Beds Phase 2
Woodeson House
Waterside Mews (Union Crane Works)
Broom Mills
Pavillion Fields
Cardigan Lane
Denison Hall
The Pudsey Centre
Hough Side Road
Boar Lane
Cloth Hall Street
Gotts Road
St Peter's Buildings
Trinity One
Sycamore Chase
Cabbage Hill
Round Foundry
Brewery Wharf
Woodlands Motel Site
Reyden Mews
Tavistock Park
York Place and Britannia Street
Upper Wortley (Wimpeys)
(Oldfield Lane)
Little Neville Street
Orchard Croft

Old Lane (Churwell)

The Intake (Mount Pleasant)

Drakes Mill
Greystone Mills
Station Road
St Georges Hospital
Haigh Court
Bruntcliffe Lane
Bruntcliffe Road
Fairfields
Fairfields (Mickletown Road)
Rein Road Phase 1
Rein Road Phase 2

● 2002
● 2003
● Proposed
■ Built-up area
— Leeds boundary

0 kilometres 5

N

Source: Bingham (2004)

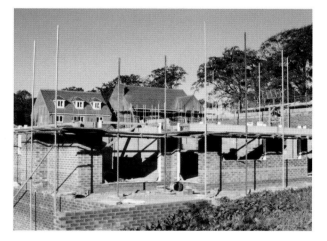

has been some attempt to provide affordable housing within these most sought-after areas, but the numbers of units are very low in proportion to the stock (see Table 14.4).

Private rented

In the UK, more than two million households are in the private rented sector and more than a third of these households live in flats; 36 per cent of households in this tenure are one-person households (ODPM, 2002). As in many parts of the UK, the private rented sector in Leeds (Figure 4.13) has been growing (Table 4.6). Renting by private owners has expanded since the growth in student numbers (from 22,000 in 1991 to 34,000 in 2001) and the imposition of tuition fees in 1998. A common model in Leeds is for parents to invest in a property in Headingley to provide conveniently-located accommodation for their own offspring while at university, an income from the other rooms that are let at commercial rents and the prospect of capital growth. The expansion of this market has created significant tensions in the area between the older-established residents and the incomers. Over half of all full-time students live in Headingley ward and one quarter of Headingley's

Houses under construction for private sale. More than 60 per cent of residential developments in Leeds District are on previously used land.

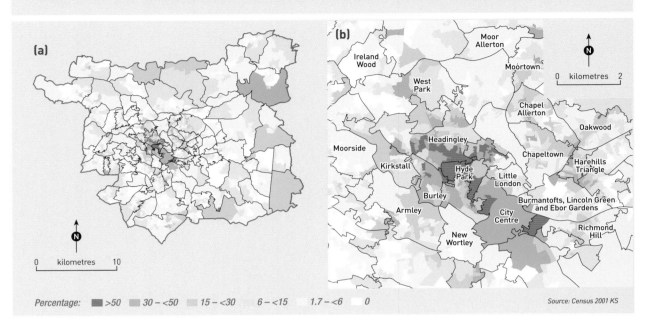

Figure 4.13 Percentage private rented by output area, (a) Leeds and (b) north and central Leeds, 2001

Percentage: ■ >50 ■ 30 – <50 ■ 15 – <30 6 – <15 1.7 – <6 0

Source: Census 2001 KS

Many terraced properties in Headingley, Hyde Park and Burley belong to landlords who often rent them out to students.

population consists of full-time students. A new policy of student housing restraint (Leeds City Council Development Department, 2003) seeks to limit further growth of this market in LS6 and redirect demand for student accommodation by encouraging provision of halls of residence in other parts of the city. A significant number of schemes have already come through the planning system and will add several thousand bed spaces.

Across Leeds, more than 250 landlords are members of the Leeds Landlords Accreditation Scheme (LLAS) covering 11,345 bed spaces. There is evidence that the scheme, which built upon the experience of the UNIPOL Code of Standards for student housing and the general Code of Standards established by the City Council, has managed to drive up standards for the housing managed by Code members, and the scheme is regarded as a leading example of its type nationally. However, only around 25 per cent of landlords in Leeds are signed up to this scheme, and it is estimated that around 50 per cent of rental properties are owned by small-scale landlords who are capitalising on opportunities presented by buy-to-let schemes.

In some areas, private renting is becoming the majority tenure, especially in areas of older back-to-back or small terraced housing (such as Cross Green, Holbeck and parts of Harehills and Beeston Hill). In such places, largely rejected by

first time buyers, the property mix and the preponderance of private renting is leading to endemic instability and lack of community links. This housing is also becoming an additional

The ODPM (2001) private landlords survey showed that nationally, nearly two-thirds of dwellings in the private rented sector are owned by private individuals. In contrast, only 7 per cent are owned by residential property companies.

Lettings to tenants on Housing Benefit account for less than a fifth of all lettings, and many landlords are reluctant to let to such tenants, yet there are some landlords who specialise in this end of the market, especially in inner city areas.

Nearly 60 per cent of private rented dwellings are dealt with by agents and these tend to be in a better state of repair than those managed by their owners. However, of those properties that are more professionally managed, nearly half fail to meet the 'decent homes' standard and written tenancy agreements are not universal.

Despite relatively low rates of return on residential investment properties in terms of income, most landlords remain committed to operating in this market on the basis that total return will prove worthwhile as property price inflation continues.

'safety net' for extremely vulnerable people, households evicted from previous accommodation and those households whom other providers are reluctant to help (for example, asylum seekers and refugees — see Chapter 3).

In addition there is increasing evidence of private landlords purchasing ex-council properties for letting (e.g. a flat to let in Marlborough Towers opposite Park Lane College at £100 per week compared with local authority rent of around £40). This has implications for estate management practices on those estates and is frustrating attempts to tackle anti-social tenants where tenants evicted can now move back into the estate by renting privately.

Social housing

The two categories of social housing are renting from the council and renting from a housing association. Council houses represented about one fifth of all dwellings in Leeds in 2001 and the spatial pattern is illustrated in Figure 4.14.

Altogether, the number of council homes declined by 30,895 between 1981 and 2001 — a reduction of 31.7 per cent. The number of homes reduced by 14,975 between 1981 and 1991; another 12,438 were sold between 1991 and 2001. Between 1980 and April 2003, 23,978 council properties were

sold under the Right-to-Buy and approximately 1,520 were sold during 2003/04. Analysis of Leeds City Council records shows that:

- 14,037 council properties were sold between 1980 and 1991 and 7,263 were sold between 1991 and 2001;

- an average of 1,058 homes have been sold each year since 1980 when the Right-to-Buy was introduced;

- the rate of sales has been rising since 1996 (622 sold); and

- the amount of homes sold each year doubled between 1998–1999 and 2003–2004.

Forty-five percent of homes sold under the Right-to-Buy since 1980 are located in outer suburban areas or villages. In Wetherby, over 40 per cent of the council housing present in 1980 has been sold and over 30 per cent has been sold in Otley, Aireborough, Horsforth, West Park, Cookridge, Garforth, Kippax and Rothwell. Many of these properties have been sold on, and while prices are substantially less than the general market rate for the surrounding area, they are still strikingly in excess of the value when sold under the Right-to-Buy. Such housing is now either providing entry level affordable housing or has been bought by private landlords for letting and provides a source of rented housing for households who would not have high priority for, or who would not personally consider applying for, social rented housing.

Conversely, less than a quarter of homes sold under the Right-to-Buy since 1980 were located in inner urban areas, and of all housing present in those areas in 1980, only 15 per cent has been sold. In Seacroft South, only 9 per cent of the council housing present in 1980 has been sold and less than 15 per cent has been sold in Lincoln Green, South Gipton, Ebor Gardens,

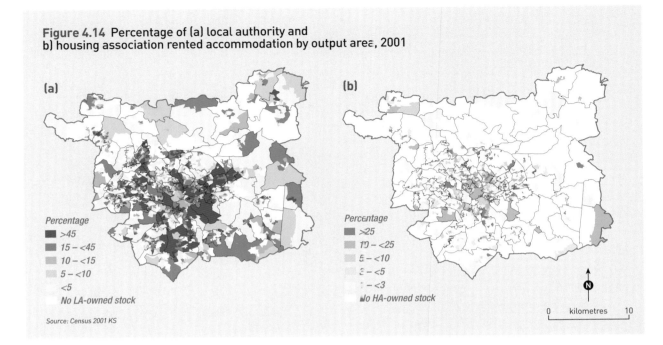

Figure 4.14 Percentage of (a) local authority and b) housing association rented accommodation by output area, 2001

(a)

Percentage
- ■ >45
- ■ 15 – <45
- ■ 10 – <15
- □ 5 – <10
- □ <5
- □ No LA-owned stock

Source: Census 2001 KS

(b)

Percentage
- ■ >25
- ■ 10 – <25
- □ 5 – <10
- □ 3 – <5
- □ 1 – <3
- □ No HA-owned stock

0   kilometres   10

Table 4.7 Local authority housing stock by property type, 2002

Type	Percentage
Houses and bungalows	59
Low rise flats	21
Multi-storey flats	11
Sheltered housing units	7

Source: LCC (2002)

Halton Moor, Armley, Belle Isle North and Little London. In these inner urban areas, there is some evidence that on resale these properties are being bought by private landlords and that this is having a negative impact on local estate management practice and action to tackle anti-social behaviour.

In addition, high levels of sales have taken place in some inner suburban areas, including North Seacroft, where 39 per cent of housing present in 1980 has been sold (possibly due to better-than-average conditions and the lack of a nearby aspirational suburban area for people to move to) and in Belle Isle South where 31 per cent has been sold. In the Burley and Headingley areas (where around 25 per cent of housing present in 1980 has been sold), ex-council homes sold on are now being bought by private landlords for letting to students.

There are many different designs of council housing, ranging from semis to highrise flats. Left: Barncroft Flats, LS14. Right, boarded up flats, LS14. Bottom, council tenants, Ramshead Gardens, LS14 .

Despite all the sales, there are still more than 66,000 council-owned properties of different types (Table 4.7) and more than 20 per cent of households remain as council tenants — a figure higher than the national average of 14 per cent (ONS, 2002). But the profile of council tenants has changed over the last 30 years: with families moving out to seek home ownership and younger people moving out for other rented housing, the remaining tenants are predominantly over 60, while the majority of people entering social housing are young. This 'hollowing out' of social housing tenant bases has led to increasing management problems and has had an impact on demand for housing in many areas.

Since the mid-1980s, council housing has become increasingly regarded as a starting place, a stepping stone or a safety net, with most of those aspirant households who are able to do so seeking and achieving home ownership. Housing association property has come to be regarded in much the same light. Demand is again not evenly spread across the available stock types and locations: a large unit in a more prosperous northern suburb is easy to let, whereas a small unit in a southern area would be hard to let. Some housing associations, targeting particular tenant groups such as black and minority ethnic households, experience high demand.

The impact of the reduction of council housing supply has been inconclusive. The number of households on the waiting list has not reduced but has stayed relatively buoyant. Some of this is probably from households seeking 'insurance' from

council housing while hoping for a better opportunity. Around 25–30 per cent of the waiting list consists of single parents but there are fewer nuclear families and a diminishing number of older people. The main new demand is from individual young people who, as tenants, may well place new demands on the community where they are allocated accommodation.

Households on the waiting list typically choose the area in which they would prefer to live and then the property type/size (although see comments below on 'innovations'.) Some areas and property types are in low demand, although some areas have seen outward moves curtailed and demand rise following regeneration work. This has been evident in areas such as Ebor Gardens and Belle Isle. But for other pockets of housing, there is little evidence of a reversal of declining demand. Indeed there are some areas of council housing where stigma, poor reputation and combinations of low demand, high turnover, high levels of crime and anti-social behaviour, and chronic social deprivation are combining to frustrate any revival in demand.

The poor condition of much of the housing stock does not enhance its popularity. The Council estimates that to bring all council homes up to the Government's minimum decency standard would require £660 million. However, to deliver the full improvement works required to bring the stock up to full modern day standards would require £1.1 billion over the next ten years (Leeds City Council, 2002).

Because of problems of structural faults and low demand, more than 7,500 properties have been demolished across the district since the mid-1980s. Clearance has been on a smaller scale than was the case in the 1960s and 1970s but substantial levels of further stock demolition are anticipated in some failing areas, especially where council housing is the sole tenure or where it is in predominance.

Recent research has suggested that there appears to be an acceptance among residents that in certain circumstances, the time may be right for demolition (Kettle *et al.*, 2004), although there is some evidence that demolition may sometimes be used to eradicate management problems rather than as a response to obsolescence. The robustness or otherwise of existing communities would appear to be crucial to the success or failure of schemes. The latest era of demolitions can at least be carried out with the benefit of hindsight, using a range of intensive and innovative community engagement techniques.

4.5 Specific policy initiatives

Communities Plan and the regional housing agenda
The 'Communities Plan', *Sustainable Communities: Building for the Future* (ODPM, 2003a) set out the Government's aim of creating and maintaining sustainable mixed-income communities across the country. Under the plan, Regional Housing Boards have been established to carry out a range of functions, including formulation and implementation of Regional Housing Strategies, allocation of a Single Regional Housing Pot to support the priorities set out in those strategies, and ensuring the linkage of the Regional Economic Strategy, the new Regional Spatial Strategy (Poxon, 2003) and the emerging Regional Housing Strategies (Watkinson, 2004).

The Regional Housing Strategy for Yorkshire and Humberside has recognised the highly polarised nature of housing markets across the region and the need to address issues of low demand, abandonment and failing markets at the same time as the apparent paradox of high demand and shortage of housing, especially affordable housing. The strategy sets out four priorities: regeneration and renewal; the provision

of new housing to help create mixed income communities; the improvement of housing to a decent standard and ensuring fair access to housing for all, and especially for vulnerable groups.

The Single Regional Housing Pot, created from the local authority Housing Investment Programme and the Housing Corporation's Approved Development Programme, is being allocated through sub-regional partnerships of local authorities and their partners to support the priorities set out in the Regional Housing Strategy.

Housing Market Renewal Fund (HMRF)

The creation of nine housing market renewal 'Pathfinders' reinforced a recognition of market failure in the North and Midlands and assumed a radical approach to market restructuring. The Pathfinders cover several contiguous local authority areas in East Lancashire, Manchester/Salford, Newcastle/Gateshead and South Yorkshire. However, West Yorkshire was not selected. Although it was recognised that there are problems in the county, the depth and severity of low demand and abandonment was substantially less than in the Pathfinder areas.

No more HMRF Pathfinders will be created, but lobbying by the West Yorkshire Housing Partnership and other areas has brought a recognition that action is required to tackle low demand in non-Pathfinder areas and it is hoped that a National Strategy for Housing Market restructuring will channel additional funding through Regional Housing Boards.

Other discretionary funding sources:
Single Regeneration Budget (SRB) and
Neighbourhood Renewal Fund (NRF)

Leeds has been successful in attracting funding through all six rounds of the SRB and these funds have been targeted to areas experiencing significant multiple deprivation. Some of the beneficiaries were housing-related schemes, including East Bank in Round 2, Chapeltown in Round 3, Beeston Hill in Round 4, and the Aire Valley in Round 6. In addition, Round 5 funds were targeted at community planning and regeneration and this inevitably impacted on housing. This funding has recently been supplemented by monies from the Neighbourhood Renewal Fund in the Neighbourhood Renewal Areas of Beeston Hill/Holbeck and Harehills, which were established through the Leeds Neighbourhood Renewal Strategy (2001). This has enabled Comprehensive Regeneration Programmes to be designed for those areas, including housing market remodelling; changes of housing mix so that needs and requirements are better matched by supply; different forms of housing to meet the specific requirements of black and minority ethnic communities in those areas and a range of housing tenures, types and costs to support a mixed income community in those areas. However, it looks likely that the discretionary funding offered through SRB and NRF and other sources will shortly end, leaving implications for the various regeneration and service initiatives funded so far.

Arms Length Management Organisations (ALMOs)

In February 2003, six Arms Length Management Organisations (ALMOs) were set up (coinciding with the boundaries of the Primary Care Trust areas — see Chapter 5) to manage the Council's housing stock and ensure that it complies with the Decent Homes Standard by 2010. All six ALMOs were inspected in the summer 2003 but only two (Leeds North East Homes and Leeds West Homes) received the two-star assessment needed to qualify for the additional funding required to enable compliance with the a multi-element standard of internal/external conditions and amenities which are currently applied

A large Victorian house divided into flats, Headingley, LS6. Many students share houses after their first year, but some student demand is being deflected to purpose-built accommodation away from LS6.

only to social housing. The remaining four received a rating of 'one star but with excellent prospects for improvement' with re-inspection in June-July 2004. The question of how or whether to seek additional funding for improvements above the Decent Homes Standard is one that the ALMOs are still considering. ALMOs will have an important role to play in dealing with the difficult issue of demolitions.

Initiatives to improve the attractiveness of social rented housing

Local authority and housing associations in Leeds have been developing and implementing a series of initiatives to improve the attractiveness of social rented housing. These include the following:

- Choice-based lettings: although allocation of housing still depends ultimately on the assessment of housing need, this policy provides opportunities for applicants to be proactive in the selection of the homes they might want to live in.

- Flexible lettings policies in low or no demand areas: where there is an over-supply of housing and little interest shown by those in housing need, properties may be offered to interested parties who may not usually qualify for them.

- Floating support provided to residents or 'supported tenancies', which provide levels of care and assistance over and above the usual tenancy management services, usually through non-statutory housing organisations and purchased through Supporting People funds.

- IN Business for Neighbourhoods — the National Housing Federation campaign to change the perception of housing associations and to gain their commitment to become key stakeholders in neighbourhoods.

- Golden triangle partnership is targeted at the very popular areas in the northern suburbs and outer areas, where

housing for purchase is expensive and where social rented homes are rarely available: this scheme aims to create vacancies in social housing by enabling aspirant households to achieve home ownership.

- Social housing for younger people is an important area where innovative practices may encourage sustainable tenancies. Issues include the need to deal with the highly mobile nature of some young people's lifestyles combined with the lack of a brand loyalty to any one tenure. There is growing evidence that the under-thirties are providing an increasing source of new tenants of social housing, and may be part of mixed age communities arising where allocations are required to some one bed flat blocks designed for older tenants. It is not generally recognised that the quality of the accommodation on offer is crucial: giving unfurnished, unsupported housing to people with no furniture, little money and little experience of independent living is destined to fail and there is a recognition of the need for packages of housing, care, support and intensive management, such as that offered by Gipsil in East Leeds.

"We must provide a range of house types that will allow aspiring people who want to do well to stay ... It's important to recognise what makes people want to stay in an area: image, availability of decent facilities and environment and jobs, but critically, education and schools that you aspire to send your children to" (Regeneration practitioner in Birmingham, quoted in Turner and Townsend Group, 2004).

4.6 Conclusions

The housing map of Leeds has changed appreciably over the last decade, fuelled by a significant shift in perceptions, expectations and aspirations of households. The tenure map has changed in particular. Local authority housing has become even more firmly rooted as a stop gap, a stepping stone or a safety net instead of the tenure of destination that it once was. Private renting has expanded rapidly, because of the boom in buy-to-let activity as well as a rapid expansion of student numbers across the range of higher education institutions. This tenure may eventually replace social housing as the dominant rented tenure. City living has transformed the market in 'town centres' across Leeds as well as in the city centre itself. Economic growth, more relaxed mortgage lending policies combined with low interest rates have driven expectations of home ownership and the increasing view of housing ownership as a form of investment. Private sector housing development will continue to be concentrated on previously developed land and the city centre market will continue to expand, diversify and mature, as sites and buildings in more fringe areas are brought into use.

The Leeds housing market has become highly polarised with around 70 per cent of neighbourhoods enjoying varying levels of affluence and high demand and the other 30 per cent suffering fragile or low demand, social and economic deprivation and increasingly obsolescent housing. Within that context, the concepts of affordability and low demand have had to change and will need to change further.

Except for a relatively small number of local authority estates, descriptions of unpopular areas as low demand areas, even where housing values are relatively low, are problematic as there is often demand for housing, albeit from low quality private landlords or speculative investors, and house prices are rising, probably as a result of speculation. In those areas, the problem is obsolescent housing, where housing types (such as back-to-back terraces in inner urban areas or one bed flats on council estates) are increasingly ill-suited to modern expectations and requirements and are being rejected by newly-forming or aspirant moving households in favour of newly-built homes or second hand homes in more desirable areas. The rejection of those areas by household types who would be expected to form the stable communities of the future is leaving some inner urban areas and social housing estates as areas that will forever cater for the needs of the highly mobile, socially excluded or highly vulnerable.

Affordability has become a rather contested concept. What is affordable or not can depend on the push and pull factors categorised. Leeds has a range of properties available at a range of prices and rents; there is a large stock of affordable housing for rent and home ownership available, but often it is located in areas which people do not find attractive and is also often of a type that does not meet households' requirements and expectations. Overall, the constrained supply of the kinds of houses people want in the kinds of areas where they want to live calls for a series of quite radical approaches, as suggested in the Barker Review (HM Treasury, 2004).

It could be concluded therefore that affordability is a subjective measure, governed by choice, aspiration, perception, and a balance of risk and benefit rather than an objective measure as defined simply by a relationship between income and price. People may choose to spend more on housing if it brings other benefits such as good schools, proximity to facilities or amenities or accessibility to family.

This all points to a time of major change in the housing landscape of Leeds over the coming years. There will be significant redevelopment and remodelling of inner urban areas and peripheral council estates, in conjunction with interventions to assist households. There will also have to be action to 'dampen' the overheating of outer areas and diversion of demand from those areas in order to create and maintain mixed income communities.

References

Anderson, I. and Sim, D. (eds) (2000) *Social Exclusion and Housing: Context and Challenges,* Chartered Institute of Housing, Coventry.

Balchin, P. and Rhoden, M. (2002) *Housing Policy: An Introduction,* (4th edition) Routledge, London.

Bruegel I. and Smith J. (1999) *Taking risks, Safe in the City,* Sustainable Communities Group, ODPM. http://www.safeinthecity.org.uk/data/downloads/taking_risks.pdf

Burt, S. and Grady, K. (1994) *The Illustrated History of Leeds,* Breedon Books, Derby.

Cole, I., Hickman, P. and Reeve, K. (2003) *The Leeds Housing Market: Perceptions of Change,* Centre for Regional Economic and Social Research, Sheffield Hallam University — report for Leeds City Council, http://www.leeds.gov.uk/pageView.asp?style=0&identifier=200379_811992825.

Crisis (2001) *Trouble at Home,* Crisis, London.

Crisis (2002) *Home and Dry?* Crisis, London.

Crisis (2003) *Homelessness Factfile 2003,* Crisis, London.

Department of Planning and Transportation, Corporation of London (2001) Development Info, period January to June 2000, http://www.cityoflondon.gov.uk/our_services/development_planning/planning/pdf/Devinfo5.pdf

Department for the Environment, Transport and the Regions (DETR) (1999) *Towards an Urban Renaissance,* final report of the Urban Task Force, DETR, London. Also at http://www.dtlr.gov.uk.

Department for the Environment, Transport and the Regions (DETR) (2000a) *Our Towns and Cities: The Future — Delivering an Urban Renaissance — The Urban White Paper,* DETR, London.

Department for the Environment, Transport and the Regions (DETR) (2000b) *Planning Policy Guidance Note 3: Housing,* DETR, London.

Dutton, P. (2003) Gentrification in context: gentrification in the regional city of Leeds, *Urban Studies,* 40(12): 2557–2572.

Fowler, F.J. (1967) Urban renewal, in Beresford, M.W. and Jones, G. R.J. (eds) *Leeds and its Region,* Leeds Local Executive of the British Association for the Advancement of Science, pp.175–185.

Fox, P. and Unsworth, R. (2003) *City Living in Leeds — 2003,* www.geog.leeds.ac.uk/publications/cityliving.

HM Treasury (2004) *Delivering Stability: Securing our Future Housing Needs* (The Barker Review of Housing Supply) http://www.hm-treasury.gov.uk/consultations_and_legislation/barker/consult_barker_index.cfm

James, K., Curteis, S., Griffiths, S. and Woodhead, J. (2003) *'Just Surviving': the Housing and Support Needs of People on the Fringes of Homelessness and/or the Criminal Justice System in West Yorkshire,* Leeds Supporting People Research and Information Team, Leeds.

Kettle, J., Littlewood, S. and Maye-Banbury, A. (2004) *Impact Evaluation of the Selected Demolition of Housing, Leeds,* CUDEM, Leeds Metropolitan University, Leeds.

Kettle, J. and Moran, C. (1999) Social Housing and Exclusion in Allmendinger, P. and Chapman, M. (eds) *Planning Beyond 2000,* John Wiley and Sons, London, pp. 225–240.

Kotkin, J. (1999) *The future of the centre: the core city in the new economy,* RPPI Policy Study No 264, http://www.rppi.org/urban/ps264.html

Leeds City Council (LCC) (2002a) *Responsive Repairs and Maintenance — May 2002,* Audit Commission, London. http://www.leeds.gov.uk/bestvalue/docs/bv49.pdf

Leeds City Council (LCC) (2002b) *Leeds Economy Handbook,* LCC, Leeds.

Leeds City Council Department of Planning and Environment (2001) *Leeds Unitary Development Plan,* LCC, Leeds.

Leeds City Council Development Department (2003) *Leeds Unitary Development Plan Review — First Deposit,* LCC, Leeds.

Leeds Housing Partnership (2001) *Neighbourhood Oriented Model of Area Demand,* October.

Leeds Housing Partnership (2002) *Decent Homes in Decent Neighbourhoods: Housing Need and Statistics Supplement,* July.

Leeds Initiative (2001) *A Neighbourhood Renewal Strategy for Leeds, Neighbourhoods and Communities Partnership,* Leeds Initiative, Leeds.

Moran, C. (1996) Social inequalities, housing needs and the targeting of housing investment in Leeds, in Haughton, G. and Williams, C. (eds) *Corporate City? Partnership, Participation and Partition in Urban Development in Leeds,* Avebury, Aldershot, pp. 277–292.

Office of the Deputy Prime Minister (ODPM) (2000) *Tapping The Potential — Assessing Urban Housing Capacity: Towards Better Practice,* ODPM, London.

Office of the Deputy Prime Minister (ODPM) (2001) *Private Landlords Survey: English House Condition Survey 2001,* ODPM, London.

Office of the Deputy Prime Minister (ODPM) (2002) Survey of English housing: provisional results 2001–02, *Housing Statistics Summary No.13,* ODPM, London.

Office of the Deputy Prime Minister (ODPM) (2003a) *The 'Communities Plan' Sustainable Communities: Building for the Future,* ODPM, London.

Office of the Deputy Prime Minister (ODPM) (2003b) *Housing Strategy Statistical Appendix,* ODPM, London.

Office of the Deputy Prime Minister (ODPM) (2004) *Land Use Change in England: Residential Development to 2003* (LUCS19), ODPM, London.

Office for National Statistics (ONS) (2003) ONS website at: http://www.statistics.gov.uk/census2001/profiles/00da.asp

Office for National Statistics (ONS) (2002) *Living in Britain: General Household Survey 2002,* ONS, London.

Poxon, J. (2003) Shaping the future: developing a regional spatial strategy for Yorkshire and the Humber, *The Yorkshire & Humber Regional Review,* 13(3): 2–4.

Robinson, D. and Coward, S. (2003) *Your Place not Mine: the Experiences of Homeless People Staying with Family and Friends,* Crisis, London.

Turner and Townsend Group (2004) *Towards More Sustainable Places: Sustainable Places, Partnership Working and Urban Regeneration,* RICS Foundation, London.

URBED (2002), *Vision for Leeds II: Lessons from Vision I,* draft report for Leeds City Council (unpublished), Leeds.

Watkinson, J. (2004) The regional housing agenda and policy initiatives, *The Yorkshire & Humber Regional Review,* 14(1): 36–37.

Yorkshire and Humber Assembly (2003) *Draft Revised Regional Planning Guidance for Yorkshire and Humber to 2016 (RPG 12),* Yorkshire and Humber Assembly, Wakefield.

5

Healthy City?
Spatial Inequalities and Health Care Provision

MYLES GOULD, AMY BURRAGE, JOHN STILLWELL & ANDY TURNER

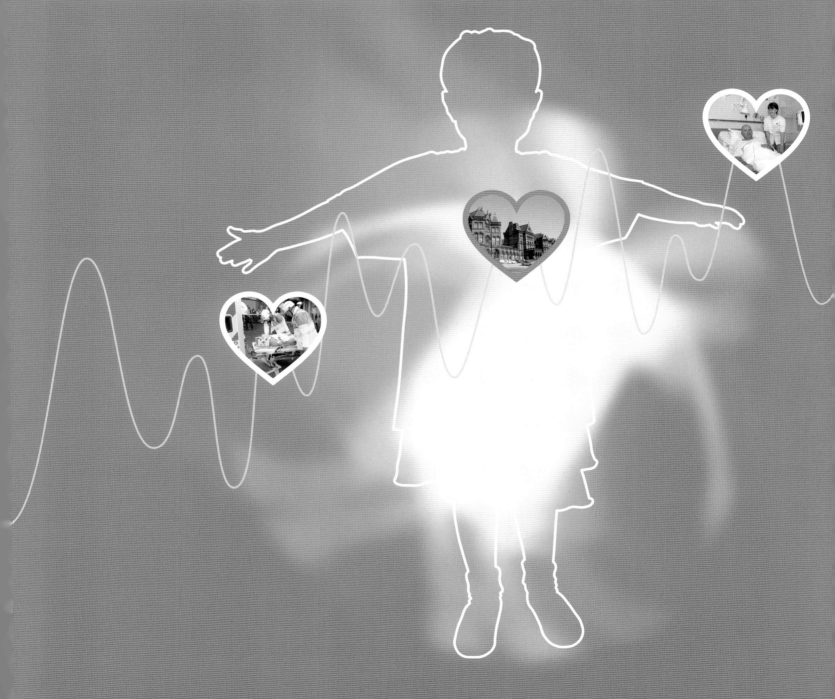

❚❚ *A healthy city for all those who live in, work in and visit, promoting fulfilling and productive lives for all.* **❚❚**

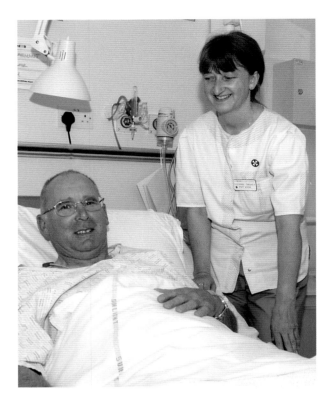

5.1 Introduction

Health is a major issue for people, planners, policy makers and academics. The health of those who live in towns and cities is largely determined by their living and working conditions and the quality of their physical and socio-economic environments, whilst individual lifestyles and circumstances and the quality and accessibility of healthcare services are also important. Health has become a subject with which everyone is engaged, and the health of cities has been examined from a range of perspectives, as documented in the case studies reported by the World Health Organisation (WHO, 1994).

Geographers and social scientists have commented on the existence of geographical and socio-economic variations and inequalities in health outcomes for several decades (Murray, 1962; Howe, 1986; Townsend *et al.,* 1988; 1992; Jacobson *et al.,* 1991). The Black Report was published in 1980 and presented evidence from a royal commission on health inequalities; it received a very frosty reception from the Thatcher Government and was buried for a number of years (Townsend *et al.,* 1992). In 1992, the Conservative Government finally began to recognize that inequalities in health outcomes and healthcare opportunities existed and a policy initiative was launched with associated targets for improving *The Health of the Nation* and reducing health inequalities (DOH, 1991; 1995). This initiative has subsequently been replaced by *Our Healthier Nation* (DOH, 1998a). Over the past 15 years, the UK, like other WHO member states, has had national targets for health issues such as heart disease, cancer, infant mortality, suicide, smoking and teenage pregnancy. The current Labour Government appointed a new independent inquiry to consider inequalities in health and has also published a White Paper containing a *Health Strategy for Saving Lives* (DOH, 1999a). Subsequently, there was an inter-departmental, cross-cutting review of initiatives and priorities for tackling inequalities in health (DOH, 1998b; DOH, 1999b; 2002). Health Action Zones and New Deal Communities are the local area-based policies that have been used to tackle health inequalities in communities that are particularly disadvantaged.

The WHO Healthy City Network for Europe was launched in 1988 (Ashton, 1992) and its strategy for action has now been superseded by *Health21,* a comprehensive policy framework centred on 21 targets for improving the health of Europeans in the twenty-first century (WHO, 1998). Although Leeds was not amongst the UK cities actively involved in the movement, the city has responded to the challenge to create "a healthy city for all those who live in, work in and visit, promoting fulfilling and productive lives for all" (Leeds Initiative, 2003). As in other cities, the local authority is in a unique position to promote health and sustainable development because it has direct responsibility for several sectors that have major impacts on health (such as environment, housing, social services, education and recreational facilities) and/or because it is able to represent locally-based agencies, citizens' groups and community organizations. Indeed, local health care organisations are expected to work closely with local authorities and other agencies in developing health improvement programmes. Consequently, Leeds has established a set of aims, as articulated in the *Vision II* strategy document (Leeds Initiative, 2004), that try to ensure that everyone is able to play as full a part in society as they wish, that health and social care

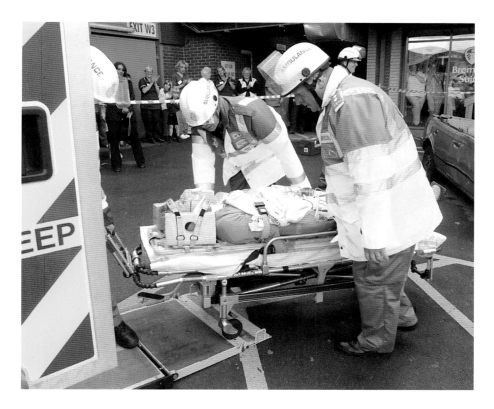

included, together with a brief discussion of the important linkages between health and lifestyle, including diet and fitness.

As indicated, this chapter attempts to bench-mark Leeds health experience with reference to Yorkshire and the Humber and England and Wales. In doing so, we make use of secondary data from official sources — the Census and ONS Vital Statistics (Moon *et al.*, 2000). The road traffic accident data are drawn from STATS19, the Department of Transport's national database containing statistics on accidents, vehicles and casualties that are used to stimulate informed debate on matters of road safety and to provide both a local and national perspective for particular road safety problems or particular suggested remedies. The data are collated from the STATS19 forms that are filled in by police personnel after any traffic accident that results in injury.

The mortality data used need careful consideration particularly when there are only a small number of deaths from a specific cause (e.g. cancer) for a specific period of time and for relatively small geographical areas such as wards (Coggon *et al.*, 1997; Gatrell, 2002; Cromley and McLafferty, 2002). It is necessary to consider standardisation to account for different populations at risk, and also to acknowledge the implications of the modifiable area unit problem. Although we present some analysis of mortality, a more detailed investigation will have to wait until the ONS links mortality data from more than one year with the Census to produce a 'stable' population base. The ONS will publish, in due course, the appropriate decennial supplement to allow more reliable and standardised comparisons (see Britton, 1990; Griffiths and Fitzpatrick, 2001, for previous examples).

West Yorkshire Metropolitan Ambulance Service covers an area with a population of 2.1 million and receives 800 calls a day. Just over 72 per cent of calls involving life-threatening conditions are responded to within 8 minutes, compared with a target of 75 per cent (2002–2003).

services are recognised for their excellence, that equality is promoted, and that social, economic and environmental conditions promote a healthy, positive society.

Given the health imperative, and also the fact that there is not very much published literature on variations in health in Yorkshire and the Humber (with the exceptions of Lister *et al.*, 1994; Manson-Siddle, 2001), we aim to provide a contemporary overview of the state of the city's health and a description of the local geography of health outcomes. In doing so, we attempt to answer the question: are the people who live in Leeds healthy in comparison to those living in neighbouring metropolitan districts, in Yorkshire and the Humber, and in the nation as a whole? This chapter focuses on self-reported measures of morbidity as recorded in the 1991 and 2001 Censuses, and also makes use of the responses to the new question about general health asked in the 2001 Census for the first time. There is also consideration of all cause mortality, deaths from chronic heart disease (CHD) and a selection of other disease-specific causes. The demographic structure and trends in casualties associated with road traffic accidents in the Leeds district are also examined. A review of health care provision is also

5.2 Key indicators

Table 5.1 shows variations in self-reported limiting long-term illness (LLTI) in 2001 for local authorities in Yorkshire and the Humber, with an additional comparison against the rate for England and Wales. We observe that rates of self-reported illness in Leeds are marginally lower than in its neighbouring districts, in the region and in the nation as a whole. Wakefield is the only adjacent metropolitan district where the percentage reporting illness is significantly higher, perhaps a legacy of the coal industry that was so important historically in this area. However, it would be wrong to conclude that Leeds is particularly healthy without making comparisons with places further afield. At the regional scale, the lowest rates of limiting long-term illness are found in the South East and London (15.5 per cent), whilst Buckinghamshire (12.8 per cent), Oxfordshire (13.4 per cent) and Surrey (13.5 per cent) enjoy some of the lowest levels amongst the counties. At a district level, the rate for Leeds is considerably lower in comparison with nation's worst districts: Easington in County Durham has 30.8 per cent of it population reporting LLTI, whilst the percentage reaches 30 per cent and 29.4 per cent respectively in the Welsh districts of Merthyr Tydfil and Neath Port Talbot.

A multi-agency regional health profile (Manson-Siddle, 2001) noted that Yorkshire and the Humber was one of the worst amongst the nine English regions, bettering only the North East and North West. Deaths from accidents amongst the under fives in the region are amongst the highest (and statistically so) for all the English regions, whilst premature death rates from cancers and circulatory diseases are the third highest. The region has the second highest perinatal death rate (i.e. still births and deaths in first week of life) and the third highest figure for low birth weight babies. Moreover, the health experiences of those in Leeds and its region should be assessed in the wider context of the persisting existence of well-known north-south gradients in health, well-being and socio-structural factors, as documented by Britton (1990), Curtis (1995), Gould and Jones (1996) and Howe (1986). We consider more local spatial variations in levels of self-reported illness between wards in Leeds in the next section and investigate whether the patterns have changed between 1991 and 2001.

It is important to appreciate that the census question on health (first introduced in 1991) asked individuals about whether they have a long-term illness, health problem or disability that limits their day-to-day activities and prevents them from working. As Dale (1993) has noted, the question has provided an unrivalled national and consistent source of information on perceived levels of morbidity and health service need that correlates well with data from other survey sources. However, other researchers have been more cautious in interpreting the variable measures: whether different individuals respond to the question in different ways (Senior, 1998) and whether the question focuses too readily on physical incapacity rather than capturing the full spectrum of (ill)health and well-being amongst individuals (e.g. mental illness). For this reason, a new question on general health was introduced in 2001 that has been a

Table 5.1 Self-reported illness in West Yorkshire districts, Yorkshire and Humber, and England and Wales, 2001

Area	Percentage reporting LLTI
Leeds	17.98
Kirklees	17.99
Calderdale	18.36
Bradford	18.49
Wakefield	22.43
Yorkshire and Humber	18.84
England and Wales	18.23

Source: Census 2001 KS

Table 5.2 Overall levels of general health, 2001

General health	Leeds	Yorkshire and Humber	England and Wales
Good	68.3	67.6	68.6
Fairly good	21.9	22.5	22.2
Not good	9.8	9.8	9.2

Source: Census 2001 KS

Table 5.3 Crude mortality rates (per 100,000) by cause and sex, 2001

	Yorkshire and Humber	UK
All people		
All causes	954	967
All circulatory diseases	378	385
All respiratory diseases	117	122
Males		
All causes	892	912
All circulatory diseases	351	367
All respiratory diseases	104	109
Females		
All causes	999	1,005
All circulatory diseases	396	395
All respiratory diseases	128	131

Source: ONS (2003)

The graveyard of the Norman church at Kippax, east of Leeds. Female mortality rates in Yorkshire and the Humber are actually lower than the UK average, despite the national upward trend.

welcome addition since it provides more information on morbidity and delivers a different perspective. The question asked respondents to rate their health over the past 12 months with respect to three reference categories: good, fairly good and not good.

The percentage of people who reported that they were in good health in Leeds is almost the same as the overall rate for England and Wales, and marginally higher than the rate for Yorkshire and the Humber (Table 5.2). When looking at the percentages of people who consider themselves not to be in good health, we see that rates are equal for Leeds and Yorkshire and the Humber, but are slightly higher than for England and Wales.

Benchmarking with other parts of the country, we find that Leeds and its region have lower rates of people not in good health than is the case elsewhere in England. For instance, there are much higher proportions of unhealthy people in the North East region (12 per cent); in the counties of Durham (13.2 per cent), Merseyside (12.6 per cent) and Tyne and Wear (12.3 per cent); and also in the South Wales districts of Merthyr Tydfil (18.1 per cent), Blaenau Gwent (16.5 per cent) and Neath Port Talbot (16.4 per cent). In contrast, the South East has the lowest rate of only 7.1 per cent of people reporting that they are not in good health, with Buckinghamshire reporting the lowest rate (5.8 per cent) of all counties.

Table 5.3 presents crude death rates in 2001 for Yorkshire and the Humber and the whole of the UK. The table provides breakdowns by sex and, in addition to providing crude deaths for all causes, it also allows comparisons with circulatory and respiratory causes of death. The importance of circulatory diseases, commonly associated with CHD, can clearly be seen as major causes of death. This is typical of communities and societies in the post-industrial developed world (Curtis and Taket, 1996; Gatrell, 2002). The table also shows that crude deaths rates for females are considerably higher (in all cases) than those for males. Interestingly, recent press reports have highlighted that rates of heart disease are falling more slowly amongst women and that they do not appreciate the risks associated with CHD (BBC, 2003). Interestingly, Lister *et al.* (1994) recognised the need in the Leeds district for targeting programmes for the prevention of CHD at women as well as men. Table 5.3 also shows that with all three causes of death (and for both sexes), crude rates per 100,000 of the population are lower in Yorkshire and the Humber than in the nation as a whole. However, it should be borne in mind that only crude death rates are presented here and that these do not take account of variations in underlying demographic structure (Moon *et al.*, 2000).

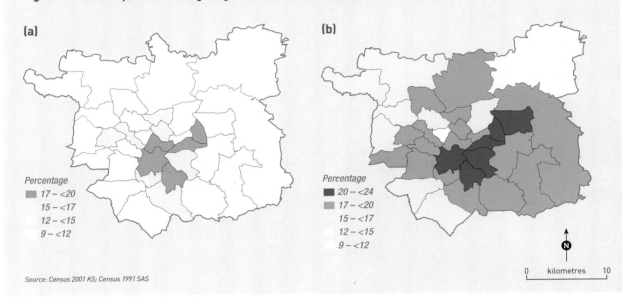

Figure 5.1 Self-reported limiting long-term illness by ward, (a) 1991 and (b) 2001

(a)

Percentage
- 17 – <20
- 15 – <17
- 12 – <15
- 9 – <12

(b)

Percentage
- 20 – <24
- 17 – <20
- 15 – <17
- 12 – <15
- 9 – <12

0   kilometres   10

Source: Census 2001 KS; Census 1991 SAS

5.3 Spatial variations in self-reported illness and general health

It is clear that rates of reported LLTI have slightly worsened amongst Leeds wards between 1991 and 2001 (Figure 5.1). There are now six wards banded with rates of illness of between 20 per cent and 24 per cent, whilst no ward had a rate greater than 20 per cent back in 1991. The six wards are Burmantofts, City and Holbeck, Hunslet, Richmond Hill, Seacroft and Whinmoor. These areas also had the highest levels of self-reported illness in 1991. The lowest rates of self-reported illness at both censuses are found in wards located in the northern part of the city region, in what are more rural and affluent areas (e.g. Wetherby, Otley and Wharfedale, and Aireborough).

In summary, Figure 5.1 shows that there is definite and distinct spatial patterning at both census dates. Rates of LLTI are higher amongst the central city wards. Rates of self-reported morbidity generally decline with distance from the wards in the city centre. There are exceptions, with areas such that Armley, Pudsey South and Wortley towards the west of city having higher rates of 17–20 per cent illness in 2001 and their health experiences appear to worsen both in absolute and relative spatial terms between 1991 and 2001.

Table 5.4 summarises the wards with the highest, lowest and median levels of limiting illness in 2001. It shows

Table 5.4 Summary of self-reported limiting long-term illness, 2001

Level	Ward	Percentage LLTI
Highest illness	Hunslet	23.78
Median illness	Harehills	18.30
Lowest illness	Headingley	10.48

Source: Census 2001 CAS

that Harehills is stereotypical in terms of its health experience with reference to other wards, and also city, regional and national rates, as indicated in Table 5.1. Headingley has the lowest rate of illness — not surprising given that its residential population is dominated young healthy students. It represents an island with much lower rates of self-reported illness in 2001 and appears to have improved its health experience since 1991.

More detailed maps of the spatial variations in levels of self-reported illness are shown in Figure 5.2 for community areas and output areas. The output area map, with community area boundaries superimposed, picks up various local hotspots for long-term illness and the upper class interval ranges are extended such

Figure 5.2 Variations in levels of self-reported limiting long-term illness for (a) community areas and (b) output areas, 2001

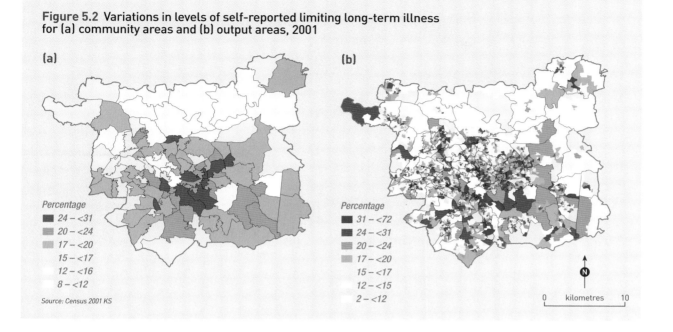

(a)

Percentage
- 24 – <31
- 20 – <24
- 17 – <20
- 15 – <17
- 12 – <16
- 8 – <12

Source: Census 2001 KS

(b)

Percentage
- 31 – <72
- 24 – <31
- 20 – <24
- 17 – <20
- 15 – <17
- 12 – <15
- 2 – <12

0   kilometres   10

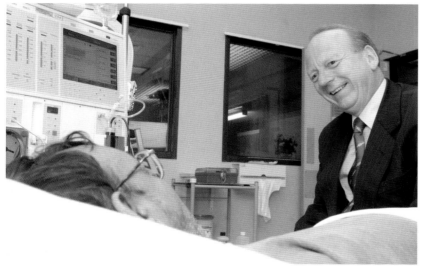

that 188 output areas are identified as having rates of self-reported illness between 31 per cent and 72 per cent.

Figure 5.2 demonstrates that many parts of Leeds are far from being homogeneous in terms of their health experiences. There is considerable variation in health experience for output areas between and within wards and community areas. For example, whilst it has already been noted that Wetherby, Otley and Wharfedale and Aireborough are wards that have

particularly low rates of LLTI, they all have output areas located within their boundaries that have high rates of self-reported illness. Similarly there are some, albeit few, output areas in inner city Leeds that have illness rates in the lowest class interval. The output areas in the North and Whinmoor wards, and also in the northern part of Barwick and Kippax, appear to be more homogeneous in terms of their health experiences. However, it should be noted that any conclusion should be drawn with caution because of the small numbers problem. Some of the output areas have rates that are 'unstable' and based upon relatively small population denominators, such that a small absolute increase in the numerator (i.e. number of people who are ill) will have considerable impact on the calculation of rates (Gatrell, 2002; Cromley and McLafferty, 2002). However, the key message is that there are some interesting local small-scale variations in health status, and further research is required based on mapping and analysis of age-standardised morbidity rates.

"And how are we feeling today?" — consultant with patient at St James's. In addition to St James's and the LGI, there are four other hospitals, plus a chest clinic and dental institute, within the Leeds Teaching Hospitals NHS Trust.

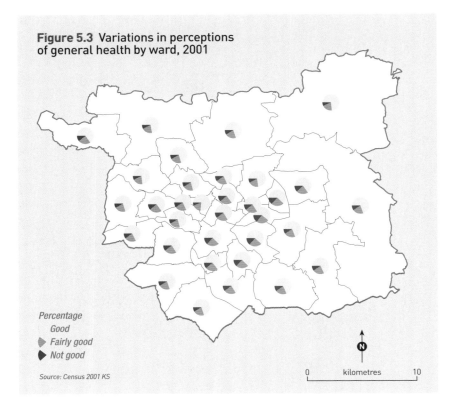

Figure 5.3 Variations in perceptions of general health by ward, 2001

Percentage
Good
Fairly good
Not good

Source: Census 2001 KS

0   kilometres   10

N

Returning to the ward level, it is apparent that variations in the three levels of general health appear remarkably constant across the metropolitan district (Figure 5.3) There are some variations, such as Headingley, with the highest percentage of people with good general health, and Burmantofts, the ward with the highest proportion of people whose general health is 'not good'. However, we can use an alternative mapping technique with the output area data to provide a continuous interpolated representation of the likely distribution of rates and overlay this with the 2001 ward boundaries. Figure 5.4 shows the areas with the highest rates of 'good' and 'fairly good' are found in the low-density areas located in the north of the city region, whilst higher rates of people who believe their health not to be good are found in central inner city areas.

The hydrotherapy pool at Chapel Allerton Hospital provides facilities for rheumatology patients to exercise safely in warm water under supervision.

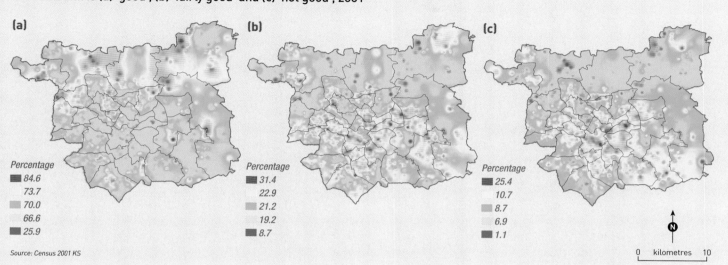

Figure 5.4 Surface maps for levels of self-reported limiting long-term illness, where health is (a) 'good', (b) 'fairly good' and (c) 'not good', 2001

(a)

Percentage
■ 84.6
73.7
■ 70.0
66.6
■ 25.9

Source: Census 2001 KS

(b)

Percentage
■ 31.4
22.9
■ 21.2
19.2
■ 8.7

(c)

Percentage
■ 25.4
10.7
■ 8.7
6.9
■ 1.1

0   kilometres   10

Table 5.5 Mortality rates by cause for all Leeds residents, 2001

	ICD codes[1]	Number	Rate per 10,000[2]	Percentage of all deaths
All causes	–	7,018	98.10	100
Malignant neoplasms	C00–C97	1,889	26.41	38
Diseases of the circulatory system	I00–I99	2,724	38.08	38
Ischaemic heart diseases	I20–I25	1,409	19.70	20
Diseases of the respiratory system	J00–J99	884	12.36	12.6
Land transport accidents	V01–V89	38	0.53	<1

Notes: [1] Based on the tenth edition of the International Classification of Disease (WHO, 1992) [2] Rounded to two decimal places
Source: ONS (2002); Census 2001 KS

5.4 Spatial variations in mortality by cause

City-wide death rates for the five main causes classified using the International Classification of Disease are shown in Table 5.5 (WHO, 1992). Death rates for all causes are also provided for comparison. Geographical variations in mortality between wards are shown in Figure 5.5 using 2001 death registrations for the numerator and 2001 Census population counts for the denominator. It is evident that diseases of the circulatory system are the main cause of death. CHD, or ischaemic heart disease to give it is correct medical name, is responsible for the

greatest proportion of deaths associated with the circulatory system. CHD involves the furring up of the arteries and reduced blood circulation and commonly results in heart attacks. Diseases of the respiratory system and CHD accounted respectively for 13 per cent and 20 per cent of all deaths in Leeds in 2001. Table 5.5 also shows that malignant neoplasms (i.e. cancers) are an important cause of death; whilst land transport accidents are relatively infrequent. In fact, they result in less than one death per hundred thousand across the city as a whole and accounted for less than 1 per cent of all deaths in 2001.

The maps in Figure 5.5 show that there is considerable variation in death rates between wards for all the different causes of mortality. Figure 5.5a shows that deaths from all causes tend to be highest in the wards located towards the centre of the city, and in the adjacent areas to the west (Pudsey

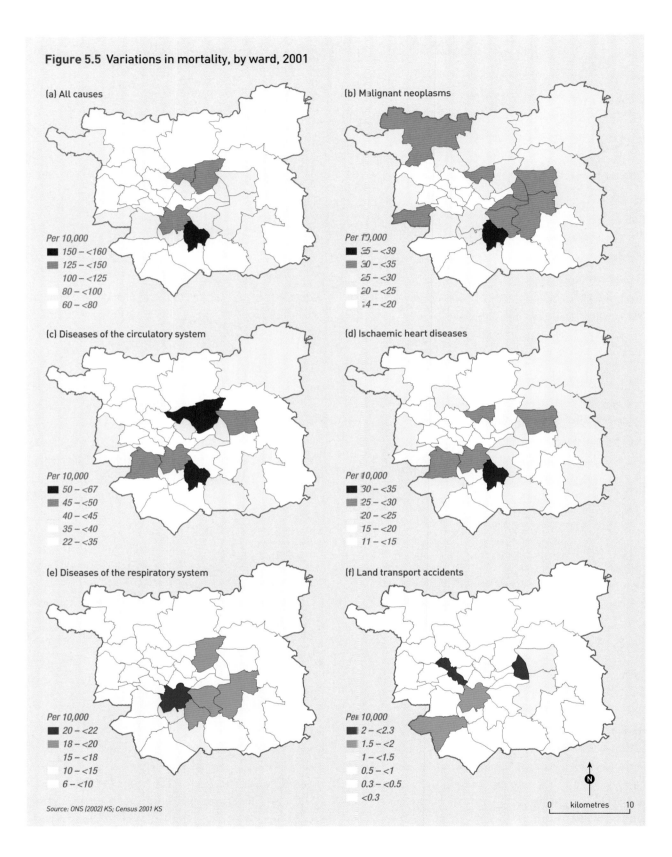

Figure 5.5 Variations in mortality, by ward, 2001

(a) All causes

Per 10,000
- 150 – <160
- 125 – <150
- 100 – <125
- 80 – <100
- 60 – <80

(b) Malignant neoplasms

Per 10,000
- 35 – <39
- 30 – <35
- 25 – <30
- 20 – <25
- 14 – <20

(c) Diseases of the circulatory system

Per 10,000
- 50 – <67
- 45 – <50
- 40 – <45
- 35 – <40
- 22 – <35

(d) Ischaemic heart diseases

Per 10,000
- 30 – <35
- 25 – <30
- 20 – <25
- 15 – <20
- 11 – <15

(e) Diseases of the respiratory system

Per 10,000
- 20 – <22
- 18 – <20
- 15 – <18
- 10 – <15
- 6 – <10

(f) Land transport accidents

Per 10,000
- 2 – <2.3
- 1.5 – <2
- 1 – <1.5
- 0.5 – <1
- 0.3 – <0.5
- <0.3

Source: ONS (2002) KS; Census 2001 KS

0   kilometres   10

Table 5.6 Wards with the highest 2001 disease-specific mortality rates, 2001

Cause	Lowest		Highest	
	Ward	Rate per 10,000	Ward	Rate per 10,000
All causes	Headingley	60.5	Hunslet	159.7
Malignant neoplasms	University	14.5	Hunslet	39.0
Diseases of the circulatory system	University	22.5	Hunslet	66.9
Ischaemic heart diseases	University	11.2	Hunslet	34.7
Diseases of the respiratory system	Headingley	6.2	City and Holbeck	21.8

Source: ONS (2002); Census 2001 KS

South, Wortley), and to the east and south east (Garforth and Swillington, Halton). There are exceptions such as Headingley, University and Burmantofts which have much lower rates compared with other city centre wards. Aireborough has a much higher overall death rate compared with other northern wards. The class intervals used in the map for malignant neoplasms (Figure 5.5b) are different and reflect the much smaller variations in death rates between wards. The spatial patterns are similar to those shown in Figure 5.5a, with the exception that Otley and Wharfedale appears to have a slightly higher rate relative to its neighbours.

The maps for diseases of the circulatory system and ischaemic heart diseases (Figure 5.5c and 5.5d) also show similar patterns to that of deaths from all causes. One exception is that Roundhay has a lower death rate from heart disease than might have been expected. Figure 5.5e shows that deaths from diseases of the respiratory system tend to be generally low across the city, although City and Holbeck, Hunslet and Roundhay do have relatively high death rates. Indeed, the first two of these areas feature as having the worst health outcomes for all the maps shown in Figure 5.5 that have been discussed so far. The number of deaths due to land transport accidents in one year is very small in comparison with the other categories and consequently the incidence shown in Figure 5.5f displays no real discernible geographical pattern. In fact, the large majority of road accidents result in injury rather than fatality.

To summarise, Table 5.6 indicates the wards which have the highest and lowest rates of death per 10,000 people, and provides a quantitative summary of the variations in death rates. Hunslet ward scores poorly on four of the key causes of

death, and is second only to City and Holbeck as the worst ward for deaths from diseases of the respiratory system. Moortown and Seacroft are examples of other wards that generally have poor mortality experiences. Headingley and University wards experience some of the lowest mortality rates across the district since, as already noted, these areas are dominated by large numbers of young and healthy university students. However, these results must be interpreted carefully as they use crude death rates that have not been standardized for age, and are also only based on death registration for a single year. The small numbers problem is not such an issue here as the population numerators for Leeds wards range from 16,155 to 29,239 residents. It is worth noting that similar and corroborative patterns and trends, albeit for different health indicators in some cases, were presented in a much earlier and now dated local report on health inequalities in Leeds (Lister *et al.,* 1994). The authors describe similar geographical patterns within Leeds for infant mortality, babies of low birth weight, hospital admiss-ions due to accidents amongst children, premature death rates amongst adults, all cause cancer rates and respiratory disease.

In 2001, there were 12 wards which had zero deaths recorded for 'land transport accidents' as the principal cause of death. These were Armley, Burmantofts, Cookridge, Harehills, Headingley, Hunslet, North, Pudsey South, Richmond Hill, Rothwell, University, and Weetwood. Ten extra deaths in any of these wards would only increase the mortality rate by approxi-mately four deaths per ten thousand population. Indeed, the largest absolute number of land transport-related deaths is four (in the City and Holbeck, Kirkstall, Morley North, and Seacroft wards). Deaths from road traffic accidents remain a relatively

rare event and we need to be very careful in drawing any conclusions from data that has been geographically aggregated for a single year. Thus, we consider spatial patterning of road traffic accidents using spatially disaggregated data for a longer time period in the next section.

5.5 Road accidents

The current STATS19 database of road accident statistics consists of an incident record, a vehicle record (for each vehicle involved) and a casualty record (for each casualty involved). STATS19 data provide a valuable framework for formulating policies and strategies to reduce injury road accidents and their resulting casualties. Since the 1992–1996 quinquennial review, there have been further reductions in fatal and serious injury road accidents but increases in slight injury road accidents in Great Britain. The data for Leeds over two periods, 1992–1996 and 1997–2001 (Table 5.7), reflect the trends apparent at the national level. The numbers of incidents involving fatality or serious injury have dropped by 5 per cent and 18 per cent respectively in Leeds whilst the number of accidents in which slight injury has occurred has risen by 22 per cent. Both the numerator and denominator are small for fatalities. These changes in the first two categories are likely to reflect improvements in vehicle

technology as well as impacts of policy initiatives such as 'Don't drink and drive' campaigns. There is no data on the number of accidents that occur without any form of injury.

The changes in casualty statistics parallel the incident data between the two periods but there are some interesting demographic variations in the probabilities of being injured, depending on the seriousness of the accident. In Figure 5.6, age probability profiles for each category of casualty are presented for males and females for the two periods concerned. The number of casualties in each five year age group in a particular category (fatal, serious, slight) are simply expressed as a proportion of all casualties in that category. Consequently, the areas under each profile sum to unity and the profiles are comparable with one another. Thus, for example, males in Leeds who die in road accidents are more likely to be in their late teens and twenties, whereas the probabilities for females have a more haphazard age pattern. Changes between 1992–1996 and 1997–2001 are evident from the profiles but the numbers of fatal casualties are relatively small and this means that interpretation of trends is less convincing than those for casualties in which injuries are serious or slight. The former show similar profiles, with probabilities for males exceeding females in the 15–29 age range in 1992–1996 but *vice versa* in the middle ages and probabilities for both males and females being higher in the older ages in 1997–2001. The profiles for males and

Table 5.7 Road accidents in Leeds, 1992–1996 and 1997–2001

Accidents	1992–1996	1997–2001	Change	Percentage change
Fatal	239	226	-13	-5.4
Serious	2,747	2,262	-485	-17.7
Slight	18,143	22,040	3,897	21.5

Source: STATS19

Figure 5.6 Accident probabilities in Leeds, 1992–1996 and 1997–2001

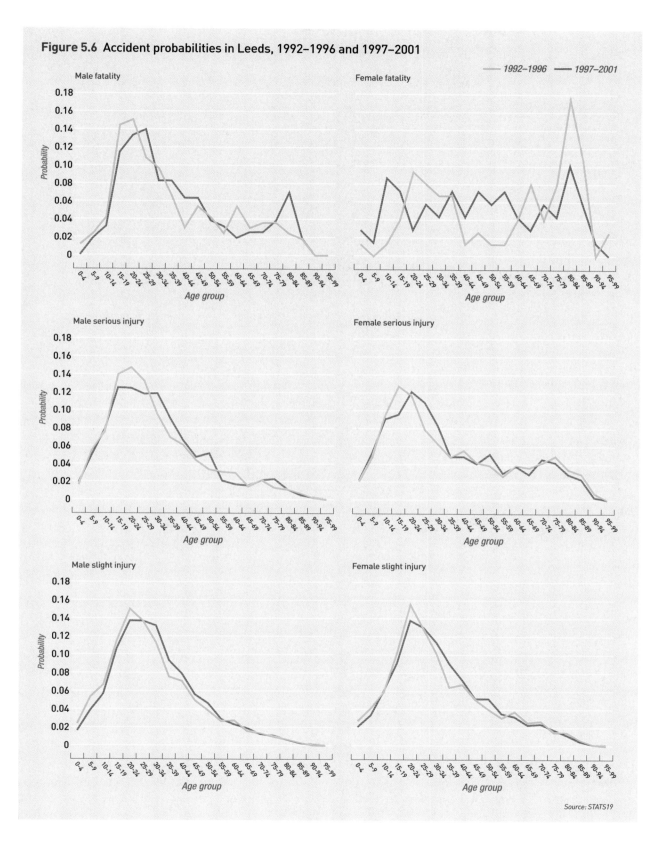

Figure 5.7 Surface representations of road accidents in central Leeds, (a) 1992–1996 and (b) 1997–2001

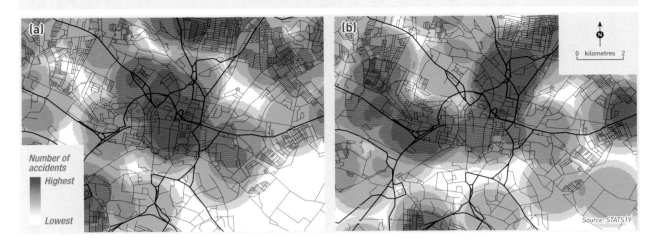

females having slight injuries are similar, both peaking in the 20–24 age group and showing probabilities declining between the two periods in the younger age groups and increasing for those aged 30–59. These profiles do not, of course, take account of the different populations at risk associated with each age-sex group.

Road accidents are also known to vary geographically (Whitelegg, 1987) and these geographical patterns change over time. In this instance, we have chosen to exemplify spatial and temporal change by presenting the distribution of personal injury road accidents in central Leeds for the two five-year time periods (Figure 5.7). Rather than show the distribution of incidents as a set of points, a surface is created using a kernel density mapping technique (Gatrell, 2002). This makes for easier comparisons between distributions (especially as many points may occur at the same locations). Effectively each point is translated into a surface that is highest at the location of the point and diminishes monotonically with distance from the point up to some distance (known as the kernel bandwidth). A composite surface is generated by adding up all the surface heights for each point in the distribution. When classified and displayed, this is known a kernel density map. The surfaces in Figure 5.7 indicate how the areas of high incidence of road accidents in the centre of Leeds have shifted to the west and to the north east between the first and second halves of the 1990s; this change is likely to be associated with the extended pedestrianisation that occurred in the city centre.

It is possible to extend or reduce the bandwidth of the kernel to obtain different representations. When a five kilometre bandwith is used for analysis of the Leeds-Bradford region, notable urban-rural variations are shown up in the incidence of road accidents involving personal injury over the last 10 years. One trend is that of an increase in accidents in more rural areas, and a decrease in more urban areas. The reasons underlying this change are complex and likely to be a function of the intrinsic risks of an accident occurring under specific environmental conditions and the change in the level of exposure to these risks. In general terms, however, road safety is improving in Leeds as it is in Great Britain as a whole.

5.5 Health care provision

As a result of recent NHS restructuring in England, primary health care is now coordinated by Primary Care Trusts (PCTs) (Higgs and Gould, 2000). Five PCTs serve the local population in Leeds (Figure 5.8). General practitioners (GPs) are responsible for providing primary care to patients resident within self-defined local catchments, making referrals to hospital and community-based secondary care services when necessary. GPs are independent NHS contractors who work in group-based practice partnerships, and are affiliated to a particular PCT. PCTs are responsible for planning and commissioning secondary health care services for their local populations, as well as improving local health needs and outcomes. The West Yorkshire

Figure 5.8 Leeds NHS primary and secondary healthcare facilities

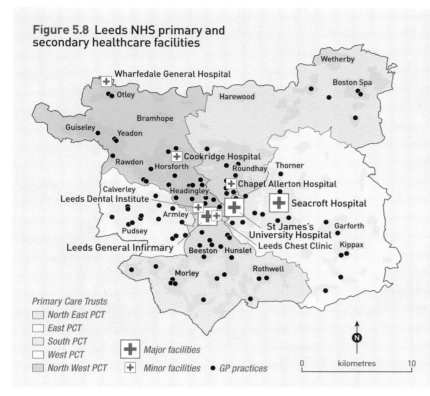

Primary Care Trusts
- North East PCT
- East PCT
- South PCT
- West PCT
- North West PCT

Major facilities
Minor facilities
GP practices

0   kilometres   10

Strategic Health Authority manages and monitors the performance of all NHS service providers in the region and also coordinates strategies for the local health services. The locations of GPs throughout the communities of Leeds are shown in Figure 5.8. Leeds appears to be reasonably well provided for with respect to primary health care, particularly so in the inner city and built-up urban areas. Primary health care facilities are not as well provided in the more rural and northerly community areas (e.g. Otley, Wharfedale and Wetherby). Some community areas towards the east (e.g. Barwick) also appear to have no GPs located within their boundaries.

Acute secondary health care is provided by the Leeds Teaching

Top, Leeds' Nuffield Hospital is a technically-advanced, not-for-profit, independent hospital. Middle, St James's University Hospital or 'Jimmys', is Europe's largest teaching hospital. Bottom, the Victorian part of the LGI was built in the 1860s to replace the eighteenth century predecessor in Infirmary Street.

Table 5.8 Average daily number of beds available and percentage occupied in Leeds Teaching Hospitals Trust, 2001–2002

	General and acute	Acute	Geriatric	Maternity	Total
Total	2,646	2,045	601	180	2,838
Percentage	84.9	81.8	95.6	63.2	83.5

Source: Department of Health

Top left, mothers and babies at a community centre. Top right, a diabetes patient arriving at the LGI. Far right, the LGI's £92 million Jubilee Wing, opened in April 1998.

Table 5.9 Accident and emergency attendances, Leeds Teaching Hospitals Trust, 2001–2002

First	Follow-up	Total
208,517	27,509	236,026

Source: Department of Health

Hospitals Trust. The location of the Trust's major and more minor facilities are also shown in Figure 5.8. The Leeds General Infirmary and Dental Institute are located next to the University of Leeds. These facilities have close partnerships with the Medical School and the School of Health Care Studies which are responsible for the education and training of medical personnel.

The photographs on pages 119 and 121 provide views of the Leeds hospitals today. They show the historical and contemporary architectural influences on NHS estate, and more importantly demonstrate the continued expansion and development of health care facilities over the past century and a half. Information about bed availability by principal health care speciality and occupation, as well as attendances at Accident and Emergency (A&E) for the Leeds Teaching Hospitals Trust, are provided in Tables 5.8 and 5.9. These help provide an indication of the size and scale of locally-based health care provision. It is also worth noting that the NHS Trusts are major local employers and are significant contributors to the local economy. Mental illness and learning disability services are provided by a separate community trust.

5.7 Lifestyle and access to healthy living

Over the past decade, health researchers and policy makers have become increasing concerned with the local characteristics of places for (re)producing health outcomes and health variations, and also supporting and reinforcing healthy living and

can, in theory, be acted upon and modified through policy interventions (DOH, 1998b; 2002). Macintyre *et al.* (1993) provide a very useful and policy relevant discussion of the relationship between place and health. They argue that place (or locality) and context make an important difference to the health of individuals. It should be noted that the importance of place in determining health outcomes has been heavily debated in the literature (Curtis, 2004). Some people have argued that it is the characteristics of people within in a place that are the key determinants of health (so called compositional explanations), whilst some believe that place and context really do matter, and others think both are important and interrelated (Jones *et al.*, 2000). Macintyre *et al.* (1993) argue that we need to consider the features of localities that might promote or damage health, including:

Top, a Leeds Lifestyle Survey in 2001 found over half of men and more than a third of women were overweight or obese — a combination of high calorie intake and lack of exercise are the main causes. Bottom, we are all recommended to eat five portions of fruit and vegetables a day.

healthy lifestyles (Jones and Moon, 1993; Curtis, 2004). Dahlgen and Whitehead (1991, cited in DOH, 1998b) provide a very useful model for considering the main determinants of health which places individuals and their characteristics right at its centre. There are, in turn, a number of 'layers of influence' that include:

- lifestyle: personal behaviour and way of life (e.g. smoking, diet and exercise);

- social and community networks: friends, relatives and mutual support;

- living and working conditions, food supplies and access to essential goods and services; and

- general societal, economic, cultural and environmental conditions.

Individual lifestyles and behaviours are seen as being embedded in social and community networks and also the workplace; although all the layers interact with each other and

Figure 5.9 Leisure facilities

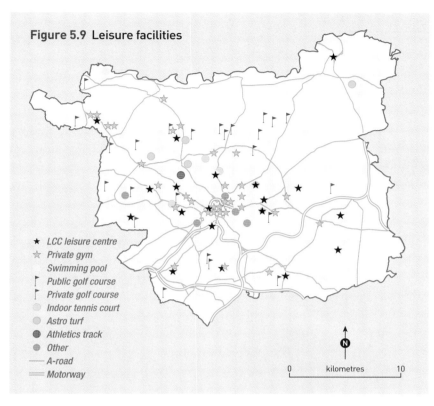

★ *LCC leisure centre*
☆ *Private gym*
   Swimming pool
⌐ *Public golf course*
⌐ *Private golf course*
◯ *Indoor tennis court*
◯ *Astro turf*
◉ *Athletics track*
◯ *Other*
── *A-road*
══ *Motorway*

0   kilometres   10

N

- physical features of the environment shared by all residents in a locality;

- availability of healthy/unhealthy environments at home, work and play;

- services provided to support people in their daily lives;

- socio-cultural features of a neighbourhood; and

- neighbourhood reputation.

The presence of pleasant open spaces and recreation facilities are seen as being important in providing opportunities for people to exercise and relax. Likewise, no one wants to live near a heavily polluted or noxious industrial plant, and such facilities can have adverse effects on psychological health (Elliott *et al.,* 1993). People tend to be happier and healthier when they perceive that they live in a neighbourhood environment that is safe, aesthetically pleasing and also has a sense of community. Access to affordable, good quality, fresh produce is seen as one important service that supports everyday healthy living (Macintyre *et al.,* 1993). A similar point was made for 'Leeds Health for All' in its call for collaborative initiatives to encourage the supply of inexpensive foodstuffs (Lister *et al.,* 1994). Similarly, access to free and affordable leisure and sports facilities is particularly important in encouraging physical activity and healthy fitness behaviour. Figure 5.10 shows the locations of a selection of sports and leisure facilities in Leeds including both private (e.g. gyms and golf courses) and public (e.g. swimming pools and municipal golf courses) facilities. Centres of population are reasonably well served, although many facilities do require a car journey. Moreover, many private facilities require membership and fees (such as private gyms and golf courses) and certain public facilities charge entrance fees that are out of reach of the poor and economically disadvantaged. This has important policy implications for improving inequalities in health.

Obesity and poor diet amongst all people, particularly children, exemplify one health and lifestyle issue that has recently received a lot of media attention (GBPHCHC, 2004).

Top, working out at the gym has become an increasingly common way for more affluent and busy members of society to keep fit. Bottom, forward defensive: competitive Airedale and Wharfedale League cricket at Guiseley provides exercise for some.

Children keep fit at an exercise class at the Footloose School of Dance in Roundhay, north east Leeds.

Poor diet and lifestyle frequently lead to being overweight and these conditions have long been implicated with some of the causes of death discussed above (i.e. CHD, stroke and certain cancers), whilst there is evidence of doctors seeing increasing incidence of diabetes in adults, and also, more worryingly, in children. Whilst information on body-mass index (BMI) is collected in the *Health Survey for England*, and a national survey of diet and nutrition amongst young people was undertaken in 1997 (Gregory and Lowe, 2000), we currently do not have comprehensive, consistent and up-to-date statistics that are routinely collected and made available at a fine spatial scale. Manson-Siddle (2001, p.59) provides a comparison of the proportion of adults who are obese (BMI >30) amongst health authority districts in Yorkshire and the Humber using data from the 1994–1996 *Health Survey for England*. Although the confidence intervals are relatively large (being based on a population survey), Leeds has the second lowest rate (bettered only by Bradford), and is lower than the average from England as a whole. Similarly, Lister *et al.* (1994) use the 1991 *Health Survey for England* to estimate that the health of 74,000 males and 72,000 females in Leeds were at risk due to being overweight and not getting enough exercise.

With increasing public concern, and plenty of anecdotal evidence from health professions, we can expect more data to be gathered and collated to help policymakers tackle issues and problems surrounding health and lifestyle. Some progress on this is already being made in some Primary Care Trusts, helping to improve local knowledge and understanding. Whatever the limitations of what we know about the incidence of obesity in Leeds (and other regions), exercise and physical activity are important in promoting healthy lifestyle, as is the consumption of healthy foodstuffs. Figure 5.9 is useful in providing a picture of the range of commercial and public sector health and fitness and associated leisure facilities throughout Leeds. The city is also renowned for the number of public parks and open spaces (many of which have tennis and basketball courts, mini-football pitches and bowling greens) and also allotment gardens. Lister *et al.* (1994) report results from a 1991 'playing pitch survey' undertaken by Leeds City Council estimating that just 23 people per 10,000 population played in a team, that membership was very locally orientated and lack of pitches was a problem. The challenge to both policy makers and the population as whole is for more people (and increasingly the young) to make increased use of all these facilities (and expand them where needed), as well as giving up the car for some relatively short journeys such as trips to school and the local convenience store, as indicated in Chapter 10, and thereby pursue a more physically active and healthy lifestyle. Schools are also being seen as important settings for encouraging health living and physical activity among the young. Access to shopping opportunities for food (and, by implication, healthy food) and the existence of 'food deserts' are described in Chapter 11.

5.8 Conclusions

Leeds appears to be generally healthy in comparison with the rest of Yorkshire and the Humber, and also England and Wales as a whole. There has been a dramatic improvement in health and well-being in Leeds (as there has been throughout the country) over the last one and a half centuries. To appreciate the full extent of this transition, one can visit the Thackray Museum (located at St James's Hospital) and witness a reconstruction of the squalor that resulted in epidemics of infectious diseases in the nineteenth century before there was sanitary and social reform.

However, this chapter has demonstrated that there is still evidence of geographical variations in health and mortality within the city, particularly at the micro-spatial scale of census output areas (in the case of morbidity), although any conclusions about these patterns should be drawn with caution. However, patterns and trends in health closely mirror those for deprivation, poverty and unemployment. There is evidence to suggest that alleviating the latter will reduce inequalities in the former (Department of Health, 1999b; 2002; Manson-Siddle, 2001). Data on self-reported limiting long-term illness contained within the 2001 Census suggest that there have been some increases in levels of poor health in absolute terms amongst wards in the city core. It is these areas that have particularly large numbers of economically deprived people. This issue of inequalities in health, together with persistent trends of increases in CHD, will continue as a challenge for public health officials and health service professionals, and is also being directly addressed by the Leeds Initiative in *Vision II* (Leeds Initiative, 2004). Similarly, we can expect to see continued health promotion campaigns to encourage the local population to pursue healthier lifestyles, maintain better diets, take more exercise, reduce smoking and alcohol consumption. Further improvements in road safety to reduce the number of accidents remains paramount.

Very much in line with central government policy, Leeds Initiative is committed to improving the community's health, improving the health of the less well off, reducing health inequalities, and ensuring accessible and high quality health services for the local population. Indeed, health issues cut across many urban and social renewal themes, as well as income, deprivation and poverty initiatives throughout the city. All five Primary Care Trusts and both NHS Trusts have now become active partners in the Leeds Initiative; they are directly involved in the Neighbourhood Renewal Area Partnerships, and also the 'Healthy Leeds' partnership (Leeds Initiative, 2004). We look forward to seeing Leeds becoming a healthier city over the next fifteen years.

References

Ashton, J. (ed.) (1992) *Healthy Cities,* Open University Press, Milton Keynes.

BBC (2003) Women unaware of heart risk, [BBC News Online] [accessed 16 March 2004] Available from http://news.bbc.uk/1/hi/health/2735677.stm

Britton, M. (1990) *Mortality and Geography: A Review in the Mid-1980s, England and Wales,* Series DS9, HMSO, London.

Cromley, E.K. and McLafferty, S.L. (2002) *GIS and Public Health,* Guilford, New York and London.

Coggon, D., Rose, G. and Barker, D. (1997) *Epidemiology for the Uninitiated,* Fourth edition, BMJ, London.

Curtis, S. (1995) Geographical perspectives on poverty, health and health policy in different parts of the UK, in Philo, C. (ed.) *Off The Map: The Social Geography of Poverty in The UK,* Child Poverty Action Group, London, pp. 153–174.

Curtis, S. (2004) *Health and Inequality: Geographical Perspectives,* Sage, London.

Curtis, S. and Taket, A. (1996) *Health and Societies: Changing Perspectives,* Arnold, London.

Dahlgren, G. and Whitehead, M. (1991) *Policies and Strategies to Promote Social Equity in Health,* Institute of Futures Studies, Stockholm.

Dale, A. (1993) The content of the 1991 Census: change and continuity, in Dale, A. and Marsh, C. (eds) *The 1991 Census User's Guide,* HMSO, London.

Department of Health (DOH) (1991) *The Health of the Nation: a Consultative Document for Health in England,* (Cmnd. 1523), HMSO, London.

Department of Health (DOH) (1995) *Variations in Health: What can the Department of Health and the NHS do?* A report produced by the Variations Sub-Group of the Chief Medical Officer's Health of the Nation Working Group, DOH, London.

Department of Health (DOH) (1998a) *Our Healthier Nation: A Contract for Health,* The Stationery Office, London.

Department of Health (DOH) (1998b) *Independent Inquiry into Inequalities in Health: Report,* The Stationery Office, London.

Department of Health (DOH) (1999a) *Saving Lives: Our Healthier Nation,* Cm 4386, The Stationery Office, London.

Department of Health (DOH) (1999b) *Reducing Health Inequalities: An Action Report,* DOH, London.

Department of Health (DOH) (2002) *Tackling Health Inequalities: 2002 Cross-cutting Review,* DOH, London.

Elliott, S.J., Taylor, S.M., Walter, S., Stieb, D., Frank, J. and Eyles, J. (1993) Modeling psychosocial effects of exposure to solid-waste facilities, *Social Science and Medicine,* 37: 791–804.

Gatrell, A.C. (2002) *Geographies of Health,* Blackwells, Oxford.

Gould, M.I. and Jones, K. (1996) Analysing perceived limiting long-term illness using UK census microdata, *Social Science and Medicine,* 42: 857–869.

Great Britain, Parliament, House of Commons, Health Committee (GBPHCHC) (2004) *Obesity: Third Report of Session 2003–04,* Vol. 1, HC 23-1, The Stationery Office, London.

Gregory, J. and Lowe, S. (2000) *National Diet and Nutrition Survey: Young People Aged 4 to 18 Years Volume 1: Report of the Diet and Nutrition Survey,* The Stationery Office, London.

Griffiths, C. and Fitzpatrick, J. (2001) *Geographic Variations in Health,* (DS No.16), HMSO, London.

Higgs, G. and Gould, M. (2001) Is there a role for GIS in the 'new NHS'? *Health & Place,* 7: 247–259.

Howe, G.M. (1986) Does it matter where I live? *Transactions of the Institute of British Geographers, New Series,* 11: 387–414.

Jacobson, B., Smith, A. and Whitehead, M. (1991) *The Nation's Health: A Strategy for the 1990s,* Second edition, King Edward's Hospital Fund for London, London.

Jones, K., Gould, M.I. and Duncan, C. (2000) Health and deprivation: an exploratory survival analysis of deaths in the Health and Lifestyles Survey, *Science and Medicine,* 50(7/8): 1059–1079.

Jones, K. and Moon, G. (1993) Medical geography: taking space seriously, *Progress in Human Geography,* 17: 515–524.

Leeds Initiative (2004) *Vision for Leeds II, 2003–2018: The Community Strategy,* Leeds Initiative, Leeds.

Lister, H., Simpkin, M. and Jones, M. (1994) *Redressing the Balance: Health and Inequality in Leeds,* Leeds Health for All, Leeds.

Macintyre, S., Maciver, S. and Soomans, A. (1993) Area, class and health: Should we be focussing on places or people? *Journal of Social Policy,* 22: 213–234.

Manson-Siddle, C. (2001) *Yorkshire and Humber Health Links,* Northern and Yorkshire Public Health Observatory, Trent Public Health Observatory, Yorkshire Forward and other organisations, Sheffield.

Moon, G., Gould, M. and Colleagues (2000) *Epidemiology: An Introduction,* Open University, Milton Keynes.

Murray, M.A. (1962) The Geography of Death in England and Wales, *Annals of the Association of American Geographers,* 52: 130-149.

Office of National Statistics (ONS) (2002) *Vital Statistics for England and Wales, 2001,* Series VS4D, HMSO, London.

Office of National Statistics (ONS) (2003) *Regional Trends 38,* HMSO, London.

Senior, M.L. (1998) Area variations in self-perceived limiting long term illness in Britain, 1992: Is the Welsh experience exceptional? *Regional Studies* 32: 265–280.

Townsend, P., Davidson, N. and Whitehead, M. (Eds.) (1992) *Inequalities In Health: The Black Report, The Health Divide,* Second edition, Penguin, Middlesex.

Townsend, P., Phillimore, P. and Beatie, A. (1988) *Health and Deprivation: Inequality and the North,* Croom Helm, London.

Whitelegg, J. (1987) A geography of road accidents, *Transaction of the Institute of British Geographers,* 12(2): 161–176.

World Health Organisation (WHO) (1992) *ICD-10: International Statistical Classification of Diseases and Health Related Problems,* Tenth Revision (Volumes 1–3), WHO, Geneva.

World Health Organisation (WHO) (1994) *Action for Health in Cities,* Regional Office for Europe, Copenhagen.

World Health Organisation (WHO) (1998) *Health21 — Health for All in the 21st Century,* European Health for All Series, No 5, WHO, Geneva.

6

The 'Haves' and 'Have-nots': Contrasting Social Geographies

JOHN STILLWELL & PETER SHEPHERD

HARVEY NICHOLS

8312 4001 1167 5432

MR A SMART

1/04

PAYING OFFICE STAMP

1 54

MR I AM BROKE
17 ST. JOHNS AVENUE   LS7 30N
HOVEL COURT
LEEDS

Department for
Work and Pensions

POST OFFICE   285323   0 00
NEWTON GROVE PO   0 34
172 CHAPELTOWN ROAD   5 30
LEEDS   2 02
7 4HP

K232030S
ways quote the above
ance Number

on other benefits

▶ PLEASE DO NOT BEND

A substantial proportion of the local population has remained excluded from the opportunities that economic growth and prosperity have brougnt.

6.1 Introduction

During the 1990s, academics and policy makers became increasingly concerned with the role played by British cities in economic competitiveness, social cohesion and environmental sustainability. The term 'social exclusion' replaced 'poverty' as the descriptor of the situation that arises when people living in parts of a city are exposed to a combination of social problems such as high long-term unemployment, low income, high crime, bad health and poor environmental conditions (Percy-Smith, 2000). In England, the Social Exclusion Unit (SEU) was set up by the Prime Minister in 1997 to research social exclusion problems in metropolitan areas such as Leeds, where the notion of a 'two-speed city' — with widening divisions between groups of socially included and excluded — had become manifest. One of the outcomes was the development of the National Strategy Action Plan, which set out an agenda and targets for narrowing the gap between neighbourhood renewal outcomes in deprived areas and the rest. At a local level, this policy was adopted by the Leeds Initiative in 2001 with the aim "to narrow the gap between the most disadvantaged neighbourhoods of Leeds and the rest of the city" (Leeds Initiative, 2001).

Encouragingly for Leeds, there is plenty of evidence to show that the city has undergone an economic renaissance over the last decade, with focus on the growing numbers of jobs in financial, legal and business services paralleled by a continued rise as a major retailing centre and a dynamic property sector (Bruff, 2002). However, there is a danger in viewing Leeds as a coherent entity and indeed in using an over-arching concept like social exclusion to explain a very diverse set of problems. A substantial proportion of the local population has remained excluded from the opportunities that economic growth and prosperity have brought. Levels of unemployment, poverty, health, crime, educational performance and environ-mental quality vary widely between localities across the city, with problems being particularly acute in some inner city areas.

This is the dichotomy that underpins this chapter and the aim here is to begin to build a detailed picture of the geography of affluence and disadvantage. This is achieved by recognising that social well-being and social exclusion are multi-dimensional concepts and a range of indicators can be defined when attempting to measure their magnitude and incidence (Percy-Smith, 2003). Typically, the economic dimen-sion is represented by variables such as unemployment, worklessness and income; the social dimension is captured by variables such as homelessness, crime levels or unwanted teenage pregnancy; the political dimension can be represented by voter turnout, or social disorder; and variables like physical degradation and decaying housing stock can be used to measure the environmental dimension. In addition, there is a range of other variables like ill-health, educational underachieve-ment and a lack of services that may be defined as contributing to social deprivation while good health, overachievement and service overprovision can reflect social advantage.

We take a selection of indicators from each of the major dimensions and examine them using recent data sources, especially the 2001 Census of Population. The mapping of crime patterns is given particular prominence because of the importance of community safety as a policy imperative, and because of the various indicators of the geography of social exclusion, crime is not covered elsewhere in this book. Some indicators are missing here because they have been covered elsewhere, while others such as homelessness and problem drug use have not been included because reliable geographic data is not available or a spatial treatment is not always appropriate.

Examples of national and local policy responses to social exclusion are included, for the most part focusing on the larger structural programmes.

6.2 Comparisons of social structure

Following a major review of governmental classifications by the Office for Population Censuses and Surveys (OPCS) during the 1990s, a new National Statistics Socioeconomic Classification (NS-SeC) was introduced in 2001. This replaced the classifica-tions of social class based on occupation (SC, formerly the

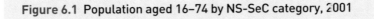

Figure 6.1 Population aged 16–74 by NS-SeC category, 2001

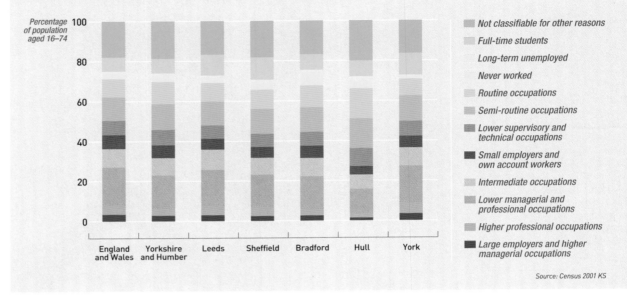

Source: Census 2001 KS

Registrar General's Social Class) and socio-economic group (SEG) and is used here for its ability, in part, to capture the economic security and prospects of economic advancement for employees.

District comparisons

Before beginning a detailed investigation of social exclusion within Leeds, it is worth reviewing how Leeds compares with similar cities, other parts of its region and the nation. The NS-SeC divides those aged 16–74 into 12 categories and Figure 6.1 compares the social structure of Leeds with that of England and Wales as a whole, Yorkshire and the Humber and the other major cities within the region. There were almost 520,500 people in Leeds enumerated by the 2001 Census in the economically active age range, the largest category (17.5 per cent) being class 3, the lower managerial and professional occupations. Leeds' profile is more akin to that of the nation than the region apart from the higher proportion of full-time students and the lower proportion of long-term unemployed (as measured on the census date, 2001). There are close similarities with the social class structure of York but clear differences from Sheffield, Bradford and Hull, all of which have lower proportions in the top three categories and higher proportions of those who have never worked or are long-term unemployed.

When Leeds' social class profile is compared with that of

other principal provincial cities (Manchester, Liverpool, Newcastle, Birmingham) (Figure 6.2), it is apparent that higher proportions of the population are classified in the more affluent categories, particularly large employers and higher managerial occupations and lower managerial and professional occupations. At the other end of the spectrum, Leeds has the lowest proportions of those who have never worked and long-term unemployed.

Local comparisons

Whilst the statistics above provide evidence of the relative affluence of the city when compared with its competitors within and outside the region, Figure 6.3 starts to provide an indication of the spatial diversity in socio-economic character that exists across the district. The percentage of those in classes 1–2 (large employers and higher managerial and professional occupations) contrasts markedly with the proportion of those in classes 7–8 (semi-routine and routine occupations). A clear north-south divide is evident. Communities including Far Headingley, Roundhay, Thorner, Collingham and Linton, and Scarcroft all have over 18 per cent of their economically active population in the top two classes, and relatively low proportions in the semi-routine and routine occupations. In contrast, places such as Cottingley, Belle Isle, New Wortley, Upper Wortley and Osmondthorpe have very low proportions in classes 1 and 2 but

Figure 6.2 Population aged 16–74 by NS-SeC category, 2001

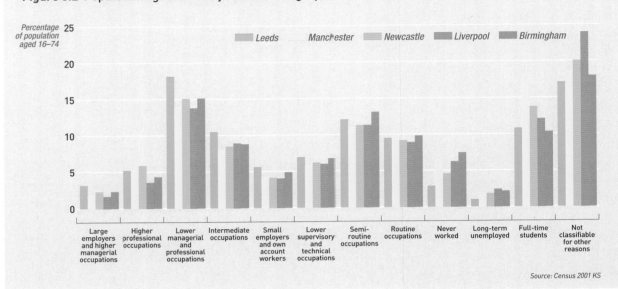

Percentage of population aged 16–74

Legend: Leeds, Manchester, Newcastle, Liverpool, Birmingham

Categories: Large employers and higher managerial occupations | Higher professional occupations | Lower managerial and professional occupations | Intermediate occupations | Small employers and own account workers | Lower supervisory and technical occupations | Semi-routine occupations | Routine occupations | Never worked | Long-term unemployed | Full-time students | Not classifiable for other reasons

Source: Census 2001 KS

Right, a life of leisure: two friends enjoy a coffee break in the Victoria Quarter during a hectic day's shopping.
Far right, *Big Issue* seller, a familiar sight in the city centre. This is one way that homeless people can start to improve their circumstances.

over a third of their 16–74 year old populations in classes 7 and 8.

The distributions shown in the maps of social class are indicative of the spatial inequalities in social structure based on occupation with which most residents of Leeds are familiar. What is highlighted is that one of the key limitations of the aggregate comparisons drawn above between Leeds and other cities is the assumption that each district is homogeneous with respect to the chosen indicator. Single measures of deprivation ignore the diversity of social conditions that exist throughout the city, as indicated in Figure 6.3.

Leeds boundary extends over a large geographical area and, consequently, it encompasses a wide spectrum of urban and rural communities and a range of better-off and worse-off areas. This situation contrasts with cities like Manchester or Liverpool, whose administrative boundaries are defined more tightly around the inner suburbs and exclude some of the more wealthy outer suburban areas that are within the commuting area. It can be argued that the heterogeneous mixture of residential environments in Leeds reduces the average scores of social indicators suggesting that Leeds is more affluent than many other places. In fact, when ranked on the basis of the overall 1998 ILD score, Leeds comes 56th amongst all local authority districts (Boyle and Alvanides, 2004) with a score of 19.06, well behind Liverpool (40.0) and Manchester (36.33).

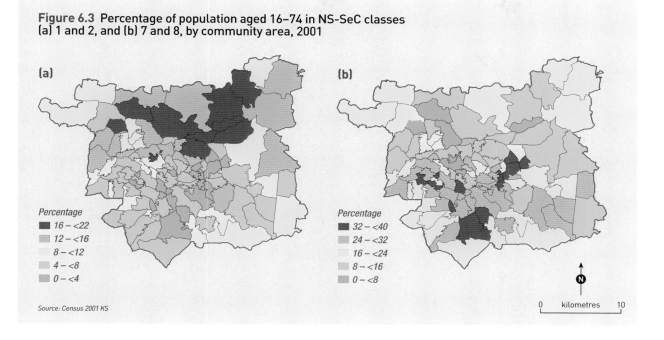

Figure 6.3 Percentage of population aged 16–74 in NS-SeC classes
(a) 1 and 2, and (b) 7 and 8, by community area, 2001

(a)

Percentage
- 16 – <22
- 12 – <16
- 8 – <12
- 4 – <8
- 0 – <4

Source: Census 2001 KS

(b)

Percentage
- 32 – <40
- 24 – <32
- 16 – <24
- 8 – <16
- 0 – <8

N

0   kilometres   10

6.3 Indicators of relative inequality

We now move on to consider other indicators of inequality and social exclusion in Leeds. In particular, we focus on temporal and spatial patterns of unemployment, car ownership (economic dimensions) and living conditions (environmental dimension).

Unemployment

One of the most common indicators of socioeconomic disadvantage is the rate of unemployment, computed by dividing the number of persons unemployed by the at risk population, those who are in the economically active age groups. This rate computation is feasible when data comes from the Census and Figure 6.4 shows the spatial patterns of male and female unemployment rates at ward level. There is a pronounced centre-periphery contrast with inner city wards of City and Holbeck, Burmantofts, Harehills and Seacroft having the highest unemployment rates, much as they did in 1991 (Stillwell and Leigh, 1996).

The difference between the rates of unemployment at these two census dates is in the magnitude rather than in the spatial pattern. Unemployment has fallen substantially over the 1990s and early 2000s, and Figure 6.5 uses data on claimant counts in 1996 and 2003, extracted from Nomisweb (an online source for labour market data), to illustrate how the pattern of unemployment inequality has been maintained despite a

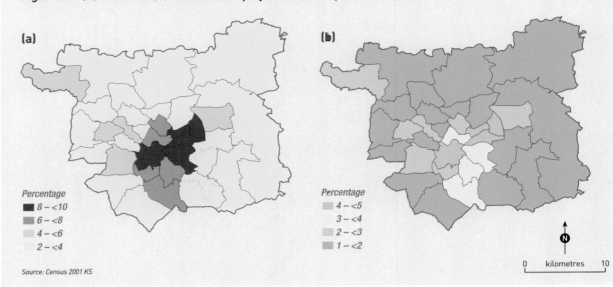

Figure 6.4 (a) Male and (b) female unemployment rates by ward, 2001

(a)

Percentage
- 8 – <10
- 6 – <8
- 4 – <6
- 2 – <4

Source: Census 2001 KS

(b)

Percentage
- 4 – <5
- 3 – <4
- 2 – <3
- 1 – <2

0   kilometres   10

reduction in claimants from 29,300 in January 1996 to 12,600 in January 2003.

The number of claimants is measured by the radius of the radar and wards are ranked according to claimants in 1996. Thus, University ward had almost 2,000 claimants in 1996 but less than half that number in 2003. As you rotate in a clockwise direction, unemployment levels decline, with the lowest value recorded for Otley and Wharfedale.

Figure 6.5 captures the extent and consistency of spatial disparity in the aggregate claimant statistics. Similar radar diagrams have been used in Figure 6.6 to contrast two particular sub-groups of unemployed persons. In Figure 6.6a, the counts of those aged 19 and under are depicted and indicate more inconsistency over time in several of the wards. In fact, the number of young claimants in Hunslet in 2003 was higher than in 1996, despite a reduction overall from 2,390 to 1,376 claimants. Figure 6.6b represents those who were claiming unemployment benefit for over 12 months. In this case, the numbers have reduced dramatically from 10,400 in 1996 to 1,534 by January 2003. In both cases, however, the wards of Harehills, Chapel Allerton, University, and City and Holbeck are amongst those with the highest numbers of claimants.

Policy from the local up to the European level realises that the provision of jobs in areas of high unemployment is one of the most important means for helping people out of poverty.

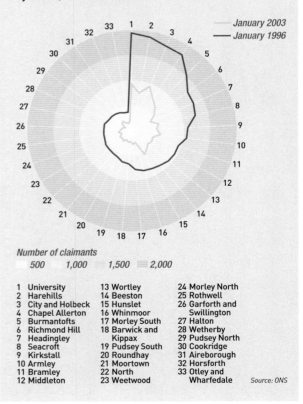

Figure 6.5 Unemployment claimants by ward, 1996 and 2003

January 2003
January 1996

Number of claimants
500   1,000   1,500   2,000

1	University	13	Wortley	24	Morley North
2	Harehills	14	Beeston	25	Rothwell
3	City and Holbeck	15	Hunslet	26	Garforth and
4	Chapel Allerton	16	Whinmoor		Swillington
5	Burmantofts	17	Morley South	27	Halton
6	Richmond Hill	18	Barwick and	28	Wetherby
7	Headingley		Kippax	29	Pudsey North
8	Seacroft	19	Pudsey South	30	Cookridge
9	Kirkstall	20	Roundhay	31	Aireborough
10	Armley	21	Moortown	32	Horsforth
11	Bramley	22	North	33	Otley and
12	Middleton	23	Weetwood		Wharfedale

Source: ONS

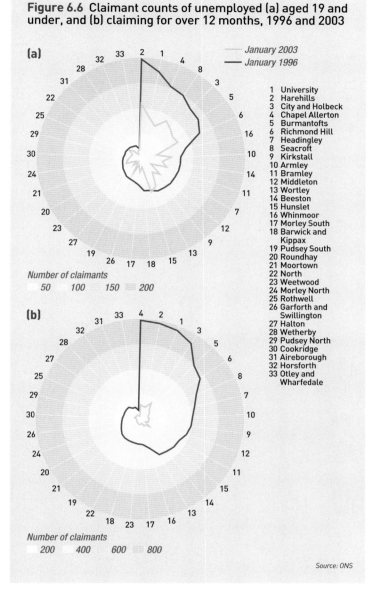

Figure 6.6 Claimant counts of unemployed (a) aged 19 and under, and (b) claiming for over 12 months, 1996 and 2003

(a)

January 2003
January 1996

Number of claimants
50   100   150   200

(b)

Number of claimants
200   400   600   800

1 University
2 Harehills
3 City and Holbeck
4 Chapel Allerton
5 Burmantofts
6 Richmond Hill
7 Headingley
8 Seacroft
9 Kirkstall
10 Armley
11 Bramley
12 Middleton
13 Wortley
14 Beeston
15 Hunslet
16 Whinmoor
17 Morley South
18 Barwick and
    Kippax
19 Pudsey South
20 Roundhay
21 Moortown
22 North
23 Weetwood
24 Morley North
25 Rothwell
26 Garforth and
    Swillington
27 Halton
28 Wetherby
29 Pudsey North
30 Cookridge
31 Aireborough
32 Horsforth
33 Otley and
    Wharfedale

Source: ONS

Money that is available to SMEs from EU Objective 2 funds is discussed in more detail in Chapter 8. Aimed at delivering economic benefits, this money is available to develop businesses in Burmantofts, Chapeltown, City and Holbeck, Harehills, Headingley and University wards. National funding through round 6 of the Government's Single Regeneration Budget (SRB) is being used to achieve social as well as economic objectives. In this way, projects such as the Aire Valley Employment Area in the south-east of the city have attracted substantial sums to help prepare previously contaminated land for development and provide grants and advice to new businesses. It is estimated that around 5,000 new jobs could be created — potentially of great benefit to the surrounding neighbourhoods of Richmond Hill, Osmondthorpe, Halton Moor, Hunslet, Belle Isle and Middleton, where unemployment is almost twice the city average.

Partnerships between local groups and business can also work together to target sustainable employment initiatives in areas of need. Seacroft is one of the 10 per cent most deprived wards in Britain and has had chronic unemployment problems. Through the efforts of the Seacroft Partnership, job guarantees were created for local people at the opening of a new Tesco Extra supermarket.

Car ownership

Car ownership features in social exclusion debates for two different reasons. On the one hand, it is often used as an indicator of income, with those living in the poorest circumstances not able to afford the costs of owning a car. On the other hand, not having personal transport can also be a barrier to finding employment, as distance and inadequate public transport connections put some job vacancies out of reach. The 2001 Census recorded just over 301,600 households in Leeds, of which 34 per cent are without a car or a van, 42 per cent have one car or van and 24 per cent have two or more cars or vans. Compared with other local authorities nationally, Leeds has a relatively high proportion of households in the no car category and a relatively low proportion in the two plus category. In fact, the district is ranked 303rd out of 376 districts in England and Wales in terms of two plus car households.

Whilst car ownership does have some currency as a measure of social affluence, the importance of car availability

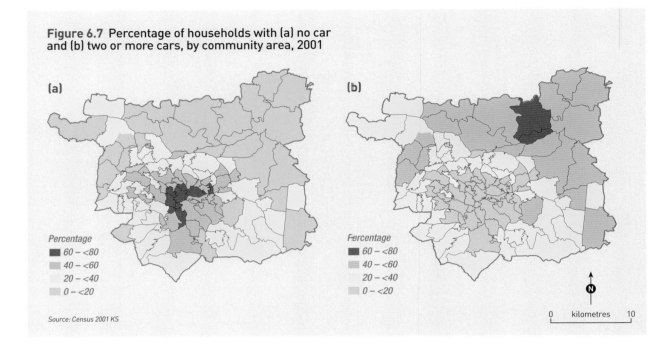

Figure 6.7 Percentage of households with (a) no car and (b) two or more cars, by community area, 2001

(a)

Percentage
- 60 – <80
- 40 – <60
- 20 – <40
- 0 – <20

Source: Census 2001 KS

(b)

Percentage
- 60 – <80
- 40 – <60
- 20 – <40
- 0 – <20

0　　kilometres　　10

N

Car ownership: a symbol of status and affluence for many. For poorer citizens, lack of access to a car limits job options.

differs according to residential location. The patterns of no car and two or more car ownership (Figure 6.7) reflect this location bias, with much higher proportions of non car ownership in the inner areas and much higher levels of two or more car ownership in the outer suburbs and rural surrounds. In certain inner city community areas, the proportion of no car households is in excess of 60 per cent. In Little London, for example, 73 per cent of households have no cars/vans and only 4 per cent have two or more vehicles. On the other hand, of the 452 households in Scarcroft, 63 per cent have two plus cars and 4 per cent have no cars.

Social exclusion policy to combat poverty and increase personal incomes will obviously bring car ownership within reach of some people. Yet, the main thrust of social exclusion policy with respect to transport provision is to provide alternatives to car ownership. Importantly, this must be to and from the places that would improve access from the poorest parts of the city to areas of employment, education, training and recreational facilities. Predicted to begin service in 2007, the Supertram network is designed to extend towards many deprived neighbourhoods, providing better access to employment and services and attracting extra investment to those areas. In the meantime, money from the Government's Urban Bus Challenge and funds from Round 6 of the SRB are helping local service provider Metro to create flexible bus services to help those living in Middleton, Belle Isle, Hunslet and Halton Moor access employment opportunities in the Aire Valley Employment Area.

Living conditions

One variable that measures deprivation in a physical way is the number of households without central heating. There are nearly 62,500 households in Leeds in this category, and in this respect, the city shows up badly compared with elsewhere. In fact, it is ranked 10th worst district in the country on this indicator. The breakdown by tenure reveals that 45 per cent of these households are owner occupied, 38 per cent are council properties, 1 per cent are other social rented and 16 per cent are privately rented. Households without central heating are found in concentrations to the north and east of the city centre (Figure 6.8), with proportions over 75 per cent in parts of the communities of Scott Hall and Miles Hill and Seacroft North. In these communities, 75.7 per cent of the properties without central heating are council properties, 1.3 per cent are other social rented, while another 6.8 per cent are privately rented.

The National Strategy Action Plan aims to bring all social housing up to a decent standard by 2010, with one third of this improvement taking place by 2004. In a housing condition survey undertaken by Leeds City Council, 55 per cent of Leeds' council homes were judged to require further work before they achieved the national decency standard. The definition of decent housing is complex and the limited variables that are available in the census can only reflect one aspect of the standard. On this

Figure 6.8 Percentage of households without central heating, by output area, 2001

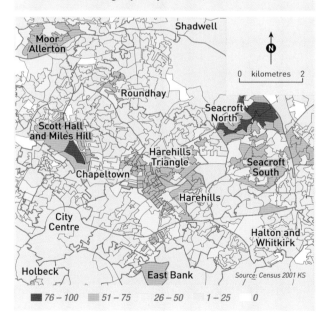

issue — effective heating — the standard places the greatest premium on the fitting of gas or oil powered central heating systems. Electric storage heaters and other heating devices are acceptable but they demand that extra levels of insulation to cavity walls and lofts (200mm) to meet energy efficiency ratings.

Energy efficiency is also a feature that is measured nationally as part of the Best Value performance system. The average performance of council housing in Leeds is broadly in line with regional and similar local authority averages, but is five percentage points lower than the national average. Transco's Affordable Warmth programme is one way in which local authorities can get assistance to install or upgrade central heating systems. The programme is essentially a leasing agreement that makes finance available for the installation of central heating systems. The Council itself is also able to offer financial support to private landlords with tenants from vulnerable groups. In 2002–2003, this amounted to around £7 million for renovation works to private owners for the benefit of applicants who include the elderly, disabled and disadvantaged people, often from the most deprived areas.

6.4 Indices of deprivation

While single indicators can provide useful insights into spatial variations in certain dimensions of social exclusion, it is of interest to know where the extremes that they collectively identify coincide geographically. For example, lone parenthood is an increasingly apparent form of household composition, so while lone parents everywhere face different problems to couple households, the problems are more significant when coincident with high levels of levels unemployment and poor housing. Various composite measures of deprivation have been derived for use in comparative research and the Government's Index of Local Deprivation (ILD) (DETR, 1998) and Index of Multiple Deprivation (IMD) (DETR, 2000) have been used frequently in policy formulation. Leeds is eligible for Neighbourhood Renewal status because the IMD 2000 put

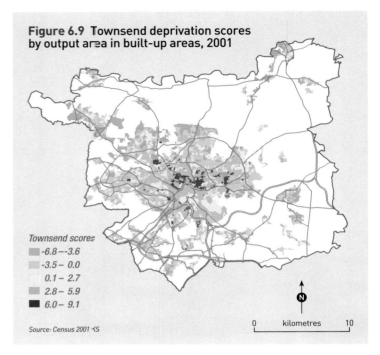

Figure 6.9 Townsend deprivation scores by output area in built-up areas, 2001

Townsend scores
- -6.8 – -3.6
- -3.5 – 0.0
- 0.1 – 2.7
- 2.8 – 5.9
- 6.0 – 9.1

Source: Census 2001 ‹S

0   kilometres   10

Leeds in the top 50 most deprived areas on one or more of the six measures that make up the index. Similar rules were also used with the ILD to determine SRB funding, for which Leeds was also eligible.

One of the more mature material deprivation measures, the Townsend index, has the advantage of being calculable for small areas and from different censuses. This in is contrast to the ILD and IMD, which are only obtainable down to ward level and may therefore mislead when a ward contains extremes of both affluence and deprivation, as frequently happens. The scores of the Townsend index are a combination of census variables measuring (no) car ownership, (non) ownership of a home, unemployment and overcrowding. High positive scores represent areas of highest material deprivation, while high negative scores represent low material deprivation.

Using the 2001 Census output areas (each zone contains an average of approximately 125 households), Figure 6.9 shows the geography of Townsend deprivation scores across residential areas of Leeds. Major transport routes are included to help orientation. The highest scores are found in areas such as Burmantofts, Wortley, Little London, Beeston Hill and Halton Moor, whilst the most affluent parts of the district include parts of Garwick in Elmet, Scholes, Horsforth, Rawdon, Shadwell and Alwoodley Park. In terms of spatial concentration, areas close to

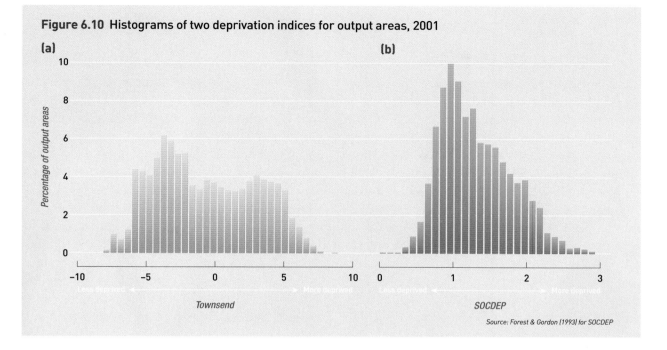

Figure 6.10 Histograms of two deprivation indices for output areas, 2001

(a)

Percentage of output areas

Townsend
Less deprived ← → More deprived

(b)

SOCDEP
Less deprived ← → More deprived

Source: Forest & Gordon (1993) for SOCDEP

the centre of Leeds' urban core exhibit the highest levels of material deprivation, with greater variation in scores in the suburban periphery. With the exception of one or two small areas in places such as Garforth and Otley, the areas to the north and east of the district are shown to be least deprived.

Looking for spatial patterns of deprivation can be complicated somewhat by land use and community consider-ations. Students, for example, rarely own their home and car ownership is also low. Areas with halls of residence, such as Boddington Hall and Beckett Park, thus stand out as areas of high material deprivation although the student population is not considered deprived in the social sense. What Figure 6.9 emphasizes at this small area scale, however, is the wide range of levels of material deprivation in Leeds, with some people prospering while others continue to struggle; the picture suggests a 'multi-speed' rather than a 'two-speed' city.

Alternatively, the notion of 'two speeds' can be investigated by visualising the distribution of deprivation index scores in the form of a histogram (Figure 6.10a). There is a peak in percentage of output areas with Townsend scores around -3, and a less clear peak for scores around +3. The fact that smaller proportions of output areas have scores between these two peaks might be interpreted as evidence of a two speed city, but there are other cities in Yorkshire and Humber region, including

Sheffield and Hull, that display a much more polarised tendency. In contrast, the histogram of SOCDEP (Forrest and Gordon, 1993) scores for Leeds (Figure 6.10b), an alternative index measuring social deprivation, has a more normal distribution. Social deprivation is more concerned with the effects of unemployment (including youth unemployment), family structure, old age and long-term illness. As such, it is more sensitive to the age distribution of the population (see Chapter 2 for further details) and in Leeds' case, would not be expected to be bimodal.

Unfortunately, major changes to the census output area geography make analysis of change in deprivation over time problematic at the small-area level. The only boundaries with complete coverage that have remained relatively unchanged in Leeds between censuses are wards (see Chapter 1). When Townsend scores are compared between 1991 and 2001, the greatest reductions in material deprivation appear in Harehills, Chapel Allerton and Middleton wards, while the greatest increases are found in City and Holbeck, Headingley and Weetwood wards. The changing size of the student population may account for some of the rises, since between 1995 and 2002 there has been a 51.7 per cent increase in higher education student registrations in Leeds (Higher Education Statistics Agency).

Car crime: while thefts of motor vehicles fell by 21 per cent in 2003–2004, joy-riding and vehicle arson are still a problem. In 2003, the City Council removed 1,782 abandoned vehicles from streets and waste ground in Leeds.

6.5 Crime and anti-social behaviour

Rightly or wrongly, crime and anti-social behaviour have become synonymous with deprivation in big cities across the UK. Collectively they represent one dimension of social exclusion and furthermore, they are a symptomatic consequence of social problems as well as a causal factor, driving out households and disincentivising private investment in the areas concerned. "Tough on crime, tough on the causes of crime" was the Government's pledge at the 1997 general election, and the Crime and Disorder Act of 1998 contains measures to try to deal with the wide-ranging problems affecting both urban and rural communities. At a local level, partnership working has been one significant result of the Act, with the police, local authorities and health authorities forming Crime and Disorder Reduction Partnerships (CDRPs). These enable closer working arrangements and encourage a more holistic, cross-cutting approach to sustainable reductions in crime, made through greater appreciation of the underlying social problems in high-crime areas. In Leeds, the CDRP is called the Leeds Community Safety Partnership (LCSP).

Thus far we have dealt mainly with data from the 2001 Census, but data on crime is altogether different and needs some introduction. Firstly, crime is categorised into different types of offence. Compared with similar local authorities such as Nottingham, Birmingham and Newcastle-upon-Tyne (all are members of the Home Office CDRP Family 4), Leeds has had less than average levels of violence, sexual offences and robbery, and above average levels of burglary and vehicle crime. Membership of the CDRP Family classification is determined by a range of variables chosen to reflect the risk of different types of crime and disorder. In Leeds, only violent crime against the person was less than the national average in the 12 months before April 2003 (Table 6.1).

Despite improvements in crime recording, evidence from the annual British Crime Survey (BCS) still suggests that there are large discrepancies between actual crime and officially recorded crime levels. For comparable crime types, the BCS estimates that only 43 per cent of crime is reported to the police (Simmons and Dodd, 2003). Theft of a vehicle is the most likely (97 per cent) to be reported followed by burglary

Table 6.1 Levels of notifiable criminal offences recorded by the police in Leeds and elsewhere, April 2002 to March 2003

	Offences recorded in Leeds	Rate per 1,000 population*		
		Leeds	CDRP Family 4 mean	England and Wales
Violence against the person	10,641	14.9	22.5	16.1
Sex offences	740	1.0	1.5	0.9
Robbery	2,650	3.7	5.0	2.1
Burglary from a dwelling	16,341	54.2	42.9*	20.2*
Theft of a motor vehicle	9,279	13.0	11.8	6.1
Theft from a motor vehicle	16,082	22.5	22.2	12.6

* Burglary rates are expressed per 1,000 households

Source: Home Office

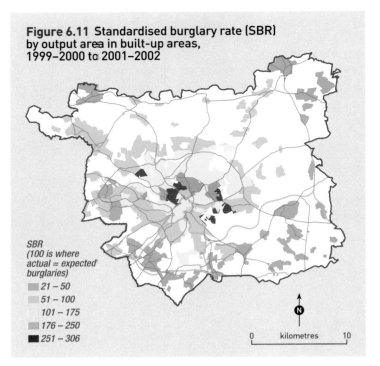

Figure 6.11 Standardised burglary rate (SBR) by output area in built-up areas, 1999–2000 to 2001–2002

SBR
(100 is where
actual = expected
burglaries)
■ 21 – 50
■ 51 – 100
  101 – 175
■ 176 – 250
■ 251 – 306

N

0   kilometres   10

where there has been a loss (87 per cent). Least likely to be reported are offences such as theft from a person (33 per cent) and vandalism (31 per cent). There are a variety of reasons for this under-reporting, with 'feelings that the police could not do anything to help' and 'dealing with the matter privately' being the most common responses given to the BCS.

The statistical analysis of spatial and temporal patterns of crime has emerged as an important field of regional science (see for example, Hirschfield *et al.*, 2001). Consequently, generic Geographical Information Systems (GIS) software as well as specialist packages, for example CrimeStat® (Levine, 1999) are being used routinely by the police and local authorities to analyse spatial patterns in crime data. In the space available here, we have chosen to use a variety of mapping techniques to analyse the geography of domestic burglary, criminal damage and anti-social behaviour.

Domestic burglary

In a three year period beginning April 1999, domestic burglary accounted for approximately 13 per cent of recorded crime in Leeds. Moreover, according to Home Office statistics (Table 6.1), 54.2 per 1,000 households were burgled in 2002–2003. As with many of the variables of social conditions across the district, Figure 6.11 shows that the district-standardised risk of domestic burglary (where 100 represents communities where the actual number of burglaries equalled the expected number, based on a district mean) varies considerably from one community to another. In particular, households in Woodhouse and Hyde Park are at a much higher risk of being victimised (SBR >100), followed closely by households in Halton Moor and Gipton South. Conversely, households in Wetherby and Otley are at a much lower risk of being burgled (SBR <100).

One of the commitments in the National Strategy Action Plan is to ensure that by 2005 burglary is reduced by 25

per cent, with no local authority area having more than three times the national average rate. In Leeds, this means aiming to keep the district rate at below 60 burglaries per 1,000 households. Additionally, the Neighbourhood Renewal Strategy for Leeds sets a floor target of a minimum 40 per cent reduction in higher crime areas. As a priority theme of the *Leeds Community Safety Strategy 2002–2005* (LCSP, 2001), a number of different approaches are being used to try and reduce burglary. The Burglary Reduction Initiative in Leeds (BRIL) has 'target hardened' over 5,000 properties across the city. Where repeat victimisation of these homes was running at 14.5 per cent, the figure is now down to 7 per cent (LCSP, 2003). Fasttrack DNA testing has also resulted in an increase of detections and prompt convictions for domestic burglary offences. Media campaigns have also sought to improve awareness of how to protect domestic properties and schemes that block off access to terrace backs (alley gating) are now starting to be implemented.

After two years of the LCSP strategy measures, it is possible to begin to evaluate their effectiveness. In 2002/03 the district-wide burglary rate was 54 offences per 1,000 households, while in 2003/04, this figure has fallen by 16 per cent, to 46 offences per 1,000 households. At ward level, 27 of the 33 wards in Leeds saw domestic burglary drop, with the largest falls in Morley North (-41 per cent) and Moortown (-46 per cent). Of those wards which saw a rise, Armley (+41 per cent) and Bramley (+25 per cent) must give special cause for concern. Indeed, this is perhaps an example of the frailty of district performance-led policies. For while the overall fall in the burglary rate should be applauded, the benefits are not being shared equally across the district.

Criminal damage

In the three year period beginning April 1999, criminal damage accounted for approximately 17.5 per cent of recorded crime in Leeds. As with domestic burglary, rates of criminal damage vary widely across the district, although it is important to bear in mind that deprived areas tend to suffer from higher levels of crime. To control for this, Figure 6.12 shows rates of criminal damage that have been standardised according to a neighbourhood classification based on the Townsend material deprivation index.

In this way, it is possible to identify areas that, even given their level of deprivation (or affluence), seem to exhibit greater or lesser amounts of criminal damage than might be expected. The city centre and Cross Green stand out as being the areas most at risk of criminal damage, but relatively low numbers of households and land use considerations affect the reliability of the standardised rates. Much more significant is the cluster of community areas in East Leeds which have high rates of criminal damage even given the levels of deprivation to be found therein. By contrast, other deprived areas with no shortage of other types of crime, such as Chapeltown and Beeston, seem less affected by criminal damage than might be expected. Thorner and Pudsey also have unexpectedly high levels of criminal damage, although in these cases, it is because deprivation is relatively low. Isolating what might be happening differently in these community areas is far from straightforward and has to take into account many factors. For example, there could be a greater propensity to report

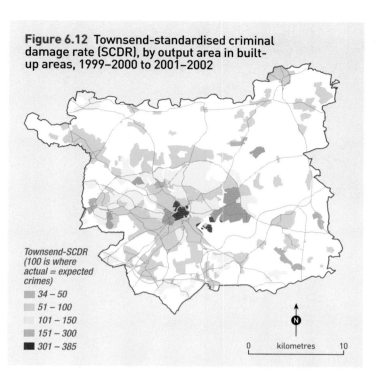

Figure 6.12 Townsend-standardised criminal damage rate (SCDR), by output area in built-up areas, 1999–2000 to 2001–2002

Townsend-SCDR
(100 is where
actual = expected
crimes)
- 34 – 50
- 51 – 100
- 101 – 150
- 151 – 300
- 301 – 385

crimes to the police in these areas, or there may be high levels of repeat offending by one or few local offenders, as was the case with arson-related incidents in Thorner between 1998 and 2001 (Yorkshire Post, 2002).

In part because of its very varied nature, criminal damage is not a specific priority theme of current community safety strategy at either local or national level. However, initiatives that ought to have an effect on offending levels are in operation and involve partners from across Leeds. For arson, the West Yorkshire Fire and Rescue Service make visits to schools to talk to young people about the dangers of fire and fire play, and a special Arson Task Force has been established in east Leeds to deal with deliberate fire starting within the Killingbeck Police Division area. Leeds City Council aims to remove abandoned and burnt-out cars within 24 hours to help reduce people's fear of crime and limit opportunities for further offending. A number of local organisations, including West Yorkshire Police and Education Leeds, help organise diversionary schemes for young people from deprived areas to keep them off the streets during school vacations and reduce the risk of them becoming a victim of crime or getting into trouble themselves.

Between 2002/03 and 2003/04, criminal damage offences rose by 9.3 per cent compared with a fall in all crime

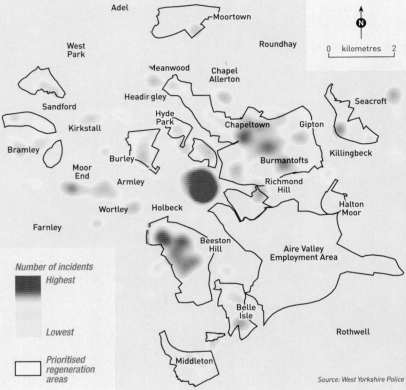

Figure 6.13 Anti-social behaviour hotspots, inner Leeds, 2000-2001

Adel
Moortown
West Park
Roundhay
0 kilometres 2
Meanwood
Chapel Allerton
Headingley
Hyde Park
Seacroft
Sandford
Kirkstall
Chapeltown
Gipton
Bramley
Burley
Killingbeck
Moor End
Armley
Burmantofts
Richmond Hill
Wortley
Holbeck
Halton Moor
Farnley
Beeston Hill
Aire Valley Employment Area
Number of incidents
Highest
Lowest
Prioritised regeneration areas
Belle Isle
Rothwell
Middleton

Source: West Yorkshire Police

Top, ASBOs are served by magistrates based on evidence gathered by Council officers or the police. 112 ASBOs were served in Leeds in the 12 months to April 2004.
Bottom, a police officer on duty in Gipton, where many ASBOS have been served.

of 1.5 per cent across the district. At a ward level, only 8 wards saw a fall in criminal damage offences. The largest falls were in University (-17 per cent) and Rothwell (-11 per cent) wards, while the largest increases were seen in Pudsey South (+33 per cent) and Armley (+31 per cent). Across England and Wales, changes to the way in which this offence is recorded have meant most police forces have seen some increase.

Anti-social behaviour

The Home Office's crime reduction website suggests 17 categories of anti-social behaviour (ASB) covering a wide range of activities from verbal abuse to harassment, from cycling on footpaths to prostitution, from racist and homophobic incidents to alcohol and solvent abuse. As such, data on ASB is both varied in nature and by the type of organisations collecting it. Data maintained by West Yorkshire Police is based upon calls for assistance or action from the public, the police and warden patrols. For the period from 1 April 2000 to 31 March 2001, this

police data has been cleaned to provide a data set of over 24,000 records (Tullett and Stillwell, 2003), which have been mapped in Figure 6.13.

This type of map is commonly referred to as a kernel-density, or 'hotspot' map, with the hotspots showing areas where there has been a clustering of ASB incidents. The city centre stands out as the area with most concentrated pattern of ASB. Elsewhere, parts of Beeston and Harehills also have high concentrations of ASB. As with other types of crime and disorder, the high values found in the city centre pose problems for trying to calculate accurate incident rates, as these are usually expressed in terms of residential population. Even if models of daytime population are used, they rarely reflect risk accurately, as patterns of offending vary season by season and by time of day (Figure 6.14).

Policy to combat ASB has received much national and local publicity and Leeds is at the forefront of developing new strategies to tackle ASB problems. The Leeds Domestic Violence

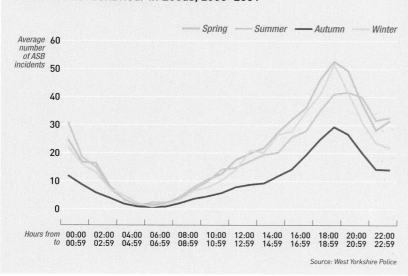

Figure 6.14 Seasonal and hourly variations in anti-social behaviour in Leeds, 2000–2001

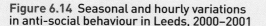

Spring — Summer — Autumn — Winter

Average number of ASB incidents

60
50
40
30
20
10
0

Hours from 00:00 02:00 04:00 06:00 08:00 10:00 12:00 14:00 16:00 18:00 20:00 22:00
to 00:59 02:59 04:59 06:59 08:59 10:59 12:59 14:59 16:59 18:59 20:59 22:59

Source: West Yorkshire Police

Woodhouse and Hyde Park are hotspots of domestic burglary, so additional secrity features are in evidence on many properties.

Cluster Court is the first of its kind in the country and ensures cases are dealt with quickly by appropriately trained staff. West Yorkshire Police have also been praised for innovative use of the new Anti-Social Behaviour Orders (ASBOs) in trying to disrupt local drugs markets, and Leeds has also been selected by the Government as a 'trailblazer' to reduce begging by 60 per cent by 2005. Yet, as cases of ASB often involve some of society's most vulnerable groups, some policies have not escaped criticism. For example, charities that support homeless and vulnerable people have been quick to point out that criminalising begging is likely to alienate vulnerable people further from society. They argue that what is required is greater and more timely provision of drug treatment and mental health services. There are also fears that there are already sufficient criminal justice powers to deal with 'aggressive begging' and that additional laws will simply tie up more police and court resources, reducing capacity to deal with more serious crimes.

6.6 Conclusions

A number of observations and conclusions have been described in the spatial evaluation of the social exclusion indicators used above. It should be stressed, however, that these findings need to be considered with a great deal of caution. By themselves, no amount of indicators will provide a complete assessment of

which parts of Leeds are suffering most from the effects of poverty, or why. Neither can an assessment of social exclusion ignore that the indicators are reflecting problems which are sometimes being addressed, and that policy responses to social exclusion have a geography too.

In essence, every city has a unique social fabric with distinctive interwoven patterns of relative affluence and deprivation. In Leeds, the extremes of society are evident and have been identified and measured in a number of different ways. The affluent suburban communities in the northern suburbs contrast starkly with those parts of the inner city where social problems across several dimensions are at their worst. Thus, it is these most disadvantaged parts of the city that have been the focus of much social policy and its associated funding. Leeds has been striving hard through its neighbourhood renewal initiatives to reduce the social and economic gap between those parts of the city most in need of 'better neighbourhoods and confident communities' (Leeds Initiative, 2003) and those areas in the outer suburbs where problems are much less acute.

Clearly the social dimension is closely connected with other dimensions (race, education, housing, health), each of which is discussed elsewhere in this volume in further detail. It is apparent, however, from the preceding analysis of variables that have been selected to represent social conditions, that longstanding and deep-rooted social and spatial divisions still remain a feature of the city in the twenty-first century, despite the plethora of policies that have been implemented to deal

Cleaning up derelict housing in Gipton. Removing old tyres and gas bottles helps to reduce opportunities for arson.

References

Boyle, P. and Alvanides, S. (2004) Assessing deprivation in English inner city areas: making the case for EU funding for Leeds City, Chapter 7 in Stillwell, J.C.H. and Clarke, G.P. (eds.) *Applied GIS and Spatial Analysis*, Wiley, Chichester, pp. 111–136.

Bruff, G. (2002) Two-speed city: narrowing the gap in Leeds, *The Yorkshire & Humber Regional Review*, 12(2): 4–6.

Department of Environment, Transport and the Regions (DETR) (1998) *1998 Index of Local Deprivation: A Summary of Results*, DETR, London.

Department of Environment, Transport and the Regions (DETR) (2000) *Indices of Deprivation*, DETR, London.

Forrest, R. and Gordon, D. (1993) *People and Places: A 1991 Census Atlas of England*, School for Advanced Urban Studies, University of Bristol, Bristol.

Hirschfield, A., Yarwood, D. and Bowers, K. (2001) Crime pattern analysis, spatial targeting and GIS: the development of new approaches for use in evaluating community safety initiatives, Chapter 17 in Clarke, G. and Madden, M. (eds.) *Regional Science in Business*, Springer, Heidelberg, pp. 323–342.

Leeds Community Safety Partnership (LCSP) (2001) *Leeds Community Safety Strategy 2002–2005*, Leeds Community Safety, Leeds.

Leeds Community Safety Partnership (LCSP) (2003) 'BRIL: Key achievements between April 2002 and End of March 2003'. Online at http://www.leeds-csp.org.uk/view.asp?level1=Burglary&level2=BRIL (Accessed 14 June 2004).

Leeds Initiative (2001) *A Neighbourhood Renewal Strategy for Leeds*, Leeds Initiative, Leeds.

Levine, N. (1999) *CrimeStat: A Spatial Statistics Program for the Analysis of Crime Incident Locations*, National Institute of Justice, Washington DC, available online at http://www.icpsr.umich.edu/NACJD/crimestat.html

Percy-Smith, J. (ed.) (2000) *Responses to Social Exclusion: Towards Inclusion?*, Open University Press, Buckingham.

Percy-Smith, J. (2003) Social exclusion in Yorkshire and Humber, *The Yorkshire & Humber Regional Review*, 13(1): 8–9.

Simmons, J. and Dodd, T. (2003) Crime in England and Wales 2002/2003, *Home Office Statistical Bulletin 07/03*, Home Office, London.

Stillwell, J.C.H. and Leigh, C.M. (1996) Exploring the geographies of social polarisation in Leeds, Chapter 4 in Haughton, G. and Williams, C. (eds.) *Corporate City? Partnership, Participation and Partition in Urban Development in Leeds*, Avebury, Aldershop, pp. 59–78.

Tullett, M. and Stillwell, J. (2003) Anti-social behaviour in Leeds, *The Yorkshire & Humber Regional Review*, 13(1): 12–13.

Yorkshire Post (2002) 'Village's arsonist jailed for six years', *Yorkshire Post Today*, article accessed 26.10.2003, available online at http://www.yorkshiretoday.co.uk/viewarticle2.aspx?ArticleID=201917&SectionID=55

with exclusion. This raises a whole series of new questions: Which policies are working? Is the gap between the haves and have nots being reduced? Is social exclusion declining? Are the streets getting safer? Are neighbourhoods getting better? Are communities gaining in confidence? These important questions imply the need for more careful monitoring and more detailed evaluation of the extent to which targets set out in strategy documents are met.

Yet, the task of evaluation is very difficult when the social problems and the policy context are complex and when the concept of 'what improvement means' will differ from person to person in the communities themselves as well as between those formulating and implementing policies and action plans and those resident in the areas at which the policies are directed. Thus, for example, whilst some regard policy initiatives in areas close to the city centre as successful if gentrification occurs and residential functions return to inner city areas, others are sceptical about the chances of creating balanced communities when it is likely that the new residents, whether young professionals or students, are likely to be more temporary and less committed to their neighbourhoods than the long-term residents who have been driven away previously.

7

Educational Attainment:
What's the Score?

ROBERT LANGLEY, HEATHER EYRE & JOHN STILLWELL

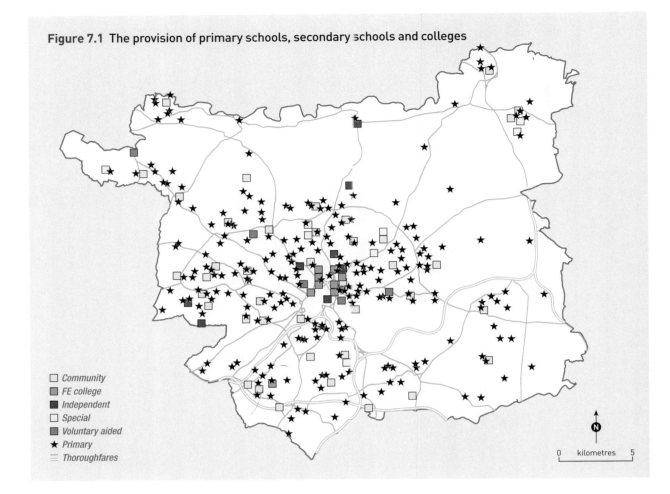

Figure 7.1 The provision of primary schools, secondary schools and colleges

□ Community
■ FE college
■ Independent
□ Special
■ Voluntary aided
★ Primary
≡ Thoroughfares

0 kilometres 5

7.1 Introduction

Education and training are vital to the future well-being of every city, particularly for enhancing the competitiveness of its workforce and ensuring that its industries, businesses and services have an ongoing supply of skilled employees in the future. In this respect, Leeds is no exception. As the city becomes more reliant on the information technology, banking and finance sectors to provide its economic wealth, a pool of labour equipped with high quality information and communication technology (ICT) and other skills is increasingly essential, enabling Leeds to compete in international markets and to deliver its economic and human development agendas.

In aggregate terms in 2001, Leeds had a population aged 0–19 of approximately 183,000 individuals (or 26 per cent of the population), some 110,000 of whom were attending local authority schools of one type or another. In 2003, there

were 294 state schools, split into primary (241) and secondary (43) phases, supported by 10 special schools. Leeds has had no middle school provision since the early 1990s. There were also a number of independent primary and secondary schools. Since April 2001, many of the functions of the local education authority (LEA) of Leeds City Council have been carried out by Education Leeds, a wholly-owned but separate company set up in order to develop the public education system. The majority of the secondary schools are community schools (Figure 7.1) that are maintained by Education Leeds who take responsibility for school admissions policy; six are voluntary-aided (VA), each with a foundation that appoints most of the governing body. Post-18 education provision is in the form of a number of further education (FE) colleges and two major higher education (HE) institutions, the University of Leeds and Leeds Metropolitan University. Each of the universities now has in excess of 30,000

Table 7.1 Comparison of the qualification levels of residents aged 16–74, 2001	Percentage with no qualifications	Percentage with highest qualification attained
England and Wales	29.08	19.76
Yorkshire and Humber	33.15	16.38
Bristol (City of)	26.08	24.50
Leeds	30.89	19.22
Sheffield	32.04	18.83
Newcastle-upon-Tyne	32.55	20.85
Nottingham	33.89	17.62
Manchester	33.95	21.42
Birmingham	37.09	16.62
Liverpool	37.82	15.24

Source: Census 2001 KS

registered students. There are therefore at least 250,000 learners in Leeds, a city of 715,000 (at the time of the 2001 Census). Education is clearly therefore a very significant part of the city's infrastructure and the lives of its citizens.

This chapter begins by exploring how educated the Leeds population is at the beginning of the twenty-first century and identifying the geographical variations which appear to exist in the success chances of the city's young people at different stages in their development. In addition to considering school attainment levels, data on pupils by their residential addresses are used initially to examine the relationship between attainment and household type and income and subsequently to support a tentative investigation of the linkage between house prices and achievement levels. Education Leeds is confronted with a number of key policy-related issues and these will be considered thereafter. In particular, demographic trends are causing falling demand for school places and the restructuring of school provision is an ongoing imperative. Unequal performance and poor attendance levels in some schools require particular policy responses and there are various curriculum developments in the pipeline (such as the proposed option to replace the current AS and A2 level examinations at the end of post-compulsory schooling) that pose challenges for the future. Finally, we demonstrate the diversity of further education provision that is available and present a short resumé of the performance of the two universities, finishing with some comments on graduate retention.

7.2 How qualified is the population?

The decennial population Census of 2001 provides information about the levels of qualification of the working age (16–74) residents of Leeds. Overall, the population is fairly typical of England and Wales as a whole, having broadly similar shares of its population with no qualifications or with the highest qualification at level four or five (i.e. first degree; higher degree; National Vocational Qualification Levels 4 and 5; Higher National Certificate; Higher National Diploma; Qualified Teacher Status; Qualified Medical Doctor, Dentist or Nurse; Midwife; Health

Degree day at the University of Leeds, 2004. Doctoral students emerge from the Great Hall with their degree certificates.

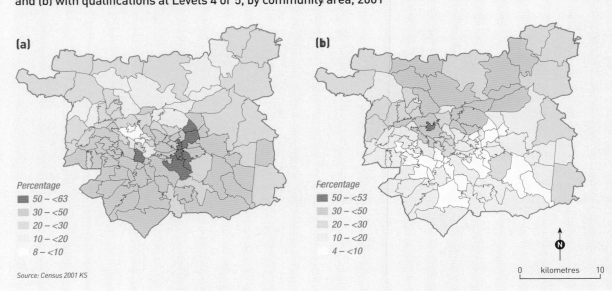

Figure 7.2 Percentage of residents aged 16–74 (a) without qualifications and (b) with qualifications at Levels 4 or 5, by community area, 2001

(a)

Percentage
- 50 – <63
- 30 – <50
- 20 – <30
- 10 – <20
- 8 – <10

Source: Census 2001 KS

(b)

Percentage
- 50 – <53
- 30 – <50
- 20 – <30
- 10 – <20
- 4 – <10

0   kilometres   10

Visitor). Leeds compares well against its region and against other core cities. In fact, as the ranking in Table 7.1 indicates, only Bristol has a lower percentage of those without qualifications, whereas at the top end of the qualification ladder Leeds comes fourth behind Bristol, Manchester and Newcastle. Of course, this may reflect differences in the age structure of the cities involved — the majority of the 16–21 age group will not yet have had opportunities to gain Level 4 or 5 qualifications. The fact that Leeds has a lower level of residents with no qualifications than any other core city except Bristol tells us that the population in general is more highly qualified at Levels 1 to 3 (single GCSE to A-Levels and equivalents). This may lead us to suggest that Leeds has a high proportion of its residents en route to higher-level qualifications. The fact that there are over 60,000 students registered at the city's two universities may bear this out.

As with other socio-economic indicators, we might expect to observe some geographical variations in the distribution of this population subset. Figure 7.2a shows the proportions of residents with no formal qualifications, by community area, highlighting the fact that there are several places where the proportion is in excess of 50 per cent, including New Wortley, Cross Green, Halton Moor, Osmondthorpe, Gipton South and Seacroft. In much of southern Leeds,

especially in the south west, the proportion is between 30 and 50 per cent. As might be expected, the student areas of Hyde Park and Headingley stand out as having relatively low shares

Subject	2001		2002		2003	
	Leeds	National	Leeds	National	Leeds	National
Reading	85	84	83	84	84	84
Writing	85	86	85	86	80	81
Spelling	76	75	79	78	–	–
Mathematics	90	91	90	90	90	90
Science	88	89	89	89	90	n/a

Source: Education Leeds (2004) (maintained schools only)

The performance of Leeds' pupils at Key Stage 1 (Table 7.2) is in line with national achievement levels. A typical seven-year-old is expected to achieve Level 2 and in 2003, the percentage of children in Leeds reaching Level 2 was 90 per cent for Mathematics and Science, 84 per cent for Reading and 80 per cent for Writing. The drop in achievement from 2002 in the latter is likely to have occurred because of the incorporation of the Spelling test into the Writing test.

The figures for the tests taken at ages 11 (Key Stage 2) and 16 (GCSE) are the most commonly used as general measures of attainment as they mark the end of primary education and the end of compulsory schooling respectively. At Key Stage 2, a typical 11 year old is expected to achieve Level 4 in English, Mathematics and Science and the results since 1996 (Figure 7.3) show increasing levels of attainment in all three subjects. On

of unqualified residents. In contrast, the pattern of those areas with high proportions of working age residents that are well qualified (Figure 7.2b) is a mirror image of Figure 7.2a, re-emphasising the north-south divide. We will return to the implications of these patterns later in the chapter.

In summary, we acknowledge that whilst the working age population of Leeds has an educational attainment profile similar to the national average and better that its region, there are very large parts of the metropolitan district where a significant number of individuals remain formally unqualified. Given this spatial pattern, we now examine the achievement levels of the young people attending Leeds' schools.

7.3 Educational attainment of school pupils

Pupils in England are now tested at various key stages in their primary and secondary school careers. These figures are traditionally used to compare schools and to give a very approximate guide to the 'quality' of a school. Educationalists would argue that examination performance is only a very small part of what makes a school good. This section examines some of the performance data for state schools in Leeds at Key Stages 1 and 2 and at GCSE.

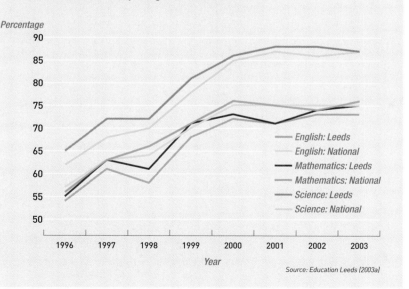

Figure 7.3 Percentages of pupils achieving Level 4 and above at Key Stage 2, 1996–2003

Source: Education Leeds (2003a)

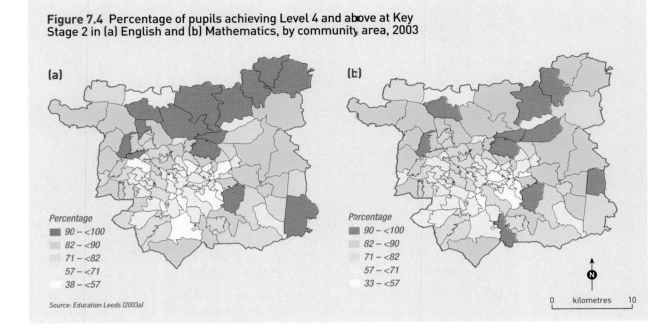

Figure 7.4 Percentage of pupils achieving Level 4 and above at Key Stage 2 in (a) English and (b) Mathematics, by community area, 2003

(a)

Percentage
- 90 – <100
- 82 – <90
- 71 – <82
- 57 – <71
- 38 – <57

Source: Education Leeds (2003a)

(b)

Percentage
- 90 – <100
- 82 – <90
- 71 – <82
- 57 – <71
- 33 – <57

0   kilometres   10

average, Leeds' schoolchildren are performing close to or just above the national average at this stage in their education.

Figure 7.4 shows the attainment of pupils in state primary schools in 2003 in English and Mathematics, two of the three main tests at Key Stage 2. The maps are based on pupil data geocoded to place of residence rather than place of school, and therefore indicate the attainment levels of those pupils who are resident in each community area, enabling us to tie the educational outcomes for pupils to the environment in which they live rather than to the school where they study.

Pupils in community areas in the north of Leeds and in the outer suburbs gain higher results in both English and Mathematics than do those who are resident in the central and southern areas, pointing up the importance of linkages between residential and home environments and educational chances. There is a clear visual correlation between the performance of youngsters at the end of primary schooling and the proportion of the population living around them who have no formal qualifications — the similarities between Figure 7.2b and Figure 7.4 are striking.

It is at GCSE when the attainment levels in Leeds start to diverge more from the national average (Table 7.3). The results for GCSE examinations and their equivalents, in the summer of 2003, expressed as the percentage of pupils achieving at least five GCSE grades at grades C and above, was 44 per cent in Leeds, some 8.5 percentage points below the national average. The proportion attaining at least five GCSEs at grades G and above (a pass) increases to 85 per cent, only 3.3 points below the national average, whilst 92.5 per cent of pupils attain at least one GCSE at grade G or above compared with the national average of 94.6 per cent. The encouraging evidence is that the GCSE results for Leeds are improving faster

Table 7.3 Percentage of pupils achieving GCSE grades, 2001–2003

Grade	2001		2002		2003	
	Leeds	National	Leeds	National	Leeds	National
5A*-C	39.6	50.0	42.4	51.6	44.2	52.6
5A*-G	86.5	88.9	85.0	88.9	85.3	88.6
1A*-G	93.4	94.5	92.1	94.6	92.5	94.6

Source: Education Leeds (2004)

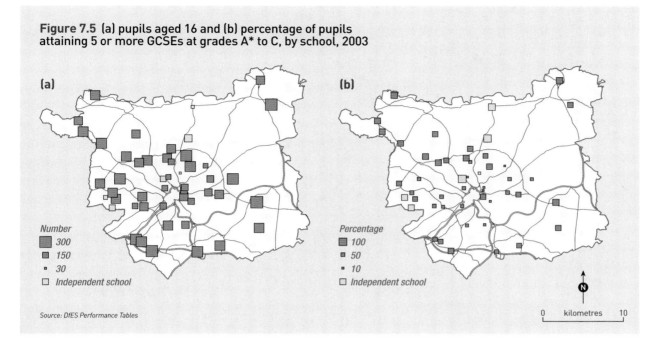

Figure 7.5 (a) pupils aged 16 and (b) percentage of pupils attaining 5 or more GCSEs at grades A* to C, by school, 2003

(a)

Number
300
150
30
Independent school

Source: DfES Performance Tables

(b)

Percentage
100
50
10
Independent school

N

0   kilometres   10

than the national rate, meaning the gap between the performance of Leeds' pupils and pupils nationally is closing.

The headline indicator for secondary school 'success' is the first of the performance measures shown in Table 7.3, the proportion of pupils aged sixteen leaving school with five or more GCSE or equivalent qualifications, at grade C or higher. The number of pupils aged 15 in each secondary school in Leeds who were entered for GCSE in 2003 and the percentage attaining five or more grades A* to C are shown in Figure 7.5. In this instance, we use data prepared for the annual school performance tables which are published by the press and which include the independent secondary schools.

There is a clear inner-outer divide in pupil attainment by school and it is not surprising to observe that schools which are in or near areas where pupils are high attaining at Key Stage 2 tend to have higher GCSE results. When comparing the performance of schools on the northern periphery, it is important to acknowledge that the data have not been controlled for 'boundary effects', i.e. there will be a number of pupils from outside Leeds attending Leeds schools and a number of pupils living within the Leeds boundary who travel to schools outside the district. This will be especially true in the north, south and west of the city, in areas that abut relatively highly-populated areas or areas which have schools that are

traditionally regarded as 'good'. This can be an important consideration in certain parts of cities, and may distort the picture we would expect to see, leaving us with schools in 'good' areas performing less well than anticipated because there is an extra-district school nearby with a better reputation.

The results shown here also display clear linkages to the educational attainment of 16–74 year-olds (Figure 7.2), suggesting that despite parents having the freedom to express a preference for the schools to which they would send their children — following the 1988 Education Reform Act — many will choose the nearest school and many may make household migration decisions based on a desire to live within reasonable commuting distance of a 'good' school. The extent to which this factor has become an important influence on residential mobility is worthy of further investigation (Dobson and Stillwell, 2000). In more detailed work in Manchester (Bradford, 1991), the link is made more explicitly between attainment and the nature of pupils' home and residential areas, showing that in fact the school itself is of relatively little importance. This may well mean that often costly migration decisions are made, particularly by middle class families, on the basis of a false sense of impact of a particular school on the examination performance of their offspring. Other studies have focused more directly on the relationship between school performance

schools in Yorkshire and Humberside in the mid-1990s.

We have chosen to explore the relationship between attainment and affluence in this section of the chapter using data on pupil performance by residential area rather than by school. This approach is facilitated by the availability of individual records for all state school pupils in Leeds with home addresses that can be geocoded and aggregated to administrative or census polygons. However, in a collaborative project for Education Leeds, Bruce-White (2003) used Demograf's geodemographic CAMEO UK classification of unit postcodes based on 1991 Census variables to explore the relationship between type of household and student attainment at GCSE level in 2002 (Table 7.4).

and social deprivation. Higgs *et al.* (1997) explored the influence of social disadvantage and attainment in Wales whilst Stillwell and Langley (1999) used the ward-based Index of Local Conditions (DoE, 1994) to demonstrate the spatial coincidence between high deprivation and under-performing

Nine CAMEO categories are shown in the second column of Table 7.4 and range from the 'young and affluent

Table 7.4 State school pupil performance at GCSE by CAMEO UK group, 2002

CAMEO code	CAMEO UK type	Total pupils	5+ A*-C	5+ A*-G	No Passes
		Percentage			
1	Young and affluent singles	1.0	64.4	93.4	4.0
2	Wealthy retired neighbourhoods	14.2	54.0	94.1	0.9
3	Affluent home owners	11.0	75.1	98.5	0.2
4	Smaller private family homes	16.5	53.3	93.5	1.9
5	Poorer home owners	24.7	43.5	92.4	2.1
6	Less affluent older neighbourhoods	2.5	50.8	94.5	1.1
7	Council tenants on family estates	12.8	25.8	83.6	3.9
8	Poorer council tenants — many single parents	13.6	22.0	79.5	4.4
9	Poorer singles	3.0	31.7	92.0	2.2

Source: Bruce-White (2003)

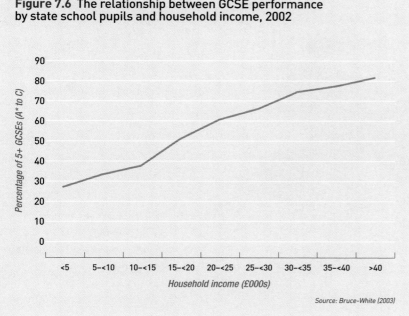

Figure 7.6 The relationship between GCSE performance by state school pupils and household income, 2002

Percentage of 5+ GCSEs (A* to C)

Household income (£000s)

Source: Bruce-White (2003)

between home and neighbourhood factors and educational outcomes is very strong, and suggests that the 'school effect' may in fact be less than is popularly supposed. Naturally it would be wrong to conclude simply that all the children of wealthier families achieve higher examination outcomes in school. The link between household income, educational background within the household and the attainment of young people is part of a complex relationship between a range of factors impacting on the educational development of young people and their eventual academic achievements. Purely financial indicators are simply crude proxies for much broader environmental factors.

singles' and 'wealthy retired neighbourhoods' down to 'poorer singles' and 'poorer council tenants'. Of course, the 7,077 pupils are not distributed evenly between these household categories in Leeds and the ranking of geodemographic groups is not directly consistent with the level of affluence in each category. However, there is a clear relationship between achievement in all three of the pupil performance indicators and the affluence characteristics of the postcode units. In areas of 'affluent home owners', three quarters of children achieve 5 or more GCSEs at grade C and over and very few young people fail to gain any GCSE-level qualifications; in areas described as 'poorer council tenants' on the other hand, only one in five reach the 5+ A*-C target and 4.4 per cent achieve no passes.

Demograf's Cameo Income classification contains nine household income categories and when pupils are classified on this basis (Figure 7.6), there is a striking and significant linear correlation with the number of pupils attaining five or more GCSEs at grade C or above. As household income rises, so does the educational attainment of young people residing in these households. Further connections can be made with the earlier figures. Those people with higher qualifications appear to have higher incomes and in turn their offspring will attain higher results in school. Clearly this is not a hard and fast rule, but is a general trend which is substantiated by these data. The link

Lawnswood School in the north of the city is one of several Leeds schools to benefit from new buildings provided under a Private Finance Initiative (PFI) which draws private funding into capital projects to enhance public services.

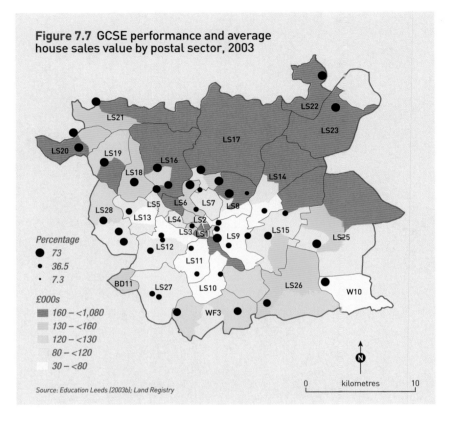

Figure 7.7 GCSE performance and average house sales value by postal sector, 2003

Percentage
● 73
• 36.5
· 7.3

£000s
▓ 160 – <1,080
▒ 130 – <160
▒ 120 – <130
▒ 80 – <120
□ 30 – <80

Source: Education Leeds (2003b); Land Registry

N

0　kilometres　10

7.4 School performance and house sales value

In this section, we discuss whether there might be an association between school performance and the housing market in Leeds. Our contention is that the price of houses may be influenced by proximity to 'good' schools and may be more expensive than similar houses elsewhere in a city. Media commentators often talk about the premium that parents will be prepared to pay to live near enough to a school to guarantee a place for their child, sometimes planning this migration several years in advance of that child reaching attendance age, though as we have seen, this belief that a 'good' school will ensure good personal examination results is likely to be misplaced. This behaviour is particularly associated with secondary schools, as there are far fewer of these and the variation in aggregate results tends to be greater than that at primary level. Langley (1997) has shown that the proportion of pupils likely to be from households in the two highest social groups (A and B) has a very strong positive correlation with the performance of the school at GCSE, while the proportion of pupils likely to be from the two lowest social groups (D and E)

is strongly positively correlated with unauthorised absence from school and negatively with GCSE performance. It is therefore certainly the case that there are social impacts on the results at a school, though again these are likely to reflect home environmental effects rather than necessarily school-specific effects.

In this section we attempt to explore whether there is any evidence that house prices measured by house sale values are higher in the areas around state secondary schools with high GCSE results and lower around schools with lower GCSE results. There are some difficulties with this exercise, not least due to the nature and quality of house sales value data which does not correspond with school catchment areas. The use of postal sectors means that some polygons are relatively large and inappropriate in this context. House price data are based only on those properties involved in transactions rather than the complete housing stock. More importantly, house prices are volatile and likely to be influenced by a range of other factors such as inflation or job opportunities. Thus, we must acknowledge that the housing market is responsive to a combination of factors that interact in a complex manner that may obfuscate any relationship with school attainment.

There are other factors to take into consideration such as the importance of changing school performance and the possibility of time lags between house price fluctuations and changes in school examination results. Furthermore, educationalists would argue that as parents become more sophisticated 'consumers' of the state education system, they become more aware of the limitations of crude school performance measures such as GCSE results being representative of school quality and therefore may be more interested in value added indicators

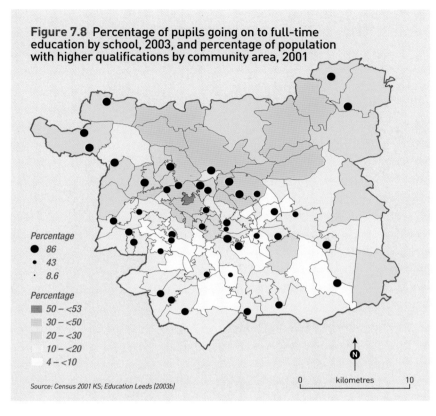

Figure 7.8 Percentage of pupils going on to full-time education by school, 2003, and percentage of population with higher qualifications by community area, 2001

Percentage
● 86
• 43
· 8.6

Percentage
50 – <53
30 – <50
20 – <30
10 – <20
4 – <10

Source: Census 2001 KS; Education Leeds (2003b)

0   kilometres   10

older population, household income and high educational outcomes of youngsters then it should logically follow that these high achievers should stay in full-time education in order to continue this cycle.

The graduated symbols in Figure 7.8 represent the percentage of pupils in state schools staying on beyond the age of 16 in full-time education whereas the choropleth shading represents the percentage reaching the top attainment levels in community areas (as in Figure 7.2b). This mapping enables some broad conclusions to be drawn about the existence of a 'cycle' of educational attainment and income within the city.

There is a strong spatial association between the two variables. Some of the aberrations can be explained by the differing geographies shown, suggesting the need for more detailed investigation of the 'home' versus the 'school' effects on pupils. However, it is clear that pupils who attend schools in areas with more highly qualified residents will tend to be more likely to remain at school post-16.

Post-16 education of an academic or vocational nature is provided through secondary schools and FE colleges. Leeds has nine FE colleges that provide educational opportunities across a range of subject areas. Several of these were founded in the early 1960s. Park Lane is the largest whilst Leeds College of Technology specialises in engineering, IT, media, printing, science, business management, health and safety and languages. Both these colleges are located near to the city centre, whereas Joseph Priestley College provides FE to people in Morley, Rothwell and Beeston in South Leeds and only gained full college status in 1988. Notre Dame Sixth Form College was formed a year later as the sixth form centre for Catholic education in Leeds. Thomas Danby College, named

rather than raw output scores. Despite these reservations, we can make a preliminary attempt to investigate whether there is any evidence of association by mapping house sales value for postal sectors against GCSE attainment by school (Figure 7.7). The results conform with what we might expect: houses in the areas with higher educational attainment appearing to be of higher sales value than those in areas with lower attainment.

It is clear from the preceding discussion that the relationship between attainment and house sale values needs more detailed research. The links between social and economic factors (at home, residential area and school level) and pupils' attainment in tests and examinations are complicated and finding a proxy for this host of complex relationships is difficult.

7.5 Post-16 education

We can also examine the relationship between residential factors and the likelihood that young people will remain in education after compulsory schooling ends. If we are to make the link suggested earlier between high education levels of the

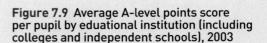

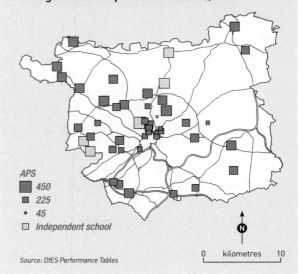

Figure 7.9 Average A-level points score per pupil by eduational institution (including colleges and independent schools), 2003

APS
■ 450
■ 225
▪ 45
□ Independent school

N

0   kilometres   10

Source: DfES Performance Tables

after the first mayor of Leeds and originally called the Branch College of Domestic Economy, is now is a Centre of Excellence for child care, social care and food-related provision. The other FE colleges are all specialist in their education provision. Leeds College of Building is the only college in the UK providing training and education for the construction industry. Leeds College of Art & Design was formerly the School of Design and dates back to 1846. It is one of the few nationally-funded independent colleges in the country specialising in the provision of art, craft and design courses. Leeds College of Music is the UK's largest music college, with some 800 full-time and over 2,000 part-time students. Finally, the Northern School of Contemporary Dance was founded in 1985 to provide vocational dance training for the many talented young dancers coming out of Chapeltown and Harehills at the time. It is now a HE college affiliated to the University of Leeds. In addition, the majority of state secondary schools have post-16 provision.

In this instance, we concentrate on academic qualifications and consider student performance at AS/A level. Data on the average GCE/VCE A/AS point scores of 16–18 year-old candidates for 2002–2003 indicate that the average points score per candidate in Leeds is 231.4 compared with the score for all schools and FE colleges in England of 257.8 and in Yorkshire and Humber of 249.4 (these figures include independent schools and FE colleges). Points are awarded as follows: an A-level A grade is worth 120 points; B 100; C 80; D 60; E 50; and an AS level is worth half an A-level. Vocational awards at this level are given equivalences to these points scores. Girls achieve higher results both locally and nationally. In Leeds, the female points score is 243.3 against the male score of 218.0, a difference of 25 points, whereas for England, girls score 268.2 points and boys score 245.9 points, a difference of 22 points.

Given that some secondary schools in Leeds do not have sixth forms and some students study for their A-levels at FE college, the average points scores for institutions across the city are presented in Figure 7.9 and indicate very considerable variation. In 2003, two schools in Leeds were amongst the top

50 comprehensives in the country, whereas a number of institutions achieved less than half of the national average. There are other factors to take into account when considering these relatively crude measures, especially at a time when the range of courses on offer is increasing. Of particular importance is the fact that the figures here include only traditional A and AS levels plus vocational A-Levels and Key Skills courses at Level 3. These are the tests which are traditionally taken into account by universities for entrance, although schools and colleges may well offer a whole range of other courses to attract and suit more learners.

7.6 Policy responses

As we have seen, there are wide variations in pupil performance across Leeds, closely tied to variations in the city's socio-economic make-up. Since Education Leeds and the City Council are committed to ensuring that all the city's schools are "good schools, improving schools and inclusive schools … places where every child and every young person can be successful and high achieving — whatever it takes" (Education Leeds, 2003b), policy formulation is critical, particularly given future demographic trends.

Added to the existing variation in outcomes for

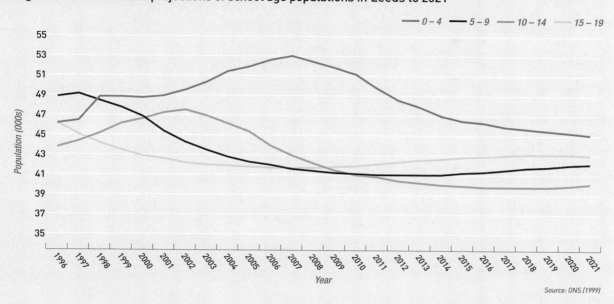

Figure 7.10 1996-based projections of school age populations in Leeds to 2021

Legend: 0 – 4 5 – 9 10 – 14 15 – 19

Y-axis: Population (000s); values 35, 37, 39, 41, 43, 45, 47, 49, 51, 53, 55

X-axis: Year; values 1996, 1997, 1998, 1999, 2000, 2001, 2002, 2003, 2004, 2005, 2006, 2007, 2008, 2009, 2010, 2011, 2012, 2013, 2014, 2015, 2016, 2017, 2018, 2019, 2020, 2021

Source: ONS (1999)

youngsters in schools, mid-year estimates show that the infant population aged under 1 and the child population aged 1–4 declined by 2,000 and 5,000 persons respectively in Leeds between 1991 and 2001. The 1996-based population projections (ONS, 1999) indicate how the decline in birth rates in the last few years has affected the size of cohorts reaching school age and the trends we can expect from now until 2021. In general terms, the 5–9 population is in a decline that will continue to 2011 (Figure 7.10); the cohorts aged 10–14 which reached a peak in 2002 are now falling sharply and this drop will continue until 2015 before they begin to level out; and the 15–19 age population will continue to grow until 2007 before it begins to diminish rapidly. The challenge posed for education Leeds by these demographic trends is to adjust education provision across the city to ensure that the supply of school places matches the age-specific demand, whilst simultaneously attempting to tackle the problem of standards at secondary level that are below the national average.

So, what does it take to address these issues? There is a range of projects in Leeds to respond to this complex agenda. One of the most high-profile is the massive programme of investment in the city's capital estate. There are currently plans, through the private finance initiative (PFI), to provide sixteen primary schools (five already open) and nine secondary schools

(three already open). In addition, through the Department for Education and Skills' 'Building Schools for the Future' programme, it is intended to fund the redevelopment or complete rebuild of a further fifteen secondary schools. This would mean the total investment in the secondary school estate of around £300 million over about five years.

In conjunction with providing state-of-the-art teaching and learning facilities across the city, in particular in the early phases in the inner city areas, the process will be running alongside other changes intended to reduce the surpluses of capacity and ensure that all the city's resources are targeted to pupils in schools. These include reducing the capacity of schools which are being rebuilt, potentially reducing the total number of secondary schools and introducing the concept of partnerships and federations of schools rather than the traditional 'one stop' school. The concept would be that pupils or students might take advantage of a range of specialisms across several schools and take parts of the curriculum in different institutions. This increasingly accords with the Government view that all schools should be specialist (in the arts, science, technology or languages, for instance) and that the increased use of modern ICT can enable teaching in increasingly individualised ways through the use of online and video-conferenced learning.

Table 7.5 Student profiles of Leeds' two universities, 2000–2001

Level/mode	University of Leeds		Leeds Metropolitan University	
	Full-time	Part-time	Full-time	Part-time
Degree	17,904	4,207	10,920	2,725
Postgraduate: taught	1,939	1,732	888	2,618
Postgraduate: research	1,365	527	61	218
Other (sub degree & FE)	–	–	3,154	16,614
Total	21,208	6,466	15,023	22,175
Percentage	77	23	40	60

Sources: University of Leeds; Leeds Metropolitan University

Together with more carefully targeted support for needy schools and associated drives to improve both attendance and behaviour in schools, the goal is that these initiatives will provide for Leeds the facilities for all of the young people to receive an excellent, modern education in the best available facilities. "Leeds is a world-class city and deserves a world-class education system" (Education Leeds, 2003b).

together with almost 7,500 staff. Leeds Met has an even larger student base which increased from around 22,500 in 1994–1995 to nearly 37,300 by 2001–2002. The data contained in Table 7.5 allows a comparison of the composition of students at the two universities during 2000–2001, showing that over three quarters of students at the University of Leeds were full-time compared with two fifths at Leeds Met, and demonstrating the relative importance of research postgraduate study at the University of Leeds and of part-time sub-degree and FE education at Leeds Met.

The two universities provide education at different levels for students from across the country. The catchment areas

7.7 Higher education and graduate retention

Leeds has two major universities, the University of Leeds, which was chartered as an independent university in 1904, and Leeds Metropolitan University, the former Leeds Polytechnic that became an independent HE corporation in 1989 and was given university status in 1992. In addition, Trinity and All Saints College is an independent Catholic found-ation that was formed by the formal merger of two existing teacher training colleges in 1980 and became a full college of the University of Leeds in 1991.

The universities are both very large and play an important role in educating the nation's undergraduates. Their existence has a massive effect on the city both through the direct effects of there being such a large body of students living and studying in the city for much of the year but also because of the contribution that the institutions make through their research activities. The University of Leeds was, in fact, the UK's most popular university in 2002–2003 with 52,521 applications for its 6,374 undergraduate places. In total, the population at the University of Leeds is approximately 31,500 full-time and part-time students, with an additional 52,100 on short courses,

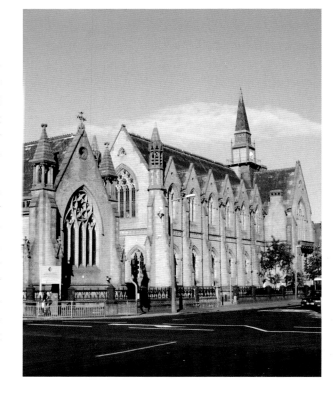

Figure 7.11 Origins of the city's full-time undergraduates, 2003–2004

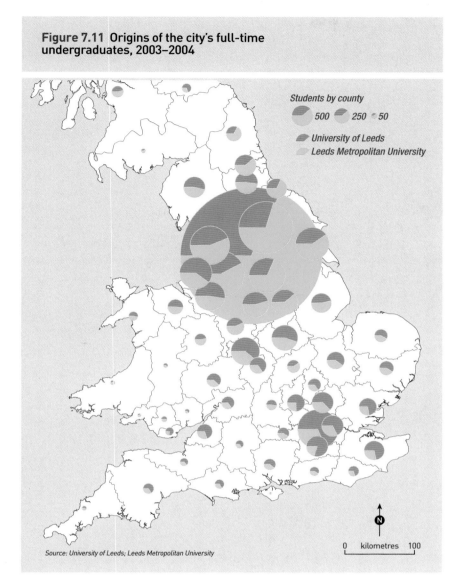

Students by county
500   250   50

University of Leeds
Leeds Metropolitan University

0   kilometres   100

Source: University of Leeds; Leeds Metropolitan University

Top, formerly Leeds Polytecnic, Leeds Metropolitan University gained university status in 1992. Bottom, located in the city centre, Leeds College of Technology has over 5,000 students on roll, studying predominantly vocational courses.

for full-time undergraduate students in the academic year 2003–2004 are shown in Figure 7.11.

So how do the two universities perform when compared with other universities in the UK? *The Sunday Times* league table of British universities and colleges, recognised as one of the most authoritative evaluations of its kind, is compiled using a formula that primarily rewards teaching excellence and the academic standard of admissions. Data on teaching quality, research quality, entry standards, graduate unemployment, the proportion of firsts and upper seconds awarded, the student/staff ratio and the dropout rates are used to calculate their league table positions. The 2002 league table was compiled using data from the Higher Education Statistics Agency (HESA), the Quality Assurance Agency for Higher Education (QAA), the national funding councils and the HE institutions themselves. Each university and college was ranked according to the total mark it achieved across the seven distinct areas indicated above. Table 7.6 indicates that out of 123 institutions in 2001, the University of Leeds is ranked 23rd and Leeds Met comes 88th. The scores are shown for each of the indicators against the top ranked university and the maximum possible mark for the first six categories is shown in brackets.

The Guardian also compiles league tables based on official information published on universities and HE colleges. This data includes teaching assessment scores from visits by Quality Assurance Agency (QAA) inspectors to departments

Table 7.6 Indicators of performance, 2001

Indicator	University of Cambridge	University of Leeds	Leeds Metropolitan University
Teaching quality (250)	236	145	45
Research quality (200)	185	127	24
A-Level/higher point (250)	248	202	128
Employment (100)	96	96	92
Firsts/upper seconds (100)	87	68	50
Staff student ratio (100)	100	99	50
Dropout rate	20	20	30
Total	972	738	419

Source: The Sunday Times University Guide 2002

during the last 10 years. Other scores are derived from figures published or provided by the HESA and by HE funding councils in the UK. In arriving at *The Guardian* teaching score for each subject, six items of data were used: a teaching assessment score; a spend per student score; a student/staff ratio score; a job prospects score; an entry qualification score; and a value added score. Details of the scoring system (available at: http://education.guardian.co.uk/universityguide2004/). In *The Guardian* league table for 2004, the University of Leeds is ranked 32nd (65.16 per cent) based on 40 subjects, whilst LMU is ranked 53rd (62.25 per cent) based on 20 subjects.

League tables based on indicators such as these are important because they provide information for students and parents in exactly the same way as school performance tables which can be used as part of the decision-making process when choosing a university. Moreover, some of the indicators used in the tables, such a research ratings, are used as performance indicators by the HE Funding Councils as a basis for resource allocation. However, Wilson (2002) argues that the variety of scores measured seems to indicate that there is no effective consensus among newspaper editors about what they are measuring. Although most league tables seek to standardise against size, the resulting indicators only tell part of the story. There is an alternative perspective that weights the quality ratings by size and so measures the quantity of quality delivered. A teaching power index can be defined that is analogous with the research power index (published in Research Fortnight and which multiplies a size measure — like number of research-active staff submitted — by the 2001 research rating on a seven point scale) by weighting teaching assessment scores by student numbers. For widening access performance, the number of students from low participation neighbourhoods and the intake of mature students are added. In each case, the numbers are factored into a 0–100 scale Table 7.7 shows the three indices separately, and combined to give a final composite score, obtained by double weighting teaching and research relative to widening access. This method produces a ranking of universities very different from the more conventional tables. New universities vie with Russell Group universities and both the universities in Leeds perform very well on certain indicators, rising to 2nd and 23rd respectively on the composite score.

The University of Leeds is among the top ten universities for research in the UK and is internationally recognised as a centre of excellence in a wide range of academic and professional disciplines. Amongst its most popular courses are

Table 7.7 Alternative league table positions, 2002

Indicator	University ranked 1st	University of Leeds rank	Leeds Met. University rank
Teaching power (100)	Manchester Met.	2nd	10th
Research power (100)	Oxford	8th	85th
Widening participation	South Bank	40th	18th
Composite index	Oxford	2nd	23rd

Source: http://www.leeds.ac.uk/media/table.htm

law, medicine, psychology, history, management studies, accounting and finance, geography and computer science. LMU has a long history of providing professional and vocational education and responding to the needs of business. Its entrepreneurial centre called Business Start-Up@Leeds Met (Robertson and Collins, 2003) reflects university policy advocating experiential learning and the development of a vocational learning curriculum in support of the widening participation agenda.

One important factor when considering the skill base of the population and the implications for economic development and the labour market is graduate retention. However, the information currently available on graduates is 'diverse and patchy' (Bolam and Gore, 2002). To what extent does Leeds retain its graduates within the district of the surrounding region? One data source is the first destination statistics collected by careers services that provide a snapshot of what graduates are doing six months after graduation. Data provided by the University of Leeds Careers Centre on first destinations of full-time graduates from the University of Leeds in 2001 and 2002 (nearly 4,500 in each year) suggest that approximately one third of graduates find employment or further study in the region and around a quarter stay in Leeds. Similar data from LMU (http://www.lmu.ac.uk/aqd/careers/fds.htm) indicate that 54.6 per cent of all graduates in 2002 entered employment

in Yorkshire and the Humber and 20.8 per cent stayed in Leeds, whereas in 2001, 44.7 per cent remained in the region and 17.3 per cent got jobs in Leeds. Unfortunately these data tell us nothing about graduate career paths so little is known about the whereabouts of Leeds' graduates in the longer term, about their sectoral concentration, or about the salaries that they receive. Given that private and public sector organisations also require basic information about the characteristics and abilities of graduates, their skills and their potentials, Bolam and Gore (2002) make the case for the development of a system that provides labour market intelligence on graduates that addresses the gaps in information provision that exist and meets the needs of the stakeholders.

7.8 Conclusions

So what's the score? Leeds appears to be doing fairly well up until the end of primary school but then a deterioration is evident in attainment levels at GCSE and A/AS level compared with the national average. This emphasises the importance of achieving the targets set out in Leeds Neighbourhood Renewal Strategy for education and skills. The targets are for all schools to have at least 25 per cent of pupils getting five GCSEs (grades A*-C), for 85 per cent of 11 year olds to achieve Level 4 or above in English and Maths by 2004 and 35 per cent to reach Level 5, and at least 20 per cent of pupils in schools in disadvantaged communities to achieve five or more GCSEs at grades A*-C by summer 2004.

This chapter has demonstrated the very distinctive geographical variations in educational performance across the city. It contains one of the first studies based on the attainment of individual pupils according to their place of residence and has demonstrated a very close relationship between educational performance at GCSE level and household income. We have argued that house prices in the vicinity of good schools are likely to be higher than elsewhere as parents seek to reside within relatively easy commuting distance, but the complex nature of the housing market means that this effect is very difficult to disentangle from the other influences on house prices and the results of the analysis of attainment and house sales value are much less clear-cut. There is also a clear suggestion that this approach by parents may not be based on a logical assessment of the impact of a school on individual children's performance. The availability of data on pupil attainment by residential location now collected regularly by Education Leeds will allow researchers to have a much better understanding of the factors that influence performance at different Key Stage levels. Not only will the data be useful to planners by informing them of the way in which school catchment areas vary across the city and change over time, but the data will also support policy makers charged with ensuring that the geographies of demand for and supply of school places are in equilibrium.

Finally, we have chosen to illustrate the size and structure of the two universities in Leeds, how they differ in their educational roles, and how they compare against other universities using a number of different criteria. In focusing primarily on the educational characteristics, we have said very little about the specific contribution that the universities make to the locality through their research, through linkages with local businesses and institutions, as providers of cultural and sporting facilities and through their contributions across a wide range of activities as indicated in the Dearing Report (National Committee of Enquiry into Higher Education, 1997) which established an agenda for HE for the twenty-first century. Furthermore, we should not neglect to acknowledge the role that both universities play internationally, both in hosting and educating a large number of students from across the world and in collaborating with partners in different countries on major research projects.

Education is clearly very important to Leeds — in direct employment terms; in terms of the development of over a third of the residents of the city at any one time; and ensuring that Leeds is in a position to ensure a continuous supply of highly-trained labour for the future. It is important therefore that the contribution of this sector to the vitality of the city be recognised and celebrated, both now and into the future.

References

Bolam, F. and Gore, T. (2002) *The Role of Graduates in the Yorkshire and Humber Labour Market,* report prepared for Yorkshire Universities and Yorkshire Futures, Policy Research Unit, Leeds Metropolitan University and Centre for Regional Economic and Social Research, Sheffield Hallam University.

Bradford, M. (1991) School performance indicators, the local residential environment and parental choice, *Environment and Planning A,* 23: 319–332.

Bruce-White, C. (2003) *Exploring the usefulness of pupil data at the individual level,* report of work placement with Education Leeds, School of Geography, University of Leeds, Leeds, pp.28.

Department of the Environment (DOE) (1994) *Index of Local Conditions: An Analysis Based on 1991 Census Data,* DoE, London.

Dobson, J. and Stillwell, J. (2000) Changing home, changing school: towards a research agenda on child migration, *Area,* 32(4): 395–401.

Education Leeds (2003a) *Primary School Performance Tables 2003 Key Stage 2 Results,* Education Leeds, Leeds.

Education Leeds (2003b) *Strategic Plan 2003–07,* Education Leeds, Leeds

Education Leeds (2004) *Governors' Bulletin,* Spring 2004, Education Leeds, Leeds.

Higgs, G., Bellin, W., Farrell, S. and White, S. (1997) Educational attainment and social disadvantage: contextualising school league tables, *Regional Studies,* 31(8): 775–789.

Langley, R. (1997) *The use and development of geographical information systems (GIS) and spatial modelling for educational planning,* unpublished PhD Thesis, School of Geography, University of Leeds, Leeds.

National Committee of Enquiry into Higher Education (1997) *Higher Education in the Learning Society,* report of the National Committee chaired by Sir Ron Dearing, http://www.leeds.ac.uk/educol/ncihe/

Office of National Statistics (ONS) (1999) 1996-based subnational population projections, England, *DNS Series PP3 No.10,* The Stationery Office, London.

Robertson, M. and Collins, A. (2003) Developing entrepreneurship: West Yorkshire universities' partnership and Business Start-Up@Leeds Met, *The Yorkshire & Humber Regional Review,* 13(2): 17–19.

Stillwell, J. and Langley, R. (1999) Information and planning in the education sector, Chapter 17 in Stillwell, J., Geertman, S. and Openshaw, S. (eds.) *Geographical Information and Planning,* Springer, Heidelberg, pp. 316–333.

Wilson, A.G. (2002) Quantity of quality — a new league table, *Financial Times,* 11 May.

8

Economic Prosperity:
Jobs, Businesses and Economic
Development Initiatives

JOHN STILLWELL & RACHAEL UNSWORTH

The disappearance of manual jobs mirrors the decline of manufacturing industry. Work for slubbers, rovers, carders and finishers in the once flourishing textile industry no longer exists. In its wake, has come the growth of the service sector and of jobs in call centres.

symbiosis between the city and its region in the development of strategies to promote economic competitiveness.

In this chapter, we attempt to provide some compositional and geographical analysis of Leeds economy by concentrating primarily on a selection of indicators that focus on the workplace. We begin by looking at the structure of employment *vis-à-vis* the region and the nation and the way this structure has changed in the four year period between 1998 and 2002, a period for which consistent data is available from the Annual Business Inquiry. Estimates of personal income for small areas are also presented since these are dependent on the jobs that people do. Thereafter, we turn attention to the establishments within which people work and examine the size characteristics of Leeds businesses, the locations of the plcs and of foreign direct investment during the 1990s. New business registrations are considered briefly before we review some of the ongoing sectoral and geographically defined projects and initiatives that constitute the implementation of *Leeds Economic Development Strategy* and the *Leeds Neighbourhood Renewal Strategy*.

8.1 Introduction

"Throughout the 1990s, Leeds had one of the fastest growing economies in the UK" (Leeds Economy Partnership, 2003, Foreword). There is justification for this assessment, since job growth has been very significant, unemployment rates have fallen, the city's gross domestic product reached £9.7 billion in 1998 and Chamber of Commerce quarterly surveys of manufacturing and services were positive during the 1990s. There is little doubt that Leeds has become a major regional centre providing retail and business services for the locality, for the region, and for the north of England. In fact, the trend in recent economic growth has been of sufficient magnitude for one group of consultants to refer to it as the "Leeds phenomenon" (Llewelyn Davies *et al.*, 2003, p.2). An earlier study by Charles *et al.* (1999) identified the distinctive roles that Leeds, as a major commercial city, plays in its region, and stresses the importance of considering the relationships and

8.2 Employment structure and dynamics

Since the end of the second world war, employment nationally has shifted from primary production and manufacturing into the service group of industries and trades. In Leeds, the effect of mechanisation of agriculture was pronounced in the immediate post-war period whilst the impact of the decline in demand for coal began to take effect in the late 1950s. Between 1949 and 1964, the number of jobs declined in all Leeds major manufacturing sectors, such as metal manufacture, engineering, vehicles, textiles, paper, printing and publishing, and in particular, clothing and footwear. This reduction was not counterbalanced by growth in new expanding manufacture (Rainnie and Wilkinson, 1967). The process of tertiarisation has continued almost unabated since then. Between 1991 and 1996, for example, as the collieries closed, the energy/water sector dropped by 42 per cent whilst manufacturing fell by 6 per

Figure 8.1 Employment structure by broad sector, 2002

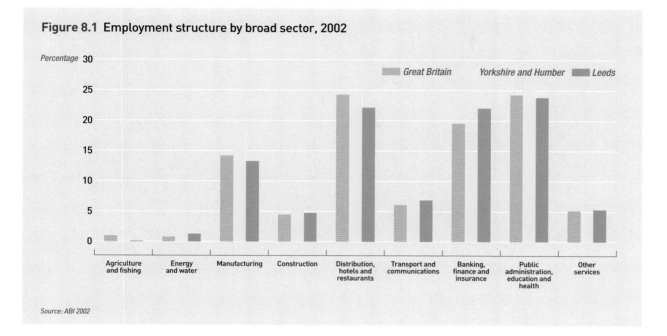

Source: ABI 2002

Figure 8.2 Employment structure by (a) sex and status, 2002, and (b) change, 1998–2002

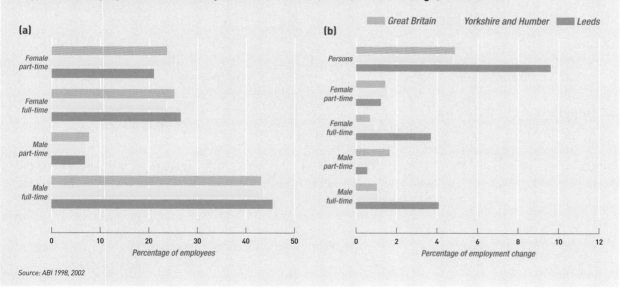

Source: ABI 1998, 2002

cent in Leeds (Leeds Development Agency, 1999). On the other hand, these declines were offset by growth in the three main service sectors — 22 per cent in finance and business services, 10 per cent in public administration and 6 per cent in distribution — resulting in overall growth of 7 per cent in the early 1990s.

The Annual Business Inquiry (ABI) now provides workplace-based data on employment, enabling the industrial structure of Leeds to be contrasted with that of Great Britain and Yorkshire and the Humber (Figure 8.1) at the start of the twenty-first century. In total, 401,000 employees were working

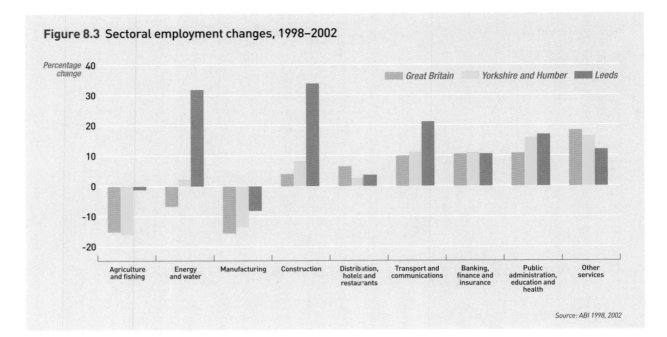

Figure 8.3 Sectoral employment changes, 1998–2002

Percentage change

Legend: Great Britain | Yorkshire and Humber | Leeds

Categories: Agriculture and fishing | Energy and water | Manufacturing | Construction | Distribution, hotels and restaurants | Transport and communications | Banking, finance and insurance | Public administration, education and health | Other services

Source: ABI 1998, 2002

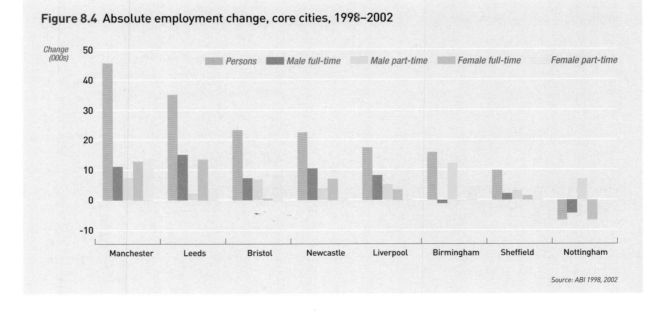

Figure 8.4 Absolute employment change, core cities, 1998–2002

Change (000s)

Legend: Persons | Male full-time | Male part-time | Female full-time | Female part-time

Cities: Manchester | Leeds | Bristol | Newcastle | Liverpool | Birmingham | Sheffield | Nottingham

Source: ABI 1998, 2002

in registered jobs in Leeds Metropolitan District in 2002; of these, almost 70 per cent were classified in three of the main industrial groups — public administration, education and health (24.7 per cent), banking, finance and insurance (23.9 per cent) and distribution, hotels and restaurants (21.4 per cent). It is the banking, finance and insurance sector where the structure of

Leeds differs most radically from its region and the nation; the ABI statistics confirm Leeds' reputation as a centre for financial and business services (see Chapter 9). This characteristic is partly responsible for the large number of jobs in distribution, hotels and restaurants, although this sector surprisingly employed a lower share of the workforce than the national

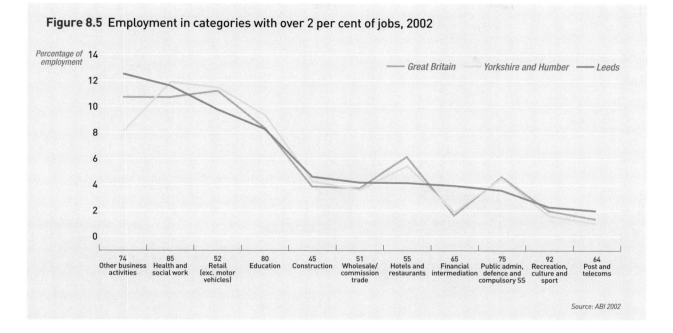

Figure 8.5 Employment in categories with over 2 per cent of jobs, 2002

Percentage of employment

— Great Britain — Yorkshire and Humber — Leeds

| 74 Other business activities | 85 Health and social work | 52 Retail (exc. motor vehicles) | 80 Education | 45 Construction | 51 Wholesale/ commission trade | 55 Hotels and restaurants | 65 Financial intermediation | 75 Public admin, defence and compulsory SS | 92 Recreation, culture and sport | 64 Post and telecoms |

Source: ABI 2002

average. A further 12 per cent of jobs were in manufacturing industry but the proportion in this sector is below the national proportion (13.4 per cent) and well below the proportion in manufacturing in Yorkshire and the Humber (16.5 per cent).

The breakdown of employment by sex and status (full-time or part-time) depicted in Figure 8.2a reveals that, in 2002, Leeds had higher proportions of male and female full-time jobs than in the region and in Great Britain, but lower proportions of part-time jobs. Moreover, the growth in overall employment of 9.6 per cent between 1998 and 2002 in Leeds, almost twice the national average (Figure 8.2b), was attributable to increases in full-time jobs for men and women. The percentage change in the four component categories of employment sum to the percentage change in total employment, the top bar of the chart in Figure 8.2b, so that the overall contribution of each component can be identified.

The change in employment in Leeds between 1998 and 2002 represented an additional 35,000 jobs, but this increase did not occur consistently across all the sectors. In absolute terms, the largest increases in new jobs occurred in public administration (14,300) and in banking and finance (9,100), with most job losses in manufacturing (4,200). The percentage changes taking place emphasise Leeds' relatively good performance across most broad sectors when compared against changes in the nation and the region (Figure 8.3). Leeds

has also performed very well in relation to other core cities (ODPM, 2004) over the period from 1998 to 2002, and is ranked second to Manchester in terms of the absolute net increase in jobs, sustaining growth in all employment status categories (Figure 8.4).

In interpreting the ABI statistics, we must be mindful of two important features: firstly, that the figures are aggregates from which the agriculture class 0100 in the 1991 Standard Industrial Classification (SIC) has been excluded; and secondly, that the data relate to employees and do not include estimates of those who work for themselves. An estimate of the latter obtained from the 2001 Census of Population indicates that there were 33,500 self-employed in Leeds on 29 April 2001 but this count is residence-based; included are those who live in Leeds and work elsewhere but not those who live elsewhere and commute into Leeds to work. The count of self-employed is approximately 10 per cent of the 322,800 total economically active residents of Leeds aged between 16 and 74.

Confidentiality constraints limit the comprehensive presentation of ABI data for more disaggregated sectors but Figure 8.5 contains the proportions of employment in SIC92 two-digit industrial categories that are over 2 per cent of Leeds total employment. These categories have been ranked and compared with the regional and national proportions. The importance of business services is evident since the category of

other business activities accounts for nearly 13 per cent of all Leeds employment. Perhaps surprisingly, Leeds is noticeably below the national average in non-vehicle retailing, hotels and restaurants and public administration but above the norm in financial intermediation, as we might expect.

8.3 Spatial variations in employment structure

So where do the workers work in Leeds, how has the distribution of employment changed over time, how does employment structure vary from one place to the next and how geographically concentrated are jobs in particular sectors? In order to answer these questions, we can make use of ABI data for 1998 and 2002 for so-called 1991-based 'frozen wards'. The distribution of jobs is highly concentrated in two wards; in 2002, there were 128,500 in City and Holbeck ward, accounting for 30 per cent of total employment in 2002, and University ward

contained nearly 34,500, or 9 per cent of total jobs in the city. No other ward had more than 4 per cent of jobs in 1998 or 2002. These statistics are largely representative of the employment status groups although Morley North and South, Hunslet and Beeston have over 4 per cent of male full-time jobs, and Horsforth had 6.2 per cent of all male part-time jobs in 1998. There is more variation between wards in the shares of their jobs in different employment categories. The wards have been ranked in Figure 8.6a according to the largest status category, male full-time employment, demonstrating that at one end of the spectrum, 63.7 per cent of workers in Richmond Hill were male full-time, in comparison with Moortown and Roundhay, both of which had less that 30 per cent of jobs taken by male full-time workers. Figure 8.6b adopts the same ward ranking to identify variations in the composition of employment in the primary, manufacturing, construction and services sectors, emphasising the predominance of service sector jobs in all

Figure 8.6 Breakdown of jobs in each ward by (a) status and (b) sector, 2002

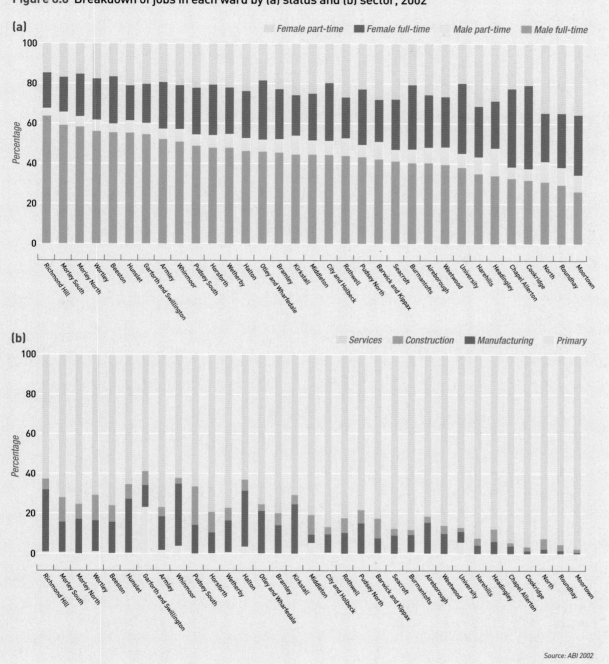

Source: ABI 2002

wards across the city but also illustrating the tendency for wards with more manufacturing to have more male full-time jobs.

The change in job distribution between 1998 and 2002 is also of interest since growth was not apparent across the whole city. As expected, over half the increase was accounted for by job growth in City and Holbeck, with 10,600 new jobs in banking, finance and insurance alone, whereas University ward actually lost 3,700 jobs in net terms, mostly in finance and

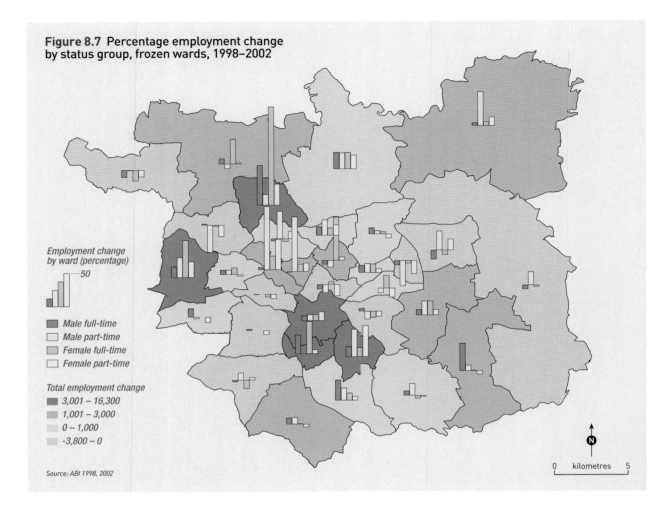

Figure 8.7 Percentage employment change by status group, frozen wards, 1998–2002

Employment change
by ward (percentage)
····50

- Male full-time
- Male part-time
- Female full-time
- Female part-time

Total employment change
- 3,001 – 16,300
- 1,001 – 3,000
- 0 – 1,000
- -3,800 – 0

Source: ABI 1998, 2002

0   kilometres   5

public administration. Policy makers will be pleased to observe that Beeston gained 3,800 jobs, many of which were in banking and finance, and Hunslet gained 3,500, including 1,000 in distribution, hotels and restaurants. On the other hand, Aireborough lost jobs as old manufacturing companies closed down and Horsforth lost over 2,200 jobs in the banking and finance sector. Figure 8.7 maps the percentage changes in employment over the four year period of employment in the four employment status categories by ward. In relative terms, the two wards experiencing the highest job growth are in the suburbs. In Cookridge, employment has doubled whereas in the Pudsey North, it has grown by 42 per cent; in both these cases, the growth of female full-time jobs has been particularly high. Seacroft, on the other hand, has experienced a 21 per cent decline in employment, due largely to the drop in part-time jobs for men and women.

Various statistics can be computed to give further measures of sectoral and spatial employment concentration. The index of localisation for each SIC92 employment 'section', for example, compares the spatial distribution of jobs in that section against those in all sections. A value of zero indicates that the two distributions are exactly the same whereas a value of one indicates maximum localisation. The index values for sectors are presented in rank order in Table 8.1 and indicate that primary sections are highly localised whereas tertiary sections such as the wholesaling and retailing have a more equal distribution of workplaces across the city and therefore a more even distribution of jobs.

Location quotients for each sector (section) in each ward measure the proportion of employment in each ward that is in each section, standardised by the proportion of total employment in that sector in Leeds. The two highest ward

Table 8.1 Indices of localisation, 2002 and change, 1998–2002

1992SIC section	Employment	Index	Change 1998–2002
Agriculture, hunting and forestry	328	0.80	0.02
Mining and quarrying	384	0.73	-0.05
Electricity, gas and water supply	4,878	0.69	0.21
Financial intermediation	29,179	0.45	0.04
Public admin/defence; social security	17,028	0.36	-0.05
Education	34,730	0.35	0.06
Health and social work	47,231	0.31	-0.02
Construction	20,947	0.23	-0.05
Manufacturing	48,076	0.23	0.00
Transport, storage and communication	24,559	0.23	-0.02
Real estate, renting, business activities	66,783	0.21	0.03
Other community, social/ personal service	20,400	0.19	0.03
Hotels and restaurants	19,115	0.17	-0.03
Wholesale/ retail trade; repair, etc.	66,826	0.11	0.01

Source: ABI 1998, 2002

quotients for each section are shown in Table 8.2. Cookridge stands out as having higher shares of employment in public administration, health and social work and real estate, Halton and Kirstall have the highest quotients for manufacturing and construction jobs are particularly important in Pudsey South and Morley South. The location quotients for the first three sections are all relatively high because of the small numbers in these sections but also because they are concentrated into a relatively small number of wards.

The structure of employment across the city is the key component for estimating income since occupation determines how much is earned. In the next section, we report on a method for estimating personal income for individuals which is residence-based rather than workplace-based.

With a growth of 6.1 per cent in construction companies (1996–2002), and the seemingly endless expansion of the housing market, the demand for skilled labour is very high in Leeds.

8.4 Estimating income for small areas using employment counts

In April 1999, just under 40,000 households in Leeds were involved in a rehearsal survey for the 2001 Census that was conducted in a sample of areas throughout the UK. The post-survey questionnaires showed that a significant proportion of

Table 8.2 Top two location quotients by 1992SIC section, 2002

1992SIC section	Ward	Location quotient	Ward	Location quotient
Agriculture, hunting and forestry	Middleton	29.10	Armley	18.70
Mining and quarrying	Garforth and Swillington	8.20	Wortley	9.50
Electricity, gas and water supply	Garforth and Swillington	21.00	University	3.80
Financial intermediation	Beeston	4.89	Pudsey North	4.32
Public admin/defence; social security	Cookridge	4.24	Wetherby	3.21
Education	Weetwood	3.37	North	3.42
Health and social work	Cookridge	5.81	Chapel Allerton	4.44
Construction	Pudsey South	3.56	Morley South	2.34
Manufacturing	Halton	2.52	Kirkstall	2.42
Transport, storage and communication	Morley South	3.81	Burmantofts	2.65
Real estate, renting, business activities	Cookridge	2.95	City and Holbeck	1.64
Other community, social/ personal service	Headingley	3.57	Wetherby	3.08
Hotels and restaurants	Rothwell	2.58	Barwick and Kippax	2.21
Wholesale/ retail trade; repair, etc.	Kirkstall	2.24	Wortley	1.83

Source: ABI 1998, 2002

people objected to the inclusion of an income question in the 2001 Census and in the light of this reaction, together with possible ambiguity over what to include as income, the Government decided against the inclusion of an income question, thus depriving researchers and policy makers of what many consider as the most useful of any socio-economic indicators for small areas. As a result, estimates of income for small areas have to be estimated (Williamson, 2000) or derived by disaggregating income data from other surveys (e.g. New Earnings Survey) at regional level.

Since the jobs that people do are largely responsible for providing their disposable income, employment data by occupation or sector can be used to estimate personal income, together with data on allowances or benefits. As indicated previously, the 2001 Census provides data on the occupation of all male and female members of the household who are in paid employment, as well as those people who are not in paid employment, i.e. the unemployed, disabled and retired. Clark (2003) has used these counts with information on occupational wage and benefit rates published by the Department for Work and Pensions (2001, 2002) to arrive at estimates of the average

income in each Leeds ward and output area. The income of a student is assumed to be the value of the full student loan (£2,170) plus a third of the average student debt (estimated at £5,961) in 2001. The income of the self-employed is taken to be £116 higher than the average employees weekly wage (Department for Work and Pensions, 2003).

The application of occupation-specific wage rates to numbers employed in each occupation in each output area has some shortcomings: no account is taken of 'non-income' benefits for those in work (e.g. child benefit) and those out of work (e.g. housing benefit) and there is the problem of excluding the income of retired people which can vary enormously between those who are living on the minimum income guarantee and those who have generous occupational or personal pension provision. Furthermore, we must remember that the ONS has randomly adjusted small counts to either 0 or 3 in order to protect individuals' privacy and these smaller counts are more likely with smaller areas. However, the methodology does provide a set of residence-based estimates of personal income for output areas in Leeds which, when mapped (Figure 8.8) and overlaid with community area

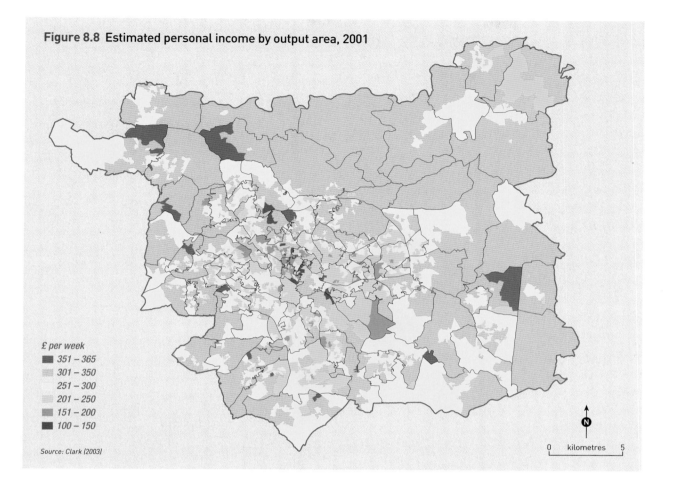

Figure 8.8 Estimated personal income by output area, 2001

£ per week
- 351 – 365
- 301 – 350
- 251 – 300
- 201 – 250
- 151 – 200
- 100 – 150

Source: Clark (2003)

0   kilometres   5

boundaries, show a pattern of relatively high incomes in the city centre surrounded by a crescent of inner city areas with lower incomes. Higher incomes are found in the outer suburban and more rural areas, although there are still some pockets of low incomes in these areas.

8.5 Workplace characteristics

Data on the number of workplaces, establishments or business units are available from the ABI as well as data on the number of jobs. The size structure of Leeds businesses can therefore be identified (Table 8.3). It is apparent that there are approximately 25,000 business units in Leeds, of which 80 per cent employ 10 or fewer people. Compared against the statistics for GB, Leeds has a lower proportion of small companies employing 1–10 and higher percentages in all the other size categories. As far as employment is concerned, the picture is

more variable. Those businesses in Leeds employing 100 or less account for 48.4 per cent of employees compared with the national figure of 58.4 per cent, whereas the businesses in Leeds employing over 1,000 employees are responsible for 16.9 per cent of jobs compared with 9.4 per cent in Great Britain. Thus, the main difference between Leeds and the whole country is that the larger firms in Leeds tend to employ, on average, fewer people than larger firms in Great Britain.

In terms of the sectoral breakdown of business units in Leeds, 27 per cent are in real estate, renting and business activities, 25 per cent are in wholesale/retail trade, repair, etc and the other large sectors with over 5 per cent of business units are other community, social/personal services (8.9 per cent), manufacturing (8.4 per cent), construction (7.9 per cent), hotels and restaurants (6.5 per cent), health and social work (5 per cent) and transport, storage and communication (5 per cent). However, the size breakdown differs from sector to sector

Table 8.3 Size structure of business units, 2002

Unit size	Leeds units	Leeds	Great Britain	Leeds	Great Britain	Leeds	Great Britain
		Percentage units		Percentage employees		Employees per unit	
1–10	19,997	79.54	83.11	15.4	20.8	3	3
11–49	3,855	15.33	13.12	21.7	25.1	23	22
50–99	660	2.63	2.11	11.3	12.5	68	69
100–499	552	2.20	1.49	28.3	24.9	206	195
500–999	38	0.15	0.12	6.4	6.7	672	669
1,000–1999	25	0.10	0.04	8.2	4.4	1,316	1,371
2,000+	14	0.06	0.02	8.7	5.6	2,498	3,258
Total	25,141	100.00	100.00	100.0	100.0	16	12

Source: ABI 2002

Figure 8.9 Size breakdown of major economic sectors, 2002

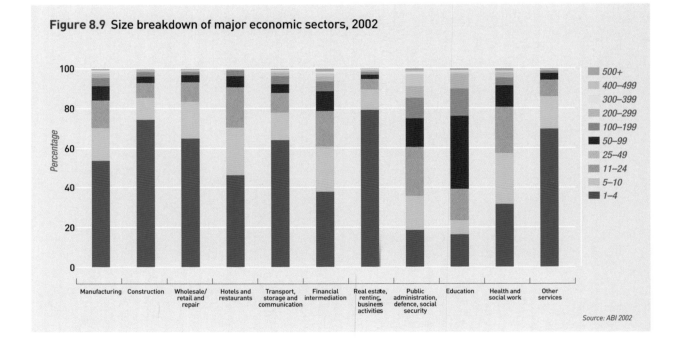

Source: ABI 2002

(Figure 8.9). The sectors with largest number of businesses have the largest proportion of small business units, whereas public administration organisations tend to have a larger proportion of units employing 11–24 persons and education and has the highest proportion of units with 25–49 employees out of all these broad sectors.

There are some relatively large businesses or organisations in Leeds. The ABI in 2002 suggests there are 77 with over 500 employees, 39 with over 1,000 employees and 14 with over 2,000 employees. Nine of the latter category are in the health and social work sector. The Leeds Economy Handbook (LCC, 2003) identifies the major employers as Leeds City Council

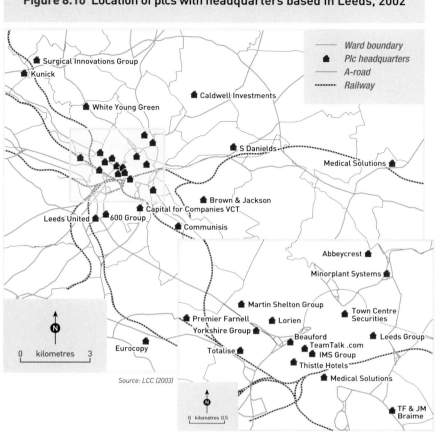

Figure 8.10 Location of plcs with headquarters based in Leeds, 2002

Ward boundary
Plc headquarters
A-road
Railway

Surgical Innovations Group
Kunick
White Young Green
Caldwell Investments
S Danields
Medical Solutions
Brown & Jackson
Capital for Companies VCT
Leeds United
600 Group
Communisis
N
0 kilometres 3
Source: LCC (2003)

Abbeycrest
Minorplant Systems
Martin Shelton Group
Town Centre Securities
Premier Farnell
Lorien
Yorkshire Group
Beauford
Leeds Group
Eurocopy
Totalise
TeamTalk .com
IMS Group
Thistle Hotels
Medical Solutions
TF & JM Braime
N
0 kilometres 0.5

gence of a regional development agency, Yorkshire Forward, with a substantial budget for use in promoting business activity and in increasing competitiveness through more innovation, more skills and improved connectivity, and a desire on behalf of the executive director to take Leeds from being a 'Premiership' city to one that is established in the 'Champions League' of cities. In 2002, there were 32 plcs with their headquarters based in Leeds (LCC, 2003), whose locations are illustrated in Figure 8.10.

Although lagging behind the best continental cities in terms of economic competitiveness, Leeds does have one of the fastest growing economies relative to other core cities in the UK. We saw earlier

and Leeds Teaching Hospitals NHS Trust, each of which employs in excess of 10,000 individuals. Amongst the other large employers are public sector organisations such as the Benefits Agency and the two universities, as well as private businesses in the financial services sector such as First Direct, Direct Line and the Halifax. British Telecommunications is another major employer in the city as is the Royal Mail, whose investment in a new site on derelict land at Stourton, where integrated mail processors sort huge volumes of mail, is a response to the city's population and commercial growth. In addition to the creation of the Leeds Mail Centre, the Royal Mail has also closed its landmark delivery office on Wellington Street, and opened a new office at the Wellington Bridge Complex.

There has long been debate about the extent to which Leeds has become a place where important development and business decisions are made. This relates in part to increasing decentralisation of central government functions and the emer-

that it is second to Manchester in terms of employment growth between 1998 and 2002. It is second to Bristol in terms of GDP *per capita* in 2001, on a par with Florence in Italy (ODPM, 2004), and is second to Birmingham in terms of the size of its manufacturing workforce.

Business success is no surprise in Leeds since it has been the starting point for many household names: Michael Marks set up his penny bazaar in Kirkgate market that became Marks and Spencer, Waddington's manufactured board games (Monopoly) for many years, and Montague Burton created the largest clothing factory in Europe. Around a third of the city's GDP is now generated by the financial and business services sector, details of which are presented in Chapter 9. Amongst other sectors of importance is printing and publishing, where there has been a longstanding tradition of successful operation. The skills and expertise available in this sector were important in attracting Mitsubishi Lithographic Presses to Leeds in 1992.

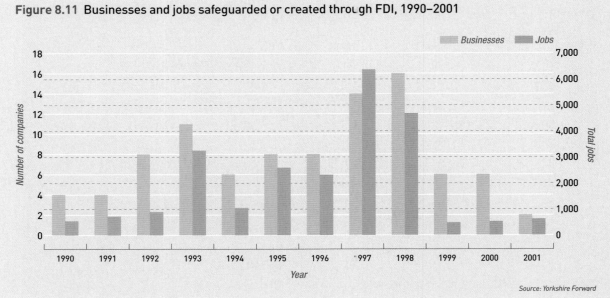

Figure 8.11 Businesses and jobs safeguarded or created through FDI, 1990–2001

Source: Yorkshire Forward

During the 1990s, Leeds has seen substantial foreign direct investment, either as new projects or acquisitions or expansions, with 1997 and 1998 being particularly good years (Figure 8.11) both in terms of the numbers of new investments and the numbers of jobs safeguarded or created. The origins of overseas inward investment are diverse but the most substantial proportion comes from the USA as Figure 8.12 indicates. Other important origins are Germany, Switzerland, Japan and France, and a significant number of these investments have locations within central Leeds (Figure 8.13).

Left, Mitsubishi Lithographic Presses at Riverside Place are suppliers of large format offset printing presses for the UK printing industry. The headquarters at Riverside Place has 50,000 square feet of showrooms, a spare parts centre, training facilities, a service centre and a rebuilding facility. Right, surveying firm Chesterton's offices in Minerva House — a late 1930s development in King Street, LS1.

Figure 8.12 Origins of foreign inward investment during the 1990s

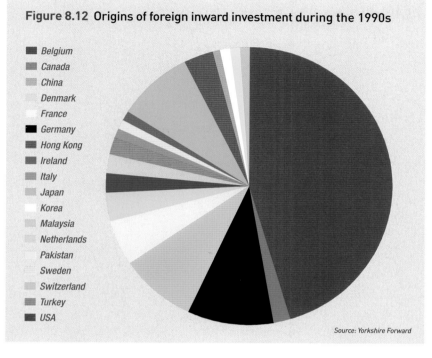

- Belgium
- Canada
- China
- Denmark
- France
- Germany
- Hong Kong
- Ireland
- Italy
- Japan
- Korea
- Malaysia
- Netherlands
- Pakistan
- Sweden
- Switzerland
- Turkey
- USA

Source: Yorkshire Forward

8.6 Business formation

Whilst most of the economic indicators for Leeds tell a positive story in the late 1990s and early years of the twenty-first century, the rate of business formation has been a cause for concern. This applies not only locally, but also at the national level. VAT registrations are a useful indicator of business formation but it should be emphasised that the data exclude firms not registered for VAT, either because they do not trade in

Figure 8.13 Locations of foreign inward investment in central Leeds

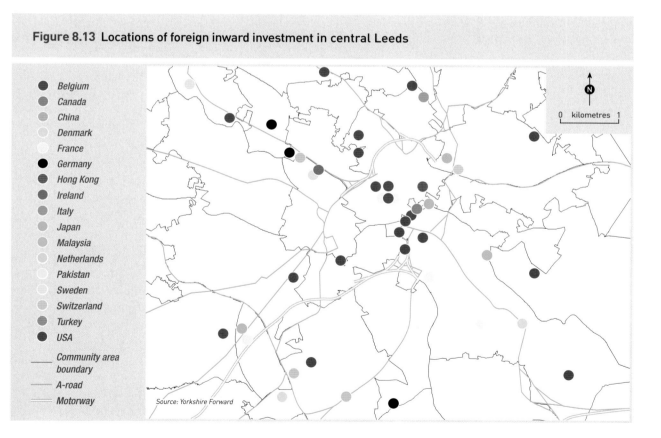

- Belgium
- Canada
- China
- Denmark
- France
- Germany
- Hong Kong
- Ireland
- Italy
- Japan
- Malaysia
- Netherlands
- Pakistan
- Sweden
- Switzerland
- Turkey
- USA
- —— Community area boundary
- —— A-road
- —— Motorway

Source: Yorkshire Forward

Table 8.4 VAT business registrations, Leeds, 1996–2001

Industrial group	Stock at end 1996	Stock at end 1996	1996–2002 change	Leeds percentage change	Great Britain percentage change
Manufacturing	2,195	1,965	-230	-10.5	-4.4
Construction	1,895	1,780	-115	-6.1	4.7
Wholesale, retail	5,040	4,480	-560	-11.1	-5.4
Hotels and restaurants	1,170	1,135	65	6.1	8.0
Transport and communications	735	830	95	12.9	7.3
Finance	175	185	10	5.7	8.7
Real estate	4,055	5,110	1,055	26.0	32.4
Public administration, other	1,320	1,485	165	12.5	9.7
Education, health	265	255	-10	-3.8	7.3

Source: VAT business registrations

VATable goods and services or because their turnover is below the registration threshold. In 2001, there were approximately 17,500 VAT registered businesses compared with the ABI figure of 25,000. Changes are positive in Leeds in five out of the nine major industrial groups between 1996 and 2001 (Table 8.4). Across GB, it was real estate where the major growth took place, increasing by 32 per cent compared with 26 per cent in Leeds. However, Leeds' business registrations in transport and communications and in public administration increased faster than the national average in this period.

8.7 Economic development policies

The changes that have taken place in the Leeds economy have, to a certain extent, been influenced by the international and national economic environment and by the policy context that has European, national and regional dimensions. In terms of EU policy, parts of Leeds have designated eligibility for Objective 2 funding from the EU Structural Funds during the period 2000–2006 and European Social Funds are available across the metropolitan district through Objective 3. On a national level, there are various Government programmes linked to competitiveness (DTI, 1998), urban renaissance (DETR, 2000) and neighbourhood renewal (Social Exclusion Unit, 2001). Under the Local Government Act 2000, councils were given scope to contribute to the economic, social and environmental

health of their areas by preparing long term 'Community Strategies' in partnership with other bodies. Leeds Initiative became the Local Strategic Partnership (LSP) for Leeds. Further-more, the Local Government Bill published in 2001 has enabled the establishment of Business Improvement Districts (BIDs) from 2004 to allow councils to work with businesses to improve town centres and commercial areas.

At the regional level, the activities of Yorkshire Forward, the regional development agency (RDA), are particularly important both in establishing the economic agenda for Leeds as the region's capital city and in taking this forward through the *Regional Economic Strategy (RES)*, reviewed in 2002 (Yorkshire Forward, 2003) and various major 'breakthrough' projects funded through the so-called Single Pot which replaces funds allocated through earlier rounds of the Single Regeneration Budget (SRB). Yorkshire Forward's annual budget is some £300 million and, while part of this funding is being used to support parts of the city doing less well, the RDA is also helping to guide a major city centre renaissance programme aiming to link the city's prime architectural areas such as Brigate, the Headrow, the Town and City Halls and Quarry Hill with high quality urban design and to link the 'high economy' centre of the city with smaller economies in suburbs like Morley and Hunslet.

So what sort of local initiatives have been underway in Leeds that support or influence economic and business

development? This section draws heavily on the 2002 Review of the *Leeds Economic Development Strategy* (Leeds Economy Partnership, 2003) where details of the initiatives and projects are more fully documented. Because of the interrelated nature of development to achieve social, environmental as well as economic sustainability, the policies range from support for regeneration in designated areas of deprivation, sector-specific initiatives (e.g. the Leeds Financial Services Initiative, Leeds Manufacturing Initiative and Leeds Media), and a host of other projects that relate to sectors such as innovation, transport and culture, all of which have a bearing on jobs and business well-being. The basic provision of financial and advisory services to start-ups and to established companies is coordinated by Leeds Business Services (LBS), working in partnership with national organisations such as the Small Business Service (Business Link for West Yorkshire). Further services and networking opportunities are provided by the Leeds Chamber of Commerce, which exists to support, promote and protect businesses in Leeds. Given the importance of Asian business in the city, an Asian Business Development Network (ASDN) was created in 1997 to support access to training and provide services for Asian companies.

Among the schemes available to encourage business start-ups are the West Yorkshire Graduate Start-up Programme (Robertson and Holt, 2002) and The Prince's Trust. The former aims to convert university students into successful entrepreneurs, a transition increasingly being recognised by politicians and policy makers as a means to generate employment growth and competitiveness (European Commission, 2003). Recent research by Robertson *et al.* (2003) shows that many students want to run their own business at some stage in their lives and that in excess of 60 per cent of students at Leeds University and Leeds Metropolitan University have aspirations as entrepreneurs (Robertson and Collins, 2003). Funding of around £3 million from Yorkshire Forward is being used to enable the creation of around 200 new businesses between 2002 and 2005. The Prince's Trust, on the other hand, has been operating since 1983 and has provided finance and mentoring to support people aged 18–30 to start up their

businesses but in this instance, target groups are young disabled people, members of ethnic minorities and ex-offenders. Between 1994 and 1999, The Prince's Trust supported 134 start-ups in Leeds. Evidence from Yorkshire and the Humber has been gathered by a survey in 2000 evaluating the business successes and the factors which have helped young people make a positive transition to self-employment (Shutt *et al.*, 2001). Two thirds of the 367 young people who were surveyed in the region reported that their business was thriving or surviving; it was also apparent that even business failure can sometimes be translated into positive, life-changing experiences for the young people involved. The research indicated that support in assisting young people to develop a business plan was critical in transforming their ideas into reality. Loans and grants are used to assemble the basic necessities for start-up and to unlock funding from other sources. Amongst the factors boosting success were more opportunities for training before start-up, more direction at the stage of product or market choice, and more help in improving the understanding of finance and business development issues.

Another initiative to support disadvantaged groups

Left, a senior process operator monitors the spray drier tanks at Yorkshire Chemicals' Leeds plant. Although the company has its roots in providing dyes for local textile manufacturers, its textile colours markets now extend worldwide. Right, the home of Tetley's bitter since the firm's creation in 1882. Carlsberg took control of Carlsberg-Tetley in 1997 and now Tetley is no longer part of the brewing giant's name.

participate in the local labour market is the EQUAL project, a European Social Fund programme that attempts to test new ways of tackling discrimination and inequality by those seeking work. Various public, private and voluntary organisations in Leeds are members of the e-Employability Development Partnership with the local authority and are trying to develop ways that enable economically and socially excluded groups to access training and jobs in the online or e-economy.

More generally, Leeds is one of the major telecommunications centres in the country and has the potential to be a leading city in the new knowledge-based economy. A feasibility study was published in 1998 by the Yorkshire and Humberside Regional Research Observatory (ReRO) that tried to evaluate the extent to which Leeds, 'the intelligent city', was "concerned with using information and communication technologies to raise awareness, promote a dynamic networking culture, and encourage good practice in their use" (ReRO, 1998, p.3). The study made various recommendations focused primarily on the removal of obstacles to the deployment of communications infrastructure. More recently, developments in the e-economy have been supported through e-HQ Leeds, a partnership that

was led initially by Leeds Development Agency and supported by Yorkshire Forward, the universities and business support services. Here the aim is to promote Leeds as a leading centre for e-business and ensure that its organisations remain up to date with e-business trends. Amongst the revolutions taking place are the adoption of 'broadband' and 'grid' technologies. Broadband represents a major transformation in the communications infrastructure and is likely to enhance competition in key markets by increasing the level of information available and thus increasing market efficiencies (Leigh, 2003). Grid technology is a form of computing that allows users to share technological resources and provide a seamless connection between people working in different locations and in different areas of work. The White Rose Grid (WRG) went live in 2002 and is currently being used by various universities and businesses (Hewitt, 2003).

Enhancing collaboration between research and policy making is the primary aim of the Leeds Initiative Knowledge NETwork (LIKNET), a project funded by the Office of the Deputy Prime Minister and which has involved using the Virtual Knowledge Park (VKP) at the University of Leeds as the computer-

Figure 8.14 VKP interface to the LIKNET book project

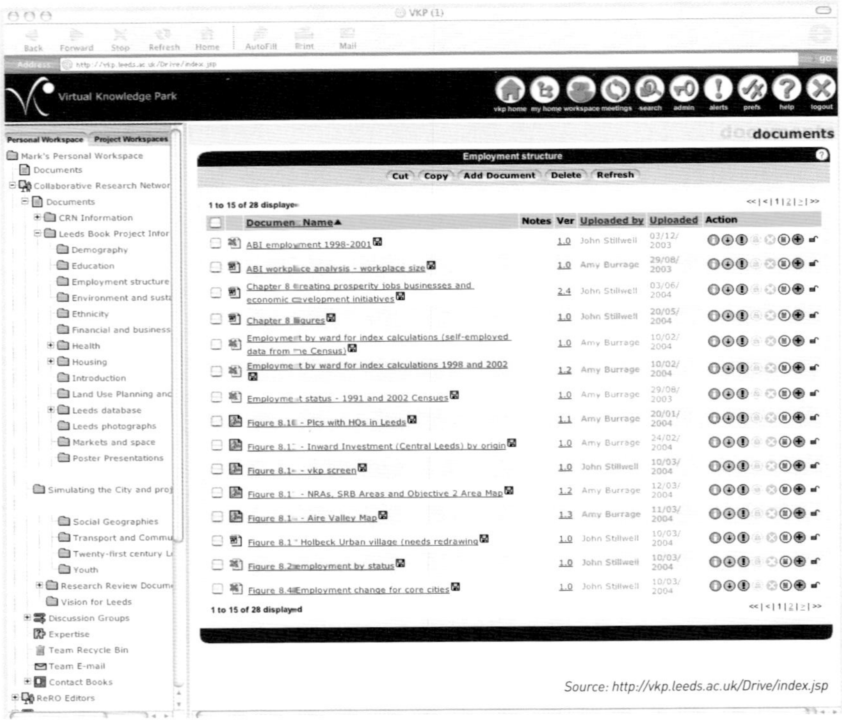

Source: http://vkp.leeds.ac.uk/Drive/index.jsp

based environment for, amongst other things, undertaking all the work associated with the preparation of this book. Figure 8.14 shows the VKP interface that collaborators have used to access the huge range of documents, data files and images that underpin this book project.

The policy initiatives that we have mentioned hitherto are not explicitly spatial, but there is a great deal of attention paid and investment directed at particular geographical areas or communities through the *Leeds Neighbourhood Renewal Strategy (LNRS)*, under the heading of regeneration. The preparation of Leeds Community Strategy, as mentioned previously, is the responsibility of Leeds Initiative. Known as *Vision II,* it follows the first *Vision for Leeds* in 1999 (Leeds Initiative, 1999) setting out proposals for long term social, environmental and economic well-being. Its intention is to address the issues of how Leeds can promote itself into the next league of international cities, how it can spread prosperity to reach those who have not benefited from the opportunities and thus narrow the gap between the haves and the have nots. In this context, the Neighbourhood Renewal Fund (NRF) is one of the most significant streams of funding to have emerged since 1999, and the LNRS was launched in 2001, establishing local targets for improving unemployment rates, crime levels, educational attainment, health and housing. It also provides a framework for agreeing priority neighbourhoods — the Neighbourhood Renewal Areas (NRAs) of Harehills, Gipton, Beeston Hill and Holbeck and the Aire Valley (Figure 8.15) — and sets out a process for agreeing how resources will be targeted in these areas.

One of the most important projects being implemented as part of the *Economic Development Strategy* is the scheme to transform the Aire Valley Employment Area into a high quality employment base. The Aire Valley Employment Area lies immediately to the south east of the city centre and extends from the Armouries and Clarence Dock eastwards towards the A1-M1 link road. The River Aire and Calder Navigation canal form a central waterways corridor through an area (Figure 8.16) where land use is diverse and contains over 300 businesses focused on the Cross Green industrial estate. There are some heavy industrial operations and some modern distribution centres. The total area covers around 1,000 hectares, of which 110 are derelict and/or contaminated and 300 have potential for development.

Leeds City Council, Yorkshire Forward, Jobcentre Plus and the private sector are the key partners in the development of the area, whose total funding requirement is estimated to be £250 million. In order to make the Aire Valley area an accessible, secure and attractive location for new investment and jobs, it is necessary to build the East Leeds Link Road to open up new sites for development, to develop integrated transport access into the area (e.g. improved buses, links with

Figure 8.15 Regeneration areas

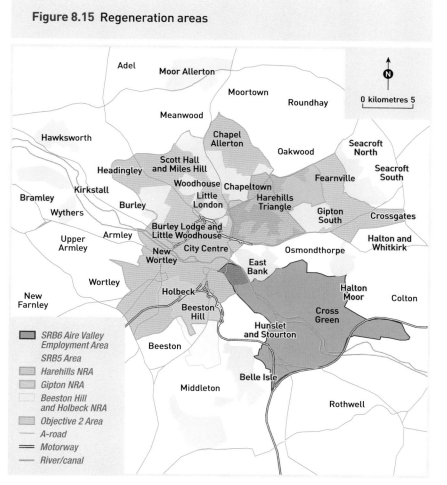

Whilst the Aire Valley is a major focus of comprehensive regen-eration, other areas have been identified in the LNRS as NRAs, including Beeston and Holbeck, which received £7.4 million in regeneration funding in 1998, Hare-hills, where unemployment and crime are major problems, and Gipton, an area that is amongst the most deprived in the country. In all these NRAs, Neighbourhood Re-newal Teams have been set up to implement a whole range of regeneration policies that include encouraging the development of community enterprises and job creation as well as promoting linkages between education, training and job opportunities. The Objective 2 Regeneration Area (Figure 8.15) covers six wards of inner city Leeds

Supertram, cycle and pedestrian routes), provide landscape and security improvements and improve the waterway corridor for recreation and leisure. A dedicated Employment Access Team has been created to work with existing businesses and inward investors to maximise employment opportunities with a view to providing 29,000 new jobs, and to work with surrounding communities (Richmond Hill, Osmondthorpe, Halton Moor, Hunslet, Middleton and Belle Isle) to identify and meet training needs to maximize access to these new jobs. Finally, a range of support for new and existing businesses has been put in place to ensure longer-term growth and sustainability. This includes a financial support package of grant aid for business expansion, property, works, security, marketing, training, consultancy, recruitment and business start-ups, a dedicated Business Adviser to liaise with local businesses and support for the Cross Green Business Association to enhance networking.

and those parts not designated as NRAs are eligible for funding from Yorkshire Forward, the EU Structural Funds and the City Council. Objective 2 is a European funding programme for 2000–2006 that aims to regenerate areas suffering from economic decline based on five Priorities. Priority 3, for example, is concerned with enabling the most deprived areas to re-engage with the local economy. Priority areas include Chapeltown, Sheepscar, Little London, Woodhouse, Mean-wood, Burley and Hyde Park and several of these areas have already received investment from the Single Regeneration Budget (see SRB 5 areas in Figure 8.15) and from the EU URBAN II initiative. Local Development and Employment Pacts (LDEPs) set out the key targets and activities to be addressed under Priority 3, for example, and projects are identified under different Measures.

Finally, we should not complete this review without

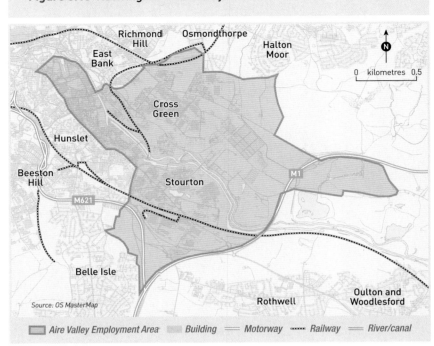

Figure 8.16 Reviving the Aire Valley

Richmond Hill · Osmondthorpe · East Bank · Halton Moor · Cross Green · Hunslet · Beeston Hill · Stourton · M1 · M621 · Belle Isle · Rothwell · Oulton and Woodlesford

Source: OS MasterMap

Aire Valley Employment Area ▪ Building ═ Motorway ∙∙∙ Railway ═ River/canal

mention of the Holbeck Urban Village, an initiative set in motion by Leeds City Council and Yorkshire Forward, aiming to deliver a sustainable urban community that deals with social exclusion but also creates jobs for people from adjacent communities. Holbeck is adjacent to where the M621 enters the city centre on the south side but is cut off by the railways and canal. It has a long industrial heritage, not least because Hol Beck was where John Marshall created the first steam-powered flax-spinning factory in the early nineteenth century. Marshall's Mill and Temple Works are both very important parts of the city's industrial architecture since they are survivals from the birth of the Industrial Revolution. The Round Foundry site on Globe Road is the sole survivor of the specialist engineering foundries which helped to kick start the Industrial Revolution. Thus, despite being formerly a scene of intense industrial activity, Holbeck became largely derelict with the factories gone and the back-to-back housing cleared away.

The concept underpinning the urban village is to create a community with a mix of uses including residential and leisure. Plans for a population of 1,000 residents, with some affordable housing for rent and sale as well as special needs accommodation are underway and some of the planned infrastructure and environmental improvements have already been put in place. Consultants were commissioned to undertake a study in 2002 and GVA Grimley's key development opportunities are indicated in Figure 8.17. The area is to become an assortment of business, good quality residential accommodation and retail services in an attractive environment, whilst preserving as much as possible of the industrial heritage. This will be Leeds' first dedicated live/work development which, it has been argued, is the ideal ingredient for attracting emergent e-businesses and e-entrepreneurs. In fact the project has been seen as an essential part of the drive to establish Leeds as a key centre for e-business and will create a distinct area where this drive can be focused. As well as the City Council and Yorkshire Forward, the partners involved in the project are British Waterways, English Heritage, Spacia and Network Rail. The Holbeck Village website (http://www.holbeckurbanvillage.co.uk/) provides current details of developments and events, indicating how the initiative has helped encourage private investors to see the potential of the area and to come forward with refurbishment schemes for some of the existing properties and new-build schemes for other sites. The Round Foundry scheme, providing apartments, eating places and shops, has demonstrated more sustainable development credentials than any other major development scheme on or near the waterfront (Millard, 2004). However, there is some concern from the Civic Trust that the type of development that will occur on sites without the strictures of listed buildings will mean that the scale of a true urban village will be lost (Leeds Civic Trust, 2000). Similar misgivings surfaced in research undertaken by Biddulph *et al.* (2003).

Figure 8.17 Holbeck Urban Village

A *Tower Works*
B *Madison Hosiery/The Antiques Centre*
C *Emco/Haynes*
D *Royal Mail/Presitage Salvage*
E *British Rail/Spacia*
F *Round Foundry*
G *Leodis Court*
H *Marshalls Mill and adjacent sites*
J *Midland Mills and adjacent sites*
K *Temple Mill and adjacent sites*
L *Vacant site*
M *Various sites on northern side of Sweet Street*
N *Jarvis Porter*
P *White Arrow Express site*
Q *Granary Wharfe*
R *Bristol Street Motors/viaduct site*
S *Landmark Bridge*

Source: http://www.holbeckurbanvillage.co.uk/

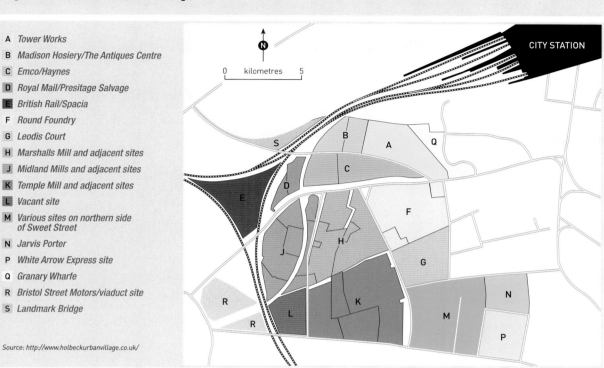

8.8 Conclusions

The evidence assembled in this chapter suggests that Leeds is making headway in its attempts to sustain its economic growth, having dealt with the industrial restructuring in many of its basic industries such as tailoring over the past 30 years. Its reaction has been astonishing and its pre-eminence over other cities in the region has been remarkable, not least because of the growth in financial and business services that will be considered in more detail in the next chapter.

Some might argue that its business diversity has been a key element in its success; others might point to its strategic location as being the catalyst; and the roles of individuals like John Trickett and organisations like the Leeds Initiative have certainly been influential. Whatever the reasons, Leeds has certainly benefited from a get-up-and-go culture (Watson, 2003). The business indicators are positive and strategic planning at sub-regional and regional levels is intent upon consolidating the city's role as regional capital and moving it forward so that it ranks alongside some of the other major cities of mainland Europe. This is a very big ask but an agenda for

core cities has been set out by the ODPM (2004) and Leeds must now consider the critical success factors — innovation, diversity, connectivity, skilled human capital, quality of life and strategic decision-making capacity — and identify those key policies that are required to further increase its competitiveness and improve productivity.

The review of policies contained in the chapter has been piecemeal rather than comprehensive. We have said little about skills or innovation, both of which are critical dimensions for successful growth. Skills in particular are central to the productivity agenda that has been outlined for the region (Riordan, 2003; Newby, 2003) and improving effectiveness of the local labour market through partnership between employers, unions, public agencies and the local Learning and Skills Council is very important. As far as innovation is concerned, Leeds has a long tradition of business innovation and entrepreneurship that moves on as times change. There is every reason to assume that new ideas will bring forth exciting new ventures and create new jobs in the future.

References

Biddulph, M., Franklin, B. and Tait, M. (2003) From concept to completion: a critical analysis of the urban village, *Town Planning Review*, 74(2): 165–193.

Clark, S. (2003) Estimating personal income for small areas, *The Yorkshire & Humber Regional Review*, 13(3): 20–22.

Charles, D., Benneworth, P., Bradley, D., Chatterton, P., Coombes, M., Cornford, J., Gillespie, A., Naylor, R., Pike, A. and Tomaney, J. (1999) *The Economic Links between Leeds and the Yorkshire and the Humber Region*, Final Report to Leeds City Council, CURDS, Newcastle-upon-Tyne.

Department of Environment, Transport and the Regions (DETR) (2000) *Our Towns and Cities: The Future — Delivering an Urban Renaissance*, CM 4911, The Stationery Office, London.

Department of Trade and Industry (DTI) (1998) *Our Competitive Future: Building the Knowledge Driven Economy*, DTI, London.

Department for Work and Pensions (2001) *Labour Market: New Earnings Survey*, Analysis by Region, Tables E9–E12.

Department for Work and Pensions (2002) *Annual Abstract of Statistics*, Table 10.15.

Department for Work and Pensions (2003) *Labour Market Trends*, September, p. 441.

European Commission (2003) *Fostering Entrepreneurship in Europe: Priorities for the Future*, European Commission, Brussels.

Hewitt, J. (2003) Research revolutionised by sharing resources, *The Yorkshire & Humber Regional Review*, 13(2): 25–27.

Leeds City Council (LCC) (2003) *Leeds Economy Handbook 2003*, http://www.leeds.gov.uk/documents/945BEA4C7BECD71880256E0000498BCA.pdf

Leeds Civic Trust (2000) *Annual Report 1999–2000*, Leeds Civic Trust, Leeds.

Leeds Development Agency (1999) Employment in Leeds, *Briefing Note Issue 7*, LDA and Leeds Training and Enterprise Council, Leeds.

Leeds Economy Partnership (2003) *Leeds Economic Development Strategy 2002 Review*, Leeds.

Leeds Initiative (1999) *Vision for Leeds*, Leeds Initiative, Leeds.

Leigh, C.M. (2003) Yorkshire and Humber: becoming an e-Region?, *The Yorkshire & Humber Regional Review*, 13(2): 28–31.

Llewellyn-Davies, Steers Davies Gleave, Jones Lang LaSalle and the University of Leeds (2003) *Leeds and Environs Spatial Strategy*, final scoping report for the Yorkshire and Humber Assembly *et al.*, Wakefield.

Millard, J. (2004) *The regeneration of sites and structures in south central Leeds: sustainable development?*, unpublished BA dissertation, School of Geography, University of Leeds, Leeds.

Newby, L. (2003) Making productivity work for people: an integrated regional approach, *The Yorkshire & Humber Regional Review*, 13(2):7–9.

Office of the Deputy Prime Minister (ODPM) (2004) *Competitive European Cities Where do the Core Cities Stand?*, Urban Research Summary 13, ODPM, London.

Rainie, G.F. and Wilkinson, R.K. (1967) The economic structure, Chapter XVIII in Beresford, M.W. and Jones, G.R.J. (eds) *Leeds and its Region*, Leeds Local Executive Committee of the British Association for the Advancement of Science, pp. 215–238.

Riordan, T. (2003) A prosperous future: closing the productivity gap in Yorkshire and the Humber, *The Yorkshire & Humber Regional Review*, 13(2): 4–6.

Robertson, M. and Collins, A. (2003) Developing entrepreneurship: West Yorkshire Universities' partnership and Business Met, *The Yorkshire &*

Humber Regional Review, 13(2): 17–19.

Robertson, M. and Holt, G. (2002) *West Yorkshire Graduate Start-up Programme*, Yorkshire Universities, Leeds.

Robertson, M., Llewellyn, D., Collins, A, Slater, J., Teal, R. and Wilson, K. (2003) *West Yorkshire Universities graduate career aspirations*, Research Working Paper, Leeds Metropolitan University, Leeds.

Shutt, J., Sutherland, J. and Koutsoukos, S. (2001) *Alive with Opportunities: Evaluating Young Business Start-up Success 1994–1999*, evidence from Yorkshire and the Humber, A Research Report for The Prince's Trust, ERBEDU, Leeds Metropolitan University, Leeds.

Social Exclusion Unit (2001) *A New Commitment to Neighbourhood Renewal National Strategy Action Plan*, Cabinet Office, London.

Watson, J. (2003) So how's business?, *The Yorkshire & Humber Regional Review*, 13(2): 2–3.

Williamson, P. (2000) *Income imputation for small areas*, project website at: ~william/income/index.html

Yorkshire Forward (2003) *Regional Economic Strategy for Yorkshire and Humber*, Yorkshire Forward, Leeds.

Yorkshire and Humberside Regional Research Observatory (ReRO) (1998) *Leeds The Intelligent City*, Report prepared for Leeds City Council, ReRO, University of Leeds, Leeds.

9

Accommodating Financial and Business Services

RACHAEL UNSWORTH & ROGER HENDERSON

The single most important issue for the future in terms of Leeds' relationship with its broader region is how to facilitate the development of the Leeds business services cluster.

9.1 Introduction

As Chapter 8 shows, services have replaced manufacturing as the principal employment sector in Leeds. Within this broad category, it is financial and business services (FBS), or producer services[1], that have expanded particularly dramatically. Their accommodation constitutes a significant feature of the urban landscape of Leeds: the city centre office stock amounts to over 1.2 million square metres and the office district has expanded beyond the confines of the traditional 'office quarter'. In addition, many firms have taken accommodation on peripheral business parks.

Whilst Leeds is a major location of FBS in England, employment in the sector is around a quarter of that in the City of London — though comparisons are difficult because the definition of the sector in Leeds is wider than that used for 'the City'. In terms of level of employment in FBS, Birmingham comes after London, with Leeds in third place (LCC, 2003a), though in terms of growth in the sector during the 1990s, Leeds was second only to London (Table 9.1). Office stock in the city centre is about one seventh of the City of London stock (Corporation of London, 2001). Leeds office take-up during the decade 1994–2003 was the sixth highest of the provincial office centres, behind Edinburgh, Manchester, Bristol, Birmingham and Glasgow (Chesterton, 2004).

Barkham (2002) devised a typology of office markets in terms of the nature of demand that includes the scope and power of occupier organisations, the diversity of activity and the size of the office stock relative to the national stock. The four levels are: international, national, regional and local. Leeds does not feature in listings of top international or even top European office locations. There are some aspects that make it an office market of national significance, such as the presence of some central government functions, the headquarters of 30 plcs (LCC, 2003a), and the offices of some professional firms of local origin that

Table 9.1 Financial services employment (SIC 7) change in the main UK conurbations/cities, 1991–1998

	Total absolute change	Percentage change	Office rents 2001 £psf
Greater London	294,454	34.2	–
Inner London	202,520	33.8	39.00
West Midlands	34,021	25.4	–
Birmingham	19,606	25.9	23.50
Greater Manchester	35,710	26.5	–
Manchester	7,634	13.4	23.75
West Yorkshire	26,510	25.7	–
Leeds	*22,957*	*40.4*	*22.50*
Clydeside	15,094	16.7	–
Glasgow	15,427	25.7	23.00
South Yorkshire	7,663	20.3	–
Sheffield	9,671	34.9	13.50
Merseyside	4,717	9.2	–
Liverpool	4,732	14.7	14.75
Tyneside	-2,741	-5.5	–
Newcastle	-1,585	-5.4	16.50
Bristol	2,274	4.0	21.00
Edinburgh	11,443	19.4	30.00
Leicester	6,211	33.3	13.50
Nottingham	5,531	29.4	14.50
Cardiff	5,396	19.9	17.75

SIC = Standard Industrial Code   Source: Gibb et al. (2001)

have extended their reach. It is clearly a strong regional service centre with many firms that run their regional business only from Leeds or with Leeds as the lead office (see Table 9.3).

In Leeds, as elsewhere, office occupier profiles, the nature of office buildings, their location and the timing of their development have always depended on a combination of six main factors:

Far left, West Riding House, a mid-1970s development, towers above Albion Street. Left, No. 1 Park Row, developed in the 1990s and occupied by law firm Pinsents — one of the 'big six' in Leeds.

- economic phases and the strength of different sectors of the national, regional and local economy, which influence the demand for buildings;

- the existing urban structure — where various uses are established and where sites are available for development/redevelopment;

- architectural fashions and building technology plus access to, and the relative prices of, building materials;

- perceptions by occupiers of acceptable locations for activities and appropriate accommodation;

- perceptions by landowners, developers, investors and their advisors of the strength and nature of demand; and

- mechanisms for controlling and stimulating renewal of the built environment (especially land-use planning and economic development strategy) and the political climate within which these mechanisms are developed and implemented.

A detailed history of the evolution of the Leeds office market is beyond our scope here but would demonstrate how these factors have interwoven over time to produce the geography that we have today and the structure within which future development will occur. In this chapter, the evolving office market is evaluated within a broad understanding of the multiplicity of factors that explain the recent expansion of the FBS sector, the changing requirements for office space, the way that the demand for accommodation has been met and the spatial patterns that have been generated and are likely to be generated into the future.

9.2 Development of the service sector and the office district

In the late eighteenth century, early service providers made a living from the financial and legal requirements of the textile trade and early industry. The local economy expanded and diversified in the nineteenth century (Bateman, 1986), requiring a wider range of services such as accountancy, architecture, surveying and broking of various kinds. As service firms became

more established and professional, so banks, insurance companies
and other professional enterprises commissioned purpose-built
offices (Black, 2000), though many small firms continued to use
rooms in converted Georgian houses. The office quarter became
established to the west of the medieval trading area of the old
town (Beresford and Unsworth, forthcoming); most FBS firms
were located within the area south of The Headrow, east of Queen
Street, north of Wellington Street and west of Albion Street.

Twentieth century inter-war and post-war offices, most of
them considerably taller than their predecessors, replaced some
of the earlier residential and warehouse buildings in this area,
and also some of the Victorian buildings, thus increasing the
density of the office district. Other buildings were refurbished or
rebuilt behind retained facades. As recently as the mid-1980s, the
office district was still more-or-less confined to its mid-nineteenth
century area, though its appearance was much transformed.

9.3 Changing role as a service sector provider

Leeds holds a pre-eminent position within a regional economy
that has shown strong growth in recent years (see Chapters 1
and 8). The reputation for prosperity has attracted further
occupiers who provide more work for existing FBS firms. By
1981, 27,000 people were employed in the FBS sector, with
banking as the core business. From the mid-1980s, banks
diversified their businesses and legal firms started to be more
significant as their corporate practices grew strongly. An article
in *The Economist* (1993) called Leeds the "pinstripe city" with
a subtitle: "less muck, more brass". By 1999, the FBS employment figure was put at 92,000 (LCC, 2001). Table 9.2 shows
both the relative importance of different sub-sectors and the
changes in the sectors 1991–1996 and 1996–2001. In the latter
period, the strongest growth has been in 'other activities',
labour recruitment, renting equipment, secretarial and trans-
lation, computing, consultancy, research and development.
Design, packaging, selling, advertising, accounting, training,
planning, banking and securities trading also contribute to the
range of activities (www.leedsfinancialservices.org.uk).

Table 9.2 Financial and business services employment change, 1991–2001

Sub-sectors	1991	1996*	Percentage change 1991–1996	1996	2001	Percentage change 1996–2001
Accountancy and book-keeping	3,700	3,200	-14	3,100	3,800	23
Advertising	950	1,500	63	1,400	1,150	-18
Architecture, engineering and technical	4,500	4,700	4	5,050	4,300	-15
Auxiliary to finance	2,950	2,850	-3	3,100	3,100	0
Business consultancy and market research	950	1,600	73	1,550	2,300	48
Computing	2,200	4,600	106	4,100	5,700	39
Financial intermediation	11,800	12,150	3	13,000	11,450	-12
Industrial cleaning	9,000	10,450	16	11,800	9,300	-21
Insurance and pension funds	4,650	4,650	0	4,550	6,000	33
Investigation and security	1,000	2,700	169	3,050	3,300	8
Labour recruitment	3,000	5,700	89	6,400	11,950	87
Legal	3,600	4,600	29	5,150	6,050	18
Management activities	300	850	180	300	350	17
Packaging	250	550	120	600	300	-49
Photographic	800	950	18	1,050	850	-19
R&D	150	500	181	500	700	40
Real estate	2,500	3,350	35	3,500	4,250	21
Rent machinery and equipment	2,850	2,550	-9	2,450	4,250	74
Secretarial and translation	600	350	-38	400	650	63
Other activities	1,200	1,700	44	1,900	5,050	165
All financial and business services	56,850	69.550	22	72,950	84,900	16

*The basis of the data changed in 1996, thus the table gives comparisons across two time periods: 1991–1996 and 1996–2001   Source: LCC (2003a)

In Leeds, financial and professional services evolved to serve home-grown industry but are now part of a more complex and large-scale division of labour that provides services beyond the city to the wider region and indeed, in the case of large firms, the whole country. The Leeds-based law firms epitomise this trend: their commercial departments expanded rapidly from 1980 onwards (Financial Times, 1995). Research for Leeds City Council (mtl Consultants, 2000) reported that Leeds-based legal and financial firms have been winning business and attracting staff from London firms. Although some nearby towns and cities have suffered through consolidation of regional service sector operations in Leeds (Tickell, 1996), researchers from the University of Newcastle argue that many of the region's business needs would now be met from London or Manchester if Leeds had not become regionally dominant (CURDS, 1999). A survey by Leeds Financial Services Initiative (LFSI) in 2000 showed that while most business was local (42 per cent) or regional (31 per cent), over 20 per cent of work comes from elsewhere in the UK or from abroad (over than 3 per cent) (LFSI/LMU 2001). LSFI member firms already have representation or business interests in over 60 countries, with Western Europe accounting for the greatest share. Expansion into European markets is seen as a future priority (LFSI, 2003).

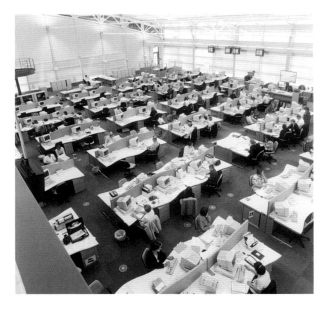

9.4 Changing office demand

The changing demand for office accommodation encompasses quantity, style and location. It reflects employment growth within existing organisations as well as new entrants. The nature of the space required relates to new ways of working (NWoW) and also to changes in fashions of architecture and design. Most firms are small or medium-sized, but of the 50 firms/organisations in Leeds employing more than 500 people, around half are classed as FBS providers (LCC, 2003a).

Economic and business change

The emerging information economy, powered and enabled by innovations in information and communications technology, is fostering NWoW which can be characterised by:

- people collaborating across geographical distance and professional boundaries;

- people working from home, on the move, and in flexible office environments;

- work being assigned to people in terms of objectives, not tasks; and

- the short timeframe of work group constellations that emerge, engage in activities, and then dissolve again, as the circumstances require (Centre for Pervasive Computing, 2003).

Predictions of a dramatic reduction in the demand for office space flowing from universal adoption of NWoW have not so far materialised, but many changes are reducing floorspace requirements.[2]

The introduction of information technology "has also created entirely new sectors of service activity such as electronic data processing, software programming, systems engineering and the handling and maintenance of electronic machines in production itself" (Martinelli, 1991, p. 23). In 2000, 'new economy' companies[3] accounted for 5 per cent of city centre take-up and 14 per cent of out-of-town office space take-up (JLL, 2001). By 2002, there were around 1,300 ICT sector businesses employing a total of 12,000 people (LCC, 2003a).

Telecommunications and computing innovations have also spawned call centres as direct customer interfaces have been replaced by centralised, remote marketing and customer services for companies with national and international coverage. In 1988, Leeds hosted the UK's first call centre when First Direct started its telephone banking service at the Arlington Business centre. The following year, the bank increased its floorspace to 6875m[2] and subsequently took an additional 9,290m[2] at Stourton. By 2002, a variety of companies employed approximately 12,000 people in 18 call centres around the city. Only four of these firms employed just call centre staff; the remainder also employed a total of approximately 8,000 staff in other capacities.

influential factors include the availability of offices at reasonable rents, a large pool of graduates, a vibrant and varied offer of city centre facilities within a compact area and the city-wide sense of innovation and creativity (JLL, 2001). As well as direct benefits, there is also a perception that reputation is enhanced by association with an emerging cluster of excellence and innovation.

No.1 Leeds City Office Park was designed to be energy efficient, making use of solar heating, natural light and ventilation. It became a customer service centre for a mobile phone company in 1998.

The attractions of Leeds

Many organisations of local origin have not taken a recent, active location decision, though when their lease expires or their business changes in size or structure, they may well have to make a decision about whether to stay. Embeddedness within the local market — including the local labour market — may well dominate the decision.

Recent factors influencing decision making are revealed in research about the location decisions of new economy companies (JLL, 2001). Connectivity was shown to be the primary requirement. Leeds is well connected to London and Scotland by rail, linked into the motorway network and accessible to inter-national destinations through Leeds-Bradford Airport. A third of internet traffic is said to be routed through Leeds (Accenture, reported in LCC, August, 2000). Leeds has more high speed ISDN lines per head of the population than any other major city (mtl Consultants, 2000). It also has the greatest uptake in the UK of ADSL, allowing copper telephone wires to carry broadband information. Leeds is thus established as a major 'new economy' hub and is increasingly acting as a focus and stimulus for the whole region. Acknowledging the potential importance of this sector, the LCC Development Department marketing budget is focused on attracting new economy incomers.

New economy companies also need to attract and retain staff, hence it is important to be in a favoured and accessible place — both for commuters and for business travellers. Other

The nature of demand — building specifications and locations

Increasingly, growing firm size, new types of businesses and new ways of working have generated demand for higher specifications, larger floorplates (the total size of office floors) which allow for open plan working or flexible reconfiguring of office units, better access and good facilities for both staff and visitors. Older buildings can be ill-suited to some current requirements and office style can have a significant influence on working cultures, productivity and the image of the firm. New economy firms often deem internal specification more important than exterior appearance of the building (JLL, 2001). Older premises do not meet all the stringent standards imposed by the 1999 and 2004 revisions to the Disability Discrimination Act 1995 (http://www.cae.org.uk/dda.html). These factors are reflected in the rental differentials and the difficulties in letting some Grade B and C space. While some private client law firms and financial institutions still feel comfortable in converted Georgian houses (Sykes, 2003), many of the recently expanded firms have been forced to move into larger premises which provide a very different kind of accommodation, often in locations that would have surprised professionals of an earlier generation. Nevertheless, a city centre location remains a priority for many:

"It is an integral part of our job to market ourselves to banks, accountancy firms and solicitors and therefore there is no other place to be but smack bang in the middle of town. We would not have opened in Leeds if we could not have opened in the city centre."

"I can certainly see the benefits of being in Leeds city centre doing business rather than working from home. It is much more difficult to market yourself working at home than it is marketing yourself from the centre of Leeds" (Swift Research, 2001).

Firms that want to be seen as major players need to occupy the most imposing space in the most prominent location attainable. Developers contrive to give their property a label of 'Number 1' wherever possible, responding to this need for accommodation to act as part of the occupier's branding.

Demand for city centre space has driven development upwards and outwards: in some cases the preference for an LS1 address has been overtaken by the need for contemporary accommodation and there is insufficient space in the traditional core (JLL, 2001).

Take-up

Office take-up in Leeds has not been at a constant level. It accelerated through the late 1980s, reaching 41,800m² in 1989,

then fell back during the recession of the early 1990s. Take-up varied during the mid-1990s, strengthened to 2000, went through a slacker period and then a recovery. This variability in the annual figures (Figure 9.1) is partly explained by the timing of completion of large buildings and therefore the possibility of major deals. For the decade 1994–2003, the average take-up was just over 40,000m² per year, and agents consider that this level will be at least maintained over the next few years as some large buildings come to the market.

Between 1992 and 2000, 33 per cent of office take-up was by the financial sector and 23 per cent by business services. By 1999, business services had taken the lead, accounting for over a third of all take-up, and financial services had slipped back to 25 per cent of the total, partly reflecting increased take-up of out-of-town property by this sub-sector. Government departments and agencies have also created significant demand: Customs and Excise, NHS Executive, Department for Work and Pensions, Inland Revenue, NHS Shared Services, Environment Agency and Yorkshire Forward.

In terms of business origins, there are several categories of occupier. The most significant of the home-grown businesses are the legal firms. Five of the 'big six' (Addleshaw Goddard, DLA, Hammond Suddards, Pinsent Curtis and Walker Morris) have moved to new premises since 1990 and Eversheds

Figure 9.1 Leeds office take-up, 1991–2003

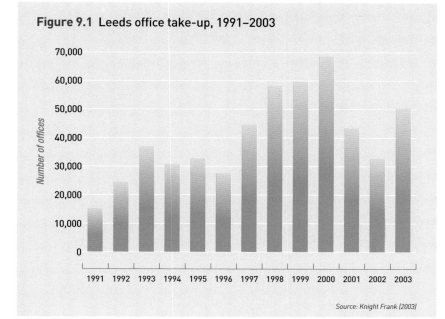

Source: Knight Frank (2003)

will move to Bridgewater Place when their current lease expires and the new property is completed. Other occupiers may be of local origin but now are partly or wholly owned by foreign-based companies (eg. Asda, Yorkshire Bank), whereas others are subsidiaries of international companies (e.g. Zurich Insurance, GE Capital). There are also representative or branch offices of national firms: Barclays Mortgage Centre; First Direct and HSBC, KPMG, Price Waterhouse Coopers). A special case is that of the Yorkshire-based Halifax Building Society, which merged with the Leeds Permanent Building Society in 1995. This enlarged institution then merged with Bank of Scotland in 2001 to create HBoS.

Table 9.3 gives evidence of the three main categories of business restructuring that have generated demand for additional/new office space. "When a firm expands it is frequently forced to move to find larger accommodation; in choosing a new address account will be taken of the organisation's pattern of internal and external linkages and ideally a location will be selected where the cost of maintaining these is at a minimum" (Goddard, 1967, p.282).

Although much publicity is given to large lettings, in recent times, only 5 per cent of applicants have required more than 5,000m^2 and the market is dominated by smaller deals. For instance, in the first

An office in or near City Square, next to the railway station, is still the first choice for many firms.

Table 9.3 Examples of office demand generated by three types of business and organisational trends

Date of news	Business re-organisation
Mergers/alliances to form larger organisations	
1995	Solicitors Eversheds associated with Hepworth & Chadwick from 1989; name changed to Eversheds in 1995. Offices in Birmingham, Cardiff, Cambridge, Manchester, Newcastle.
1996	Wilson Braithwaite Scholey (Leeds) merged with Learoyd & Longbottom (Harrogate) to form one of the region's largest independent firms of accountants.
1997	Accountants Arthur Andersen merged with Binder Hamlyn; firmed moved to 1 City Square in 1998.
1997	Accountants Price Waterhouse merged with Coopers Lybrand.
2000	Lawyers Hammond Suddards merged with a Birmingham firm to become Hammond Suddards Edge. Later merger with Hausmann et Associes, opening offices in Munich and Berlin.
2000	HLB Kidsons merged with Grant Thornton to create the 6th largest accountancy firm in UK.
2001	Pinsent Curtis merged with City of London firm Biddle to form Pinsent Curtis Biddle (eighteenth largest law firm in UK). Later changed to 'Pinsents'.
2001	BWD Securities bought London-based broking business Dennis Murphy Campbell.
2003	Cobbetts (northern firm) merged with Lee Crowder (Birmingham) to create one of the largest regional law firms.
2004	Lawyers Gordons merged with Nelson & Co.
Consolidation of local firms and those already in Leeds, previously spread over several buildings and requiring larger premises	
1987	Asda (supermarket): previously in eight locations; moved to Great Wilson Street.
1996	Allied Dunbar (financial advisor): previously in three core area offices; moved to Granary Wharf.
1999	Pinsent Curtis moved out of several offices in and around Park Square; moved to 1 Park Row.
2002	WS Atkins (engineers) moved from two central offices to Thorpe Park.
Establishing/strengthening of regional presence in Leeds, including closing of offices in some cities around the north	
1990	Accountants KPMG moved staff from City Square, and also from Huddersfield and Bradford, to new offices Neville Street.
1995	Loss adjustors Robins strengthened Leeds, Hull and Middlesbrough, and closed Sunderland, Grimsby and York.
1996	BWD Rensburg moved from Park Row and amalgamated Leeds, Bradford and Huddersfield offices at Granary Wharf.
2000	Capita Business Services opened regional offices East Quay.
2000	Daiwa Kasei (car components) opened a European sales office.
2001	Insurance, financial and business services provider, Ward Evans Group, moved corporate HQ from York to Leeds; already had call centre in West Riding House.
2001	Handelsbanken (Swedish) opened branch at 100 Wellington Street as part of expansion into UK.
2001	JDA (direct marketing) moved 55 staff from Bradford to Albion Court, Armley.
2001	Inland Revenue took space at White Rose Office Park as a regional HQ.
2002	Everywhere! Broadband relocated HQ from Harrogate to Leeds.
2003	Accountants Baker Tilly moved to Whitehall II as West Yorkshire HQ; 100 staff moved from Bradford.
2004	International architects Aedas took space at Brewery Wharf; relocated 80 architects from Leeds and Huddersfield offices.

six months of 2001, over 50 per cent of the space taken was in units of less than 1,000m² (JLL, 2001). But a high proportion of take-up is accounted for by a small number of large deals.

LCC Development Department handles many enquiries from firms needing office accommodation, although the majority of requirements go straight to commercial surveyors, who are much more numerous than they were. Most enquiries come from within the city itself and a relatively small proportion concern long distance relocation from the South East (Table 9.4).

The Lyons Review identified potential for relocation of government functions from the South East — up to 300,000m² of office space could be vacated. But the implications for the regional office markets are far from clear, not least because the 2004 budget included an announcement of up to 42,000 civil service job cuts by 2008 (CBRE, 2004). The Department of Transport is already known to be seeking space in Leeds.

9.5 New shape of the office market

The office quarter has expanded to accommodate the growing demand for space, and offices have changed from being predominantly cellular to being open-plan on larger floorplates.

Expansion beyond the traditional office core

From 1994 to 2004, Leeds City Council recorded £569 million of office property investment, of which 63 per cent is accounted for by city centre developments (Leeds Economy Briefing Note Issue 24). Almost all the rest was in the south-ern and western sectors, though Quarry House was developed on council-owned land to the east. The central Leeds office market now encompasses a much wider area than the traditional 'office quarter' as defined in the Unitary Development Plan (see Chapter 14). The original office area has proved inadequate in both quantity and type of stock: redevelopment opportunities are restricted by lease structures, listed buildings (Figure 14.5) and site configurations. In the 1970s and 1980s, new developments took place north of The Headrow. From the late 1980s, opportunities arose to the south and west as economic restructuring released former industrial, warehousing and railway sites. These locations allow construction of buildings with larger floorplates and higher car parking ratios. Figure 9.2 shows the expanded city centre office area and indicates the sequence of development of the 63 largest schemes (over 4,000m²). Postcode district LS1 accounts for around 55 per cent of the space

Table 9.4 Property enquiries to Leeds Development Department, 2002–2003

Year	From within Leeds		From the South East		All
	Number	Percentage	Number	Percentage	Number
2000	747	51	92	6.3	1,455
2001	753	59	57	4.4	1,284
2002	841	61	52	3.7	1,388
2003	927	62	54	3.6	1,494

Source: LDA

developed since 1987, but the map also shows a tendency for the most recent schemes (including those yet to be built) to be located further out from the traditional core.

The 42 completed developments shown in Table 9.5 account for only about half of the floorspace in major new schemes; the seven that are under construction and the further 14 that are 'in the pipeline' will add more than 300,000m².

Rapid change started in the late 1980s at the time of the Leeds Development Corporation (LDC) (see Chapter 14). Initially, KPMG and Asda were thought daring to venture south of the river, but soon others followed. Research during 2000 indicated that occupiers located south of the traditional core area were very satisfied with their location and their accommodation (Melville, 2000). These findings suggest that there is unlikely to be a reverse move by these businesses back into the traditional core, nor are they likely to move further out.

The traditional core is evolving in character as some secondary offices that did not match occupier needs have been converted to residential and leisure uses (see Chapter 4). With rents in central Leeds almost steady at under £20psf in the 1990s, and secondary space commanding only a half or a third of prime rents, developers favoured

Figure 9.2 Major city centre office developments (over 4,000m²), 1998–2004

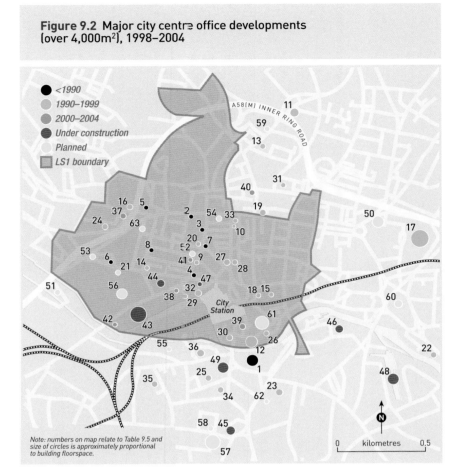

Note: numbers on map relate to Table 9.5 and size of circles is approximately proportional to building floorspace.

Table 9.5 Major city centre office schemes (4,000m² or larger), completed, under construction and planned, 1987–2004 *(continues on page 204)*

No.*	Property	Address	Postcode	Completion date/stage	Floorspace (m²)
1	Asda House	South Bank, Great Wilson Street	LS11	1987	18,580
2	Headrow Court	Headrow/Park Cross Street	LS1	1988	4,130
3	–	10–12 East Parade	LS1	1988	4,150
4	–	40–50 Wellington Street	LS1	1988	4,620
5	Westgate Point	Westgate	LS1	1988	5,000
6	–	Wellington Street/Lisbon Street	LS1	1988	7,618
7	Minerva House	King Street	LS1	1989	6,131
8	–	27 Park Place	LS1	1989	4,080
9	King's Court	King Street/Quebec Street	LS1	1990	4,370
10	Park Row House	19–20 Park Row	LS1	1991	4,180
11	Leeds Permanent House (Halifax)	1 Lovell Park Road	LS2	1991	19,497
12	Embankment development	Sovereign Street	LS1	1991	19,000
13	Brunswick Point	Merrion Street/Claypit Lane	LS1	1991	7,620
14	–	78 Wellington Street	LS1	1991	5,020
15	No. 1 Trevelyan Square and Ambler House	Trevelyan Square	LS1	1992	7,535
16	–	2 Park Lane	LS3	1992	5,950
17	Quarry House	Quarry Hill	LS2	1993	41,805
18	The Bourse	Boar Lane	LS1	1993	5,382
19	Headrow House	Headrow	LS1	1993	8,360
20	–	1 East Parade	LS1	1994	4,550
21	Tower Square	Wellington Street	LS1	1995	6,500
22	Rose Wharf (conversion)	East Street	LS9	1995	4,000
23	Leeds City Office Park Phase I	Meadow Lane	LS11	1995	7,432
24	Blenheim House	Duncombe Street	LS1	1995	7,430
25	Halifax Direct	Water Lane	LS11	1995	10,787
26	Sovereign House	Sovereign Street	LS1	1997	7,000
27	–	1 City Square	LS1	1997	10,400
28	–	1 Park Row	LS1	1997	7,430
29	Whitehall Phase I	Aire Street	LS1	1997	4,834
30	Privilege Insurance	Victoria Gate	LS1	1998	6,967
31	Fairfax House (refurbishment)	Merrion Street	LS2	1998	4,738
32	Princes Exchange	Prince's Square	LS1	1999	9,962
33	–	Victoria Square	LS1	1999	9,290
34	Victoria Place	Victoria Road	LS11	1999	10,666
35	Marshall Mills (conversion)	Marshall Street Holbeck	LS11	1999	9,290
36	*Multiple buildings*	Granary Wharf	LS11	1993–2000	9,950
37	–	1 Park Lane	LS3	2001	7,430
38	Whitehall Phase II	Aire Street	LS1	2002	7,426
39	–	1 Sovereign Street	LS1	2003	10,220
40	The Qube (conversion)	Albion Street/Great George Street	LS2	2003	5,250
41	Bank House (refurbishment)	27 King Street	LS1	2003	5,328
42	Riverside West	Whitehall Road	LS1	2004	4,650
43	Whitehall Riverside	Whitehall Road	LS1	U/C	53,480
44	West Central	Wellington Street	LS1	U/C	13,380
45	Velocity (formerly City Walk)	Sweet Street	LS11	U/C	8,955
46	Brewery Wharf	Bowman Lane	LS10	U/C	7,150
47	City Square House	City Square/Aire Street	LS1	U/C	12,350
48	Clarence Dock	Chadwick Street	LS10	U/C	18,580
49	Bridgewater Place	Victoria Road	LS11	U/C	20,790

Table 9.5 Major city centre office schemes (4,000m² or larger), completed, under construction and planned, 1987–2004 *(continued from page 203)*

No.*	Property	Address	Postcode	Completion date/stage	Floorspace (m²)
50	Quarry House	Quarry Hill	LS2	Planned	24,600
51	The Crescent	Gotts Road	LS12	Planned	4,830
52	City Point	29 King Street	LS1	Planned	6,085
53	Bridge House/Compton House	Wellington Street	LS1	Planned	5,574
54	Phoenix House/Fountain House	125–141 Headrow	LS1	Planned	9,290
55	Tower Works	Globe Road	LS11	Planned	4,650
56	Wellington Place Phase III	Wellington Place	LS1	Planned	21,367
57	City One	Meadow Lane	LS11	Planned	37,160
58	Lateral	Sweet Street	LS11	Planned	9,290
59	Hepworth House	Claypit Lane	LS1	Planned	7430
60	Howarth Timber site	East Street/Crown Point	LS9	Planned	n/a
61	Criterion Place	Sovereign Street	LS1	Planned	27,870
62	Leeds City Office Park Phase II	Meadow Lane	LS11	Planned	4,535
63	Brotherton House	Little Queen Street	LS1	Planned	6,500

* Corresponding number in Figure 9.2

Total 658.424m²

Park Row (east side) has been extensively redeveloped: some buildings remain as offices; others have been converted into apartments.

other types of development. Although 50 schemes up to 2003 involved conversion of office buildings, this is not as dramatic a loss of office stock as it might seem: 36 schemes are conversions of offices in LS1 but only 12 of these involve substantial buildings in the traditional office quarter. In total, around 75,000m² of office space has been lost to residential schemes, amounting to around 7 per cent of the total office stock. The most concentrated area of conversion is around Park Row, until the end of the twentieth century the prime office street in Leeds. Already, six buildings have been converted and two more are to follow.

New types of accommodation

Although the first serviced office accommodation was available in a converted warehouse in Sovereign Street from 1980, it was not until the late 1990s that a number of national operators opened premises in Leeds. By 2001, there were 16 serviced office buildings in Leeds, amounting to around 16,000m². Although comprising less than 2 per cent of the office stock, the availability of small units on flexible terms, with all additional services as optional extras, appeals to a variety of office occupiers such as IT firms, head-hunters and financial services companies setting up operations. It provides an easy way for new firms, especially those from outside the city, to establish a

Figure 9.3 Office park locations

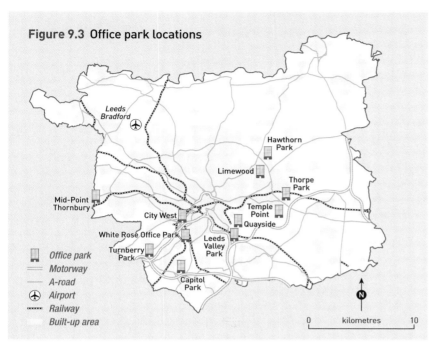

Office park
Motorway
A-road
Airport
Railway
Built-up area

0   kilometres   10

presence from which they can later move to more traditional accommodation. In May 2004, there were ten schemes in LS1 and another ten elsewhere in Leeds (www.office broker.co.uk) and occupancy levels remain high.

Office parks have added a relatively new dimension to the Leeds office market. The early examples of Lawnswood (now completed) and Arlington Business Centre (now White Rose Office Park) have been joined by 10 other sites (Table 9.6) totalling nearly 200 hectares. Most are adjacent to, or within easy reach of, a motorway (Figure 9.3) and there is still a large reserve of land yet to be developed: a total of around 400,000m² is built or planned. Since 2000, development activity has increased and in 2002, for the first time, the take-up of out-of-town space exceeded the city centre figure (LCC, December 2003).

There is concern that the city centre market might be undermined by occupiers choosing locations that are more accessible by road, have better parking facilities and large floor-plates. Nevertheless, while the rental differential is narrowing, it seems that the two types of location are complementary and

Business parks offer a different combination of locational advantages. Top, Arla Foods at Leeds Valley Park; bottom left, buildings under construction at Capitol Park; and bottom right, a building nearing completion at Thorpe Park.

Table 9.6 Major business park developments (actively under construction)

Business park	Location	Site size (ha)	Development size (m²)	Rent (m²)
Thorpe Park, LS15	North east Leeds — J46 M1	109	167,225	£16.50
Capitol Park, LS27/WF3	Century Way, M62 Tingley	22.25	46,451	£17.50
Leeds Valley Park, LS26	J44 M1 (junction with M621)	20.24	67,820	£17.50
City West, LS12	J1 M621	8	24,870	£17.50
White Rose Office Park, LS11	Southern Ring Road/A653	8	18,200	£17.00
Temple Point, LS26	South west of J46 M1	6.5	13,100	£16.50
Mid Point, Thornbury, BD3	Leeds/Bradford border	4.5	21,925	£14.50
Quayside, LS10	Thwaite Gate, Hunslet	4	18,950	£14.50
Turnberry Park, LS27	A650/M621	3	10,855	£16.50
Hawthorn Park, LS14	Whinmoor, north east Leeds	1.2	4,665	£16.00
Limewood Business Park, LS14	Whinmoor, north east Leeds	<1	2,787	£14.75
Total development size			*396,848*	

Figure 9.4 Thorpe Park Masterplan

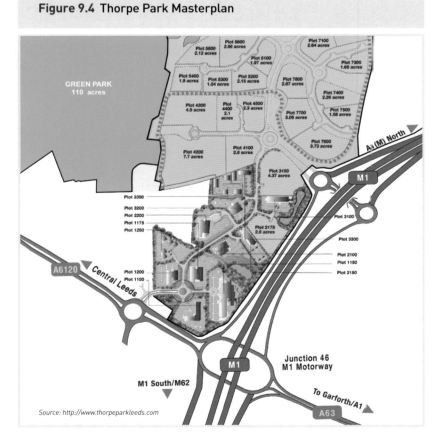

Source: http://www.thorpeparkleeds.com

that the overall Leeds economy is strengthened by the greater availability and range of property. So far, occupiers on office parks have not included professional firms such as lawyers and accountants. Instead, the construction and engineering sector is well-represented, there are hybrid light production/administration facilities and some public sector functions.

Thorpe Park (Figure 9.4) is by far the largest business park, strategically located adjacent to the M1. It includes a University of Leeds satellite known as the 'Knowledge Economy Campus', which aims to strengthen the park as a location for hi-tech businesses (http://www.thorpeparkleeds.com/university.asp).

As well as serviced offices, business park buildings and new developments in and adjacent to the city centre, there have been opportunities for reusing redundant buildings such as Marshall's Mill and Rose Wharf.

9.6 Main influences on the shape of the market

Property industry

In a constantly changing business climate, with new businesses being formed, and established ones growing and reinventing themselves, accommodation supply rarely matches occupiers' requirements. Property developers, investors, surveyors and other players in the industry supplying accommodation for producer services attempt to respond to the changing quantity and nature of demand and renew office accommodation where and when it is possible to acquire sites and raise funding.

The vast majority of office development in Leeds has been carried out by Leeds-based development companies or national companies with strong local representation.

Property developers in Leeds have usually been reluctant to build purely speculative developments, even in times of high demand, because of funding constraints or high perceived risk. A few institutions have directly funded office schemes (such as Norwich Union's 1 City Square, Nat West's 1 Park Row, and Hermes Pension Fund's Wellington Place), but in the case of property development companies, the preference is for pre-lets of at least 40 per cent of the space. Developers may enter into deals with potential occupiers of new buildings, agreeing to take responsibility for remaining leases, thus releasing occupiers to move and delivering to the developer a further investment/development opportunity.

The constant delivery of space to the market and steady take-up has meant that Leeds has avoided the 'boom and bust' of sharp rental growth and then decline or stagnation. Rents for top quality space touched £19psf in 1991 and then moved down to £16.75 by 1993 (Knight Frank, 2003). £20.00psf was reached in 1999 and Grade A offices can now cost £23–24psf.

The 'Leeds Look' (see Chapter 14) schemes of the 1980s and early 1990s gave way to a more international look in the late 1990s — such buildings as Princes Exchange and 15–16 Park Row. Mixed use schemes are now being devised and these will again change the character of the office district (see Chapter 14).

The scale of office developments and the occupier profile of Leeds has attracted investment institutions. Investment ownerships peaked in 1996 (91 properties worth £374 million); by 2002, there were 63 institutionally-owned

properties with a total value of £463 million (IPD, 2003). Knowledge that large lots can be sold on to investors helps to fuel the continuing progress of development and redevelopment in Leeds. The large mixed-use schemes in the pipeline, previously viewed with suspicion by investing institutions, are highly likely to find favour in the future.

Public sector

The public sector influence on the evolving office market mainly consists of the strategic planning framework, decisions on planning permissions (see Chapter 14) and the actions of bodies aiming to maximise inward investment and activity levels. National, regional and local public sector bodies also constitute a significant element of demand for office space, although no total is available.

It is not possible to calculate the effect of public sector effort in attracting occupiers to Leeds, but a keen awareness of the changing context of the city and the need to renew the built environment, infrastructure and services has been a significant element in Leeds' continuing ability to retain a position near the top of the urban hierarchy.

Public-private sector co-operation

Under the overall banner of the Leeds Initiative, the Leeds Financial Services Initiative (LFSI) was launched in November 1993 with the aim of fostering co-operation between financial companies in the city, promoting the city as a financial centre and representing the interests of the financial sector within the city. It demonstrated early success in addressing these aims (Tickel, 1996) and continues to perform as a successful public-private partnership. In 2002, there were over 120 members of the LFSI (LFSI, 2003), from an increasingly wide spectrum of business types. In terms of accommodation for the sector, dialogue between the private sector and LCC Development Department has facilitated a more proactive approach to bringing sites forward for development, ensuring modernisation of more of the office stock than might otherwise have been the case.

9.7 Future office demand and supply

The future shape of the office market in Leeds will reflect the way that the set of six factors listed at the outset evolve and

Completed in 1997, Whitehall Quay Phase I stood alone on the land to the south west of the traditional office core. Mixed use schemes by Paramount, KW Linfoot and Town Centre Securities have since claimed the whole river frontage.

interact. The FBS sector is likely to grow and therefore to require further accommodation. The preferred locations of development and the way that buildings are constructed and operated will depend particularly on the relative importance accorded to a city centre location and also to the thoroughness with which sustainable development concepts are worked into public and private sector thinking and action.

Clustering versus dispersal

A key area of uncertainty is the way that the costs and benefits of locating in the city centre will be weighed against those of other locations by different kinds of office users. Even in the 1960s, researchers studying the Leeds office market suggested that "much of the functional clustering may well, to some extent, be a relic of Victorian times rather than a present day necessity, although no-one would dispute the convenience of proximity for face-to-face contact" (Facey and Smith, 1968, p.106). It was the financial and professional service firms that had the greatest intensity of contacts across a range of customers/clients, other professional firms, competitors/similar firms, business suppliers, firms and organizations in London and other cities.

For some time, the rationale for clustering in city centres has been weakened. ICT innovations are gradually loosening the bonds of face-to-face contact, though not as rapidly or as thoroughly as had been predicted (see Chapter 10). Diseconomies associated with large urban areas (pollution, congestion, crime, fiscal instability) can outweigh the original agglomeration economies that pulled people and economic activities together (Gordon et al., 1998; Glaeser, 1998). In the USA, much office-based economic activity has located at freeway intersections and along beltways (Knox, 1993; Garreau, 1991). There are well-established 'edge cities' around Washington DC, Boston, New Jersey, Detroit, Atlanta, Phoenix and San Fransisco. Many businesses in the UK have at least partially decentralized (Cowan, 1969; Gillespie and Richardson, 2000; Schiller, 2001) and office-based activities now cluster on the edges of many towns, especially at key motorway junctions.

On the other hand, although predictions were made that computers, mobile telecommunications and the Internet would make us a placeless society (Huws et al., 1990), the irony is that these innovations in some ways make place more important than ever (Kotkin, 2000). While in theory people can

Bridgewater Place — a significant new landmark of the early twenty-first century, just to the south of Granary Wharf. The eight lower floors of the 30-storey tower are offices.

now work anywhere and be connected globally, top level knowledge workers still value a central location that is well-connected both physically and electronically. ICTs can substitute for some face-to-face contact but their role is more to increase efficiency and turn-around times. People still place a value on meeting business associates and on being 'in the swim of things'. While their virtual reach is more extended, their work is still grounded in hubs of activity and connectivity, of which Leeds is an appealing one. Central city areas hold a comparative advantage for labour-intensive activities and peripheral locations for capital-intensive ones. In many service industries, time replaces weight as a force for agglomeration. Complex

service products require multiple inputs and it is more efficient to outsource to conveniently located providers (Sassen, 1995).

Although it is unclear how these centrifugal and centripetal forces will balance in terms of the relative locational demands by different types of organisation, it seems likely that less contact-dependent activities will locate at settlement edges rather than centres but that there will still be significant numbers of particular types of office workers in city centre accommodation, especially in cities with at least a regional role. Edge cities in the American style will simply not be widely feasible in the more constricted landscape of Britain, especially since changes in planning regulations during the 1990s (Gibb *et al.*, 2001).

property sector. If followed, office developments should integrate economic, social and environmental considerations. This has implications for location in relation to transport networks, for car parking provision, for landscaping and for other aspects of the relationship of the development to the natural, built and social environment. At the level of individual buildings, adherence to these relatively new principles should mean delivery of "a new form of office space which provides a flexible, healthy workplace, which takes into account the desires of its inhabitants and their concern for wider environmental issues, and which avoids ostentatious statements which evoke a culture of excess, is being increasingly demanded" (Guy, 2002, p. 263).

So far in Leeds, there have been few examples of buildings deliberately designed according to sustainable development criteria, apart from the Leeds City Office Park building,

It is also likely that teleworking, video-conferencing and other innovations will eventually fulfil some of the potential which has long been (prematurely) predicted for reducing the need for all high level knowledge workers to commute daily to a fixed workstation at an employer's office. But again, the technological possibilities and changing patterns of work and travel will not entirely erase the significance of real places which have a concentration of people, activities and facilities.

Sustainable development

New concerns have emerged which are influencing urban development and regeneration as well as office design. The principles of sustainable development (see Chapter 13) are now supposed to be guiding principles of all public sector decision making and are increasingly being incorporated into private sector strategy and actions, including those of the

eventually let to BT Cellnet. It was designed to be energy-efficient, using natural lighting and ventilation instead of relying on artificial light and internal atmosphere controls. The building did not immediately find a tenant — an indication that occupiers are still not sufficiently interested in or motivated towards giving priority to the environmental performance of buildings.

Leeds Valley Park offers a current example of design according to sustainable development best practice, with a high rating achieved on the Building Research Establishment Environmental Assessment Method (BREEAM). However, there is still a long way to go to ensure that the office stock and its associated activities adhere closely to principles of sustainable development. Changes in the national legislative framework are needed to stimulate better practice in the construction and running of new and refurbished buildings (Sustainable Buildings Task Group, 2004).

The future of the FBS sector

"The single most important issue for the future in terms of Leeds' relationship with its broader region is how to facilitate the further development of the Leeds business services cluster, for this is the main motor of economic dynamism which the region possesses" (CURDS, 1999). Cambridge Econometrics' forecast that 28,000 additional jobs will be generated in FBS between 2004 and 2014, with professional services leading the way. The sector will account for nearly all the total net employment growth in Leeds (LCC, April 2004). A study for LFSI and Yorkshire Forward (Business Strategies/Experian, 2004) reinforces the view that the dynamic FBS sector will be the main driver of the local economy, expanding more rapidly in Leeds than in other regional cities.

LFSI and Leeds Development Department will continue to work to retain the organisations that are currently located in Leeds, and to maximise the attractions of the working and living environment such that other businesses will consider Leeds to be an appealing option. Nurturing home-grown businesses, facilitating business start-ups and enabling a rational city-regional spread of activity is considered to be a sounder approach than trying to attract large occupiers from other locations.

A note of warning must be sounded about one element of the FBS sector: call centre jobs are not necessarily a secure element of the market. Already many have been relocated from the UK, especially to India, and it is expected that up to 100,000 more jobs will be lost to offshore locations by 2008 (LCC, June 2003). Leeds will not be immune to this trend: less skilled call centre work is likely to move to the periphery both within the city region and more widely across the world, and Leeds, as the core city of its region, is likely to focus on retaining higher value-added types of work rather than fighting to keep lower order jobs (Henderson, 2003).

9.8 Conclusions

As in other cities, providers of commercial space in Leeds will have to be increasingly responsive to the changing and more demanding needs of occupiers since "with the emergence of an increasingly complex system of global capital, and with manufacturing industry reorganised on a world-wide scale, the

spatial-temporal context of commercial activity is undergoing rapid transformations. Flexibility provides the defining logic of these economic shifts. International corporations are having to become increasingly sensitive to the fast-changing demands of world markets in the accelerated, more competitive environment created by the internationalisation of trade and services. As the commercial strategies of businesses are re-ordered, so their occupational requirements will be similarly remodelled. This will result in a fast-changing demand profile for commercial property. Space requirements are likely to ebb and flow, with the desired floorspace, specification and location of new buildings altering dramatically" (Guy and Harris, 1997, p.126). Individual localities will be increasingly vulnerable to decisions made in more distant boardrooms.

In Leeds, redevelopments and refurbishments of stock in the expanded city centre will continue. Further large developments will be added to the south west and south of the old office quarter, and eventually, some of these buildings will in turn be redeveloped to meet future occupier requirements for space configuration and building services. Developments on the various office parks near motorway junctions will be heavily influenced by the opportunities for pre-letting, with speculative office starts being restricted to times of acute supply shortage. At the other end of the spectrum, the serviced office sector will evolve, providing flexible accommodation for various new, mobile and agile businesses, many of whom will have few permanent, full-time employees. Individual buildings may specialise in providing appropriate space for particular sub-sectors, creating miniature clusters.

Elsewhere, there will be a growing range of hybrid space and mixed developments. Apartments and houses will have space and facilities to allow home-working. There will be residential components of both city centre and more peripheral office developments. The separation of work and non-work time and space will blur.

Much more detailed work is needed to ascertain how the office space in the city centre is actually used (as was done by Sydney City Council, 1997) and how closely the supply fits the demand. A related research area has already been identified (Llewelyn-Davies et al., 2002): how will the different locational factors be weighed up by occupiers in making future office location decisions and how will this influence where they locate? Will the city centre continue to command a premium, reflecting continuing pressure of demand from service sector firms?

Notes

1   Producer services are those that are sold to other businesses rather than to the general public. They consist of financial, legal and general management matters, innovation, development design, administration, personnel, production technology, maintenance, transport, communications, wholesale distribution, advertising, cleaning services for firms, security and storage. Central components of the producer services category are a range of industries with mixed business and consumer markets. They are insurance, banking, financial services, real estate, legal services, accounting and professional associations (Sassen, 1995, p. 56).

2   See for example: Futurespace, Building 12.1.01 which discusses the implications of the cordless workstation: http://www.barbourexpert.com/archive/archiveStory.asp?storyCode=1002857

3   This label encompasses technology, media and telecommunications; web support services and web-based advertising and publishing; web-based financial services; internet service providers and others involved in selling/developing internet infrastructures; e-retailers.

References

Barkham, R. (2002) Market research for office real estate, in Guy, S. and Henneberry, J. (eds) *Development and Developers: Perspectives on Property,* Blackwell Science, Oxford, pp. 53–72.

Bateman, M. (1986) Leeds: a study in regional supremacy, in Gordon, G. (ed) *Regional Cities in the UK 1890-1980,* Harper and Row, London, pp. 99–115.

Beresford, M.W. and Unsworth, R. (forthcoming) Locating the early service sector of Leeds: the origins of an office district, *Journal of Historical Geography.*

Black, I.S. (2000) Spaces of capital: bank office buildings in the City of London 1830–1870, *Journal of Historical Geography,* 26(3): 351–375.

Business Strategies/Experian (2004) *The Leeds Financial and Business Services Sector,* report for LFSI and Yorkshire Forward, Leeds?

CB Richard Ellis (CBRE) (2004) *The Lyons Review and the Regional Office Markets,* May 2004 http://www.cbre-emea-research.com/publications/Lyons_Regional_Brief_May_04.pdf

Centre for Pervasive Computing (2003) *New Ways of Working — NWOW,* http://www.pervasive.dk/resAreas/NWOW/NWOW_summary.htm

Centre for Urban and Regional Development Studies (CURDS) (1999) *The Economic Links between Leeds and the Yorkshire and Humber Region, Final Report,* unpublished report commissioned by Leeds City Council.

Chesterton (2004) *City Centre Office Markets,* Chesterton, London.

Corporation of London Department of Planning and Transport (2001) *Office Stock in the City of London,* November, http://www.cityoflondon.gov.uk/NR/rdonlyres/C1D29546-0495-4F27-AD56-F62FC3E1F6F1/0/offstock_complete.pdf

Cowan, P. (1969) *The Office: A Facet of Urban Growth,* Heinemann, London.

Facey, M.V., and Smith, G.B. (1968) *Offices in a Regional Centre: A Study of Office Location in Leeds,* Research Paper no.2, Location of Offices Bureau, London.

Financial Times (1995) *Survey: Leeds and the North,* 20 June.

Garreau, J. (1991) *Edge City: Life on the New Frontier,* Doubleday, New York.

Gibb, K., Lever, W. and Kasparova, D. (2001) *The Future of UK Cities: Measurement and Interpretation,* RICS Foundation Report Series, December.

Gillespie, A. and Richardson, R. (2000) Teleworking and the city: myths of workplace transcendence and travel reduction, in Wheeler, J., Aoyama, Y. and Warf, B. (eds) *Cities in the Telecommunications Age: The Fracturing of Geographies,* Routledge, London, pp. 228–245.

Glaeser, E.L. (1998) Are cities dying?, *Journal of Economic Perspectives,* 12(2): 139–160.

Goddard, J.B. (1967) Changing office location patterns within central London, *Urban Studies,* 4(3): 276–285.

Gordon, P., Richardson, H.W. and Yu, G. (1998) Metropolitan and non-metropolitan employment trends in the US: recent evidence and implications, *Urban Studies,* 35(7): 1037–1057.

Guy, S. (2002) Developing interests: environmental innovation and the social organisation of the property business, in Guy, S. and Henneberry, J. (eds) *Development and Developers: Perspectives on Property,* Blackwell Science, Oxford, pp. 247–266.

Guy, S. and Harris R. (1997) Property in a global-risk society: towards marketing research in the office sector, *Urban Studies,* 34(1): 125–140.

Henderson, R. (2003), India answers the call: globalisation and the Indian call centre challenge to financial services, *Yorkshire Post,* 14 October.

Huws, U., Korte, W.B. and Robinson, S. (1990) *Telework: Towards the Elusive Office,* John Wiley and Sons, Chichester.

Investment Property Databank (IPD) (2003) *Key Centres Report 2003,* IPD, London.

Jones Lang LaSalle (JLL) (2001) *Leeds in the New Economy,* UK Regional Research Report, March.

Knight Frank (2003) *Leeds Office Market Overview,* unpublished report.

Knox, P. (1993) *The Restless Urban Landscape,* Prentice-Hall, Englewood Cliffs, New Jersey.

Kotkin, J. (2000) *The New Geography: How the Digital Revolution is Reshaping the American Landscape,* Random House, New York.

Leeds City Council (LCC) (from mid-1990s) *Leeds Economy Bulletins,* LCC, Leeds.

Leeds City Council (LCC) (2003a) *Leeds Economy Handbook,* LCC, Leeds.

Leeds City Council (LCC) (2003b) *Leeds — The e-location for 2003,* LCC, Leeds.

Leeds City Council (LCC) (2003c) *Local Economic Development Strategy: 2002 Review,* LCC, Leeds.

Leeds Financial Services Initiative (LFSI)/Leeds Metropolitan University (2001) *Annual Survey of the Leeds Financial Services Industry,* January 2001.

Leeds Financial Service Initiative (LFSI) (2003) *Financial Services see Europe as Key Priority for Leeds,* news release, April.

Llewelyn-Davies, Steer Davies Gleave, Jones Lang LaSalle and University of Leeds (2002) *Leeds and Environs Spatial Study,* final scoping report for Yorkshire and Humber Assembly, November.

Martinelli, F. (1991) Producer services' location and regional development, in Daniels, P.W. and Moulaert, F. (eds) *The Changing Geography of Advanced Producer Services: Theoretical and Empirical Perspectives,* Belhaven Press, London, pp. 70–90.

Melville, H. (2000) *Is there a continuing rationale for office development in Leeds?,* unpublished undergraduate dissertation, School of Geography, University of Leeds, Leeds.

mtl Consultants (2000) *Anticipation of Change: Investigating Future Challenges facing Key Service Sectors in Leeds,* report on behalf of Leeds TEC Ltd, Leeds Development Agency and The Leeds Initiative, Leeds.

Sassen, S. (1995) Urban impacts of economic globalisation, in Brotchie, J., Batty, M., Blakely, E., Hall, P. and Newton, P. (eds) *Cities in Competition: Productive and Sustainable Cities for the 21st Century,* Longman, Australia, pp. 36–57.

Schiller, R. (2001) *The Dynamics of Property Location,* Spon Press, London.

Sustainable Buildings Task Group (2004) *Better Buildings — Better Lives,* Report to ODPM, Defra and DTI, www.dti.gov.uk/construction/sustain/EA_Sustainable_Report_41564_2.pdf

Swift Research (2001) *Leeds City Centre Audit Public Perceptions Market Research Survey: Senior Business People Depth Interviews Summary Report,* prepared for Leeds Development Agency.

Sykes, K. (2003) *Leeds: a provincial financial and legal centre,* unpublished BSc Dissertation, University of Loughborough Department of Geography, Loughborough.

Sydney City Council (1997) *Floorspace and Employment Survey,* unpublished data.

The Economist (1993) *Leeds: pinstripe city,* 15/5/93.

Tickell, A. (1996) Taking the initiative: the Leeds financial centre, in Haughton, G. and Williams, C. (eds) *Corporate City? Partnership, Participation and Partition in Urban Development in Leeds,* Ashgate, Aldershot, pp. 103–118.

10

Providing for Mobility:
Transport Planning Under Pressure

DAVE MILNE, GUENTER EMBERGER, JOHN STILLWELL & RACHAEL UNSWORTH

II ... the range and quality of national and international transport links are often given as principal factors contributing to Leeds' economic success. II

10.1 Introduction

Demand for motorised mobility rose steeply during the twentieth century and shows no signs of abating, despite the advent of technology that allows substitutes for face-to-face contact. Mobile phones, email, the internet and video links have all begun to act as complements to physical travel but have not so far resulted in reduced average person-kilometres (Graham, 1998). Regardless of the rise of the so-called 'weightless economy' (selling services such as banking and insurance and non-material items such as phone ring tones and music), continuing economic growth means that there is still increasing demand for movement of people and physical materials in geographical space, using the transport infrastructure that has evolved over time.

This chapter reviews the extent and structure of transport networks in Leeds and examines the relative importance of the different transport media. The supply of infrastructure and service provision that we see today is both a response to demand in the past and an anticipation of demand in the future. With this in mind, we consider trends in travel behaviour, focusing in particular in Section 10.3 on the journey to work and examining geographical variations in the origins of commuting flows by mode of transport.

Transport policy makers have to cope with the political, financial and practical difficulties of meeting the demand for fast, efficient travel in circumstances where there is pressure not to devalue the urban landscape by taking ever more land for infrastructure, and where there is an urgent need to minimise damage to the natural environment and to health. In addition, transport has a critical role to play in wider social planning, facilitating the economic regeneration of run-down areas and helping to improve opportunities for members of the community who may have restricted access to goods and services. In Section 10.4, we look at recent and potential future policy interventions and commercial innovations that show how planning is responding to the increasingly complex challenges of achieving this wider, in some cases conflicting, set of objectives. As a prosperous city with large numbers of commuters, but also extensive areas that are in need of regeneration, Leeds exemplifies very clearly the tensions and dilemmas involved.

Computer-based models are commonly used to support transport decision making. In Section 10.5, selected examples of these tools are presented to show how they are being applied to evaluate various transport policy options in Leeds, including the adoption of a road pricing cordon to deter drivers from entering the city centre, although it is important to note that Leeds City Council has no proposals to introduce such a cordon at present. As policy objectives have become more complex, it has become necessary to adopt an interdisciplinary approach, taking on board ideas from beyond the traditional economics and engineering-based transport disciplines, such as geography, civic design and environmental management. Thus, existing transport modelling tools are being expanded to incorporate this broader knowledge base. We illustrate progress in this respect through an application of the MARS suite of models that attempt to link transport with land-use changes.

10.2 Development of the transport network

Leeds' location at a major crossing point of the River Aire became a regular trading place for wool producers and merchants from the twelfth century and provided the basis for a growing settlement. The expansion of that trade over the centuries made Leeds an increasingly significant nodal point. Growing prosperity both required and enabled investment to enhance efficiency in transporting materials and goods, as demonstrated by improvements to the navigability of the River Aire (Aire-Calder navigation completed 1699), the investment in turnpike roads (from the mid-seventeenth through to the late nineteenth centuries) and the construction of the Leeds-Liverpool canal (completed in 1816) (Burt and Grady, 2002). In turn, the improvements in transport efficiency significantly enhanced the pace of growth as the industrial age began (Harvey, 1989). Leeds was at the forefront of rail development (the Middleton Colliery Railway being the first line to be established by Act of Parliament

Figure 10.1 The primary transport network

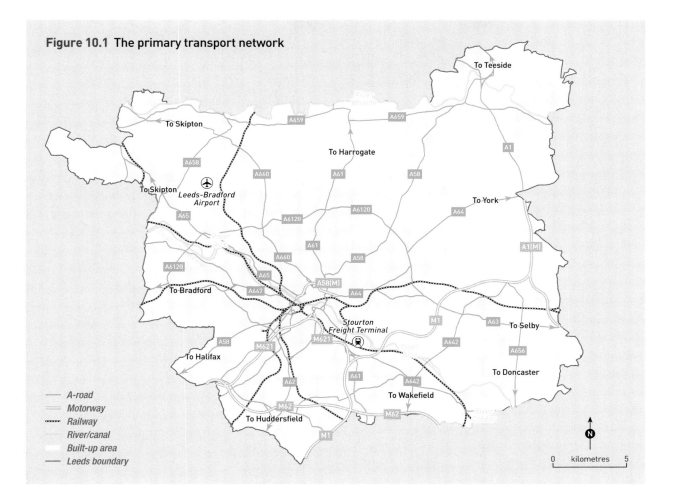

in 1758 and the first to operate locomotives commercially from 1812) and was already well connected into the railway network by the 1850s, with much land in the city given over to railway lines, goods facilities and stations.

Internal transport was revolutionised in the late nineteenth century by the advent of electric trams (1891), allowing urban growth to spread to areas previously inaccessible from the centre. However, despite having one of the most advanced tram networks in Europe in the 1930s, policy favoured the greater comfort and flexibility of newer vehicles powered by the internal combustion engine after World War II and trams were completely superseded by road buses in 1959 (Dickinson, 1967).

Throughout the twentieth century, as car ownership and use grew, there was huge national and local investment in roads and related infrastructure. The completion of the M1 in

the early 1960s made Leeds one of the first UK cities to be connected into the motorway network and, along with the addition of the M62, gave rise to the proud slogan 'Motorway city of the 1970s'. Internally, existing roads were remodelled and widened and the outer and inner ring roads were added (in the 1930s and 1960s, respectively). During this period, Leeds was one of the case study cities presented in the Buchanan Report: 'Traffic in towns'. The aim of the Buchanan Working Group was to study the long term development of roads and traffic in urban areas and their influence on the urban environment. The report presented alternative approaches for dealing with the steep expected increase in demand for access and parking in ways that would also take environmental quality into account (Buchanan, 1963). The problem, it was clear, could only be tackled within an overall strategy for urban design which might well have very radical implications for the

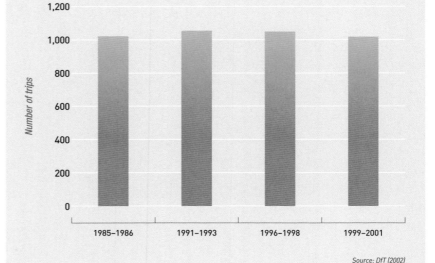

Figure 10.2 Number of trips per person and year, national trends, 1985–2001

Source: DfT (2002)

reconfiguration of the built environment (Tetlow and Goss, 1968). Although the city did not implement all the suggestions contained in Buchanan, the ideas were influential in later policy development (Judge and Hick, 1996).

Leeds-Bradford International Airport started life as Yeadon Aerodrome in the 1930s and began offering commercial flights within the UK as early as 1935. However, it was in the post-war period that civil aviation really took off, with the first international flights in 1955, daily services to London and Dublin in 1960 and the first chartered holiday flights, to the Iberian Peninsula, in 1976. Runway and terminal facilities have been expanded and improved continuously during the airport's existence and have facilitated the growth of Leeds-Bradford to become a significant regional access point to the international air network, particularly since the extension of the main runway to accommodate Jumbo jets from 1984 (LBIA website, 2004). However, the range of destinations accessible directly from Leeds-Bradford remains rather limited and its potential for growth is always likely to be constrained by limitations of space, a reputation for being regularly fog-bound at certain times of year and the proximity of a major international airport in Manchester with a direct rail link to the centre of Leeds. Its role within Yorkshire may also change in future with the planned creation of a new international airport at the former Finningley RAF base near Doncaster.

Figure 10.3 Modal split in national travel behaviour, 1985–2001

Source: DfT (2002)

Today, the range and quality of national and international transport links are often given as principal factors contributing towards Leeds' economic success and providing connections to several holiday destinations (for example,

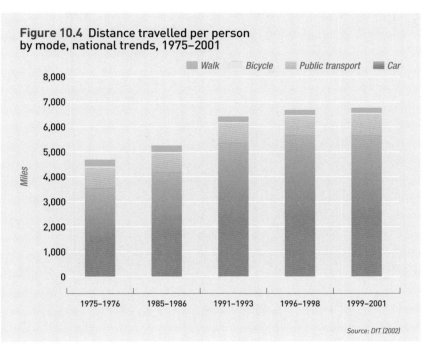

Figure 10.4 Distance travelled per person by mode, national trends, 1975–2001

Legend: ■ Walk   Bicycle   Public transport   ■ Car

Y-axis: Miles (0 to 8,000)

X-axis categories: 1975–1976, 1985–1986, 1991–1993, 1996–1998, 1999–2001

Source: DfT (2002)

www.uksfavouritecity.com). Figure 10.1 presents the primary land transport network within the Leeds District, showing that rail and motorway links tend to be concentrated to the south of the city, away from the main residential areas to the north. This means that rail plays a relatively minor role in travel within the district and that a large proportion of drivers wanting to access the motorway network need to travel across the city or through the centre to do so.

10.3 Trends and patterns in personal travel

General trends

Four interesting trends are evident nationally. First, in terms of daily behaviour, time spent travelling has not changed significantly in Great Britain during the last two decades — on average people spend around one hour per day in transit. Second, according to the National Travel Survey in 2002 (www.transtat.dft.gov.uk), the number of trips per person per year (Figure 10.2) has stayed nearly constant over the same period, suggesting that total travel demand in future may change as a function of demographic change (i.e. related to the size and spatial distribution of the population).

Third, the share of trips made by car has continued to increase (Figure 10.3). In addition to higher incomes and related higher vehicle ownership rates (and maybe also a perceived deterioration of quality and increase of cost of public transport), this is due to the increasing volume of road infrastructure and changing patterns of land use, including the decentralisation of activities such as shopping centres, leisure complexes and housing. The survey statistics indicate the extent to which healthy and environmentally friendly walking trips have been replaced by private car trips since the mid-1980s.

Fourth, annual distance travelled per person has also increased continuously over time (Figure 10.4), a trend that is directly related to the increasing share of private car use. Although more mileage may suggest that individuals are fulfilling their own personal desires and realising more opportunities, this increase is associated with detrimental effects of congestion, environmental degradation and, for non-car users, inequality of access.

Commuting to work in Leeds

The most important travel activity for most residents of Leeds is the journey to work. The 2001 Census records 322,830 individuals who live within the district boundary aged 16–74 either travelling to work or working at home. There are, additionally, significant flows between Leeds and its adjacent districts: the 1991 Census indicated that almost 60,000 people commuted in from Harrogate, Selby, Bradford, Calderdale, Kirklees and Wakefield (Stillwell and Duke-Williams, 2003). Geographical variations in commuting flows for this wider catchment area by social class and gender in 1991 have been examined by Harland (2001). Here, we focus on the mode of transport. As in other big cities, the majority of commuters resident in Leeds in 2001 travelled by car (60 per cent) either as drivers or passengers (Figure 10.5). Relatively small

proportions of commuters travelled by bus or coach (17 per cent) or on foot (11 per cent) and only 1.5 per cent travelled by train. Approximately 7.5 per cent of residents worked mainly at or from home in 2001.

There are distinct geographies of car ownership across Leeds that have been discussed in Chapter 6. Households that do not have a car tend to be concentrated in the inner parts of the city because they do not have sufficient income to own a vehicle, because public transport is adequate or because facilities are within walking and cycling distance. The percentage of households who own just one car, on the other hand, tends to be fairly uniform across the city, while the proportion who own two or more vehicles is lowest in the inner city areas and

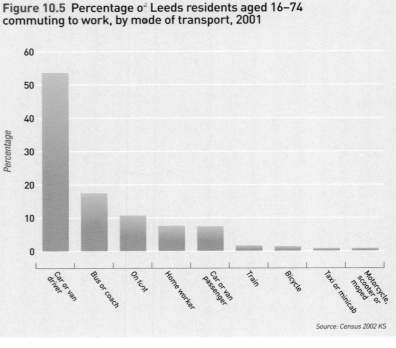

Figure 10.5 Percentage of Leeds residents aged 16–74 commuting to work, by mode of transport, 2001

Source: Census 2002 KS

highest in the outer suburbs, particularly in the north and north east of the district. In these areas, the locations of facilities and services are more dispersed and make the car a necessity for accomplishing the activities of daily living. It is not surprising

Left, the A1-M1 link provides better intra- and inter-regional connections. Right, the outer ring road reduces the amount of through traffic in the city centre but it is not continuous dual carriageway and has been pieced together over 70 years. There are plans for improvement but no definite schedule for implementation.

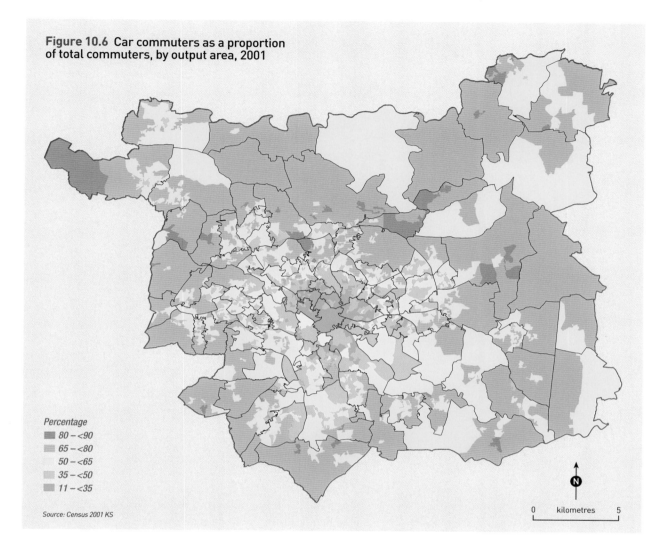

Figure 10.6 Car commuters as a proportion of total commuters, by output area, 2001

Percentage
- 80 – <90
- 65 – <80
- 50 – <65
- 35 – <50
- 11 – <35

N

0   kilometres   5

Source: Census 2001 KS

that the geographical pattern of travel to work at output area level, either as a car driver or passenger (Figure 10.6), reflects that pattern of car ownership. The map shows car drivers and passengers as a percentage of all commuters leaving from each output area, with higher percentages evident in the outer suburban and rural areas. Community area boundaries have been overlaid to provide some orientation. This pattern of trip origins generates a large number of journeys, particularly at morning and evening peak times.

Figure 10.7 shows an output of the SATURN model (Van Vliet, 1982) that estimates traffic flows and delays within the Leeds network for different periods of the day. The plot shows current morning peak travel conditions across the developed urban area, with the width of the green bands, by direction, correspond-

The bus and taxi interchange outside Leeds railway station was opened in 2004, occupying land used previously as a car park.

Source: SATURN

ing to the volume of traffic flow in passenger car equivalent units (PCUs), which allow different types of vehicles to be combined into a single flow measure. The highest flows are those travelling towards the city centre on the M1 from the south east (5,000–7,000 PCUs per hour, depending on section), the M621 from the south west (3,500–4,000 PCUs per hour) and those circulating around the centre on the inner ring road (2,000–4,000 PCUs per hour). Flows on the major radials to the north of the city increase closer to the centre (typically peaking at 1,500–2,500 PCUs per hour just outside the inner ring road). The other main traffic carrier is the orbital outer ring road (800–2,000 PCUs per hour), which caters for both cross-city movements and regional through traffic. The function of the model and examples of its application are considered later in the chapter.

The car is, of course, not the only means of travel to work. In 2001, around 56,000 Leeds residents travelled to work by bus or coach each day and 5,000 travelled by train. The percentages of commuters using each of these modes of transport are mapped by output area in Figure 10.8. Commuting by

bus tends to be high where car commuting is low and, as with the rail network, the bus network is focused on the city centre with much less provision of cross-suburban orbital services. Trains are really only an important mode of travel for those living in locations served by a railway station. The inequality in rail service provision across Leeds is evident from the map of the percentage of total commuters that use the train in Figure 10.8b.

Figure 10.8 (a) Bus and (b) train commuters as a percentage of total commuters, by output area, 2001

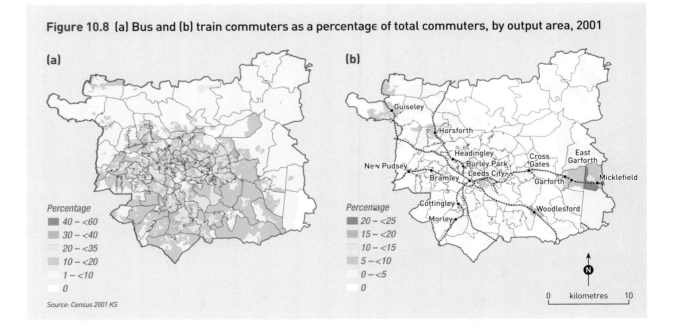

(a)

Percentage
■ 40 – <60
■ 30 – <40
  20 – <35
  10 – <20
  1 – <10
  0

Source: Census 2001 KS

(b)

Percentage
■ 20 – <25
■ 15 – <20
  10 – <15
  5 – <10
  0 – <5
  0

Guiseley
Horsforth
Headingley
New Pudsey
Burley Park
Bramley
Leeds City
Cross Gates
East Garforth
Garforth
Micklefield
Cottingley
Morley
Woodlesford

N

0   kilometres   10

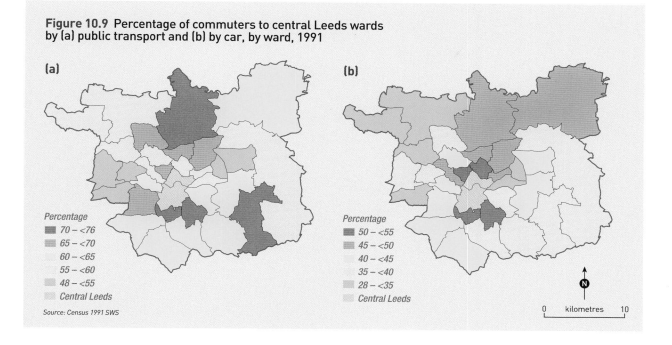

Figure 10.9 Percentage of commuters to central Leeds wards by (a) public transport and (b) by car, by ward, 1991

(a)

Percentage
- 70 – <76
- 65 – <70
- 60 – <65
- 55 – <60
- 48 – <55
- Central Leeds

Source: Census 1991 SWS

(b)

Percentage
- 50 – <55
- 45 – <50
- 40 – <45
- 35 – <40
- 28 – <35
- Central Leeds

For many suburban commuters, the decision whether to travel by public transport or by car is dependent on factors such as car parking provision at the workplace destination as well as the cost and quality of the public transport that is available. Like most UK cities, approximately half of all car parking spaces in the city centre are privately owned non-residential, in the hands of the business community and typically provided free or at low cost to employees (Ghali *et al.*, 2000). A high proportion of public transport commuters are those who work in the city centre. Data on flows by ward of origin and destination are not yet available for 2001 but equivalent data for 1991 can be used to illustrate this. The maps in Figure 10.9 show, for car and public transport respectively, the flows from each ward to central Leeds (defined as City and Holbeck and University wards in this instance) expressed as a percentage of total flows by mode out of each ward to central Leeds. In total, there were almost 173,000 commuting flows between wards in Leeds in 1991, of which 106,000 travelled by car and 50,000 by public transport (bus and train). Almost 41 per cent of inter-ward car commuters made journeys to the two central wards, whereas 61 per cent of public transport journeys terminated in City and Holbeck and University wards. In the case of public transport, there are some wards where almost three quarters of all commuters leaving the ward work in the

city centre, although in Pudsey and Bramley in the west and in Whinmoor and Seacroft in the east the percentage falls to below 55 per cent. Bradford is likely to be an important commuting destination for residents in west Leeds, be they public transport or car users. In fact the percentage using cars

After twice being rebuilt — in 1937 and 1967 — Leeds City Station has undergone a £245 million modernisation that will accommodate more and faster trains.

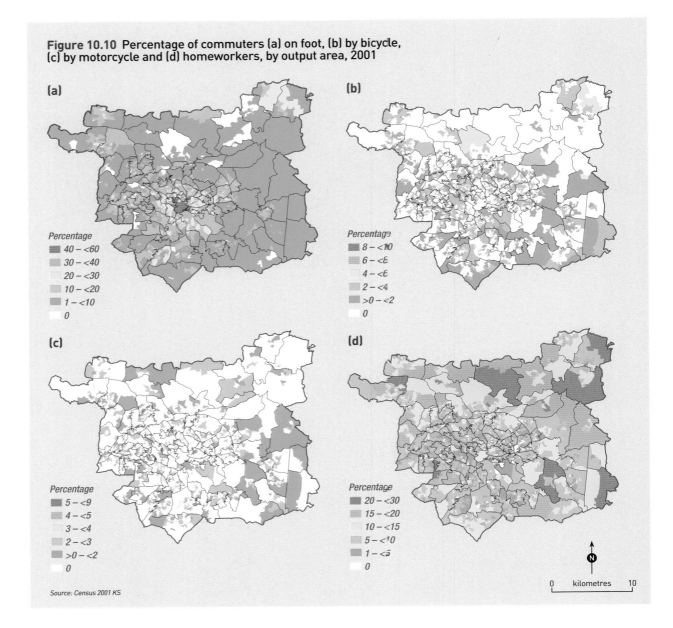

Figure 10.10 Percentage of commuters (a) on foot, (b) by bicycle, (c) by motorcycle and (d) homeworkers, by output area, 2001

(a)

Percentage
- 40 – <60
- 30 – <40
- 20 – <30
- 10 – <20
- 1 – <10
- 0

(b)

Percentage
- 8 – <10
- 6 – <8
- 4 – <6
- 2 – <4
- >0 – <2
- 0

(c)

Percentage
- 5 – <9
- 4 – <5
- 3 – <4
- 2 – <3
- >0 – <2
- 0

(d)

Percentage
- 20 – <30
- 15 – <20
- 10 – <15
- 5 – <10
- 1 – <5
- 0

0   kilometres   10

Source: Census 2001 KS

falls to 28 per cent in Aireborough, although the existence of a railway station in Guiseley is also likely to be a significant factor affecting mode choice (as is evident in Figure 10.8).

Whilst private car and public transport are the major modes of travel to work, some people choose to commute either on foot, bicycle or motorbike and others avoid commuting by working at or from home. Figure 10.10 illustrates the spatial patterns of the percentages of total commuters in each of these categories by output area in 2001. The incidence of those who cycle to work or who use a motorbike or scooter is

sporadic, whereas journeys on foot are most concentrated in the city centre. A survey by Fox and Unsworth (2003) showed that 90 per cent of city centre residents who work within postal district LS1 and 78 per cent of those working in LS2 walk to work. A third of respondents used cars to get to work (mostly to workplaces beyond the city), but car ownership is well below national levels: only 43 per cent of the sample owned at least one car. Nearly half the survey sample lived in an apartment without an associated parking space — a feature that can add between £15,000 and £20,000 to the price of a city centre apartment.

There are other ways of avoiding commuting journeys. Homeworking, or 'telework' is an increasingly widespread phenomenon: at least 7.4 per cent of the UK workforce works from home at least one day a week and the numbers have grown at about 13 per cent a year since 1997 (ONS, 2002). The geographical distribution in Leeds suggests that it is most common in the outer suburbs of the north and east. There are pockets in the inner suburbs where home-working is not a feature. The census data on homeworking, as with the other data on commuting by mode, provide only a snapshot at the time of the Census (April 2001) and this issue raises questions about the seasonality of commuting behaviour that require further research.

10.4 Transport policy

Transport policy is concerned with providing for the present and future transport needs of society. As in other major UK cities, transport policy in Leeds is the responsibility of the locally elected City Council and covers the construction, maintenance and management of infrastructure for drivers, cyclists and pedestrians. In addition, West Yorkshire Metro, the regional passenger transport authority (PTA) oversees the provision of public transport services (both bus and local rail) across the city by private commercial operators, though its powers are limited in a privatised and deregulated environment. In particular, it has no control over public transport fares and limited influence on services. Other non-local bodies, too numerous to describe here, are also involved in transport policy through the provision of inter-urban road and rail-based transport that interacts with the Leeds area.

The traditional policy response to increasing demand has involved the construction of more and more transport infrastructure. This expansionist 'predict and provide' philosophy characterised planning from the emergence of the internal combustion engine and continued throughout most of the twentieth century. However, the result was to encourage further transport growth, leading to higher levels of congestion (SACTRA, 1994; Black, 2001). Recognition of the concept of

sustainability (Brundtland and World Commission on Environment and Development, 1987) has resulted in a 'new realism' in transport planning (Goodwin, 1991), which acknowledges that allowing (or, worse still, actively encouraging) private car travel to grow unchecked is unsustainable. The benefits of increasing mobility on economic prosperity need to be balanced against the problems of negative side-effects, such as congestion, environmental degradation (including air pollution, noise and safety), increasing car dependency (and, thus, inequality of access for those without a car) and, over time, increasing urban sprawl.

In recognition of these negative impacts, the UK 1998 Transport White Paper (DETR, 1998) advocated the use of integrated transport strategies and promoted techniques for managing travel demand and providing effective alternatives, as ways of achieving the Government's sustainability objectives in urban areas. That approach was subsequently reinforced in the Government's guidelines on local transport plans, which all local government authorities outside London submitted in 2000, and in the Planning Policy Guidance 13 document, which details the transport requirements for new land developments (DETR, 2001). Particular attention is focused on changing the relative attractiveness of different modes of transport, by combining infrastructure, management and pricing measures. There are also links into land-use policy, including the priority now being given to redevelopment of brownfield sites that are accessible by public transport (see Chapters 4 and 14), therefore reducing the need for more private car travel.

Current transport policy in Leeds has evolved over more than a decade and many of the ideas it includes are older still. The *Leeds Transport Strategy* (Leeds City Council and West Yorkshire PTA, 1991) identified three priorities from public consultation:

· providing an efficient public transport system;

· improving safety for transport users and pedestrians; and

· providing a clean environment for the city.

Table 10.1 Infrastructure-based measures employed as part of recent Leeds transport policy (continues on page 227)

Measure	Summary of Leeds experience	Policy themes				
Infrastructure-based measues		Economy	Environment	Efficiency and access	Integration	'Liveability'
Walking and cycling						
Pedestrianisation	Gradual removal of motor vehicles from CBD since 1970s; two central public squares enlarged by road closure since 2000.	●	●			●
Cycle lanes and routes	Piecemeal addition of cycle lanes on some major corridors since 1990s; small number of coherent routes using minor roads; first Leeds cycle map produced late 1990s; little supporting infrastructure (e.g. cycle parking in CBD or at transport hubs).		●	●		
Public transport						
New railway stations	A number of new local railway stations (e.g. Burley Park, East Garforth) opened since 1980s, providing increased opportunities for use of rail for city centre related travel.	●	●	●	●	
Public transport box	Dedicated orbital route for buses within CBD, allowing access closer to centre by public transport than by private car; fully implemented 2000.		●	●		
New bus/coach station	Creation of single terminus and unification of bus and coach networks; still some way from railway station; completed late 1990s.		●	●	●	
Central railway station redevelopment	Expansion and upgrade of main rail terminus to reduce congestion, increase number of platforms and improve standard of facilities; £165m Leeds 1st project completed 2002, related development continuing.	●	●	●	●	
New bus/rail inerchange	Provision of bus stops at station entrance, allowing convenient access to select number of services; completed 2004.		●	●	●	
Bus priority	Gradual provision of bus lanes and preferential treatment for public transport at traffic signals, to allow buses to escape the worst pockets of congestion; continuous implementation since 1980s; HOV lane (described in more detail below) also assists buses; bus priority schemes have resulted in increases in patronage.	●		●		
Guided bus	Provision of separate tracks alongside congested road sections, allowing specially equipped buses to bypass delays; three routes implemented since late 1990s.	●		●		

Measure	Summary of Leeds experience	Policy themes				
Infrastructure-based measues		Economy	Environment	Efficiency and access	Integration	'Liveability'
Public transport continued from page 226						
Park and ride	Circa 70 per cent of people working in centre live within Outer Ring Road, so limited scope for park and ride; one permanent site at end of guided bus line to north of city.	•		•	•	
Quality Bus Partnership	Mechanism to allow public investment in infrastructure, in collaboration with privatised and deregulated bus operators; helped to fund guided bus infrastructure, but also new, improved shelters across the city; operating since 1990s.		•	•	•	
Private road traffic						
Inner Ring Road	Main orbital route around city centre; north and west sections built 1960s; south and east sections formed by improving existing roads over time; east still to be completed.	•		•		
City centre loop	One-way system around CBD, designed to remove cars from centre; fully implemented 2000.	•	•	•		
Parking restrictions	Gradual regulation and removal of on-street parking in the city centre since 1970s to create Restricted Parking Zone across CBD and areas immediately beyond.		•	•		
Parking signage	Electronic message signs to show availability of off-street parking in city centre, reducing circulating traffic; implemented 1990s.			•		
HOV lane	Dedicated lane for use only by High Occupancy Vehicles (buses and cars with at least two people in) during peak hours; introduced late 1990s during ICARO research project.		•	•		
Traffic calming	Physical interventions (e.g. speed humps, chicanes etc.) to slow down traffic in residential areas; implemented gradually in sensitive locations since late 1980s; comprehensive scheme, backed up by 20mph speed limit, implemented across Hyde Park district in 2000.		•			•
Home Zone	Area in which people have formal priority over motorised vehicles, for which there is a 20mph speed limit; incorporates traffic calming; idea originally Dutch; The Methleys formed UK pilot scheme from 1996.	•	•			•

These principles were subsequently combined with priorities in other policy areas to produce an integrated *Vision for Leeds* (Leeds City Council, 1999) and the first *West Yorkshire Local Transport Plan* (West Yorkshire Passenger Transport Executive *et al.,* 2000) which covered proposed transport investments for 2001–2006. Consistent policy themes for transport underlying the more detailed aims outlined in these documents include promoting economic prosperity, providing a safe and pleasant urban environment, providing efficient transport with good access for everybody, integration (both within the transport system and between transport and other policy areas) and maintaining and enhancing quality of life. While increasing economic prosperity through efficient transport has always been a key policy objective, issues relating to the environment, equity of access and integration have been gaining ground in recent years as part of the new realism referred to above. This has led to a broad range of measures being implemented and considered to achieve transport objectives, in addition to traditional infrastructure investment. These are discussed in more detail below.

Transport policies pursued by the Council within the city also need to be consistent with the actions of external organisations responsible for strategic, inter-urban transport links. In recent years, the Highways Agency has completed the M1-A1 link, providing a new orbital route around the south east of the city, Railtrack (and subsequently Network Rail) has invested £245 million in the redevelopment of Leeds City Station, to ease congestion, increase the number of platforms and improve passenger facilities, and Leeds Bradford International Airport has invested £22 million in a new passenger terminal and is continuing to expand its facilities. These measures might be expected to have enhanced Leeds' connections to other cities, both within the UK and internationally, and to have contributed to economic prosperity.

Recent transport innovations

Tables 10.1 and 10.2 summarise the range of transport measures employed in Leeds and attempt to illustrate how they

contribute to the themes of transport policy described above under five headings. 'Economy' is defined as making a contribution to promoting the economic prosperity of the city; 'environment' covers contributions to protecting and improving both the natural environment and man-made urban form; 'efficiency and access' refers to meeting travel requirements both in terms of demand and social need; 'integration' means improving coherence and compatibility both within the transport system and between transport and the human activities it supports; and 'liveability' may be defined as a contribution to protecting and improving the quality of human life beyond the most easily quantifiable economic and environmental criteria (e.g. disposable income or exposure to air pollution). These themes attempt to summarise the main aims of transport policy in Leeds, as set out in the key policy documents, while linking in to formal transport policy objectives described elsewhere (May, 2003). Of course, policy themes are not mutually exclusive and many measures may contribute to more than one. A further theme of transport policy that has not been considered here is safety, as this tends to be an important issue for all measures. Also, more detailed policy analyses may

Table 10.2 Soft measures employed in Leeds transport policy

Measure / Soft measues	Summary of Leeds experience	Economy	Environment	Efficiency and access	Integration	'Liveability'
Public transport ticketing	West Yorkshire METRO provides frequent user tickets covering all public transport modes, but harder in privatised and deregulated environment to offer uniform tickets for individual trips.	●			●	
Green travel plans	Travelwise Campaign; plans drawn up with larger employers to encourage staff to choose more sustainable travel options, in response to central government guidelines contained in PPG 13 (DETR, 2001).		●		●	
Parking pricing	Increase in short-stay capacity for shoppers, while strict control of long-stay spaces for commuters, since mid-1990s.	●		●		
Leeds City Car Club	Cars for hire to members when required, removing the need for ownership and providing cost savings for infrequent drivers; initiative started 2003; relatively limited impact so far; relaunched summer 2004, including provision of reserved on-street city centre parking.		●	●		
G-Wiz electric cars	Two-seater, low energy vehicles available for hire for £1 per hour; initiative started 2003; relatively limited impact so far.		●			

choose to use rather longer lists of more subtly distinguished themes than was judged to be appropriate in this context. Exercises of this nature are inevitably subjective, so should be considered as indicative and a starting point for debate rather than a definitive assessment.

In Table 10.1, focusing on infrastructure-based measures, it can be seen that the primary focus is on contributing to efficiency and access. However, many measures also contribute to environment. Although making improvements to efficiency, access and environment would be expected to have knock-on benefits for the economy, rather fewer of the measures might be expect to impact on it directly. Measures that promote integration are primarily those related to public transport, which are typically attempting to make buses and trains a more attractive option than the private car, while those that contribute directly to liveability are largely concerned with improving conditions for pedestrians and cyclists and/or constraining the private car.

Table 10.2 focuses on soft measures, covering all aspects of transport policy that are not concerned with the provision of basic infrastructure, dealing instead with issues of regulation, pricing and management. Although public transport ticketing and parking charges are long-standing policy issues, the others are relatively recent innovations that have had somewhat limited impact so far. In addition, approaches to public transport ticketing in the UK have tended to lag behind the state of the art in many other European cities, particularly in terms of attractiveness to travellers. This is, at least in part, the result of widespread privatisation and deregulation in the UK public transport industries that has made it more difficult to offer common, integrated tickets between (and even within) modes.

Table 10.3 Future transport policy options for Leeds

Measure All measues	Summary of Leeds experience	Policy themes				
		Economy	Environment	Efficiency and access	Integration	'Liveability'
Supertram	Tram to replace/supplement buses on three radial corridors (see Figure 10.12); four associated park and ride sites; considered since 1980s but finally gained national government support late 1990s; main infrastructure scheme in 2001–2006 West Yorkshire Local Transport Plan; ongoing funding problems.	●	●	●		●
Completion of Inner Ring Road	Improvement to east section, identified in Table 10.1; infrastructure scheme in 2001–2006 West Yorkshire Local Transport Plan.	●		●	●	
Extension of quality bus initiatives	Extension of bus priority and guided bus measures; development of real time information systems; aim to be complete by 2011.			●	●	
Smartcard ticketing for public transport	Introduction of electronic smartcards to make public transport more user-friendly and increase integration of ticketing between modes and across a wider area; aim to introduce by 2006.			●	●	
East Leeds link road	New route between M1-A1 link and inner ring road, through area requiring redevelopment; additional access to city to relieve existing radial routes; infrastructure scheme in 2001–2006 West Yorkshire Local Transport Plan.	●		●		
Improvements to Outer Ring Road	Major infrastructure plan to upgrade northern section abandoned due to loss of national government support during 1990s; new, more diverse strategy to resolve specific problems; issue for 2006–2011 West Yorkshire Local Transport Plan.	●		●		
City centre road pricing cordon	Ideas developed during TRANSPRICE research project and proposals included in draft of 2001–2006 West Yorkshire Local Transport Plan; immediate plans shelved when Supertram received full financial support from national government, but remains an option in the longer term.	●	●	●		●

Future transport policy options

Table 10.3 summarises the policy options planned and under consideration in Leeds. As the number of entries is significantly smaller than in the case of recently applied measures, infra-structure-based and soft measures have not been separated. It should be noted that this summary covers only a selection of major measures and that more detailed plans are described elsewhere (Transport Leeds, 2002). Comparing the potential contributions of these measures to policy themes with those already implemented, it is clear that there is a strong focus on efficiency and access and on promoting the local economy.

The centrepiece of future transport policy in Leeds is the proposed Supertram, which has initially been planned to run along three major corridors (shown in Figure 10.11) and has been a key aspiration of local planners since it was first conceived in the late 1980s. Although an important objective of re-installing trams in the city might be to encourage more car users to change mode on the basis of perceived improvements to public transport quality, requirements for financial success have dictated that the first routes to be built would be those that currently have the highest bus patronage rather than those through the most car-dependent suburbs. Thus, most pass-engers might be expected to come from bus routes that have been replaced, although the creation of four associated park and ride sites may encourage more mixed mode trips made by people who live beyond the outer ring road. Another issue is that the north route, past the university campuses and through Headingley, is likely to be complex to build as it involves a mixture of on- and off-road sections. This has led to increasing construction cost estimates that have put the whole scheme in doubt. Taking these issues together, critics would argue that the transport benefits of the tram could be matched, maybe even exceeded, by cheaper schemes such as bus priority and guided bus. However, there is still a feeling among policy makers that trams can achieve rather more in changing the image of public transport and, therefore, the attitudes of travellers towards using it. At the time of writing, the Supertram proposal is under review to ensure that it is still the most appropriate public transport scheme and to reduce the risks of failure by re-considering the previous logistical arrangements for funding it.

The other most interesting proposal is the consideration of a city centre road pricing cordon, which was included explicitly in the draft of the 2001–2006 *West Yorkshire Local Transport Plan,* but only alluded to briefly in the final document (West Yorkshire Passenger Transport Executive *et al.,* 2000). This option was investigated as part of the TRANSPRICE research project (Ghali *et al.,* 2000) and its potential impacts are discussed further in Section 10.5. The original motivation was for a 'parking cordon' around the centre, to replace traditional on and off-street charges, with the aim of ensuring that commuters with access to free private spaces at workplaces were treated the same as those without such privileges and not discouraged from using public transport as a result. However, as national proposals to road pricing schemes were developed (DETR, 1998), this evolved to a more conventional peak hour charge to access the city centre, designed to reduce car use and provide revenues for investment in the transport system. Although it might be attractive to see a cordon as having the potential to provide funds to help meet construction costs of the Supertram, this link has so far been discounted. It is widely agreed that the success of cordon pricing schemes may depend on the availability of suitable alternative options for people who would be affected. On this basis, Leeds City Council has given a

There have been some improvements in facilities for cyclists, but more needs to be done to increase the attractiveness of commuting to work by bike.

Figure 10.11 The proposed Supertram network

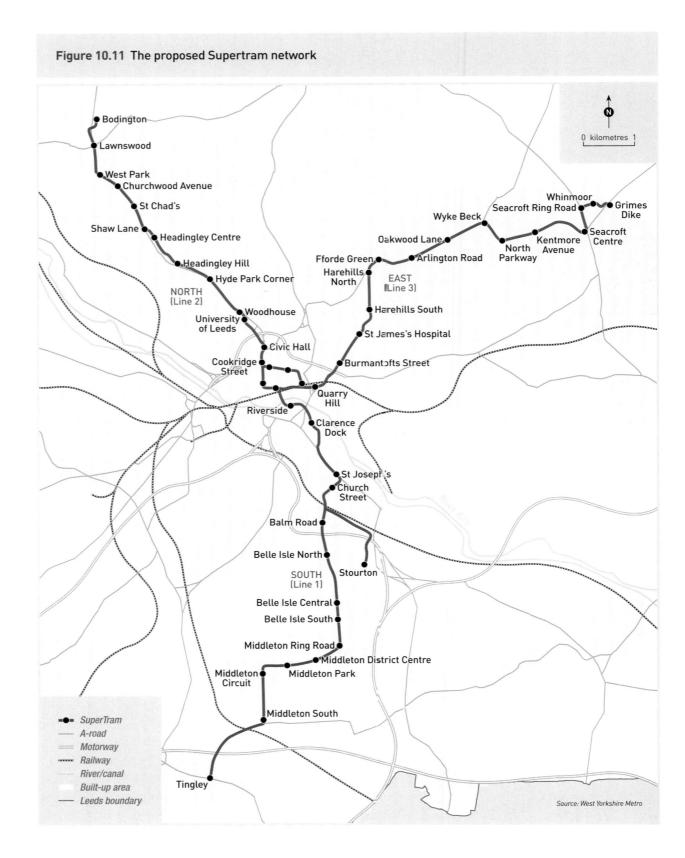

Source: West Yorkshire Metro

SuperTram
A-road
Motorway
Railway
River/canal
Built-up area
Leeds boundary

within the West Yorkshire conurbation, its neighbours (Bradford, Wakefield, Huddersfield and Halifax) are mainly independent urban centres rather than subordinates within a metropolitan hierarchy. In addition, the existence of major trans-Pennine road and rail links through West Yorkshire means that the level of interaction between Leeds and Greater Manchester is higher than with many other parts of Yorkshire. Elsewhere in Europe, strong regional government agencies commonly oversee the provision of integrated transport across areas that encompass the bulk of regular travel activity relating to a city. In the UK, this is not the tradition and, even with consideration of a new regional assembly for Yorkshire, the complex geography makes it uncertain how effective regional integration will be achieved.

"Leeds Supertram will be a 28km light rail network providing state-of-the-art public transport services that will run at frequent intervals" (www.leeds supertram.co.uk).

political commitment that city centre cordon charges will not be introduced until both the Supertram (providing improved public transport) and the final sections of the inner ring road (providing better orbital road capacity around the centre) are complete. These three schemes may be seen, therefore, in some respects as forming an integrated package of measures to change city centre commuting travel patterns in Leeds.

Integration is an increasingly important theme of policy in the early twenty-first century. In transport planning, this means that much greater emphasis is being placed on the roles that transport plays in the economy, the locations of activities and the wider management of human and natural environments through formulation of a coherent regional spatial strategy that brings together policies from different planning spheres (Government Office for Yorkshire and the Humber, 2001). In the context of Leeds, there are challenges to be met at different levels in order to improve the integration of transport planning.

At the local level, policies to integrate urban transport within Leeds continue to be hindered by the spatial dislocation of the central rail and bus terminals, meaning that the city lacks a single, central public transport hub that allows convenient interchange and the concentration of accompanying passenger services at one point.

At the regional level, the city sits within a complex and diverse landscape. Although Leeds is the largest urban area

10.5 Transport policy tools and their applications

Since the early 1960s, computer-based modelling tools have been used to help design effective transport policy. The development of these tools has evolved continuously in response to growing demand for methods to address an increasingly diverse range of transport-related issues, advances in understanding of the key relationships involved and huge technological advances in computing power. Figure 10.12 provides an overview of computer-based modelling tools currently used to inform transport policy and classifies them into ten categories, based on the scope and complexity of the real situation being addressed, in terms of the volume of subsystems and the interrelationships between them (vertical axis), and the level of detail of the modelled representation (horizontal axis). An increase in either of these dimensions leads to a greater demand for input data and, therefore, an increase in the model setup time, run time and maintenance effort. The models towards the bottom left of the plot are very simple. Categories of model further away from the origin are more complex and comprehensive in their characteristics.

A number of computer-based modelling tools have been developed at the Institute for Transport Studies in Leeds and used to support decision making. Two examples of more sophisticated

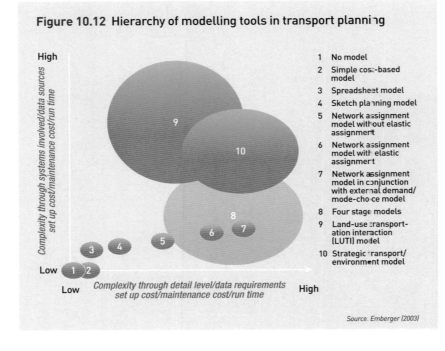

Figure 10.12 Hierarchy of modelling tools in transport planning

High

Complexity through systems involved/data sources
set up cost/maintenance cost/run time

9

10

8

5

6   7

3   4

1   2

Low

Low   Complexity through detail level/data requirements   High
set up cost/maintenance cost/run time

1   No model
2   Simple cost-based
     model
3   Spreadsheet model
4   Sketch planning model
5   Network assignment
     model without elastic
     assignment
6   Network assignment
     model with elastic
     assignment
7   Network assignment
     model in conjunction
     with external demand/
     mode-choice model
8   Four stage models
9   Land-use transport-
     ation interaction
     (LUTI) model
10   Strategic transport/
     environment model

Source. Emberger (2003)

models which have been applied to aid transport policy formulation in Leeds are SATURN, a class 5/6 network assignment model, and MARS, a class 9/10 land-use transport interaction model.

Using SATURN to represent a city centre road pricing cordon

SATURN is a network assignment model that was originally designed during the 1970s and 1980s for representing the impacts of urban traffic management schemes, such as the signalisation of road junctions (Van Vliet, 1982). Over time, the model's capabilities have been expanded to allow its use for investigating the network effects of addition or contraction of road capacity, changes in the level and pattern of travel demand and, more recently, policies that affect road travel decisions, such as parking charges or road pricing (May and Milne, 2000). The main function of the model is to demonstrate how a pre-determined volume of drivers might be expected to choose routes through a road network (normally referred to as 'assignment'), based on the concept of economic 'generalised cost', which represents travel behaviour through a weighted combination of travel time, travel distance and monetary cost. In addition, it has the capability to show how the volume of travel demand may change in response to changes in road travel cost, through an own-price elasticity relationship

(normally referred to as 'elastic assignment') (Hall *et al.*, 1992). In Leeds, SATURN was used during the late 1990s to conduct a series of tests of a central road pricing cordon as part of the EU TRANSPRICE project (Ghali *et al.*, 2000). This was purely an academic research study and is not part of Leeds City Council's present transport policy proposals. Nevertheless, it provides a good illustration of the contribution modelling tools can make to policy formulation.

Figure 10.13 shows the proposed location for the Leeds road pricing cordon, arrived at through testing a number of alternatives within the SATURN model. The key feature of the cordon is that, from a route choice viewpoint, it falls largely within the inner ring road and, thus, avoids the question of whether to charge for access to one of the most heavily used routes in the city and risk diverting

Figure 10.13 Proposed location of city centre road pricing cordon

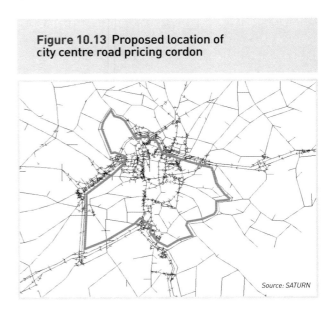

Source: SATURN

Figure 10.14 Key congestion points in current year morning peak

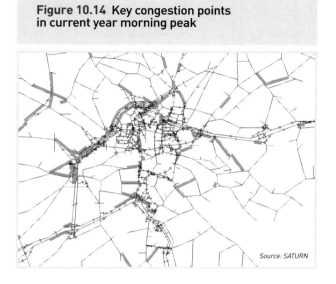

Source: SATURN

Figure 10.15 Key congestion points in morning peak with £2 cordon charge

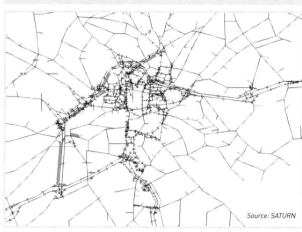

Source: SATURN

traffic onto lower capacity, more environmentally sensitive roads. The small extension of the cordon to the north west, covering the university campuses, does not imply the need to charge traffic on the inner ring road (as the map might suggest) because that section of the orbital route runs through tunnels below ground level.

Figures 10.14 and 10.15 show the key congestion points in and around the city centre of the Leeds network, as estimated by SATURN, with and without the road pricing cordon. In this context, congestion has been defined as those links in the network where the traffic flow arriving at the downstream junction during the morning peak hour is at least 90 per cent of the maximum available capacity, so that significant queues might be expected to start developing. The plots show that, currently, many links in and around the centre are congested, with particular problems on the northern section of the inner ring road. However, if a £2 cordon charge is added, the number of congestion hot-spots reduces considerably.

Figure 10.16 illustrates the estimated differences in flow between the current situation and the scenario with the road pricing cordon. The blue bars show where peak hour traffic flows fall as a result of the cordon, while green signifies higher flows. The width of the bars corresponds to the magnitude of change. As might be expected, imposing a £2 charge across the proposed cordon tends to reduce traffic flows, especially within the city centre. However, there are also a number of links that experience significant flow increases. These are predominantly

Figure 10.16 Differences in traffic flows with and without road pricing cordon

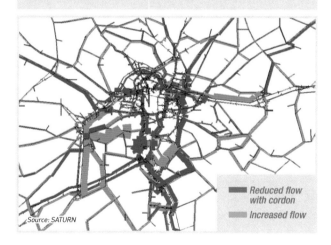

Source: SATURN

Reduced flow with cordon

Increased flow

roads carrying orbital traffic that is diverted around the cordon, but there are also a number of access points to the CBD, within the cordon, that are predicted to become more popular, maybe as a result of general reductions to congestion in the city centre (referring back to Figures 10.14 and 10.15).

While estimates of traffic flows and associated predictions of congestion tend to be the most useful outputs of SATURN for transport planners attempting to manage the road network, examining routes to which drivers are assigned for particular journeys in the model can be a powerful tool for understanding

Figure 10.17 North to south route in current morning peak (a) and with road pricing cordon (b)

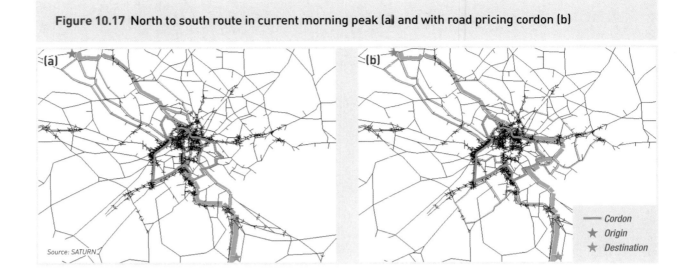

Source: SATURN

Cordon
★ Origin
★ Destination

Figure 10.18 City centre north to south route in current morning peak (a) and with road pricing cordon (b)

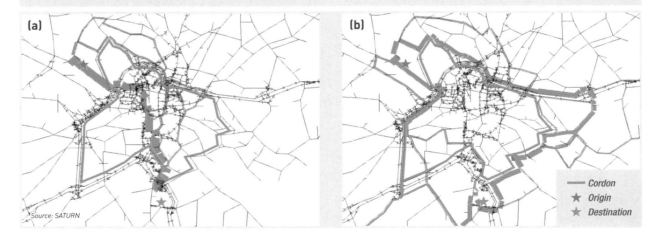

Source: SATURN

Cordon
★ Origin
★ Destination

the impacts of policy. Figures 10.17 and 10.18 show the predicted route choice effects of the road pricing cordon for two typical journeys in the Leeds network during the morning peak.

In Figure 10.17, we observe the likely routes for trips from a northern residential suburb, just within the outer ring road, to the M1 south of the city. This may represent a reasonably common cross-city commute. The relative thickness of the green bars shows the proportions of flows using each road link. In the current situation, all trips travel through the city centre, using roads contained within the proposed road pricing cordon. However, once a charge of £2 is applied,

these drivers are predicted to reroute almost in their entirety around the perimeter of the cordon, in the area of the unfinished eastern sections of the inner ring road. This helps explain the policy link between completion of the inner ring and the introduction of the cordon.

Figure 10.18 focuses on a much shorter urban journey, from a mixed business and residential area next to the university campuses to a business area on the southern fringes of the city centre. This may represent a short business or delivery trip. Again, in the current situation, all drivers are predicted to go through the centre, although there are some more circuitous routes that attempt to avoid congestion on the most direct links. However, with the £2 cordon charge almost all drivers choose to switch to orbital routes (and particularly the inner ring road), avoiding the need to make payments but resulting in significant increases to the distances they travel. This is, potentially, an unwelcome side-effect of cordon charging that may be identified in a model and addressed in the detailed design of a scheme.

Using MARS to represent long-term land-use trends

MARS (Metropolitan Activity Relocation Simulator) is a land-use and transport interaction (LUTI) model that can represent responses to a range of both demand-side (land use) and supply-side (transport) policy instruments. Its main strengths are the ability to test the impacts of combinations of land-use and transport policy instruments simultaneously and to optimise them with reference to pre-defined targets. MARS was developed within a series of EU funded research projects at the Technical University of Vienna (Pfaffenbichler, 2003) and has been applied in Leeds to identify optimal combinations of public transport fares, public transport frequencies, city centre cordon charges and some modest adaptation of the existing road capacity.

Figure 10.19 shows predicted changes for a number of key land-use indicators at electoral ward level, based on a 30 year forecast run of the Leeds-MARS model. The left-hand column of maps illustrates the change in resident population, number of workplaces in the production sector, number of workplaces in the service sector and the ratio of workplaces to resident population for a 'do-nothing' scenario, based on land use changes that are expected in the *Leeds Unitary Development Plan* (LCC Development Department, 2001). The central column of maps depicts trends in spatial development for the same set of indicators for a 'do-something' scenario, in which both transport and land-use policy measures were included. Finally, the right-hand column of maps show percentage differences between the 'do-nothing' and 'do-something' scenarios. The colours show the magnitude of changes compared to the current situation (for the left-hand

and central columns) and between the two predicted future scenarios (for the right-hand column).

In the 'do-something' scenario, the transport measures comprised: public transport fare reductions (50 per cent); public transport service level increases (tripling); a cordon charging scheme (similar to that investigated in SATURN); and minor changes to road network capacity through optimised traffic signalling. The land use element comprised a strategy to increase the density of development within the outer ring road.

In the 'do-nothing' case, the model suggests a trend for people and workplaces to move from the inner to the outer wards. The highest growth in population and workplaces occurs in the eastern zones of the city. In other words, the MARS model predicts that Leeds is heading towards greater suburban sprawl if no action is taken. In the 'do-something' case, similar trends are observed, suggesting that the policy combination tested is insufficient to prevent the forces in favour of decentralisation. However, the difference maps show that the policy measures do have some impacts. In particular, they appear to discourage depopulation of a number of wards close to the centre and to reduce decentralisation of jobs in the production sector quite significantly. A fuller description of the model and results from the Leeds 'Optimal Strategies' research are available elsewhere (Emberger *et al.*, 2003).

10.6 Conclusions

Throughout this chapter, a recurring theme has been the tension that exists in transport planning between catering for increasing motorised mobility, which has been a significant factor associated with economic growth and prosperity since the Industrial Revolution, and the more recently developed awareness of the negative impacts that continuous motorised travel growth is having on both the human and natural environments. In Leeds, this has been responsible for the policy shift from self-proclaimed 'motorway city of the 70s' to the current focus on providing alternatives to the car, especially through improved public transport (e.g. bus priority, guided bus and, potentially,

Figure 10.19 Projected ward land-use changes under different scenarios over a 30-year period

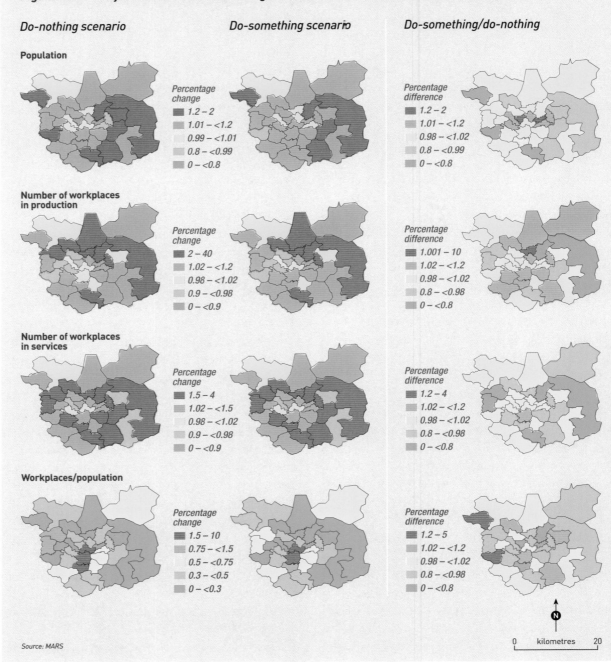

Do-nothing scenario

Do-something scenario

Do-something/do-nothing

Population

Number of workplaces
in production

Number of workplaces
in services

Workplaces/population

Source: MARS

Supertram). So far, as the 2001 Census illustrates, there has been little success in influencing long-term mobility trends, resulting in parallel consideration of more radical approaches to discourage car use (e.g. the city centre road pricing cordon investigated during academic research in the 1990s). However, even if such a scheme were to be introduced, it would only have a direct effect on journeys interacting with a limited area of the city during certain hours of the day. In addition, promoting economy and access through expansion and upgrade of road infrastructure continues to be part of proposed future policy measures. So, we should conclude that existing transport plans for Leeds are unlikely to bring about a major shift in travel patterns across the city in the foreseeable future and that the dilemmas of meeting conflicting demands for economic growth and improved environments are likely to trouble decision makers for many years to come. Indeed, it may be that measures beyond the local level, such as the growing number of proposals to replace annual vehicle licensing with some form of nationwide distance-based road pricing (CfIT, 2002; Grayling et al., 2004), will ultimately be the mechanism through which significant changes to travel patterns occur, once appropriate technology becomes available for widespread application (currently estimated to be a decade away).

Another recurring theme, during discussion of transport policy, has been the challenge of integration, which manifests itself in various ways. In particular, there is now a well recognised need to integrate transport policy with other planning decisions that affect the locations of activities and land uses, all of which have transport implications. This is complicated by the fact that, over time, development of faster transport has allowed the spatial scope of regular journeys that interact with the city to far outgrow traditional administrative boundaries. Thus, a significant proportion of journeys to workplaces within the Leeds district may originate in commuter towns beyond (e.g. Harrogate), while the wide range of retail, cultural and entertainment opportunities that the city offers may attract customers from throughout West Yorkshire and further afield. Indeed, decisions to locate developments close to major transport links on the edge of town (e.g. the White Rose Centre) may be aimed explicitly at regional markets. Although planning guidance from central government now includes procedures to bring transport and development policies together and there is ongoing debate about the formation of a Yorkshire Assembly which may provide stronger regional coordination of policy, the UK lags behind many parts of Europe on these issues.

A significant barrier to increased integration of planning is the lack of effective powers to allow government agencies to shape development within their jurisdictions. Furthermore, the spatial division of a region into a number of administrative areas, all within regular travel range of the same population, may actually encourage competition between authorities and place too much bargaining power in the hands of private developers. An additional dimension affecting transport planning is the fact that responsibility for strategic routes through local areas and control of budgets for all major investments within them normally falls to national agencies, so there are likely to be significant influences from institutions motivated by issues unrelated to regional requirements. Therefore, it is necessary to conclude that improving integration of planning will be a long process that is currently in its very early stages.

Focussing on integration at the lower level of the Leeds transport network, key issues include the dislocation of the main bus and rail terminals in the centre and the lack of high quality public transport links to developments around the periphery of the city, such as Leeds-Bradford International Airport and the White Rose Centre. At present, there are no firm proposals to address these problems (although approaches to improve airport access are being considered). Therefore, they will continue to contribute to the predominance of the car as the travel mode of convenience across the district.

Despite these somewhat pessimistic conclusions, it is important to acknowledge that Leeds has long been a pioneer in transport (having been at the forefront of canal, rail, tram and motorway development) and that this tradition continues through the city implementing the first high occupancy vehicle lane in the UK, being among the leaders in developing guided bus schemes and providing the original pilot study for the Home Zones concept, as well as being one of only a handful of urban areas outside London to consider road pricing as part of its 2001–2006 local transport plan. Leeds' current strength in transport planning may prove to be the variety of measures that it has been prepared to explore and implement, so that the city's decision makers are potentially better placed than those elsewhere to make informed long-term choices between alternative policy options.

References

Black, W.R. (2001) An unpopular essay on transportation, *Journal of Transport Geography,* 9: 1–11.

Brundtland and World Commission on Environment and Development (1987) *Our Common Future,* Oxford University Press, Oxford.

Buchanan, C. (1963) *Traffic in Towns: A Study of the Long-term Problems of Traffic in Urban Areas,* HMSO, London.

Burt, S. and Grady, K. (2002) *The Illustrated History of Leeds,* Second Edition, Breedon Books, Derby.

Commission for Integrated Transport (CfIT) (2002) *Paying for Road Use,* report for Department for Transport, at: www.cfit.gov.uk

Department of Environment, Transport and the Regions (DETR) (1998) *A New Deal for Transport: Better for Everyone,* White Paper, DETR, London.

Department of Environment, Transport and the Regions (DETR) (2001) *Transport,* PPG 13, DETR, London.

Department for Transport (DfT) (2002) *National Travel Survey 2002,* available at: www.transtat.dft.gov.uk

Dickinson, G.C. (1967) Passenger transport developments, in Beresford M.W. and Jones, G.R. J. (eds) *Leeds and its Region,* Leeds Local Executive Committee of the British Association for the Advancement of Science, pp.167–174.

Emberger, G. (2003) *Local Transport Plans Guidance: Forecasting and Appraisal, Task 3 Report, Scoping Study for Simplified Modelling Approaches,* report for the DfT by the Institute for Transport Studies, University of Leeds, Leeds.

Emberger, G., May, A.D., and Shepherd, S.P. (2003) Method to identify optimal land use and transport policy packages: introduction of an indicator/target based appraisal approach, paper presented at CUPUM'03, *8th International Conference on Computers in Urban Planning and Urban Management,* Sendai, Japan.

Fox, P. and Unsworth, R. (2003) *City Living in Leeds 2003,* K W Linfoot plc and School of Geography, University of Leeds, Leeds, Also at: www.geog.leeds.ac.uk/publications/cityliving

Ghali, M.O., Pursula, M., Milne, D., Keranen, M., Daleno, M. and Vougioukas, M. (2000) Asessing the impact of integrated trans modal urban transport pricing on modal split, in Ortúzar, J. de D. (ed) *Stated Preference Modelling Techniques,* PTRC, London.

Goodwin, P.B. (1991) *Transport: The New Realism,* University of Oxford Transport Studies Unit, Oxford.

Government Office for Yorkshire and the Humber (2001) *Regional Planning Guidance for Yorkshire and the Humber (RPG12),* The Stationery Office, London.

Graham, S. (1998) The end of geography or the explosion of place? Conceptualising space, time and information technology, *Progress in Human Geography,* 22(2): 165–185.

Grayling, T., Sansom, N. and Foley, J. (2004) *In the Fast Lane: Fair and Effective Road User Charging in Britain,* report for Institute for Public Policy Research at: www.ippr.org.uk

Hall, M.D., Fashole-Luke, T., Van Vliet, D. and Watling, D.P. (1992) *Demand responsive assignment in SATURN,* proceedings of Seminar E, PTRC 20th Summer Annual Meeting, University of Manchester Institute of Science and Technology (UMIST).

Harland, K. (2001) Commuting to Leeds: social and gender divides, *The Regional Review,* 11(2): 13–14.

Harvey, D. (1989) *The Urban Experience,* Blackwell, Oxford.

Judge, E. and Hick, D. (1996) Transport and personal accessibility in Leeds, in Haughton, G. and Williams, C. (eds) *Corporate City? Partnership, Participation and Partition in Urban Development in Leeds,* Avebury, Aldershot, pp.235–252

Leeds City Council (LCC) (1999) *Vision for Leeds,* LCC, Leeds.

Leeds City Council and West Yorkshire PTA (1991) *Leeds Transport Strategy,* LCC, Leeds.

Leeds City Council Development Department (2001) *Unitary Development Plan,* LCC, Leeds.

LBIA website http://www.lbia.co.uk/airportinformation_airporthistory.php.

May, A.D. (2003) *Developing Sustainable Urban Land Use and Transport Strategies: A Decision Makers' Guidebook,* report developed for the EC PROSPECTS project, Institute for Transport Studies, University of Leeds, Leeds.

May, A.D. and Milne, D.S. (2000) Effects of alternative road pricing systems on network performance, *Transportation Research Part A,* 34: 407–436.

Office of National Statistics (ONS) (2002) *Labour Market Trends,* June and October.

Pfaffenbichler, P.C. (2003) *The strategic, dynamic and integrated urban land use and transport model MARS (Metropolitan Activity Relocation Simulator),* Technische Universitaet Wien, Vienna.

Standing Advisory Committee on Trunk Road Assessment (SACTRA) (1994) *Trunk Roads and the Generation of Traffic,* HMSO, London.

Stillwell, J.C.H. and Duke-Williams, O. (2003) A new web-based interface to British census of population origin-destination statistics, *Environment and Planning A,* 35: 113–132.

Tetlow, J. and Goss, A. (1968) *Homes, Towns and Traffic,* Faber and Faber, London.

Transport Leeds (2002) *Integrated Local Transport for Leeds,* Leeds Integrated Transport Partnership, Leeds.

Van Vliet, D. (1982) SATURN — a modern assignment model, *Traffic Engineering and Control,* 23(12): 578–581.

West Yorkshire Passenger Transport Executive, City of Bradford Metropolitan District Council, Calderdale Council, Kirklees Council, Leeds City Council and City of Wakefield Metropolitan District Council (2000) *West Yorkshire Local Transport Plan 2001–2006,* West Yorkshire Passenger Transport Executive, Leeds.

11

Shopping Around:
The Development of Suburban
and City Centre Retailing

GRAHAM CLARKE, RACHAEL UNSWORTH & HILLARY SHAW

9 780853 162425

> ▌▌ *Cities are no longer seen as landscapes of production, but as landscapes of consumption.*[1] ▌▌

11.1 Introduction

Leeds is typical of most post-industrial cities in its determination to reinvent itself. An essential element of securing economic turnaround is seen as maximising the 'offer' to consumers — of goods and leisure experiences. The simple assertion is that as a city becomes more attractive, increasing numbers of people will come and spend more money. Activity to attract consumers has focused especially on the city centre, with its legacy of retail space, historic buildings and public spaces and there has evidently been considerable success in achieving the aim of appealing to consumers: Leeds city centre's Prime Shopping Quarter (see Figure 14.3), with its 1,000 shops, is rated the third most attractive shopping location in the UK, after London's West End and Glasgow's city centre (LCC, 2003a)[2]. Other recent surveys have consistently ranked Leeds amongst the top six shopping centres[3]. The city has a growing range of cultural venues and events, many of which draw large crowds. Leeds appeals to shoppers, tourists, residents and businesses and therefore also to retailers, hotel owners and leisure operators providing for these consumers. Thus, a seemingly virtuous circle of economic prosperity is achieved.

But city centre retailing is only part of the picture. The aim of this chapter is to review the dynamics of the retail and leisure sectors across the city since the 1960s. We have chosen this date because the 1960s witnessed the start of the major transformation from the 'corner shop' environment to the 'supermarket' environment, with the retail scene increasingly dominated by large new 'cathedrals of consumption'.

We have already seen in Chapter 8 the growth in the service economy, in which retailing plays a significant role. Over 40,000 people now work in retailing in Leeds — 75 per cent of these in places other than the city centre. In Section 11.2, we explore the dynamics of retailing in the suburbs. We outline a number of phases of development: the demise of many traditional ribbon developments in the inner city, the growth of

out-of-town superstores, new planned suburban shopping centres, retail warehouses, retail parks and most recently, new regional malls. Then, in Section 11.3, we explore change in the city centre, which is partly driven by changes in suburbia, or reactions to these changes.

11.2 Suburban change

The retail geography of suburban Leeds is a product of long-term change and especially of changes that have taken place since the 1960s. This section is divided into five parts. First, we look briefly at the pre-supermarket era of suburban Leeds up to and including the 1960s. Second, we consider the period of the late 1960s and early 1970s, as this was a key time for suburban developments as well as the period of the arrival of the supermarket. The third section deals with the mid-1970s to mid-1980s when new supermarkets were built and retail warehouses came on the

Figure 11.1 Surburban shopping centres

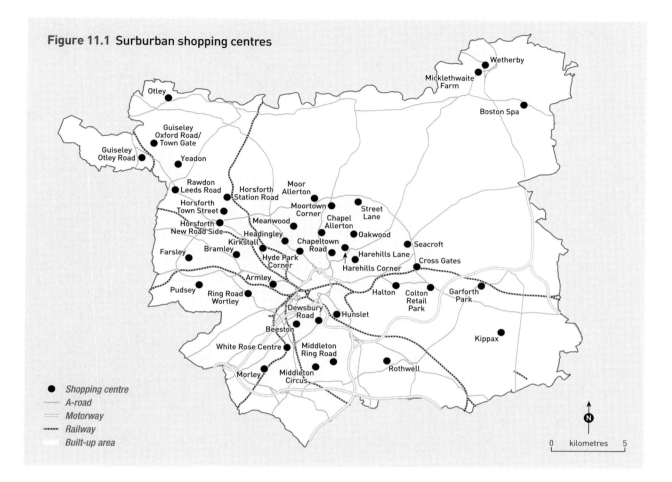

- Shopping centre
- A-road
- Motorway
- Railway
- Built-up area

scene. The fourth section examines the period from the 1990s, as supermarkets and retail warehouses have been superseded by hypermarkets, retail parks and regional shopping centres. The final section speculates briefly on future trends.

The early 1960s

Figure 11.1 shows the main pattern of suburban shopping centres in Leeds since the 1960s. All the major retail centres (such as Pudsey, Crossgates, Armley, Headingley) had developed in parallel with their post-war growth in catchment area populations and were sizeable centres even by 1960. Suburban retail facilities within these well-established centres were supplemented by a number of major 'ribbon' developments stretching along the main roads which radiated from the city centre. These included Kirkstall Road to the west, Chapeltown Road to the north, Hunslet Road to the south-east, Dewsbury Road to the south-west and York Road to the east.

One of the few remaining local shops in South Parkway, LS14. By 1983, less than 30 greengrocers were in business in the northern suburbs of Leeds compared with around 300 in the 1950s.

By 1960, however, these ribbon developments constituted some of the oldest and most blighted retail configurations in the city (Davies, 1974). They had been built in areas of dense housing in inner city areas, where a large and generally poor population provided the clientele. Many of these areas had their origins in nineteenth century urban growth, although as Cox (1968) notes, they were still significant enough to drain off large shares of the market from the city centres in the 1960s, especially for foodstuffs. In their prime, in the middle of the twentieth century, such developments could provide continuous belts of shops up to two miles long. In the northern inner city area of Leeds alone in the late 1950s, there were almost 1,000 shops, of which 300 were grocers or greengrocers (Leeming, 1959). Although a number of these types of development survive today (notably Dewsbury Road and York Road) many have been demolished as inner city housing has been bulldozed. Others have simply closed, failing to compete in the new supermarket era. By 1983, in the same area of inner northern Leeds mentioned above, the number of shops was less than 150 and only 28 sold fresh food produce (Clarke, 1984).

Mid-1960s to mid-1970s

The character of suburban retailing began to change radically in most British cities from the mid-1960s onwards. The first major innovation was the planned shopping centre. The concept of the planned centre was becoming widespread following the publication of the influential book *British Shopping Centres* by Wilfred Burns in 1959. This suggested the planning of a hierarchy of centres akin to the concepts of classic central place theory (Christaller, 1966): a city should have a city centre, regional centres (serving 50,000–80,000), district centres (25,000–50,000), neighbourhood centres (10,000–25,000) and local centres (5,000–10,000).

The first centres in Leeds to benefit from such investment were those in east Leeds. The area had grown rapidly since the second world war and retail facilities were clearly poor by the mid-1960s. Crossgates saw the most

fundamental change. Promoted to 'regional centre' status, it became one of the first suburban centres in the UK to have a precinct format, with all the major stores under one roof. In addition, 'magnet' stores were encouraged such as Tesco and the Hamilton and Bell Department store (later sold to Boots). Other leading retailers (or the 'multiples', as they have become known) were also encouraged to locate in these centres. CALUS (1975) reported that such regional centres were likely to have 80 per cent of floorspace occupied by multiples. Thus, the Arndale development at Crossgates became one of the first pedestrianised shopping parades in the UK. (See Jones, 1969, for comparisons with other similar developments elsewhere).

The second centre to emerge in east Leeds was that of Seacroft: a completely new, purpose-built, pedestrianised shopping centre built by the local authority in 1965. It contained 40 major stores, two public houses and a bus station. This development came under the banner of 'district centre', built to serve the large post-war council estate at the eastern city edge. Similar upgrades to district centre status were identified in 10 other centres across the city (see below). However, a major

Morrisons, Hunslet, opened in the mid-1980s. Under charismatic chairman, Ken Morrison, the company grew from a small local to a major national supermarket player, acquiring the Safeway chain in 2003.

additional development after 1965 was the anchoring of such developments with a large superstore. Supermarkets (465–740m²) had been common in Britain since the 1950s. Building on the success of their American counterparts, British supermarket companies grew rapidly from the 1950s onwards as they gained economies of scale through increased size, self-service, greater purchasing power, and the routinisation of day-to-day management. Superstores, however, were larger still, averaging 1,860–2,790m². They became more possible and likely after retail price maintenance was abolished in 1964, allowing retailers to pass on those greater economies of scale to their customers through cheaper prices. Two of the retailers to benefit most from these developments in Leeds were the local organisations, ASDA and Morrisons (headquarters in Leeds and Bradford respectively).

Although the growth of the superstore was rapid across the UK, there were fierce critics amongst local trading councils and chambers of commerce given their potential impacts on small shops. The legacy of the superstore in Leeds is described in a later section. However, even in the early 1970s, there were concerns that the loss of small grocery stores could leave a less affluent, less mobile community vulnerable to a decline in accessibility to fresh foods (Hillman, 1973). A compromise seems to be offered by the UK Government's Planning Policy Guidance Note 13 (PPG13: first of many drafts!) which stressed the benefits of a superstore incorporated within a planned centre (as described above) rather than as a single store operation. This advice was adopted by Leeds City Council.

The consequence of accepting PPG13 was that the new district centres in Leeds all incorporated a new superstore, with Morrisons and ASDA especially prevalent. (For a review of the growth of Morrisons and ASDA see Jones, 1981; Seth and Randall, 1999). These centres included Armley, Pudsey, Bramley, Holt Park, Horsforth, Kirkstall, Chapel Allerton, Beeston and Headingley (Figure 11.1). At the same time, the older ribbon developments were beginning to decline rapidly. Hunslet Road, for example, had become an almost obsolete trading area having undergone drastic surgery following the inner city clearance programmes (and, in this instance, road improvement/widening schemes).

Mid-1970s to mid-1980s

The end of the 1970s saw the continuation of the phase of district/planned centres including a major superstore. An interesting new development was Hunslet in south Leeds. This was built to replace the many shops lost in the old ribbon developments around Hunslet Road. It was also a good example of a large superstore built in a very low income area — a rare event in many UK cities after 1975. As the 1970s drew to a close, Leeds City Council was facing mounting pressure for a new superstore in north Leeds. In 1980, Sainsbury's was granted permission to build a new district centre at Moor Allerton, a site surrounded by some of the most affluent suburbs of Leeds including Roundhay, Adel and Moortown.

The suburban retail landscape of the 1970s and 1980s was also influenced by the development of the retail warehouse. This was the non-food equivalent of the superstore. These tended to be 930–1,860m² stores and were often located

firms became particularly adept at beating the planning system through both the sheer number of applications put forward and their skill at manipulating the appeal process. When combined with even greater economies of scale as power steadily switched from manufacturers to retailers, this marked a 'golden age' for superstore development (Wrigley, 1987). In the non-food markets the retail warehouse estates, in former warehouses or cinemas, were being replaced by retail parks with modern, purpose-built megastores and ample parking. The Armley site in Leeds was replaced by the new Aireside Centre built on the old railway sidings close to

in former warehouses, converted mills or old cinemas/bingo halls (Jones, 1984). The advantage of these sites was the space inside for large amounts of stock and the space outside for car parking. The early pioneers came from five major retail warehouse sectors: DIY/home improvement (B&Q, Wickes, Dodge City); furniture/carpets (MFI, Harris/Queensway); electrical goods (Comet, Bridges); household goods (Reading Warehouses); leisure equipment (Blacks) (URPI, 1981). Although retailers wished for similar locations to superstore operators, many local authorities favoured more 'fringe, brownfield locations'. They also tended to identify large blocks of adjacent brownfield sites so that retail warehouses could form some kind of retail estate. The implication of this sort of policy was to see the first retail warehouse estate developed between Leeds and Armley, close to the Leeds-Bradford major trunk road. By 1980 this site housed B&Q, Comet and MFI. By the mid-1980s, however, dissatisfaction with the size of units put pressure on the City Council to find a new site.

The early 1980s was also a time when the retail planning regime was beginning to change very radically. The new Conservative Government elected in 1979 was much more pro-*laissez-faire* and retailers were beginning to become much cleverer at obtaining planning permission (see Davies, 1984; 1986 for details of the changing planning regime). This was more evident in some retail sectors than others. The grocery

of 20 years of uneven superstore development across Leeds. The food desert concept developed from the fact that the golden age of superstore retailing was largely aimed at middle class England. Companies such as Tesco and Sainsbury's were keen to have access to the more affluent consumers with their greater spending power. Hence, many of their urban superstores are closer to the more affluent suburbs (see Guy, 1996, for a comparative analysis of superstore development in Cardiff).

To some extent, the gap in provision in less affluent suburbs was filled during the 1980s and 1990s by the arrival of the discount retailers. The first major discount retailer in the UK was Kwik Save. From its base in North Wales it very successfully targeted the poorer suburbs of towns and cities across the north of England, before heading south to the Midlands and London (Sparks, 1990). By 1995, Kwik Save had opened stores (mainly smaller stores of around 930m²) in Holbeck, Crossgates,

Top, the 1960s Seacroft retail development was demolished and replaced with a new development, opened in 1999. Bottom, Kwik Save was the first major discount retailer in the UK, trading from its base in North Wales.

the main city station. (This in turn will be swept away when a large, mixed redevelopment of Wellington Place takes place — see Table 14.5).

Mid-1980s onwards

The new developments in Leeds after the mid-1980s could simply be described as 'bigger and brighter', although there is the arrival of some new forms of retailing. The new supermarkets built tended to be 2,790m² plus. The two ASDA stores, one at Pudsey and the other at Killingbeck, are good examples of bright modern, purpose-built hypermarkets (the latter term associated with larger superstore developments). Even in these examples, however, the stores are not single store operations. ASDA Pudsey is joined by a large Marks and Spencer store, whilst ASDA Killingbeck is amongst a number of smart new retail warehouses. The most recent hypermarket opening has come at Seacroft in east Leeds. The purpose-built centre described above was completely demolished after years of neglect, decay and urban crime. The new Tesco store was built in what has been labelled as an urban 'food desert', the legacy

Figure 11.2 Retail grocery provision

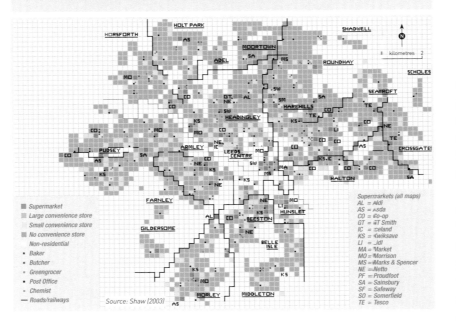

Source: Shaw (2003)

Legend:
- Supermarket
- Large convenience store
- Small convenience store
- No convenience store
- Non-residential
- · Baker
- · Butcher
- · Greengrocer
- · Post Office
- · Chemist
- — Roads/railways

Supermarkets (all maps)
AL = Aldi
AS = Asda
CO = Co-op
GT = GT Smith
IC = Iceland
KS = Kwiksave
LI = Lidl
MA = Market
MO = Morrison
MS = Marks & Spencer
NE = Netto
PF = Proudfoot
SA = Sainsbury
SF = Safeway
SO = Somerfield
TE = Tesco

according to the nature of shopping provision. Light orange squares have no retail grocery provision and clusters of such squares can be termed 'urban food deserts', some examples of which are listed in Table 11.1.

Clarke *et al.* (2002) modelled accessibility to shopping facilities in Leeds using a suite of spatial interaction models (and the performance indicators produced by the models). These models allow scores to be produced based on the size and quality of all nearby facilities rather than the more usual and simple measure of distance to nearest store. Seven areas were identified as having particularly low accessibility/provision scores: Cookridge, Garforth, Guiseley, Middleton, Rothwell, Roundhay and Seacroft (prior to Tesco new store). Of these, Seacroft and Middleton were deemed to be the most

Harehills, Dewsbury Road and York Road, some of the poorest districts of the city (and in areas formerly characterised by ribbon developments). However, the arrival of the limited assortment discounters (LADs) from overseas had an even greater impact in Leeds. Buoyed by high profit margins in the UK compared with the rest of Western Europe (Burt and Sparks, 1995) these stores began to appear in the heartland of Kwik Save, and to a lesser extent ASDA and Morrisons. The first LAD store was that of Netto in Halton. This Scandinavian company then opened stores in Seacroft, Meanwood, Beeston and Kirkstall. Aldi located soon after in Cottingley and Meanwood, whilst Lidl entered the very lowest income areas of Gipton and Hunslet. More recently, increasing price competition on basic foodstuffs from the other major grocery firms has put some pressure on the discounters. By 2003, Netto had closed its stores in Halton (sold to the Co-op), Armley (currently vacant) and Beeston (converted into an Asian supermarket).

Despite the presence of discount retailers in less affluent urban areas, many communities still had relatively poor access to top quality fresh food and vegetables (see also Bromley and Thomas 1993). Shaw (2003) looked at food deserts in Leeds from a micro perspective. Figure 11.2 shows Leeds divided into 250 x 250 metre grid squares and classifies each square

The White Rose Centre opened for business in 1997 and attracts customers from across the whole district, 90 per cent of which come by car.

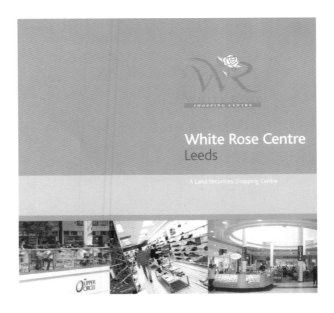

Table 11.1 Classification of urban food deserts

Type of area	Examples in Leeds	Key groups affected
City centre fringe	'The Calls' and new riverside developments	Young, single executives
Inner city areas *White* *Ethnic* *Student*	East Park (York Road) Beeston, Chapeltown Hyde Park	Elderly; mothers with children Poorer ethnic minority residents Poor students and some pensioners
Peripheral council estates	Gipton, Seacroft	Poor residents (high unemployment, low car ownership)
Wealthy suburbs	Roundhay, Cookridge	Wealthier residents (high car ownership)

Source: Shaw (2003)

problematic areas since they contained high percentages of residents with low incomes and low car ownership levels.

Following the findings of the research by Clarke *et al.* (2002), a research agenda was formulated concerning the consumption patterns of a sample of households in Seacroft in Leeds (Wrigley *et al.*, 2002a; Whelan *et al.*, 2002). This allowed a much clearer and more detailed picture of life in a food desert; in particular, income, shopping habits, diets and travel patterns. In many cases, it made for grim reading in terms of a healthy lifestyle. For example, Whelan *et al.* (2002) found that in the Seacroft sample, 40 per cent of residents earn less than £10,000 per annum, 61 per cent live on benefits of some kind and 30 per cent labelled themselves as heavy smokers.

The authors go on to report that many consumers have a high intake of fast foods and there was a notable lack of fruit and vegetables in daily diets. The authors were able to do a follow-up survey of the same households once the new Tesco was operating in 2001. This provided a unique opportunity to examine the extent and manner of switching behaviour between different types of household (Wrigley *et al.*, 2003). Such evidence showed that the switching behaviour could put financial pressure on a number of surrounding stores. If these subsequently close, new micro deserts may form causing new access problems for the least mobile.

Away from grocery retailing *per se,* there have also been some spectacular new developments in Leeds since the mid-1980s. The largest retail park was constructed at Crown Point (south of the city centre in Hunslet). This was a former industrial area close to the large Tetley Brewery. The site benefited from the amount of space available, allowing 20,440m² of modern, quality retail warehouses and car parking for over 200 vehicles. These new retail parks also began to house traditional high street retailers keen to introduce the warehouse unit to their portfolios (Guy, 1998). The other major development was the White Rose Shopping Centre opened in 1997. Advertised as 'West Yorkshire's Premier shopping experience', the White Rose Centre is situated 4 miles south west of Leeds city centre between Junction 28 of the M62 and Junction 1 of the M621. The 60,400m² building, with two 'anchor stores' (Sainsbury's and Debenhams) and around 80 other retail outlets and a food court, is surrounded by 4,800 car parking spaces. This modern 'regional centre' is one of many new large-scale, edge-of-town retail developments of the 1980s and 1990s (Lowe, 2000). Other larger examples in the UK include Metro Centre (Gateshead), Lakeside (Thurrock), Merry Hill (Dudley), Meadowhall (Sheffield) and the Trafford Centre (Manchester) (Rushton, 1999). When the White Rose centre was opened, there was great concern about the impacts on existing non-food retailing in the city centre. In reality, the impact has probably been greatest in surrounding suburban centres such as Morley, Armley and Beeston. These smaller market towns are in turn trying to reinvent themselves. Morley, for example, is working on the idea of a specialist market to attract new visitors, possibly based on antiques or books.

11.3 City centre dynamics

Much of the investment in building, rebuilding and maintaining the city centre comes from the private sector, but the framework of national and local public sector policy and actions is important in explaining the overall configuration and functioning of the city centre. Also, the City Council has been instrumental in levering funds from a variety of sources to pay for both physical development and the cultural activities within buildings and spaces of the city centre.

Concern about urban vitality and viability arose during the 1990s when it became clear that traditional town and city centres had been adversely affected by the planning policies and decisions of retailers during the 1970s and the 1980s. As we have seen in Section 11.2, there had been a relaxation of control on development on greenfield sites outside town and city centres and also a change in the kinds of development that were permitted on land previously designated for industrial use; now there could be retail and business parks in locations convenient for motorways and other main routes. As car ownership rose, these locations were increasingly advantageous. This meant that many developers took the easier option of building on edge-of-town and out-of-town sites instead of tackling redevelopment of constrained central sites that had inadequate nearby parking facilities. Two thirds of shopping floor space opened between 1987 and 1990 was out-of-town. These developments detracted from the intensity of activity in town and city centres and in some cases had very serious repercussions for viability. More on the general impacts of out-of-town developments on town and city centres can be found in Thomas and Bromley (1993) and DETR (1998). Case studies showed that the impact of out-of-town centres on traditional retail environments could be immense. Rowley (1993), for

example, plots the number of vacant properties in the centre of Sheffield in the early 1990s, following the opening of the large Meadowhall Centre adjacent to the M1 motorway at the edge of Sheffield.

Since the early 1990s, central government policy has placed a strong emphasis on improving the state of town and city centres — improving vitality and viability. Vitality is measured by the numbers of people, the amount of activity, the range of opportunities for consumers, through the day, across the week, throughout the year. Viability means the financial stability and outlook for businesses operating in town centres — the ability of a centre to attract continuing investment (URBED 1994). Research for the Department of the Environment (DoE) by URBED in 1994 made recommendations for re-orientating development towards central areas. For metropolitan cities (the category into which Leeds fits), the priorities were seen as:

- counteracting dispersal of people and activities;

- restoring image;

- developing mixed use buildings and localities;

- improving public transport;

- developing distinct quarters; and

- making visitors more welcome.

Enhancing conditions for business enables them to survive and to be more profitable. Vitality contributes to achieving viability: more people and a greater intensity of activity make it more likely that new businesses will be encouraged to locate in town centres, and the vicious circle of decline can be broken. Policies to attract more people are therefore crucial.

First, it is useful to explore the national framework on policy change. By 1996, the DoE had revised its Planning Policy

Figure 11.3 City centre retail area: 'Prime Shopping Quarter'

Main shopping centres

(2000) discuss the operation and success of such schemes in north-west England in more detail. All these agencies have been keen to ask the question: 'what makes a successful city centre'? (see National Retail Planning Forum, 1996, for one set of answers).

In Leeds, recent policy developments have been very significant. The city is trying to make itself known as a world class city that maximises opportunities for its people while protecting the environment (LCC, 1999).

"Changing consumer habits, perceptions regarding access, congestion, security and the environment, combined with increased competition from developments designed to suit the car user, can all have an effect on the viability of existing centres. Conversely, the location of a wide range of cultural facilities, entertainment and tourism destinations can significantly add to the centre's attractiveness" (LCC, 1998, p14).

Leeds City Council, in partnership with other organisations in the city, has attempted to put in place or facilitate the elements that add up to a vital and viable city centre. LCC does not own much property in the city centre and funds for enhancement of public areas are of course limited. However there are many elements of policy and a variety of actions that help to nurture a successful city centre.

Apart from the land-use planning system, the other major tool for encouraging improved vitality and viability is the City Centre Management Initiative, formed in 1999. This brought together the Leeds City Centre Initiative (formed 1993) and the City Centre Management Unit so that strategic and operational matters are handled by one body. With the full

Guidance note on retail development (PPG6) with a view to ensuring that local plans reworked policies so as to sustain and enhance the vitality and viability of town centres. PPG6 was followed by the publication of the Urban Task Force's report (1999) and the subsequent Urban White Paper (DETR, 2000) which brought together many strands of urban policy and particularly emphasised the need for mixed use, compact and lively city centres (see Chapter 4 for the effect of these policies on the housing market). These various elements of policy have had an effect on retail development location: a report by surveyors CB Hillier Parker in May 2001 showed that high street shopping centre proposals accounted for over 90 per cent of the floorspace in the UK retail development pipeline, up from 37 per cent in 1998 and 45 per cent in 1999. In addition, we have witnessed a steep increase in town centre management schemes. The first began in 1987 and the number had reached 300 by 1999. Warnaby *et al.* (1998) and Warnaby and Medway

Table 11.2 Summary of perceptions of shopping in Leeds

Swift Research (2001) showed that 50 per cent of Leeds residents interviewed in the city centre go there at least once a week and younger people are the most frequent visitors. Shopping is the primary draw (for 82 per cent of respondents). The majority of respondents who work in the city centre also shop there or visit pubs/clubs/bars and restaurants/cafes, a number of them even coming in specially on Sundays.

Respondents appreciate the mix of shops in Leeds city centre and the range of places to eat and drink. Also attracting positive comments were the restaurants, pubs and bars, pedestrian areas, the range of activities and the markets area. In this survey, respondents mentioned the cosmopolitan atmosphere of the city centre — a point that was not raised in an earlier survey in 1997. Overall, the quality of the environment was rated as more important than was the case in 1997 and despite some continuing problems, public transport was thought to have improved.

Negative comments were limited mainly to issues about parking, traffic congestion and late night transport. Residents and workers were most likely to mention public conveniences. The presence of *Big Issue* sellers is a tiresome feature for many who come to the city centre.

"All groups commented that Leeds city centre had changed a great deal over the last few years and that these changes were generally positive. The types of changes noted included new buildings, restoration of existing buildings, increased leisure and entertainment facilities, more high profile shopping opportunities and improvements to the road system" (Swift Research, 2001, p.8).

Source: Swift Research (2001)

participation of relevant partners, the aims are to monitor the health of the city centre, devise strategies for improvement of appearance, function and facilities and implement changes to enhance vitality and viability. There was also a significant investment in Leeds city centre retail property from the late 1980s, following on from the city's boom in financial services: shopping centres, arcades and the market were refurbished and many run-down streets were smartened up. It is estimated that £1.8 billion was invested in Leeds city centre between 1992 and 2001, with £277 million of this going into major retail and leisure schemes and £37 million being invested during 2001 alone.

So what are the key features of the structure and dynamics of Leeds city centre? There are around 1,000 shop units in the city centre catering for the whole of the Leeds population as well as the 100,000 people that work in the city centre (14,000 in retailing alone). In a typical week, over 700,000 people enter the Prime Shopping Quarter (Figure 11.3). Market research in 1996 showed that about 80 per cent of Leeds shoppers were from Leeds postcode districts; 10 per cent were from Wakefield postcode districts and the remaining 10 per cent were from a mixture of other places. Most of the money spent in the city centre comes from people classed as 'locals' as opposed to those classed as 'visitors', although this is changing rapidly. Table 11.2 presents a synopsis of public perceptions of shopping in Leeds in 2001.

Since the 1960s, the retail core has been dominated by fashion and comparison good outlets, but there has been a decline in outlets which provide goods such as food, furniture, carpets, DIY, textiles, hardware and motor accessories. Such products are now found at retail warehouse parks outside the city centre and in suburban supermarkets in the case of food (see Section 11.2). Also under-represented are chemists, florists, charity shops and convenience goods shops, though Kirkgate Market provides a range of food and low price goods (which are not included in the official count of individual outlets). However, even in activities such as fashion retailing there are significant changes. Today, the town or city centre is increasingly segregated into high and low income fashion areas, with the former dominated by major multiples such as GAP, Diesel and Next. Crewe and Lowe (1995) suggest that within core urban areas, the identity and image of particular streets has changed rapidly with new cultures and images of high fashion. The knock-on effects of the presence of these new fashion retailers is to push up rents and rates in these streets

Table 11.3 Catering and entertainment in LS1 and LS2

Type of outlet	Number in 1991	Number in 2003
Restaurants	50	80
Bars and public houses	55	110
Cafés	61	110
Hotels	11	17
Nightclubs and casinos	13	21

Source: LCC 2003)

of outlet, with the only significant change over recent years being the advent of mobile phone shops.

Another key development in Leeds city centre — as in many other cities — has been the growth in leisure and entertainment businesses. In addition to new pubs and clubs, there has also been a significant rise in the number of restaurants and cafes. Altogether, leisure and entertainment premises now account for around 20 per cent of all units in the city centre. Table 11.3 indicates the numbers in 1991 and 2001. The latter includes organisations such as Starbucks, which supposedly appeal to a new breed of consumer keen to watch the streetscape as they sip their coffee (Smith, 1996).

Hannigan's *Fantasy City* provides an overview of the growth of leisure facilities in contemporary cities (Hannigan,1998). The trend is driven by a number of factors, not least a place marketing strategy which has encouraged the idea of the 'party city'. However, the increase in young people (including students) and tourists is also important. Chatterton and Hollands (2002) explore the contemporary culture of clubbing, and the resulting change in 'nightscapes', in a number of UK cities. The sector has diversified, adding jazz and

Café Rouge is one of many new café bars to open since the early 1990s. The area near the Corn Exchange has a high concentration of leisure venues.

and force other retailers to relocate to cheaper urban areas. In some of the larger centres (and increasingly in Leeds), these top fashion retailers are made up of international fashion players (see Fernie *et al.*, 1997 for a good illustration of this in London's West End). There is a rapid turnover of retail occupiers in the city centre, though analysis of occupier types shows that there is a remarkably constant mix of the main different types comedy venues, and there is more blurring of venue types: pubs/clubs, cafés/bars. More pubs, clubs and health and fitness centres will be provided as part of mixed use developments that are in the pipeline (see Chapter 12 for a critique of this aspect of the city centre). In Leeds, the concept of the 24-hour city has been widely promoted. Whilst it is probably true that Leeds is still a long way from being 'open all hours', the night-time population has been expanded by more liberal opening hours in many bars and clubs as well as retail outlets themselves. The 'live after five' initiative introduced late night (Thursday-Saturday) and Sunday trading for all the main shops around the core Briggate area.

Local Leeds pub, club and café clientele is increasingly supplemented by visitors, many more of whom can now stay in relative comfort in city centre hotels. Although there were only 850 hotel rooms in central Leeds in 1989, by 2002 developments had brought the total number of rooms to 2,045. If all proposed schemes are delivered, by 2005 there will be 4,250 bed spaces — five times the hotel capacity that existed in 1989. Leeds is an important destination for both business and cultural tourism. The tourism industry in Leeds has developed rapidly and substantially in recent years, generating an estimated £735 million in 2000 alone for the city's economy — this was an increase of 25 per cent on 1998. The expenditure supports in excess of 19,000 full-time equivalent jobs. The 2003 City Centre Audit reported that

- there were 1.43 million 'staying' trips to Leeds (a 20 per cent increase on 1994), generating an estimated £189 million (26 per cent of all visitor spending in Leeds);

- there were over 18 million visitor day trips to the city, generating expenditure of £546 million, accounting for 74 per cent of all tourism spend in the city; and

- visitors to Leeds spend over three-and-a-half times the national average, a sum of £48.35 a day (LCC, 2003b).

The number of 'shopping breaks' booked has increased sharply, especially in October and November (Leeds City Centre Management Initiative, 2003). In 1999, Leeds won the 'England for Excellence Award' for its 'Clubbing Breaks' marketing initiative, developed in partnership with Leeds hotels and clubs. During 2000–2001, Leeds was promoted as a destination by P&O North Sea Ferries throughout Holland and Belgium. The city was also included as a clubbing break destination by a tour operator in Holland.

The *Cultural Strategy*, launched in early 2003, addresses arts, sport, tourist facilities and libraries across the city, including the city centre. Until this point, arts and cultural activities had been organised in a rather *ad hoc* fashion, with no overall strategic idea of where the city should be going and how arts and culture fitted with other policy areas, such as regeneration (Strange 1996). Now there is a deliberate attempt to ensure that excellent cultural opportunities, experiences and facilities are provided for everyone (Leeds Cultural Partnership, 2003c). Arguably this enables a more proactive approach and increases Leeds' chances of winning new high profile facilities and events. There is also attention to the need to continue to stimulate and support community level activities and participation, not just pursue the winnings from the so-called 'visitor economy' (Chatterton and Unsworth, forthcoming).

Aggregate attendance at the city's three theatres

Table 11.4 Regional prime rents

	£ per square foot				
	1998	1999	2000	2001	2002
Leeds	190	190	260	260	275
Birmingham	335	335	335	335	335
Manchester	250	275	300	300	302
Newcastle	300	300	310	320	320
Glasgow	200	210	210	210	210
Edinburgh	220	220	230	240	230

Source: LCC (2003b)

Top, Albion Place has been a busy shopping area since it was laid out in the early nineteenth century. Middle, King Edward Street — an early twentieth century addition to the city centre retail area. Bottom, Allders department store on The Headrow was built as a Lewis's store in 1931, and at that time was reputedly the largest store outside London.

These developments in Leeds' cultural sector have continued to make the city centre an attractive location for many comparison goods and leisure retailers. This is reflected in buoyant rates and rents (Table 11.4). Leeds has the highest retail rents in Yorkshire and the Humber and the fourth highest rents of the main regional cities. Within

decreased by 2 per cent in the year to March 2002, but the total figure was still 27 per cent higher than the attendance in the year ending March 1998. The Henry Moore Institute is seeing increasing visitor numbers while the number of people visiting the Art Gallery has dropped from a peak in 1999. Visitor numbers at The Royal Armouries picked up after admission charges were dropped in 2001. The City Museum is currently closed but will reopen in the former Civic Theatre in 2007.

the city centre, Commercial Street and Briggate are the prime areas: this is where the highest rents are paid, reflecting the greatest intensity of trading (Commercial Street £250 per square foot; Briggate £225 per square foot). The arrival of Harvey Nichols in 1996 gave a boost to Leeds' image and lifted the Victoria Quarter. The east side of the city centre has experienced rent rises with some high profile tenants taking space along Vicar Lane.

Table 11.5 Shopping centres in the Prime Retail Quarter

(1) Merrion Centre: built 1963 by Town Centre Securities on the site of housing, brewery and a synagogue; refurbished 1985; to be redeveloped. When built, it was the largest commercial redevelopment ever carried out and included the first multi-storey car park in Leeds. In 1998, TCS bought the freehold from the Council. There are 50 shops, a supermarket, three cafes, four restaurants, five bars, two clubs, a hotel, a bowling alley and a comedy store.

(2) Leeds Shopping Plaza: formerly the Bond Street Centre; built 1977; refurbished 1988 and again in 1997. A large delivery area was eliminated and two new floors were created, with 49 units formatted on three floors. New entrance to City Square has improved access and footfall figures have increased dramatically. Adjoins planned Trinity Quarter. Owned by Tops Estates.

(3) St John's Centre: built in 1985. 40 units. Owned by Hermes (BT Pension Fund).

(4) Headrow Centre: formerly Schofields from 1989; refurbished 1996 and name changed. 40 units. Owned by Hermes (BT Pension Fund).

(5) Victoria Quarter: built 1898–1900; refurbished 1980s. Sold by Prudential to Highstone Estates 2001. Refurbishment 2002 to provide some larger units and flats on upper floors. 72 units.

(6) The Light: opened 2001; formerly office blocks with ground floor retail on Headrow side. Open 19 hours a day. 24 shopping units; a 13-screen, 2,900 seat multiplex cinema; a 300 cover restaurant and a 150-bed, four-star hotel. Owned by Halifax and Clerical and Medical.

(7) Corn Exchange: built 1863; converted into a shopping centre 1990. 36 units and 30 extra stalls at the weekend. Owned by Threadneedle Property Investments.

Table 11.6 The traditional market

Kirkgate Market has 390 traders and a total of around 2,000–2,500 people directly employed on the stalls. Visitor numbers dipped in the late 1990s but have recently stabilised and there are rarely vacant stalls. Swift Research (2001) found that it is still regarded positively as a shopping facility, especially by older people and those in social groups D and E. While there are many regular market customers, a higher proportion of city centre shoppers never use the markets.

The managers are keen to ensure that the Markets have a role in the future of the city. The stalls are not just a source of cheap goods for people on low incomes (and in any case, the discount supermarkets can do this more effectively); they also have a role to play in providing business opportunities — possibly a stepping stone to a larger retailing presence (after all, Marks & Spencer did it!). There are proposals to offer training in business planning and management in exchange for special deals on taking a stall — helping to encourage viable business start-ups — all part of 'closing the gap' (*Vision II* theme).

Some elements of strategy are:

• to encourage more fresh produce: fresh produce gets the biggest rental discount;

• for 10 x10-foot stalls in the 1976 and 1981 areas to amalgamate — it is considered that there are too many of this size. There are bigger discounts for the larger stalls;

• the managers would like at least some parts of the market to be open on Sundays. In the city centre as a whole, 20–25 per cent of trade is taking place on Sundays. Traders remain resistant, presumably because they are mostly small family businesses and need to have a day off. Even a suggestion to have a rota of opening by different kinds of stalls has not been accepted. Indeed, there is still strong support for the half day closing on Wednesday; and

• city centre residents would no doubt use the Markets for food purchases if there was late opening, but there has been strong resistance to this idea from traders.

There are some in the Council who think that the market is bigger than is really required and that the 1976 and 1981 areas should be redeveloped as part of the Union Street/Templar Street development that is planned. The Markets manager argues that there is a demand for the goods offered across the whole market. If there were not, more vacancies would occur more frequently and stalls would be harder to re-let. However, recent rent rises have caused a good deal of bad feeling and may result in some traders not renewing their leases.

The Farmers' Market has been held at Kirkgate on the first Sunday of every month since 1999 — one of 450 such markets that have been established in the UK since 1997. At first there were around 30 stalls; now there are 75–80 stalls each time. Customers clearly do more than just load up with organic and home-made produce, meat, fish and dairy produce, crafts and flowers: the manager of Allders on the Headrow reports a 20 per cent increase in takings on the Sunday when the market operates.

Commercial agents report that there is demand from 200 retailers for units in the city centre, mainly for larger units (Estates Gazette, 24 May 2003). Vacancy levels of 14 per cent (early 2003) are largely concentrated in areas of the city centre that are subject to potential redevelopment. (The national average vacancy rate was 11 per cent in early 2003).

Future developments are likely to secure growth in the city. A further £3.4 billion is said to be in the pipeline (URBED, 2002) including two large developments:

- Hammerson and Town Centre Securities plan a joint £400 million, 92,900m², mixed regeneration scheme covering a large site on both sides of Eastgate. Work is progressing to try to ensure that the final form of the development not only secures the success of the scheme itself but also helps to connect that side of the city centre to the adjacent areas.

- The Universities Superannuation Scheme is to fund the re-development of Trinity Quarter to provide 27,870m² of retail space.

The shops beneath West Riding House on Albion Street are likely to be redeveloped and the Merrion Centre is due for redevelopment. In both cases, larger units will be created. There will be significant amounts of new retail space at Clarence Dock (near the Royal Armouries). Kirkgate still awaits the much-needed boost that will be provided by the redevelopment of the site that includes remnants of the eighteenth century White Cloth Hall.

It is clear that in order to increase the attractiveness of the retail environment, it has also been necessary to improve the safety and comfort of shopping. Thus, much effort has gone into reducing crime and the fear of crime, and reducing noise, litter, air pollution and waste output. Nineteen CCTV cameras were put in place in 1996; further cameras were later installed. Overall crime levels fell by 10 per cent in the year to March 2003, but crimes against the person rose by 29 per cent. The City Council is working with the police to reduce the incidence of crime in the city centre (LCC, 2003a) and newly appointed street wardens began duties in early 2003.

To address the issue of consumer comfort, pedestrianisation started in the early 1970s and included provision of new/improved road crossings. Pedestrianisation of Briggate was completed in 1997 (and with funding from Yorkshire Forward, further improvements are planned); Vicar Lane may follow. Pedestrianisation is generally reckoned to improve retail prosperity by making shoppers feel that they are in a friendlier environment and reducing the resistance to crossing the street to visit shops on the other side. City Centre yards and arcades are receiving attention and Lands Lane and Kirkgate are scheduled for improvement. Other areas of environmental improvement include new lamp standards, benches, paving and other aspects of street styling, inspired by what the Council leader of the time had seen and admired in Barcelona. The development of a database for reporting faults to relevant Council departments (Highways Maintenance, Street Cleansing and Leisure Services) also helped in the removal of graffiti and chewing gum and the encouragement of design that minimises maintenance.

11.4 Conclusions

This chapter has sought to examine changes in retail patterns across suburban and central Leeds since the 1960s — a case study of retail change rarely seen in the literature. The story is one of a dramatic transformation in the urban landscape as waves of development have brought a massive increase in floorspace. These developments closely mirror, and are indeed shaped by, changing national and local planning legislation.

The move away from allowing out-of-town development has meant that since 2000, more shop floorspace has been opened in town centres than in out-of-town centres and retail warehouse parks put together (The Guardian, 2004). Any new retail developments are likely to continue to be based in town centres or on improvements or extensions to existing suburban centres, such as the recent Seacroft superstore described in Section 11.2. Grocery retailers in particular may be especially keen to persuade the local planners in Leeds that more Seacroft-type developments are needed in other food desert locations. The planning guidelines on retail development are under revision in 2004, but despite renewed pressure from major retailers such as Ikea and ASDA-Wal-Mart for a relaxation of the ban on out-of-town retailing, the Office of the Deputy Prime Minister is likely to maintain its determination to limit this kind of development (personal communication; Association of Town Centre Managers).

What about the future of the city centre? It is clear that the city centre will continue to reinvent itself and new retail goods and services will replace those activities which begin to struggle on the high street. Predicting which ones will fade and die is not easy. For example, Cope (1996) predicted that by 2005 there would be few travel agents and banks on our high streets. This prediction was driven by the rise in e-commerce and the use of the Internet for shopping purposes. Despite the fact that Cope's prediction has clearly been somewhat premature, all analysts remain convinced that e-commerce will become a much more significant player in the market over the next ten years. The greatest problem for Internet retailers is likely to be the 'e-gap' which exists both in access to the

Shoppers' delight: the Victoria Quarter, Leeds' premier retail area, combines the unique charm of late-Victorian architecture with the latest fashion boutiques.

Internet and desire to use it. This gap currently lies between the young, professional, well-educated consumers and the urban poor and excluded living in the worst of the council estates. Birkin *et al.* (2002) estimate the nature of this gap for consumers in Leeds using data obtained from lifestyle surveys. The 'connected' north and west of the city contrasts starkly with the 'unconnected' south and east. If the Internet offers the potential to eradicate urban food deserts such as Seacroft in Leeds, then schemes to provide public access to technology need to be found (see Davies, 1985 for details of a scheme perhaps ahead of its time!)

Other analysts have also been happy to try and predict the future high street. Field (1997), Fernie (1998) and Markham (1998) all provide interesting end-of-century forecasts of the forthcoming retail environment and Wrigley *et al.* (2002b) discuss the relationship between traditional retailing and 'e-tailing'. Field (1997) and Fernie (1998) talk of more automation on the high street, as retailers swap staff for computer-based electronic ordering, in the form of interactive kiosks. These rely on the consumer's willingness to press buttons and interact with a terminal. Although to many retailers such kiosks are only part of the new marketing mix, there is interest in providing stand-alone kiosks to reach new customers (possibly in remote locations). It is difficult to envisage a high street with too many automated kiosks. High-level service is also likely to be a key feature of the future high street, thus preventing automation becoming too widespread. Treanor (2004) reports that many banks are now deciding to reverse their longstanding branch de-staffing strategies in order to provide more customer service and advice in their leading high street branches (despite the in-roads made by electronic banking). While stores with off-the-peg clothes will continue to attract customers who want to see and try on before buying, there will also be special services for made-to-measure clothes, with computers used to gather data to send on to low-wage workshops outside Britain. It is likely that people will still want to browse for gifts and novelties and will continue to enjoy the shopping

experience, mixed with other leisure activities, that cannot be completely replicated on the Internet.

We can perhaps be more certain of some future changes in Leeds. The fifth Leeds City Centre Audit (LCC, 2003b) gives us to some guidelines to priority areas. These include improving accessibility for all: working on matching job seekers in inner city areas to available city centre jobs; improving aspects of physical access; improving family-friendliness of the city centre and ensuring that there are no sections of the population who feel that the city centre does not offer them what they want and can afford. The City Council also plans to place more emphasis on street life: there is scope for increasing entertainment, building on the success of existing events and festivals. But it seems that the major developments may come in the form of further 'landmark buildings' and visitor attractions to complement retailing (see Chapter 16). The city centre will continue to be a dynamic place, with rapid turnover of occupiers, plenty of visitors and concerted partnership between public and private sectors to ensure continuing vitality and viability.

Notes

1   Quote from Zukin, S. (1998).
2   Experian Goad ranking based on a range of indicators including total floorspace, numbers of different types of retailers, vacancy rate and presence of outlets vulnerable to out-of-town and e-tail competition (LCC, 2003a).
3   Verdict Research; Hiller Parker National Survey of Local Shopping Patterns (LCC, 2003a).

References

Birkin, M., Clarke, G.P. and Clarke, M. (2002) *Retail Geography and Intelligent Network Planning,* Wiley, Chichester.

Bromley, R.D.F. and Thomas, C. (1993) The retail revolution, the carless shopper and disadvantage, *Transactions, Institute of British Geographers,* 18: 222–236.

Burns, W. (1959) *British Shopping Centres: New Trends in Layout and Distribution,* Leonard Hill, London.

Burt S. and Sparks, L. (1995) Understanding the arrival of limited-line discount stores in Britain, *European Management Journal,* 13: 110–119.

CALUS (1975) *Rent Assessment and Tenant Mix in Planned Shopping Centres,* Centre for Advanced Land Use studies, Reading.

Chatterton, P. and Hollands, R. (2002), *Urban Nightscapes: Youth Cultures, Pleasure Spaces and Corporate Power,* Routledge, London

Chatterton, P. and Unsworth, R. (forthcoming) Making space(s) for alternative cultures, Local Economy.

Christaller, W. (1966) *Central places in Southern Germany,* translated by C.W. Baskin, Prentice-Hall, Englewood Cliffs, New Jersey.

Clarke, G.P. (1984) *The changing expression of small-scale retailing in Leeds, 1960–1983,* Working Paper, School of Geography, University of Leeds, Leeds.

Clarke, G.P., Guy, C.M. and Eyre H. (2002) Deriving indicators of access to food retail provision in British Cities; studies of Cardiff, Leeds and Bradford, *Urban Studies,* 39: 2041–2060.

Cope, N. (1996) *Retail in the Digital Age,* Bowerdean, London.

Cox, R.K. (1968) *Retail Site Assessment,* Business Books, London.

Crewe, L. and Lowe, M. (1995) Gap on the map? Towards a geography of consumption and identity, *Environment and Planning A,* 27: 1877–1898.

Davies, R.L. (1974) Nucleated and ribbon components of the urban retailing system in Britain, *Town Planning Review,* 45: 91–111.

Davies, R.L. (1984) *Retail and Commercial Planning,* Croom Helm, London.

Davies, R.L. (1985) The Gateshead shopping and information service, *Environment and Planning B,* 12: 209–220.

Davies. R.L. (1986) Retail planning in disarray, *The Planner,* 72: 20–22.

Department of Environment, Transport and the Regions (DETR) (1998) *The Impact of Large Foodstores on Market Towns and District Centres,* DETR, London.

Department of Environment, Transport and the Regions (DETR) (2000) *Urban White Paper,* http://www.regeneration.detr.gov.uk/policies/ ourtowns/cm4911/pdf/

Department of the Environment (DoE) (1996) *Planning Policy Guidance Note 6: Town Centres,* DoE, London.

Fernie J. (ed, 1998) *The Future for UK Retailing,* Financial times Retail and Consumer Publishing, London.

Fernie, J., Moore, C., Lawrie, A. and Hallsworth, A. (1997) The international-isation of the high fashion brand: the case of Central London, *Journal of Product and Brand Management,* 6: 151–162.

Field, C. (1997) *The Future of the Store: New Formats and Channels for a Changing Retail Environment,* FT Retail & Consumer Publishing, London.

The Guardian (2004) Storing up trouble, *The Guardian,* 24 March.

Guy, C.M. (1996) Corporate strategies in food retailing and their local impacts: a case study of Cardiff, *Environment and Planning A,* 28: 1575-1602.

Guy, C.M. (1998) 'High street' retailing in off-centre retail parks, *Town Planning Review,* 69(3): 291–313.

Hannigan, J. (1998) *Fantasy City,* Routledge, London.

Hillman, M. (1973) The social costs of hypermarket developments, *Built Environment,* 2: 89–91.

Jones, C.S. (1969) *Regional Shopping Centres: Their Location, Planning and Design,* Business Books, London.

Jones, P. (1984) Retail warehouse developments in Britain, *Area,* 16(1): 41–47.

Leeds City Centre Management Initiative (2003) *Annual Report 2002,* LCC, Leeds.

Leeds City Council (LCC) (1998) *Vision for Leeds — Draft Report,* Leeds Initiative, Leeds.

Leeds City Council (LCC) (1998) *City Centre Audit: 1st Annual Report,* LCC, Leeds.

Leeds City Council (LCC) (1999) *Vision for Leeds,* Leeds Initiative, Leeds.

Leeds Cultural Partnership (2003c) *The Cultural Strategy for Leeds,* Leeds?

Leeming, F. (1959) An experimental survey of retail shopping and service facilities in part of North Leeds, Transactions, *Institute of British Geographers,* 26: 133–152.

Lowe, M. (2000) Britain's regional shopping centres: new urban forms? *Urban Studies,* 37: 261–274.

Markham, J. (1998) *The Future of Shopping — Traditional Patterns and Net Effects,* MacMillan Business Press, Basingstoke.

National Retail Planning Forum (1996) *A Tale of Three Cities: What Makes a Successful City Centre,* National Retail Planning Forum, London.

Rowley, G. (1993) Prospects for the central business district, in Bromley, R.D.F. and Thomas, C.J. (eds) *Retail Change: Contemporary Issues,* UCL Press, London, pp.110–125.

Rushton, P. (1999) *Out of Town Shopping: The Future of Retailing,* The British Library, London.

Shaw, H. (2003) *The ecology of food deserts,* unpublished PhD thesis, School of Geography, University of Leeds, Leeds.

Smith, M.D. (1996) The empire filters back: consumption, production and the politics of Starbuck's coffee, *Urban Geography,* 17: 502–524.

Sparks, L. (1990) Spatial-structural relationships in retail corporate growth: a case study of Kwik Save group PLC, *The Services Industries Journal,* 10: 25-84.

Strange, I. (1996) Pragmatism, opportunity and entertainment: the arts, culture and urban economic regeneration in Leeds, in Haughton, G. and Williams, C. (eds) *Corporate City? Partnership, Participation and Partition in Urban Development in Leeds,* Avebury, Aldershot, pp. 135–152.

Swift Research (2001) *Leeds City Centre Audit: Public Perceptions Market Research Survey* (prepared for Leeds Development Agency).

Thomas, C.J. and Bromley, R.D.F. (1993) The impact of out-of-centre retailing, in Bromley, R.D.F.and Thomas, C.J. (eds) *Retail Change: Contemporary Issues,* UCL Press, London, pp. 126–152.

Treanor, J. (2004) From local branch to wine bar and back again? *The Guardian: Business,* Tuesday 8 June, p.15.

Unit of Retail, Planning and Information (URPI) (1981) *DIY Retail*

Warehouses, report of an URPI workshop, URPI U21, Reading.

Urban Task Force (1999) *Towards an Urban Renaissance,* final report of the Urban Task Force chaired by Carol Rogers of Riverside, DETR, London.

URBED (1994) *Vital and Viable Town Centres: Meeting the Challenge,* HMSO, London.

URBED (2002) *Vision for Leeds II: Lessons from Vision I.* Draft report for LCC (unpublished).

Warnaby, G., Alexander, A. and Medway, D. (1998) Town centre management in the UK: a review, synthesis and research agenda, *International Review of Retail, Distribution and Consumer Research,* 8(1): 15–31.

Warnaby, G. and Medway, D. (2000) *Competitive responses by town centres to off-centre retail developments,* paper presented to CIRM 2000 Conference, Department of Retail marketing, Manchester Metropolitan University.

Whelan, A., Wrigley, N., Warm, D.L. and Cannings, E. (2002) Life in a 'food desert', *Urban Studies,* 39: 2083–2100.

Wrigley, N. (1987) The concentration of capital in UK grocery retailing, *Environment and Planning A,* 19: 1283–1288.

Wrigley, N., Guy, C.M. and Lowe, M. (2002a) Urban regeneration, social inclusion and large store development: the Seacroft development in context, *Urban Studies,* 39: 2101–2114.

Wrigley, N., Lowe, M. and Currah, A. (2002b) Retailing and e-tailing, *Urban Geography,* 23(2): 180–197.

Wrigley, N., Warm, D.L. and Margetts, B. (2003) Deprivation, diet and food retail access: findings from the Leeds 'food desert study', *Environment and Planning A,* 35: 151–188.

Zukin, S. (1998), Urban lifestyles: diversity and standardisation in spaces of consumption, *Urban Studies,* 35(5–6): 825–839.

12

The London of the North?
Youth Cultures, Urban Change and Nightlife

PAUL CHATTERTON & ROBERT HOLLANDS

While one might initially be quick to applaud the development of urban nightlife, our aim is to look beyond the hubbub of self-congratulation to a number of crucial elements that are often overlooked.

Right, It could be London, but it's Leeds: one of the new-style café bars that have appeared in central Leeds over the last decade, giving it a more cosmopolitan feel. Far right, traditional pubs, such as The Ship face competition from new-style venues.

12.1 Introduction

Who could fail to notice that Leeds' centre has been comprehensively transformed over the last decade or so? Examples of key changes are described in Emmett (1998), Simpson (1999) and Fox and Unsworth (2003). A once semi-derelict city centre, known more for its ugly decaying buildings and a smattering of rough pubs and discos, has been redeveloped into what people call the 'London of the North', replete with imposing new office blocks, pavement cafés and cutting edge bars and cool clubs, playing music late into the night. Yet scratch the surface and there is another face to the city centre: stark contrasts between wealth and poverty, homelessness, increases in firearms offences, racist attacks and violence towards women. Understandably then, there is also a sense of unease that accompanies Leeds' success story, which

asks who are the winners and losers in the recent drive for the city to become more cosmopolitan? The tensions between what the city is striving for, what it has consigned to the past, and what it chooses to ignore are vividly illustrated in its nightlife. Like many UK cities, branded corporate theme and style bars are now commonplace, aimed at 'cash-rich' groups while traditional and alternative venues have either closed down, been marginalised or transformed into trendy restaurants or style bars (Chatterton and Hollands, 2002; 2003).

This chapter is an attempt to explain many of the transformations in nightlife culture in Leeds. It is structured around three main sections to develop an understanding of young people's use of nightlife. First, we highlight the expanding role of large national/international corporate nightlife operators taking over the city. Next, we examine the

planning of nightlife through the activities of the police, magistrates and the local state. Finally, we look at the consumption of nightlife spaces by exploring young adults' own 'lived experience' of Leeds. Before that, it is worth explaining some of the transformations which have been affecting both cities and young people, and some recent changes in Leeds.

Changing youth, changing cities

First, we are concerned with the dramatic and forceful changes which have occurred within many British cities over the last few decades. Since the 1970s, they have experienced decline and deindustrialisation, due to a suburbanisation of employment,

depopulation, a move to home-based leisure, national-local political wrangling and marginalisation by multi-national capital. The result has been widespread unemployment, physical and social decay, crime, homelessness and dereliction (Hudson and Williams, 1995). Over the last two decades attempts have been made to tackle this predicament facing British 'core' cities and remodel them as places to live, work and be entertained. A whole host of city marketeers has been active in promoting a new identity and 'cultural brand' for cities. British cities in general have borrowed both from the excesses of the North American model of casinos, multiplexes and malls (Hannigan, 1998) and the continental European model of 'café society' and socially inclusive city centre living (Landry, 2000).

This move back to the city is part of a wider process of social and economic change within the UK. For example, the political project since the Thatcher years eroded the established masculine and labourist city strongly connected to its industrial past, in favour of private/corporate capital, knowledge-based activities, 'feminised' and middle-class consumption and an entrepreneurial turn in urban governance aimed at attracting and satisfying the demands of highly mobile global capital (Jessop, 1997). This 'return to the centre' has come of age through a reinvention of city centres (O'Connor and Wynne, 1995) which focuses on business service employment and city centre living, and a greater economic role for leisure and consumption-based, rather than production-based activities (Zukin, 1995). Further, all metropolitan centres now point towards the vibrancy of their nightlife, and 24-hour activity, as a growing economic sector and a key indicator of a healthy economy and population.

While one might initially be quick to applaud the development of urban nightlife, our aim is to look beyond the hubbub of self-congratulation to a number of crucial elements that are often overlooked. For example, little is said about who owns the night-time economy: many large national operators are dominating city centre landscapes and lifestyles and smaller, local independent operators are being squeezed out, unable to compete with the bids made for sites and tenancies by larger

companies. Additionally, many of Britain's core cities are pursuing a rather off-the-shelf approach to developing the night-time economy through multiplexes, theme pubs and casinos, which begs the question in whose interest and for whom is the city being developed? Current trends suggest that many of our cities are becoming havens for high value-added entertainment for the cash rich, at the expense of a diverse and locally embedded range of activities for the majority, including the urban poor.

Second, we are concerned with the shifting identities and life-worlds of young people (Miles, 2000). In particular, growing up in many western countries has been extended due to exclusion from the labour market, increased participation in education, lower marriage rates and greater dependency on the family household. As a result, there is evidence of a period of extended or post adolescence, in which an array of youthful lifestyles and identities are visible much longer. It is this group who are targets for future nightlife provision. Further, for many young adults, consumption, especially based in city centres, is becoming a more influential element in the formation of youth identity (Hollands, 1995). Feminisation of the youth labour market has also had an impact on the public presence of young women in city centres, at work and at play (Pattison, 2000).

It is also important to stress that significant differences are still visible, between, for example, unemployed young people or those dependent on welfare benefits or unstable employment, university students and those in high-level training, and young professionals in stable, well-paid jobs. These differences are reflected in the nightlife, e.g. the growing number of young people working in an unstable labour market, whose participation in city centre nightlife is curtailed by poverty (MacDonald, 1997). At the same time, numbers of university students have substantially increased in Britain since 1992 and identifiable swathes of all cities are devoted to meeting their educational, housing and entertainment needs, offering a host of promotional nightlife discounts. Finally, many young people emerging from higher education are able to enter a world of relatively stable employment and consumer lifestyles. These young urban service workers, knowledge

professionals and cultural intermediaries are often heralded as the saviours of the city's new night-time and cultural economy.

Growth and change in the corporate city

Leeds has had a more effective make-over than many other post-industrial cities. The city's marketers have been successful in persuading both the travel industry and the general public that it is an attractive tourist and leisure destination with a strong European-style café society. The City Council's strategy to develop Leeds as a cosmopolitan, 24-hour, European city, was initiated by John Trickett, council leader in the mid-1990s (Trickett, 1994). Since then, a liberal attitude to licensing has allowed a vibrant late-night economy to flourish. Led by independent operators initially, the city centre has been transformed into one of the liveliest, most cosmopolitan and progressive late-night entertainment areas in the country. However, more recently, there have been concerns that the city has arguably reached saturation point (Chesterton, 2003) due to the rapid growth of nightlife venues dominated by large-scale corporate investments.

There is also another side to this story of prosperity, especially in the areas surrounding the city centre: many

13

How Green is My City?
Environment and Sustainability:
Status, Policy and Prospects

GORDON MITCHELL & RACHAEL UNSWORTH

depopulation, a move to home-based leisure, national-local political wrangling and marginalisation by multi-national capital. The result has been widespread unemployment, physical and social decay, crime, homelessness and dereliction (Hudson and Williams, 1995). Over the last two decades attempts have been made to tackle this predicament facing British 'core' cities and remodel them as places to live, work and be entertained. A whole host of city marketeers has been active in promoting a new identity and 'cultural brand' for cities. British cities in general have borrowed both from the excesses of the North American model of casinos multiplexes and malls (Hannigan, 1998) and the continental European model of 'café society' and socially inclusive city centre living (Landry, 2000).

This move back to the city is part of a wider process of social and economic change within the UK. For example, the political project since the Thatcher years eroded the established masculine and labourist city strongly connected to its industrial past, in favour of private/corporate capital, knowledge-based activities, 'feminised' and middle-class consumption and an entrepreneurial turn in urban governance aimed at attracting and satisfying the demands of highly mobile global capital (Jessop, 1997). This 'return to the centre' has come of age through a reinvention of city centres (O'Connor and Wynne, 1995) which focuses on business service employment and city centre living, and a greater economic role for leisure and consumption-based, rather than production-based activities (Zukin, 1995). Further, all metropolitan centres now point towards the vibrancy of their nightlife, and 24-hour activity, as a growing economic sector and a key indicator of a healthy economy and population.

While one might initially be quick to applaud the development of urban nightlife, our aim is to look beyond the hubbub of self-congratulation to a number of crucial elements that are often overlooked. For example, little is said about who owns the night-time economy: many large national operators are dominating city centre landscapes and lifestyles and smaller, local independent operators are being squeezed out, unable to compete with the bids made for sites and tenancies by larger

planning of nightlife through the activities of the police, magistrates and the local state. Finally, we look at the consumption of nightlife spaces by exploring young adults' own 'lived experience' of Leeds. Before that, it is worth explaining some of the transformations which have been affecting both cities and young people, and some recent changes in Leeds.

Changing youth, changing cities

First, we are concerned with the dramatic and forceful changes which have occurred within many British cities over the last few decades. Since the 1970s, they have experienced decline and deindustrialisation, due to a suburbanisation of employment,

companies. Additionally, many of Britain's core cities are pursuing a rather off-the-shelf approach to developing the night-time economy through multiplexes, theme pubs and casinos, which begs the question in whose interest and for whom is the city being developed? Current trends suggest that many of our cities are becoming havens for high value-added entertainment for the cash rich, at the expense of a diverse and locally embedded range of activities for the majority, including the urban poor.

Second, we are concerned with the shifting identities and life-worlds of young people (Miles, 2000). In particular, growing up in many western countries has been extended due to exclusion from the labour market, increased participation in education, lower marriage rates and greater dependency on the family household. As a result, there is evidence of a period of extended or post adolescence, in which an array of youthful lifestyles and identities are visible much longer. It is this group who are targets for future nightlife provision. Further, for many young adults, consumption, especially based in city centres, is becoming a more influential element in the formation of youth identity (Hollands, 1995). Feminisation of the youth labour market has also had an impact on the public presence of young women in city centres, at work and at play (Pattison, 2000).

It is also important to stress that significant differences are still visible, between, for example, unemployed young people or those dependent on welfare benefits or unstable employment, university students and those in high-level training, and young professionals in stable, well-paid jobs. These differences are reflected in the nightlife, e.g. the growing number of young people working in an unstable labour market, whose participation in city centre nightlife is curtailed by poverty (MacDonald, 1997). At the same time, numbers of university students have substantially increased in Britain since 1992 and identifiable swathes of all cities are devoted to meeting their educational, housing and entertainment needs, offering a host of promotional nightlife discounts. Finally, many young people emerging from higher education are able to enter a world of relatively stable employment and consumer lifestyles. These young urban service workers, knowledge

professionals and cultural intermediaries are often heralded as the saviours of the city's new night-time and cultural economy.

Growth and change in the corporate city

Leeds has had a more effective make-over than many other post-industrial cities. The city's marketers have been successful in persuading both the travel industry and the general public that it is an attractive tourist and leisure destination with a strong European-style café society. The City Council's strategy to develop Leeds as a cosmopolitan, 24-hour, European city, was initiated by John Trickett, council leader in the mid-1990s (Trickett, 1994). Since then, a liberal attitude to licensing has allowed a vibrant late-night economy to flourish. Led by independent operators initially, the city centre has been transformed into one of the liveliest, most cosmopolitan and progressive late-night entertainment areas in the country. However, more recently, there have been concerns that the city has arguably reached saturation point (Chesterton, 2003) due to the rapid growth of nightlife venues dominated by large-scale corporate investments.

There is also another side to this story of prosperity, especially in the areas surrounding the city centre: many

citizens of Leeds have not participated in these rapid changes. One third of wards in Leeds are within the worst 10 per cent of wards nationally (see Chapter 6). The segmented nature of the labour and entertainment market has resulted in a a multi-speed city, where groups, mainly in the outer areas, are not able to keep up with the pace of current developments. As a result, many young people are relegated to either unemployment or low level positions in the labour market and are in general non-participants in the city's vibrant nightlife. Statistics show consistently that the majority of city residents are not receiving the full benefits of Leeds' burgeoning success. Because of this, perhaps the 'classic corporate approach' to development needs rethinking if the city wants to increase inclusivity and access for all residents.

12.2 Producing the night-time economy

Production of alcohol and ownership of pubs were subject to restructuring and concentration over the course of the twentieth century. While in 1930 there were 559 brewery companies in the UK, by 1998, there were only 59 (BLRA, 1999). One company, Scottish-Courage, runs a near-monopoly on the domestic supply of beer, while a small number of chain pub companies now dominate the ownership of pubs and bars. Much of this dramatic shift in ownership came about through the 1989 Monopolies and Mergers Commission report and subsequent Beer Orders Act, which aimed to break the monopoly ownership of pubs by national brewers (Mason and McNally, 1997). Since then, there has been an acceleration of mergers within the brewing and pub industry. Scottish and

A traditional pub in a Briggate yard, Whitelocks was first granted a licence in 1715. Since being rebuilt in the 1860s, it has changed little, though new corporate owners have brought in changes that have excited negative reactions from traditional pub-goers.

Table 12.1 Change in pub ownership
in the UK, 1989–2000

	1989	Jan 2000	July 2000
National brewers			
Tenanted	22,000	2,724	1,000
Managed	10,000	7,336	2,300
Sub total	32,000	10,060[1]	3,300[2]
Regional brewers			
Tenanted	9,000	5,939	5,939
Managed	3,000	3,498	3,498
Sub total	12,000	9,437	9,437
Non-brewers			
Single site	16,000	18,098	18,098
Multi-site pubcos	–	24,196	30,956
Sub total	16,000	42,294	48,392
Total	60,000	61,791	61,791

[1] *Bass, Scottish & Newcastle, Whitbread* [2] *Scottish & Newcastle only*
Source: The Publican (2000)

In Lower Briggate and the Call Lane area there is a cluster of pubs and new-style venues. The Viaduct was a Tetley pub, serving the beer brewed just across the River Aire. It was one of many taken over by a pubco in the early 1990s.

all pubs and bars. Nightclubs are currently experiencing a similar level of merger activity with the emergence of mega operators such as the PoNaNa Group and Luminar Leisure — the largest nightclub operator in the UK.

Branding has become a key part of this restructuring with 8 per cent of all pubs in the UK (4,776 outlets) branded using one of 206 brands, with the top five pub operators controlling 63 per cent of branded pubs (The Publican, 2000). Pub branding exploded during the 1990s through the emergence of Aussie, Irish and sports themed bars which came under heavy criticism from consumer groups and publicans alike due to their role in eroding the identity of the traditional British pub and its clientele (Everitt and Bowler, 1996). For many companies, branding is the backbone of maintaining shareholder profits.

Newcastle, Interbrew, Carlsberg-Tetley and Guinness control 81 per cent of beer sales in the UK, while the number of large pub chains (or 'pubcos') has flourished by buying-up outlets from former brewers. Pubcos, which owned 16,000 outlets in 1989, now own around 48,000 pubs — many of them multi-site (accounting for nearly 80 per cent of the market) (Table 12.1).

Many of these pub companies, such as JD Wetherspoons, the Punch Group, Spirit and PubMaster, have shown remarkable levels of growth. Overall, the Beer Orders legislation largely had the opposite effect of reducing the monopoly in the sector as pub ownership by a small number of large brewers has now been replaced by monopoly ownership by a small number of pub companies. For example, the top 10 leading UK pub operators now account for nearly 50 per cent of

Figure 12.1 Change in pub ownership, 1950–2000

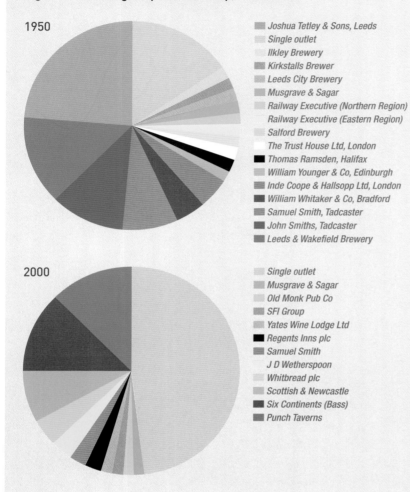

1950

- Joshua Tetley & Sons, Leeds
- Single outlet
- Ilkley Brewery
- Kirkstalls Brewer
- Leeds City Brewery
- Musgrave & Sagar
- Railway Executive (Northern Region)
- Railway Executive (Eastern Region)
- Salford Brewery
- The Trust House Ltd, London
- Thomas Ramsden, Halifax
- William Younger & Co, Edinburgh
- Inde Coope & Hallsopp Ltd, London
- William Whitaker & Co, Bradford
- Samuel Smith, Tadcaster
- John Smiths, Tadcaster
- Leeds & Wakefield Brewery

2000

- Single outlet
- Musgrave & Sagar
- Old Monk Pub Co
- SFI Group
- Yates Wine Lodge Ltd
- Regents Inns plc
- Samuel Smith
- J D Wetherspoon
- Whitbread plc
- Scottish & Newcastle
- Six Continents (Bass)
- Punch Taverns

Figure 12.2 illustrates the distribution of ownership in city centre pubs, bars and night clubs. National operators own twice as many venues as their independent and local/regional competitors combined. Their respective territories divide the city: the corporate heavyweights hold sway in the station, university, Headrow and Greek Street areas, whilst the single-site, independent operators dominate the areas around The Calls and Corn Exchange. The Call Lane area is a particular focus of growth in independent bars, thanks to cheap rents and a lack of interest from other commercial sectors. With the backing of brewery loans, the 'independents' have been able to colonise this previously disused area.

Leeds has also moved heavily down the branded nightlife route.

Current patterns of provision in Leeds' nightlife

Over the last 10 years, Leeds has seen a remarkable growth in nightlife venues. Between 1994 and 2001, licensed premises increased by 53 per cent and special hours certificates (post 11pm) increased by 155 per cent. By 2001, the city centre had 121 pubs and bars and 18 nightclubs. New licence applications constantly come forward. At the same time, the ownership of pubs in Leeds has changed dramatically since 1950 (Figure 12.1). There has been a move away from local and regional-based brewers (especially Joshua Tetley, who owned one quarter of all city centre pubs), towards a more diffuse pattern of ownership in which large pubcos and corporate operators vie with smaller independent companies.

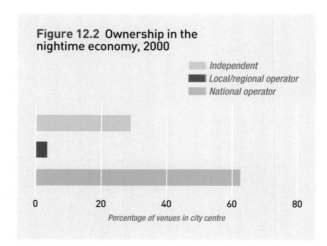

Figure 12.2 Ownership in the nightime economy, 2000

- Independent
- Local/regional operator
- National operator

Percentage of venues in city centre

Café bars, nightclubs and pubs all have their place in the diverse array of venues. Some transform themselves from daytime café bars to dimly-lit late night bars with loud music. Others are dedicated late night venues opening their doors as the pubs close. Bands play at some pubs, such as the Duck and Drake in Kirkgate, which features jazz.

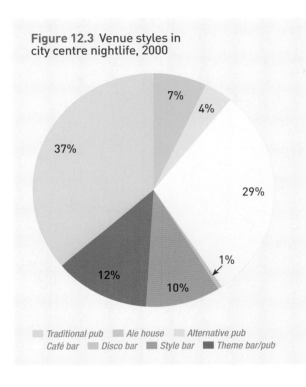

Figure 12.3 Venue styles in city centre nightlife, 2000

7%
4%
37%
29%
1%
12%
10%

Traditional pub ☐ Ale house ☐ Alternative pub
Café bar ☐ Disco bar ☐ Style bar ☐ Theme bar/pub

Most of these large branded venues have been established in Leeds since 1999, taking advantage of the availability of large empty buildings such as banking halls.

Traditional pubs face stiff competition

Over one quarter of city centre pubs are branded. As Figure 12.4 shows, branded pubs and bars, with themed bars such as Walkabout and Springbok, are concentrated around the universities. Greek Street and South Parade also have several branded outlets which are predominantly aimed at the after-work, office market such as All Bar One and Casa. There is also a cluster of branded establishments near the station and along Boar lane which attracts the more 'townie' crowd. Several branded venues have emerged around the Corn Exchange such as Pitcher and Piano and Café Rouge aiming for the daytime café bar crowd and the more sophisticated evening market.

Figure 12.3 highlights the different styles of venues in Leeds. While traditional pubs still make up one third of Leeds' pubs and bars, café and style bars have grown rapidly, comprising nearly 40 per cent of Leeds' licensed premises. These are clustered around the Greek Street — Park Lane area and in Calls and Corn Exchange area. Alternative venues, marked by

Figure 12.4 Branding of nightlife venues, 2000

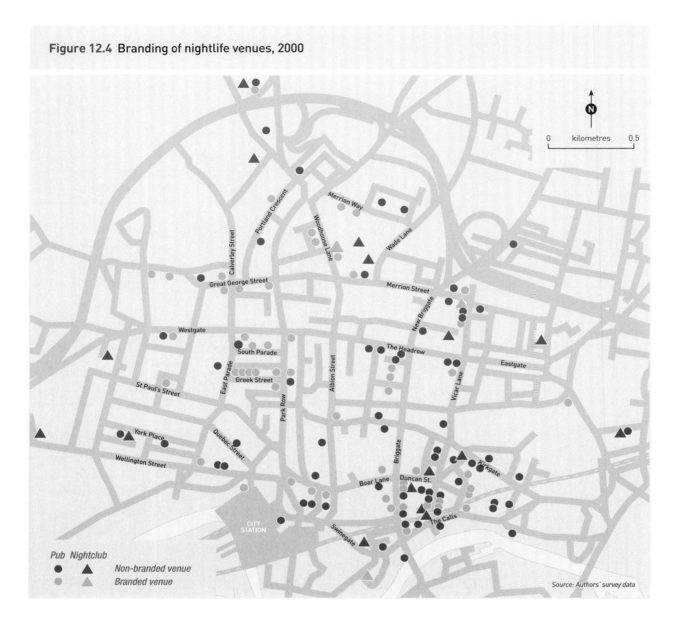

Pub Nightclub
●   ▲   *Non-branded venue*
●   ▲   *Branded venue*

Source: Authors' survey data

their individuality, and catering for smaller sub-cultural groups, are one of the smallest segments by type within city centre Leeds, accounting for 4 per cent of venues, and are scattered around the edges of the core area. Ale houses, or market taverns, comprise 7 per cent of venues. These are clustered around the market area and are a dying element within the city's nightlife. The key question to ask is how such places can survive in the post-industrial corporate city? A notable feature of the new wave of nightlife venues are multi-purpose bars offering food and coffee during the day and DJs and dance floor

space in the evening. Many are no longer pubs but wider lifestyle venues. New monikers such as 'cantina and bar' or 'urban hang suite' are often used to identify them.

Since the heady days of the dance music explosion of the early nineties, Leeds has gained a well-deserved reputation as one of the UK's leading clubbing destinations outside of London; Leeds is also synonymous with pioneering club nights such as Back to Basics and Speed Queen. The City Council has played a role in developing this aspect of Leeds' culture, as it was the first to promote clubbing breaks including Friday or

Figure 12.5 Ownership of nightlife venues, 2000

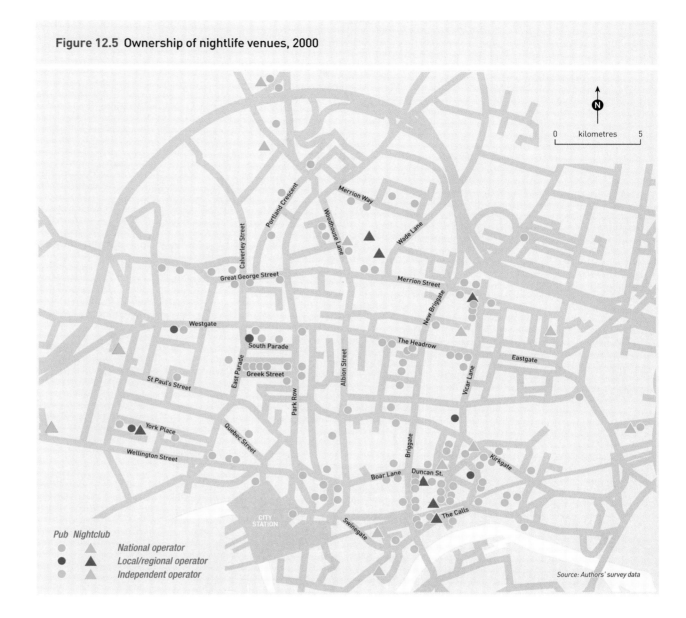

Pub   Nightclub

National operator

Local/regional operator

Independent operator

Source: Authors' survey data

Saturday night accommodation in a luxury city centre hotel, with late checkout along with entry into a nightclub of choice.

Historically, Leeds has had a strong clubbing scene with the Music Factory starting in the early 1990s and a pedigree of credible music nights such as Up Yer Ronson, I-Spy, Vague and Speed Queen. In May 2001, there were 19 nightclubs in Leeds with a combined capacity of 15,642. This nightclub infrastructure is increased by late bars with dance floors serving alcohol after 11.00pm, which have blurred the boundaries between traditional nightclubs and pubs.

Much of this rapid growth of late-night bars has been unplanned, and as a response to this, the Leeds Nightclub Association (LNA) was established between the city's nightclubs. Reasons for the creation of LNA are manifold: on the one hand there was a desire from the City Council to have a representative group that they could liaise with and which could be represented on the City Centre Management Board. On the other hand, LNA emerged from the needs of venues to have their voice heard. As one nightclub owner said to us: "something I'd learned long ago, if you try and do something

as an individual, nothing happens. If you try and do it as an association or whatever, people take notice". LNA now acts as the official voice of Leeds' nightclubs, both large and small, and is currently chaired by the manager of Creation, one of Leeds' largest nightclubs. It stages events to promote the city's nightlife sector such as the annual 'Leeds Bars and Clubs Awards and the Leeds Nightclub Association Awards and co-produces the NorthNights Discount Card, offering discounts to nightlife venues. On a more cautionary note, considering the overall makeup of nightclubs in Leeds in terms of capacity and ownership, and the links of the current chairperson of the LNA, the Association may represent particular interests more than others.

There is little doubt that the provision of city centre nightlife has changed dramatically over the last 20 years: from the decline in the male-dominated ale houses and working men's clubs of the 1970s, the lager-fuelled discos and pubs in the 1980s and 1990s, to the development of a more diverse and cosmopolitan night-time environment in the twenty-first century. However, underneath this façade of diversity, a drab uniformity of branded bar experiences is increasing.

Whilst there may appear to be a greater variety of provision, Leeds nightlife has largely developed a non-local 'experience' which is eroding many of its distinctive elements. Nevertheless, these types of venues do remain popular, and the fact that they continue to be in business demonstrates that demand does exist. However, it is important to look at what other types of provision could be offered, and whether consumers are simply consuming because there is little choice. Other types of less profit-focused provision might be just as popular, but due to high entry costs, they do not feature in city centres. There is a lack of places where people can hear themselves speak, or hear live music; places where they can play various games and sports; places where the consumption of alcohol, *ad nauseum,* is discouraged.

Top, Students form a significant element of the term-time market. Female alcohol consumption has risen as youth culture has changed and venues have made women more welcome. Leeds is trying to bring in measures that will discourage irresponsible selling and consumption of alcohol.

12.3 Regulating the night-time economy

To fully understand the regulation of nightlife, it is necessary to consider a number of different dimensions: legal, technical, economic, social and cultural. Legal forms include legislation laid down to regulate nightlife activity. Technical forms include the use of CCTV and radio-nets to monitor behaviour. Economic forms include pricing policies of drinks and door entry. Social and cultural regulations include more informal aspects such as dress codes, style and music, which are largely enforced through door staff. There are also many different players involved in the regulation of nightlife such as licensing magistrates, fire departments, local authorities, the police, door staff, residents' groups, local authorities, and a growing number of public-private partnerships and 'cultural intermediaries'.

What is evident is that the regulation of nightlife activity is currently in the midst of a significant transition. Historically, the night-time drinking economy was characterised by monopoly ownership of beer production and distribution aimed at a relatively homogenous clientele whose activities were carefully regulated through the curtailment of opening hours to ensure that workers' leisure did not interfere with their productivity. However, the 1980s saw a shift towards a 'new entertainment economy' in cities (Hannigan, 1998) which entails forging new sets of relations between the state, capital and consumers. In particular, the role of the local state has largely shifted from managing the city to encouraging and supporting entrepreneurialism (Harvey, 1989). As a result, large industrial cities, facing problems of declining populations and tax bases, are aligning themselves with private capital in the development of urban nightlife. For example, the idea of the '24-hour city' was designed to break away from the industrial city with its emphasis on manufacturing production and its strict temporal and spatial ordering. The number of pubs continues to grow. Licensed premises have increased by almost 30 per cent in the last twenty years and today the pub and club industry has a turnover of around £22 billion — equal to around 3 per cent of the UKs GDP (Hobbs *et al.,* 2000). Major national changes are also under way through the Government's recent White Paper to create a genuine 24-hour licensing system (Home Office, 2000).

Yet, there have been problems with building a new regulatory environment. While the Beer Orders legislation was intended to break down monopoly and increase diversification, it merely shifted control from the breweries to the large pub chains which have pioneered much more aggressive approaches to marketing their nightlife brands as a lifestyle. The increase in both numbers of places and late licences has also led to more public disorder in town centres. These images have become commonplace in the media, leading to discussions about shutting down 'thug pubs' and curtailing drink-fuelled violence and vandalism and issuing anti social behaviour orders. Below we look at some of these issues in Leeds.

Regulating nightlife in Leeds

City centre managers and the Council have worked with the magistrates and police to generate a more relaxed attitude to the granting of late-night licences. An important part of the initiative was improvement in street lighting, installation of CCTV and promotion of the 24-hour city. This set in train a large number of changes and improvements in the city centre. However, these rapid changes have occurred against a backdrop of regulation from a number of traditional power brokers in the night-time economy.

Magistrates, police and bouncers

Historically the power to regulate night-time activity through liquor licensing has rested with licensing magistrates and despite their non-elected and non-representative status they wield considerable power to control the night-time economy, guided by moral and social concerns (Justices' Clerks' Society, 1999) when deciding on new licences. This role of the licensing magistrates has recently come under scrutiny. The Justices' Clerks' Society issued a Good Practice Guide (1999), which set out a number of recommendations to standardise the work of licensing committees, which were interpreting national laws in different ways, in different areas.

Since the 1990s, there has been a growing determination that licensing committees should not refuse liquor licences on the grounds that there is no need or demand for more venues in a specific area. In particular, it was felt that licensing magistrates should not make decisions based on trade protection or attempts to reduce unfair competition. Increasingly, licensing issues revolve around balancing economic development agendas with anxieties about potential disorder and disruption to residents. As a result, the once all-important role of the magistrates and their licensing committees, has greatly diminished in line with the increasing attention paid to market forces. Licensing magistrates in Leeds, then, have seen their powers diminish and have largely embraced arguments for expanding nightlife.

The police have a dual role in the night-time economy: advising magistrates on the suitability of applicants and applications for licences and policing nightlife activity. Caught up in the city's desire for rapid growth, police are in a difficult position because their powers to object to the granting of new licences solely on the grounds that there is no 'need' is now under scrutiny. From a policing point of view, the growth of nightlife venues in Leeds has both dispersed as well as increased violence and disorder 'flashpoints'. The sheer numbers of people using Leeds city centre, often in excess of 100,000 during weekend evenings, has resulted in an increase of some anti-social behaviours, while others have declined. While the number of arrests in the city centre has been fairly stable in recent years, there has been an increase in assaults in particular (Table 12.2). However, if we put these figures into the context of the ongoing increases in terms of people living in, and using, the city, then such increases in crime are less worrying.

Despite this, the ambition to create a 24-hour city is still strong in Leeds, and generally this drive has the support of the police. As one inspector commented: "It's a dynamic city. It's a forward-looking city. You know, we want to go with that from a police perspective, but of course it does have implications for us as a police service. I think we're about a 20-hour city at the moment. We just need those few more hours, to push forward. That's the way the entertainment seems to be going now".

The police, then, are enthusiastic about the 24-hour city initiative, because their initial anxieties about the unmanageable volume of drunkenness and public disorder have not been realised, and they have introduced a number

Every late-night venue has door staff. It is bouncers rather than the police who do most of the work of keeping order within and around the pubs and clubs. They also have a role in vetting potential customers and can reject those who are deemed not to be suitably dressed, though stylishly scruffy is now accepted.

Table 12.2 Alcohol-related arrests involving violence, drugs or disorder, 1998–2001

Arrest	1998–1999	1999–2000	2000–2001
Drunk and disorderly	771	705	753
Public Order (4 and 5)	207	176	229
All assaults	556	710	761
Drug offences	580	520	386
Total	2,114	2,111	2,129

Source: Performance Management Team, Milgarth Police Station, West Yorkshire Police

of complementary policing methods such as professional door supervisors, CCTV cameras and staggered opening hours. In addition, smaller bars/cafés tend to encourage self-regulation by attracting a specific type of customer and ensuring that the door staff-to-client ratio is significantly higher than that of the super clubs.

Door supervisors, or bouncers, also play a key role in regulating the night. Leeds now administers a scheme which requires individuals who wish to work as door supervisors to undertake training, wear identity cards and the submit details of any criminal convictions. Not all of the people we interviewed were happy with the system. One major complaint against the Door Registration Scheme would seem to be the ease with which a registration badge can be obtained. Furthermore, there is a frustration amongst the police, who feel that they have only partial access to the scheme.

Yet, with tens of thousands of people using the city on an average weekend, the police freely admit that they could not cope without what amounts to a private police force of bouncers in the city centre. Door security in Leeds is mainly provided by a small number of door staff firms, although Leeds

appears to have had very little history of protection rackets, organised crime or drug trafficking amongst door staff teams. In the end, growing competition between pubs and clubs in Leeds has become so great that the public simply will not tolerate being treated rudely by door staff. If bouncers are unwelcoming or intimidating, customers can easily move on somewhere else. Increasingly, door staff and managers are under pressure to attract customers and it is not uncommon in Leeds for door staff to invite people into a pub or club as they are passing. Seemingly, without exception, the bouncers in Leeds are friendly, chatty and pleasant.

Finally, the whole idea of enforcing simple dress codes in Leeds has shifted, due to the style explosion in the city and the decline of traditional 'shirt and shoes' dress codes. Thus, many door staff show evidence of a more people-centred approach. Existing door policies, based primarily on clothing, are being replaced by more sophisticated style decisions through the introduction of 'door pickers' or 'selectors'. Through style selection, the ambience of a venue is carefully monitored *vis-à-vis* the type of person allowed entry, with regard to the social, ethnic and gender mix.

The changing role of the local state

Local authorities in England have long had a role to play in the planning and development of cities. Traditionally, they have not been involved in the activities of local businesses or tried to inhibit or encourage private enterprise, unless firms breached planning regulations. Recently, their role of managing the local state has been broadened to include promoting urban regeneration in partnership with private capital. The shift to a more pro-active attitude to mainstream economic development now extends to the cultural, entertainment and night-time economies.

Leeds has embraced this entrepreneurial approach, much of which was associated with the desire to revamp Leeds' decaying centre. With the decline of manufacturing, factories and warehouses became derelict and throughout the 1970s the urban infrastructure deteriorated. Very few people used to live in the city centre and most business and retail premises there closed around 5pm, so that the area became depopulated in the early evening and at night. By the 1980s, leisure, entertainment and nightlife became recognised as key vehicles for regenerating the city centre, and as mentioned earlier, the City Council took a lead in developing such ideas, especially through the idea of the European city, 24-hour activity, café culture and city living. The 5pm exodus has to some extent been reversed or extended by the opening of pubs, clubs and café-bars, which remain open late.

The City Centre Management Team has recognised nightlife as a core part of the commercial success of the central area. The growth of nightlife has been an important source of financial stability for the Council which has also encouraged further investment of private capital, changed the appearance and atmosphere of the city centre, provided many jobs in the service sector, and created a more buoyant evening culture. However, many people felt that outside the growth of nightlife, the city centre lacked some important aspects: "I am not aware that there is anything particularly in terms of public facilities apart from just the normal cultural facilities that we have got here. I do not think there is anything particularly for people who

are 15–16. They like to come in at the weekends and hang out, and there are loads of them around on Saturdays" (City Centre Management Team representative).

The obvious advantages of the 24-hour initiative, then, must be balanced against its disadvantages. If the nightlife infrastructure becomes a drain on public resources, it is likely to cause resentment amongst those who are excluded, by choice or necessity, from the nightlife, but who pay taxes. They may have very different and equally legitimate needs that are neglected, or suffer the nuisance and inconvenience of late night noisy revellers. There is much that can be done by large nightlife operators, individually and through associations, to solve the problems that stem directly from their profit-making activities, such as drunkenness and disorder. It is vital that the City Council and the police look at ways of making such groups more accountable in terms of the wider effects of the nightlife which they provide.

Part of the urban regeneration process is the huge increase in city centre residents and clearly, this residential and nightlife growth in Leeds' city centre is storing up tensions between residents and revellers (see Chapter 14). Noise pollution at night, in particular, threatens much of the new living accommodation in the city centre. However, since the resident city centre population has largely grown up in tandem with the recent developments in nightlife, actual disputes have been fairly low. In many ways, the new residents in the city centre are a self-selected group, whose lifestyles may be more accepting of night-time activity. However, city centre housing is currently aimed at wealthier social groups and issues of social mix and diversity have to be addressed through future housing developments (see Chapters 4 and 14).

12.4 Consuming the nightlife

As a backdrop for understanding how nightlife is consumed, it is worth highlighting a number of wider social trends and changes that are affecting the lives of young people and their nightlife activities: youthful behaviour extends beyond that of a

teenager in a period of post-adolescence; young people are seeking to redress the balance between work and play, and many continue to face social and economic problems such as unemployment and low wages. Despite this latter fact, nightlife activity is a significant part of most young people's lives in Britain. With around two-thirds of city-centre populations aged 15–44 (Mintel, 2000a), cities are reasserting themselves as leisure and entertainment hubs for young people. Visiting pubs and clubs is a core element of young people's lifestyles. Eighty per cent visited pubs and clubs in 1999, an increase of 12 per cent over five years (Mintel, 2000b). Clubbing has become a way of life for many young people, largely through the advent of dance music and club cultures over the last two decades (Bennett, 2000; Thornton, 1995).

Pub-going has also been transformed, as the traditional experience based around dingy, male-dominated ale houses has largely been replaced by style bar and café-bar culture. Some pubs and bars have matured into pre-club venues — hybrid half-club, half-pubs — which may have eroded the popularity of more traditional night clubs. Motivations for nightlife activity today are wide and complex: a desire for a good time or letting go, socialising with friends and/or work-

mates, or seeking casual sex. City centres remain highly segmented and socially divided spaces when it comes to nightlife, highly structured around drinking circuits or areas each with their own set of codes, dress styles, language and tastes. This is particularly evident in Leeds. Furthermore, city nightlife continues to face challenges from home-based activities, financial constraints, the increased cost of city entertainment and issues of safety, travel and access.

More than many other countries in Europe, the consumption of alcohol, and increasingly drugs, shapes young people's nightlife activities in Britain. Estimated alcohol consumption in the UK increased from 5.07 litres in 1957 to 9.44 litres in 1998. Moreover, 36 per cent of males and 25 per cent of females aged 16–24 drank over the selected weekly limit of alcohol (21 units for men, 14 units for women) in 1998–1999 (General Household Survey, 1999). Such problems are confounded by the current licensing laws which condense drinking into a few hours and promote binge drinking and aggressive behaviour. In terms of young people's drinking habits, in the 1930s under-24-year-olds were the lightest drinkers in the population. By the 1980s, this situation had reversed (Institute for Alcohol Studies, 2000). The role of

drinking alcohol has also changed from a largely male ritual to a broader lifestyle phenomenon associated with fun, hedonism and courtship, mainly for the young. In this context, concern has been raised over public disorder and yobs. Alcohol consumption has also shifted towards designer drinks, especially through the growth in popularity of wine, spirits, bottled beers and alcopops and has been decreased in the wake of dance and drug culture. Illegal drugs — especially cannabis, amphetamines and ecstasy — are now a common part of youth consumption (Coffield and Gofton, 1994).

Experiencing Leeds' nightlife

Nightlife in Leeds is spread across a number of distinct areas, used by certain social groups, each with their own social codes and styles. Below we sketch these out.

Mainstream Leeds

A dominant feature of parts of most British towns and cities every weekend evening is the drunken hedonism which flows from pubs and clubs onto the streets. We have labelled this 'the mainstream', which is characterised by established gender roles and working cultures, pleasure-seeking, hedonism and excessive drinking which can sometimes lead to outbursts of violence. The heart of the commercial mainstream in Leeds centres upon the Boar Lane/City Square area and is home to venues such as Square on the Lane, Yates Wine Lodge, The Observatory, The Bondi Beach Bar and Majestyk. Bars here are large, normally over 500 capacity, have strict dress codes, loud music and drinks promotions. One person commented to us: "We have Majestyk, Club Europa, Club Heaven and Hell. Yippee! I attempt to enter but am turned away by a Neanderthal doorman who doesn't understand the concept of man with long hair or a girl in trousers. For the fun, I don a pair of white chinos and obligatory Timberland sweater. Hey presto, they let me in. It's packed, as the mainstream clubs often are. If you can be bothered queuing for half an hour for an overpriced drink" (Ian).

Many groups referred to a distinctive type of consumer in the mainstream — the townie. People had quite specific views on townies, seeing them as a group who made a real effort dress-wise when they went out at the weekend, yet also associated them with drink-fuelled, sexually-charged environments with loud pumping cheesy music. There is a specific dress code, involving making a conscious effort to conform to door policies, such as wearing shoes and smart attire.

The mainstream, then, comprises a significant infra-structure in the city and is consumed by a relatively large group of people. It is also increasingly popular, not unproblematically, with stag and hen parties (Bellamy, 2001). Many people are attracted by smart venues, branded drinks, loud recorded music and the glamour of sharing the evening with local celebrities or footballers. Many consumers here still share traditional ideas about social roles, courtship and gender relations and often regard the 'weekend' as a sacred time for letting go and self-

Top left, many new venues have carefully decided on their target market and aim to ofer drinks, food, style and atmosphere that match their customers' aspirations. Bottom, downing pints with mates is a main activity, whether students or townies, mainstream or on the margins.

indulgence, which is a reward for the time and effort spent in work during the week. Entertainment offered in the mainstream consists of an opportunity to dress up, meet like-minded people and join a large crowd bent on getting drunk and strutting their stuff to the latest dance tunes.

Attempts to move upmarket

Leeds has pioneered new types of nightlife venues based upon more European café and style bar venues. The Calls, recently marketed as the Exchange Quarter, is the centre of Leeds' style bar explosion. Many offer quirky styles, relaxed atmospheres during the day, often serving food, attracting more sophisticated clientele, operating with relaxed dress codes described as stylishly scruffy. The emergence of more exclusive, stylish forms of nightlife, then, signifies a new consumption experience in Leeds. Style venues imply rising prices, new forms of dress codes and a more divisive atmosphere. While originally fuelled by local creative independent entrepreneurs, a number of these venues face competition from national corporate operators, or have been bought up by them, threatening Leeds' reputation of nightlife distinctiveness. There are also limits to the style revolution. Exclusive members club Teatro, which closed down in June 2001 after attracting only 80 members to pay its £250 annual membership fee, shows the limitations of creating nightlife for a chosen elite.

On the margins: alternative Leeds

Although the city centre is known for young Goths hanging out outside the Corn Exchange and skaters practising in the revamped Millennium Square, the city centre has a few alternative spaces — here defined as more individualised, one-off venues catering for particular youth or sub-cultural styles and tastes. Many alternative promoters are price-sensitive and can only afford venues on the city's fringes. But they are also aware that using the city's fringe distances them from problems associated with the city centre's mainstream. Promoters offering alternative events in the city centre have found it more difficult as mainstream musical styles such as house and garage take priority. We found clear differences of opinion between those on the margins and those in the mainstream. Alternative clubbers view the mainstream large clubs with suspicion, being

Leeds does not have such a high profile gay scene as Manchester, but many bars and pubs around the Calls area are gay-friendly, and gays report that they feel more relaxed in the city centre than was the case a decade ago.

aware of not just the difference in music policy, but attitudes, people attending and producer motivation: "These conveyor belt clubs, lovely venues though some of them are, are designed for one thing and one thing only: promotion. Be it for the latest alcopop or breezer style drink or be it the music which has been thrust into the public domain by the amount of finance behind it as opposed to actual musical talent" (Jack, alternative clubber and promoter).

Views about Leeds' new Millennium Square perhaps summed up many people's dissatisfactions with the lack of genuine public places. Many skateboarders are angry at being evicted from this 'multi-million pound patio' which despite being dubbed the people's square and being financed through public money, is subject to high entry prices and is often fenced off during events. Many people rarely venture into the city centre, often for reasons of price, but also because of a feeling that there is little for them. In the face of these limitations, one group of people, the A-Spire collective, have been opening up free, community-run alternative spaces in derelict sites adjacent to the city centre. They describe their spaces in the following way: "It is a place where people can go during the day or night

and socialise away from the buy, buy, buy mentality that is present day capitalism. Once there you can do pretty much whatever you want to (within reason)." (www.a-spire.org.uk).

Many young people were frustrated at the commercial priorities of the City Centre Management Team — that simply 'hanging out' was bad for business or seen as a threat to the commercial viability of the city centre. Clearly, Leeds city centre has a long way to go before it offers a diverse range of provision during the night.

Gay Leeds

One of the distinctive features of the city's nightlife is its variety of gay pubs and clubs. There are several new gay venues, and some older established ones (O'Neill, 2003), but unlike Manchester, Leeds does not have an area with a self-consciously gay image. However, the new style bars in the Calls area are regarded as gay-friendly. In contrast to the situation a decade ago, many young gay consumers now say they feel relaxed and safe in the city centre. However, hesitance is still expressed about walking though other areas in the city, which are not perceived to be as safe and liberal. Of particular concern

for gay consumers are the more mainstream nightlife areas adjacent to the Calls, such as City Square and the market. Criticism about Leeds' gay venues is centred on the lack of choice after 11pm, with only two regular gay club nights — SpeedQueen at the Warehouse and Poptastic at the Cockpit. A further criticism is the lack of locally-owned gay venues which are better able to respond to the needs of the gay community.

Suburbanisation of nightlife

Over the course of the 1980s and 1990s, much entertainment and leisure activity was suburbanised through the growth of out-of-town entertainment destinations, video shops and off licences. More recently, the rapid growth of nightlife activity has saturated many city centres and has led to a flight of entrepreneurs out of them in search of new profits, cheaper venues and less restrictive licensing. Suburban areas have benefited from this shift, with the growth of new nightlife concepts moving along major arterial routes leading to city centres. Such a shift has also been a response to the constraints of city centre consumption such as high costs, overcrowding, violence and problems of late night travel.

The most obvious examples of this type of development in Leeds are the Headingley and Hyde Park areas of the city. Headingley in particular is becoming one of the city's new nightlife hot spots, much of which is fuelled by the growth in numbers of students and young professionals. Yet many local people are concerned at several new applications for new licensed premises by large corporate operators keen to get into this lucrative market. This area, then, once known for its trad-itional, community-based atmosphere, is showing signs of being overrun by new style bars and firms eager to cash in on the student pound.

Student Leeds

All British cities have experienced a rapid growth of in-migrant higher education students, who have imprinted a striking mark on the urban fabric since the early 1990s. Leeds is no exception. Students have come to play an important role in the city, not

just educationally but also in terms of stimulating and maintaining nightlife activity. In 2002, there were around 65,000 students at the two universities in Leeds — a market segment that makes a significant impact upon city centre leisure provision. One way in which this is felt is through their spending impact. Average student expenditure in Britain in 1995–1996 was estimated at £5,091 with one fifth, or £1,187, spent on entertainment. (Callender and Kempson, 1996). Based on 1995 spending figures, the 65,000 higher education students in Leeds have an annual spending power of over £330 million and spend nearly £77million on entertainment alone. However, the replacement of grants by loans and the increasing incidence of student debt and part-time working, has brought new restraints on student nightlife. Despite this, students remain important consumers of nightlife activity.

The distinguishing features of student life are its rhythms and rituals where leisure time is structured around particular times and places such as the pub, student digs, shared housing and student parties. On arriving in Leeds, most first years follow a set routine through the Leeds' nightlife, influenced by the

Celebrating the Millennium New Year's Eve at The Majestyk in City Square. Up to 3,000 people can fit into this former cinema.

marketing efforts of venues and promoters and advice gathered from Freshers' Week and other students. A popular, and notorious tradition amongst Leeds students is a specific pub-crawl known as 'The Otley Run' consisting of around 16 pubs which are visited on the same night. While students' unions traditionally catered for the entertainment needs of students, the students' unions in Leeds are facing increasing competition. For example, four large branded pubs, with a combined capacity of over 10,000 and late licences, are situated in an area of about 100 metres between the city centre and the two universities. Students are seen by large national nightlife operators as a key new target audience: "I'd rather have students than the trash of the locals. Students can be arseholes, but they tend to come in, have a good night and go away again. You don't have the trouble, fights or drug problems with students that you do get with locals" (City centre pub staff).

However, there are mixed feelings about the relationship students have with locals in the city. For example, the balance between rented and owner-occupied residential housing, and between locals and students in Headingley is now seriously jeopardised by the increase in student numbers and the activities of landlords keen on maximising rental returns. Further, local townies, who are out in the city centre at week-ends, are generally perceived by many students to be territorial, forcing students to stick to student-only areas at weekends.

After hours Leeds

Leeds has a reputation as a place where you can continue partying after the traditional nightclub closing times. In 2001, there were four unlicensed venues in the city centre which were open throughout Saturday night selling soft drinks, smoothies and coffee: Casa Loco, Classhouse, Kahuna, Soul Kitchen. Clearly, the fact that there are those able and willing to continue dancing until 8 or 10 the next morning, implies that this clientele comes from the more drug and dance music-oriented cultures than the mainstream, 'drink and pull' scene. Some venue managers feel that issuing such licences encourages drug use; however, there is also a feeling that young people would take drugs anyway and this is just catering to demand.

style and original features, are often in need of redecoration, and are situated in run down areas, serving a loyal, regular clientele. Established perceptions stop most people from entering such places: regulars who are unwelcoming of strangers, intolerant of minority groups and hostile towards women. What some people call 'scratters', are a widely recognised group here: "Nasty, horrible creatures of society, who crawl out from under their stone on Thursday cos its dole day ... Mainly seen wearing the PVC skirts and boob tubes, which are too tight, sort of sagging and not nice. The over forties, who still think that they are teenagers" (Mark).

Age would also seem to be a key issue, in a society obsessed with youth and beauty, hence scratters are seen as middle-aged, working class and undignified, the very embodiment of failure. Most perceptions however, are based upon myths about the venues, and the people who frequent them, largely supported by real first-hand experience. Despite these negative images, the loss of such places would sever the links between city

Residual Leeds

Working class, local and community pubs, many of which hark back to an era of ritualisec session drinkers, form a residual and endangered element of city centre nightlife. The city centre still has such pubs, in spite of the growth of national branded pubs and style bars. 'Ale houses' are pubs that maintain a traditional

centres and traditional community-based pubs and would represent a replacement of the local with the consumption experience of the non-local branded or style bar. Moreover, it would force out those consumption groups who do not want to, or cannot afford to, engage with the boisterousness of the new corporate world of Leeds' glitzy style bars and cafés.

12.5 Issues in the night-time economy

Making room for independent bars and creativity in the corporate playground

"I just think in Leeds it is a fine line between... dirty nasty places and really trendy dressy places. Like on a Friday and Saturday night, it is hard to find a middle ground" (Julie, young profess-ional). Leeds' nightlife has been comprehensively revamped over the last 10 years. While early growth was based upon clusters of small, independent bars, more recent transform-ations have been led by large corporate chain bars who want a slice of the action (and profits) and are able to pay higher rents for properties. As one bar owner commented: "If you look around in cities you will find a handful of people involved in setting up bars and the rest of it is just the corporates. But then the corporates come straight in afterwards and if you're setting up a bar and struggling to make a living and somebody comes along and says well we'll give you half a million, you take it and run" (Independent bar owner).

In response, the Leeds Café Bar Association was set up by some of the early independent pioneers to give a collective voice to the concerns facing the independent bar owners to check the development of large sites into bars by corporate companies. While some might argue that such competition is healthy, others suggested to us that the pendulum has swung too far towards corporate provision and that city nightlife had reached saturation point. Additionally, in terms of safety and regulation of premises, one bar owner expressed that smaller independent premises encourage individuality and intimacy: "I mean if you've got a small bar that you know is going to be run individually and you get rid of the social problems associated with the anonymity of the larger places which are just about consumption".

For the future, Leeds' nightlife will continue to balance precariously between independent and corporate activity. Close attention from the police, magistrates and Council is needed to ensure that corporate brands do not become too dominant and erode the strong reputation which Leeds has built up in terms of a vibrant and diverse independent bar scene. Left unchecked, nightlife in Leeds will become more mono-cultural and dominated by outside interests, catering to the whim of shareholders rather than local diversity or creativity.

Leeds: late night and laid back — licensing and beyond

Those in charge of regulating nightlife in Leeds have largely adopted a hands-off attitude to its development. Later/ staggered drinking hours have been successful in changing some behaviour. One of the key insignias of modern day Leeds has been the extension of activity well after the traditional '5pm flight'. The expansion of nightlife has also expanded opportunities for other retail activities. However, key parts of the late night infrastructure need addressing to ensure that there is a variety of activities late into the night and not just those associated with alcohol, dancing and drugs (Chesterton, 2003). A more continental approach needs to be adopted, including the granting of more children's licences, and the development of more family-friendly venues, which may change drinking habits. For the future, those implementing regulatory laws should pay more attention to the type rather than just the amount of new activity to ensure that a balance is struck between a range of activities rather then an alcohol monoculture driven by large non-local corporate developers. Clearly, a much wider range of activities needs to be encouraged away from the youth-oriented drinking monoculture.

Leeds: Barcelona, Paris, London of the North?

To what extent does Leeds stand out from other neighbouring industrial cities? Has it really thrown off its old hard, smoke stack image and replaced it with a new chic culture? Major changes in going-out cultures have happened over the last 10 years in Leeds. A handful of rough pubs and clubs have been replaced by countless new style bars and larger branded corporate pubs. No doubt in response to these changes, the night-time clientele have adapted their tastes and preferences and a host of new younger and wealthy revellers have been

the needs of under-18s, families, older people and those on low incomes could be catered for more in the new glitzy world of branded café and style bars, especially by providing more varied early evening entertainment.

These issues need urgent attention if comparisons with European cities are to have any substance. The qualities of European cities are often-used benchmarks for many ailing British cities. These qualities are hard to define and even harder to attain. But in general they include: a more balanced housing provision between social and private housing; denser and more varied central populations; a greater number and diversity of local services in central areas; a stronger sense of civic pride and culture reinforced by more pubic space; higher levels of public land ownership and a more equal relationship and greater dialogue between local authorities and communities in central areas; more family-oriented and less profit-oriented patterns of property ownership often existing in smaller units (such units are more difficult to merge into larger units which then become popular to large, external developers). All of this is underpinned by more financially stable local authorities on the European continent which have not experienced the large exodus of people, industry and taxes occurring in British cities.

attracted to Leeds from all over the region and the country. Leeds, then, feels very different on a night from how it felt 10 years ago. However, Leeds is not yet a mini-London and the Calls area is not Soho, neither is it a city like Barcelona which has successfully used culture and nightlife to move up the urban hierarchy. This is wishful thinking from the city marketers, and says little about the day-to-day life in Leeds. Looking at the itinerary of some of the Leeds United players on their infamous drinking binge nights reveals that they prefer the much more traditional circuit of 'booze and birds' taking in DV8 table dancing bar, the Observatory disco bar and Majestyk night club. The city's nightlife remains tainted by its hard-edged image and high profile cases of racist assaults.

Moreover, it is important to keep in mind that not everyone has been caught by the rising tide of Leeds' growing economy and cultural infrastructure. As one person commented to us: "A rising tide lifts all boats, but if you haven't got a boat, you've had it". While some opportunities have opened up in terms of low paid service work in call centres and the hospitality industry, many of the people in the outlying estates and inner city areas have been left behind by much of the development in this 'corporate city'. In particular, the new breed of style bars simply prices out many people from the city centre. In many ways, then, the city centre is becoming more of a ghetto for cash-rich groups (Wynne and O'Connor, 1998), whether young professionals or wealthy students. In particular,

12.6 Conclusions

Leeds has transformed its urban core into a busy business and cultural destination. This has been aided by a prosperous population catchment, a strong role as regional employment centre, the established cosmopolitan nature of its centre, the strategic leadership shown by the local state, and significant growth in service sector professionals which has fuelled demand for entertainment goods and services. The recent good times for the city centre, then, have stimulated the growth of corporate and branded entertainment based around a range of upmarket bars, clubs and restaurants, which in some cases has

also created opportunities for the independent sector.

Yet it is important not to take such success stories at face value and to recognise that many young people are disenfranchised from such prosperity and that the urban night-time fabric is increasingly socially and geographically divided. Further, many independent entrepreneurs may face limited options in the light of the growth of large corporate players. Many of these latter type continue to focus upon profit maximisation through beer sales which undermines attempts to create more tolerant and plural nightlife spaces and creates problems of social disorder. Alcohol consumption is still often the *raison d'être* of a night out and issues of disorder, sexism, violence and drunkenness remain. Our analysis suggests that a solution to many of these problems does not rest with the development of large corporate-owned licensed themed venues, but more local coalitions of producers/consumers/cultural entrepreneurs. Upgrading the city centre largely means pricing trouble out of the market, which only happens at the expense of excluding the city's poorer residents. Finally, the dominant audience for nightlife is increasingly mainstream, higher spending, consumption groups such as young professionals, aspiring townies and university students. Other groups of young people are disenfranchised within the current range of nightlife provision on the basis of price, style, dress or demeanour such as alternative cultures, groups of teenagers, or those with few resources.

Whether we are looking at Leeds, Glasgow or Manchester, there appears to be an air of inevitability in the way in which urban nightlife will develop. However, there are a number of different choices and ways forward. First, Leeds could simply become 'Anywheres-ville UK' and continue to accommodate and embrace the global corporate world hoping that it can continue to remain capital's 'flavour of the month'. This very much appears to be the current trend. By bending over backwards trying to attract major global pubcos it will sideline smaller, locally owned nightlife and the city will lose its uniqueness and distinctive flavour. Balancing the global, national and the local is a second scenario. This would involve the City Council working together with all interested parties in the night-time economy. In such a context, there is a need for the local state to help strike a balance between commercial and local need. Finally, the City Council and other regulators could be more radical in their orientation and begin to actively promote local nightlife cultures, emphasising diversity, creativity and social cohesion.

To encourage this latter model, mechanisms would need to be established to favour certain types of nightlife activity, create more opportunities for local entrepreneurs and massage property markets in their favour. It would also involve more support and training for young cultural entrepreneurs and the provision of affordable premises for those in the creative industries (Chatterton and Unsworth, forthcoming). More fundamentally, it would point to a change in cultural values and philosophies based on an inclusive urban realm, giving space to dissenting voices, and encouraging the mixing of different age groups and night-time activities in which alcohol consumption, on its own, played a much smaller role.

The future direction of the city is still up for grabs. However, what is painfully evident is that Leeds is losing its soul, its creativity and its identity. Currently caught up in the desire for corporate glam and pandering to wealthy in-migrants and tourists, Leeds has a long way to go before it can boast anything like a diverse, European, 24-hour nightlife.

References

Bellamy, A. (2001) Just hen-joy yourselves, *Absolute Leeds,* 26 June

Bennett, A. (2000) *Popular Music and Youth Culture: Music, Identity and Place,* Macmillan, Basingstoke..

Brewers and Licensed Retailers Association (BLRA) (1999) *Statistical Handbook,* BLRA, London.

Brewers and Licensed Retailers Association (BLRA) (2000) http://www.blra.co.uk/

Callender, C. and Kempson, E. (1996) *Student Finances. The Real Costs of Being a Student: Where the Money Comes From and Where it Goes,* PSI, London.

Chatterton, P. and Hollands, R. (2002) Theorising urban playscapes: the production, regulation and consumption of youthful nightlife spaces, *Urban Studies,* 39(1): 95–116.

Chatterton, P. and Hollands, R. (2003) *Urban Nightscapes: Youth Cultures, Pleasure Spaces and Corporate Power,* Routledge, London.

Chatterton, P. and Unsworth, R. (forthcoming), Making space for culture(s) in Boomtown. Some alternative futures for development, ownership and participation in Leeds city centre, *Local Economy.*

Chesterton (surveyors) (2003) *Leeds Evening and Night-time Economy Study,* draft final report for Leeds City Council, Leeds.

Coffield, F. and Gofton, L. (1994) *Drugs and Young People,* Institute for Public Policy Research, London.

Emmett, A. (1998) Leeds on the rebound: a city with a feast of follies: who needs Florence, Venice and Verona when you've got West Yorkshire?, *The Independent,* 3 October.

Fox, P. and Unsworth, R. (2003) *City living in Leeds — 2003* http://www.geog.leeds.ac.uk/publications/cityliving/

General Household Survey (1999) *Living in Britain 1998,* HMSO, London.

Hannigan, J. (1998) *Fantasy City. Pleasure and Profit in the Postmodern Metropolis,* Routledge, London.

Harvey, D. (1989) From managerialism to entrepreneurialism: the transformation of urban governance in late capitalism, *Geografiska Annaler,* 71B(1): 3–17.

Hobbs, D., Lister, S., Hadfield, P. and Hall, S. (2000) Receiving shadows: governance, liminality in the night-time economy, *British Journal of Sociology,* 51(4): 701–717.

Hollands, R. (1995) *Friday Night, Saturday Night: Youth Cultural Identification in the Post-Industrial City,* Newcastle University, Newcastle.

Home Office (2000) *Time for Reform: Proposals for the Modernisation of Our Licensing Laws,* Cm 4696, TSO, London.

Hudson, R. and Williams, A. (1995) *Divided Britain,* 2nd Edition, John Wiley, Chichester.

Institute for Alcohol Studies (1999) *Alcohol and Young People,* IAS Factsheet, IAS, London.

Jessop, B. (1997) The entrepreneurial city: reimagining localities, redesigning economic governance or restructuring capital, in Jewson, N. and McGregor, S. (eds) *Transforming Cities,* Routledge, London.

Justice Clerks' Society (1999) *Good Practice Guide,* Justice Clerks' Society, London.

Landry, C. (2000) *The Creative City. A Toolkit for Urban Innovators,* Earthscan, London.

MacDonald, R. (1998) *Youth, the 'Underclass' and Social Exclusion,* Routledge, London.

Miles, S. (2000) *Youth Lifestyles in a Changing World,* Open University Press, Buckingham.

Mintel (2000a) In versus Out-of-town, *Leisure Intelligence,* March.

Mintel (2000b) Pre-family Leisure Trends, *Leisure Intelligence,* January.

O'Conner, J. and Wynne, D. (1995) *From the Margins to the Centre,* Arena, London.

O'Neill, L. (2003) *Factors Influencing the Leeds Gay Scene: Past and Future Changes,* unpublished BA dissertation, School of Geography, University of Leeds, Leeds.

Pattison, G. (2000) Young women drink to the age of equality, *The Journal,* 4 November.

Simpson, D. (1999) A short break in Leeds: the inhabitants of the formerly industrial city work hard at being stylish and having fun', *The Independent,* 21 March.

The Publican (2000) *Pub Industry Handbook 2000,* Quantum Publishing, Surrey.

Thornton, S. (1995) *Club Cultures,* Polity, Cambridge.

Trickett, J. (1994) The 24-hour city: retailing as animation, *Regenerating Cities,* 1(6): 9–11.

Wynne, D. and O'Conner, J. (1998) Consumption and the postmodern city, *Urban Studies,* 35(5–6): 841–864.

Zukin, S. (1995) *The Cultures of Cities,* Blackwell, London.

The economy transformed: Top, call centre on a former coal staithe, Canal Basin; Bottom, reflection in the River Aire — Addleshaw Goddard's offices on the site of warehouses.

13.1 Introduction

Charles Dickens once described Leeds as "the beastliest place, one of the nastiest I know" (Lewis, 2001). Industrial development and rapid population growth occurred within a context of weak national and local environmental controls, leading to unhealthy and dangerous working and living conditions for the majority and to degradation of the natural environment. Until the late Victorian era, Leeds was clearly far from being a sustainable city. Eventually, driven by public health concerns, enabling legislation led to practical actions to improve the environment. These included sewer construction, development of water supplies from Eccup, the River Wharfe and the Washburn valley, and the first sewage treatment works in 1897 (Sellars, 1997). These actions led to a much cleaner city, though environmental costs were often simply moved outside Leeds. Further progress was made in the twentieth century through a combination of economic restructuring (see Chapter 8), further legislation (national and European) and technological advances.

However, whilst the worst excesses of the Victorian industrial city are gone, and substantial recent progress has been made, much remains to be done to deliver a city which is economically and socially viable, and which develops within the constraints set by the natural environment. In this chapter, we consider environmental sustainability in Leeds. First, we examine the drivers for urban environmental improvement in the UK, then we present an overview of the state of the Leeds environment focused on six core issues and associated policy and practice. We conclude by outlining what we perceive to be the key challenges and prospects for future environmentally sustainable development in Leeds.

13.2 Impulses for change: incorporating environment into urban policy

Until well into the twentieth century, environmental issues were largely the concern of an enlightened minority, but today more people value the natural environment, and environmental issues are now in the political mainstream. Urban environmental concerns, which started with attention to acute health problems associated with severe pollution, have developed to encompass a greater awareness of city impacts on ecosystems and the natural resource base. There is an increasing recognition that economic development, characterised by production, consumption and exchange of goods and services, is ultimately supported by the natural environment, acting as a source of materials and a sink for waste and pollution. Major cities, like Leeds, typically draw on these ecosystem services at local, regional and global scales, and impacts have consequences for both current and future generations, presenting a complex and significant challenge to those seeking to promote environmentally sustainable urban development.

Growing awareness of the links between economic development, social welfare and environmental quality, and of the need to think at more extensive spatial and temporal scales has led to a formulation of ideas for sustainable development, classically defined in the Brundtland report as "Humanity has the ability to make development sustainable — to ensure that it meets the needs of the present without compromising the ability of future generations to meet their own needs" (WCED, 1987, p. 8), and by the IUCN *et al.* (1991) as "development that improves the quality of human life while living within the carrying capacity of supporting ecosystems". This discourse has become manifest in policy at the highest level, with sustainability principles at the core of international and national policies, including the UN Agenda 21 Programme (UNCED, 1992), the EU Fifth Environmental Action Programme (European Commission, 1992) and the UK Sustainable Development Strategy (DoE, 1994; DETR, 1999a; under review in 2004).

Although these policy statements are national or international in scope, they all stress the local scale as the main

Leeds Local Agenda 21 drew together many strands of effort on sustainable development.

geographical level for policy intervention, as the local state has unique capacity, legitimacy and experience in articulating and delivering the goals of sustainable development (Selman, 1999). In the UK, as elsewhere, local authorities are required to develop local policies and strategies in response to national policy initiatives, and their own bottom-up perspectives, as prompted by the Local Agenda 21 programme, which in Leeds, was incorporated into the wider *Vision for Leeds* exercise (Leeds Initiative, 1999) addressing the strategic development of the city to 2020. Local indicators and targets are set within a wider, nationally-agreed framework which recognises that each locality is unique, with its own set of actors, comprising public, private and voluntary sectors that act and react in ways that reflect local social and political characteristics and contexts (DETR, 2000a). Thus, each place has a unique history of, and potential for, conflict and compromise between economic, social and environmental interests.

When local authorities first addressed the sustainable development agenda, there were often difficulties in promoting a conception of the environment as something other than parks, litter and dog fouling. Whilst some people still hold this view, gradual progress was made in raising awareness amongst officers, politicians and electors of a broader conceptualisation of environmental issues, including recognition of the wider global agenda, and linkage of environmental issues to social and economic plans and policies. The 1990s saw a heyday when Local Agenda 21 officers were recruited and, with support from the Local Government Management Board (now IDeA), made headway in mainstreaming environmental concerns in local public administration. Local Agenda 21 officers were instrumental in spreading the notion that all policies and activities should be viewed from a sustainable development perspective, with explicit consideration of impacts on the 'triple bottom line' of social, economic and environmental impact (Elkington, 1998). Still, in many places, Local Agenda 21 amounted to little more than re-branding of existing social, economic and environmental policies (Mittler, 2001). In Leeds, the outcomes are arguably more positive, with the development of a genuinely new culture in thinking and working such that longer-term, more holistic approaches are now the norm and it has become second nature to engage stakeholders in finding appropriate ways forward across the range of policy areas.

Since the late 1990s, the UK has experienced a reformulation of modernised local government (see Chapter 1). This has had several implications for the way in which environmental issues are addressed at the local level. First, local government has undergone a reorganisation intended to facilitate community planning, in which greater decision-making power is given to local people. Community planning requires that local authorities consult local people over investment and management priorities, and involve citizens and all relevant stakeholders in formulating and delivering policy. A second implication is that the new focus on delivering services which give 'best value' to communities implies a move away from services based largely on lowest cost towards those that offer value across a wider range of functions. Best value criteria include an explicit consideration of whether the service is delivered in such a way that the natural and built environment is enhanced and protected. Finally, the modernisation of local government has given local authorities the power to promote local social, economic and environmental well-being (as well as the duty to produce community strategies)[1]. Pinfield and Saunders (1999) argue that whilst this may appear a minor development, it can be interpreted powerfully, suggesting that sustainable development becomes the central driving force of local authority policy development and implementation.

Despite having apparently positive implications, these changes are not without risk for the environment. The modernisation process has been criticised for moving the focus of service delivery down to the local level, following a period of public consultation and community plan formulation. The concern is that community strategies result in fragmentation and that action on the environment will again be focused solely on local and possibly parochial concerns, such as graffiti, litter and dog-mess, to the exclusion of more pressing long-term non-local environmental problems. Thus Selman and Parker (1999, p.12) warned "The challenge for sustainable development practitioners may well be to ensure that the principles inherent in sustainable development (including environment, futurity and global concern) are not forgotten in the dash for community planning", whilst from an analysis of Leicester's experience of developing environment policy, Roberts (2000, p.26) concludes that "community-led development and sustainable development are not necessarily the same things".

This micro-level planning and service delivery tends naturally to focus on improvements to local quality of life. Nevertheless, the community plan reviews (LCC, 2003) show evidence of a joined-up approach encompassing issues of green space, health and fitness, community safety, leisure opportunities, building refurbishment and improved recycling facilities. Some community planning actions undoubtedly further sustainable development goals, but the explicit consideration of the wider environmental implications of action, welcomed by most people at the local level, is not always clear. However, community planning does take place within an overarching, area-wide policy framework addressing issues such as transport, land use, housing, economic development, and waste management, all of which have the potential to reduce resource inputs, waste and pollution, whilst improving local quality of life in other ways.

Left, Ferrybridge power station, seen from Great Preston. In 2002, it became the first UK power station to use renewable sources of fuel, which it 'co-fires' with coal. Right, In 2000, the River Aire was one of many rivers that burst its banks after a prolonged period of exceptionally heavy rain.

The community planning approach also operates within a regional policy framework for Yorkshire and the Humber that addresses environmental concerns via its recognition of the *2003 Regional Sustainable Development Framework*. Environmental concerns are also recognised in the *Regional Economic Strategy (2003–2012)* that has been subject to a sustainability appraisal (Yorkshire Forward *et al.*, 2002), and in the new *Regional Spatial Strategy* that replaces and enhances the scope of Regional Planning Guidance, and which will explicitly consider environmental issues within the regional land-use plan. Nevertheless, there is a danger that in considering environmental issues within community or regional planning, where concerns and spatial scales are very broad, the specific focus on environmental issues in Leeds will be lost. Thus, this chapter aims to examine the environmental progress made by the city of Leeds, and the challenges that remain to be faced.

13.3 Leeds — Environment City?

In 1993, Leeds was one of four UK cities named as a BT 'Environment City' (see Wood, 1995, for a review of the programme). This national competitive award recognised the progress Leeds had made in mobilising stakeholders to address environmental challenges, and thus recognised potential for delivering environmental sustainability. In an attempt to

identify the extent to which this potential has been realised, we present an overview of the current state of the environment in Leeds, focused upon the environmental indicators recommended to local authorities by Government, in its 'local quality of life counts' guidance (DETR, 2000a). These indicators address the themes of prudent use of natural resources (energy, water and household waste) and protection of the environment (air pollution, river pollution and biodiversity).

Energy use

In the 1970s, the Club of Rome was a strong advocate of energy conservation, on the grounds that by the turn of the century, demand would begin to outstrip supply, placing severe limits on further economic growth. Today, energy conservation is a major goal of developed countries, but motivation for conservation comes not from a declining resource base, but from the adverse impacts arising from the burning of fossil fuels, and principally the emission of carbon dioxide (CO_2), the dominant greenhouse gas. It is likely that impacts of climate change are now being felt in the UK, particularly as an increase in the frequency and severity of extreme climatic events. In Yorkshire, for example, severe flooding occurred in several towns in 1998 and 2000, whilst

summer droughts occurred in 1976, 1984 and 1995.

Given the scale at which climate change operates, it is difficult to reconcile local environmental impacts to local actions, hence local action on greenhouse gas reduction is largely the product of national government policy. The UK emits 2 per cent of global anthropogenic CO_2, and under the Kyoto Protocol, has a legally binding commitment to cut greenhouse gas emissions by 12.5 per cent by 2008 from a 1990 base. (The domestic target is a more ambitious 20 per cent cut by 2010, and 60 per cent by 2050). Britain is currently performing well with respect to its Kyoto commitments, but this is largely a consequence of a decline in the more energy-intensive manufacturing industries and a switch from coal to gas. Energy demand is actually rising due to changing lifestyles, particularly greater travel and elevated rates of household formation (due to declining family size), threatening the past gains in emission reduction. There is, therefore, a need to develop renewable energy supplies (the UK has a target of 10 per cent of electricity from renewable sources by 2010) and to encourage further energy conservation. This can be achieved through measures such as building design and refit, energy-sensitive spatial planning to reduce travel demand or provide opportunities for renewable energy and combined heat and power sources, and by provision of energy efficiency advice to homeowners and businesses.

In Leeds, the City Council has taken a lead in promoting energy efficiency. In 1991, the Council's Green Strategy (LCC, 1991a) expressed a desire to implement practical actions of the kind cited above, and in 1992, an energy working group was established to formulate an overall city energy policy. In 1995, the Council made a further commitment to energy conservation, aiming to achieve, by the year 2005, a 30 per cent reduction from 1990 levels of CO_2 emissions due to energy and transport use in the local authority area. There was a recognition that the target could only be achieved through a combination of local actions and new policy measures from national government.

The Council, itself one of the city's largest consumers, reduced its own energy use by 24 per cent by 2003 following an environmental audit and follow-up action, whilst a recent contract to secure a third of its electricity from renewable supplies should see the Council achieving the 30 per cent reduction target. However, the aspiration for a 30 per cent cut city-wide, as expressed in the 1991 Green Strategy, appears optimistic. Measures to encourage energy efficiency include the opening of an energy advice office, an energy information service to local businesses, and the development of *Warm Homes, Cool Planet* (LCC, 1996), the Council's home energy conservation plan developed in response to the Home Energy Conservation Act 1995. Over the period 1996–2002, this plan led to a reduction in energy use in the public and private sector housing of 7 per cent (equivalent to circa 250,000 tonnes of CO_2) (HECA, 2002) and identified ways to address fuel poverty in local authority housing.

These actions are encouraging. However, it is not clear that the energy efficiency aspirations expressed in the early Green Strategy have been realised. EMAS accreditation (gained in 2002) shows that the Council has been highly successful in setting its own house in order, but wider progress across the city appears less substantial. For example, the 7 per cent reduction in housing energy use (8.4 per cent by 2003) appears less significant in the context of the Government target for Leeds of a 30 per cent cut by 2011 (Objective ES2 of the Home Energy Conservation Act 1995), a problem complicated by the need to ensure that fuel poverty issues are adequately addressed. Energy conservation does not feature strongly in the spatial planning of Leeds, and CO_2 emission from transport is forecast to grow 76 per cent over the period 1993–2015 (Mitchell *et al.,* 2003), although this growth would be slowed following the introduction of the Supertram. Regionally, only 1.5 per cent of electricity is supplied from renewable sources, and whilst this capacity is forecast to grow (to 9.4 per cent by 2010 and 22.5 per cent by 2021) (AEAT, 2002), little of this capacity looks likely to be provided in the Leeds area, partly because much of the capacity is forecast as offshore wind. (One CHP plant and a few landfill gas generators currently exist in Leeds).

Water use

Water is often taken for granted in northern counties like Yorkshire, where resources are commonly perceived to be abundant. The reality is that, whilst Yorkshire does have significant water resources, the county also has a large population with a *per capita* demand that is amongst the highest in Europe. The excess of supply over demand is actually rather small, and in the past, supply has been threatened following very dry summers. After the droughts of 1976 and 1984, Yorkshire Water improved its regional distribution network, but in 1995 was nevertheless still reliant on a fleet of road tankers to import supplies from outside the region. With projected wetter winters and drier summers (DoE, 1996), water stress induced by climate change is likely to increase.

There is a limit to the extent that new resources can be developed. Physical constraints and very high cost mean that few opportunities exist for building new reservoirs, whilst sufficient water must be left in rivers to ensure that they maintain their ecological and amenity value. The solution to water stress is now widely regarded as demand management, yet in Yorkshire, demand is forecast to increase steadily for several decades. The picture for Leeds is less certain, largely because, like energy, resource appraisals are made on a regional rather than city basis. However, from forecasts made for Yorkshire Water, it is possible to gain some insight into the impact that Leeds may have on the future regional pattern of water sustainability.

Mitchell *et al.* (2000) forecast demand in nine non-household sectors in Yorkshire, addressing agriculture, industry and services. They forecast non-household demand in the region to grow by about 0.75 per cent per annum to 2025,

In 1996, the reservoir at Eccup, north of Leeds, was still very low after the record drought of 1995. Water had to be brought by tanker from Northumberland to supply the Leeds area.

The city aims to expand the community forest as part of its regeneration programme, which will have benefits of increasing CO_2 sequestration. However, currently planned expansion is unlikely to make a significant change in the net CO_2 budget for the city.

Whilst appraisals of urban use of regional resources are hampered by scale issues, it is apparent that no serious attempt has been made to assess the energy efficiency of the city, and neither energy use nor CO_2 emissions are included as a *Vision for Leeds* indicator (Leeds Initiative, 2001). The ten-year *Vision for Leeds* strategy (Leeds Initiative, 1999) devoted just a few lines to energy — surprising given that the City Council had previously aimed to develop an overall energy policy for the city, and identified a series of wide-ranging energy efficiency objectives in its 1991 Green Strategy. Thus, once the easy wins derived from past industrial restructuring and the 'dash for gas' have faded, Leeds may find that the absence of a strategic energy policy makes it increasingly difficult to fuel the city in a sustainable manner, where economic growth is decoupled from environmental impact. In this respect, much is resting on the implementation of the *Vision II* strategy, published in 2004, in which more robust action plans on energy and greenhouse gases are expected (Kelly, personal communication).

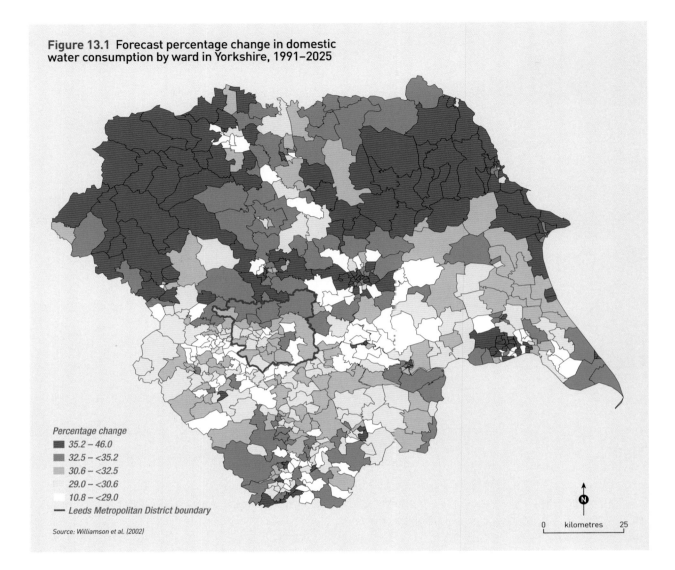

Figure 13.1 Forecast percentage change in domestic water consumption by ward in Yorkshire, 1991–2025

Percentage change
- ■ *35.2 – 46.0*
- ■ *32.5 – <35.2*
- ▨ *30.6 – <32.5*
- *29.0 – <30.6*
- □ *10.8 – <29.0*
- — *Leeds Metropolitan District boundary*

Source: Williamson et al. (2002)

0　　kilometres　　25

driven by economic growth and falling water prices (revised price limits). The majority of growth is in the service sector (business services and the public sector) and in food, drink and manufacturing, where annual demand is forecast to grow by 2.0 and 0.8 per cent respectively for the region. Leeds has a strong representation of these activities (a leader in business services — see Chapter 9, second largest manufacturing employer outside London — see Chapter 8) and hence it is reasonable to conclude that the Leeds economy will have a disproportionate and growing share of impacts on regional water resource sustainability. Water prices are likely to rise in 2004 following the periodic review, but these increases are not likely to reverse the upward trend in demand fuelled by

economic growth and restructuring.

Turning to household water use (Figure 13.1), we find that demand in Yorkshire is likely to increase by 30 per cent over the period 1991 to 2025 (Williamson *et al.,* 2002). Of this increase, approximately one quarter will be accounted for by increases in population, with the remainder arising from changes in water consuming behaviour (e.g. smaller household size, greater ownership of dishwashers, power showers and other water-intensive appliances). Within Yorkshire, however, this increase will vary greatly spatially, with the change by ward ranging from +11 to +46 per cent. The greatest increases are expected in affluent areas characterised by households with large gardens and high forecast rates of water appliance ownership. In contrast, inner city areas, including those of Leeds, Bradford and Sheffield, are forecast to experience some of the lowest demand increases, due to the predominance of poorer households in areas of below average population growth. With the exception of its inner city areas, Leeds may again be expected to exert a disproportionately large impact on future regional water resource sustainability, given that it is a city characterised by its leafy suburbs and growing affluence.

Raising water prices can reduce demand. However, most household demand in the UK is not charged for on a unit basis, in part due to concerns over the ability of poorer households to pay for water. In addition, the last decade has seen little in the way of real price increases as the regulator has felt that prices for water services were in general too high. Given this context, measures to reduce demand preferentially address processes (leakage reduction, waste minimisation) or new technology (e.g. water efficient appliances, rainwater harvesting, grey water recycling). Leeds has seen some activity in these areas, particularly in leakage reduction and in implementation of waste minimisation practices in local industries, under a pioneering pilot scheme promoted by CEST (Edwards and Johnston, 1996). Leeds City Council has achieved a reduction (1992–1999) in water use in its own buildings, but recent years have seen a gradual increase, hence the *Energy and Water Management Plan* (LCC, 2003b) has set a target of reducing demand by 5 per cent over the period 2003–2008. On a more strategic level, Leeds has given relatively little attention to water resource issues when considering future infrastructure development, and has implicitly taken a 'predict and provide' approach to water resource provision. Leeds is not alone in this respect, and the Government's own Sustainable Communities plan (ODPM, 2003a) has been severely criticised for failing to give adequate consideration to water resource issues in development planning (ODPM, 2003b). The incorporation in the 2004 revised Unitary Development Plan of draft supplementary planning guidance on sustainable urban drainage (which addresses resource issues to a limited degree) illustrates some progress in this direction.

It is true that city authorities have little direct control over water resource management, which is the responsibility of the privatised utilities (regulated by Ofwat) and the Environment Agency. This may explain why water resource management has received little attention in the environmental policy documents of the City Council. However, greater attention to water resource issues might be expected in the Leeds *Vision* (a city as opposed to City Council strategy), given that it is a forward-looking initiative developed by an extensive group of local stakeholders, including those with responsibilities for water management.

Household waste arising and recycling

"Sustainable waste management means using material resources efficiently, to cut down on the amount of waste we produce... and dealing with it in a way that actively contributes to the economic, social and environmental goals of sustainable development" DETR (1999b, p.9). In practice, this seemingly simple aspiration is impeded by technical, economic and institutional barriers that make delivery of sustainable waste management one of the greatest challenges facing cities today. One of the areas where waste strategy is focussed is household waste, which accounts for 89 per cent of municipal waste[2] though for only 7 per cent of total waste arising in the UK (DEFRA, 2003b). In 2002, UK households generated 26 million tonnes of waste, up 1.7 per cent from 2001, of which 12 per cent was recycled or composted, with most of the remainder going to landfill (DEFRA, 2003a), a finite capacity that merits conservation like any other non-renewable resource.

At the heart of the UK's waste management strategy (DETR, 2000b), driven by EU and UK legislation (EC, 1991; DoE, 1995), is the waste hierarchy: reduce, re-use, recover energy and dispose the remainder as locally as possible to the source. The strategy has been implemented via the landfill tax to encourage waste reduction and other disposal routes; the Waste and Resources Action Programme to develop markets for recycled materials; the Landfill Tax Credit Scheme to generate funds for re-use and recycling projects; producer responsibility legislation to increase packaging recycling; and the setting of statutory local authority waste recycling targets. Despite these measures, the UK is not on target to meet its statutory EU commitment to cut biodegradable waste going to landfill by two thirds by 2020, whilst performance against the 25 per cent household waste recycling/composting target for local authorities has been so poor that the target has been set back five years. Whilst Europe incinerates 18 per cent of its waste, public concern over emissions (Davoudi, 2001) means that incineration accounts for just 2 per cent of UK waste. New facilities are urgently needed if targets for diverting waste from landfill are to be met (ICE, 2004).

As a unitary authority, Leeds City Council is responsible for both waste collection and disposal, and has thus developed an integrated waste management strategy (LCC, 2003d) dealing with all municipal waste, not just that from households. The strategy sets targets for waste arising in Leeds: growth should be limited to 3 per cent a year from 2001–2005, falling to 0.5 per cent growth by 2016. The strategy includes a clear statement of the need to break the link between economic growth and solid waste production and to deal with waste in the most responsible manner possible. The proportion of household waste going to landfill fell from 91 per cent to 85 per cent between 1998 and 2002 as waste recycling and composting grew. However, over the same period, household waste arising grew by over 6 per cent per annum, twice the national average, due to strong economic growth, and hence the total volume of waste going to landfill is increasing by 4 per cent a year. Half of this is disposed of in sites within the metropolitan boundary, but current capacity is expected to be exhausted in 10–20 years (LCC, 2000a). The Council is exploring possible alternatives.

Leeds is aiming for recycling (including composting) of 21 per cent of household waste by 2005–2006 (33 per cent by 2015) (LCC, 2003d). There are 340 recycling drop off sites (bottles and other materials) and ten household waste recycling centres (which are being redeveloped to improve capacity and provide on-site compaction). However, participation in recycling is greatest with kerbside collection (Gandy, 1994), hence the SORT scheme (Separate Out Recyclables Today), in which residents are provided with separate bins for dry recyclables (not glass), putrescibles and non-recyclables is a key component of waste strategy. Starting with a 4,000 household trial in 1989, the scheme will cover 250,000 households by 2004, with recycling facilities provided to a further 10,000 households in multi-storey flats or with shared yards. This means that nearly every property that could have waste separation at source will have been included. The programme was supported in 1993 by the development of a materials recovery facility at Kirkstall to enable further waste separation.

SORT recycling rates were initially high, and Leeds still has a good performance compared with other cities (Best Value Inspection Service, 2001), but rates have declined as the scheme has expanded. Recycled materials are no longer collected weekly, but monthly, and collection of putrescible material for composting has ceased due to contamination with glass. Provision for composting is made through disposal of garden waste at civic amenity sites, and through subsidy of home composting bins. Around 20,000 households now have a composting bin, but this is well short of the Government's 40 per cent household target, equivalent to 119,000 households in Leeds.

Trends for waste arising and recycling in Leeds suggest that current policies and initiatives will not be quite sufficient to meet targets for reducing household waste (2 per cent growth 2006–2010; 1 per cent for the following five years and then 0.5 per cent growth up to 2020) and reducing waste to landfill. Actions in hand to raise awareness amongst the public of the seriousness of the waste disposal problem may lessen apathy and antipathy towards recycling, but it is far from certain that a change in attitude would produce the required change in behaviour (Blake, 1999). Real changes in amounts of household waste going to landfill seem more likely to arise as a result of external drivers. First, the 2003 Household Waste Recycling Bill places a duty on local authorities to provide a collection of at least two types of recyclable waste from 2010 for every household in the country. Whilst Leeds already has a scheme in place, the duty on authorities to provide kerbside collection for all households is expected to change the economics of recycling nationally, making it more effective. Second, Leeds spends £23 million a year on waste management (£75 per household), with costs increasing by £500,000 annually due to the landfill tax (currently £15 per tonne eventually rising to £35 per tonne) (HM Treasury, 2002). Continuing to service such costs from council taxation may prove increasingly unpopular, and householders may ultimately be persuaded to switch to payment on a cost per unit waste basis, where the lower cost for recycled waste provides an incentive to recycle. In the meantime, the principal

goal of waste management in Leeds is to reduce net growth in waste arising. This may be an ambitious target under present circumstances, yet paints a rather pessimistic picture in which sustainable waste management will still seem a distant goal to the next generation.

Air quality

Urban air quality in Britain has improved dramatically since the first half of the last century, when coal burning led to major smogs in the nation's industrial centres. Air pollution continues to diminish, and for most of the time urban air quality is good. However, whilst visible air pollution is largely a thing of the past, less visible air pollutants remain at sufficiently high concentrations to ensure that air quality remains a major environmental concern. For example, the European Environment Agency concluded that across Europe's 115 largest cities, 40 million people were exposed annually to air quality that breached current health-based standards (EEA, 1998), whilst in the UK, poor urban air quality is responsible for bringing forward 12–24,000 deaths each year and accounts for 3–6 per cent of all hospital admission for respiratory illness (DoH, 1998). Other problems associated with atmospheric emissions and poor air quality include disruption of natural processes (acidification, ozone depletion, climate change) and nuisance (soiling of buildings, odour).

The principle EU legislation intended to combat these problems is the Air Quality Framework Directive (96/62/EC). The directive defines minimum quality standards, and the target dates by when they must be met, but it is up to member states to decide how best to achieve the objectives. The UK response is defined by the 1995 Environment Act and the subsequent National Air Quality Strategy (NAQS) (DETR, 2000c) which defines procedures for air quality review and assessment, and identifies those responsible for implementation of the strategy. Local authorities have a major part to play in delivery of the NAQS, and are responsible for air quality review and assessment, and establishment of air quality management areas (AQMAs) and associated action plans for

Spires on Woodhouse Lane. In the nineteenth century, air pollution turned stonework black within four years. Air quality is now much improved: the freshly cleaned spire will not blacken rapidly. The church on the left has been converted into a nightclub — plus points for the re-use of a building, though sound pollution may be an issue.

those places where there is a danger of not meeting air quality standards by the 2005 target date.

Judging from city centre monitoring, air quality in Leeds has been improving in recent years (Table 13.1). The local authority's NAQS Stage 1 and 2 reviews have also found that concentrations of four NAQS pollutants (carbon monoxide, benzene, 1,3-butadiene and lead) are unlikely to exceed standards anywhere in the city (LCC, 1999). Under the Stage 3

assessment (LCC, 2001), emission and dispersion modelling was conducted to forecast future concentrations of sulphur dioxide, nitrogen dioxide and fine particulates (PM_{10}), pollutants for which the earlier reviews had indicated the possibility of non-compliance with the required standards for 2005. Whilst smoke control orders have effectively limited sulphur dioxide (SO_2) emission in Leeds, a potential problem was identified with the grounding of plumes from the Aire

Table 13.1 Days of moderate or high pollution in Leeds city centre

Pollutant	1993	1994	1995	1996	1997	1998	1999	2000	2001	2002
Carbon monoxide (CO)	0	0	0	0	0	0	0	0	0	0
Nitrogen dioxide (NO₂)	0	3	1	0	1	0	0	0	0	0
Fine particulates (PM₁₀)	42	42	37	47	49	13	12	1	6	6
Ozone	3	5	21	12	9	3	27	8	10	5
Sulphur dioxide (SO₂)	19	23	15	9	11	6	6	1	3	1
Total (Leeds)[1]	64	73	74	68	70	22	45	10	19	12
Total (UK urban average)[2]	59	n/a	n/a	48	38	22	28	21	25	20

Source: [1]LCC (1999, 2000c, 2001); [2]DEFRA (2001b, 2002)

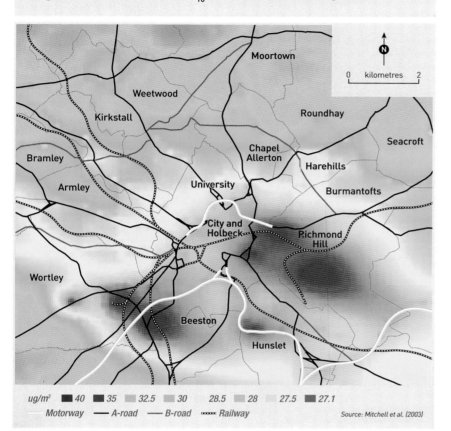

Figure 13.2 Annual mean PM$_{10}$ concentration in Leeds, 2005

ug/m^3 ■ 40 ■ 35 ▨ 32.5 ▨ 30   28.5   28   27.5 ■ 27.1
— Motorway — A-road — B-road ▨▨▨ Railway   Source: Mitchell et al. (2003)

action must address road traffic, the main source of nitrogen oxides (NO$_x$).

The 2000 fuel crisis provided a graphic example of how traffic reduction could deliver air quality benefits in Leeds. During the crisis, average daily traffic fell by 24 per cent, and NO$_2$ concentrations by 30 per cent, a decline sufficient to ensure compliance with NAQS objectives. However, a sustainable strategy clearly requires that traffic reductions are achieved in other ways. Leeds has been active in developing appropriate measures, including introduction of electric vehicles within the City Council and investment in public transport and traffic restraint (see Chapter 10).

In collaboration with the City Council, Mitchell *et al.* (2003) investigated the impact of a variety of strategic traffic management measures on urban air quality in Leeds, using a series of linked models of traffic assignment, pollutant emission and dispersion. The study illustrated that a modest road user distance charge (2 pence per kilometre), levied for travel within the outer ring road, was the only strategy of the 16 tested that ensured air quality standards were met, whilst also ensuring trips were shorter and faster. In contrast, seven kilometres of network development (including the East Leeds Link road) induced additional traffic and led to localised reductions in air quality. The 'business as usual' strategy indicated that, with no interventions to the transport system, vehicle trips in Leeds will become slower and that total vehicle kilometres travelled in the city will increase (by 2.5 per cent per year) as travel demand grows. Fleet turnover and continual improvement in emission technology means that emissions of most pollutants continue to decline, but the growth in trips ensures that total vehicle

Valley power stations on those infrequent occasions when an easterly wind blows. However, the Environment Agency. responsible for regulating these sources, indicates that an emission improvement programme will have been implemented by 2005, ensuring that breaches of the 15-minute SO$_2$ standard are eliminated.

The Stage 3 modelling did, however, predict exceedences of annual mean standards for nitrogen dioxide (NO$_2$) and PM$_{10}$ and hence, in July 2001, AQMAs were designated (these were later confirmed by a subsequent stage 4 review). One AQMA was designated in Micklefield to address PM$_{10}$ derived from a high incidence of domestic coal burning. This problem is relatively simple to address (e.g. householders can be given incentives to switch from coal to gas). However, for the other AQMAs, which address forecast exceedences of the NO$_2$ standard near main roads (A58M Inner Ring Road, York Road, Dewsbury Road), action planning is more complex, as remedial

emission of PM_{10} increases. As the PM_{10} standard is to be halved to 20 g/m³ as an annual mean from 2010 (DEFRA, 2001b), the increase in particulate emission from transport represents a major problem for Leeds (and most other major UK cities), as much of the city centre will be in breach of the standard (Figure 13.2). Implementation of the local transport plan, and particularly the Supertram system, may be effective in securing the required air quality, although the full air quality implications of these measures have yet to be assessed.

Air quality in Leeds has improved markedly in recent years, and is now of a consistently high standard. There is, however, no room for complacency. New evidence of the health effects of air pollutant exposure (e.g. long-term effects) is likely to lead to new and tighter standards, as has recently occurred with PM_{10}, necessitating further improvements in air quality management. Localised areas of poor air quality do occur, and if present traffic growth goes unchecked, more people will be adversely affected. Finally, ground level ozone, a pollutant that commonly breaches standards, presents a further challenge. Due to the way in which it is formed (a photolytic reaction product of VOC and NO_x), ozone is not a responsibility of local authorities, but through a wider collaborative network, they undoubtedly have a significant role to play.

Water quality

In 1694, Leeds became one of the first towns in Britain to have a piped water supply, when the lower Briggate station first pumped water from the River Aire. By 1841, however, the river was so polluted from industrial discharges and surface drainage rich in human effluent that this source was abandoned. Before 1870 there were few sewers but growing access to piped water sources led to an acceleration of sewer construction, and the discharge of untreated sewage direct to the River Aire

Table 13.2 River water quality in Leeds Metropolitan District (percentage length by class), 1990–2002

	Biological water quality				Chemical water quality				N	P
	Good	Fair	Poor	Bad	Good	Fair	Poor	Bad	High	High
1990	34	7	10	49	38	31	29	2	–	–
1995	40	33	26	1	29	51	16	4	28	57
2000	39	26	28	7	28	57	14	1	28	65
2002	40	27	25	7	29	50	20	1	25	68

Table refers to rivers Aire, Wharfe and Calder, and tributaries with mean annual flow > 1m³/sec   *Source: DEFRA (2003b)*

(Sellars, 1997). These actions improved public health considerably, but they also ensured that the quality of the river remained exceedingly low. Even after the city's first sewage treatment works was built (at Knostrop in 1877), the Aire, once one of the best salmon rivers in England, remained devoid of life.

Over the last decade, the quality of the rivers in Leeds (Table 13.2), particularly the Aire, has improved significantly, largely due to capital investment in sewage and industrial effluent treatment, driven by the EU urban waste water treatment directive. This has allowed coarse and game fish to return to the river, whilst otters, top predators and a key indicator of river health, have also been reported in the Aire east of Leeds. The improved water quality has not only benefited wildlife, but has contributed substantively to efforts to regenerate the waterfront area in central Leeds, and has presented new recreational opportunities, such as angling and canoeing.

The post-industrial recovery of water quality in the region's rivers represents one of the world's most successful environmental clean-ups. However, the recovery is incomplete and large stretches of the Aire continue to be graded as 'poor'. The most urgent problem is that of combined sewer overflow (CSO). Before the 1950s, sewers were built to convey both sewage and surface runoff, and at times of high rainfall, effluent may by-pass the treatment works and be discharged direct to rivers. This is a major cause of downgrading of water quality in the Aire, but is soon to be tackled through further capital investment by Yorkshire Water. Non-point source discharges, such as that draining roads and built areas, is also a significant source of pollutant loads to rivers in the region, and in future is likely to be the single most important reason for rivers like the Aire failing to achieve their water quality objectives. This type of

pollution can be tackled using sustainable urban drainage systems, such as swales and filter strips, but it is important that these devices are not just built in new developments, but are also installed in those parts of the city that already generate high loads. A national project to develop a means of identifying these urban diffuse load 'hot-spots' has now been completed, using the Aire and Calder Basin as the pilot region (Mitchell, 2001).

Micro-organic pollutants (e.g. pesticides, fungicides, PAHs, PCBs) present another problem. The concentration of these chemicals is particularly high in the Humber rivers, and levels in sediment, not normally monitored, are sufficient to exert adverse ecotoxicological effects (Neal *et al.*, 2000). There is also concern over levels of oestrogen compounds that interfere with reproduction in fish, as high and persistent levels have been found in the Aire (FWR, 1995). Whilst some oestrogenic compounds used in industry are being phased out, the evidence base on the source, fate and impact of these compounds remains very limited. The growing demand for water, exacerbated by climate change, can also compound water quality problems of the city's rivers, as in meeting the demand for water, the flow available to dilute pollution is reduced.

Past improvement in local water quality has been achieved through a combination of legislative pressure (especially EU directives), and an active multi-partner approach to river management involving Yorkshire Water, the Environment Agency, the Council, local business and the voluntary sector. The effectiveness of this approach has been shown by initiatives such as the Aire and Calder waste minimisation project, that demonstrated how industry could save money through reducing discharges, and whose lead has been followed throughout the country. The Eye on the Aire, a

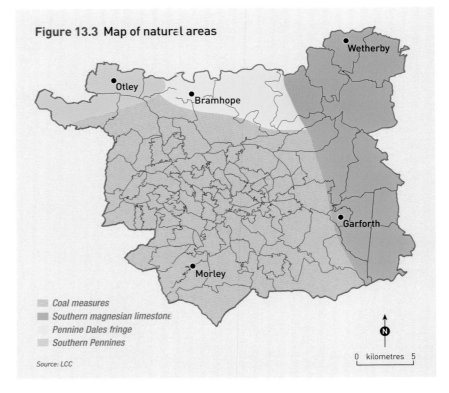

Figure 13.3 Map of natural areas

- Coal measures
- Southern magnesian limestone
- Pennine Dales fringe
- Southern Pennines

Source: LCC

respected local lobby group, has also proved effective in mobilising support for improvement initiatives (e.g. Rodley and Shipley wildlife reserves) and provides a model for other groups such as Calder Futures whose work upstream of Leeds will influence the quality of rivers in the Leeds area.

In 2004, the local stakeholder organisations formed a new State of the River Management Partnership, designed to co-ordinate the development of the River Aire and its tributaries, for the benefit of the city's environment and local communities. One of the key aims is to make sure that the public benefits from and becomes actively involved in making the best use of the river and its environment. It remains to be seen whether ambitious goals, such as 'day lighting' and restoration of the city's becks, abstraction for potable water downstream of Leeds, and ultimately recovery of the rivers' pre-industrial status, can be met. Such initiatives suggest that prospects for further improvement of the city's waterways are good.

Biodiversity conservation

Cities are not often thought of as places with a rich biological diversity. It is true that dense urban centres have impoverished fauna and flora, but wider urban areas collectively make an important contribution to national biodiversity. Leeds is notable in this respect, as over two thirds of the area is countryside. A varied geology and topography produces four main natural areas in the district (Figure 13.3): coal measures covering much of the built area, southern magnesian limestone to the east, the Pennine Dales fringe to the north and a small part of the southern Pennines around Otley.

These distinct areas provide the basis for significant local biodiversity, whose importance is recognised through the designation of statutory protected areas. Leeds has six Local Nature Reserves, 17 Sites of Special Scientific Interest (SSSIs), 33 Sites of Scientific Interest (SSIs), 43 Sites of Ecological or Geological Importance (SEGIs). There are also 116 Local Nature Areas as shown in Figure 13.4, together with around 2,600 hectares of woodland — mostly broadleaved — of which over 40 per cent are on Council-owned land. Some of these designated special areas overlap, as in the case of the River Wharfe along the northern extremity of the district.

Leeds is one of around 160 UK areas with a formal local *Biodiversity Action Plan (BAP)* (LCC, 2000b). These BAPs represent local implementation of the national BAP, developed to address Britain's commitment to the 1992 International Convention on Biological Diversity (which requires creation and enforcement of national biodiversity protection strategies). The Leeds BAP focuses on four habitats and six species where protection is most needed, and where resources are expected to have the greatest effect (Table 13.3). The Leeds BAP describes the current status of these species and habitats (extent, trend and importance), factors causing their loss or decline, and a management plan specifying actions, responsibilities and measurable targets.

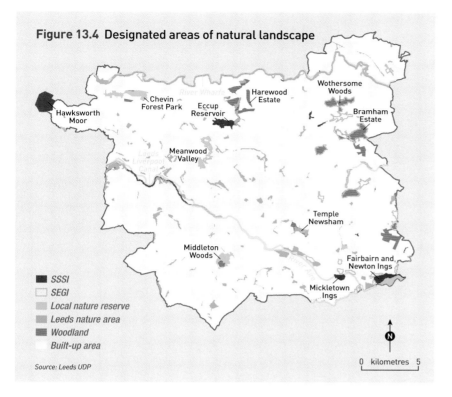

Figure 13.4 Designated areas of natural landscape

Wothersome Woods

Harewood Estate

Chevin Forest Park

Eccup Reservoir

Hawksworth Moor

Bramham Estate

Meanwood Valley

Temple Newsham

Middleton Woods

Fairbairn and Newton Ings

Mickletown Ings

- SSSI
- SEGI
- Local nature reserve
- Leeds nature area
- Woodland
- Built-up area

Source: Leeds UDP

0   kilometres   5

The UK approach to biodiversity action planning is based on five key principles: decision making based on sound information; establishment of measurable conservation targets; policy integration with other sectors; public awareness and action; and a broad partnership approach. These attributes are evident in the *Leeds Nature Conservation Strategy* (LCC, 1991b), developed in response to the 1987 DoE circular on nature conservation. For example, under the strategy, biological surveys ensured that ecologically sensitive areas were given protection from development in the Unitary Development Plan process, whilst conservation objectives, including raising public awareness, were pursued in partnership with statutory groups (e.g. English Nature, NRA/Environment Agency) and voluntary groups such as the Yorkshire Wildlife Trust and RSPB.

Biodiversity links to other policy areas have subsequently been strengthened, via, for example, the City Council's forest and countryside strategies, and their procurement policy which is reducing its use of peat and hardwoods. The BAP does, however, demand a more quantitative approach than previously seen in Leeds, with a series of measurable outcomes with target dates established for each of the ten priority areas. These relate not just to ends,

for instance population status by 2010, but also to means. For example, the Leeds BAP identifies 18 actions intended to reverse decline of the thistle broomrape, a nationally important plant now only found in Yorkshire. Lead agencies responsible for these actions (such as land management, research and monitoring, awareness raising) are identified, but there are strong concerns over how these actions will be resourced. This is not simply a Leeds issue. A national survey of local BAP officers found that the most important constraint to achieving plan targets was a lack of funding (Entec, 2003). Lead agencies identified limited research and surveying as the key barrier, but this is also clearly linked to available resources.

Biodiversity management is, however, unlikely to receive direct funding sufficient to implement the monitoring and action plans that conservationists would like. Ecological organisations such as West Yorkshire Ecology (the county's ecological database and advisory service based in Leeds) have been established recently, and have a lead role to play in monitoring progress toward BAP targets, but successful protection depends on actions elsewhere. Policy and practice in related areas (e.g. land-use planning, infrastructure development, agricultural practice, pollution control) must be sensitive to biodiversity goals, while strong partnerships of statutory, voluntary, business and academic sectors will be required to champion biodiversity. There is evidence of policy integration and partnership building in Leeds (including explicit attention to the Leeds BAP in the *Vision II* process), but it is too early to judge how effective these factors will be in ensuring that the BAP is implemented and its goals met.

Table 13.3 Leeds Biodiversity Action Plan priorities

Priority: (H) Habitat; (S) Species	Status, trends and targets
Magnesian Lowland Grassland (H)	15 small isolated sites; declining nationally due to under grazing, development and management cost; aim to increase area by 50 per cent by 2005, and ensure populations of key species stable by 2008.
Reedbed (H)	Small area only (Micklefown Ings SSSI); nationally declining at an unknown rate; threatened by water pollution and abstraction; aim to increase area from 6–100 hectares of reedbed by 2020.
Lowland wet grassland (H)	No detailed inventory but several known areas in Aire and Wharfe floodplains; threatened by water pollution and abstraction; aim to produce a baseline survey and maintain existing habitat.
Hedgerow and Field Margin (H)	Little detailed local information, and none on quality or total length; threats from agricultural practice and infrastructure development; aim to conduct baseline survey and set replanting targets.
Pasqueflower (S)	Nationally scare; once common in Yorkshire but only one plant remains, and threatened by collectors or chance loss; aim to increase to 400 plants at four sites in 10 years.
Thistle Broomrape (S)	Nationally scarce with key sites in Yorkshire; factor causing decline not well understood; aim to reverse decline by 2003.
Harvest Mouse (S)	Various sites around Leeds, marking the territorial limit of the species; declining due to habitat loss from agriculture and development; aim to assess population and set expansion target.
Pipistrelle Bat (S)	Around 500 animals recorded in Leeds urban areas; national decline (70 per cent 1978–1993); aim to extend survey, improve foraging habitat in key roost areas and support national target of pre-1970 population.
Atlantic Stream Crayfish (S)	Found within Wharfe and Aire catchments, but declining nationally; main threats are other crayfish species, habitat degradation and disease; aim to increase population and reduce that of other species.
Great Crested Newt (S)	Only 97 animals recorded in Leeds at six sites since 1998; fastest UK decline of any reptile or amphibian due to pond drainage, pollution and predation; aim for 200 newts at 12 sites by 2010.

Source: LCC

Table 13.4 The state of the Leeds environment

Indicator	Trend		Target
CO_2 emission	?	Uncertain city wide due to limited data; falling in housing, but rising in transport.	Commitment to 30 per cent reduction in housing sector (1996–2011) and agreement to aim for 30 per cent city-wide cut from 1990 base (LCC/FoE); aspiration to collect data to permit city wide assessment.
Renewable energy use	✓	Increasing but from very low level (1.5 per cent in region).	Not set; future regional capability is estimated at 22.5 per cent by 2021.
Air quality	✓	Improving and of high quality.	Air quality management areas designated to eliminate standard exceedences by 2005.
Domestic waste arising	X	Domestic waste increased 24 per cent 1997–2001.	Reduce annual growth rate to 3 per cent by 2005, and 0.5 per cent by 2020.
Domestic waste recycling	✓	Increased from 8 per cent in 1997 to 15.7 per cent in 2003.	Recycle 19.6 per cent of all city waste by 2004, and 30 per cent of household waste by 2010.
Brownfield use	✓	Achieved 86 per cent in 2003.	Local Public Service Agreement target of 82 per cent in 2004.
River water quality	✓	Improving, but much of Leeds water courses are of 'poor' quality (Table 13.2).	Compliance with statutory water quality objectives.
Water demand	X	Rising by c. 1 per cent year.	No target set for region.
Noise and other nuisances	?	Uncertain, due to limited data.	No targets, although noise reduction targets may be required following EU directive.
Environment and deprivation	X	27 per cent of households in fuel poverty in 2002.	National target to eradicate fuel poverty in vulnerable households by 2010 and in all households by 2018.
Biodiversity	?	Decline in key species and habitats.	Various (see Table 13.3 and the Leeds Biodiversity Action plan).
Built heritage	?	Unknown; buildings at risk register recently established.	Removal of five buildings per year from the seriously at risk register.

Source: LCC (2003a); Kelly (personal communication, 2004)

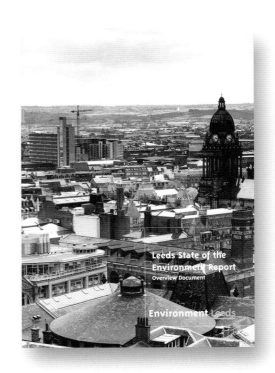

The *Leeds State of the Environment Report*, published in 2003, indicates that the city has a long way to go before it can claim to be environmentally sustainable.

13.4 Environmental progress and prospects

Leeds: environment city — sustainable city?

Over the last few decades, great improvements in the quality of air and water in Leeds have been achieved, and the city is very different from the grossly polluted place that Dickens found so terrible. However, expectations today are greater than in Dickens' time, and the environmentally sustainable city is one that must perform well across a wider range of criteria than just those important to public health. Our review of key environmental issues identified by *Local Quality of Life Counts,* and summary (Table 13.4) of the recently released city State of the Environment report (LCC, 2003a), shows that the environmental performance of Leeds is at best patchy. Air and water quality are improving, but waste arising and water demand are not yet on a sustainable trajectory, and in other key areas, performance against targets is very slow or difficult to evaluate due to a lack of available data.

The environmental improvements that have occurred in Leeds over the last twenty years or so have been made at a time of substantial economic growth. However, the improvements are not obviously a consequence of a richer city flexing its financial muscle to benefit its citizens by raising environmental quality. Rather, these improvements might well have occurred anyway in response to a range of external drivers including a shift to a less polluting service economy; implementation of EU and national legislation (e.g. Waste Water directive, Air Quality Framework directive); technology development (e.g. less polluting vehicles, lead free petrol) and business efforts to 'go green' so as to avoid prosecutions, make cost savings and improve their image (e.g. water industry privatisation, CEST Aire and Calder waste minimisation project). Indeed, economic growth has generated new environmental concerns, particularly those arising from traffic growth (noise, particulate pollution), pressures on green space, waste arising and resource consumption. The acute pollution problems of a hundred years ago are gone, but there is little evidence that Leeds has made progress in breaking the link between economic growth and its wider impacts on the regional and global environment.

Whilst external drivers have arguably been the dominant influence on environmental quality in Leeds, many important initiatives have been developed, led by the City Council and its partners (Table 13.5 and While *et al.,* 2002). These initiatives, and particularly the consensual approach to city management, have ensured that Leeds has a favourable environmental and sustainability image. However, as our limited review, and the Environment City Partnership's *State of the Environment Report* suggest, this image is not necessarily a reflection of real delivery of a more environmentally sustainable city, and a number of challenges remain. Several of these are in key sector areas, such as waste arising, which we have addressed above, or in transport (see Chapter 10). Other challenges, more generic in nature, are discussed below.

Key environmental challenges

Of all the environmental challenges facing Leeds, perhaps the most prosaic, yet important, is that of adequate environmental reporting. A state of the environment (SOE) report fulfils several functions providing a baseline assessment of current status and recent trends in environmental quality; identifying key pressures and possible future problems; identifying locations of

Table 13.5 Landmarks in the environmentally sustainable development of Leeds

Year	Environmental landmark
1990	The Leeds Initiative, the city's main public-private partnership, set up to address a wide range of common objectives, including environmental performance.
1991	The City Council publishes the Leeds Green Strategy, a 155 objective action plan to improve council environmental performance across all its services (LCC, 1991); Leeds Nature Conservation Strategy (LCC, 1991b) published, followed by Woodland Strategy (LCC, 1992).
1992	Leeds Environmental Business Forum formed to raise business awareness of environmental issues (70+ members); Leeds Environmental Action Forum formed: an umbrella group of community and voluntary sector organisations (80 members).
1993	The city wins the RSNC/BT Environment City title, one of four awards made nationally to local authorities. The award recognised commitment to environmental improvement through mobilising stakeholders around environmental issues.
1994	Environment City Unit established.
1995	Countryside strategy established
1996	A Leeds Initiative-led *Vision for Leeds* exercise was conducted, the largest public consultation ever in Leeds, canvassing citizens on aspirations for the city.
1997	Leeds City Council Environmental Policy established; *Sustainable Development Design Guide* (LCC, 1998) published to supplement planning guidance.
1998	Draft Local Agenda 21 strategy and action plan published; Biodiversity action plan published.
1999	Environment recognised as a core value in the City Council's Corporate Plan 1999–2002, but is secondary to best value, community planning, democratic renewal and regeneration; *Vision for Leeds* strategy for 1999–2009 published, incorporating Agenda 21.
2000	The city was a finalist in the international ICLEI 'Global-Local' initiative, that recognised excellence in 'governance for sustainable development' based on the *Vision for Leeds.*
2002	Leeds City Council achieved EMAS status, the largest public sector organisation in Europe to gain this independently verified EU environmental audit accreditation; the Environment City Partnership release an environment and education plan; integrated waste management strategy (draft) and Biodiversity Action Plan published.
2003	*Vision for Leeds II* exercise conducted; The Environment City Partnership release the city's first 'State of the Environment Report'. Revision of Leeds City Council Environment Policy under way — direct and indirect effects of council activity.
2004	*Vision for Leeds II 2004–2020* published.

greatest concern; fostering interaction with stakeholders; supporting evaluation of the effectiveness of existing policies and
assisting policy makers to make
more informed decisions about
the city. The production of a SOE
report for Leeds was an objective
of the 1991 Green Strategy, but
limited resources delayed its
publication and mean that it is
not the comprehensive document that is ideally required. It is
long on context and short on
actual information about Leeds (summarised in Table 13.4), with
little appraisal of trends against targets, and nothing on spatial
variation. There is an awareness within the Council both that the
report is less than ideal and that a different approach should be
taken to the compilation and production of future reports. There
is also a need to ensure that the information is used by decision
makers. Development of a robust SOE report for Leeds is essential
to guide progress, and to complement the *Vision for Leeds*
headline indicators, of which only two (waste and air quality)
address the environment.

A second challenge is the reconciliation of future
growth with environmental limits. Leeds is perhaps unusual in
not having had any major environmental conflicts in the past,
which While *et al*. (2002) attribute to the personalities of city
leaders who have not adopted a 'growth at all costs' strategy.
However, they also point out that major infrastructure
development has yet to be constrained by environmental
concerns. The major regeneration efforts of the early 1990s
were focussed along the waterfront, coinciding with and
contributing to river clean up. Brownfield land has not been in
short supply, and even the A1-M1 motorway link was largely
unopposed, as it did not cross areas of significant wildlife or
landscape value. As Leeds grows, however, environmental
limits may become more obvious, and city leaders may face

greater difficulty in reconciling potentially competing goals.
Unless there is some radical intervention, the expansion of the
retail core (see Chapter 11), with ever greater chances for
consumption, is arguably at variance with recent attempts to
rethink consumption and re-orientate behaviour (DEFRA,

Figure 13.5 Kirkstall Valley Park proposals

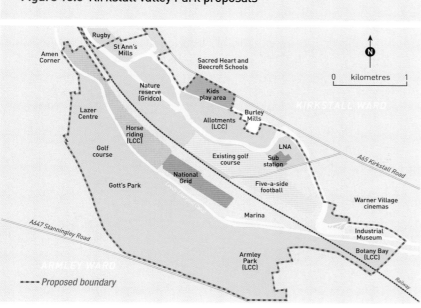

Walker, 2003), indicates that one ward in Leeds is a national 'environmental inequality' hotspot.

Perhaps the most significant challenge facing the environment of Leeds is to ensure that environmental goals are valued equally with social and economic goals. Sustainability objectives have permeated many areas of local policy formulation and action planning, and are central to both the *City Council Plan 2003/2004* (LCC, 2003e) and Leeds Initiative's *Vision II* strategy (Leeds Initiative, 2004). It is clear, however, that social regeneration and economic development are the top priorities of the Leeds Initiative, whilst priorities of the City Council's corporate plan are best value, community planning, democratic renewal and regeneration. The environment is a 'core value', although key council activities are limited to EMAS, green purchasing, implementation of the waste management strategy and air quality review and assessment. Interestingly, these last two address the *Vision II* headline environmental indicators, and illustrate the problem of preferentially addressing those issues for which performance indicators are used.

While *et al.* (2002) note that, whilst difficult to develop, high profile city-wide environmental projects are needed to act as a catalyst for environmental progress, and give new focus to the role of the Environment City Partnership, the city's champions of the environment. One major project (though not city-wide), is the proposed Kirkstall Valley Park, a site of about 150 hectares in the river valley west of the city centre (Figure 13.5).

Enhanced nature conservation will be combined with improved access and new leisure and employment opportunities. Innovative ideas relating to multi-stakeholder involvement in planning and delivery (e.g. using probationers to cultivate organic produce for disadvantaged people) are also being developed. If

2003c). Expansion of services at Leeds-Bradford Airport and improved connections to the city centre — seen as vital by the business community — are at odds with wider concerns about fossil fuel consumption and CO_2 emissions.

A related challenge is the adequate integration of environmental issues with developing social and economic policy. This is important in terms of reducing impact upon the environment, but also in recognising the positive contribution the environment can make to social and economic goals. In some areas, there is evidence that this is achieved effectively. For example, air quality goals feature significantly in the development of local transport plans, and we have seen how regeneration of the city centre was helped by cleansing of the River Aire. In other areas, there is high level recognition of the importance of links between policy domains, but policy development and action plans need to address these links more explicitly (Ove Arup, 2003). For example, whilst livelihood, housing and crime are likely to remain top social exclusion issues, it is evident that one aspect of the Leeds 'two-speed' city problem is the relationship between social deprivation and low environmental quality (pollution, access to green space and so on), particularly given the implications over health inequalities. This issue is a growing concern nationally (SDC, 2002; Chalmers, 2003), and recent evidence (Mitchell and successful, the park will deliver significant social and economic benefits, whilst also representing the most significant addition of new public open space in the city for a century.

13.5 Conclusions

Over the last decade, Leeds has gained a reputation for excellence in governance, and a high profile for its efforts to develop sustainably. The rhetoric of environmental policy making remains strong, and key officers and politicians are committed to environmentally sustainable development. Many new environmental initiatives are planned (e.g. with respect to energy, 2004 sees new working groups on climate change and on housing energy, and a sustainable design and construction guide will be produced to help developers and architects produce more energy-efficient buildings).

Nevertheless, an assessment of the current state of the Leeds environment suggests that the city has perhaps not fully lived up to the early promise recognised by its Environment City award. Real progress is, however, difficult to assess, as a state of the environment report has not been attempted until very recently and is not comprehensive. Arguably, the greatest progress has been achieved through external levers such as legislation (air quality review and assessment, waste water treatment directive, etc.) and economic imperatives (land restoration via commercial development), rather than through pro-active management within Leeds. In future, these external levers (including forthcoming initiatives such as revision to building regulations, green taxes, the 'strategic environmental assessment' directive and the Aarhus Environment convention) are likely to remain the dominant drivers of environmental improvement in Leeds. Indeed, policy leaders within the city need to be vocal in pressing for changes at national and international level that will more strongly support their local efforts.

Governance structures in Leeds are certainly good, hence the mechanisms for ensuring that environmental issues are adequately addressed are largely in place. However, in mainstreaming sustainability in the decision-making process, there is a danger that environmental issues will not receive the attention they deserve, and Leeds will be slow to re-orient its development to an ecologically sustainable trajectory. However, the current *Vision for Leeds* recognises that 'business as usual' is not an option and that there should be efforts to try to do things better and differently: "It is about achieving social, environmental and economic objectives at the same time, and not at the expense of each other. We need to link these objectives together and recognise that the decisions we take in Leeds affect the rest of the world and our children. The *Vision for Leeds* emphasises the need for people to be involved in the decisions which affect them. We aim to challenge and change the way we do things now and in the future" (Leeds Initiative, 2004, p.75). If Leeds really does work in this way, a Leeds version of sustainable development will be evident, with environment fully taken into consideration at every turn.

We stress, however, that whilst the City Council and the Leeds Initiative have taken a strong lead on sustainable development, there are many actors who are not fully 'signed up' to improved environmental performance. The admirable governance structures that now exist must be exploited to the full and further enhanced, so that all stakeholders can and do contribute to the transformation of the city. Ultimately, the success of the *Vision for Leeds* sustainability exercise will be judged by the delivery of tangible results. In the environmental area, this can be particularly difficult, as targets are set not just through a community dialogue (as with social and economic themes), but must often address physical thresholds and capacities of the natural environment, which are hard to define and do not have such immediate resonance with citizens. But failure to deliver on these environmental goals will amount to failure of the wider sustainability strategy.

The University of Leeds Environment Policy is available at: http://www.leeds.ac.uk/estate_services/pages/06_corp/environ/06cenv9.htm

Notes

1   See Local Government Act 2000 explanatory note at:
     http://www.hmso.gov.uk/acts/en/2000en22.htm
2   Municipal waste includes household waste and any other waste
     collected by a waste collection authority (such as Leeds City Council) or
     its agents. Non-municipal waste is that collected from commerce and
     industry, construction and demolition.

References

AEAT (2002) *Development of a Renewable Energy Assessment and Targets for Yorkshire and Humber,* Main Report 1 of Final Report to the Government Office Yorkshire and Humber, Leeds.

Best Value Inspection Service (2001) *Leeds City Council: Refuse Collection and Waste Management — Best Value Inspection,* LCC, Leeds.

Blake, J. (1999) Overcoming the 'value-action gap' in environmental policy: tensions between national policy and local experience, *Local Environment,* 4(3): 257–278.

Chalmers, H. (2003) *Environmental Equality Research, Policy and Action,* first report of the Environment Agency environmental equality steering group, Environment Agency, Bristol.

Davoudi, S. (2001) Planning and Sustainable Waste Management, in Layard, A., Davoudi, S. and Batty, S. (Eds.) *Planning for a Sustainable Future,* Spon Press, London, pp.193–209.

Department of Environment (DoE) (1994) *Sustainable Development, The UK Strategy,* DoE, HMSO, London.

Department of Environment (DoE) (1995) *Making Waste Work: A Strategy for Sustainable Waste Management in England and Wales,* DoE, London.

Department of Environment (DoE) (1996) *Review of the Potential Effects of Climate Change on the United Kingdom: Conclusions and Summary,* HMSO, London.

Department of Environment (DoE) (1998) *Quantification of the Health Effects of Air Pollution in the United Kingdom. DoH Committee on the Medical Effects of Air Pollution,* The Stationery Office, London.

Department for Environment, Food and Rural Affairs (DEFRA) (2001a) *The Environment in Your Pocket,* DEFRA, London.

Department for Environment, Food and Rural Affairs (DEFRA) (2001b) *Consultation on Proposals for Air Quality Objectives for Particles, Benzene, CO and PAHs,* DEFRA, London.

Department for Environment, Food and Rural Affairs (DEFRA) (2002) Air Quality, press release May 2002, DEFRA, London.

Department for Environment, Food and Rural Affairs (DEFRA) (2003a) *Municipal Waste Management Statistics 2001–02,* http://www.defra.gov.uk/environment/statistics/wastats/index.htm

Department for Environment, Food and Rural Affairs (DEFRA) (2003b) *Digest of Environmental Statistics,* The Stationery Office, London.

Department for Environment, Food and Rural Affairs (DEFRA) (2003c) *Changing Patterns: UK Government Framework for Sustainable Consumption and Production,* DEFRA Publications, London http://www.defra.gov.uk/environment/business/scp/

Department of Environment, Transport and the Regions (DETR) (1999a) *A Better Quality of Life: A Strategy for Sustainable Development in the UK,* HMSO, London.

Department of Environment, Transport and the Regions (DETR) (1999b) *Away with Waste: A Draft Waste Strategy for England and Wales Part I,* HMSO, London.

Department of Environment, Transport and the Regions (DETR) (2000a) *Local Quality of Life Counts,* DETR, London.

Department of Environment, Transport and the Regions (DETR) (2000b) *Waste strategy 2000: England and Wales Parts I and II,* DETR, London.

Department of Environment, Transport and the Regions (DETR) (2000c) *The Air Quality Strategy for England, Scotland, Wales and Northern Ireland: Working Together for Clean Air,* DETR, London.

Edwards, A.M.C. and Johnston, N. (1996) Water and waste water minimisation: the Aire and Calder project, *Journal of the Chartered Institute of Water and Environmental Management,* 10(4): 227–234.

Elkington J. (1998) *Cannibals with Forks: The Triple Bottom Line of 21st Century Business,* New Society Publications, London.

European Commission (EC) (1991) European Community Framework Directive on Waste 75/442/EEC as amended by 91/156/EEC and 91/962/EEC.

European Commission (EC) (1992) *Towards Sustainability. A European Community Programme of Action in Relation to Environment and Sustainable Development (Fifth Environmental Action Programme),* Com (92), EC, Brussels.

European Environment Agency (EEA) (1998) *Europe's Environment: The Second Assessment,* EEA, Copenhagen.

Entec (2003) *Millennium Biodiversity Report — Independent Evaluation of Progress,* Entec Ltd, Leamington Spa.

Foundation for Water Research (FWR) (1995) *Effects of Trace Organics on Fish,* Phase II, FWR, London.

Gandy, M. (1994) *Recycling and the Politics of Urban Waste,* Earthscan, London.

Home Energy Conservation Act (HECA) (2002) *Home Energy Conservation Act: 6th Progress Report,* DEFRA, London, http://www.ukace.org/campaign/HECA2002/HECA2002figures.pdf

HM Treasury (2002) *Pre-budget report 2002,* http://www.hm-treasury.gov.uk/pre_budget_report/prebud_pbr02/report/prebud_pbr02_repchap7.cfm

Institute of Civil Engineers (ICE) (2004) *The State of the Nation Report,* ICE, London, http://www.ice.org.uk/downloads//SoN_2004.pdf

IUCN-UNEP-WWF (1991) *Caring for the Earth: Second Report on World Conservation and Development,* Earthscan, London.

Leeds City Council (LCC) (1991a) *Leeds Green Strategy,* LCC, Leeds.

Leeds City Council (LCC) (1991b) *Leeds Nature Conservation Strategy,* LCC, Leeds.

Leeds City Council (LCC) (1992) *Woodland Strategy,* LCC, Leeds.

Leeds City Council (LCC) (1996) *Warm Homes, Cool Planet,* LCC, Leeds.

Leeds City Council (LCC) (1998) *Sustainable Development Design Guide,* LCC, Department of Planning, Leeds.

Leeds City Council (LCC) (1999) *Air Quality Review and Assessment: Stage 1,* LCC, Leeds.

Leeds City Council (LCC) (2000a) *Leeds Local Agenda 21: Draft Strategy Statement and Action Plan,* LCC, Leeds.

Leeds City Council (LCC) (2000b) *Biodiversity Action Plan for Leeds,* LCC, Leeds.

Leeds City Council (LCC) (2000c) *Air Quality Review and Assessment: Stage 2,* LCC, Leeds.

Leeds City Council (LCC) (2001) *Air Quality Review and Assessment: Stage 3,* LCC, Leeds.

Leeds City Council (LCC) (2003a) *The Leeds State of the Environment Core Document,* April 2003, Environment City Office, LCC, Leeds.

Leeds City Council (LCC) (2003b) *Energy and Water Management Plan 2003–2008,* LCC, Leeds.

Leeds City Council (LCC) (2003c) *Community Plan Reviews covering 15 out of the 16 Community Involvement Team Areas,* LCC, Leeds.

Leeds City Council (LCC) (2003d) *Integrated Waste Management Strategy 2003–2006,* LCC, Leeds.

Leeds City Council (LCC) (2003e) *Council Plan 2003/2004: Closing the Gap,* LCC, Leeds.

Leeds Initiative (1999) *Vision for Leeds: A Strategy for Sustainable Development,* Leeds Initiative, Leeds.

Leeds Initiative (2001) *Making Progress: Indicators for the Vision for Leeds,* Leeds Initiative, Leeds.

Leeds Initiative (2004) *Vision for Leeds 2004 to 2020,* Leeds Initiative, Leeds.

Lewis, M. (2001) *The Urban Geography of Leeds: An Historical Analysis of Urban Development,* Department of Geography, Northamptonshire Grammar School, Northampton.

Mitchell, G. (2001) Assessing a pointless pollution hazard, *Geo:Connexion,* 1(1): 2–5.

Mitchell, G., McDonald, A., Williamson, P. and Wattage, P. (2000) A SIC-coded strategic planning model of non-household water demand for UK regions, *Journal of the Chartered Institution of Water and Environmental Management,* 14(3): 226–232.

Mitchell, G. and Walker, G. (2003) *Environmental Quality and Social Deprivation. Phase I: A Review of Research and Analytical Methods,* R&D Project Record E2-067/1/PR2, The Environment Agency, Bristol.

Mitchell, G., Namdeo A., May T., and Milne D. (2003) The air quality implications of urban road user charging, *Traffic Engineering and Control, The International Journal of Traffic Management and Transportation Planning,* 44(2): 57–62

Mittler, D. (2001) Hijacking sustainability? Planners and the promise and failure of Local Agenda 21, in Layard, A., Davoudi, S. and Batty, S. (eds.) *Planning for a Sustainable Future,* Spon Press, London, pp.53–60.

Neal, C., House, W., Leeks, G., Whitton, B. and Williams, R. (2000) Conclusions to the special issue of Science of the Total Environment concerning 'The water quality of UK rivers entering the North Sea', *Science of the Total Environment,* 251/252: 557–573.

Office of the Deputy Prime Minister (ODPM) (2003a) *Sustainable Communities: Building for the Future,* ODPM, London

Office of the Deputy Prime Minister (ODPM) (2003b) *Planning for Sustainable Housing and Communities: Sustainable Communities in the South East,* eighth report, ODPM: Housing, Planning, Local Government and the Regions, London.

Ove Arup (2003) *Sustainable Development Appraisal of Draft Leeds Vision II: Final Report,* Ove Arup and Partners Ltd, Leeds.

Pinfield, G. and Saunders, J. (1999) Community planning and LA21, *Local Government Voice,* 9–12 September.

Roberts, I. (2000) Leicester environment city: learning how to make Local Agenda 21, partnerships and participation deliver, *Environment and Urbanisation,* 12(2): 9–26.

SDC (2002) *Vision for Sustainable Regeneration. Environment and Poverty — Breaking the Link?,* The Sustainable Development Commission, London.

Sellars, D. (1997) *Hidden Beneath our Feet: The Story of Sewerage in Leeds,* LCC, Department of Highways and Transportation, Leeds.

Selman, P. (1999) *Planning Sustainability,* Routledge, London.

Selman, P. and Parker, J. (1999) Tales of local sustainability, *Local Environment,* 4(1): 47–60.

United Nations Conference on Environment and Development (UNCED) (1992) *Earth Summit 1992 (Agenda 21) UNCED,* The Regency Press Corporation, London.

World Commission on Environment and Development (WCED) (1987) *Our Common Future (The Brundtland Report),* WCED, Oxford University Press, Oxford.

While, A., Gibbs, D. and Jonas, A. (2002) Environment as good governance: sustainability and the Vision for Leeds, *Governance and Regulation in Local Environmental Policy Making, Case-study Working Paper Number 5,* Department of Geography, University of Hull.

Williamson, P., Mitchell, G. and McDonald, A.T. (2002) Domestic water demand forecasting: a static microsimulation approach, *Journal of the Chartered Institution for Water and Environmental Management,* 16(4): 243–248.

Wood, C. (1995) *Painting by Numbers,* British Telecom/Royal Society for Nature Conservation, London.

Yorkshire Forward, Regional Assembly for Yorkshire and the Humber and Government Office for Yorkshire and the Humber (2002) *Sustainability Appraisal of Regional Economic Strategy for Yorkshire and Humber,* Final Report November 2002, Entec UK Ltd, London.

14 Form, Movement, Space and Use: Land-Use Planning and Urban Design

RACHAEL UNSWORTH & LINDSAY SMALES

15 Simulating the City and Alternative Futures

JOHN STILLWELL, MARK BIRKIN, DIMITRIS BALLAS,
RICHARD KINGSTON & PHIL GIBSON

16 Twenty-First Century Leeds

JOHN STILLWELL, RACHAEL UNSWORTH, PAUL STEPHENS & GORDON CAREY

14

Form, Movement, Space and Use: Land-Use Planning and Urban Design

RACHAEL UNSWORTH & LINDSAY SMALES

In Leeds, the Civic Trust, the Victorian Society, Eye on the Aire and other groups have worked actively to try to ensure that buildings and other elements of the landscape are protected and that the developer's 'bottom line' is not the only consideration to influence decisions.

14.1 Introduction

Land is mostly a finite resource. It is usually in demand — often from competing potential users — and this is especially so in a city like Leeds, where economic development creates pressures for commercial, residential and transport development. But as well as wanting mobility, a job, somewhere to live and a range of other facilities, all of which take up land, many people also appreciate open countryside and areas of natural beauty and wildlife interest. They value urban open space and the heritage of older buildings that make up the character of their locality. So there is political pressure both to allow for development and also to restrict it to certain locations and particularly to focus it at some strategic points — either where demand is especially strong or in areas where there is a need for regeneration.

The planning system exists to attempt to reconcile the different demands and preferences over what should happen to land and property and to achieve certain strategic goals in respect of economic and social development. A series of Acts of Parliament over the course of the twentieth century set a framework within which private and public interests are mediated, land is earmarked for future development and regeneration, and other buildings and areas are protected from development pressures (Cherry, 1996; Rydin, 1993). Planning officers follow guidance from central government, responses from public consultation and their own professional knowledge and judgement in devising strategies for reshaping and conserving the built and natural environment. The resulting plan, consisting of written policies and corresponding maps, is then used as a reference against which the development control officers determine planning applications. On major schemes, the elected councillors have the final say as to whether planning permission is granted, though in Leeds, 90 per cent of decisions are delegated to officers. Applicants can go beyond the local authority and appeal to the Secretary of State if their applications are turned down.

Transport infrastructure also has to be strategically planned and this is partly a task for transport specialists concerned with different modes of transport, traffic flows and

the engineering of infrastructure, and partly for land-use planners who have to take into account the linkages between different land uses, provision for transport-related land uses, the social and economic impact of transport options and the overall environmental quality of different parts of the district (see Chapter 10). In the city centre, around two thirds of the area is the responsibility of highways officers (now within the Development Department — see Table 1.3).

ensure that buildings and other elements of the landscape are protected (Ravetz, 2000) and that the developer's 'bottom line' is not the only consideration to influence decisions. The Trust scans all planning applications and engages in "constructive and critical dialogue" with planners and developers over all major proposals (Leeds Civic Trust, 2000, p.1).

In the years since the 1947 Town and County Planning Act, major changes have occurred in the approach to planning Leeds and massive changes have been brought about in the urban landscape (Smales and Whitney, 1996). The changes that have taken place since the turn of the millennium and those that are now in the pipeline amount to dramatic reworking of large swathes of the city. This chapter briefly sketches the context within which the planning and design of Leeds takes place, summarises the process by which the latest land-use plan was produced, summarises other key policy initiatives, comments on some of the main achievements and conflicts relating to planning and urban design policy and then turns to a consideration of future directions for the planning of the city.

14.2 Legacy of earlier periods of planning policy priorities and development pressures

The Industrial Revolution created wealth, grand civic buildings and prosperous suburbs in many UK cities, but it also left slum dwellings, narrow streets that could not handle growing traffic flows, and noxious and noisy industry mingled unhealthily with residences. Twentieth century town planning sought to rectify these problems by encouraging development of low density housing areas and new styles of housing (see Chapter 4), by widening existing roads and cutting new thoroughfares, and by separating uses (Hall, 2001a). Post-war population growth and economic prosperity meant that growth management was at the centre of planning. Correcting the legacy of earlier times and accommodating growth resulted in greatly extended built-up areas, new concrete structures and inner ring roads that created a new set of problems; of buildings that at first looked impressive but deteriorated rapidly; of socially and spatially

In many parts of the country, there have been bitter conflicts over land-use and transport planning proposals. The conflicts in Leeds have been relatively low key by comparison (While *et al.*, 2002), but rarely do any major developments occur without debates between interest groups — over the use(s) of a site, building scale, design or landscape impact. In Leeds, the Civic Trust (founded in 1965), the Victorian Society, Eye on the Aire and other groups have worked actively to try to

industrial cities and were contentious agencies (Haughton, 1999), not least because they displaced local authority control over local development. A UDC not only acted as the planning authority for its defined territory; it also deployed a budget to 'pump-prime' the area and attract private investment. Some successes were achieved (Robson *et al.*, 1998) and in Leeds, the South Central UDC area was substantially transformed between 1988 and 1995. Within Leeds, there is a sense that the regeneration was starting to occur just at the point when the UDC came into being but that there were some positive benefits to having a

isolated communities without a focus and of landscapes dominated by cars. Leeds has had its fair share of such problems (Smales and Whitney, 1996).

In the 1980s, new policies were aimed at rectifying the mistakes of the post-war period and dealing with the uncomfortable economic transformation to a post-industrial age. In order to stimulate new activity, national planning regulations were relaxed and the market was allowed to take the lead in deciding the location of new development. Large out-of-town business parks and shopping developments were the most prominent results of this approach, though Leeds has not hosted a regional shopping centre of the scale of the Metro Centre or Meadowhall and the business parks have developed only gradually. Indeed, the growth of the financial and business services sector from the mid-1980s stimulated a new round of city centre retail and office developments. Many of the office buildings are notable for exemplifying what came to be known as 'the Leeds Look', a term coined to describe the bland reinterpretation of former warehouse style with multi-coloured brick and slate roofs (Smales and Whitney, 1996). The style was dismissively criticised as "the offence of the inoffensive" (Powell, 1989, p. 124).

There were special measures to deal with selected areas of severe industrial decline: Urban Development Corporations (UDCs) were imposed on swathes of many

Top left, a 1960s
building being
demolished,
Kirkstall Road.
Top right, a failed
urban design concept:
abandoned escalator
that formed part of
an incomplete
pedestrian route.
Bottom left, a block
to be redeveloped at
the north end of
Albion Street.
Bottom right,
rebuilding in the
city centre.

The report of the Government's wide-ranging Urban Task Force (1999) was carried forward into the Urban White Paper (DETR, 2000), drawing together many aspects of urban planning and development thinking and setting an agenda for an urban renaissance (LCC, 2003c). A crucial assertion in the policy is that "the compact, many-centred city of mixed uses which favours walking, cycling and public transport, is the most sustainable urban form" (Urban Task Force, 1999, p.40). Arguments still continue about the desirability and feasibility of increasing urban densities and whether this is effective as a way to reduce travel and energy use (Hall, 2001b). However, it is agreed that integrating land-use and transport planning and implementing a variety of changes that improve the quality of places can have a beneficial effect on urban vitality and viability (see Chapter 11 for more on this concept). A major strand of policy is to increase densities along public transport corridors.

bounded area within which investment was concentrated. Former warehouses and derelict industrial sites on 'the wrong side of the tracks' became the locations for high quality offices and housing. This new land-use phenomenon no doubt helped to convince those drafting the new plan for the city (see Section 14.4) that there should be a wider definition of the city centre.

14.3 National planning framework: recent innovations

"Leeds is not an island. Events in Leeds are shaped by social, economic and environmental forces which combine to affect the way in which land is used. These forces operate at local, regional, national or international levels" (Leeds City Council, 2001, p.11). From the early 1990s, there has been a plan-led system and the adoption of more holistic approaches to planning and development that take into account social as well as economic problems. In 1998, the Government published proposals aimed at modernising planning: to make it fairer, more open and accountable, providing a framework within which competing demands can be balanced and resolved in an efficient and effective way (DETR, 1998a). There has been a rolling programme of revisions to Planning Policy Guidance Notes (PPGs) to reflect changing and new priorities.

14.4 Local land-use planning policy

The evolution of land-use planning in Leeds up to the mid-1990s was set out in Smales and Whitney (1996). Here, we pick up the themes developed in that work and summarise the way that land-use planning and urban design have developed since that time.

Leeds Unitary Development Plan

In the late-1980s, central government required large metropolitan areas to develop a new type of plan: a Unitary Development Plan (UDP). Instead of the previous two-tier arrangement of structure plans and local plans, there was to be a single plan covering the whole district. The UDP process began in Leeds in 1992 and went on to dominate the entire decade. The main reason for this lengthy process (Table 14.1) was that Leeds

Table 14.1 The UDP process in Leeds *(continues on page 326)*

Date	UDP stages
Sept 1989	Secretary of State issues a commencement order.
1991	LCC produces reports on key issues; out to consultation.
1992	Draft UDP; consultation May–July.
July 1992 to mid-1993	Results of consultation worked into draft UDP.
Mid-1993	Revised draft produced (RDUDP) Aim: to manage change by providing for needed development while still conserving heritage; provide a framework for a balanced pattern of development. The key points are: • Most new development is proposed in or adjoining the main urban areas. • The countryside is protected for its own sake and to protect the special identity of towns and communities. • The quality of life for city dwellers is promoted by protecting urban green space, renovating older housing and industrial areas, and improving the quality of new building • Visitors will find it a welcoming and interesting place and facilities provided for visitors will also benefit local people. • The transport strategy promotes an integrated system, including a choice of public transport, with supertram, rail, and bus and a road network that puts Leeds right at the heart of Britain. • Pedestrians should enjoy safer roads, and residential areas are protected from the effects of rat-running. • The RDUDP provides an imaginative plan for business and industrial development to attract the inward investment that the city needs. The Plan tries to promote the interests of disadvantaged people in terms of housing, access to shopping facilities, leisure and recreation, transport and jobs. A key part of the vision for the future is a city which has education and training as its heart and has a lively cultural life. The RDUDP is designed to provide guidelines for change to lead Leeds into the twenty-first century as a true European city.
Mid-1993 to mid-1994	Over 21,000 representations received, of which 19,763 were objections.
October 1994 to July 1996	Public Inquiry Proposed changes published in four stages during the inquiry and reactions to these were in turn considered by the inspectors.
February 1999	Inspector's Report into objections to the RDUDP received by LCC; corrections made and further document received July 1999.

Table 14.1 The UDP process in Leeds *(continued from page 325)*

Date	UDP stages
After receipt of Inspector's report	LCC accepted 93 per cent of the Inspector's recommendations and incorporated modifications into plan: • extension of the timescale of the Plan from 2001 to 2006; • a target of land for 28,500 dwellings to be made available within this period; • the strategic principles guiding the distribution of housing land (SP3 and SP5) subject to minor wording changes to strengthen the link between development sites and public transport and to suggest only limited additional provision in areas of high demand; • no need for new settlement either now or at first review; • the distribution (Strategic Principle SP6) and scale of employment provision (although with a different package of sites — Parlington and M62 Junction 30 sites rejected and replaced by land at Skelton and adjoining the East Leeds Radial); and • support for the city centre/town centres as the focus of retailing and other commercial activity (SP7) and for the regional role of the city centre (SP8).
12 July 2000	The Council's response to the UDP Inspector's Report, including proposed modifications, approved by the Executive Board.
14 August 2000	Modifications 'went on deposit'; public comments analysed.
Early 2001	UDP adopted.

Source: http://www.leeds.gov.uk/lcc/planning/udp/udp_fr.html

Two thirds of the land area within Leeds Metropolitan District is green belt, which is a mixture of farmed and natural areas. The UDP includes policies relating to all land-use types.

Metropolitan District consists not just of a large and complex city but also includes many quasi- or completely separate surrounding settlements. Previously, the area had been covered by a total of nine local plans. Leeds was not alone in the protracted timescale of UDP production (Thomas and Roberts, 2000), but this was probably the longest process in the UK.

The printed map that accompanies the UDP measures 182 by 137 centimetres, so it is impossible to include it in its entirety, even in a fairly large-format book! Consequently, four sample segments from the UDP map (LCC, 2003b) are presented in Figure 14.1 to illustrate the style and content of the document and to show the range of categories of land-use planning designations across the district. The four samples illustrate parts of Otley, Wetherby, Alwoodley and Rothwell and demonstrate both designations relating to preservation of existing land uses and features and also land parcels picked out for potential future

Figure 14.1 Excerpts from UDP map (a) Otley, (b) Wetherby, (c) Alwoodley and (d) Rothwell

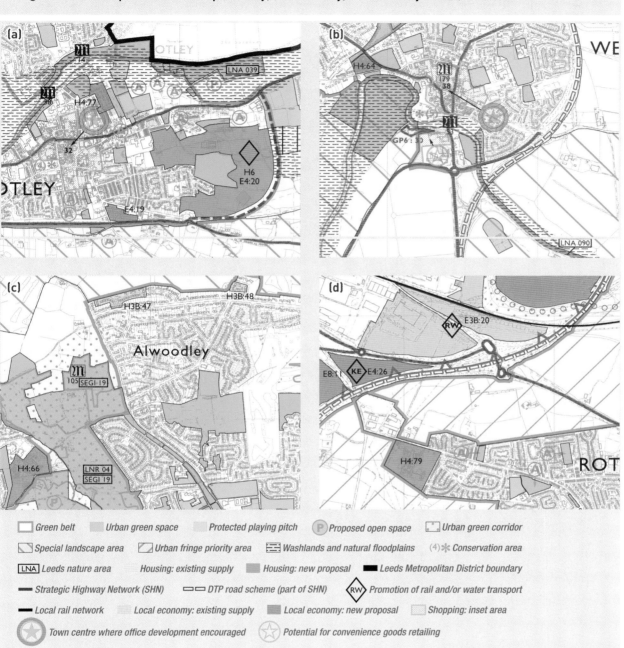

☐ Green belt	▨ Urban green space	▨ Protected playing pitch	Ⓟ Proposed open space	⬚ Urban green corridor
◩ Special landscape area	▨ Urban fringe priority area	▤ Washlands and natural floodplains	(4)✳ Conservation area	
[LNA] Leeds nature area	Housing: existing supply	▨ Housing: new proposal	▬ Leeds Metropolitan District boundary	
▬ Strategic Highway Network (SHN)	▭▭ DTP road scheme (part of SHN)	⬦RW⬦ Promotion of rail and/or water transport		
▬ Local rail network	Local economy: existing supply	▨ Local economy: new proposal	▦ Shopping: inset area	
★ Town centre where office development encouraged	★ Potential for convenience goods retailing			

development. The whole map is now held on a geographic information system (GIS) in LCC Development Department.

The UDP Review (LCC, 2003a) is limited in scope, mainly because the new Local Development Framework will create a new context for planning (see Section 14.7). The Review focuses particularly on housing, in response to the revised Planning Policy Guidance Note 3 (DTLR, 2000) requiring a new approach to housing land.

Table 14.2
Planning decisions made by Leeds City Council, 1991–2003

Year	Number of planning decisions
1991	6,010
1992	4,985
1993	4,818
1994	4,957
1995	4,671
1996	4,744
1997	4,723
1998	4,753
1999	4,795
2000	4,841
2001	5,692
2002	6,811
2003	7,258

Source: LCC

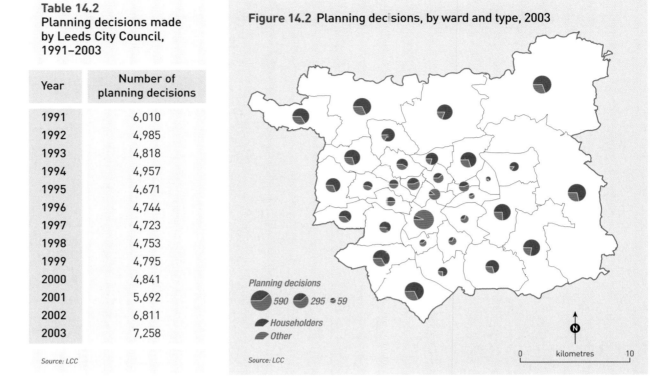

Figure 14.2 Planning decisions, by ward and type, 2003

Planning decisions
590   295   59

Householders
Other

Source: LCC

0   kilometres   10

The number of planning applications has risen steeply since the turn of the century and this is reflected in the total number of decisions made (Table 14.2). Figure 14.2 shows how the volume and type of decisions vary across the city, with the majority of planning issues in City and Holbeck relating to non-householder matters (over 6 per cent of the total decisions in 2003), and the greatest volume of householder matters relating to the outer suburbs and freestanding settlements.

The number of planning decisions translates into large sums of physical investment. Table 14.3 shows that the city

Table 14.3 Value of property investment (£000), 1991–2004

	City centre	East	South	West	North
Offices	1,267,400	434,500	321,400	125,000	2,148,300
Apartments	1,115,300	75,800	27,000	57,900	1,276,000
Infrastructure and public sector	444,800	658,400	12,900	50,100	1,166,200
Mixed use	866,000	n/a	n/a	48,000	914,000
Retail	673,050	54,200	119,500	66,100	912,850
Leisure	552,400	89,100	63,400	120,000	824,900
Manufacturing	11,000	41,500	334,550	42,800	429,850
Total	4,929,950	1,353,500	878,750	509,900	7,672,100

Source: LCC

Figure 14.3 Area designations in the city centre

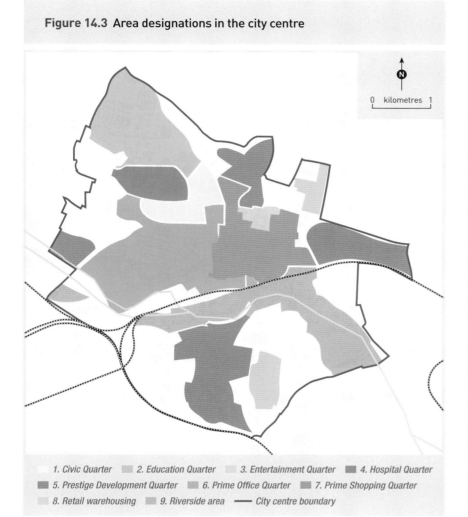

0 kilometres 1

N

1. Civic Quarter   2. Education Quarter   3. Entertainment Quarter   4. Hospital Quarter
5. Prestige Development Quarter   6. Prime Office Quarter   7. Prime Shopping Quarter
8. Retail warehousing   9. Riverside area   —— City centre boundary

centre accounts for 64 per cent of large development schemes involving properties with value of at least £1 million. However, there are many other property developments that are valued at less than £1 million.

For the purposes of planning the city centre, the area was divided into various 'quarters', riverside areas, and areas designated for prestige development or retail warehousing (Figure 14.3).

The distribution of listed buildings across Leeds by ward and by grade is illustrated in Figure 14.4. The city centre is the part of Leeds that has the greatest concentration of listed buildings (designated by English Heritage) (Figure 14.5). These structures create both problems and opportunities: site assembly for large-scale redevelopment is limited by the location of features that have to be retained. But the protection afforded by listed building status ensures that elements of the city's past are carried through into later eras, resulting in a richer mix of styles and facilities than might be the case if there were no such conservation measures.

Supplementary guidance —
sustainable development and urban design

The production of the UDP was a fixed procedural system, so it was hard to incorporate evolving ideas on land-use planning into the UDP document itself. Instead, several documents of supplementary guidance were produced. Two of the most significant are those on sustainable development and urban design, and we consider each of these in the following two sub-sections.

The view to the west from Victoria Bridge: the River Aire and Canal Basin are in the foreground and behind the railway lines are some of the new mixed use developments along Whitehall Road and Wellington Street.

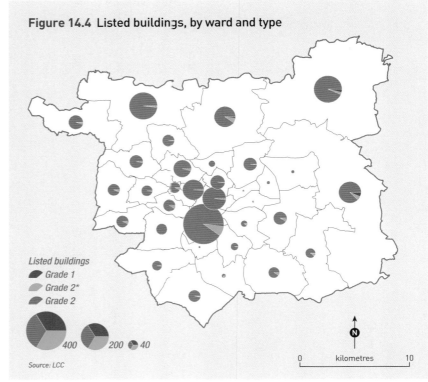

Figure 14.4 Listed buildings, by ward and type

Listed buildings
- Grade 1
- Grade 2*
- Grade 2

400   200   40

Source: LCC

N

0   kilometres   10

Sustainable development design guide

As mentioned in Chapter 1 and further explained in Chapter 13, sustainable development principles have been incorporated across the whole range of government policy since the early

Figure 14.5 Listed buildings in the city centre

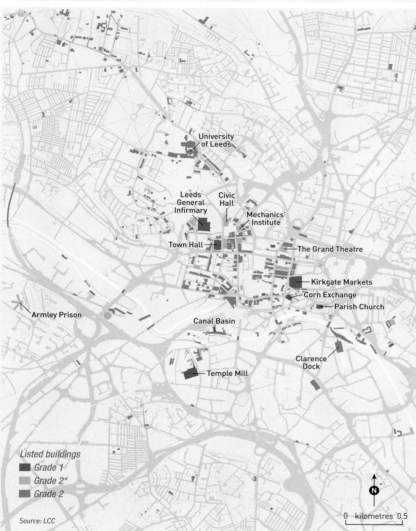

University of Leeds

Leeds General Infirmary

Civic Hall

Mechanics' Institute

Town Hall

The Grand Theatre

Kirkgate Markets

Corn Exchange

Parish Church

Armley Prison

Canal Basin

Clarence Dock

Temple Mill

Listed buildings
- Grade 1
- Grade 2*
- Grade 2

Source: LCC

0 kilometres 0.5

N

themselves (construction methods, building materials and energy efficiency). If the principles in this guide were closely followed, all property developments in the city would be of a high calibre in terms of environmental performance; they would use minimum quantities of resources from sustainable sources and create the lowest possible environmental impact in use. But the document is not sufficiently angled towards the kinds of major schemes that have been coming through the planning system since the late-1990s; its illustrations relate to residential schemes of modest proportions. Also, there is no monitoring of the extent to which the guide is in fact used and interviews with developers (Millard, 2004) indicate that although there is generally good understanding of the issues and some effort to make buildings energy efficient, there are still perceptions that building according to the most stringent sustainable development criteria presents an

1990s and local authorities are responsible for ensuring that all local policies are devised and all decisions are made in such a way that social, economic and environmental considerations are integrated (DETR, 1998b).

One of the main responses from Leeds City Council Planning Department was the publication of a *Sustainable Development Design Guide* (LCC, 1998), believed to be the first of its kind in the country. It covers issues relating to the development site (appraisal, layout, biodiversity, natural resources and waste management) and also the structures

unacceptable commercial risk. No cases are known of a proposal being turned down on grounds of not having taken sustainable development criteria sufficiently into account (Millard, 2004). There is some way to go before it is generally the case that "architecture is enlivened and generated by sustainable development considerations" (Peter Clegg, 25 March 2004 — 4 X 4 debate, Leeds). In the past, sustainable development has been addressed in terms of balancing social, economic and environmental considerations. But with this approach, there are bound to be winners and losers in respect of each development.

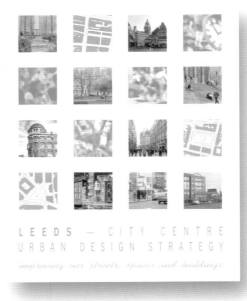

The UDP Review adds to planning policy in Leeds the overarching concept that all development should aim to integrate rather than just balance social, economic and environmental considerations. This will not be easy to achieve, but without the aim, there is always a likelihood of the environment coming a poor third in calculations of relative costs and benefits.

In addition, it is proposed that a sustainability assessment should be submitted with planning applications for 'major development', defined in Circular 15/92 as a development comprising of:

- ten or more dwellings or where the site area is 0.5 hectares or more;

- other types of development where the floorspace to be created is 1,000m² or more, or where the site area is one hectare or more;

- all mineral workings; and

- all waste developments including the treating, storing, processing or disposing of refuse or waste materials.

Urban design

Planning applications for major developments are subject to negotiations between the developers and planners before permission is granted and these discussions always include a design dimension — related to the design policies of the UDP (Section 5.3). But in the era when development schemes were of limited scale, the issues were limited to the way in which an individual building fitted within its immediate context. With the latest generation of large-scale schemes that have such a potentially high impact on the urban landscape, there is a need to integrate thinking about architecture, land-use planning, landscaping, transport and pedestrian linkages, and also to include consideration of how economic prosperity and social cohesion can be maximised by improvement of the quality of

places. This approach is more holistic, with professionals from a range of specialisms involved in the production and reproduction of the city contributing to concepts for regenerating urban landscapes in creative, practical ways that create a coherent, economically-viable place which is more than a collection of buildings and spaces of different eras and purposes.

The Leeds Architecture and Design Initiative (LADI) was set up in 1994 under the umbrella of the Leeds Initiative as a partnership between the City Council, the universities, relevant professional institutes and the private sector. The principal aim is to raise the quality of the built environment in Leeds. By holding proactive design workshops on large development proposals, before designs are worked up in detail, LADI has succeeded in raising expectations about design quality and helped the city to move forward from its 'Leeds Look' period.

Across the country, there has been more overt attention to design issues in recent years (Punter, 1999). This has particularly been the case since the Commission for Architecture and the Built Environment (CABE) was set up in 1997 by the Department of Culture, Media and Sport (DCMS). The Commissioners, appointed from the professions of architecture, planning, engineering, quantity surveying, housing design and built environment education, review the design of all major planning proposals — schemes that cover large areas of city centres and/or include tall buildings. The Commission is closely involved in the design of a large site between Whitehall Road

The Northern Ballet School development has flats wrapped round the performing space, enabling it to work as a commercial venture. Cultural investments worth in excess of £140 million will be implemented over the next few years.

Figure 14.6 Design guide excerpts

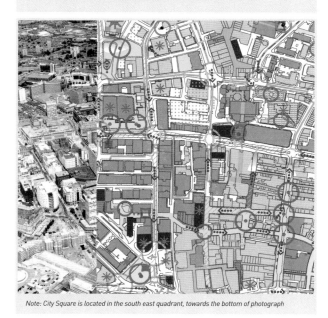

Note: City Square is located in the south east quadrant, towards the bottom of photograph

encourages a masterplanning approach to development (CABE, 2004) in which overall design of large sites is considered as thoroughly as possible.

Though there is some discomfort in Leeds about the term 'masterplanning', holistic approaches to urban design were in evidence before CABE's pronouncements on the matter. The *City Centre Urban Design Strategy (CCUDS),* first mooted in 1996 and published in 2000, was developed in collaboration with academics and students at Leeds Metropolitan University. Inspired by the writings of key urban design academics and practitioners (Smales and Burgess, 1999), the strategy examines the treatment of form, movement, space and use; it considers overall quality, distinctive qualities — including listed buildings and dealing with low quality areas. There is also consideration of views, landmarks, gateways and 'quarters' where certain uses predominate. The detailed analysis of existing conditions, together with examples of good practice, are intended to stimulate a more holistic approach to future development of the central area. As Councillor Minkin said in her foreword to the strategy: "Using the established character of the city centre as a starting point, developers, architects and designers can produce original buildings which reinforce and develop the individuality of Leeds" (LCC, 2000, p.1). Indeed, recent planning proposals have been drawn up with reference to the strategy, for instance, the large-scale proposal around Eastgate.

Figure 14.6 illustrates the kind of analysis included in the CCUDS, showing categorisation of landmarks, streets, spaces and uses (LCC, 2000, p.73 for explanation of the symbols).

Greater influence can be brought to bear on design in the few cases where City Council sites are offered to the market and a development brief is drawn up. But design issues have also been elements in negotiations for planning consents for privately-owned sites.

and Wellington Street. Its predecessor, The Royal Fine Arts Commission, insisted on significant changes to the original designs for Princes Exchange (featured on the front cover of this book). CABE

Another significant feature of recent years has been the widening of the Civic Architect's role from that of designing public buildings to a much broader involvement in thinking through the complex process of reconfiguring elements of the city, especially in the central area. The current Civic Architect, John Thorp, has now become something of a civic lynchpin, actively engaged in joining up the thinking between land and property, design, physical environment and social and economic regeneration. This is the kind of work that is needed to overcome the problems of lack of coherence that are inevitable in a market-led, piecemeal approach to producing and reproducing the city (Smales and Burgess, 1999). A creative and lateral approach is taken to regeneration opportunities — collective improvisation involving planning, architecture, politics and finance. On the one hand, property that could have value added by the private sector is released from Council occupation for new commercial uses and on the other hand, gaps and disorderly elements of the urban structure have been attended to — "missing and bad teeth have been repaired", as John Thorp puts it — and wherever possible, gains have been secured for the 'public realm'.

This process has been especially intensive in the Civic Quarter north of the Headrow and west of Woodhouse Lane. LCC departments were tenants in Dudley House (now reborn as K2) and parts of the Headrow properties that were to become The Light. To accommodate staff displaced from these buildings, two old school buildings between Rossington Street and Great George Street were refurbished and the empty site on the

international panel of architects to understand the way that Leeds works and to suggest ways of attending to gaps in strategy. The first focus was on connections between the city centre and the contiguous areas, many of which contrast very sharply with the prosperity of the city centre (see especially Chapters 4 and 6). The avowed priority of Leeds Initiative to 'close the gap' is being taken literally in this case, with a variety of ideas for enabling people to move more easily back and forth across the intimidating elements of the transport network that separate the city centre and the inner city. A particularly promising opportunity will arise with the development of the Union Street/Templar Street area on each side of Eastgate. An

corner near the old Civic Theatre was filled in with a new office (the Leonardo Building) linking to one of the older buildings. Millennium Square, re-developed partly with lottery money, was intended to enhance the setting of some of the monumental and grand buildings around its perimeter, and also to provide performance space with a capability for a mix and range of events, including entertainment, civic celebrations, ceremonies and community life. Though the square has not met with universal approval (Sandle, 2001), it has stimulated major economic regeneration of the area.

These and other substantial changes to the city centre have been achieved within the broad framework of the UDP and the concepts in the CCUDS, but there has been pragmatism in deciding on courses of action as opportunities have arisen and connections could be made between one element of regeneration and another. When the UDP was first drafted, there could have been little idea of the extent to which city centre sites and buildings would be in demand for residential and mixed use schemes. Planning permissions have been forthcoming nevertheless.

Yorkshire Forward considers that over and above the level of strategy applied through reference to the UDP, there should be a greater breadth of vision guiding the planning of the city centre and its role in the wider regeneration of the city. To this end, an Urban Renaissance Visioning Steering Group and a Panel were set up in 2003. The Civic Architect worked with an

Figure 14.7 Petal diagram: connecting the city centre to the inner city

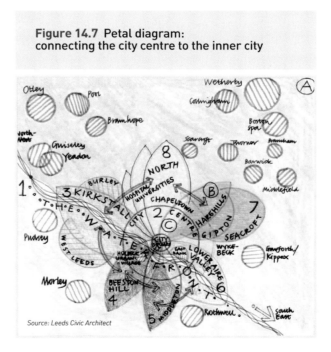

Source: Leeds Civic Architect

Waterfront development is one of the success stories of redevelopment, though there are continuing disagreements about its form and function.

essential element of this scheme would enable links to be made to the east and north east. Elsewhere, additional footbridges over the river are also part of the aspiration for connecting the city centre with the surrounding inner city. (Figure 14.7).

As well as looking for opportunities for connectivity, the Urban Renaissance Visioning Panel sought potential improvements to public space, especially chances to provide covered space that increases functionality throughout the year. There are proposals to use planning agreements more flexibly, with transference of advantages between sites rather than delivery of planning gain in or adjacent to the scheme that gives rise to the agreement. All in all, the aim is to latch onto nucleus elements of regeneration around which and from which other elements of renaissance can spring.

The involvement of Yorkshire Forward in demanding this more integrated approach to city centre planning is indicative of a general trend towards considering urban issues within a wider planning framework. Leeds is the acknowledged core city of a region that comprises ten local authorities (see Chapter 1) and there is pressure from national level to develop strategies that will enable Leeds to maximise its potential as main driver of this city region. This in turn will enable Leeds to maximise its contribution to UK plc.

14.5 Achievements of land-use planning and urban design policy

How influential is the planning system in affecting the urban landscape? The fact is that although land-use planning has become more innovative and holistic, there is a limit to what can be achieved. The system has weaknesses, does not produce all the strategic effects that are its aims and there is a range of unintended and inappropriate outcomes (Rydin, 1993). Planning may help to limit the extent to which the rich and powerful can gain even more wealth and power through the way that land is used, and may help to protect the interests of the less powerful and preserve elements of the natural and built landscape, but there is still a tendency for the strongest interests to prevail. At

the strategic level, limits can be placed on what may or may not happen on different categories of sites and a clear indication is given of areas where development can most effectively be concentrated, but there are inadequate powers to ensure certain outcomes on most individual sites. At the development control level, negotiations over applications can bring about some modifications to proposals that happen to be forthcoming. The location, form and content of larger development proposals depend on land owners', developers' and funders' perceptions of what is likely to be profitable at any given time.

In a plan-led system, such as has operated in Britain since the early 1990s, if a proposal is broadly in keeping with the policies set out in the plan, it is likely to gain permission (usually with various conditions attached). Even where a publicly-owned site is offered to the market with a development brief to show what will be acceptable and preferred, there is no guarantee that the brief will be fulfilled as set out. Negotiations may well erode some of the ideals, such as the inclusion of public open space, affordable housing or other social benefits — as happened at Clarence Dock. In the case of competition for a site, the local authority is usually under pressure to accept whichever proposal will generate the most income and will therefore secure the highest price for the land, though other factors can be taken into account. Where there is competition for sites in a vibrant market, there is a chance for more onerous planning obligations (also known as Section 106 agreements) to

Top, re-use of former industrial buildings has been widely welcomed as an enhancement of the landscape.
Bottom, K2, a new landmark — an office block transformed into apartments with offices at lower levels.

(concert hall, arena, exhibition space) and major new public spaces — elements of the urban landscape that either do not generate income or are notoriously difficult to maintain as going concerns. In the absence of large-scale public sector involvement, planning agreements have been used extensively to try and ensure that private development projects also deliver elements of benefit to the public, such as art and improved access.

All in all, then, the landscape is influenced but by no means determined by land-use planning. Planners argue that they are often caught between the various interest groups and are limited by both their statutory responsibilities and relative lack of proactive powers. They set the framework, argue in favour of the overall strategic aims and high quality design, but even detailed negotiations cannot guarantee an optimum outcome.

But there have been some notable successes where physical and economic regeneration have worked together to deliver benefits to the city — as in the example of Millennium Square discussed above. More widely across the city centre, the concept of the 24-hour city, pioneered in Manchester in the early 1990s (Heath, 1997), was soon to be picked up in Leeds (Lewis, 1997). Though there are problems associated with the realisation and management of the concept (see Chapter 12), many redundant or under-used sites and buildings have found a new lease of life.

Waterfront redevelopment, so successfully started under the UDC (see Section 14.2), picked up new momentum at the turn of the millennium. There is now an almost continuous string of residential and mixed use schemes — some completed, others in progress or planned — along the whole length of the River Aire from Gotts Island in the west almost to Accommodation Road bridge in the east. Rather belatedly, a *Waterfront Strategy* (LCC, 2002) was developed by representatives of the City Council, Leeds Initiative, Leeds Civic Trust, British Waterways and other organisations. The aims were to identify key components for generating an attractive, vibrant, safe and sustainable waterway corridor; provide a framework to guide future development, management or improvement proposals; and co-ordinate marketing efforts.

be attached to planning consents (Campbell *et al.*, 2001). But planning applications from a myriad of sources are lodged in no logical order and the planners are not in a position either to fully assess the likely impact of each and every application or to predict the total impact in landscape, economic and social terms of the ensemble of effects from the long run of planning decisions. The pressure to speed up the planning system does not always give the best possible outcomes because the majority of decisions are pushed through the system without detailed critical assessment.

Regeneration of the city has been almost entirely delivered by the private sector. As a result of the need to maximise profits, there has been a lack of cultural facilities

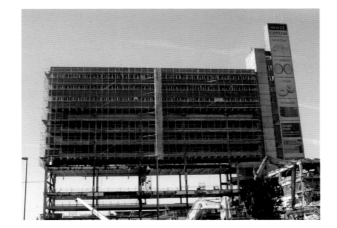

Much effort and attention is focused on the city centre, but as Figure 14.2 and Table 14.3 show, there is a good deal of development activity beyond the city centre. The guide to residential development design (LCC, 2003d) will strengthen the quality of urban design across the district.

14.6 Examples of conflict over land, property and spaces

A question of values?

There have been several recent examples of disagreement over the future development of some key city centre sites. Proposals for the remaining land on Quarry Hill, the Sovereign Street site and Warehouse Hill have all been criticised for being too commercially-led: the winning schemes have fitted the greatest amount of floorspace onto the available land area. Land values have been maximised while public open space has been squeezed to a minimum (Leeds Civic Trust newsletters and reports, 1998–2004). In the case of the Warehouse Hill proposal, the Civic Trust argues that several of the main principles of the *Waterfront Strategy* have been ignored. The proposals for Eastgate, while broadly welcomed for giving more productive use and greater aesthetic appeal to an area long dominated by surface car parks, are criticised for the extensiveness of proposed demolition. The Civic Trust believes, in this case as in others, that "stitching new development into valued existing city fabric is more sensitive and ultimately more successful that wholesale clearance which destroys city image and collective memory along with the fabric" (Leeds Civic Trust Newsletter, June 2004, p.4).

There has been much bad feeling over the closure of the International Pool on the west side of the city centre. A new facility is to be provided in south Leeds, but protesters, who consider that the new pool will be too inaccessible, believed that the original pool could have been refurbished and that it

Mixed use: mixed blessing?

By March 2004, planning permissions had been granted for around 140 city centre residential schemes (many of which are mixed use schemes that include flats) and 75 of these schemes had been completed (see Chapter 4). The addition of residential uses has helped to fulfil the aim of creating a diverse 24-hour city and those choosing this new lifestyle option have the benefit of short distances between home, work, shops and leisure time activities. People will want to be where there is the highest density of activity (Jacobs, 1961; Marsh, 1999; Glaeser, 2000), but short distances between different urban functions can create some discomforts as well as benefits (Hayes, 2001). Even young people do not appreciate noise pollution from 24-hour city activities such as bars, nightclubs and rubbish clearing. Smells and noise from restaurant extraction systems are also intrusive.

Strict controls are applied in respect of noise from bars and clubs within the city centre. Developers have had to spend large sums attempting to design out the possible problems associated with nearby noise sources, but the measures have not always been entirely successful and increasingly, developers are looking for ground and lower ground floor uses that are more sympathetic to the presence of residents.

It seems that the concept of the 24-hour city may not be operationally practical or realistically achieveable, and in future, there will have to be a more co-ordinated and careful approach to the juxtaposition of different uses (Chesterton, 2003). Leeds City Council Environmental Health Department is keen to ensure that even more issues are dealt with at the planning stage rather than after construction, when it may be costly or even impossible to make changes.

was the prospect of both income from sale of the site and the provision of a new facility through Sport England that made this an irresistible move for the Council, regardless of strong public opinion and the less-than-coherent arrangement of land uses that is emerging in south Leeds.

In conjunction with every new planning application, there are questions about the extent to which the building designs will help to give Leeds a stronger identity, a more up-market image or more dramatic skyline. The UDP actively encourages "good contemporary design" (Policy N13, p.60), but also insists that such buildings should be sympathetic or complementary to their setting. Impressive buildings that are parachuted into an intricate patchwork of familiar landmarks of all ages may upstage rather than enhance the overall scene, though arguably, buildings by nationally- or internationally-renowned architects can help to lift a city beyond its regional status. Over time, even a building that breaks with the past and upsets public opinion may come to be a cherished element of the built heritage. Respect for the past has to be balanced against the benefits of innovation: some truly unusual buildings would add to the image of the city.

14.7 Current and future issues

Local Development Frameworks

It has been recognised by Government that the UDP approach to planning was far from perfect. Plans took too long to prepare and have an inherent inflexibility that militates against creative interaction between strategy and opportunity. A new system of two levels of planning is to be applied across the whole country (ODPM, 2003); each region will have a Regional Spatial Strategy within which each area is to have a Local Development Framework. It is suggested that most authorities will find it more effective to produce a range of documents that can be developed gradually and therefore more flexibly than was the case with the former all-encompassing local or unitary plans which have often taken so long to go through all their stages. The Local Development Framework must connect up with each local area's Community Strategy and help deliver the policies it contains — thus effectively widening the scope of land-use planning and improving the ability of planning to deliver sustainable development. The framework is intended to include a clear set of criteria by which a local authority will be able to steer development and use growth to deliver the vision for their area. Each Local Development Framework will consist of:

- a concise statement of core policies setting out the local authority's vision and strategy to be applied in promoting and controlling development throughout its area;

- more detailed action plans for smaller local areas of change, such as urban extensions, town centres and neighbourhoods undergoing renewal; and

- a map showing the areas of change for which action plans are to be prepared and existing designations, such as conservation areas.

It is considered that this approach will provide business with greater certainty. In addition, business planning zones will allow planning controls to be lifted where they are not necessary. Under the present system, it has not been easy to deal with major development proposals. With the new system, masterplanning of major sites can proceed as the need arises. This will help developers plan for higher quality development in partnership with local authorities, but it does assume that local authorities have the staff and skills to do this. Another potentially very influential element of the new proposals is that

Table 14.4 Major city centre developments in progress and in the pipeline, 2004

Name of scheme	Site size (ha)	Usage	Date
Brewery Wharf	8.00	7,150m² offices, 305 apartments, hotel	Started 2002
Clarence Dock	6.00	18,580m² offices, 600 apartments, hotel, retail, leisure	Started 2002
Bridgewater Place	0.60	20,800m² offices; 200 apartments	Started 2004
Whitehall Riverside	2.43	13,380m² offices, 351 apartments, retail, leisure	Started 2000
West Central	0.80	46,450m² offices	Started 2003
Quarry Hill	3.20	49,238m² office, retail, leisure, residential	Preferred developer selected 2003
Wellington Place	5.70	105,900m² office, retail, leisure, residential	Outline permission 2004
Trinity Quarter	4.00	27.870m² retail	Permission 2004; completion 2008
Harewood Quarter, Eastgate	8.15	92,900m² retail, leisure, residential	Application 2004
International Pool site	1.20	Mixed-use scheme	Development brief 2004
Criterion Place, Sovereign Street	–	2 office towers: 47 storeys and 29 storeys	Developers chosen 2003
East Street	–	Several residential and mixed-use schemes	Some under construction
Globe Road	2.50	600 apartments; offices, restaurants and shops	Proposed

councils are to have discretion to sell land that is worth less than £2 million at less than the full market value without referring to the Secretary of State, if this will result in promotion or improvement of the economic, social or environmental well-being of the area.

Most people's involvement with the planning system is restricted to objections to strategic proposals while plans are being formulated, and objections to individual applications. It is almost wholly a negative involvement. The *Vision for Leeds* process and the community planning exercise have attempted to overcome this problem by trying to draw out what people do want. Under the new regime of Local Development Frameworks, the local authority will be encouraged to work with the Leeds Initiative (the Local Strategic Partnership) to establish effective mechanisms for community involvement, building on their work preparing the *Vision for Leeds*. All sectors within the local community will have to be involved, including local business, residents, tenants and voluntary groups.

The Civic Trust suggests that more people would be actively involved in the planning process if there was better access to planning applications. Much more detail should be available on the web (Leeds Civic Trust, 2003). As e-government becomes a reality, this is one element of interaction between

government and citizens that should be greatly enhanced (ODPM, 2004a). Elected councillors serving on planning committees are often insufficiently well trained to undertake their important duties and there is a proposal to improve both officer and councillor understanding of relevant issues (ODPM, 2004b).

Planning for future housing demand and delivering housing

"Housing issues are amongst the most important, and certainly the most contentious, of those considered by the UDP" (LCC, 2001, p.125). There has been much debate nationally about the process and implications of the predictions made about housing demand (Breheny, 1999; Holmans, 2001), but it has been widely recognised that provision must be made for growth in the numbers of households. Although the population as a whole will grow at around 2 per cent over the first decade of this century, there will be a 5–7 per cent increase in household numbers (Gibb *et al.*, 2001).

The planning process is required to set the framework for ensuring an adequate supply of housing in appropriate locations by designating which parcels of land are suitable for housing. But the actual provision relies on a wide range of

Table 14.5 Affordable housing delivery from 2001 onwards

	2001–2002	2002–2003	2003–2006
Number of sites	11	14	30
Social rented	32	48	101
Discounted for sale	37	24	81
Sub-market rented	18	15	81
Other categories	0	0	48
Total affordable units	87	87	301

Source: Bingham (2004)

suppliers, mostly in the private sector. The local authority is now in the role of enabler: "setting a strategic framework, exploring new partnerships and initiatives, levering in private finance, and achieving housing provision and renewal through other agencies" (Moran, 1996, p.281).

The decision about the pace of housing development in the district is now made at the regional level, not in Leeds itself. The RPG for Yorkshire and the Humber (Yorkshire and Humber Assembly, 2001) sets out a requirement for Leeds to make sure that there is enough land available to provide 1,930 dwellings a year — totalling 29,000 in the period up to 2016. But it is also a national requirement that this total should not be slavishly pursued independently of other considerations. There is to be a managed approach: all sites identified for immediate release as potential housing sites are brownfield sites. In a second phase, after 2011, land in east Leeds will be released. If, after phase 2, the quantity of housing land is judged to be inadequate, development on greenfield sites may be supported, but each case will be critically assessed.

The Council estimates that identified sites have a potential capacity of 40,000 dwellings — well above the RPG requirement. Additional 'windfall 'sites on previously developed land are expected to come forward for consideration as housing sites during the plan period, helping to stave off the eventual need to bring forward greenfield sites.

Development must contribute through good design to the quality of the built environment. All developments must reflect sustainability considerations, including linkages to public transport and provision of affordable housing for those in housing need but who cannot compete in the mainstream rental or owner occupier market.

There have been adverse comments about the elitist nature of much of the city centre residential development. But the city and its region would be disadvantaged by not enabling the provision of accommodation for top companies and high earners. Prices for prime property are inevitably pushed up by such incomers, but there is a positive contribution to the wider economy. So far, since 2001, there has been a low level of delivery of affordable housing as part of private sector development, but new rules and a firmer approach by the council is helping to increase the numbers of units that will in future be available to tenants or purchasers (Bingham, 2004). In addition to the sites included in Table 14.5 (and mapped in Fig. 4.12), there are seven 'strategic sites' across the city that have the potential to deliver up to 1,500 affordable units (East Otley, Holbeck Urban Village, Hunslet Riverside, Middleton, Thorp Arch, Micklefield and Allerton Bywater).

14.8 Conclusions

The pace of change in Leeds during a prolonged period of economic growth has tested the capacity of the planning system in a number of ways. Though private sector actors are wont to complain about delays, planning obligations and perspectives that do not match their own, the reality is that a perennially understaffed planning department has overseen and helped to enact far-reaching changes in the city. The changes are widely admired, even though there are gripes about the realisation of individual schemes and an understanding that there is still much to be done to bring about a thorough transformation of urban quality. Design issues are now much more to the forefront, starting with the strategies of the UDP, receiving a very significant boost with the creation of CCUDS, and now being taken a step further with the Urban Renaissance Visioning exercise.

References

Bingham, B. (2004) *Mapping Affordable Housing and Assessing its Delivery within Leeds*, unpublished report for Leeds City Council Department of Neighbourhoods and Housing, School of Geography, University of Leeds, Leeds.

Breheny, M. (1999) People, households and houses: The basis to the "great household debate" in England, *Town Planning Review*, 70(3): 275–293.

CABE (2004) *Creating Successful Masterplans: A Guide for Clients*, http://www.cabe.org.uk/pdf/CreatingSuccessfulMasterplans-nav.pdf

Campbell, H., Ellis, H., Henneberry, J., Poxon, J., Rowley, S. and Gladwell, C. (2001) *Planning Obligations and the Mediation of Development*, RICS Foundation, London.

Cherry, G.E. (1996) *Town Planning in Britain since 1900: The Rise and Fall of the Planning Ideal*, Blackwell, Oxford.

Chesterton (2003) *Leeds Evening and Night-time Economy Study*, draft final report for Leeds City Council, June.

Department of Environment, Transport and the Regions (DETR) (1998a) *Modernising Planning: A Policy Statement by the Minister for the Regions*, HMSO, London.

Department of Environment, Transport and the Regions (DETR) (1998b) *Planning for Sustainable Development: Towards Better Practice*, DETR, London.

Department of Environment, Transport and the Regions (DETR) (2000) *Our Towns and Cities: The Future*, Urban White Paper http://www.regeneration.detr.gov.uk/policies/ourtowns/cm4911/pdf

Department for Transport, Local Government and the Regions (DTLR) (2000) *Planning Policy Guidance Note 3: Housing*, DTLR, London.

Fox, P. and Unsworth, R. (2003) *City living in Leeds — 2003*, Leeds.

Gibb, K., Lever, W. and Kasparova, D. (2001) *The Future of UK Cities: Measurement and Interpretation*, RICS Foundation Report Series, December.

Glaeser, E.L. (2000) Demand for density? The functions of the city in the 21st century, *Brookings Institution Review*, 18(3): 10–13.

Hall, P. (2001a) *Cities of Tomorrow*, Blackwell, Oxford.

Hall, P. (2001b) Sustainable cities or town cramming? in Layard, A., Davoudi, S. and Batty, S. (eds) *Planning for a Sustainable Future*, Spon Press, London, pp.101–114.

Haughton, G. (1999) Trojan horse or white elephant? The contested biography of the life and times of Leeds Development Corporation, *Town Planning Review*, 70(2):173–190.

Hayes, H. (2001) 'Managing the stress of mixing uses' (balancing residential amenity and the vibrancy of the street in the growing 24-hour economy in city centres), *Urban Environment Today*, 134(8 November): 10–11.

Heath, T. (1997), The 24 city concept: a review of initiatives in British cities, *Journal of Urban Design*, 2(2): 193–204.

Holbeck Urban Village (2003) *Newsletter 01*, February.

Holmans, A. (2001) *Housing Demand and Need in England 1996–2016*, Town and Country Planning Association, London.

Jacobs, J. (1961) *The Death and Life of Great American Cities*, Random House and Vintage Books, New York.

Leeds City Council (LCC) (1998) *Sustainable Development Design Guide* (Supplementary Planning Guidance), LCC, Leeds.

Leeds City Council (LCC) (2000) *Leeds — City Centre Urban Design Strategy: Improving Our Streets, Spaces and Buildings* (Supplementary Planning Guidance), LCC, Leeds.

Leeds City Council (LCC) (2001) *Leeds Unitary Development Plan*, Leeds City Council Department of Planning and Environment, LCC, Leeds.

The housing development on the former Yorkshire Water filter beds site in Far Headingley includes 24 affordable units (12 houses and 12 flats) managed by Yorkshire Metropolitan Housing.

In future, it will continue to be the market, not the planning system, that identifies and reacts to the gaps in property provision, both in terms of sectors and geographical location, though the private sector will be guided by evolving spatial policy from national, regional and local levels. There is a prospect of greater co-operation between public and private sectors through the Property Forum, established in 2003. This body, led by the Chamber of Commerce and Leeds City Council Development Department, brings together people involved in land-use planning, urban design and economic regeneration. The aim is to identify and move forward on a wide range of projects for the city centre (and beyond) and there is great capacity within the assembled group of people for innovative thinking to maximise the benefits from a more coherent and holistic approach to land and property development: enhanced value, job opportunities, environmental quality, community involvement. It is to be hoped that under the new system of Local Development Framework in conjunction with the Local Community Strategy (*Vision II*), the non-specialists of Leeds will also be more actively involved in positive work on regeneration.

Leeds City Council (LCC) (2002) *Leeds Waterfront Strategy* (Supplementary
 Planning Guidance), LCC, Leeds.
Leeds City Council (LCC) (2003a) *Leeds Unitary Development Plan Review,*
 First Deposit, Leeds City Council Development Department, LCC, Leeds.
Leeds City Council (LCC) (2003b) *Revised Draft Proposals Map,* Leeds UDP, LCC
 Department of Planning, Leeds.
Leeds City Council (LCC) (2003c) *Leeds Economy Handbook,* LCC, Leeds
Leeds City Council (LCC) (2003d) *Neighbourhoods for Living: a Guide for
 Residential Design in Leeds,* LCC, Leeds.
Leeds Civic Trust (1998–2004) *Newsletters,* Leeds Civic Trust, Leeds.
Leeds Civic Trust (2000) *Annual Report 1999/2000,* Leeds Civic Trust, Leeds.
Leeds Civic Trust (2003) *Annual report 2002/2003,* Leeds Civic Trust, Leeds.
Lewis, R. (1997) How conversions can help put life back into city centres,
 Urban Environment Today, 9 January.
Marsh, G. (1999) Millennium property survey, *Estates Gazette,* December.
Millard, J. (2004) *The regeneration of sites and structures in South Central
 Leeds: sustainable development?* unpublished BA dissertation, School of
 Geography, University of Leeds, Leeds.
Moran, C. (1996) Social inequalities, housing needs and the targeting of
 housing investment in Leeds, in Haughton, G. and Williams, C. (eds)
 *Corporate City? Partnership, Participation and Partition in Urban
 Development in Leeds,* Avebury, Aldershot, pp. 277–292.
Office of the Deputy Prime Minister (ODPM) (2002) *Sustainable
 Communities — Delivering through Planning,* July 2002, http://www.
 info4local.gov.uk/searchreport.asp?id=7358&heading=e-mail+alert
Office of the Deputy Prime Minister (ODPM) (2004a) *Community involvement
 in planning: the government's objectives,* http://www.odpm.gov.uk/stellent/
 groups/odpm_planning/documents/page/odpm_plan_027497.pdf
Office of the Deputy Prime Minister (ODPM) (2004b) *Delivering Skills for
 Sustainable Communities: Egan Skills Review,* http://www.odpm.gov.uk/
 eganreview
Powell, K. (1989) The offence of the inoffensive, *The Architects' Journal,*
 189(18): 124–126
Punter, J. (1999) Aesthetic Control in the United Kingdom, *Urban Design
 International,* 4(1/2): 67–76.
Ravetz, A. (2000) *Millennium Square: A Historical Context,* Millennium
 Intervention Group, April 2000, http://www.pavilion.org.uk/consights/
 papers/ravetz.pdf
Robson, B., Bradford, M., Deas, I., Fielder, A. and Franklin, S. (1998)
 *The Impact of Urban Development Corporations in Leeds, Bristol and
 Central Manchester,* DETR, London.
Rydin, Y. (1993) *The British Planning System: An Introduction,* Macmillan, London.
Sandle, D. (2001) Millennium Square Leeds Civic Space, Public Arts and Social
 Facilitation, paper given to the international conference, *Waterfronts of
 Art II — The Arts in Urban Development,* Universitat de Barcelona, October.
Smales, L. and Burgess, M. (1999) Tapping into local talent: the production of
 the Leeds City Centre Urban Design Strategy, *Built Environment,* 25(4):
 300–316.
Smales, L. and Whitney, D. (1996) Inventing a better place: urban design in
 Leeds in the post-war era, in Haughton, G. and Williams, C. (eds)
 *Corporate City? Partnership, Participation and Partition in Urban
 Development in Leeds,* Avebury, Aldershot, pp.199–218.
Thomas, K. and Roberts, P. (2000) Metropolitan strategic planning in England,
 Town Planning Review, 71(1): 25–49.
Urban Task Force (1999) *Towards an Urban Renaissance,* final report of the
Urban Task Force chaired by Lord Rogers of Riverside, DETR, London.
Walsh, B. (1998) The 24-hour city — do we really want it?, *Urban Environ-
 ment Today,* 24 November.
Yorkshire and Humber Assembly (2003) *Draft Revised Regional Planning
 Guidance for Yorkshire and the Humber to 2016 (RPG12),* Yorkshire and
 Humber Assembly, Wakefield, http://www.goyh.gov.uk/rpg/acrobat/
 documents/Draft per cent20Revised per cent20RPG per cent2012.pdf

15

Simulating the City and Alternative Futures

JOHN STILLWELL, MARK BIRKIN, DIMITRIS BALLAS, RICHARD KINGSTON & PHIL GIBSON

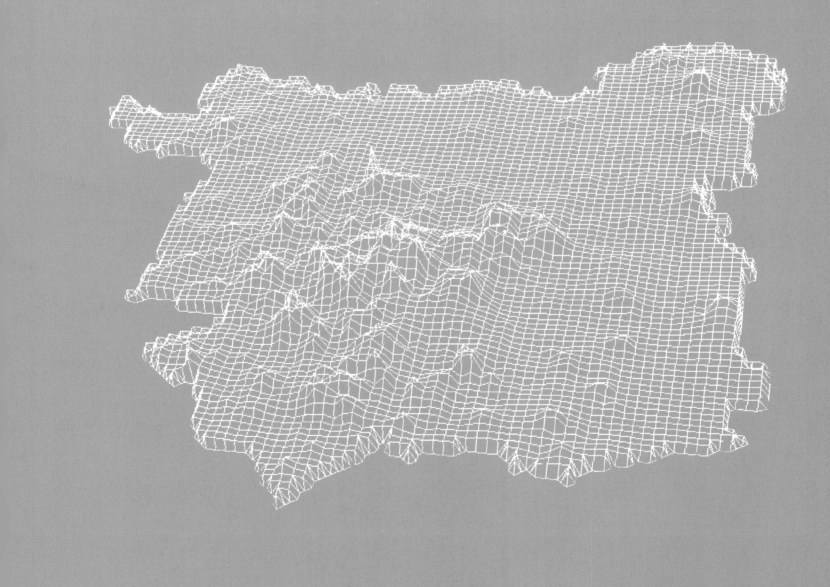

15.1 Leeds modelling tradition

Thirty years ago, a group of researchers in the School of Geography at the University of Leeds, under the direction of Alan Wilson, pioneered a new kind of regional geography, the development of a suite of quantitative methods for urban and regional analysis. The underpinning theoretical concepts and the mathematical models formulated to simulate the urban system and its various components (residential location, workplace location, shopping, utilisation of services, transport, economic activities) had been articulated in seminal texts by Wilson (1970; 1974). Leeds and West Yorkshire were used as the geographical laboratory for the empirical calibration and testing of these new, innovative approaches to understanding the way in which cities and their regions functioned and *Models of Cities and Regions* (Wilson *et al.*, 1977) demonstrated the state of the art as far as the application of the techniques was concerned. Leeds was proclaimed as one of the international centres of excellence in urban and regional modelling and remained steadfast in its commitment to quantitative geography throughout the 1970s despite fierce critiques of the approach (Lee, 1973; Sayer, 1976) and the desertion of some key figures in the sub-discipline as documented by Johnston (1996).

During the following decade, rapid and remarkable developments took place in the field of computer technology and, more specifically, with the emergence of geographical information systems (GIS). The ability of computers and software to rapidly process large quantities of data, paved the way for a resurgence of interest in modelling methods and this was matched with a new found enthusiasm in the discipline of Geography at Leeds to solve real location problems in fields such as health, education, retailing, transport and deprivation analysis. With hindsight and an appreciation of the scale of funding required to develop applications, it is perhaps easier to understand why it was that the commercial business community rather than the public sector became the primary clients for 'intelligent GIS' (Birkin *et al.*, 1996). Such was the commercial interest in model-based systems that Alan Wilson and Martin Clarke created a university company (GMAP) in the late 1980s which has since

successfully provided geographical modelling tools to a range of client organisations including supermarkets, high street multiples, out-of-town retailers, travel agents, petrol companies, banks and automotive manufacturers and distributors. Details of the range of commercial applications developed by GMAP are described elsewhere (Birkin *et al.*, 1996, 2002; Clarke and Clarke, 2001) and a compendium of recent examples of applied GIS and spatial analysis across a much wider set of contexts has been assembled by Stillwell and Clarke (2004).

In this chapter, we present two projects that demonstrate how the modelling expertise available in the School of Geography is currently being used to support urban and regional planning and policy making in Leeds. The first of these has been funded by Leeds Initiative and makes use of a microsimulation modelling technique that was rediscovered by Wilson in the 1970s and is being used currently as a planning support system to simulate the populations of individual people and households in Leeds in 2001 and into the future. The system, known as Micro-MaPPAS is outlined and some of the simulated results for the base year are presented. The use of the system to provide future simulations and to undertake impact analysis is discussed. The second project was funded by the Yorkshire and Humber Regional Assembly and uses aggregate spatial interaction modelling methods to identify the potential impacts on housing provision in Leeds under different projected employment growth scenarios.

15.2 Microsimulation and the Micro-MaPPAS system

What is microsimulation?

Traditionally, confidentiality constraints mean that demographic and socio-economic data on individuals, despite being collected from censuses and surveys, are not available for researchers. Microsimulation is a methodology that attempts to reproduce the demographic and socio-economic characteristics of human behaviour of individual people or households (Clarke, 1996).

Ballas and Clarke (2003) have recently provided a detailed review of the development of the methodology from Orcutt's original work in the 1950s (Orcutt, 1957). Thus, a micro-simulation model for Leeds aims to construct a list of 715 thousand individuals along with their associated attributes for any point in time, past or future. There are various different ways of calibrating the model but the results are particularly valuable because they combine data from different sources to provide estimates of the probabilities that individuals or households will have particular characteristics and thus create new population cross-classifications unavailable from published sources. So, for example, it becomes possible to identify individuals with the characteristics of being aged 18, a lone parent, unemployed and living in private accommodation in an area prone to high levels of crime. Alternatively, households can be identified in the outer suburbs that contain five persons and have a head of household who is a professional working in another city and earning over £50,000 per year. Once the long list of individuals and their attributes has been simulated, the individuals and households (and the attributes which they possess) can be aggregated to any geographical scale which is deemed appropriate such as output areas, wards or postal sectors for example, or more specific areas designed for policy implementation such as regeneration areas.

The modelling approach

The model that has been developed in this instance is a microsimulation model that implements a combinatorial optimisation approach to generating spatially disaggregated population and household microdata sets at output area (OA) level for the metropolitan district of Leeds as defined in 2001. The modelling involves the construction of micro-level population using existing 2001 Census Key Statistics (KS) tables for population and household characteristics of all 2,439 OAs in Leeds together with sample data from the British Household Panel Survey (BHPS), a national microdata set of household characteristics. The BHPS contains data on different variables (such as income) for households and their occupants that can

be used to derive estimates of 'new' variables for OAs. The technique adopted is known as 'simulated annealing' and is distinguished from other methods such as iterative proportional fitting (Norman, 1999; Ballas and Clarke, 2001). Simulated annealing involves reweighting the microdata sample from the BHPS so that it fits OA data for Leeds from the Census. In the first instance, the BHPS microdata set has been reweighted to estimate its parent population at the micro-spatial scale. The BHPS provides a detailed record for a sample of households and all of their occupants. The reweighting method can enable the sampling of this universe of records to find the set of household records that best matches the population described in the KS tables for each OA.

The actual procedure works as follows. First, a series of Census (KS) tables that describe the small area of interest must be selected. The next step is to identify the records of the BHPS microdata that best match these tables. However, there are a vast number of possible sets of households that can be drawn from the BHPS sample. Clearly, it would be impractical to exhaustively consider all possible sets so this is where the simulated annealing[1] (Ballas *et al.*, 1999; 2003) is used to find a set that fits the target tables well. The Micro-MaPPAS simulation model builds on previous computer software known as SimLeeds (Ballas, 2001) and uses the tenth wave of the BHPS to provide a detailed record for a sample of households and all of their occupants.

A simple example can be described for clarification. Let us assume that, according to the Census, in a particular OA there are 100 households, of which 60 are owner occupiers, 10 are renting from a local authority (LA) or housing association (HA), and the remaining 30 are privately rented. The simulated annealing procedure would select a combination of BHPS households that would have tenure characteristics as close as possible to the actual data. An exact match would be possible if the tenure KS table is the only 'constraint' in the procedure. However, the purpose of using a combinatorial optimisation technique is to select households that match several KS table constraints. Let us assume that we introduce the number of cars

Table 15.1 Calculating the absolute error

	Household car ownership characteristics			Household tenure characteristics		
	1 car	2+ cars	No car	Owner-occupied	LA/HA rented	Other
Simulation	27	24	49	39	17	44
Census	50	20	30	60	10	30
Absolute error	23	4	19	21	7	14

by household KS table as a further constraint and that our OA contains 50 households with one car, 20 households with two or more cars; and 30 households with no car. The aim of the annealing would now be to find a set of 100 BHPS households that best fit both tenure and car ownership constraints. To do this, an initial random sample of records is selected from the BHPS until sufficient households are represented (i.e. if there are 100 households in the OA, then 100 households will be selected at random). These records are used to create tables that match the selected target KS tables. An initial random selection of 100 BHPS households could result in the distribution described in the first row of Table 15.1. The total absolute error of 88 is the sum of the differences between the simulated and the actual Census values on the bottom row.

The task in the simulated annealing procedure is to minimise the total absolute error. In order to do so, a record in the originally selected household set is then selected at random and replaced with one chosen at random from the universe of records. The error is recalculated and the change in error (Δe) is calculated where t = the temperature or annealing parameter. If Δe is less than zero, then there has been an improvement and the change is accepted; if not, then exp(-(Δe/t)) is compared to a random number between 0 and 1. If it is greater than the random number, then the change

is accepted; otherwise the change is rejected and reversed. So, in the above example, a randomly selected household out of the 100 originally sampled would be swapped with another household. Let's assume that a LA/HA renting household is swapped with an owner occupier household from the BHPS. This would result in the reduction of error by 1, as the new owner occupier simulated total would be 40 (not 39) and therefore closer to the actual Census total (60 households) and the LA/HA rented total would be 16 (not 17), which is closer to the Census actual total of 10. This household swap would therefore be accepted. Conversely, if the change increased the error, it would be rejected and another household selected. It is evident from this example that the model is very computationally intensive, particularly when several table constraints are introduced.

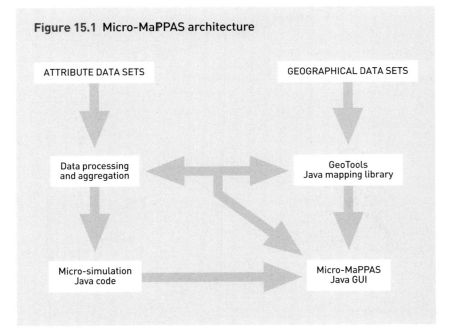

Figure 15.1 Micro-MaPPAS architecture

Figure 15.2 Model controller interface

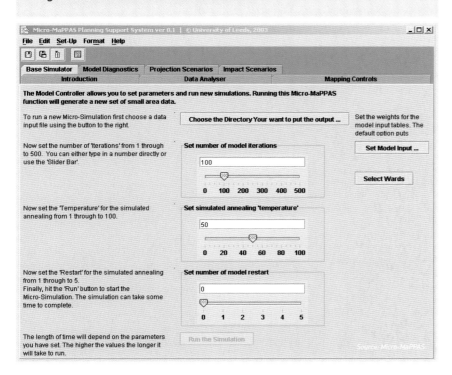

(minimum, maximum, absolute mean, mean, standard deviation) and also the percentages of values that have been over-predicted and under-predicted. Each simulation generated has a corresponding model diagnostics table and Figure 15.4 illustrates the statistics associated with the single year of age variables from 0 to 15. The mean error is lowest (closest to zero) for those aged 10 and highest for those aged 12, for example.

The Micro-MaPPAS system

The Micro-MaPPAS software is written in the Java programming language version 1.4, which means that it can be installed and operated on any computer system and platform. A default set of simulations generated for OAs is loaded when the system is booted up. The structure of the Micro-MaPPAS system is illustrated in Figure 15.1. Through the graphical user interface (GUI), the user has access to various modules: the model controller, the model diagnostics, the data analyser, the mapping controller and the scenario builders.

Model controller: This module allows the user to set the parameters for a small area simulation. The user can set the temperature, the number of model iterations and the number of restarts (Figure 15.2) and also apply weights to input tables (Figure 15.3) using slider bars. A simulation can take several hours to run if results are required for all OAs in Leeds and if relatively high temperature and large number of iterations or restarts are selected. It is also possible to run the simulation model for OAs contained within individual wards or community areas.

It compares the simulated data for OAs with the actual census variables and produces a set of basic statistics

Figure 15.3 Weights controller interface

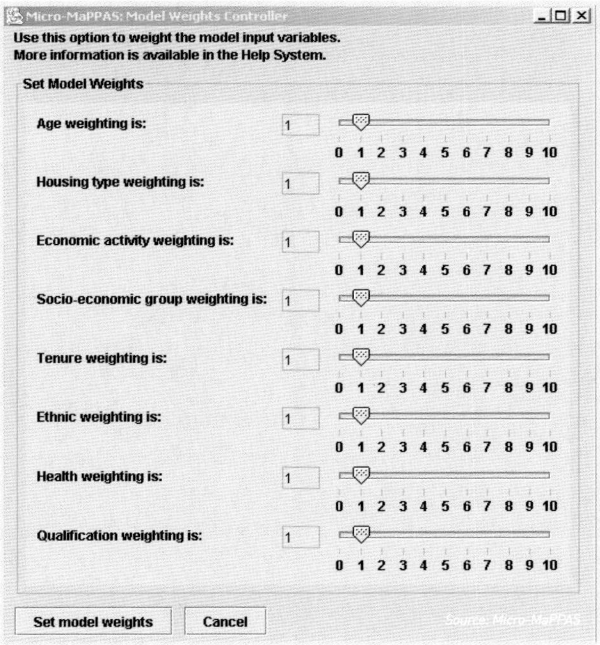

Figure 15.4 Model diagnostics table for simulated data for OAs

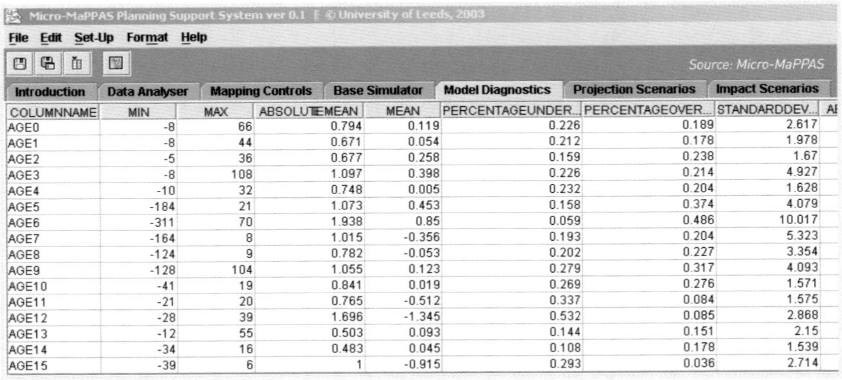

COLUMNNAME	MIN	MAX	ABSOLUTEMEAN	MEAN	PERCENTAGEUNDER...	PERCENTAGEOVER...	STANDARDDEV...
AGE0	-8	66	0.794	0.119	0.226	0.189	2.617
AGE1	-8	44	0.671	0.054	0.212	0.178	1.978
AGE2	-5	36	0.677	0.258	0.159	0.238	1.67
AGE3	-8	108	1.097	0.398	0.226	0.214	4.927
AGE4	-10	32	0.748	0.005	0.232	0.204	1.628
AGE5	-184	21	1.073	0.453	0.158	0.374	4.079
AGE6	-311	70	1.938	0.85	0.059	0.486	10.017
AGE7	-164	8	1.015	-0.356	0.193	0.204	5.323
AGE8	-124	9	0.782	-0.053	0.202	0.227	3.354
AGE9	-128	104	1.055	0.123	0.279	0.317	4.093
AGE10	-41	19	0.841	0.019	0.269	0.276	1.571
AGE11	-21	20	0.765	-0.512	0.337	0.084	1.575
AGE12	-28	39	1.696	-1.345	0.532	0.085	2.868
AGE13	-12	55	0.503	0.093	0.144	0.151	2.15
AGE14	-34	16	0.483	0.045	0.108	0.178	1.539
AGE15	-39	6	1	-0.915	0.293	0.036	2.714

Figure 15.5 Data analyser and query interface with age drop down menu in use

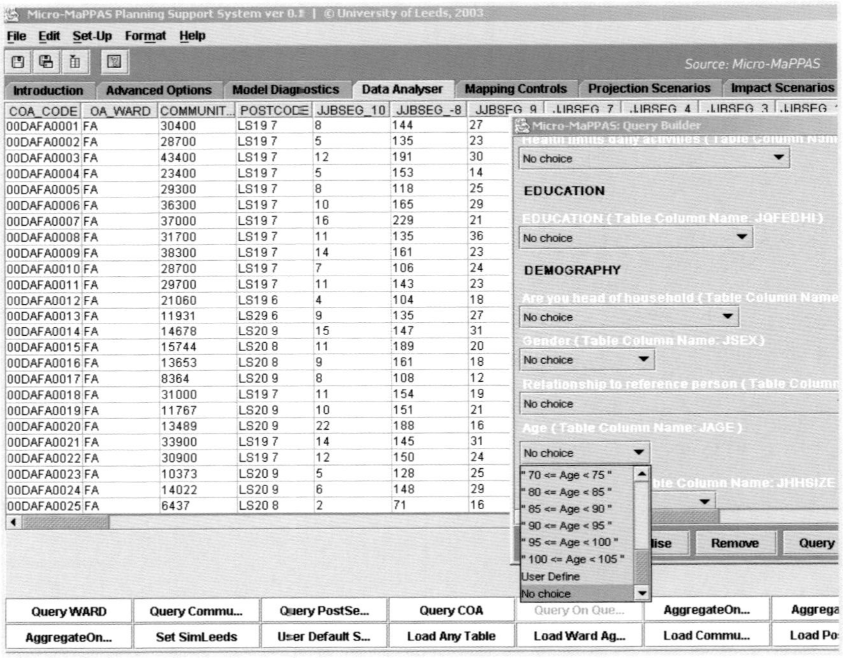

Data analyzer: The model generates a simulated set of data of individuals but these are never visible through the interface. The simulated data are aggregated to OAs and the data analyser provides a table view of this information (Figure 15.5). Below the table are a number of buttons that enable the user to run queries on the OA data to select the information required but also to aggregate the data to another spatial scale if required. The query builder interface is shown in Figure 15.5 and, once a query has been constructed, the results are returned to a table in the bottom half of the data analyser window. As an example, a query is undertaken which selects the number of individuals in each ward aged 20–30 whose household income is between £20,000 and £30,000. The results of the query are then shown in the bottom section of the data analyser and these can then be mapped.

Mapping controller: The mapping module allows the user to select a variable from a query and map the results at any of the geographical scales of OA, community area, ward or postal sector. Figure 15.6 illustrates the mapping of the query relating to persons aged 20–30 with incomes of £20,000 to £30,000. Mapping functions include panning and zooming and symbology editing.

Scenario builders: The system is being developed to provide facilities to design and run simulations for future scenarios based upon different assumptions about population change in the future, and also to undertake some evaluation of 'what if' scenarios. The interfaces of these components are not illustrated here; we choose instead to present some example results of model simulations in the next section.

Figure 15.6 Results of the query as shown in the mapping controller

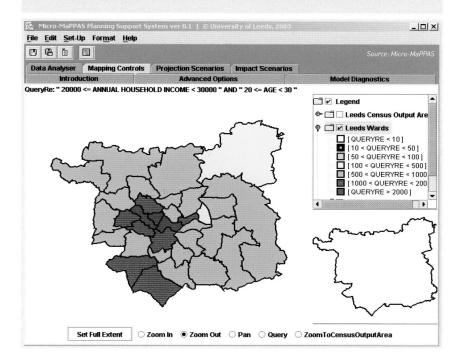

15.3 Some simulation results

Base period simulations

The Micro-MaPPAS system has been designed to create sets of simulations for 2001 as the base period. Three examples of sub-group distributions generated by the Micro-MaPPAS query are presented by way of illustration at two different spatial scales. These examples are all produced from the simulation that gives equal weight to all the tables used in the simulation. The first two queries provide more detailed information about the locations of disadvantaged groups. Figure 15.7 shows the distribution of female lone parents with dependent children, where the household income is less than £10,000 per year. The query has been carried out at the scale of community areas and the distribution demonstrates the concentration of this particular subgroup in areas to the east of the city centre (Chapeltown, Burmantofts, Harehills and Seacroft South) and to the south (Beeston Hill, Belle Isle and Middelton).

The second query identifies children aged 0 to 15 in households where income is less than £10,000. The distribution of this subgroup has been mapped for output areas in inner Leeds (Figure 15.8) and community area boundaries have been overlaid to aid orientation. The largest numbers of children in poor families are found in

Figure 15.7 Simulated distribution of female lone parents with dependent children in households with low income by community area, 2001

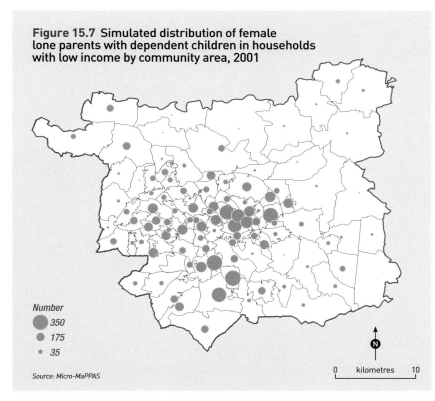

Number
350
175
35

Source: Micro-MaPPAS

0   kilometres   10

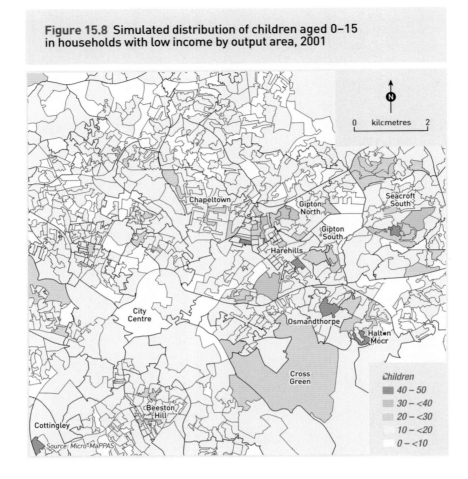

Figure 15.8 Simulated distribution of children aged 0–15 in households with low income by output area, 2001

Children
- 40 – 50
- 30 – <40
- 20 – <30
- 10 – <20
- 0 – <10

Source: Micro-MaPPAS

Leeds population in future years. The method we are adopting is to build a crude projection model for aggregate ward populations and then to use these totals to constrain more detailed projections generated by the Micro-MaPPAS model. In other words, we apply the Micro-MaPPAS reweighting methodology to readjust the weights of BHPS households so that they fit small area constraint data in any projection year.

It is important to recognise that, currently, there is no provision of small area projections by a single agency in Britain. The ONS is responsible for producing sub-national population projections for England, as indicated in Chapter 2, but these are only produced for local authority areas and on a relatively infrequent basis. A comparison of the projected population for Leeds in 2001 from the latest (1996-based) set of ONS sub-national projections (ONS, 1999) with the mid-year estimate for 2001 (extracted from NOMIS) indicates an over-projection of nearly 16,000 persons overall. Figure 15.10 shows the differences between projected counts and estimates for males, females and persons; most of the over-projection has occurred for males and females (to a lesser extent) aged 35 to 54 and these differences offset under-projections of females in their 20s and early 30s.

The lessons we take from the comparison are to recognize that even short-term projections for certain age groups in relatively large areas may be error-prone and it might not be wise to use the 1996-based district projections as constraints for all age groups. Consequently, the first step in our methodology is to project the numbers of households and individuals for every year into 2021 by ward within the district

pockets to the east of the city centre in community areas like Halton Moor, Harehills, Gipton North, as well as Seacroft South, with pockets also in Cottingley and Belle Isle in the south.

The third example involves households at the other end of the social spectrum. Figure 15.9 shows the distribution by output area (with community areas overlaid) across the whole of the metropolitan district of those individuals living in two person households with no dependent children and with a household income in excess of £50,000. These are the so-called DINKies and their spatial incidence is observed across the north of the district, particularly in the outer suburbs of Harewood and Arthington and Pool in the north and Calverley in the west, but also in pockets in the south.

Future simulations

In addition to modelling the population in 2001, micro-simulation can be used to predict the characteristics of the

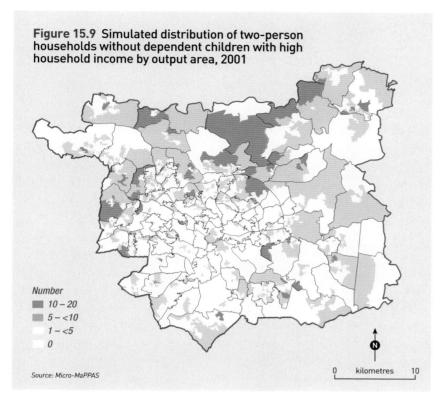

Figure 15.9 Simulated distribution of two-person households without dependent children with high household income by output area, 2001

Number
- ▓ 10 – 20
- ▓ 5 – <10
- ░ 1 – <5
- ☐ 0

Source: Micro-MaPPAS

0   kilometres   10

ward the annual rates of change between 1991 and 2001 for households and individuals and apply these to successive years after 2001 to give ward-based population totals up to 2021. The percentage changes between 2001 and 2011 in the ward populations of those aged 65 and over, for example, are presented in Figure 15.11 and illustrate the clear distinction between increasing numbers of elderly in the outer wards and declining numbers in the inner wards.

The projection of the disaggregated counts of the population in future years according to marital status, socio-economic group, number of cars owned, etc., is undertaken by applying annual rates of change between 1991 and 2001 in exactly the same way as with the aggregate populations. The projection of these counts

independently. In order to do this, we make the simple assumption that the annual rate of change between 1991 and 2001 will continue until 2021. Therefore, we calculate for each

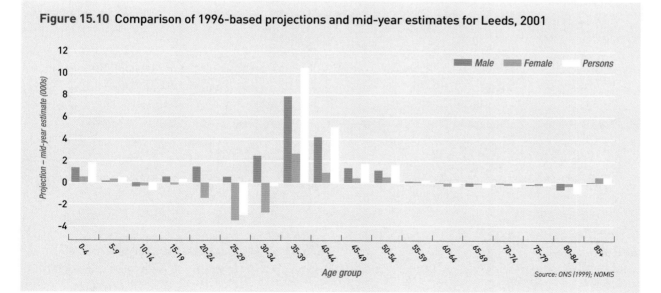

Figure 15.10 Comparison of 1996-based projections and mid-year estimates for Leeds, 2001

Source: ONS (1999); NOMIS

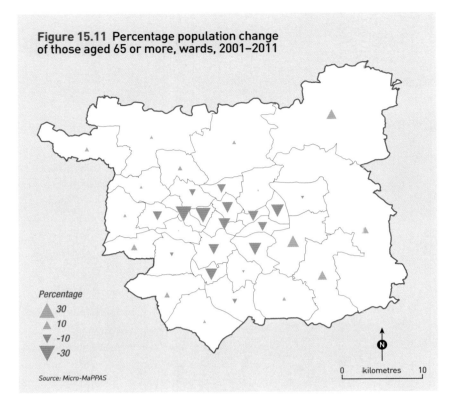

Figure 15.11 Percentage population change of those aged 65 or more, wards, 2001–2011

Percentage
▲ 30
▲ 10
▼ -10
▼ -30

Source: Micro-MaPPAS

proportions of all car ownership categories in each ward based on 2001 or making assumptions about how these proportions might change in the future. These proportions are then applied to the projected numbers of households by ward. In this way, we ensure that the sum of all cars by household categories adds up to the aggregate household projection. The same method can be applied for all other household (e.g. tenure) and individual (e.g. ethnic group) variables.

The above discussion implicitly assumes that the 1991 Census recorded accurately the populations living in Leeds wards. However, over 2 per cent of the population was missed overall in 1991 and this under-enumeration did not occur uniformly across all areas or age-sex groups (ONS, 2001). Furthermore, the 1991 Census did not

is necessary given that these variables are used as constraints in the simulated annealing household reweighting procedure. So, for example, having projected the car ownership characteristics by household, the next step involves calculating the

Table 15.2 Part of the travel-to-work ward to ward probability matrix for 1991

	Aireborough	Armley	Barwick and Kippax	Beeston	Bramley
Aireborough	0.46	0.01	0.00	0.01	0.01
Armley	0.01	0.16	0.00	0.03	0.04
Barwick and Kippax	0.00	0.01	0.16	0.02	0.00
Beeston	0.00	0.01	0.00	0.16	0.01
Bramley	0.01	0.09	0.00	0.02	0.12
Burmantofts	0.00	0.01	0.00	0.02	0.00
Chapel Allerton	0.01	0.00	0.00	0.01	0.01
City and Holbeck	0.00	0.04	0.00	0.06	0.01
Cookridge	0.02	0.01	0.00	0.02	0.02
Garforth and Swillington	0.00	0.01	0.04	0.01	0.00

Figure 15.12 The effect of plant closure on annual income by enumeration district

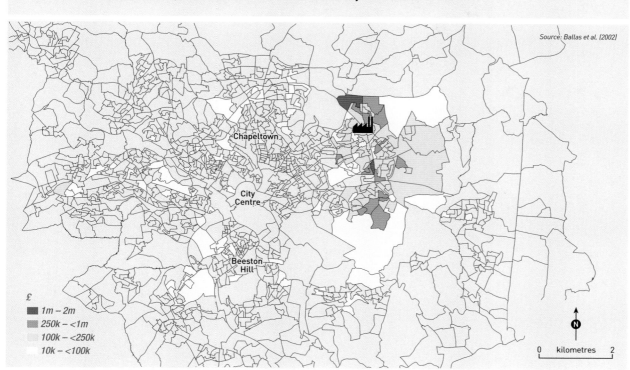

Source: Ballas et al. (2002)

£
- ■ 1m – 2m
- ■ 250k – <1m
- ▢ 100k – <250k
- ▢ 10k – <100k

0   kilometres   2

record the number of students, which is quite large in some electoral wards such as Headingley. In order to deal with these problems, the following strategies were adopted. To tackle the problem of the undercount in 1991, the ward populations in 1991 can be readjusted on the basis of alternative assumptions on the extent of the undercount. For instance, if it is assumed that the Leeds population in 1991 was underestimated by 4 per cent, the 1991 population numbers can be increased by this rate and the projection procedure described above is applied using the annual rates of change recomputed on this basis. A reasonable solution to the problem of not counting the students in the 1991 Census is to estimate their numbers on the basis of 2001 proportions. For instance, according to the 2001 Census, students in Headingley comprise 54.5 per cent of the total population and this proportion can be added to the published 1991 population total.

Impact analysis

One of the important features of the system is to construct interactive facilities to assess the impact of particular scenarios that may be policy-related. What is the employment impact across the city on the closure of a factory or the opening of a new supermarket, for example? This type of scenario requires some measure of the interaction between where people work and where they live. In order to model scenarios such as these, the system uses interaction statistics from the 1991 Census to estimate the commuting trip for every economically active individual in the database. Interaction data for 2001 will be used once it becomes available. In particular, all simulated individuals will be assigned workplaces (at ward level) on the basis of Monte Carlo sampling from probabilities based on the Census journey to work flows. These probabilities, as shown by a subset of probabilities from the full 33 x 33 matrix (Table 15.2), can be used to assign each simulated individual in the database to a workplace ward. Thus, for instance, 46 per cent of economically active individuals residing in Aireborough in 1991 also worked in Aireborough whilst 1 per cent travelled to work in each of the wards of Armley, Beeston and Bramley. No one commuted to work from Aireborough to Barwick and Kippax.

Table 15.3 Employment change, 1991–2000

Local authority area	Employees 2000	Numerical change 1991–2000	Percentage change 1991–2000
Leeds	386,800	60,000	18
Edinburgh	293,400	33,900	13
Kirklees	151,800	14,100	10
Cardiff	168,000	13,600	9
Glasgow	366,400	27,000	8
Bristol	232,600	14,700	7
Leicester	165,600	8,800	6
Bradford	194,900	7,200	4
Sheffield	227,000	8,300	4
Nottingham	174,700	6,300	4
Newcastle	163,500	4,700	3
Manchester	283,400	7,400	3
Birmingham	475,800	-4,100	-1
Liverpool	196,700	-4,200	-2

Source: LCC (2003)

Once workplace has been assigned, it is then possible to estimate the spatial and socio-economic impacts of events in the local economy such as plant closures or new developments by altering the number of jobs in the workplace ward. For instance, Ballas *et al.* (2001; 2002) have demonstrated how it is possible to analyse the spatial impact of a hypothetical plant closure in Leeds. In particular, they estimated the multiplier effects of a closure assuming that the plant had suppliers in various locations around the city. The spatial distribution of the workforce laid off when the plant and its suppliers closed is simulated and the subsequent income effect estimated. Figure 15.12 depicts the spatial distribution of the total annual income loss by enumeration district that resulted from the plant closure. As would be expected, the areas around the plant location were most affected. Nevertheless, there are other localities in the city which experience second order effects, caused by the job lay-offs of the plant suppliers (Ballas *et al.,* 2002).

15.4 Modelling the impact of economic growth on the housing market

In this section of the chapter we report on a project which has been supported by the Yorkshire and Humberside Regional Assembly as part of a strategic review of the future economic development of the region (Llewellyn-Davies *et al.,* 2002). One of the major issues faced by the region is the buoyancy of the Leeds economy over the last two decades. Data from the Annual Business Inquiry (Leeds City Council, 2003) shows Leeds as leader in the league table of growth rates for major UK cities in the 1990s (Table 15.3). A major strategic question for planners in the region is whether a continuation of this growth is both desirable and sustainable. A particular concern is the lack of balanced growth between the metropolitan areas of West Yorkshire, as illustrated in Table 15.4.

Baseline economic forecasts produced on behalf of Yorkshire Forward, the regional development agency, by Cambridge Econometrics (LCC, 2003) show an expectation of 36,000 new jobs in Leeds in the next ten years. In the following sections, we describe a modelling approach which evaluates the effect of these changes on the housing market of Leeds. The approach is based on a series of 'what if?' simulations following employment changes in the city. We begin with a discussion of the methodology adopted, and the calibration of a baseline labour market model. Journey-to-work data is again a very important data component. Thereafter, we review the pressures on the sub-regional housing market which are induced by projected employment growth. In particular, we argue that different policy responses can generate significant alternative future development paths for the local economy, and that a simulation of these processes can add significant insights for planners and decision makers.

The origins of this type of modelling framework lie in the family of spatial interaction models championed by Wilson as described in the introduction. As researchers, we argue whilst the theory of these models has been studied extensively, their empirical validity has been subjected to far less scrutiny and only by moving into an applied research environment can we expose and surmount the major obstacles which constrain

Table 15.4 Sectoral employment distribution by district in West Yorkshire, 2001

	Percentage distribution 2001						Percentage change 1996–2001
	Manufact-uring	Distribution	Business services	Public services	Other services	All industries	All industries
Bradford	24	22	17	23	18	21	+2
Calderdale	11	7	6	7	8	8	-7
Kirklees	24	15	13	18	15	17	+8
Leeds	29	40	56	39	47	42	+10
Wakefield	12	15	8	14	12	13	+9
Total	100	100	100	100	100	100	+6

Source: LCC (2003)

Figure 15.13 Alternative modelling structures

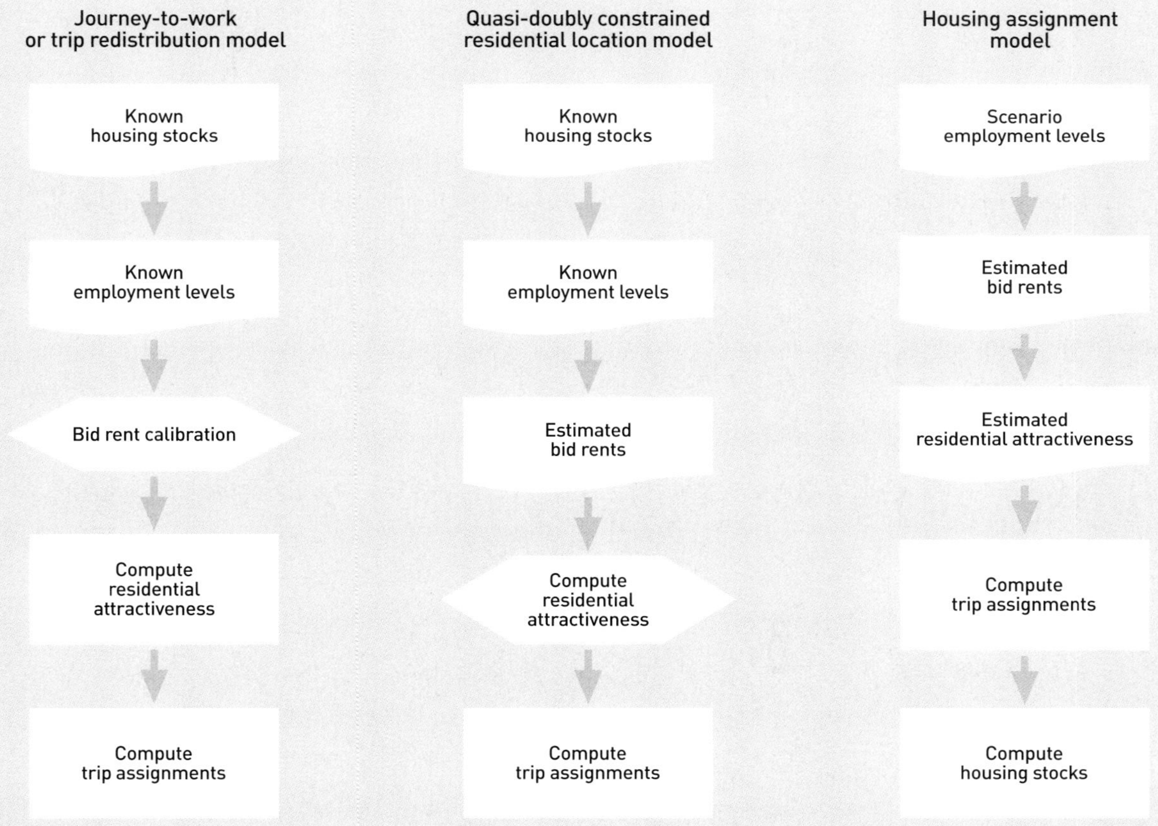

Journey-to-work or trip redistribution model

Known housing stocks → Known employment levels → Bid rent calibration → Compute residential attractiveness → Compute trip assignments

Quasi-doubly constrained residential location model

Known housing stocks → Known employment levels → Estimated bid rents → Compute residential attractiveness → Compute trip assignments

Housing assignment model

Scenario employment levels → Estimated bid rents → Estimated residential attractiveness → Compute trip assignments → Compute housing stocks the provision of effective decision support tools for planners and policy makers (Birkin *et al.*, 1996; 2002).

As a starting point, we take the residential location model presented by Senior and Wilson (1974). The structure of the model is outlined schematically on the left hand side in Figure 15.13. This model assumes that we know the number of houses in each residential area (split into different types, e.g. 'detached', 'terraced') and the number of jobs in each employment zone (split by social class or skill level, e.g. professional, manual, clerical). The unknowns in the model are the bid rents which balance the costs of land and housing in each area against the desire of the different social groups for short trips to their places of employment. In effect, this model says that the journey-to-work flows between a residential area and a workplace area will tend to be highest where there is a lot of housing, a large number of jobs and not much physical separation between the jobs and the homes. For example, we would expect large commuter flows into the city centre where most jobs are located from inner urban residential neighbourhoods like Burmantofts and Armley. The model is 'calibrated' by finding a set of bid rents which generates commuting flows that match the known trip patterns of the different social groups.

Two important features of the model are worthy of further comment. Firstly, it is assumed that both housing and employment totals for small areas are known. Thus the problem is to determine the most likely set of journey-to-work flows associated with this distribution. To the extent that these flows are moderated through a congested transport network in which both the real and invisible financial costs of trips are variable, then this model has obvious applications to transportation planning. Secondly, the attractiveness of residential areas is determined by a 'bid rent' process through which individuals offset the price of housing and the costs of transportation against their available expenditure for housing. For the purposes of this applied research, we have found it necessary to adapt both of these features. The fundamental question can be posed as: where is the best place to put

housing to support 36,000 new jobs in Leeds? Since it makes no sense to take housing counts as fixed, we address this problem through a re-specification of the model in a 'quasi-doubly constrained' form, replacing the balancing factors at each residential location with an 'attractiveness' factor. The model is described as quasi-doubly constrained because it can be calibrated in such a way that the number of workers allocated to each residential area balances the available housing stock in that zone. In other words, given that we know the bid rents from our previous set of calculations, we now want to determine a level of 'attractiveness' for each housing type in the different zones which is consistent with the overall distribution of housing across the city (Figure 15.13).

In order to implement this model, we now wish to express the attractiveness of each residential area in terms of factors which make that area a pleasant place in which to live. We selected four variables from which to compute this attractiveness index: population density, crime rate, educational performance and degree qualifications. Population density and degree qualifications were both derived from the 1991 Census, educational performance from published school league tables, and crime rates from publicly available reports. The other model ingredients were initialised or calibrated using a combination of data from HM Land Registry (house prices), Family Expenditure Survey (housing expenditure), National Transport Statistics (travel expenditure), Annual Business Inquiry (employment statistics), and Census data (housing stock). The model recognises four different types of housing — detached, semi-detached, terraced and flats — for which both the stocks and prices are known (from the Census and HM Land Registry respectively). Local authority wards are used as the spatial zones.

The results from the attractiveness calculations are shown in Table 15.5. The four variables described above were forced into a multiple regression model for each of the four housing types. Population density and crime were both associated with a negative correlation against attractiveness, so that housing is seen as less desirable in areas of high density and high crime rates. Degree qualifications and school

Table 15.5 Regression coefficients and goodness-of-fit statistics for the housing model

Housing type	School performance coefficient	Population density coefficient	Crime coefficient	Degrees coefficient	Goodness-of-fit (R^2)
Detached	64.490	-44.20	-8.66	18.076	0.730
Semi-detached	11.160	-6.82	-2.60	5.342	0.856
Terraced	9.125	-6.20	-2.82	4.019	0.765
Flats	7.506	-6.76	-14.58	1.671	0.472

performance are both positively correlated, so that housing is more desirable within the catchment areas of high quality schools. In relation to education, it is the magnitude rather than the sign of the coefficients which is most significant. Thus well-educated employees exhibit a strong preference for high quality, detached residences. Elsewhere, the pattern of the coefficients is broadly as one would expect, with the largest coefficients for both school performance and population density occurring in the detached housing category. Perhaps the main surprise is that the attractiveness of flats has the highest coefficient for crime rates. This may be in part a reflection that flats are most numerous in the high crime inner city areas, and that the impact of crime is therefore the strongest differentiator for these neighbourhoods. On the other hand, the possibility of inter-correlation amongst the variables should not be neglected (i.e. the crime rate in these areas could be a proxy for other effects).

Each of the housing sub-models was found to be statistically significant, explaining more than 70 per cent of the variance for each of the three housing types, and just over 47 per cent of the attractiveness for flats (as noted above, this group tends to have the greatest level of spatial concentration which probably explains why it is hardest to predict). What this may in turn imply is that it is possible to build predictive models of the attractiveness of areas based on their constituent characteristics, and perhaps to look at the effect of changes in these components on neighbourhood attractiveness. However these processes like rising crime and changing school performance will typically operate over relatively long time periods, and this is not the purpose of the present exercise. Rather, our aim is to demonstrate that the attractiveness terms within our model are intuitively sensible, and that it is therefore

reasonable to use such measures as neighbourhood attractors within a 'what if?' simulation of changing housing requirements in response to growth in employment. Thus we use a third type of model (Figure 15.13, right hand side) which can be described as 'attraction-constrained', in building housing market scenarios. In this case, we have calculated both the bid rents (in relation to known trip patterns) and the attractiveness of different locations (in relation to population density and social factors), and these can be used as the basis to demonstrate the housing preferences of the population for any given employment distribution. The baseline distributions of housing and employment are mutually consistent, i.e. given the starting set of employment totals, the calibration of the bid rents and residential attractiveness is such that the model 'predicts' the starting distribution of housing stocks.

In building scenarios of future changes in the local housing market, two possibilities were considered:

- Following the introduction of 36,000 new jobs, where are the ideal places to allocate new housing developments in order to provide residences for these workers?

- If there is no increase in the provision of housing, what would be the effect of employment growth on house prices within the city?

In order to answer either of these questions, we need to make specific assumptions about the nature and location of the new jobs to be created. As noted above, the magnitude of the increase in employment follows the ten-year projections of Cambridge Econometrics (CE). According to the Leeds Economy Handbook (LCC, 2003), following CE, these new jobs will be taken up by commuters from outside the city region, but this is a remarkably simplistic view. The Leeds Urban Development

Figure 15.14 Scenarios of alternative housing by ward

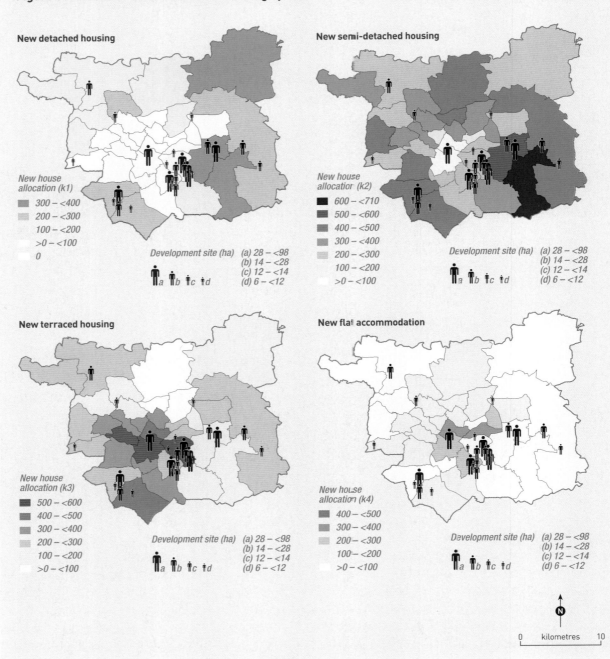

New detached housing

New house allocation (k1)
- 300 – <400
- 200 – <300
- 100 – <200
- >0 – <100
- 0

Development site (ha)
(a) 28 – <98
(b) 14 – <28
(c) 12 – <14
(d) 6 – <12

New semi-detached housing

New house allocation (k2)
- 600 – <710
- 500 – <600
- 400 – <500
- 300 – <400
- 200 – <300
- 100 – <200
- >0 – <100

Development site (ha)
(a) 28 – <98
(b) 14 – <28
(c) 12 – <14
(d) 6 – <12

New terraced housing

New house allocation (k3)
- 500 – <600
- 400 – <500
- 300 – <400
- 200 – <300
- 100 – <200
- >0 – <100

Development site (ha)
(a) 28 – <98
(b) 14 – <28
(c) 12 – <14
(d) 6 – <12

New flat accommodation

New house allocation (k4)
- 400 – <500
- 300 – <400
- 200 – <300
- 100 – <200
- >0 – <100

Development site (ha)
(a) 28 – <98
(b) 14 – <28
(c) 12 – <14
(d) 6 – <12

N

0   kilometres   10

Plan (LCC, 2001) was used to identify all of the major sites which are zoned as 'employment land', and new employment was allocated to these locations in proportion to the size of each site. The major development sites are related to the new A1-M¯ link road to the south and east of the city centre, and also in the vicinity of the White Rose retail and office park, and in the town of Otley. Furthermore, however, it was assumed that City and Holbeck ward, which accounts for nearly one-third

Figure 15.15 Scenarios of new alternative housing allocations by ward,
(a) detached, (b) semi-detached, (c) terraced and (d) flats

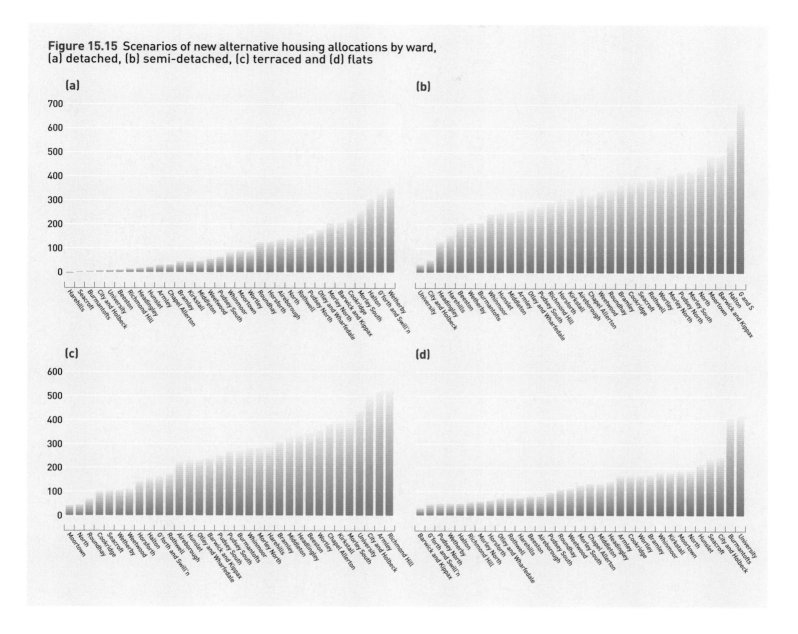

of all jobs in Leeds, would continue to account for a constant share of employment. In terms of the composition of jobs, we followed CE in assuming that 75 per cent of all new employment will be in 'Finance and Business'. The remainder were allocated in proportion to the existing employment mix of individual wards.

For the purposes of the first simulation, the attractiveness of each residential area is held constant in relation to the constituent area profiles as discussed above. The net effect in relation to the provision of detached housing is that although

most of the new jobs are created in the centre and in the south-east, the ideal place for new executive homes is in the Wetherby area to the north-east of Leeds (Figure 15.14 and 15.15). However, the wards of Halton and Garforth, which are both moderately attractive and highly accessible, also suggest strong development potential. In the case of terraced housing, access to jobs is a more important consideration (as one would expect), and in this case the pressure for new housing is distributed within the City and Holbeck, and its neighbours Armley to the west and Richmond Hill to the east.

Figure 15.16 House price inflation, fixed housing stocks by ward

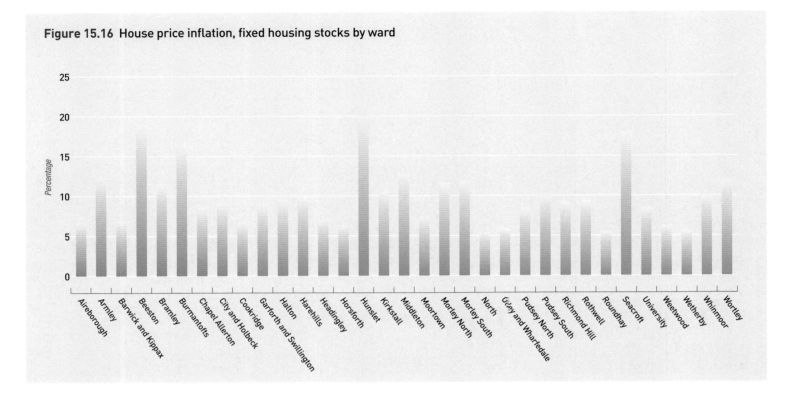

The results of the first simulation are intended to stimulate further consideration of planning design scenarios, in particular relating to the balance between zoning for employment and housing. The major development areas for housing according to the UDP are spread across the city, with many developments planned in the west and north west of the city (LCC, 2001; see Chapter 4). This looks to be less than ideal in terms of the kinds of patterns which have been analysed above, and it may be that some of the areas currently designated for employment to the south and east might usefully be re-designated for housing, and *vice versa* to the north-west. Such alternative scenarios could easily be explored within the simulation framework described here, although this capability has not been demonstrated explicitly as yet.

In a second simulation, we explore an extreme scenario in which the housing market is unable to respond to employment growth, perhaps because of a lack of availability of suitable land for development. If the housing stock is fixed, then the alternative response which is embedded within the model is for 'bid rents' to increase in order that a balance be maintained. In effect, because trip costs are held constant this means that house prices have to increase. The average increase in house prices across Leeds wards under this scenario is shown in Figure 15.16. Unsurprisingly, perhaps, house price inflation is most marked in those locations previously identified as either accessible to new employment growth, or with desirable physical and social properties.

Whilst this latter simulation of fixed housing stocks is perhaps unrealistic, the future probably contains elements of both of the scenarios introduced here. Thus since new housing will not miraculously appear in exactly the right locations, there will be an element of differential response within house prices in order to compensate. Further exploration of such scenarios, in which planners and policy makers can explore the implications of different plans and zoning regulations on the need for housing, and on regulation of the market through house price adjustments, are presented here as a means for improving both the effectiveness and efficiency of local planning processes.

15.5 Conclusions

Envisioning and predicting the future is a challenging task. The complexities of the sub-systems that constitute the urban system and the ways in which they interact with one another through markets and across space are difficult enough to understand in the past, let alone to predict in the future, yet it is the future on which we must concentrate. The simulation modelling methods that have been presented in this chapter provide examples of the application of tools that are now becoming available to help us evaluate the scenarios that we envisage under particular sets of assumptions. It is the latter that are key and whose specification poses the greatest challenge. Can we assume the continuation of past trends or will circumstances arise that mean radical changes will take place?

Far from developing a comprehensive model as posited by Lowry 40 years ago (Lowry, 1964), the approach has focused on particular urban components — people, households, jobs and housing — and the use of microsimulation and spatial interaction models to help guide our thinking about the implications of change. Whilst apparently rather dissimilar, at a deeper level the two approaches are in fact highly complementary. It is well-known that spatial interaction models can be derived via statistical averaging from the behaviour of a large population of individuals under appropriate constraints (Wilson, 1970). The models can then be used to address structural issues, such as retail profitability and saturation, or locations for new residential development, as discussed in Section 15.4. The principal drawback with these models is that they become hard to disaggregate. Thus, once the definition of neighbourhoods or zones becomes detailed, or the characteristics of the target population are considered at high resolution, then the approach quickly becomes unmanageable.

The strengths and weaknesses of the microsimulation approach are almost a mirror image of the spatial interaction models. Microsimulation and related agent-based approaches are enormously flexible in their ability to represent individuals and households in great detail. Where appropriate behavioural data is available, then each of the agents may be assigned detailed and realistic activity patterns. The difficulty lies in relating behavioural variations to underlying statistical variations. For example, suppose that 80 per cent of individuals in Leeds have a preference for a four bedroom detached property, yet 80 per cent of the housing stock is comprised of three bedroom semi-detached houses. This situation can only be regulated through some market-clearing mechanism which cannot be represented through existing microsimulation structures.

In summary, therefore, microsimulation approaches are excellent at regulating individual characteristics and behaviours in great detail. The strength of spatial interaction models lies in their ability to regulate supply and demand within local markets. Future research which integrates the two approaches will have considerable value (Nakaya et al., 2003; Birkin, 2004).

As with all modelling, there is room for improvement in the models that have been reported in this chapter. Our approach to population projection in the microsimulation model for Leeds, for example, is very crude and highlights the need for a more sophisticated small area population projection methodology that ages cohorts through time and which accounts for births, deaths and migrations into and out of the study area in a comprehensive manner. Likewise, the commuting data sets on which the impact analyses are reliant, date back to the 1991 Census; their reliability for representing interactions in the twenty-first century will only be revealed when the 2001 journey-to-work data become available.

Yet despite shortcomings such as these, the gathering recognition of the value of the modelling tools that are now being developed, particularly when linked to user-friendly planning support systems, bodes well for the future. In the same way that private business has begun to exploit the potential of the geotechnology to support strategic decision making for location choice, so local and regional planning agencies and practition-ers must recognise that the role that robust simulation models can play in supporting the decisions that need to be taken now that will determine the future geographies of our populations, economies, transport infrastructures and land uses.

Note

1   Annealing is a physical process in which a solid material is first melted in a heat bath by increasing the temperature to a maximum value at which point all particles of the solid have high energies and the freedom to randomly arrange themselves in the liquid phase. This is then followed by a cooling phase, in which the temperature of the heat bath is slowly lowered. The particles of the material attempt to arrange themselves in a low energy state during the cooling phase. When the maximum temperature is sufficiently high and the cooling is carried out sufficiently slowly then all the particles of the material eventually arrange themselves in a state of high density and minimum energy.

References

Ballas, D. (2001) *A spatial microsimulation approach to local labour market policy analysis,* unpublished PhD thesis, School of Geography, University of Leeds, Leeds.

Ballas, D. and Clarke, G.P. (2000) GIS and microsimulation for local labour market policy analysis, *Computers, Environment and Urban Systems,* 24: 305–330.

Ballas, D. and Clarke, G.P. (2001) Towards local implications of major job transformations in the city: a spatial microsimulation approach, *Geographical Analysis,* 31: 291–311.

Ballas, D. and Clarke, G.P. (2003) *Microsimulation and regional science: 30 years of spatial microsimulation of populations,* paper presented at the 50th Annual North American Meeting of the Regional Science Association International, Philadelphia, 19–22 November.

Ballas, D., Clarke, G.P. and Dewhurst, J. (2002) *A spatial microsimulation approach to the analysis of local multiplier effects,* paper presented at the 32nd Regional Science Association, RSAI — British and Irish Section Conference, The Dudley Hotel, Brighton and Hove, 21–23 August.

Ballas, D., Clarke, G.P., Dorling, D., Eyre, H., Rossiter, D. and Thomas, B. (2003) *SimYork: Simulating Current and Future Trends in the Life of Households in York,* report to the Joseph Rowntree Foundation, May.

Ballas, D., Clarke, G.P. and Turton, I. (1999) *Exploring microsimulation methodologies for the estimation of household attributes,* Paper presented at the 4th International Conference on GeoComputation, Fredericksburg, Virginia, 25–28 July.

Birkin, M. (2004) Location planning, chapter in Maguire, D. Goodchild, M. and Batty, M. (eds) *GIS, Spatial Analysis and Modelling,* ESRI Press, in press.

Birkin, M., Clarke, G.P., Clarke, M. and Wilson, A.G. (1996) *Intelligent GIS: Location Decisions and Strategic Planning,* GeoInformation, Cambridge.

Birkin, M., Clarke, G.P., and Clarke, M. (2002) *Retail Geography and Intelligent Network Planning,* Wiley, Chichester.

Clarke, G.P. (1996) Microsimulation for Urban and Regional Analysis, *European Research in Regional Science 6,* Pion, London.

Clarke, G.P. and Clarke, M. (2001) Applied spatial interaction modelling, in Clarke, G.P. and Madden, M. (eds) *Regional Science in Business,* Springer, Berlin.

Johnston, R.J. (1996) *Geography and Geographers,* 5th edition, Edward Arnold, London.

Lee, D.B. (1973) Requiem for large scale models, *Journal of the American Institute of Planners,* 39: 163–78.

Leeds City Council (LCC) (2001) *Leeds Urban Development Plan,* at www.investmentpropertyuk.com/downloads/Leeds per cent20Property.pdf, accessed September 2003.

Leeds City Council (LCC) (2003) *Leeds Economy Handbook 2003,* at www.eeds.gov.uk/ documents, accessed February 2004.

Llewellyn-Davies, Steers Davies Gleave, Jones Lang LaSalle and University of Leeds (2002) *Leeds and Environs Spatial Strategy,* final scoping report for the Yorkshire and Humber Assembly and others.

Lowry, I. (1964) *A Model of Metropolis,* RM-4035-RC, Rand Corporation, Santa Monica.

Nakaya, T., Yano, K., Koga, S., Fotheringham, A.S., Ballas, D., Clarke, G. and Hanaoka, K. (2003) *Retail Interaction Modelling Using Meso and Micro Approaches,* paper presented at the 33rd Annual Conference of Regional Science Association International British and Irish Section, St. Andrews, Scotland.

Norman, P. (1999) Putting iterative proportional fitting on the researcher's desk, *Working Paper 99/3,* School of Geography, University of Leeds, Leeds.

Orcutt, G.H. (1957) A new type of socio-economic system, *The Review of Economics and Statistics,* 39: 116–123

Office of National Statistics (ONS) (1999) *1996-based Subnational Population Projections — England,* Series PP3 no. 10, The Stationery Office, London.

Office of National Statistics (ONS) (2001) *Census 2001: A Guide to the One Number Census,* ONS on-line document: http://www.statistics.gov.uk/census2001/pdfs/oncguide.pdf

Sayer, R.A. (1976) A critique of urban modelling, *Progress in Planning,* 6: 187–254.

Senior, M.L. and Wilson, A.G. (1974) Exploration and syntheses of linear programming and spatial interaction models of residential location, *Geographical Analysis,* 6: 209–238.

Stillwell, J. and Clarke, G.P. (eds) (2004) *Applied GIS and Spatial Analysis,* Wiley, Chichester.

Wilson, A.G. (1970) *Entropy in Urban and Regional Modelling,* Pion, London.

Wilson, A.G. (1974) *Urban and Regional Models in Geography and Planning,* John Wiley, Chichester.

Wilson, A.G., Rees, P.H. and Leigh, C.M. (eds) (1977) *Models of Cities and Regions Theoretical and Empirical Developments,* John Wiley, Chichester.

16
Twenty-First Century Leeds

JOHN STILLWELL, RACHAEL UNSWORTH, PAUL STEPHENS & GORDON CAREY

The chapters of this book have revealed much about the city of Leeds at the beginning of the twenty-first century that we can be proud of ... But there remains much of concern...

16.1 Introduction

Is life in Leeds getting better or worse? What will the city be like 20 years from now? These are difficult questions to answer directly. Better or worse for whom, and in what respects? It seems that expectation of life is improving, yet drug-related illness continues to increase and many people fear the consequences of venturing from their homes after dark. We know that disposable income is rising, yet indebtedness has spiralled and a huge number of people remain multiply deprived. The material quality of life has improved, yet divorce has accelerated, generations live increasingly separate lives and more individuals experience social isolation. The economy flourishes in some sectors and in some places, yet traffic congestion has reached epidemic proportions on certain routes and economic growth has not been sufficiently decoupled from environmental impact. Technology is moving dramatically onward, yet major skill shortages are manifest. Planning tools have evolved, huge investment has been made and experience has accumulated, yet geographies of disparity remain a marked feature of the urban reality (Ward, 2003).

The answer to the initial question depends partly, of course, on the time perspective that we wish to adopt. After visiting Leeds, Friedrich Engels confirmed the view described in the Artisan in 1845 that "... the low-lying districts along the river and its tributary becks are narrow, dirty and enough in themselves to shorten the lives of the inhabitants, especially

An 1870s print of Leeds. The city grew rapidly as thousands of people came to work in the many factories. Land development was largely uncontrolled, air and water pollution were at high levels and health was poor.

Print by J. Stephenson published between 1870 and 1875 by T. Baines in *Yorkshire Past and Present*, Vol. 2.

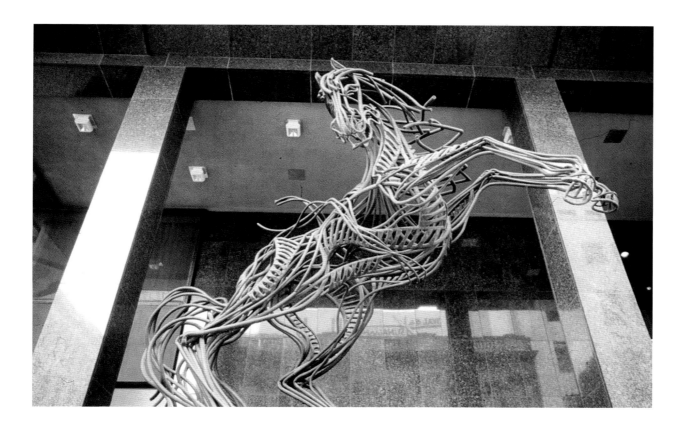

Peter Tysoe's
The Black Horse —
a skeletal sculpture
made from mild steel
tubing — was
installed for Lloyds
Bank outside their
prestigious Yorkshire
and Humberside
Regional Offices in
Park Row in 1976.
Despite its hollow
section construction,
The Black Horse still
weighs in at a hefty
1.5 tonnes.

the little children. Added to this, the disgusting state of the working men's districts about Kirkgate, Marsh Lane, Cross Street and Richmond Road, which is chiefly attributable to their unpaved, drainless streets, irregular architecture, numerous courts and alleys, and total lack of the most ordinary means of cleanliness..." (Engels, 1845, p.80). There is no doubt that since Engels observed the situation in Leeds (the long term), there have been significant improvements in most of the indicators that might be used to measure economic, social or environmental conditions. However, the short-term perspective is much less easy to evaluate. In this last chapter of the book, we draw some conclusions and look ahead. Some of the key issues and messages about Leeds at the beginning of the twenty-first century that have emerged from the preceding chapters are summarised in Section 16.2 before a consideration of how, in the short term, the city retains its role and maintains its forward momentum. The focus shifts to the longer term in Section 16.4 with a presentation of two extreme scenarios and discussion of some potential influences of major importance that are likely to impact on the city. The concluding section envisages what Leeds might really look like in 2020.

16.2 Some key messages

The chapters of this book have revealed much about the city of Leeds at the beginning of the twenty-first century that we can be proud of: sustained economic growth; very strong legal, financial and business services sector; relatively low unemployment overall; vibrant city centre; positive population change; rich mix of cultures; centre of learning; dynamic regional capital with a positive image. But there remains much of concern: not everyone has benefited from the economic success and there are many areas with high levels of deprivation, relatively high unemployment, high incidence of crime and anti-social behaviour and poor education attainment after primary level. The patterns of demographic, socio-economic and urban morphology have been illustrated through a range of mapped indicators that highlight the geographical diversity that is, in itself, such an important characteristic of Leeds.

As a way of summarising the various socio-demographic geographies that have been evident for different thematic areas in earlier chapters, we refer to a new national classification of 2001 Census output areas (OAs), developed by researchers in the School of Geography at the University of

OA classification
1. City centre melting pot
2. Typical traits
3. Inner city multicultural blend
4. Blue-collar communities
5. The rural idyll
6. Older struggling estates
7. Comfortable suburban estates

Source: Census 2001

0   kilometres   5

Leeds in conjunction with the Office of National Statistics (Vickers, 2004). The process of geographical classification is carried out by clustering OAs according to their values for 41 Census variables and the resulting groups are therefore a representation of the social make-up of the city based on criteria applied nationally. Figure 16.1 shows the distribution of the seven groups of the national classification within the Leeds area. Group 1 is referred to as the 'city centre melting pot' and OAs in this category are found mainly in the centre of the city and running into the main student areas of Hyde Park and Headingley. The group is characterised by a young single population of which the majority live in flats. OAs in group 2, 'typical traits', are found in suburban areas of the city mainly to the south but also in significant amounts in Aireborough and Wetherby. This group is characterised by its averageness, with most people living in semi-detached or terraced housing and with populations that are distinctly middle-aged.

Group 3 contains the 'inner city multicultural blend' OAs which are predominantly found to the north east of the city centre. This group is characterised by a high proportion of non-whites, with almost 40 per cent of population being of black, Asian or mixed ethnicity The characteristic housing for this group is mainly terraced and flats. Group 4 is known as 'blue collar communities' and contains OAs that are well spread across the city though with concentrations in the south. OAs in this group are characterised by having almost all terraced and semi-detached housing, and employment in routine and semi-routine occupational categories. Group 5, 'the rural idyll', is the group of OAs that surround the city's urban extent to the north and the east. This category is characterised by a low population

Figure 16.2 Contrasting Leeds with other core cities using a national OA classification, 2001

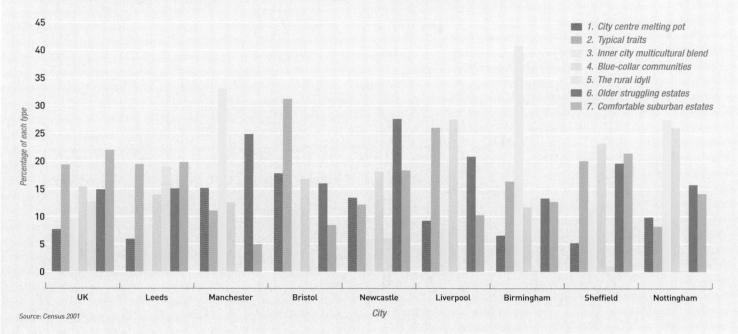

Source: Census 2001

density, high car ownership, detached housing, an older middle age population and the presence of agricultural employment. In contrast, group 6 consists of 'older struggling estates'. In the main this group surrounds the city centre enclosing groups 1 and 3 and is characterised by an ageing population, poor health and housing mainly in flats but with some terraces and semis. Nearly 50 per cent of homes are council rented; there is very low car ownership; and the unemployment rate is double the national average. Finally, group 7, 'comfortable suburban estates', are OAs that represent the urban extent of the city to the north and the east, also with areas in Aireborough and Wetherby. These OAs have predominantly married white couples with children, low unemployment, managerial and professional employment, detached and semi-detached housing and many households with two or more cars.

Throughout the book, authors have drawn comparisons between Leeds and the nation, the region, the other districts in the region or the set of core cities of which Leeds is a member (ODPM, 2004a). What is striking is the similarity that is apparent when we compare the percentages of OAs in the seven categories of the national classification with those across the whole of the UK (Figure 16.2). The main difference in Leeds'

profile is the proportion of OAs defined in the 'rural idyll' category, a difference that also distinguishes Leeds from the other core cities whose profiles are also graphed in Figure 16.2. Manchester, Birmingham and, to a lesser extent Nottingham, all have relatively high percentages in the 'inner city multicultural blend' category whilst Bristol is dominated by 'typical traits'. OAs classified as 'older struggling estates' are particularly evident in Newcastle, whereas the highest percentages of OAs in Liverpool and Sheffield are classified as 'blue collar communities'. The analysis on which the profiles shown in Figure 16.2 is based re-emphasises the need to treat comparisons between the core cities with caution. In other words, one of the reasons that Leeds is different from elsewhere is because its administrative boundaries circumscribe a relatively wide area well beyond the limits of the built up area.

Cities in late capitalist economies are undergoing extensive changes in a range of different ways and Leeds' renaissance exemplifies many of the processes that urban commentators have identified as occurring elsewhere. In terms of economic activities, Leeds' declining manufacturing sector and increasing service sector jobs are a reflection of how the global economic system is restructuring. The increasing mobility

of capital and the declining role of manufacturing are allowing many cities to re-emerge with new roles in the global system. Leeds' success in this respect is partly due to its spectacular growth in legal, financial and business services but also because of its redefinition as a city of consumption rather than production, though these two processes are not mutually exclusive. The increase in workers in the professional services sectors has created a huge demand for new accommodation, as evidenced by the increased demand for city centre apartments, and has highlighted the city centre as a target for profitable investment. As commerce and retailing have expanded and as major names have been attracted to the high street, there has been expanded demand for cultural activities to improve the quality of life for residents and visitors.

Property development in the city centre is seen as a key part of the new urban regeneration with new offices and apartment blocks signifying the transition from industrial city (much of the development is taking place on former industrial sites) to international service economy, a representation of success in the physical fabric of the city. The creation of the City Centre Management Team in 1998 is an important develop-

ment as is the emphasis on building design, ensuring that a 'modern' city is created with an innovative blend of old Victorian and new landmark buildings. Many cities have engaged in the promotion of cultural consumption as a means of place marketing, attempting to carve out a market niche on an international level. Whilst there is no doubt that Leeds has moved forward in this respect, there are serious deficiencies in the current provision of cultural facilities and John Trickett's vision of Leeds as a 24-hour European city has yet to be realised. The presence of large numbers of students from the city's two universities has contributed to the demand for cultural consumption as well as to Leeds' positive image, and major investment in cultural facilities is in the pipeline. However, much remains to be done to attract sub-groups of the population into the city centre other than professional workers and students. Not only is it necessary to create affordable homes, but also to provide all the services that are required to support families.

An important dimension of Leeds' image in the past, particularly at a global scale, is that associated with prowess in major sporting activities. This is perhaps best exemplified by the footballing achievements of Leeds United in both domestic and

European competitions and with the use of Headingley as a venue for test match cricket since 1899. Whilst the effects of relegation in 2004 from the Premiership on incoming revenue and local morale are very difficult to predict, the city can only benefit from its soccer team's rapid return to the top flight and the re-instatement of Elland Road as an attractive venue for soccer fans from across the world. During the 1990s, there was much debate about the future of Headingley stadium for cricket and rugby, given the demands for refurbishment and the lack of car parking provision. In 1999, strategic plans for the comprehensive redevelopment of Headingley were prepared, including a £32m project to rebuild the Western Terrace. The new West Stand with seating for 7,500, was officially opened in 2001 and now Headingley is the home of three world-class teams: Yorkshire Cricket, Leeds Tykes, and Leeds Rhinos. It will be crucial for the city to secure the future of Headingley Stadium as a regional and international sporting facility and this implies further improvements for spectator and visitor facilities as well as appropriate consideration of the views and needs of local residents.

Much has been made in the press of Leeds' image as a 'two-speed city' in which those working centrally in white collar

occupations and reaping the consumption benefits which are available in the city centre are contrasted with those confined to deprived inner city and suburban neighbourhoods who tend to be excluded from the benefits of development. The mapping of different indicators of life expectancy, ethnicity, housing tenure, social class, unemployment, car ownership, criminal damage, anti-social behaviour, educational attainment, employment change and income have all demonstrated the extent of disparity and emphasised the complexity of the spatial variations that exist. Whilst it is clear that the city has much to do to improve conditions in many of its poorer communities, it seems fallacious to think that the population is polarised only between those who have and those who do not. The variety of demographic structures, ethnic groups, social classes and occupational groups living and working in different environments is indicative of a vibrant city of individuals operating at different speeds.

Overall, many of the problems that Leeds experiences are similar in nature if not in extent to the problems of cities in general: social disparities, ethnic conflict, crime and drug abuse, transport congestion, environmental degradation. These are all 'big' problems that are slow to arrive and will probably be even slower to solve. It is therefore imperative that we recognise the trend towards short-sightedness associated with market economies and political structures that has tended to characterise much thinking and decision making in recent times and that we attempt to confront the challenge of providing a longer term perspective. The role of governance at all levels and of individuals to set goals to solve these problems will involve consistency and patience because the problems are complex and difficult in a world that increasingly seeks immediate restorative solutions. Brand (1999) refers to the ancient Greek terms 'kairos' and 'chronos' to distinguish respectively between the opportunity-grabbing now and the all-inclusive longer term, arguing forcefully for us all to take a much deeper responsibility for the latter. Yet there is a sense of urgency in a competitive world to find rapid solutions that will help 'Leeds plc' to keep up with or pull ahead of its competitors.

16.3 Remaining the UK's favourite city

Nick Falk, whilst working on *Towns and Cities: Partners in Urban Renaissance* (URBED, 2002) stated that "towns and cities are essentially organic and should not be seen as just a set of problems or machines to be fixed with a 'toolkit' of short term projects". So what are the key issues that are important for the future success of Leeds? If we use the three dimensions of the sustainability framework, the aims for Leeds would include maintaining a vibrant economy; creating a healthy, safe, diverse and inclusive society; and ensuring a quality environment. In fact, the assessment of Leeds' successes, failures, strengths and weaknesses has led to identification of three main themes for future strategy that form the objectives of *Vision II* (Leeds Initiative, 2004). The first of these is that Leeds needs to 'go up a league' when compared with other cities nationally and internationally; the second is for Leeds to 'narrow the gap', spreading the city's prosperity to those who have yet to gain benefit; the third is for Leeds to 'develop its role as the regional capital'. These aims, all of which have been mentioned at various times in several of the preceding chapters, are to be achieved through a wide range of measures enacted by the newly re-organised Council departments, with active co-operation from the organisations that have been brought into the partnership arrangements of the Leeds Initiative. It is important to re-emphasise that the strategy for Leeds does not operate in a vacuum. Thus, in terms of economic development, for example, Leeds should align with Government focus on regional productivity and the key areas of competitiveness — innovation, connectivity, skills and governance — as set out in the Core Cities programme (ODPM, 2004a) and embraced by Yorkshire Forward in the Regional Economic Strategy (Yorkshire Forward, 2003).

Simulations of the Leeds economy are produced annually by Cambridge Econometrics and those for Spring 2004 predicted employment growth of 6.3 per cent between 2004 and 2014, a net increase of 27,700 jobs largely due to the continued expansion of financial and business services (LCC, 2004). Yet, if Leeds is to maintain its vibrant economy and be

... towns and cities are essentially organic and should not be seen as just a set of problems or machines to be fixed with a 'toolkit' of short term projects.

a Champion's League business capital, it requires support to provide enterprising opportunities for all so as to turn good ideas into good earners, to equip businesses to go global, to develop a more skilled workforce, to utilise the benefits of its two major universities to better effect, to minimise red tape for small businesses and reduce business crime whilst simultaneously fostering an approach in which businesses demonstrate far greater concerns about the environment. Organisations such as Leeds Cares and Business in the Community are actively campaigning to address these issues. Moreover, strategies for waste management and pollution reduction are part of the need to match sustainable economic growth with a sustainable environment.

Achieving sustainable development includes mixed land use, attending to deprivation and reducing the resource-intensity of development, economic output and consumption. A critical question is how to reconcile these aims with efforts to increase consumption in the city centre. On the subject of sustainability, there is an argument that familiar and longstanding problems are unlikely to be overcome without some serious changes that might include major shifts in public subsidies away from roads, oil, and centralised energy; giving real power to the local level through neighbourhood assemblies; taking seriously the idea of bio-city regions and self-sufficiency in food and energy production and off the grid technologies; meeting basic housing needs through self build; and developing a solidarity economy, (through credit unions, local food production and green jobs, for example) not as a bolt-on but as a serious counterpart to the existing neo-liberal economy (Chatterton, 2002).

Transport improvements must be at the top of the priority agenda for economic and environmental reasons but also simply to provide individuals with the connections they require whenever they need to travel. There is much to admire in the integrated public transport systems that appear to function so effectively in parts of mainland Europe. It seems unfortunate that with so many sectoral or local planning strategies dovetailing with the Supertram proposals, its future

remains in doubt after such a long period of gestation. Some might argue that the expansion of Leeds-Bradford International Airport (LBIA) is likely to be more important in the overall scheme of things, particularly if it can be connected more directly through rapid links with the main business centres that it services. LBIA has in place a 25-year expansion programme, creating 5,000 new jobs over and above the current 1,800 so that it can accommodate seven million passengers by 2030. The development of Doncaster-Finningley airport, with its long haul potential, could open up further opportunities, especially for the east and south sides of Leeds.

Boosting the city's image is another key requirement for maintaining success. The creation of City Image Task Group with an innovative marketing strategy and promotion campaign (www.uksfavouritecity.com) has been long overdue, as has the establishment of a Cultural Facilities Task Group in 2003 to address the issue of new cultural facilities and to commission feasibility studies as required. It is a widely held view that 'league promotion' will require an increase in the range and quality of functions performed in Leeds (Hillman, 2002; Leeds Civic Trust, 2003). It is argued that additional facilities are required to 'round out' the range of commercial and leisure activities that can be hosted by the city, boosting the city's image, attracting more visitors and generating spin-offs that will have positive impacts on employment and prosperity. Leeds has to find ways to be considered as a top ranking destination, and it cannot do this if there are still gaps in its functional offer that make it seem less appealing than some other cities of a similar size. A major gap that has been identified is that of concert/arena/exhibition/conference facilities (Millard, 2004) and work has begun to try to identify suitable sites, make a business case for development and address funding issues.

But more than this will be needed. There will have to be further visitor attractions that appeal to a wide market — in terms of catchment area, age, socio-economic and ethnic group — and more intangibly than this, attention will need to be paid to creating the kinds of environment and conditions in which

the most innovative people will want to live and work —
newcomers, Leeds graduates and those born and bred in the
area. Creative industries already employ over 12,000 people
(Taylor, 2003) but the numbers did not increase over the years
1998-2001. What can be done to improve the chances of new
business start-ups and growth of existing businesses that will
add to this crucial well spring of creativity?

In the short term, the city's image will be boosted by
the quality of the developments that are already in prospect,
since these will transform the physical form and function of the
city over the next 10 years. Previous chapters have summarised
various of the developments that have taken place recently and
that are in the pipeline. Amongst developments worth more
that £1 million, a total of £2.4 billion-worth have been constructed since 1991 (LCC Development Department database).
There are many large and imposing buildings which have

recently been added to the skyline and there are some
particularly tall ones still to come, including the tower at
Bridgewater Place and the so-called 'Crystal Towers', a 47-
storey, heart-of-Leeds glass tower on the former Queens Hall
site, along with a smaller 29-storey neighbour building. Such
developments will put Leeds more nearly on a par with
Manchester with its own 47-storey tower.

There is creative tension between carrying forward the
strengths and achievements of the past — in institutions and
elements of the landscape — and adapting to new
opportunities and creating them. In the annual report of the
Leeds Civic Trust for 1998–1999, there was the seemingly
oxymoronic suggestion that the city should take various actions
in order to be assured of a place in the 'future history' of the
country (Leeds Civic Trust, 1999). As Peter Hall argues in *Cities
in Civilisation* (Hall, 1998), the character of cities both shapes

16.4 Less certain futures

The longer term future is difficult to predict. "Possible futures emerge from the turbulent interplay of current trends and emerging issues of change" (Schultz, 2002, Slide 3). Some aspects of the future, such a population changes, we can be more certain about because of the natural process of demographic development and our sensible judgements about fertility, mortality and migration. Other futures are much less certain. Economic forecasts tend to be much less reliable because of the unpredictability of factors outside of local or even regional control. Leeds is not an island and consequently will feel the disruptive effects of downturns or upturns in global and international economies, though the city has a history of weathering periods of recession remarkably well. It is immensely hard to make judgements about the economic impact on the city of the expansion of the European Union, or of the effects of the instability in the Middle East on ethnic relations in the city in 20 years time. However, any organisation (such as Leeds Initiative) trying to think even 20 years ahead is compelled to grapple with these major

and is shaped by the prevailing civilisation — and if they work well, so does the civilisation of which they are part. Civilisation/culture is part of the deep structure of cities. It is healthy that there are elements of the city fighting to retain connections to the past amidst the flurry of fashionable changes (Brand, 1999). A city that has no past is bland and characterless. But equally, "cities that hold their ranking over the long term ... do so by continuing to capture propulsive industries" (Storper and Walker, 1989, p.33). So there has to be a constructive interplay between holding onto that which is valuable from the past and making space(s) for new activities, enterprises, lifestyles, interactions and exchanges (Chatterton and Unsworth, forthcoming). "Continuity and perpetual renewal go together" (Brand, 1999).

international factors as well as the long-term needs such as an educated workforce and a sustainable regional economy referred to previously. In the longer-term perspective, we cannot predict as such. There are bound to be significant trends and events that no-one can foresee, so long-range forecasts are probably a complete waste of time. At this time scale, we enter the realm of scenario planning and the contemplation of alternative futures. Somewhere within the range of all possible futures are the more probable ones, and within those are the preferable ones that we would like to work towards (Schultz, 2002). Long-term scenarios can be beneficial if used in the right way; they may not generate consensus but they do allow different parties to agree about the possible futures to be faced in a collective way. The good and bad scenarios of Leeds

Figure 16.3 Leeds in 2033 under a good scenario

TAKE THE TOUR — KNOW YOUR CITY

Jane Murgatroyd
at Leeds International Airport

On landing at Leeds International Airport in the latest stealthair people carrier, the tour whisks you through the Lawnswood Country Park by smartshuttle, allowing you to catch glimpses of the wildlife that flourishes in this well managed 'wilderness' area.

You are soon in the city centre — the historic core ringed by modern landmark buildings, a sign of the city's desire to look to the future, but respecting and building on the past. The city centre has a vibrant and international feel to it. There is a wide range of quality facilities, yet it is human in scale, open and inclusive.

The focus of the tour is the city's new 'Knowledge Centre' where you can conduct your own interactive online discussion with LEO, the local knowledge engineer, a robot who is able to answer questions about how the city has managed to achieve its successful trajectory over the last 30 years.

LEO will tell you about the following: demographic changes and migration rates; the number of new businesses and the levels of inward investment; the growth and changing structure of employment and homeworking; the continued investment in property, cultural and tourist developments; the renewal of the built environment; and the revitalisation of the transport network. LEO will inform you about all the international events, sporting and cultural, taking place in the city's arena and concert venues. LEO will show you what public services are on offer and how they have been improved year on year. LEO's vast database is updated hourly and provides information immediately which can be visualised using charts and maps. If you have time to spare, you can use LEO to show you what the city might look like in ten years time if all the current growth trends continue.

After lunch in one of the new glasshouse cafés on Millennium Square, take the Supertram to the south east of the city centre to one of the main employment areas developed over the past 30 years. There has clearly been a high level of investment with a continuing high quality of maintenance of the built environment. Non-polluting and quieter forms of private transport together with demand management and investment in mass transit have had a major impact on environmental quality.

Before returning to the airport you should ensure you pass through one of Leeds' more deprived neighbourhoods. Here unemployment and crime rates are running at twice the city average, but that is still lower than 30 years ago. The quality of the housing stock is good and local people will confirm the high quality of local services and good access to quality local amenities. They will also confirm that ethnic groups can living together in relative harmony.

Your trip back to the airport is via the eastern and northern orbital — one of the key elements of the new rapid transit infrastructure developed some ten years ago.

See Leeds Online's Around the World in 8 Hours Stealthair Trip for Two competition on page 356

presented in Figures 16.3 and 16.4 are sufficiently thought-provoking to enhance participation in the processes that will determine what the future holds.

One vision that has captured much attention since its announcement in early 2004 is John Prescott's concept of a super-city of the north, stretching from Liverpool to Hull, from Sheffield to Newcastle, and encompassing Leeds (Figure 16.5). The so-called 'Northern Way' (ODPM, 2004b) would act as a rival to London in terms of size and economic power, attracting large numbers of people northwards to take up new jobs and in so doing, relieving the South East in particular of the pressures on land for new housing developments. Prescott's vision, which has appeared at a time when the Government is considering the potential transfer of a further 20,000 public sector jobs from London to the regions (study by Sir Michael Lyons), is in many respects a scenario that builds on the concept

Figure 16.4 Leeds in 2033 under a bad scenario

LEEDS POST   5 February 2033

50 DEAD IN CITY RIOTS

Investigation reveals causes of unrest during Leeds' darkest hour

**Bill Openshaw
at Leeds City Hall**

On the weekend of 28th and 29th August 2032, over 50,000 people took part in the civil unrest and disturbances in Leeds. At least 50 people were killed, and many hundreds injured. The cost of the damage to property is estimated to run into many hundreds of millions of euros. Property was destroyed, businesses looted and their premises severally damaged or gutted. Civic buildings were occupied and the police withdrew from much to the city. Even now, some six months later, the authorities are not in full control of the city.

An investigation into the underlying factors which led to the civil unrest and destruction of property has been in progress this week. The city authorities have been receiving evidence from many people — individual residents, businesses, government agencies and a wide range of other groups and organisations.

A key question and focus of this investigation has been to understand the factors that have turned Leeds from a prosperous, vibrant and growing city at the turn of the century to the declining, decaying and divided city of today — a city which is eligible for the highest level of European aid. It is apparent that: businesses have closed, people have moved away, visitors and students no longer come to the city, disinvestment and dereliction is widespread, crime levels are high and increasing, poverty, deprivation and ill-health are widespread, culture facilities and visitor attractions are closing and public services are poor.

The investigating committee came to the following conclusions:

• Increasing congestion in the city centre in the early 2000s, the delays to the tram project and its final abandonment resulted in businesses beginning to leave the city centre. This trend accelerated following the worsening of the rail service to London, and increasingly poor connection to other UK cities and to Europe.

• The deteriorating quality of the built environment and the worsening pollution made the city less attractive for both residents and visitors. Retail spending fell with a knock-on-effect for the leisure and tourism industries in the city.

• The inability to tackle crime has led to business closures or relocations, and to the abandonment of large swathes of housing. Disinvestment and dereliction have become widespread.

• Skilled and professional workers have been the first to leave, reversing the trend of the late 1990s and early 2000s. This has exacerbated the scale of deprivation and disadvantage, and reinforced the divide between the 'haves' and 'have-nots'.

• Public services have been unable to cope with the scale of the problem, and have also been beset by staff shortages and poor leadership.

• The strong local authority leadership of the late twentieth century and the innovative partnership arrangements have fallen apart as political tensions and fundamental disagreement emerged between partners about the city's future. The increasing emphasis on regional and sub-regional arrangements has resulted in a shift of power away from the city, and hence uncertainly over its future role.

Local government leaders are expected to comment today.

of the Transpennine Corridor that has been considered by various commentators for many years (Robson *et al.,* 1995, for example) and has been facilitated by European INTERREG 2 funding (Hebbert, 2000). Figure 16.5 indicates that seven of the nine new housing market renewal pathfinders and five of the provincial core cities span the existing transport corridors that link the northern conurbations. Leeds sits at the fulcrum of the proposals and would play a key role at the hub of this megalopolis.

One of the most important contributions of visionary exercises of this type is that they provoke local and regional

configured open spaces, new public art and street furniture and greater priority for pedestrians, cyclists and public transport. The 3,300 listed buildings, as documented at the turn of the century, will have been augmented by a number of late twentieth and early twenty-first century structures as the city endeavours to preserve representative features of all eras of architectural heritage. This will create both problems and opportunities as ways have to be found to work around the elements of structures that have to be preserved and buildings judged to have aesthetic/historic value are put to new uses rather than being replaced outright. There will be a fusion of historic settings and state-of-the-art products and services creating unique consumption opportunities (Zukin, 1995).

Where there are fewer strictures in terms of preserving existing structures, the scale and nature of development will be bolder. Low rise buildings that are not of special architectural merit will give way to new buildings with higher plot ratios. Bridgewater Tower and the glass tower on Sovereign Street will not be the only new towers to pierce the skyline. The success of these skyscrapers will convince developers, planners, citizens and their representatives that other high rise buildings should be constructed in the expanded city centre of this core city in

the Northern Growth Corridor. This in turn will intensify the density of commercial and residential occupation and mean that a wider range of services can be supported within the regenerated areas. Retail and service outlets in the city centre will configure and deliver highly differentiated, customised goods. A new generation of cafés, bars, restaurants, nightclubs and virtual reality micro-cinemas will have opened their doors in the main retail area. Some of these specialist micro-quarters will have new roofing that can be used to shield them from the elements when necessary. A new, tourist-orientated smart bus will carry passengers free of charge round a city centre in which most streets and squares are not open to through traffic (Alcantara de Vasconcellos, 2004), and where a series of ornamental drinking fountains will play to the accompaniment of various kinds of live and recorded sounds.

Whilst a new City Museum in the old Leeds Institute will be attracting visitors wanting to know what Leeds used to be like, other historic structures such as the Dark Arches, St Paul's House, the 1860s section of Leeds General Infirmary and Temple Mill may well be housing more specialist commercial or manufacturing collections with interactive leisure elements. Maybe the Town Hall, newly redundant when a large concert

arena complex opens, can host the European version of the Clock of the Long Now — a project that aims to give everyone a heightened sense that the present encompasses the past and the future (Brand, 1999). The Town Hall is the most potent symbol of Leeds' connection with its past; such a project would give it a long, long lease of life and also make Leeds a unique European city. There is potential to connect the Town Hall, the City Library and the Art Gallery (appropriately renamed after the insufficiently celebrated Henry Moore), and reconfigure the space to the south to create a truly world class collection of buildings, spaces and facilities.

On the topic of lease of life, the demographic complexion of the city will change as the number of older people increases, but older people will not be confined to the suburbs and 'rural idyll' locations. Greater numbers of 'empty-nesters', retired people and those with extended careers characterisec by flexible, multi-stranded working patterns will make their home in the city centre, actively involving themselves in economic and voluntary activity that will help to reinvigorate their own lives and the life of the city. Certain parts of suburban Leeds such as the universities, hospitals, retail centres and business parks will remain much as they are now,

though with new/renewed structures interspersed. But manufacturing, once the backbone of Leeds, will comprise an even smaller element of the economy and the landscape. Those firms that do survive and the new ones that form will be highly specialised, automated and mainly in the sectors encouraged and supported within the city-region planning process. The demise of more manufacturing firms will make yet more brownfield sites available for re-use. There will be a re-sorting of economic activity so that organisations that do not require the benefits of a city centre location will increasingly avoid the additional costs and locate in business parks on the eastern, south-eastern and southern sides of the city. This will be encouraged by the pricing cordon that will surround the city centre and the universities and associated improvements in public transport.

Some areas of low demand housing will have been demolished and either redeveloped or given over to new uses, including ecologically-sound open space with tree-surrounded pools and lakes where topography allows. Ethnic minorities will remain concentrated, but over larger areas of the city as their populations expand through natural increase. Many of the failing schools of the early twenty-first century will have been

II We hope that our successors reading this volume at the start of the twenty-second century will be able to reflect with pride on the Leeds' achievements in the previous 100 years. II

closed and new ones will have been built to fit better with the reconfiguring of the population. Crime and anti-social behaviour will remain the major social problem and CCTV will have spread beyond the highest value and highest risk areas. Some of the notorious areas of multiple deprivation that haunted the policy makers at the opening of the twenty-first century will have been shrunk by a combination of enlightened intervention and natural evolution; other areas will have expanded as they accommodate people still trapped without a full role in the society of the time.

Throughout the city, businesses will operate in ways that are more environmentally sound than is the case in 2004, as Leeds maintains its leading role as a city serious about aiming for sustainability and demonstrating both the methods of reducing resource use and pollution output and also the benefits of a cleaner, less resource-intensive way of life that respects the natural environment. Many of the new buildings will have been constructed according to best practice in terms of site selection in relation to other land uses and to transport networks, sources of materials and environmental performance of the building in use. Even quite small projects will have to be subjected to environmental assessment, the criteria for which will have become much more stringent.

A network of three Supertram lines will be in place and the success of this public-private mass transit venture will mean that two further routes are under construction, together with developments of the existing road and rail infrastructure and the designation of more land use for car parking adjacent to tram stops in the outer suburbs. Independent cycle lanes will have been created to allow access to areas of open recreational space both within the built up area and beyond. The continuous process of re-planning and re-configuring the city will itself create a significant number of new jobs. Both the river and the canal will be in use to bring people from desirable residential areas beyond the city centre. Other river-based activities will include canoeing, narrow boat activity, private moorings, festivals and child-orientated leisure uses, including a specially designed pedalo fleet.

Local developer-investors will continue to be the major players in the Leeds scene, though national house builders and both national and international commercial developers will play a role in some of the largest property schemes as Leeds succeeds in the aim of encouraging world class architecture. Although the number of properties owned by large investing institutions has fallen somewhat from the late 1990s peak (IPD, 2004),[1] it is expected that major national and international property-owning institutions will buy into some of the properties that will change the Leeds skyline over the next few years. This will reflect both the growing status of Leeds as a major city, the increased scale and quality of property development and the changing nature of the product with its potential for maintaining and enhancing value by internal restructuring as demand changes.

Leeds will no doubt continue to reinvent itself in ways that are largely home-grown, though increasingly influenced by the wider world. The majority of occupiers of new commercial and residential schemes will mainly be new generations of companies and employees who are of Leeds origin, but the nature of their businesses and lifestyles will be more cosmopolitan, more closely linked into networks that span the globe, with inputs, throughputs and outputs structured in ever-more complex and ingenious ways. Geographers seem to be agreed that there is a crucial paradox for cities: the more interconnected the world becomes, the more the particularities of place have importance for individuals and commercial organisations. The less it matters where you carry out business, the more it matters that the place where you happen to locate should deliver all that is vital for a high-quality lifestyle (Glaeser, 1998; Harris, 1999; Scott, 2001; Townsend, 2001). As described in Newsweek, cities are less frequently where people stay to lead the good life, and more often way stations for people in pursuit of it. Cities are now junctions in the flows of people, information, finance and freight, nodes of nomadism linked by high speed trains and cheap flights (Power, 2002). In the old days, hard location factors, such as the presence of a harbour, a river, a bridge or a crossroads, determined whether the place

House boats moored at Calverley on the Leeds-Liverpool canal. The canal and the river, once crucial to the Leeds economy, are valuable landscape, environmental and leisure assets that can be better integrated into the life of the city.

succeeded as a city. These days, attractions of the natural and cultural environment determine where firms are located (Amin and Thrift, 2002; Power, 2002; Gopal, 2003) and therefore how a city like Leeds rates in the urban hierarchy. Further attention will have to be paid to weaknesses in Leeds' economy, such as the relatively low level of business start-ups and the lack of research and development activity (outside the universities).

Whatever the future may have in store, we must learn to use our knowledge and experience of the past more effectively, in other words, to use the technology to store and provide access to what has worked in the past, what has been good, successful and valuable practice in dealing with the

problems of the past. Policy and plan evaluation is inherently difficult to carry out successfully and we are only beginning to learn how to do this effectively.

We hope that each of the chapters of this book conveys to each reader something valuable or interesting about the city of Leeds. It is imperative that we preserve the Leeds heritage because it nurtures our culture. The accumulated past is life's best resource for future innovation and this will help Leeds to become an even better place. We hope that our successors reading this volume at the start of the twenty-second century will be able to reflect with pride on Leeds' achievements in the previous 100 years.

Evening light on The Royal Armouries, which houses the national collection of armour and weaponry. The Armouries is an integral part of planned waterfront development to the south-east of the city centre.

Note

1 Investment Property Databank tracks holdings and performance of institutionally-owned property across the UK.

References

Alcantara de Vasconcellos, E. (2004) The use of streets: a reassessment and tribute to Donald Appleyard, *Journal of Urban Design,* 9(1): 3–22.

Amin, A. and Thrift, N. (2002) *Cities: Reimagining the Urban,* Polity Press, Cambridge.

Brand, S. (1999) *The Clock of the Long Now Time and Responsibility,* Phoenix, London.

Burt, S. and Grady, K. (1994) *The Illustrated History of Leeds,* Breedon Books, Derby.

Chatterton, P. (2002) 'Be realistic: Demand the impossible' Moving towards 'strong' sustainable development in an old industrial region?, *Regional Studies,* 36(5): 552–561.

Chatterton, P. and Unsworth, R. (forthcoming), Making space for culture(s) in Boomtown. Some alternative futures for development, ownership and participation in Leeds city centre, paper submitted to *Local Economy.*

Engels, F. (1845) *The Condition of the Working Class in England,* edited with a foreword by Victor Kiernan, Penguin, Harmondsworth (published in 1987).

European Commission (1999) *ESDP European Spatial Development Perspective, Towards Balance and Sustainable Development of the Territory of the European Union,* prepared by the Committee on Spatial Development, European Commission, Luxembourg.

Glaeser, E.L. (1998) Are cities dying?, *Journal of Economic Perspectives,* 12(2): 139–160.

Gopal, K. (2003) Great cities, *Yorkshire Business Insider Magazine,* June 2003: 20–22.

Hall, P. (1998) *Cities in Civilisation,* Weidenfield and Nicolson, London.

Harris, R. (1999) *The office and working practice in 2010,* paper delivered to The Property Forum, September 1999 (unpublished).

Hebbert, M. (2000) Transpennine: imaginative geographies of an interregional corridor, *Transactions Institute of British Geographers New Series,* 25: 379–392.

Hillman, J. (2002) *The city international: raising the profile,* paper prepared for Vision for Leeds II: Lessons from Vision I, draft report for Leeds City Council by URBED (unpublished).

Investment Property Databank (2004) *Key Centres Report,* IPD, London.

Leeds City Council (LCC) (2004) *Leeds Economy Bulletin,* LCC, Leeds.

Leeds Civic Trust (1999) *Annual Report,* Leeds Civic Trust, Leeds.

Leeds Civic Trust (2003) *Newsletter, December 2003,* Leeds Civic Trust, Leeds.

Leeds Initiative (2004) *Vision for Leeds 2004 to 2020,* Leeds Initiative, Leeds.

Millard, J. (2004) *The regeneration of sites and structures in South Central Leeds: sustainable development?* unpublished BA dissertation, School of Geography, University of Leeds, Leeds.

Office of the Deputy Prime Minister (ODPM) (2004a) *Competitive European Cities: Where do the Core Cities Stand?,* ODPM, London.

Office of the Deputy Prime Minister (ODPM) (2004b) *Making it Happen: The Northern Way,* ODPM, London.

Power, C. (2002) Putting the city in motion, *Newsweek,* 23 September: 74–75.

Robert Huggins Associates (2001) *Research Journal No.2 High Technology Clusters and Network Capital,* available at: http://www.hugginsassociates.com/product_info.php/cPath/22/products_id/37

Robson, E., Hebbert, M., Handley, J, Mackie, P., Tweddle, G., Richardson, T., Baker, M., Franklin, S. and Perry, D. (1995) *Regions in Partnership: The Transpennine Corridor Study,* report by the Universities of Manchester and Leeds to the Transpennine Steering Group, Transpennine Ltd, Hebden Bridge.

Schultz, W. (2002) *Emerging Change and the Arts of the Future: Using Futures Studies to Explore Possible Developments in Arts and Crafts,* available at: www.infinitefutures.com/essays/prez/iarts/index.htm

Scott, A.J. (2001) *Global City-regions: Trends, Theory, Policy,* OUP, Oxford.

Storper, M. and Walker, R. (1989) *The Capitalist Imperative: Territory, Technology, and Industrial Growth,* Blackwell, Oxford.

Taylor, C. (2003) *Creative Industries in Leeds,* presentation to Leeds Arts Partnership, November.

Townsend, A.M. (2001) The internet and the rise of the new networked cities 1969–1999, *Environment and Planning B,* 28: 39–58.

URBED (2002) *Towns and Cities: Partners in Urban Renaissance,* URBED, London.

Vickers, D (2004) *The UK national area classification of 2001 Census output,* paper presented at the Annual Conference of the British Society for Population Studies, University of Leicester, 13–15 September.

Ward, K. (2003) The limits to contemporary urban redevelopment: 'doing' entrepreneurial urbanism in Birmingham, Leeds and Manchester, *City,* 7(2): 199–211.

Yorkshire Forward (2003) *Regional Economic Strategy: Ten Year Strategy for Yorkshire and Humber 2003–2012,* Yorkshire Forward, Leeds.

Zukin, S. (1995) *The Cultures of Cities,* Blackwell, Oxford.

Sunset over the Pennines from Arthington. There will be 3,652 sunsets between the 2001 and 2011 Censuses. This book will have a long life.